Citroën BX Owners Workshop Manual

I M Coomber

Models covered
Citroën BX Hatchback & Estate models with petrol engines
(inc. GTi, 16 valve & special/limited editions)
1360 cc, 1580 cc & 1905 cc

Does not cover Diesel engine variants or 4x4 models

(908-4V9)   ABCDE
FGHI

2

Haynes Publishing Group
Sparkford Nr Yeovil
Somerset BA22 7JJ England

Haynes Publications, Inc
861 Lawrence Drive
Newbury Park
California 91320 USA

Acknowledgements

Thanks are due to Champion Spark Plug, who supplied the illustrations showing spark plug conditions, to Holt Lloyd Limited who supplied the illustrations showing bodywork repair, and to Duckhams Oils, who provided lubrication data. Certain other illustrations are the copyright of Citroën (UK) Limited, and are used with their permission. Thanks are also due to Sykes-Pickavant Limited, who provided some of the workshop tools, and to all those people at Sparkford and Newbury Park who helped in the production of this manual.

© **Haynes Publishing Group 1993**

A book in the **Haynes Owners Workshop Manual Series**

Printed by J. H. Haynes & Co. Ltd, Sparkford, Nr Yeovil, Somerset BA22 7JJ, England

ISBN 1 85010 905 2

British Library Cataloguing in Publication Data
A catalogue record for this book is available from the British Library

Restoring and Preserving our Motoring Heritage

Few people can have had the luck to realise their dreams to quite the same extent and in such a remarkable fashion as John Haynes, Founder and Chairman of the Haynes Publishing Group.

Since 1965 his unique approach to workshop manual publishing has proved so successful that millions of Haynes Manuals are now sold every year throughout the world, covering literally thousands of different makes and models of cars, vans and motorcycles.

A continuing passion for cars and motoring led to the founding in 1985 of a Charitable Trust dedicated to the restoration and preservation of our motoring heritage. To inaugurate the new Museum, John Haynes donated virtually his entire private collection of 52 cars.

Now with an unrivalled international collection of over 210 veteran, vintage and classic cars and motorcycles, the Haynes Motor Museum in Somerset is well on the way to becoming one of the most interesting Motor Museums in the world.

A 70 seat video cinema, a cafe and an extensive motoring bookshop, together with a specially constructed one kilometre motor circuit, make a visit to the Haynes Motor Museum a truly unforgettable experience.

Every vehicle in the museum is preserved in as near as possible mint condition and each car is run every six months on the motor circuit.

Enjoy the picnic area set amongst the rolling Somerset hills. Peer through the William Morris workshop windows at cars being restored, and browse through the extensive displays of fascinating motoring memorabilia.

From the 1903 Oldsmobile through such classics as an MG Midget to the mighty 'E' Type Jaguar, Lamborghini, Ferrari Berlinetta Boxer, and Graham Hill's Lola Cosworth, there is something for everyone, young and old alike, at this Somerset Museum.

Haynes Motor Museum

Situated mid-way between London and Penzance, the Haynes Motor Museum is located just off the A303 at Sparkford, Somerset (home of the Haynes Manual) and is open to the public 7 days a week all year round, except Christmas Day and Boxing Day.

Contents

Spark plug condition and bodywork repair colour pages between pages 32 and 33

4

Citroën BX 16

About this manual

Its aim

The aim of this manual is to help you get the best value from your vehicle. It can do so in several ways. It can help you decide what work must be done (even should you choose to get it done by a garage), provide information on routine maintenance and servicing, and give a logical course of action and diagnosis when random faults occur. However, it is hoped that you will use the manual by tackling the work yourself. On simpler jobs it may even be quicker than booking the car into a garage and going there twice, to leave and collect it. Perhaps most important, a lot of money can be saved by avoiding the costs a garage must charge to cover its labour and overheads.

The manual has drawings and descriptions to show the function of the various components so that their layout can be understood. Then the tasks are described and photographed in a step-by-step sequence so that even a novice can do the work.

Its arrangement

The manual is divided into Chapters, each covering a logical sub-division of the vehicle. The Chapters are each divided into Sections, numbered with single figures, eg 5; the Sections are divided into paragraphs, or into sub-sections and paragraphs.

It is freely illustrated, especially in those parts where there is a detailed sequence of operations to be carried out. There are two forms of illustration: figures and photographs. The figures are numbered in sequence with decimal numbers, according to their position in the Chapter – eg Fig. 6.4 is the fourth drawing/illustration in Chapter 6. Photographs carry the same number (either individually or in related groups) as the Section and paragraph to which they relate.

There is an alphabetical index at the back of the manual as well as a contents list at the front. Each Chapter is also preceded by its own individual contents list.

References to the 'left' or 'right' of the vehicle are in the sense of a person in the driver's seat facing forwards.

Unless otherwise stated, nuts and bolts are removed by turning anti-clockwise, and tightened by turning clockwise.

Vehicle manufacturers continually make changes to specifications and recommendations, and these, when notified, are incorporated into our manuals at the earliest opportunity.

We take great pride in the accuracy of information given in this manual, but vehicle manufacturers make alterations and design changes during the production run of a particular vehicle of which they do not inform us. No liability can be accepted by the authors or publishers for loss, damage or injury caused by any errors in, or omissions from, the information given.

Introduction to the Citroën BX

The Citroën BX was introduced in France in October 1982 and became available in the UK in September 1983. The original models available in the range were the BX, BX 14 E and BX 14 RE, the BX 16 RS and BX 16 TRS. The engine, transmission and equipment fitted being dependent on the model. In March 1984 the BX 19 RD (diesel version) became available in the UK, but this is not covered in this manual.

For the 1985 model year, the BX 19 GT (petrol version) became available for the customer requiring a higher performance version of the model.

In 1985 the BX Leader replaced the BX and BX 14 models, the Leader being fitted with the same engine and transmission as the BX 14 model.

The BX Estate was introduced in the second half of 1985, two versions being available, the BX 16 RS Estate and the BX 16 TRS Estate.

Changes for the 1987 model year included the introduction of the

BX 19 GTi (with fuel injection), the BX 19 GTi with 16 valve engine and Motronic fuel injection/ignition system, and the replacement of the BX 19 GT by the BX 19 TRS. In early 1990, the BX 19 TZi models became available equipped with catalytic converters. Details of these and other changes will be found in the Supplement at the end of the manual.

On all models, the engine and transmission unit is mounted transversely and drives the front wheels through two driveshafts. The gearbox available (depending on model) is a four- or five-speed manual or a four-speed automatic.

The models are extremely comfortable to ride in, thanks to the hydropneumatic suspension and luxurious interior trim. The unique design suspension is self-levelling and the ride height is maintained automatically over all road conditions. A ground clearance lever inside the car may be used to adjust the ride height when travelling over rough ground, and also makes changing a roadwheel much simpler.

General dimensions, weights and capacities

Dimensions
Overall length
Hatchback .... 4230 mm (166.7 in)
Estate .... 4394 mm (173.1 in)

Overall width .... 1660 mm (65.3 in)

Overall height*
Hatchback .... 1358 mm (53.4 in)
Estate .... 1428 mm (56.2 in)

Ground clearance* .... 160 mm (6.3 in)
* *Engine running – normal setting*

Weights
Kerb weight
BX, BX 14 .... 900 kg (1984 lb)
BX 16 .... 950 kg (2094 lb)
BX 16 Estate .... 998 kg (2200 lb)
BX 19 .... 1000 kg (2205 lb)
BX 19 Estate .... 1037 kg (2286 lb)
BX 19 GTi .... 1025 kg (2260 lb)
BX 19 GTi 16V .... 1070 kg (2359 lb)

Maximum towing weights
BX, BX 14 .... 1000 kg (2205 lb)
BX 16 .... 1100 kg (2425 lb)
BX 16 Estate .... 1100 kg (2425 lb)
BX 19 .... 1100 kg (2425 lb)
BX 19 Estate, BX 19 GTi, BX 19 GTi 16V .... 1100 kg (2425 lb)

Maximum roof rack load
All Hatchback .... 75 kg (165 lb)
Estate .... 100 kg (220 lb)

Capacities
Engine
BX 14 (XY6 engine) .... 4.5 litres (7.9 pints)
BX 14E and RE (XY6 engine) .... 5.0 litres (8.8 pints)
BX 14 (K1G or TU3 engine) .... 3.5 litres (6.2 pints)
BX 16 and BX 19 (except GTi 16V) .... 5.0 litres (8.8 pints)
BX 19 GTi 16V .... 5.3 litres (9.3 pints)

Gearbox
BX 14, 14 E and RE (XY6 engine) .... combined with engine
BX 14 (K1G or TU3 engine) .... 2.0 litres (3.5 pints)
BX 16 and BX 19:
    BE1/5 manual gearbox models................................ 2.0 litres (3.5 pints)
    BE3/5 manual gearbox models................................ 1.8 litres (3.2 pints)
BX 16 (automatic transmission):
    Drain and refill .... 2.5 litres (4.4 pints)
    Total refill .... 6.5 litres (11.4 pints)

Cooling system
BX and BX 14 .... 6.5 litres (11.4 pints)
BX 16 and BX 19 .... 6.5 to 7.0 litres (11.4 to 12.3 pints)

Fuel tank
BX and BX 14 .... 44 litres (9.7 gallons)
BX 16 and BX 19 .... 52 litres (11.4 gallons)

Jacking and towing

Jacking

To change a roadwheel the vehicle must be parked on firm level ground. Fully apply the handbrake (operates the front wheels only), run the engine at idle speed and set the ground clearance selector lever to the maximum height setting position. If the front of the vehicle is to be raised, firmly chock the rear wheels.

Open the tailgate and, using the wheelbrace stored in the recess on the right-hand side of the luggage compartment, loosen the roadwheel bolts on the wheel to be removed.

Again using the wheelbrace, unscrew the spare wheel retainer bolt in the middle of the luggage compartment floor at the rear and lower the spare wheel carrier (photo). About 6 to 8 turns will lower the carrier enough to allow the spare wheel to be withdrawn. Lift the wheel carrier to swing the catch clear to remove the spare wheel.

Remove the jack from the recess in the spare wheel and securely locate it in the side jacking point beneath the body sill. Raise the vehicle by winding up the jack using the wheelbrace so that the wheel to be removed is clear of the ground, then undo and remove the wheel bolts and remove the wheel.

Fit the spare wheel using a reversal of the removal procedure. Remember to reset the ground clearance lever to the normal driving position before moving off.

When jacking-up the car with a trolley jack, or supporting the vehicle on safety stands, locate them only at the specified support points indicated in the accompanying illustration. Always ensure that they are securely located and the vehicle firmly supported before working underneath the vehicle.

Towing

A single towing eye is provided at the front of the vehicle whilst the rear end has two towing eyes, one each side (photos).

It is preferable to tow BX, BX 14, Leader and all automatic transmission models with the front wheels clear of the ground. If this is impossible, restrict towing speed to 30 mph and distance towed to 30 miles maximum. Automatic transmission must be in position N. Disregard of these instructions may cause transmission damage.

To raise the front of the vehicle for a suspended tow, attach the lifting sling hooks to the suspension arms each side and, to protect the underside of the vehicle from damage, locate a piece of suitable wood between the vehicle and the lift sling. If possible remove the front bumper or protect it from damage with rags or similar.

If towing with the rear wheels lifted clear of the ground apply the same protective measure as for the front end, but attach the lifting hooks to the axle crossmember. Towing by this method is only permitted on BX 16 and 19 models with manual transmission.

When being towed, the hydraulic circuit must be pressurized wherever possible, but if this is not possible reduce the towing speed and if available use a towing bar. **Caution:** *Once the reserve of hydraulic pressure has been exhausted, the footbrake will not work and the handbrake will have to be used instead. Power steering assistance (when applicable) will also be lost.*

Use wheelbrace to operate spare wheel retainer

Towing eye – front

Towing eye – rear

8

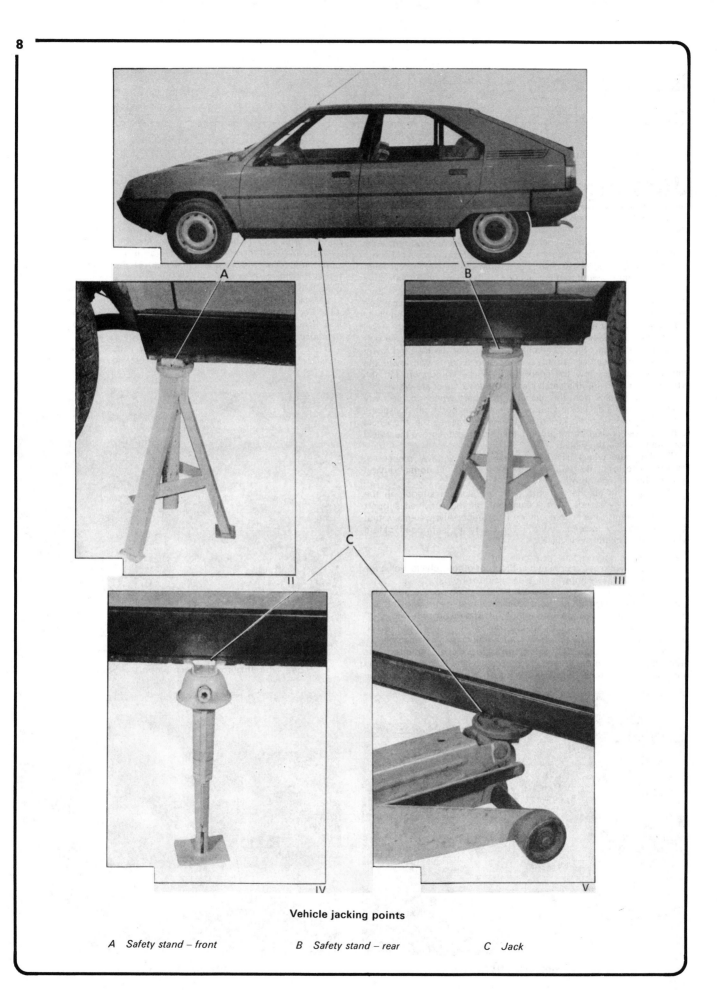

Vehicle jacking points

A   Safety stand – front   *B   Safety stand – rear*   *C   Jack*

Buying spare parts
and vehicle identification numbers

Buying spare parts

Spare parts are available from many sources, for example: Citroën garages, other accessory shops and motor factors. Our advice regarding spare parts is as follows:

Officially appointed Citroën garages – This is the best source for parts which are peculiar to your car and otherwise not generally available (eg, complete cylinder heads, internal transmission components, badges, interior trim etc). It is also the only place you should buy parts if your car is still under warranty; non-Citroën parts may invalidate the warranty. To be sure of obtaining the correct parts it will always be necessary to give the storeman your car's engine and chassis number, and if possible, to take the old part along for positive identification. Many parts are available under a factory exchange scheme – any parts returned should always be clean. It obviously makes good sense to go straight to the specialists on your car for this type of part, for they are best equipped to supply you.

Other garages and accessory shops – These are often very good places to buy materials and components needed for the maintenance of your car (eg, oil filters, spark plugs, bulbs, drivebelts, oils and grease, touch-up paint, filler paste etc.) They also sell accessories, usually have convenient opening hours, charge lower prices and can often be found not far from home.

Motor factors – Good factors stock all of the more important components which wear out relatively quickly (eg, clutch components, pistons and liners, valves, exhaust systems, brake pipes/seals and pads etc). Motor factors will often provide new or reconditioned components on a part exchange basis – this can save a considerable amount of money.

Vehicle identification numbers

Modifications are a continuing and unpublished process in vehicle manufacture, quite apart from major model changes. Spare parts manuals and lists are compiled upon a numerical basis, the individual vehicle numbers being essential to correct identification of the component required.

When ordering spare parts, always give as much information as possible. Quote the car model, year of manufacture, body and engine numbers as appropriate.

The *car identification plate* is in the engine compartment on the right-hand side wheel arch.

The *engine number* location depends on the engine type. On BX and BX 14 models it is located on the bottom left-hand side of the engine. On BX 16 and BX 19 models it is located on the top right-hand side of the engine.

The *gearbox number* is stamped on the gearbox casing.

The *chassis number* is stamped into the manufacturer's plate in the engine compartment on the front panel.

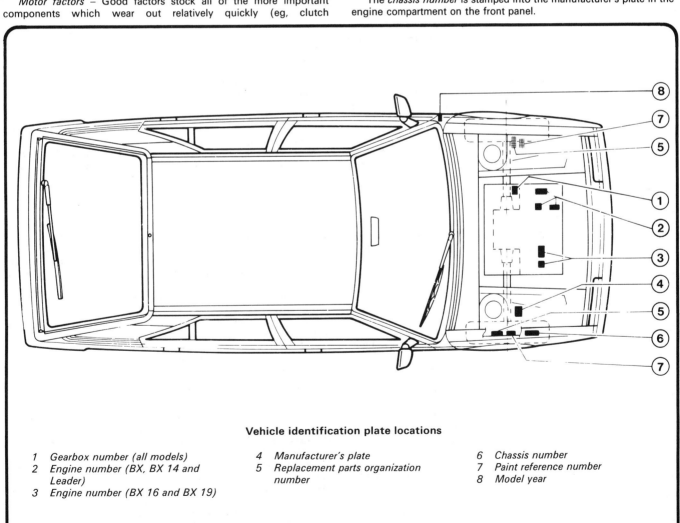

Vehicle identification plate locations

1 Gearbox number (all models)
2 Engine number (BX, BX 14 and Leader)
3 Engine number (BX 16 and BX 19)
4 Manufacturer's plate
5 Replacement parts organization number
6 Chassis number
7 Paint reference number
8 Model year

General repair procedures

Whenever servicing, repair or overhaul work is carried out on the car or its components, it is necessary to observe the following procedures and instructions. This will assist in carrying out the operation efficiently and to a professional standard of workmanship.

Joint mating faces and gaskets

Where a gasket is used between the mating faces of two components, ensure that it is renewed on reassembly, and fit it dry unless otherwise stated in the repair procedure. Make sure that the mating faces are clean and dry with all traces of old gasket removed. When cleaning a joint face, use a tool which is not likely to score or damage the face, and remove any burrs or nicks with an oilstone or fine file.

Make sure that tapped holes are cleaned with a pipe cleaner, and keep them free of jointing compound if this is being used unless specifically instructed otherwise.

Ensure that all orifices, channels or pipes are clear and blow through them, preferably using compressed air.

Oil seals

Whenever an oil seal is removed from its working location, either individually or as part of an assembly, it should be renewed.

The very fine sealing lip of the seal is easily damaged and will not seal if the surface it contacts is not completely clean and free from scratches, nicks or grooves. If the original sealing surface of the component cannot be restored, the component should be renewed.

Protect the lips of the seal from any surface which may damage them in the course of fitting. Use tape or a conical sleeve where possible. Lubricate the seal lips with oil before fitting and, on dual lipped seals, fill the space between the lips with grease.

Unless otherwise stated, oil seals must be fitted with their sealing lips toward the lubricant to be sealed.

Use a tubular drift or block of wood of the appropriate size to install the seal and, if the seal housing is shouldered, drive the seal down to the shoulder. If the seal housing is unshouldered, the seal should be fitted with its face flush with the housing top face.

Screw threads and fastenings

Always ensure that a blind tapped hole is completely free from oil, grease, water or other fluid before installing the bolt or stud. Failure to

do this could cause the housing to crack due to the hydraulic action of the bolt or stud as it is screwed in.

When tightening a castellated nut to accept a split pin, tighten the nut to the specified torque, where applicable, and then tighten further to the next split pin hole. Never slacken the nut to align a split pin hole unless stated in the repair procedure.

When checking or retightening a nut or bolt to a specified torque setting, slacken the nut or bolt by a quarter of a turn, and then retighten to the specified setting.

Locknuts, locktabs and washers

Any fastening which will rotate against a component or housing in the course of tightening should always have a washer between it and the relevant component or housing.

Spring or split washers should always be renewed when they are used to lock a critical component such as a big-end bearing retaining nut or bolt.

Locktabs which are folded over to retain a nut or bolt should always be renewed.

Self-locking nuts can be reused in non-critical areas, providing resistance can be felt when the locking portion passes over the bolt or stud thread.

Split pins must always be replaced with new ones of the correct size for the hole.

Special tools

Some repair procedures in this manual entail the use of special tools such as a press, two or three-legged pullers, spring compressors etc. Wherever possible, suitable readily available alternatives to the manufacturer's special tools are described, and are shown in use. In some instances, where no alternative is possible, it has been necessary to resort to the use of a manufacturer's tool and this has been done for reasons of safety as well as the efficient completion of the repair operation. Unless you are highly skilled and have a thorough understanding of the procedure described, never attempt to bypass the use of any special tool when the procedure described specifies its use. Not only is there a very great risk of personal injury, but expensive damage could be caused to the components involved.

Tools and working facilities

Introduction

A selection of good tools is a fundamental requirement for anyone contemplating the maintenance and repair of a motor vehicle. For the owner who does not possess any, their purchase will prove a considerable expense, offsetting some of the savings made by doing-it-yourself. However, provided that the tools purchased meet the relevant national safety standards and are of good quality, they will last for many years and prove an extremely worthwhile investment.

To help the average owner to decide which tools are needed to carry out the various tasks detailed in this manual, we have compiled three lists of tools under the following headings: *Maintenance and minor repair*, *Repair and overhaul*, and *Special*. The newcomer to practical mechanics should start off with the *Maintenance and minor repair* tool kit and confine himself to the simpler jobs around the vehicle. Then, as his confidence and experience grow, he can undertake more difficult tasks, buying extra tools as, and when, they are needed. In this way, a *Maintenance and minor repair* tool kit can be built-up into a *Repair and overhaul* tool kit over a considerable period of time without any major cash outlays. The experienced do-it-yourselfer will have a tool kit good enough for most repair and overhaul procedures and will add tools from the *Special* category when he feels the expense is justified by the amount of use to which these tools will be put.

It is obviously not possible to cover the subject of tools fully here. For those who wish to learn more about tools and their use there is a book entitled *How to Choose and Use Car Tools* available from the publishers of this manual.

Maintenance and minor repair tool kit

The tools given in this list should be considered as a minimum requirement if routine maintenance, servicing and minor repair operations are to be undertaken. We recommend the purchase of combination spanners (ring one end, open-ended the other); although more expensive than open-ended ones, they do give the advantages of both types of spanner.

Combination spanners - 10, 11, 12, 13, 14 & 17 mm
Adjustable spanner - 9 inch
Engine sump/gearbox/drain plug key
Spark plug spanner (with rubber insert)
Spark plug gap adjustment tool
Set of feeler gauges
Brake bleed nipple spanner
Screwdriver - 4 in long x $^1/4$ in dia (flat blade)
Screwdriver - 4 in long x $^1/4$ in dia (cross blade)
Combination pliers - 6 inch
Hacksaw (junior)
Tyre pump
Tyre pressure gauge
Oil can
Fine emery cloth (1 sheet)
Wire brush (small)
Funnel (medium size)

Repair and overhaul tool kit

These tools are virtually essential for anyone undertaking any major repairs to a motor vehicle, and are additional to those given in the *Maintenance and minor repair* list. Included in this list is a comprehensive set of sockets. Although these are expensive they will be found invaluable as they are so versatile - particularly if various drives are included in the set. We recommend the $^1/2$ in square-drive type, as this can be used with most proprietary torque wrenches. If you cannot afford a socket set, even bought piecemeal, then inexpensive tubular box spanners are a useful alternative.

The tools in this list will occasionally need to be supplemented by tools from the *Special* list.

Sockets (or box spanners) to cover range in previous list
Reversible ratchet drive (for use with sockets)
Extension piece, 10 inch (for use with sockets)
Universal joint (for use with sockets)
Torque wrench (for use with sockets)
'Mole' wrench - 8 inch
Ball pein hammer
Soft-faced hammer, plastic or rubber
Screwdriver - 6 in long x $^5/16$ in dia (flat blade)
Screwdriver - 2 in long x $^5/16$ in square (flat blade)
Screwdriver - 1$^1/2$ in long x $^1/4$ in dia (cross blade)
Screwdriver - 3 in long x $^1/8$ in dia (electricians)
Pliers - electricians side cutters
Pliers - needle nosed
Pliers - circlip (internal and external)
Cold chisel - $^1/2$ inch
Scriber
Scraper
Centre punch
Pin punch
Hacksaw
Valve grinding tool
Steel rule/straight-edge
Allen keys
Selection of files
Wire brush (large)
Axle-stands
Jack (strong trolley or hydraulic type)

Special tools

The tools in this list are those which are not used regularly, are expensive to buy, or which need to be used in accordance with their manufacturers' instructions. Unless relatively difficult mechanical jobs are undertaken frequently, it will not be economic to buy many of these tools. Where this is the case, you could consider clubbing together with friends (or joining a motorists' club) to make a joint purchase, or borrowing the tools against a deposit from a local garage or tool hire specialist.

The following list contains only those tools and instruments freely available to the public, and not those special tools produced by the vehicle manufacturer specifically for its dealer network. You will find occasional references to these manufacturers' special tools in the text of this manual. Generally, an alternative method of doing the job without the vehicle manufacturers' special tool is given. However, sometimes, there is no alternative to using them. Where this is the case and the relevant tool cannot be bought or borrowed, you will have to entrust the work to a franchised garage.

> Valve spring compressor
> Piston ring compressor
> Balljoint separator
> Universal hub/bearing puller
> Impact screwdriver
> Micrometer and/or vernier gauge
> Dial gauge
> Stroboscopic timing light
> Dwell angle meter/tachometer
> Universal electrical multi-meter
> Cylinder compression gauge
> Lifting tackle
> Trolley jack
> Light with extension lead

Buying tools

For practically all tools, a tool factor is the best source since he will have a very comprehensive range compared with the average garage or accessory shop. Having said that, accessory shops often offer excellent quality tools at discount prices, so it pays to shop around.

There are plenty of good tools around at reasonable prices, but always aim to purchase items which meet the relevant national safety standards. If in doubt, ask the proprietor or manager of the shop for advice before making a purchase.

Care and maintenance of tools

Having purchased a reasonable tool kit, it is necessary to keep the tools in a clean serviceable condition. After use, always wipe off any dirt, grease and metal particles using a clean, dry cloth, before putting the tools away. Never leave them lying around after they have been used. A simple tool rack on the garage or workshop wall, for items such as screwdrivers and pliers is a good idea. Store all normal wrenches and sockets in a metal box. Any measuring instruments, gauges, meters, etc, must be carefully stored where they cannot be damaged or become rusty.

Take a little care when tools are used. Hammer heads inevitably become marked and screwdrivers lose the keen edge on their blades from time to time. A little timely attention with emery cloth or a file will soon restore items like this to a good serviceable finish.

Working facilities

Not to be forgotten when discussing tools, is the workshop itself. If anything more than routine maintenance is to be carried out, some form of suitable working area becomes essential.

It is appreciated that many an owner mechanic is forced by circumstances to remove an engine or similar item, without the benefit of a garage or workshop. Having done this, any repairs should always be done under the cover of a roof.

Wherever possible, any dismantling should be done on a clean, flat workbench or table at a suitable working height.

Any workbench needs a vice: one with a jaw opening of 4 in (100 mm) is suitable for most jobs. As mentioned previously, some clean dry storage space is also required for tools, as well as for lubricants, cleaning fluids, touch-up paints and so on, which become necessary.

Another item which may be required, and which has a much more general usage, is an electric drill with a chuck capacity of at least 5/16 in (8 mm). This, together with a good range of twist drills, is virtually essential for fitting accessories.

Last, but not least, always keep a supply of old newspapers and clean, lint-free rags available, and try to keep any working area as clean as possible.

Spanner jaw gap comparison table

Jaw gap (in)	Spanner size
0.250	1/4 in AF
0.276	7 mm
0.313	5/16 in AF
0.315	8 mm
0.344	11/32 in AF; 1/8 in Whitworth
0.354	9 mm
0.375	3/8 in AF
0.394	10 mm
0.433	11 mm
0.438	7/16 in AF
0.445	3/16 in Whitworth; 1/4 in BSF
0.472	12 mm
0.500	1/2 in AF
0.512	13 mm
0.525	1/4 in Whitworth; 5/16 in BSF
0.551	14 mm
0.563	9/16 in AF
0.591	15 mm
0.600	5/16 in Whitworth; 3/8 in BSF
0.625	5/8 in AF
0.630	16 mm
0.669	17 mm
0.686	11/16 in AF
0.709	18 mm
0.710	3/8 in Whitworth; 7/16 in BSF
0.748	19 mm
0.750	3/4 in AF
0.813	13/16 in AF
0.820	7/16 in Whitworth; 1/2 in BSF
0.866	22 mm
0.875	7/8 in AF
0.920	1/2 in Whitworth; 9/16 in BSF
0.938	15/16 in AF
0.945	24 mm
1.000	1 in AF
1.010	9/16 in Whitworth; 5/8 in BSF
1.024	26 mm
1.063	1 1/16 in AF; 27 mm
1.100	5/8 in Whitworth; 11/16 in BSF
1.125	1 1/8 in AF
1.181	30 mm
1.200	11/16 in Whitworth; 3/4 in BSF
1.250	1 1/4 in AF
1.260	32 mm
1.300	3/4 in Whitworth; 7/8 in BSF
1.313	1 5/16 in AF
1.390	13/16 in Whitworth; 15/16 in BSF
1.417	36 mm
1.438	1 7/16 in AF
1.480	7/8 in Whitworth; 1 in BSF
1.500	1 1/2 in AF
1.575	40 mm; 15/16 in Whitworth
1.614	41 mm
1.625	1 5/8 in AF
1.670	1 in Whitworth; 1 1/8 in BSF
1.688	1 11/16 in AF
1.811	46 mm
1.813	1 13/16 in AF
1.860	1 1/8 in Whitworth; 1 1/4 in BSF
1.875	1 7/8 in AF
1.969	50 mm
2.000	2 in AF
2.050	1 1/4 in Whitworth; 1 3/8 in BSF
2.165	55 mm
2.362	60 mm

Conversion factors

Length (distance)

Inches (in)	X	25.4	= Millimetres (mm)	X 0.0394	= Inches (in)
Feet (ft)	X	0.305	= Metres (m)	X 3.281	= Feet (ft)
Miles	X	1.609	= Kilometres (km)	X 0.621	= Miles

Volume (capacity)

Cubic inches (cu in; in³)	X	16.387	= Cubic centimetres (cc; cm³)	X 0.061	= Cubic inches (cu in; in³)
Imperial pints (Imp pt)	X	0.568	= Litres (l)	X 1.76	= Imperial pints (Imp pt)
Imperial quarts (Imp qt)	X	1.137	= Litres (l)	X 0.88	= Imperial quarts (Imp qt)
Imperial quarts (Imp qt)	X	1.201	= US quarts (US qt)	X 0.833	= Imperial quarts (Imp qt)
US quarts (US qt)	X	0.946	= Litres (l)	X 1.057	= US quarts (US qt)
Imperial gallons (Imp gal)	X	4.546	= Litres (l)	X 0.22	= Imperial gallons (Imp gal)
Imperial gallons (Imp gal)	X	1.201	= US gallons (US gal)	X 0.833	= Imperial gallons (Imp gal)
US gallons (US gal)	X	3.785	= Litres (l)	X 0.264	= US gallons (US gal)

Mass (weight)

Ounces (oz)	X	28.35	= Grams (g)	X 0.035	= Ounces (oz)
Pounds (lb)	X	0.454	= Kilograms (kg)	X 2.205	= Pounds (lb)

Force

Ounces-force (ozf; oz)	X	0.278	= Newtons (N)	X 3.6	= Ounces-force (ozf; oz)
Pounds-force (lbf; lb)	X	4.448	= Newtons (N)	X 0.225	= Pounds-force (lbf; lb)
Newtons (N)	X	0.1	= Kilograms-force (kgf; kg)	X 9.81	= Newtons (N)

Pressure

Pounds-force per square inch (psi; lbf/in²; lb/in²)	X	0.070	= Kilograms-force per square centimetre (kgf/cm²; kg/cm²)	X 14.223	= Pounds-force per square inch (psi; lbf/in²; lb/in²)
Pounds-force per square inch (psi; lbf/in²; lb/in²)	X	0.068	= Atmospheres (atm)	X 14.696	= Pounds-force per square inch (psi; lbf/in²; lb/in²)
Pounds-force per square inch (psi; lbf/in²; lb/in²)	X	0.069	= Bars	X 14.5	= Pounds-force per square inch (psi; lbf/in²; lb/in²)
Pounds-force per square inch (psi; lbf/in²; lb/in²)	X	6.895	= Kilopascals (kPa)	X 0.145	= Pounds-force per square inch (psi; lbf/in²; lb/in²)
Kilopascals (kPa)	X	0.01	= Kilograms-force per square centimetre (kgf/cm²; kg/cm²)	X 98.1	= Kilopascals (kPa)
Millibar (mbar)	X	100	= Pascals (Pa)	X 0.01	= Millibar (mbar)
Millibar (mbar)	X	0.0145	= Pounds-force per square inch (psi; lbf/in²; lb/in²)	X 68.947	= Millibar (mbar)
Millibar (mbar)	X	0.75	= Millimetres of mercury (mmHg)	X 1.333	= Millibar (mbar)
Millibar (mbar)	X	0.401	= Inches of water (inH₂O)	X 2.491	= Millibar (mbar)
Millimetres of mercury (mmHg)	X	0.535	= Inches of water (inH₂O)	X 1.868	= Millimetres of mercury (mmHg)
Inches of water (inH₂O)	X	0.036	= Pounds-force per square inch (psi; lbf/in²; lb/in²)	X 27.68	= Inches of water (inH₂O)

Torque (moment of force)

Pounds-force inches (lbf in; lb in)	X	1.152	= Kilograms-force centimetre (kgf cm; kg cm)	X 0.868	= Pounds-force inches (lbf in; lb in)
Pounds-force inches (lbf in; lb in)	X	0.113	= Newton metres (Nm)	X 8.85	= Pounds-force inches (lbf in; lb in)
Pounds-force inches (lbf in; lb in)	X	0.083	= Pounds-force feet (lbf ft; lb ft)	X 12	= Pounds-force inches (lbf in; lb in)
Pounds-force feet (lbf ft; lb ft)	X	0.138	= Kilograms-force metres (kgf m; kg m)	X 7.233	= Pounds-force feet (lbf ft; lb ft)
Pounds-force feet (lbf ft; lb ft)	X	1.356	= Newton metres (Nm)	X 0.738	= Pounds-force feet (lbf ft; lb ft)
Newton metres (Nm)	X	0.102	= Kilograms-force metres (kgf m; kg m)	X 9.804	= Newton metres (Nm)

Power

Horsepower (hp)	X	745.7	= Watts (W)	X 0.0013	= Horsepower (hp)

Velocity (speed)

Miles per hour (miles/hr; mph)	X	1.609	= Kilometres per hour (km/hr; kph)	X 0.621	= Miles per hour (miles/hr; mph)

Fuel consumption*

Miles per gallon, Imperial (mpg)	X	0.354	= Kilometres per litre (km/l)	X 2.825	= Miles per gallon, Imperial (mpg)
Miles per gallon, US (mpg)	X	0.425	= Kilometres per litre (km/l)	X 2.352	= Miles per gallon, US (mpg)

Temperature

Degrees Fahrenheit = (°C x 1.8) + 32

Degrees Celsius (Degrees Centigrade; °C) = (°F - 32) x 0.56

*It is common practice to convert from miles per gallon (mpg) to litres/100 kilometres (l/100km), where mpg (Imperial) x l/100 km = 282 and mpg (US) x l/100 km = 235

Safety first!

Professional motor mechanics are trained in safe working procedures. However enthusiastic you may be about getting on with the job in hand, do take the time to ensure that your safety is not put at risk. A moment's lack of attention can result in an accident, as can failure to observe certain elementary precautions.

There will always be new ways of having accidents, and the following points do not pretend to be a comprehensive list of all dangers; they are intended rather to make you aware of the risks and to encourage a safety-conscious approach to all work you carry out on your vehicle.

Essential DOs and DON'Ts

DON'T rely on a single jack when working underneath the vehicle. Always use reliable additional means of support, such as axle stands, securely placed under a part of the vehicle that you know will not give way.

DON'T attempt to loosen or tighten high-torque nuts (e.g. wheel hub nuts) while the vehicle is on a jack; it may be pulled off.

DON'T start the engine without first ascertaining that the transmission is in neutral (or 'Park' where applicable) and the parking brake applied.

DON'T suddenly remove the filler cap from a hot cooling system – cover it with a cloth and release the pressure gradually first, or you may get scalded by escaping coolant.

DON'T attempt to drain oil until you are sure it has cooled sufficiently to avoid scalding you.

DON'T grasp any part of the engine, exhaust or catalytic converter without first ascertaining that it is sufficiently cool to avoid burning you.

DON'T allow brake fluid or antifreeze to contact vehicle paintwork.

DON'T syphon toxic liquids such as fuel, brake fluid or antifreeze by mouth, or allow them to remain on your skin.

DON'T inhale dust – it may be injurious to health (see *Asbestos* below).

DON'T allow any spilt oil or grease to remain on the floor – wipe it up straight away, before someone slips on it.

DON'T use ill-fitting spanners or other tools which may slip and cause injury.

DON'T attempt to lift a heavy component which may be beyond your capability – get assistance.

DON'T rush to finish a job, or take unverified short cuts.

DON'T allow children or animals in or around an unattended vehicle.

DO wear eye protection when using power tools such as drill, sander, bench grinder etc, and when working under the vehicle.

DO use a barrier cream on your hands prior to undertaking dirty jobs – it will protect your skin from infection as well as making the dirt easier to remove afterwards; but make sure your hands aren't left slippery. Note that long-term contact with used engine oil can be a health hazard.

DO keep loose clothing (cuffs, tie etc) and long hair well out of the way of moving mechanical parts.

DO remove rings, wristwatch etc, before working on the vehicle – especially the electrical system.

DO ensure that any lifting tackle used has a safe working load rating adequate for the job.

DO keep your work area tidy – it is only too easy to fall over articles left lying around.

DO get someone to check periodically that all is well, when working alone on the vehicle.

DO carry out work in a logical sequence and check that everything is correctly assembled and tightened afterwards.

DO remember that your vehicle's safety affects that of yourself and others. If in doubt on any point, get specialist advice.

IF, in spite of following these precautions, you are unfortunate enough to injure yourself, seek medical attention as soon as possible.

Asbestos

Certain friction, insulating, sealing, and other products – such as brake linings, brake bands, clutch linings, torque converters, gaskets, etc – contain asbestos. *Extreme care must be taken to avoid inhalation of dust from such products since it is hazardous to health.* If in doubt, assume that they *do* contain asbestos.

Fire

Remember at all times that petrol (gasoline) is highly flammable. Never smoke, or have any kind of naked flame around, when working on the vehicle. But the risk does not end there – a spark caused by an electrical short-circuit, by two metal surfaces contacting each other, by careless use of tools, or even by static electricity built up in your body under certain conditions, can ignite petrol vapour, which in a confined space is highly explosive.

Always disconnect the battery earth (ground) terminal before working on any part of the fuel or electrical system, and never risk spilling fuel on to a hot engine or exhaust.

It is recommended that a fire extinguisher of a type suitable for fuel and electrical fires is kept handy in the garage or workplace at all times. Never try to extinguish a fuel or electrical fire with water.

Note: *Any reference to a 'torch' appearing in this manual should always be taken to mean a hand-held battery-operated electric lamp or flashlight. It does NOT mean a welding/gas torch or blowlamp.*

Fumes

Certain fumes are highly toxic and can quickly cause unconsciousness and even death if inhaled to any extent. Petrol (gasoline) vapour comes into this category, as do the vapours from certain solvents such as trichloroethylene. Any draining or pouring of such volatile fluids should be done in a well ventilated area.

When using cleaning fluids and solvents, read the instructions carefully. Never use materials from unmarked containers – they may give off poisonous vapours.

Never run the engine of a motor vehicle in an enclosed space such as a garage. Exhaust fumes contain carbon monoxide which is extremely poisonous; if you need to run the engine, always do so in the open air or at least have the rear of the vehicle outside the workplace.

If you are fortunate enough to have the use of an inspection pit, never drain or pour petrol, and never run the engine, while the vehicle is standing over it; the fumes, being heavier than air, will concentrate in the pit with possibly lethal results.

The battery

Never cause a spark, or allow a naked light, near the vehicle's battery. It will normally be giving off a certain amount of hydrogen gas, which is highly explosive.

Always disconnect the battery earth (ground) terminal before working on the fuel or electrical systems.

If possible, loosen the filler plugs or cover when charging the battery from an external source. Do not charge at an excessive rate or the battery may burst.

Take care when topping up and when carrying the battery. The acid electrolyte, even when diluted, is very corrosive and should not be allowed to contact the eyes or skin.

If you ever need to prepare electrolyte yourself, always add the acid slowly to the water, and never the other way round. Protect against splashes by wearing rubber gloves and goggles.

When jump starting a car using a booster battery, for negative earth (ground) vehicles, connect the jump leads in the following sequence: First connect one jump lead between the positive (+) terminals of the two batteries. Then connect the other jump lead first to the negative (–) terminal of the booster battery, and then to a good earthing (ground) point on the vehicle to be started, at least 18 in (45 cm) from the battery if possible. Ensure that hands and jump leads are clear of any moving parts, and that the two vehicles do not touch. Disconnect the leads in the reverse order.

Mains electricity and electrical equipment

When using an electric power tool, inspection light etc, always ensure that the appliance is correctly connected to its plug and that, where necessary, it is properly earthed (grounded). Do not use such appliances in damp conditions and, again, beware of creating a spark or applying excessive heat in the vicinity of fuel or fuel vapour. Also ensure that the appliances meet the relevant national safety standards.

Ignition HT voltage

A severe electric shock can result from touching certain parts of the ignition system, such as the HT leads, when the engine is running or being cranked, particularly if components are damp or the insulation is defective. Where an electronic ignition system is fitted, the HT voltage is much higher and could prove fatal.

Routine maintenance

For modifications, and information applicable to later models, see Supplement at end of manual

Maintenance is essential for ensuring safety and is desirable for the purpose of getting the best in terms of performance and economy from the car. Over the years the need for periodic lubrication – oiling and greasing – has been drastically reduced, if not totally eliminated. This has unfortunately tended to lead some owners to think that because no such action is required the components either no longer exist or will last for ever. This is a serious delusion. If anything, there are now more places, particularly in the steering and suspension, where joints and pivots are fitted. Although you do not grease them any more you still have to look at them – and look at them just as often as you may previously have had to grease them. It follows therefore that the largest initial element of maintenance is visual examination. This may lead to repairs or renewal.

Top view of the engine and associated components (BX 16) with the air filter removed for clarity

1 Battery	7 Radiator filler cap	11 Spark plug	15 Distributor
2 Bleed screws – radiator	8 Alternator	12 Diagnostic socket	16 Ignition coil
3 Clutch cable	9 Hydraulic system reservoir	13 Fuel pump	17 Windscreen washer reservoir
4 Dipstick	10 Rear window washer reservoir	14 Dipstick – alternative position	18 Front suspension unit – left side
5 Oil filler cap			
6 Carburettor			

Underside view of the engine and associated components (BX 16)

1 Exhaust system
2 Suspension arm

3 Driveshaft intermediate
   bearing – right-hand side
   (BX 16 and 19 only)

4 Sump
5 Drain plug
6 Differential housing

7 Gearbox
8 Brake unit
9 Track rod

Underside view at rear (BX 16)

1 Fuel filler pipe
2 Rear suspension arm
3 Fuel tank

4 Exhaust system and heat
  shield

5 Rear suspension unit
6 Spare wheel

18

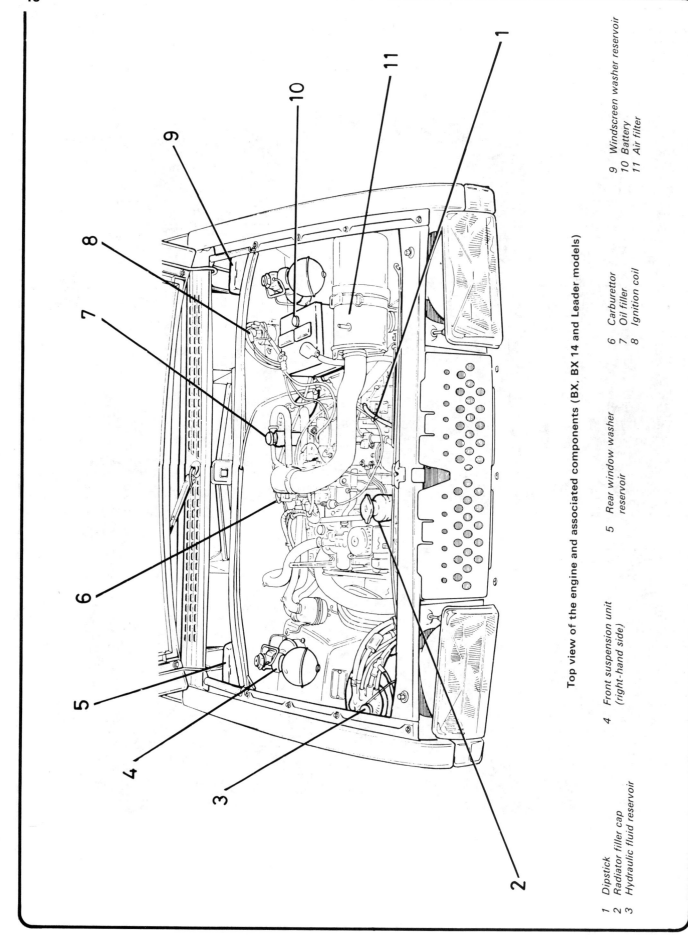

Top view of the engine and associated components (BX, BX 14 and Leader models)

1 Dipstick
2 Radiator filler cap
3 Hydraulic fluid reservoir

4 Front suspension unit (right-hand side)
5 Rear window washer reservoir

6 Carburettor
7 Oil filler
8 Ignition coil

9 Windscreen washer reservoir
10 Battery
11 Air filter

Every 250 miles (400 km) or weekly – whichever comes first

Steering
Check the tyre pressures (Chapter 7)
Examine the tyres for wear or damage (Chapter 7)

Lights, wipers and horns
Do all the lights work at the front and rear?
Are the headlamp beams aligned properly?
Check the windscreen washer fluid level. If necessary, top up the reservoir and include a screen wash, such as Turtle Wax High Tech Screen Wash

Engine
Check the level of the oil, top up if necessary (Chapter 1)
Check the level of the electrolyte in the conventional type battery and top up the level as necessary (Chapter 12)
Check coolant level and top up if necessary (Chapter 2)

Every 6000 miles (10 000 km) or every six months – whichever comes first

Engine
Change engine oil and renew filter element (Chapter 1)
Clean air filter element (Chapter 3)

Hydraulic system
Check the fluid level in the reservoir (Chapter 8)

Transmission
Check the automatic transmission fluid level and top up if necessary (Chapter 6)
Check and if necessary adjust the clutch (Chapter 5)

Brakes
Check disc pads for wear (Chapter 9)
Check brake hydraulic circuit for leaks, damaged pipes etc (Chapter 9)
Check handbrake and adjust if necessary (Chapter 9)
Check the discs for condition (Chapter 9)

Steering
Check front wheel alignment and adjust if necessary (Chapter 10)
Check for security and condition of steering gear and balljoints, and condition of rubber bellows and dust excluders (Chapter 10)

General
Examine exhaust system for corrosion and leakage (Chapter 3)
Lubricate all controls, linkages, door locks and hinges
Check all hydraulic lines for conditions and security

Every 12 000 miles (20 000 km) or annually – whichever comes first

Engine
Clean battery terminals (Chapter 12)
Check drivebelts tension and adjust if necessary (Chapters 8 and 12)

Renew spark plugs (Chapter 4)
Clean the crankcase ventilation hoses, renew if necessary
BX, BX 14 and Leader: Check and if necessary adjust the valve clearances (Chapter 1)
Check and if necessary adjust the engine idle speed (Chapter 3)
Renew fuel filter (BX 16 RE)

Clutch
Lubricate the clutch pedal and cable pivot points with grease

General
Check wiper blades and renew if necessary (Chapter 12)
Check seat belts and anchorages
Check front suspension lower balljoints (Chapter 10)
Check the condition of the wheel bearings (Chapter 7)

Every 18 000 miles (30 000 km) or every eighteen months – whichever comes first

Renew the air filter element (Chapter 3)
Clean the hydraulic system filters (Chapter 8)
Renew the air cleaner element (fuel injection engines)

Every 36 000 miles (60 000 km)

Drain and renew the hydraulic system fluid (Chapter 8)
Drain the cooling system and refill using new antifreeze (Chapter 2)
Drain and renew the automatic transmission fluid (Chapter 6)
Renew the camshaft drivebelt – not applicable to models with the type 150 engine (Chapter 1 or 13). **Note:** *Although this task is not specifically required by the manufacturers, it is recommended that the belt be renewed at this mileage, as a precaution against engine damage should the belt fail in service.*

Every 48 000 miles (80 000 km)

Renew the fuel filter – fuel-injected BX 16 models

Every 60 000 miles (100 000 km)

Drain and renew the manual transmission oil – BX 16 and BX 19 models (Chapter 6)
Renew the fuel filter – fuel-injected BX 19 models

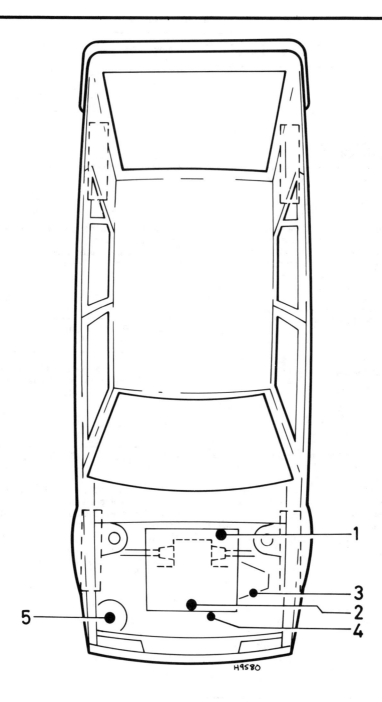

Recommended lubricants and fluids

Component or system	Lubricant type/specification	Duckhams recommendation
1 Engine/gearbox (BX and BX 14, up to August 1988)	Multigrade engine oil, viscosity SAE 15W/40 or 20W/50	Duckhams Hypergrade
2 Engine (BX 14, August 1988 on, BX 16 and BX 19)	Multigrade engine oil, viscosity SAE 15W/40 or 20W/50	Duckhams Hypergrade
3 Manual gearbox (type BT, BL, BN and MA)	Gear oil, viscosity SAE 75W/80W	Duckhams Hypoid PT 75W/80
4 Automatic transmission	Dexron IID type ATF	Duckhams Uni-Matic or D-Matic
5 Hydraulic system	Green LHM fluid	Duckhams LHM fluid

Fault diagnosis

Introduction

The vehicle owner who does his or her own maintenance according to the recommended schedules should not have to use this section of the manual very often. Modern component reliability is such that, provided those items subject to wear or deterioration are inspected or renewed at the specified intervals, sudden failure is comparatively rare. Faults do not usually just happen as a result of sudden failure, but develop over a period of time. Major mechanical failures in particular are usually preceded by characteristic symptoms over hundreds or even thousands of miles. Those components which do occasionally fail without warning are often small and easily carried in the vehicle.

With any fault finding, the first step is to decide where to begin investigations. Sometimes this is obvious, but on other occasions a little detective work will be necessary. The owner who makes half a dozen haphazard adjustments or replacements may be successful in curing a fault (or its symptoms), but he will be none the wiser if the fault recurs and he may well have spent more time and money than was necessary. A calm and logical approach will be found to be more satisfactory in the long run. Always take into account any warning signs or abnormalities that may have been noticed in the period preceding the fault – power loss, high or low gauge readings, unusual noises or smells, etc – and remember that failure of components such as fuses or spark plugs may only be pointers to some underlying fault.

The pages which follow here are intended to help in cases of failure to start or breakdown on the road. There is also a Fault Diagnosis Section at the end of each Chapter which should be consulted if the preliminary checks prove unfruitful. Whatever the fault, certain basic principles apply. These are as follows:

Verify the fault. This is simply a matter of being sure that you know what the symptoms are before starting work. This is particularly important if you are investigating a fault for someone else who may not have described it very accurately.

Don't overlook the obvious. For example, if the vehicle won't start, is there petrol in the tank? (Don't take anyone else's word on this particular point, and don't trust the fuel gauge either!) If an electrical fault is indicated, look for loose or broken wires before digging out the test gear.

Cure the disease, not the symptom. Substituting a flat battery with a fully charged one will get you off the hard shoulder, but if the underlying cause is not attended to, the new battery will go the same way. Similarly, changing oil-fouled spark plugs for a new set will get you moving again, but remember that the reason for the fouling (if it wasn't simply an incorrect grade of plug) will have to be established and corrected.

Don't take anything for granted. Particularly, don't forget that a 'new' component may itself be defective (especially if it's been rattling round in the boot for months), and don't leave components out of a fault diagnosis sequence just because they are new or recently fitted. When you do finally diagnose a difficult fault, you'll probably realise that all the evidence was there from the start.

Electrical faults

Electrical faults can be more puzzling than straightforward mechanical failures, but they are no less susceptible to logical analysis if the basic principles of operation are understood. Vehicle electrical wiring exists in extremely unfavourable conditions – heat, vibration and chemical attack – and the first things to look for are loose or corroded connections and broken or chafed wires, especially where the wires pass through holes in the bodywork or are subject to vibration.

All metal-bodied vehicles in current production have one pole of the battery 'earthed', ie connected to the vehicle bodywork, and in nearly all modern vehicles it is the negative (–) terminal. The various electrical components – motors, bulb holders etc – are also connected to earth, either by means of a lead or directly by their mountings. Electric current flows through the component and then back to the battery via the bodywork. If the component mounting is loose or corroded, or if a good path back to the battery is not available, the circuit will be incomplete and malfunction will result. The engine and/or gearbox are also earthed by means of flexible metal straps to the body or subframe; if these straps are loose or missing, starter motor, generator and ignition trouble may result.

Assuming the earth return to be satisfactory, electrical faults will be due either to component malfunction or to defects in the current supply. Individual components are dealt with in Chapter 12. If supply wires are broken or cracked internally this results in an open-circuit, and the easiest way to check for this is to bypass the suspect wire temporarily with a length of wire having a crocodile clip or suitable connector at each end. Alternatively, a 12V test lamp can be used to verify the presence of supply voltage at various points along the wire and the break can be thus isolated.

If a bare portion of a live wire touches the bodywork or other earthed metal part, the electricity will take the low-resistance path thus formed back to the battery: this is known as a short-circuit. Hopefully a short-circuit will blow a fuse, but otherwise it may cause burning of the insulation (and possibly further short-circuits) or even a fire. This is why it is inadvisable to bypass persistently blowing fuses with silver foil or wire.

Spares and tool kit

Most vehicles are supplied only with sufficient tools for wheel changing; the *Maintenance and minor repair* tool kit detailed in *Tools and working facilities*, with the addition of a hammer, is probably sufficient for those repairs that most motorists would consider attempting at the roadside. In addition a few items which can be fitted without too much trouble in the event of a breakdown should be carried. Experience and available space will modify the list below, but the following may save having to call on professional assistance:

Spark plugs, clean and correctly gapped
HT lead and plug cap – long enough to reach the plug furthest from the distributor
Distributor rotor and distributor cap
Drivebelt(s) – emergency type may suffice
Spare fuses
Set of principal light bulbs
Tin of radiator sealer and hose bandage
Exhaust bandage
Roll of insulating tape
Length of soft iron wire
Length of electrical flex
Torch or inspection lamp (can double as test lamp)
Battery jump leads
Tow-rope
Moisture dispersant aerosol such as Holts Wet Start
Litre of engine oil
Sealed can of hydraulic fluid
Emergency windscreen
Worm drive clips

Carrying a few spares can save a long walk!

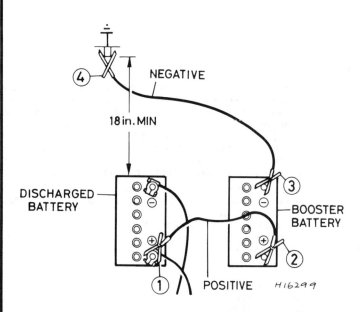

Jump start lead connections for negative earth vehicles –
connect leads in order shown

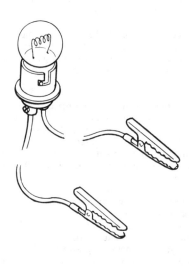

Simple test lamp is useful for tracing electrical faults

If spare fuel is carried, a can designed for the purpose should be used to minimise risks of leakage and collision damage. A first aid kit and a warning triangle, whilst not at present compulsory in the UK, are obviously sensible items to carry in addition to the above.

When touring abroad it may be advisable to carry additional spares which, even if you cannot fit them yourself, could save having to wait while parts are obtained. The items below may be worth considering:

Clutch and throttle cables
Cylinder head gasket
Alternator brushes
Tyre valve core

One of the motoring organisations will be able to advise on availability of fuel etc in foreign countries.

Engine will not start

Engine fails to turn when starter operated
Flat battery (recharge, use jump leads, or push start)
Battery terminals loose or corroded
Battery earth to body defective
Engine earth strap loose or broken
Starter motor (or solenoid) wiring loose or broken
Ignition/starter switch faulty
Major mechanical failure (seizure)
Starter or solenoid internal fault (see Chapter 12)

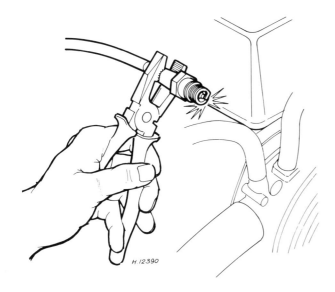

Crank engine and check for spark. Note use of insulated tool

Starter motor turns engine slowly
Partially discharged battery (recharge, use jump leads, or push start)
Battery terminals loose or corroded
Battery earth to body defective
Engine earth strap loose
Starter motor (or solenoid) wiring loose
Starter motor internal fault (see Chapter 12)

Starter motor spins without turning engine
Flywheel gear teeth damaged or worn
Starter motor mounting bolts loose

Engine turns normally but fails to start
Damp or dirty HT leads and distributor cap (crank engine and check for spark)

No fuel in tank (check for delivery at carburettor or fuel filter, as applicable)
Excessive choke (hot engine) or insufficient choke (cold engine)
Fouled or incorrectly gapped spark plugs (remove, clean and regap)
Other ignition system fault (see Chapter 4)
Other fuel system fault (see Chapter 3)
Poor compression
Major mechanical failure (eg camshaft drive)

Engine fires but will not run
Insufficient choke (cold engine)
Air leaks at carburettor or inlet manifold
Fuel starvation (see Chapter 3)
Ignition fault (see Chapter 4)

Engine cuts out and will not restart

Engine cuts out suddenly – ignition fault
Loose or disconnected LT wires
Wet HT leads or distributor cap (after traversing water splash)
Coil failure (check for spark)
Other ignition fault (see Chapter 4)

Engine misfires before cutting out – fuel fault
Fuel tank empty
Fuel pump defective or filter blocked (check for delivery)
Fuel tank filler vent blocked (suction will be evident on releasing cap)
Carburettor needle valve sticking, where applicable
Carburettor jets blocked (fuel contaminated), where applicable
Other fuel system fault (see Chapter 3)

Engine cuts out – other causes
Serious overheating
Major mechanical failure (eg camshaft drive)

Engine overheats

Ignition warning light not illuminated
Coolant loss due to internal or external leakage (see Chapter 2)
Thermostat defective
Low oil level
Brakes binding
Radiator clogged externally or internally
Electric cooling fan not operating correctly
Engine waterways clogged
Ignition timing incorrect or automatic advance malfunctioning
Mixture too weak

Note: *Do not add cold water to an overheated engine or damage may result*

Low engine oil pressure

Gauge reads low or warning light illuminated with engine running
Oil level low or incorrect grade
Defective gauge or sender unit
Wire to sender unit earthed
Engine overheating
Oil filter clogged or bypass valve defective
Oil pressure relief valve defective
Oil pick-up strainer clogged
Oil pump worn
Worn main or big-end bearings
Note: *Low oil pressure in a high-mileage engine at tickover is not necessarily a cause for concern. Sudden pressure loss at speed is far more significant. In any event, check the gauge or warning light sender before condemning the engine.*

Engine noises

Pre-ignition (pinking) on acceleration
Incorrect grade of fuel
Ignition timing incorrect
Distributor faulty or worn
Worn or maladjusted carburettor, where applicable
Excessive carbon build-up in engine

Whistling or wheezing noises
Leaking vacuum hose
Leaking carburettor or manifold gasket, as applicable
Blowing head gasket

Tapping or rattling
Incorrect valve clearances
Worn valve gear
Worn timing chain or belt
Broken piston ring (ticking noise)

Knocking or thumping
Unintentional mechanical contact
Peripheral component fault (alternator, water pump etc)
Worn big-end bearings (regular heavy knocking, perhaps less under load)
Worn main bearings (rumbling and knocking, perhaps worsening under load)
Piston slap (most noticeable when cold)

Chapter 1 Engine

For modifications, and information applicable to later models, see Supplement at end of manual

Contents

Specifications

General (all engines)
Engine type .... Four-cylinder, in-line, ohc, water cooled, transverse mounting

Engine type reference
BX .... 150 A (XY6C)
BX 14 .... 150 C (XY6D)
BX 16 .... 171 B or C (XU5S)
BX 19 .... 159 A (XU9S)

General details

	150 A	150 C	171 B and C	159 A
Bore (mm)	75	75	83	83
Stroke (mm)	77	77	73	88
Cubic capacity (cc)	1360	1360	1580	1905
Maximum power DIN (BHP)	62 at	72 at	92 (94*) at	105 at
	5500 rpm	5750 rpm	6000 rpm	5600 rpm
Maximum torque DIN (lbf ft)	79.4 at	79.4 at	96.9 at	88.1 at
	2500 rpm	3000 rpm	3500 rpm	2000 rpm
Compression ratio	9.3:1	9.3:1	9.5:1	9.3:1

* 171 C engine from October 1984

Location of No 1 cylinder .... At clutch end of block
Firing order .... 1 - 3 - 4 - 2
Direction of rotation .... Clockwise viewed from pulley end
Lubricant type/specification .... Multigrade engine oil, viscosity SAE 15W/40 or 20W/50 (Duckhams Hypergrade)

Engine type 150
Cylinder head
Type .... Aluminium alloy, bi-spherical combustion chambers, offset valves and five bearings for the camshaft
Maximum allowable distortion .... 0.05 mm

Valves

	Inlet	Exhaust
Head diameter (mm)	36.8	29.3
Stem diameter	8	8
Seat contact surface width – maximum (mm)	1.45	1.80
Seat angle	120°	90°
Valve length (mm)	113.19 to 113.63	113.11 to 114.01
Valve springs:		
Wire diameter (mm)	4.3	4.3
Length under load (mm/kg)	41/26	30/77

Valve timing

	150 A engine	150 C engine
Valve lift (mm)	7.25	8.25
Camshaft identification mark	A	S
Inlet valve opens*	4° ATDC	0° ATDC
Inlet valve closes*	29° ABDC	42° ABDC
Exhaust valve opens*	30° BBDC	43° BBDC
Exhaust valve closes*	5° BTDC	1° BTDC

*with valve clearance of 0.7 mm

Valve rocker clearance (cold)

Inlet (mm)	0.10 to 0.15
Exhaust (mm)	0.20 to 0.30

Camshaft

Endfloat (mm)	0.07 to 0.17

Crankshaft and main bearings

Number of bearings	Five
Crankshaft endfloat (mm)	0.07 to 0.27
Thrust washer thicknesses (mm)	2.40, 2.50, 2.55, 2.60
Minimum allowable ovality of crankpins and journals (mm)	0.007
Main bearing journals:	
Standard diameter (mm)	49.981 to 49.965
Regrind diameter (mm)	49.681 to 49.665
Crankpins:	
Standard diameter (mm)	45

Connecting rods

Small-end bush diameter (mm)	19.463 to 19.476
Big-end diameter (mm)	48.655 to 48.671

Cylinder liners

Type	Cast iron, wet type
Grades:	
Piston:	
A	One file mark
B	Two file marks
C	Three file marks
Cylinder liner base seal	O-ring
Liner protrusion – clamped or without seal (mm)	0.10 to 0.17
Maximum allowable projection difference between two liners (mm)	0.05
Piston offset (mm)	1.0

Pistons

Type	Aluminium alloy, two compression and one oil control ring. Gudgeon pin free in piston, interference fit in connecting rod
Piston fitting direction	Arrow mark on crown points to the timing gear (DT)
Gudgeon pin classes	Three, colour-coded to marks on piston crown
Running clearance (mm)	0.07 to 0.09

Lubrication system

Minimum oil pressure at 4000 rpm	3 bar	
Low pressure warning	0.6 bar	
Oil capacity:	**150 A**	**150 C**
New or reconditioned engine	5.0 litres (8.8 pints)	5.5 litres (9.7 pints)
After draining	4.5 litres (7.9 pints)	5.0 litres (8.8 pints)
Dipstick minimum to maximum	1 litre (1.76 pints)	1 litre (1.76 pints)
Oil filter (up to July 1988)	Champion C204	Champion C204

Oil pump

Maximum lobe-to-body clearance (mm)	0.064

Torque wrench settings

	kgf m	lbf ft
Rocker cover	1.0	7.2
Rocker adjuster screw locknuts	1.7	12.3
Camshaft retaining plate bolt	1.8	13.0
Cylinder head bolts:		
Stage 1	5.0	36.1
Stage 2	7.75	56.0
Crankshaft pulley nut	14.0	101.2
Timing cover bolts	1.2	8.6
Timing chain guide plate bolts	0.6	4.3
Timing chain tensioner (both types)	0.6	4.3
Camshaft sprocket bolt	7.5	54.2
Oil pressure switch	2.0	14.5
Coolant temperature sender unit	4.5	32.5
Sump	1.0	7.2
Sump drain plug	2.8	20.2
Oil suction strainer bolts	1.0	7.2
Clutch casing bolts	1.0	7.2
Flywheel bolts	6.8	50.0
Connecting rod big-end cap bolts	3.75	27
Gearbox to engine	1.5	11.0
Engine mountings – refer to Fig. 1.16:		
A	5.0	36.1
B	2.2	16.0
C	3.5	25
Main bearing/casing bolts:		
Stage 1	3.75	27.1
Stage 2	5.25	38
Crankcase flange housing bolts	1.0	7.2

Engine type 171
Cylinder head
Type .... Aluminium alloy, in-line valves and five camshaft bearings
Maximum allowable distortion .... 0.05 mm

Valves

	Inlet	Exhaust
Head diameter (mm)	40	32
Stem diameter (mm)	7.98 to 7.83	7.96 to 7.81
Seat angle	90°	90°
Valve guide bore diameter (mm)	8.0 to 8.022	8.0 to 8.022
Valve length (mm)	107.49 ± 0.1	106.92 ± 0.1
Valve springs:		
Wire diameter:	4.4 mm	4.4 mm
Length under load (mm/kg)	40.5/41	30.0/80

Valve timing
Valve lift (mm) .... 10.4 or 9.7 (from December 1983)
Inlet valve opens* .... 0° 48' BTDC
Inlet valve closes* .... 37° ABDC
Exhaust valve opens* .... 35° 36' BBDC
Exhaust valve closes* .... 2° 12' ATDC
*with valve clearance of 1.0 mm

Valve clearances (cold)
Inlet (mm) .... 0.15 to 0.25
Exhaust (mm) .... 0.35 to 0.45
Valve clearance adjustment shim thickness .... 2.225 mm to 3.025 mm (in steps of 0.025 mm)
3.100 mm to 3.550 mm (in steps of 0.075 mm)

Camshaft
Endfloat (mm) .... 0.07 to 0.16

Crankshaft and main bearings
Number of bearings .... Five
Crankshaft endfloat (mm) .... 0.07 to 0.27
Thrust washer thickness (mm) 2.30, 2.35, 2.40, 2.45, 2.50
Maximum allowable ovality of crankpins and journals (mm) 0.007
Crank journal dimensions:
    Standard diameter (mm) .... 60.0 to 59.981
    Regrind diameter (mm) .... 59.7 to 59.681
Standard main bearing thicknesses (mm) 1.842
Replacement main bearing thickness after regrind (mm) 1.992
Crankpin dimensions:
    Standard diameter (mm) 45
    Regrind diameter (mm) 44.7
    Standard bearing thickness (mm) 1.817
    Replacement bearing thickness after regrind (mm) 1.967

Connecting rods
Small-end bore diameter (mm)	22
Small-end to gudgeon pin (mm)	0.020 to 0.041
Big-end bore diameter (mm)	48.655

Cylinder liners
Type	Cast iron, wet type
Grades:	
Piston:	
A	One file mark
B	Two file marks
C	Three file marks
Cylinder liner base seal	O-ring
Liner protrusion – damped or without seal (mm)	0.08 to 0.15
Maximum allowable projection difference between two liners (mm)	0.05
Piston offset (mm)	1.5

Pistons
	As engine types 150 A and 150 C

Lubrication system
Oil pressure at 4000 rpm	3.5 bar
Oil pressure switch calibration:	
Operates between	0.44 and 0.58 bar
Stops operating at	0.8 bar (maximum)
Oil capacity:	
New or reconditioned engine	5.2 litres (9.1 pints)
After draining	5.0 litres (8.8 pints)
Dipstick minimum to maximum	1.5 litres (2.6 pints)
Oil filter	Champion F104

Torque wrench settings
	kgf m	lbf ft
Cam cover	1.0	7.2
Camshaft bearing cap bolts	1.5	11.0
Camshaft sprocket	8.0	58.0
Camshaft stop (thrust plate)	1.5	11.0
Camshaft inner cover	0.7	5.0
Exhaust manifold	2.2	16.0
Inlet manifold	2.2	16.0
Spark plugs	1.8	13.0
Timing covers	0.8	5.7
Mounting bracket	2.0	15.0
Cylinder head bolts:		
Stage 1	6.0	43.0
Stage 2 (after slackening)	2.0	15.0
Stage 3:		
Hexagon headed bolts	Tighten a further 120°	Tighten a further 120°
Torx headed bolts	Tighten a further 300°	Tighten a further 300°
Timing belt tensioner	1.6	11.5
Timing belt tensioner lock cam (Interlock plunger)	1.5	11.0
Crankshaft pulley	11.0	80.0
Crankshaft main bearing cap bolts	5.3	38.0
Connecting rod big-end cap bolts	4.9	35.4
Sump bolts	1.9	13.7
Sump drain plug	3.0	21.7
Suction drain pipe nuts	0.5	3.6
Oil pump bolts	1.9	13.7
Crankshaft front cover	1.6	11.5
Flywheel bolts	4.9	35.4
Coolant temperature sender units	1.8	13.0
Engine mountings – refer to Fig. 1.54:		
A	3.5	25.0
B	2.8	20.0
C	2.3	16.6
D	4.5	33.0
E	1.8	13.0
F	5.0	36.0
G	2.0	15.0

Engine type 159
    The engine specification details are similar to those given for the 171 type engine except for the following items

Valves
	Inlet	Exhaust
Head diameter (mm)	39.5	33
Valve lift (mm)	10.3	10.3

Valve timing

Inlet valve opens*	–3° BTDC
Inlet valve closes*	46° ABDC
Exhaust valve opens*	40° BBDC
Exhaust valve closes*	2° ATDC

*with valve clearance of 1.0 mm

PART A: 150 ENGINE

1 General description

The 150 series engine fitted to the Citroën BX and BX 14 models is a four-cylinder, in-line, overhead camshaft engine. The engine is mounted transversely.

A manual gearbox is bolted to the bottom of the engine and uses a common oil system. The final drive to the roadwheels is via a differential unit on the front of the gearbox. Drive to the gearbox is via conventional clutch on the left-hand side of the engine, through an input pinion free-running on the crankshaft and located between the clutch and the engine block.

All the major casings and housings are manufactured from pressure die-cast aluminium alloy. The cylinder block has removable wet cylinder liners which are centrifugally cast from special iron alloy and the main bearing caps are made of cast iron. The cylinder head has bi-spherical squish effect combustion chambers, each having one exhaust valve, one inlet valve, and a taper seated spark plug location. Single springs are fitted to the valves which are operated by rockers, each incorporating an adjustable screw and locknut for valve clearance setting.

The aluminium alloy pistons are fitted with three rings, two compression and one 'perfect circle' scraper. The pistons are assembled to the forged steel connecting rods by a gudgeon pin which is a force fit in the connecting rod small-end.

The crankshaft is carried in five main bearings and the flywheel and clutch are bolted to its rear end in conventional manner. The other end is keyed to drive the camshaft chain sprocket and also a shaft by which the oil pump, fuel pump and distributor are driven.

Special notes

Because of the unusual layout of the engine and transmission systems, extra care and attention are necessary during maintenance and overhaul procedures which, in many instances, differ from more conventional systems.

Read through the various Sections concerned before tackling any job, and analyse the instructions, so that any snags or possible difficulties can be noted in advance. Because the sub-assembly castings are made from aluminium alloy it is of utmost importance that, where specified, all fastenings are tightened to the correct torque and, in some instances, in the correct sequence.

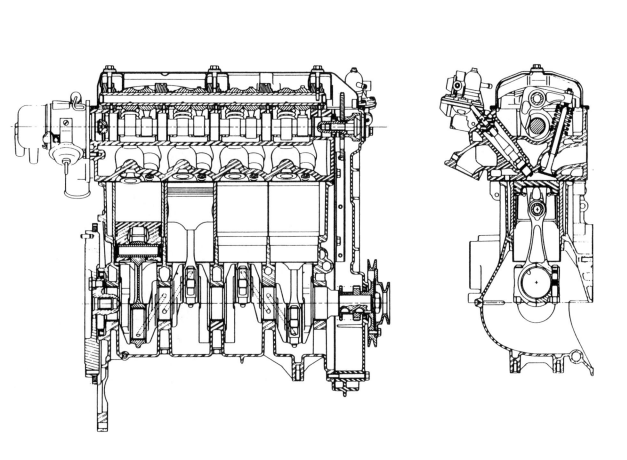

Fig. 1.1 Sectional view of the 150 engine (Sec 1)

2 Routine maintenance

The following maintenance procedures must be carried out at the specified intervals given at the front of this manual.

1 **Engine oil level check:** The engine oil level check must be made with the vehicle parked on level ground. If possible, allow the engine to cool off before checking the oil level which must be kept between the minimum and maximum markings on the dipstick. Withdraw the dipstick, wipe it clean and fully reinsert it. Withdraw the dipstick and now observe the oil level reading. If required top up the oil level through the filler neck on the rocker cover. Do not overfill.

2 **Engine oil change:** Position a suitable container beneath the sump drain plug (raise the vehicle to its full height setting to allow improved clearance and support it on axle stands). Unscrew the plug and allow the oil to drain into the container (photo).

3 Refit and tighten the plug when draining is completed. If the oil filter is to be renewed, do this before topping-up the engine/transmission oil. Use only the correct grade and quantity of oil.

4 **Oil filter renewal:** Renew the oil filter at the specified intervals, referring to Section 4 for details.

5 **General:** Occasionally check the engine and associated components for signs of oil, fuel and coolant leaks and make any repairs as necessary.

6 Remove the oil filler cap and hoses and wash through in petrol.

3 Lubrication system – description

1 A forced feed lubrication system common to engine and transmission is employed and is shown in Fig. 1.3. The oil pump is attached to the crankcase in the lower section of the timing chest and it incorporates the pressure relief valve. The pump is driven by gears from the crankshaft.

2 Oil from the pump passes via an oilway to the oil filter, and thence to the crankshaft main bearings, connecting rod bearings and transmission components. Another oilway from the filter delivers oil to the overhead camshaft and rocker components. Oil from the cylinder head passes to the transfer gear housing and then back to the sump contained within the transmission housing.

3 Apart from the standard replaceable canister filter located on the outside of the crankcase there is a gauze filter incorporated in the oil pump suction intake.

4 The oil level must be correctly maintained by reference to the dipstick. The oil filler cap is in the rocker cover. An oil pressure warning switch is fitted which illuminates a warning light in the instrument panel should a drop in pressure occur.

4 Oil filter – removal and refitting

1 The oil filter is contained in a canister mounted just above the alternator and is renewed as a complete assembly when a filter change is due.

2 To remove the filter canister a strap or chain wrench is necessary, but if one of these is not available, pierce the side of the canister with a long pointed tool and use this as a lever to unscrew the canister from its mounting. Be prepared for oil spillage.

3 The new filter will be supplied with a new oil seal mounted in it. Before fitting the filter, carefully remove the seal and apply a little clean engine oil between the seal and canister, then refit the seal.

4 Clean the outer face of the seal and its contact face on the engine and screw the canister down by hand only, until the seal contacts the face. Then tighten it a further $3/4$ of a turn (photo).

5 After renewing a filter always check for oil leaks when the engine is next run and top up the engine oil.

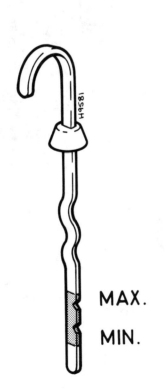

Fig. 1.2 Engine oil level dipstick. Oil requirement if at minimum level is 1.0 litre (1.76 pints) (Sec 2)

2.2 Sump drain plug (150 engine)

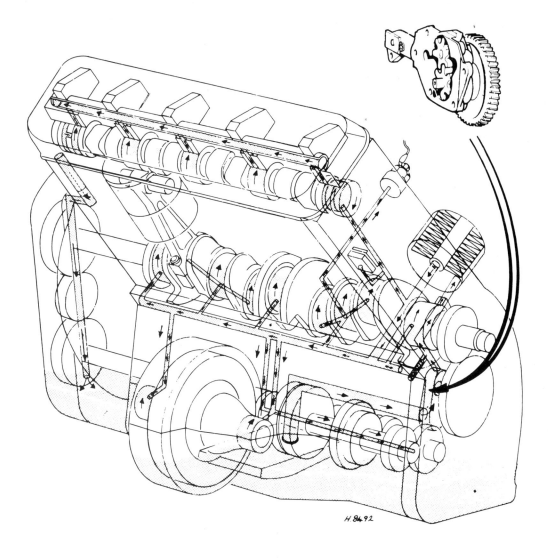

Fig. 1.3 Lubrication system (150 engine) (Sec 3)

4.4 Fitting the oil filter cartridge (150 engine)

5 Major operations possible with engine installed

The following operations are possible with the engine in the vehicle:

(a) *Removal and refitting of the cylinder head*
(b) *Removal and refitting of the clutch unit*
(c) *Removal and refitting of the engine mountings*
(d) *Removal and refitting of the timing case*

Note: *some tasks can only be achieved with the aid of special Citroën tools.*

6 Major operations requiring engine removal

The engine must be removed for the following operations:

(a) *Removal and refitting of the transmission unit*
(b) *Removal and refitting of the crankshaft and main bearings.*
(c) *Removal and refitting of the piston and connecting rod assemblies*
(d) *Renewal of the big-end bearings*

7 Valve rocker clearances – checking and adjustment

1   This operation is the same whether carried out with the engine installed or on the bench. If installed it must only be done when the engine is cold. The importance of correct rocker arm clearances cannot be overstressed as they vitally affect the performance of the engine. If the clearances are too big, engine efficiency is reduced as the valves open too late and close too early. On the other hand inadequate clearances may prevent the valves closing when the engine is warmed up, resulting in burnt valve seats and possible warping.

2   If the engine is in position in the vehicle, remove the rocker cover.

3   The engine will need to be progressively turned over when checking the rocker/valve clearances. To do this, raise the front of the vehicle so that a roadwheel is clear of the ground, then turn the roadwheel with 4th gear engaged and turn the engine over as required. Removal of the spark plugs when checking and adjusting its clearances will allow the engine to be turned over more easily.

4   It is important that the clearance is set only when the rocker of the valve being adjusted rests on the heel of the cam; that is, directly opposite the peak of the cam. This can be ensured by carrying out the adjustments in the following sequence, which also avoids turning the engine more than necessary:

Valve fully open	Adjust valve numbers
1 exhaust	*3 inlet and 4 exhaust*
3 exhaust	*4 inlet and 2 exhaust*
4 exhaust	*2 inlet and 1 exhaust*
2 exhaust	*1 inlet and 3 exhaust*

The correct clearances are listed in the Specifications. The valve locations can be determined from the position of the manifolds.

5   Set the clearances by positioning a valve fully open and inserting a feeler gauge in the gap between the rocker arm and valve stem of the appropriate valve. Loosen the locknut with a spanner and turn the adjuster screw with a screwdriver (photo). Adjust the screw so that the feeler gauge slides in the gap with a slight drag. Tighten the locknut, recheck the clearance and readjust if necessary. Repeat until all clearances have been set.

6   Checking and setting the valve clearances must always be carried out after removing and refitting the cylinder head and also whenever the cylinder head bolts are retightened following overhaul (see Section 8).

7   Check that the rocker cover seal is in good condition, renewing it if in doubt, and refit the cover. Fit new sealing washers under the retaining bolts and tighten the bolts. Refit the air cleaner on an installed engine.

7.5 Adjusting a valve rocker clearance

8 Cylinder head – removal and refitting (with engine installed)

1   The cylinder head can be removed and refitted with the engine in position in the vehicle, but a Citroën special tool will be required to hold the camshaft sprocket and prevent the timing chain from falling down into the timing case. This tool is part number 7012-T and comprises three items referred to as N1, N2 and N3. If possible borrow or hire this tool.

2   When the cylinder head is being removed there is a risk of disturbing the wet liners in their locations. Because of this certain checks are necessary to confirm that the liners are correctly located. If it is found that they are not within permissible limits, new O-rings will have to be fitted between the liners and the cylinder block. *This job will entail removal of the engine/transmission unit from the car and the virtual complete dismantling of the unit on the bench.* It can be seen that removing the cylinder head on this engine, when installed, should only be undertaken if full facilities are available to remove and dismantle the engine – even though they may not be required. Alternatively, be prepared to have the car towed to your Citroën agent if the liner O-rings have to be removed.

3   First disconnect the battery earth lead.

4   Drain the cooling system, referring to Chapter 2 for further details if necessary.

5   Drain the engine/gearbox oil.

6   Raise and support the vehicle on safety stands.

7   From underneath the vehicle, undo the two retaining nuts and disconnect the exhaust downpipe at the ball socket connection. Disconnect the warm air feed pipe.

8   Disconnect the following hoses, referring to Fig. 1.5, and position them out of the way:

   (a) *Heater hoses at the bulkhead*
   (b) *Water pump hoses, or unbolt the water pump*
   (c) *Cylinder head hose*
   (d) *Thermostat hose*
   (e) *Heater hoses to the carburettor*
   (f) *Carburettor fuel feed and return hoses. Plug or clamp these hoses*

9   Disconnect the ignition HT and LT wiring from the plugs and distributor. Position the wiring harness out of the way.

10   Remove the spark plugs using the spanner supplied with the vehicle.

11   Disconnect the accelerator cable from the carburettor and position it out of the way.

12   Remove the cooling system de-aerator unit.

13   Remove the hose carrier from the timing cover.

14   Unbolt and remove the fuel pump and withdraw the operating rod (Chapter 3).

15   Remove the distributor, as described in Chapter 4.

16   Unbolt and remove the rocker cover.

17   Disconnect the following items, noting their connections:

   (a) *Idle cut-off lead from the carburettor*
   (b) *Water temperature sensor lead*
   (c) *Earth cables to the cylinder head*
   (d) *The econoscope vacuum hose on the inlet manifold*

18   Referring to Fig. 1.6, unscrew and remove the extended head bolt (12) and the end plate (13) which is secured by two bolts. Loosen but do not remove the extended head bolt (11).

19   Unscrew and remove the bolt retaining the timing gear to the end of the camshaft. Do not disturb the gear as the bolt is withdrawn.

20   Lubricate the special tool (7012-T) with oil and fit it into position. Fit the clamp onto the timing case, but do not fully tighten the bolts. The mandrel groove must engage with the fuel pump control cam pin. Tighten the mandrel onto the camshaft. The camshaft and mandrel grooves must be in alignment (Fig. 1.7). Mark the relative positions.

21   Turn the engine over slowly so that the mandrel groove mark can be seen to be positioned within the upper quarter of the timing cover face. In this position fully tighten the clamp bolts.

22   Loosen the camshaft retaining plate bolt and withdraw the plate from its groove, then retighten the bolt.

23   Position a piece of modelling clay or similar compound under the front left-hand cylinder head nut to keep it in position when the bolt is

Are your plugs trying to tell you something?

Normal.
Grey-brown deposits, lightly coated core nose. Plugs ideally suited to engine, and engine in good condition.

Heavy Deposits.
A build up of crusty deposits, light-grey sandy colour in appearance.
Fault: Often caused by worn valve guides, excessive use of upper cylinder lubricant, or idling for long periods.

Lead Glazing.
Plug insulator firing tip appears yellow or green/yellow and shiny in appearance.
Fault: Often caused by incorrect carburation, excessive idling followed by sharp acceleration. Also check ignition timing.

Carbon fouling.
Dry, black, sooty deposits.
Fault: over-rich fuel mixture.
Check: carburettor mixture settings, float level, choke operation, air filter.

Oil fouling.
Wet, oily deposits. Fault: worn bores/piston rings or valve guides; sometimes occurs (temporarily) during running-in period.

Overheating.
Electrodes have glazed appearance, core nose very white – few deposits. Fault: plug overheating. Check: plug value, ignition timing, fuel octane rating (too low) and fuel mixture (too weak).

Electrode damage.
Electrodes burned away; core nose has burned, glazed appearance. Fault: pre-ignition. Check: for correct heat range and as for 'overheating'.

Split core nose.
(May appear initially as a crack). Fault: detonation or wrong gap-setting technique. Check: ignition timing, cooling system, fuel mixture (too weak).

WHY DOUBLE COPPER IS BETTER FOR YOUR ENGINE.

Unique Trapezoidal Copper Cored Earth Electrode — 50% Larger Spark Area — Copper Cored Centre Electrode

Champion Double Copper plugs are the first in the world to have copper core in both centre and earth electrode. This innovative design means that they run cooler by up to 100°C – giving greater efficiency and longer life. These double copper cores transfer heat away from the tip of the plug faster and more efficiently. Therefore, Double Copper runs at cooler temperatures than conventional plugs giving improved acceleration response and high speed performance with no fear of pre-ignition.

Champion Double Copper plugs also feature a unique trapezoidal earth electrode giving a 50% increase in spark area. This, together with the double copper cores, offers greatly reduced electrode wear, so the spark stays stronger for longer.

 FASTER COLD STARTING

 FOR UNLEADED OR LEADED FUEL

 ELECTRODES UP TO 100°C COOLER

 BETTER ACCELERATION RESPONSE

 LOWER EMISSIONS

 50% BIGGER SPARK AREA

THE LONGER LIFE PLUG

Plug Tips/Hot and Cold.
Spark plugs must operate within well-defined temperature limits to avoid cold fouling at one extreme and overheating at the other.
Champion and the car manufacturers work out the best plugs for an engine to give optimum performance under all conditions, from freezing cold starts to sustained high speed motorway cruising.
Plugs are often referred to as hot or cold. With Champion, the higher the number on its body, the hotter the plug, and the lower the number the cooler the plug.

Plug Cleaning
Modern plug design and materials mean that Champion no longer recommends periodic plug cleaning. Certainly don't clean your plugs with a wire brush as this can cause metal conductive paths across the nose of the insulator so impairing its performance and resulting in loss of acceleration and reduced m.p.g.
However, if plugs are removed, always carefully clean the area where the plug seats in the cylinder head as grit and dirt can sometimes cause gas leakage.
Also wipe any traces of oil or grease from plug leads as this may lead to arcing.

CHAMPION

DOUBLE ◀◀ COPPER

1

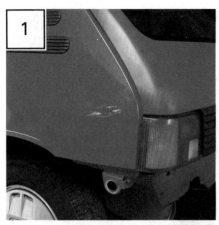

This photographic sequence shows the steps taken to repair the dent and paintwork damage shown above. In general, the procedure for repairing a hole will be similar; where there are substantial differences, the procedure is clearly described and shown in a separate photograph.

2

First remove any trim around the dent, then hammer out the dent where access is possible. This will minimise filling. Here, after the large dent has been hammered out, the damaged area is being made slightly concave.

3

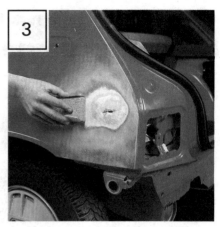

Next, remove all paint from the damaged area by rubbing with coarse abrasive paper or using a power drill fitted with a wire brush or abrasive pad. 'Feather' the edge of the boundary with good paintwork using a finer grade of abrasive paper.

4

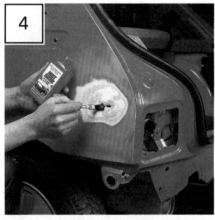

Where there are holes or other damage, the sheet metal should be cut away before proceeding further. The damaged area and any signs of rust should be treated with Turtle Wax Hi-Tech Rust Eater, which will also inhibit further rust formation.

5

For a large dent or hole mix Holts Body Plus Resin and Hardener according to the manufacturer's instructions and apply around the edge of the repair. Press Glass Fibre Matting over the repair area and leave for 20-30 minutes to harden. Then ...

5A

... brush more Holts Body Plus Resin and Hardener onto the matting and leave to harden. Repeat the sequence with two or three layers of matting, checking that the final layer is lower than the surrounding area. Apply Holts Body Plus Filler Paste as shown in Step 5B.

5B

For a medium dent, mix Holts Body Plus Filler Paste and Hardener according to the manufacturer's instructions and apply it with a flexible applicator. Apply thin layers of filler at 20-minute intervals, until the filler surface is slightly proud of the surrounding bodywork.

5C

For small dents and scratches use Holts No Mix Filler Paste straight from the tube. Apply it according to the instructions in thin layers, using the spatula provided. It will harden in minutes if applied outdoors and may then be used as its own knifing putty.

6

Use a plane or file for initial shaping. Then, using progressively finer grades of wet-and-dry paper, wrapped round a sanding block, and copious amounts of clean water, rub down the filler until glass smooth. 'Feather' the edges of adjoining paintwork.

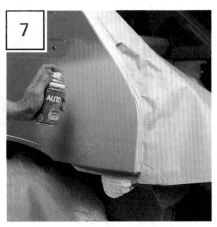

Protect adjoining areas before spraying the whole repair area and at least one inch of the surrounding sound paintwork with Holts Dupli-Color primer.

Fill any imperfections in the filler surface with a small amount of Holts Body Plus Knifing Putty. Using plenty of clean water, rub down the surface with a fine grade wet-and-dry paper – 400 grade is recommended – until it is really smooth.

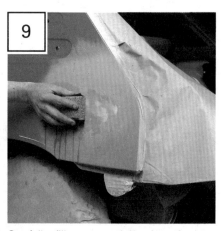

Carefully fill any remaining imperfections with knifing putty before applying the last coat of primer. Then rub down the surface with Holts Body Plus Rubbing Compound to ensure a really smooth surface.

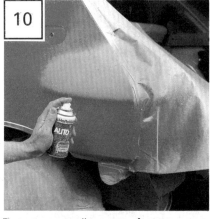

Protect surrounding areas from overspray before applying the topcoat in several thin layers. Agitate Holts Dupli-Color aerosol thoroughly. Start at the repair centre, spraying outwards with a side-to-side motion.

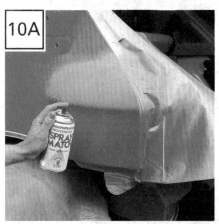

If the exact colour is not available off the shelf, local Holts Professional Spraymatch Centres will custom fill an aerosol to match perfectly.

To identify whether a lacquer finish is required, rub a painted unrepaired part of the body with wax and a clean cloth.

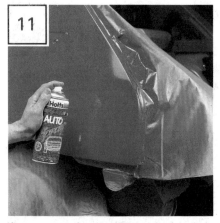

If *no* traces of paint appear on the cloth, spray Holts Dupli-Color clear lacquer over the repaired area to achieve the correct gloss level.

The paint will take about two weeks to harden fully. After this time it can be 'cut' with a mild cutting compound such as Turtle Wax Minute Cut prior to polishing with a final coating of Turtle Wax Extra.

When carrying out bodywork repairs, remember that the quality of the finished job is proportional to the time and effort expended.

HAYNES No1 for DIY

Haynes publish a wide variety of books besides the world famous range of *Haynes Owners Workshop Manuals*. They cover all sorts of DIY jobs. Specialist books such as the *Improve and Modify* series and the *Purchase and DIY Restoration Guides* give you all the information you require to carry out everything from minor modifications to complete restoration on a number of popular cars. In addition there are the publications dealing with specific tasks, such as the *Car Bodywork Repair Manual* and the *In-Car Entertainment Manual*. The *Household DIY* series gives clear step-by-step instructions on how to repair everyday household objects ranging from toasters to washing machines.

Whether it is under the bonnet or around the home there is a Haynes Manual that can help you save money. Available from motor accessory stores and bookshops or direct from the publisher.

Fig. 1.4 Exhaust downpipe ball socket connection (Sec 8)

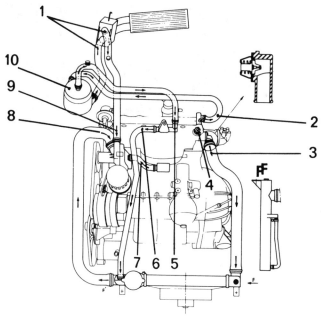

Fig. 1.5 Cylinder head removal – engine in vehicle.
Disconnect the items indicated (Sec 8)

1	Heater hoses	6	Carburettor hose
2	Cylinder head hose	7	Water pump hose
3	Thermostat hose	8	Water pump hose
4	Water temperature sensor	9	Water pump hose
5	Carburettor hose	10	De-aerator unit

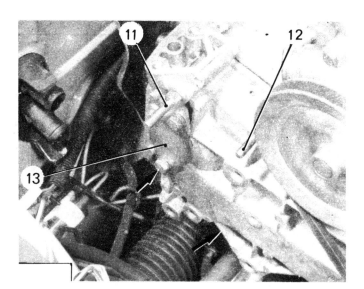

Fig. 1.6 Extended head bolt (12), end plate (13) and
extended head bolt (11) (Sec 8)

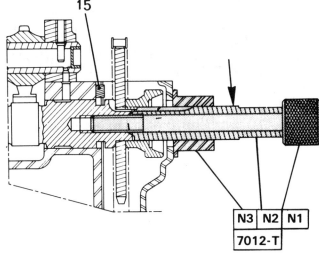

Fig. 1.7 Sectional view showing fitting position of Citroën
special tool 7012-T in camshaft. The camshaft retaining
plate is indicated (15) (Sec 8)

removed. Following the tightening sequence in reverse (see Fig. 1.9) progressively loosen the 10 cylinder head bolts; as they are loosened, the rocker shaft assembly will lift under the influence of the valve springs. Remove the bolts and the rocker shaft assembly.

24 Loosen the special tool (N1) from the camshaft and slide the camshaft away from the gear by hand. When the camshaft is clear of the gear the cylinder head can be removed. If it appears to be stuck, insert two bars into cylinder head bolt holes, taking care not to damage the head, and rock it free of the block. Don't, on any account, hammer on the cylinder head as it can be damaged very easily. Fit temporary restraining straps made of strip material to the block to keep the cylinder liners in position; secure them with bolts and nuts in the

cylinder head bolt holes. To dismantle and overhaul the cylinder head refer to Section 15.

25 Carefully cut and remove the upper, exposed portion of the timing case gasket level with the face of the cylinder block. Clean the mating faces of the block, cylinder head, and timing case free of all jointing materials. Do not use emery cloth or sharp-edged tools as the surfaces must be free of all traces of scores, burns, or impact damage.

26 If there is likely to be an appreciable time lapse before reassembly, cover the exposed parts of the engine internals with clean, fluff-free rag.

27 Before refitting the cylinder head, check the cylinder liner protrusions, as described in Section 19.

Fig. 1.8 View showing dowel stop rod (4), guide pins (5) and timing cover extended screw locations (a) (Sec 8)

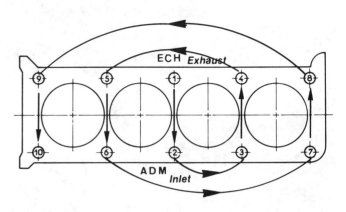

Fig. 1.9 Sequence for tightening the cylinder head bolts (Sec 8)

8.33A Lower the cylinder head into position ...

8.33B ... then fit the rocker assembly onto the cylinder head

28 Check that the location dowels are in position in the cylinder block top face and to prevent the rear dowel from being pushed down when fitting the cylinder head, insert a suitable rod into the hole in the crankcase side wall directly beneath the dowel.

29 Locate two guide pins in the cylinder block (Fig. 1.8). The pins should be 11 mm in diameter and no more than 95 mm long.

30 Lubricate the cylinder walls with engine oil. Remove the cylinder liner retaining straps.

31 Locate the new cylinder head gasket. It must be fitted dry and the arrow mark must point towards the front of the engine. Smear the timing cover mating faces with a suitable sealant.

32 Loosen the rocker adjustment screws.

33 Carefully lower the cylinder head into position on the block and then fit the rocker assembly into position on the cylinder head (photos). Fit the cylinder head bolts and nuts but leave them untightened for the moment. Remove the guide pins and the dowel support rod.

34 Locate the timing cover extended head bolt into position at 'a' (Fig. 1.8), but do not fully tighten it yet.

35 Align the grooves of the camshaft and the mandrel and tighten it into position. Push the timing gear and the camshaft together ensuring correct engagement. If necessary tap the rear end of the camshaft with a soft-faced mallet.

36 Fit the camshaft retaining plate into its groove and tighten the bolt to the specified torque.

37 Tighten the cylinder head bolts in the sequence shown in Fig. 1.9. The bolts must be tightened in two stages to the torque settings given in the Specifications (photo).

38 Remove the special tool (7012-T) then refit the gear/camshaft retaining bolt and tighten it to the specified torque.

39 Refit the timing cover bolts and tighten them to the specified torque. Before refitting the timing case closing plate smear the mating edges with sealant.

40 Adjust the rocker/valve clearances, as described in Section 7.

41 Refitting of the remaining components is a reversal of the removal procedure, but note the following special points:

  (a) Tighten fasteners to the specified torque setting where these are listed in the Specifications
  (b) Refill the cooling system and top up the engine/gearbox oil
  (c) Before restarting the engine, check that all tools and equipment are removed from the engine compartment
  (d) Check the ignition timing (Chapter 4) and, when the engine is warmed up, adjust the idle speed (Chapter 3)
  (e) After starting the engine, check for leaks and then run it until the electro-magnetic fan engages. Stop the engine and when it is cool top up the cooling system

(f) *After the engine has been allowed to cool for at least two hours the cylinder head bolts must be retightened. First remove the rocker cover and, following the sequence in Fig. 1.9, slacken the first bolt and then retighten it to the Stage 2 specified torque. Then slacken the second bolt and retighten it, and so on until all bolts have been separately retightened.*

(g) *Following the retightening of the cylinder head bolts the inlet and exhaust valve clearances must be reset.*

8.37 Tightening the cylinder head bolts

9 Engine and transmission – removal and refitting

1   The engine and transmission unit must be removed as a complete assembly and cannot be separated until removed. The combined weight of the two components is not great due to the extensive use of aluminium alloy, but certain operations are awkward and care must be taken not to damage adjacent components in the engine compartment, especially during removal, as space is limited in which to manoeuvre the assembly out. It therefore pays to have an assistant on hand whenever possible. Start by removing the bonnet, as described in Chapter 11.

2   Chock the rear wheels then raise the vehicle at the front so that the front roadwheels are clear of the ground and support on safety stands. Unbolt and remove the roadwheels.

3   Disconnect the positive and negative leads from the battery.

4   Disconnect the earth wires from the cylinder head.

5   Remove the battery from the engine compartment. Also remove the battery plastic tray.

6   Detach and remove the air cleaner unit, referring to Chapter 3 if necessary.

7   Referring to Fig. 1.10, disconnect the following:

(a) *The HT lead at the coil*
(b) *The diagnostic plug negative and positive wires at the coil*
(c) *The wiring connector at the distributor*
(d) *The econoscope wiring harness*
(e) *The econoscope vacuum inlet tube*

8   Disconnect the clutch inner cable from the operating lever clevis.

9   Undo and detach the speedometer drive cable at its transmission connection. Fold the cable back out of the way.

10 Disconnect and remove the air intake duct from the wing panel.

11 Disconnect the choke cable and the accelerator cable at the carburettor.

12 Detach the fuel feed hose from the petrol pump and the fuel return hose from the carburettor. Plug the hoses and connections to prevent excessive leakage and the ingress of dirt.

13 Drain the cooling system, as described in Chapter 2.

14 Disconnect and detach the heater flow and return hoses at the water pump, the inlet manifold heater hose and the cylinder head-to-radiator coolant hose.

15 Disconnect the wiring connectors from the cooling fan temperature sensor and the coolant level sensor at the radiator.

16 Undo the five radiator top panel retaining bolts, then remove the panel and the radiator; taking care not to damage its core as it is lifted out.

17 Detach and remove the de-aeration chamber from its support on the right-hand side of the engine compartment.

Fig. 1.10 View showing items to be disconnected (Sec 9)

4 Coil HT lead   7 Econoscope connector
5 Coil leads   8 Econoscope tube
6 Distributor connector

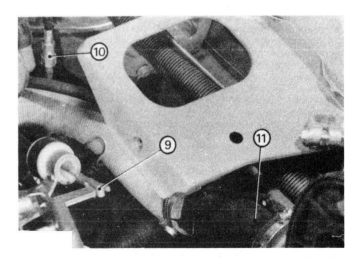

Fig. 1.11 Disconnect the clutch cable (9), speedometer cable (10) and air intake duct (11) (Sec 9)

Fig. 1.12 View showing the reversing lamp switch (7), wiring harness clip (8) and sump drain plug (9) (Sec 9)

Fig. 1.13 Disconnect the oil suction pipe (1) from the HP pump (Sec 9)

Fig. 1.14 Disconnect the oil return pipe (3), the outlet pipe (2) and securing lug at the pressure regulator unit (4) (Sec 9)

18 Position a suitable container under the sump then remove the drain plug and drain the engine oil.

19 Detach the reversing lamp switch leads and detach the wiring harness from the retaining clip.

20 Release the pressure from the hydraulic system, referring to Chapter 8, Section 2 for details.

21 Disconnect the oil suction pipe from the high pressure (HP) pump. Clean the connections and plug the ports to prevent the ingress of dirt.

22 Referring to Fig. 1.14, disconnect the oil return pipe and outlet pipe from the pressure regulator unit. Clean the connectors and plug the ports to prevent the ingress of dirt.

23 Disconnect the hydraulic outlet pipe from its location lug and the two pipes from the lugs on the engine front face.

24 Disconnect the link rods from the gearbox.

25 Disconnect the exhaust downpipe at the balljoint.

26 The steering link rods and lower wheel arm balljoints must now be separated. Loosen the retaining nuts and use a suitable separator to disconnect the joints (see Chapter 10 for details).

27 Pull the driveshafts outwards and release them from the transmission. Support the shafts so that they are out of the way without damaging their rubber gaiters or straining their joints.

28 Connect a sling to the lift brackets at each end of the cylinder head. Lift and just take the weight of the engine/transmission unit.

29 Unscrew and remove the engine mounting nuts.

30 Check that the engine and associated components are fully disconnected and positioned so that they will not be damaged or interfere with the engine/transmission removal.

31 Lift the engine/transmission unit clear of the mountings then guide the unit upwards out of the engine compartment. An assistant will be necessary to steady the unit as it is removed.

32 On removal from the vehicle, the engine and transmission can be cleaned externally then moved to the work area for dismantling and overhaul.

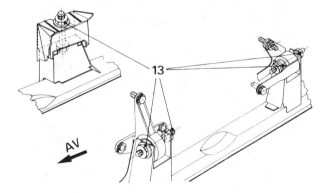

Fig. 1.15 Undo the engine mounting nuts indicated (13) (Sec 9)

Refitting

33 The refitting of the engine and transmission unit is, in general, the reverse of the removal procedure, but note the following special points.

34 Check that the lift sling is securely located before lifting the unit into position.

35 Check that all loose hoses, wires, hydraulic pipes and components in the engine bay are moved back out of the way as the unit is lowered into position.

36 When reconnecting the driveshafts take care not to damage the oil seals and ensure that the shafts are fully located.

37 Renew the engine mounting self-locking nuts, also those of the lower wheel arm and steering link rod balljoints.

38 Tighten all mounting and connecting bolts and nuts to the specified torque settings (Fig. 1.16).

39 Refer to Chapter 3 when reconnecting the choke and accelerator cables.

40 Connect and adjust the clutch cable, as described in Chapter 5.

41 Check that the cooling system, fuel system and hydraulic system hoses are in good condition before reconnecting them.

42 Check that all electrical connections are correctly and securely made.

43 Top up the cooling system, as described in Chapter 2.

44 Top up the engine/transmission oil level.

45 Retighten the hydraulic system pressure regulator bleed screw and top up the hydraulic fluid level as necessary (see Chapter 8). The system will need to be repressurized as soon as the engine is started.

46 Go carefully round the engine to make sure that all reconnections have been made. Especially check that the electrical earth connections are made, the drivebelts are correctly tensioned, the carburettor controls are connected and that there are no apparent oil or coolant leaks. Remove all loose tools, rags, etc.

47 Refit the battery and secure with its clamp plate. Reconnect the battery leads and check the operation of the electrical circuits.

48 The engine is now ready for its initial start-up – further details of which are described in Section 22.

10 Engine dismantling – general

1 A good size clean work area will be required, preferably on a bench. Before moving the engine and transmission assembly to the work area it should be cleaned to remove road dirt, oil and grease.

2 During the dismantling process care should be taken to avoid contaminating the exposed internal parts with dirt. Although everything will be cleaned separately before reassembly, road dirt or grit can cause damage to parts during dismantling and could also affect inspection and checks.

3 A good proprietary grease solvent will make the job of engine/transmission cleaning much easier but if this is not available use paraffin. With a solvent the usual procedure is to apply it to the contaminated surfaces and, after a suitable soaking period has elapsed, to wash it off with a jet of water. Where the grease or oil and dirt mixture is encrusted the solvent should be worked in using a stiff brush.

4 After rinsing off the solvent and dirt, wipe down the exterior of the assembly and then, only when it is clean and dry, the dismantling process can be started.

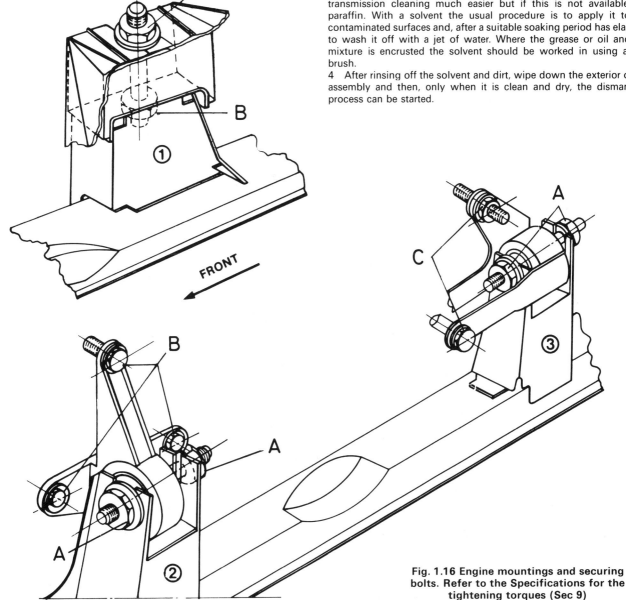

Fig. 1.16 Engine mountings and securing bolts. Refer to the Specifications for the tightening torques (Sec 9)

5   As the unit is stripped, the individual parts should be examined before being washed in a bath of paraffin and wiped dry. The examination need only be cursory at this stage but it is sometimes helpful as the cleaning procedure might wash away useful evidence of running conditions. Avoid immersing parts with internal oil passages, such as the crankshaft and the timing case, in paraffin. To clean such parts use a paraffin-damped rag and clean out the oilways with wire. If an air supply is available the oilways can be blown through to clear them.

6   The re-use of old gaskets or old oil seals is a false economy and can lead to fuel, oil or coolant leaks, if nothing worse. To avoid the possibility of such problems, always use new gaskets throughout.

7   Don't throw away the old gaskets, as it sometimes happens that an immediate replacement is not available and the old gasket is then useful as a template. Hang up the old gaskets as they are removed on a suitable hook or nail.

8   A suggested procedure for dismantling is to remove the clutch assembly and then the timing mechanism (this order could be reversed if required) followed by the transmission, cylinder head and finally the crankshaft and piston assemblies. A supply of wooden blocks of varying sizes will be useful in supporting the assembly as it is being worked on.

9   Wherever possible refit nuts, bolts, and washers finger tight from wherever they were removed as this helps avoid later loss or muddle. If they cannot be refitted, lay them out in such a fashion that it is clear where they came from. Make sketches or notes if you think you may forget the position of washers etc.

11 Engine dismantling – ancillary items

1   Irrespective of whether you are going to dismantle the engine completely and rebuild it, or are simply going to exchange it for a new or reconditioned unit, the ancillary components will have to be removed.

2   The only possible method of determining the exact condition of the engine and assessing the extent of reconditioning required is to dismantle it completely. If, having done this, it is decided that a reconditioned short block is needed then the unit can be loosely reassembled, but check that a replacement is available first.

3   Refer to the relevant Chapters, if necessary, and remove the following components or assemblies:

   (a) Distributor (Chapter 4)
   (b) Fuel pump and operating plunger (Chapter 3)
   (c) Carburettor (Chapter 3)
   (d) Inlet and exhaust manifolds (Chapter 3)
   (e) Coolant pump and drivebelt (Chapter 2)
   (f) Alternator and starter motor (Chapter 12)
   (g) Diagnostic socket and wiring harness
   (h) Coolant temperature sender (Chapter 2)
   (j) Oil pressure sender
   (k) Thermostat and housing (Chapter 2)
   (l) Oil filter and dipstick tube
   (m) Clutch assembly (Chapter 5)
   (n) Hydraulic system HP pump unit (Chapter 8)
   (o) Pressure regulator unit (Chapter 8)
   (p) The support mounting

4   If the engine is to be exchanged, check what ancillary items are included in the exchange unit. Make sure that the old engine is cleaned before being exchanged.

12 Engine and transmission – separation

1   If the engine is to be dismantled for overhaul, refer to the previous Section and remove the items listed, then in addition remove the flywheel, as described in paragraph 3 below.

2   If the two units are to be separated but the engine is not being dismantled, remove the items indicated in Fig. 1.17, referring to the relevant chapters concerned for details where necessary.

Fig. 1.17 Items to be disconnected to separate engine from gearbox if engine is not being dismantled (Sec 12)

1 Engine support mounting
2 Starter motor
3 Dipstick tube
4 Alternator and HP pump drivebelts
5 HP pump unit
6 Pressure regulator unit
7 Fuel pump

Fig. 1.18 Engine-to-transmission securing bolts (1) and nut (2) at the flywheel end (Sec 12)

Fig. 1.19 Engine-to-transmission securing bolts (arrowed) – inlet side (Sec 12)

Fig. 1.20 Engine-to-transmission securing bolts (arrowed) – exhaust side at timing cover end (Sec 12)

Fig. 1.21 Engine-to-transmission securing bolts (arrowed) – exhaust side at flywheel end (Sec 12)

3   When the clutch unit is removed, unbolt and remove the flywheel. The retaining bolts' positions are not symmetrical so there is no need to mark the fitted position of the flywheel.
4   Unscrew and remove the two bolts and the single nut securing the engine and transmission joint faces at the flywheel end (Fig. 1.18).
5   If still in position, unbolt and remove the rocker cover.
6   Unbolt and detach the HP pump drive pulley from the crankshaft inner pulley. Undo the central retaining bolt and remove the crankshaft pulley. To prevent the crankshaft from turning when undoing the bolts, fit two flywheel bolts into the crankshaft rear end and jam a bar diagonally between the bolts.
7   Unscrew and remove the timing cover retaining bolts. As they are withdrawn note the respective bolt sizes and fitted positions to ensure correct refitting.
8   Carefully remove the timing cover. If it is stuck, gently break the joint by tapping it free with a soft-faced hammer, but do not use

excessive force as the light alloy casing can easily be damaged. Remove the timing cover gasket (this must be renewed when reassembling). Retrieve the petrol pump pushrod.
9   Unscrew and remove the engine-to-transmission retaining bolts on each side.
10 Support the engine, then prise the transmission away from the engine using a suitable length of wood. Take care not to damage the casings. If the two assemblies are reluctant to part check that there are no retaining bolts or nuts left in position.

13 Engine – complete dismantling

1   Support the engine on the bench or strong table. If such facilities are not available then it will have to be dismantled on the floor, but at

Fig. 1.22 Loosening the first type chain tensioner (Sec 13)

least cover the floor with a sheet of hardboard.
2   Remove any remaining engine ancillary items.
3   Loosen the timing chain tensioner. One of two types will be fitted.
With the first type retract the tensioner by turning the lock in an
anti-clockwise direction (Fig. 1.22). With the second type, use a
screwdriver as shown and press down the tensioner to release it
(Fig. 1.23).
4   Unbolt and remove the chain tensioner.
5   Unbolt and remove the chain guide plate.
6   Unscrew the camshaft sprocket bolt. The crankshaft must be held
against rotation for this operation. Do this by screwing two bolts into
the flange and passing a long lever between them.
7   Remove the fuel pump eccentric cam.
8   Remove the oil pump socket-headed screws. Some of these are
accessible through the holes in the oil pump driven gear.
9   Remove the oil pump and backplate.
10 Withdraw the camshaft sprocket, timing chain and crankshaft
sprocket with Woodruff key.

**Fig. 1.23 Method used to release the second type chain
tensioner (Sec 13)**

Fig. 1.24 Oil pump and backplate removal (Sec 13)

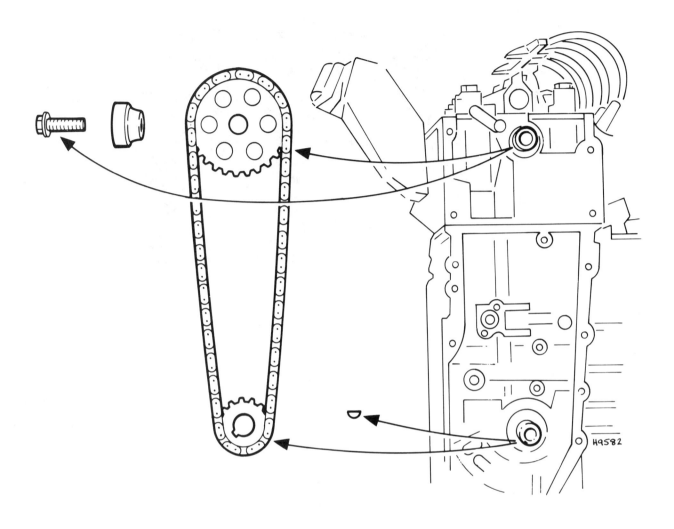

Fig. 1.25 Timing chain and sprockets removal (Sec 13)

11 Unscrew and remove the spark plugs using the special spanner supplied with the vehicle.
12 Remove the cylinder head bolts by unscrewing them in the reverse order to that shown in Fig. 1.9.
13 Lift off the rocker assembly.
14 Drive down a cylinder head positioning dowel so that the cylinder head can be swivelled rather than lifted from the block. This is to prevent disturbing the cylinder liner base seals. If the liners are to be removed then obviously this precaution is not necessary, neither is the need to fit cylinder liner clamps to hold the liners down once the cylinder head has been removed.
15 Dismantling the cylinder head and removal of the camshaft is covered in Section 15.
16 Unscrew and remove the bolts which hold the crankcase half sections together. Split the crankcase and keep the main bearing shells with their crankcase web recesses if the shells are to be used again.
17 Remove the crankshaft oil seal.
18 Mark the rim of the cylinder liners in respect of position in the block and orientation.
19 Mark the big-end caps and the connecting rods so that they can be refitted in their original sequence and the correct way round. A centre punch or hacksaw blade is useful for this purpose.
20 Unscrew the big-end nuts, remove the caps. If the bearing shells are to be used again, keep them taped to their respective cap or connecting rod.

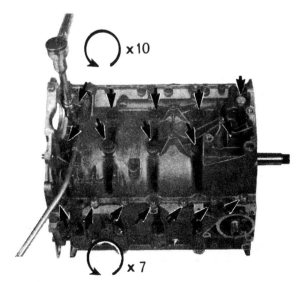

Fig. 1.26 Crankshaft half casing retaining bolt locations – arrowed (Sec 13)

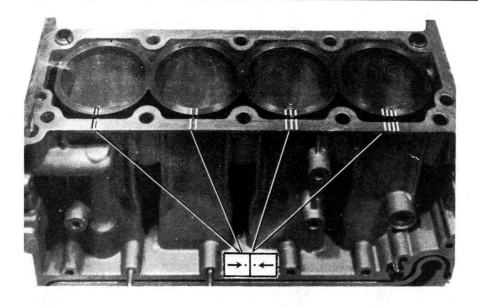

Fig. 1.27 Cylinder liners and block match marks (Sec 13)

21 Lift the crankshaft from its crankcase half section, keep the shell bearings in their original web recesses if they are to be used again and retrieve the semi-circular thrust washers from either side of Number 2 web.
22 Remove each liner/piston/connecting rod as an assembly from the crankcase. Use a plastic-faced or wooden mallet to tap the liners out if necessary. Make sure that the liners and their respective piston rod assemblies are marked as to position in the block and orientation. A spirit marker is useful for this purpose.
23 Discard the liner base seals which must be renewed.

14 Engine components – examination and renovation (general)

1 With the engine dismantled, all components must be thoroughly cleaned and examined for wear, as described in the following Sections.
2 If a high mileage has been covered since new or the last engine rebuild, and general wear is evident, consideration should be given to renewing the engine with a reconditioned one.
3 If a single component has malfunctioned and the rest of the engine is in good condition endeavour to find out the cause of its failure if not readily apparent. For example, if a bearing has failed, check that the adjoining oilways are clear; the new bearing will not last long if it is not being lubricated.
4 If uncertain about the condition of any components, seek a second opinion, preferably from a Citroën dealer/mechanic who will obviously have an expert knowledge of your model and be able to advise on the best course of action.
5 Check on the availability of replacement parts before discarding the old ones. Check the new part against the old to ensure that you have the correct replacement.
6 Some of the measurements required will need the use of feeler blades or a micrometer, but in many instances wear will be visually evident or the old component can be compared with a new one.
7 When cleaning old sealant and/or gaskets from mating faces take care not to damage the surfaces.

15 Cylinder head – dismantling, decarbonising and reassembly

1 Having removed the cylinder head, place it onto a clean workbench where it can be dismantled and examined. Unbolt the retaining plate (if necessary) and withdraw the camshaft (photos).

2 Remove each valve and spring assembly using a valve spring compressor. Extract the split collets from between the spring retaining cup washer and valve stem (photo).
3 Progressively release the tension of the compressor until it can be removed, the spring and retainer withdrawn, and the valve extracted from the guide (photos).
4 As the valves are removed, keep them in order by inserting them in a card having suitable holes punched in it, numbered from 1 to 8. Discard the valve stem oil seals.
5 Wash the cylinder head clean and carefully scrape away the carbon build-up in the combustion chambers and exhaust ports, using a scraper which will not damage the surfaces to be cleaned. If a rotary wire brush and drill is available this may be used for removing the carbon.
6 The valves may also be scraped and wire-brushed clean in a similar manner.
7 With the cylinder head cleaned and dry, examine it for cracks or damage. In particular inspect the valve seat areas for signs of hairline cracks, pitting or burning. Check the head mating surfaces for distortion, the maximum permissible amount being 0.05 mm (0.002 in).
8 Minor surface wear and pitting of the valve seats can probably be removed when the valves are reground. More serious wear or damage should be shown to your Citroën dealer or a competent automotive engineer who will advise you on the action necessary.
9 Carefully inspect the valves, in particular the exhaust valves. Check the stems for distortion and signs of wear. The valve seat faces must be in reasonable condition and if they have covered a high mileage they will probably need to be refaced on a valve grinding machine; again, this is a job for your Citroën dealer or local garage/automotive machine shop.
10 Insert each valve into its respective guide and check for excessive side play. Worn valve guides allow oil to be drained past the inlet valve stem causing a smoky exhaust, while exhaust leakage through the exhaust valve guide can overheat the valve guide and cause sticking valves.
11 If the valve guides are to be renewed this is a job best left to your Citroën agent who will have the required specialist equipment.
12 Assuming the valves and seats are in reasonable condition they should be reseated by grinding them using valve grinding carborundum paste. The grinding process must also be carried out when new valves are fitted.
13 The carborundum paste used for this job is normally supplied in a double-ended tin with coarse paste at one end and fine at the other. In addition, a suction tool for holding the valve head so that it may be rotated is also required. To grind in the valve, first smear a trace of the

coarse paste onto the seat face and fit the suction grinder to the valve head. Then with a semi-rotary motion grind the valve head into its seat, lifting the valve occasionally to redistribute the grinding paste. When a dull matt continuous line is produced on both the valve seat and the valve then the paste can be wiped off. Apply a little fine paste and finish off the grinding process, then remove all traces of the paste. If a light spring is placed over the valve stem behind the head this can often be of assistance in raising the valve from time to time against the pressure of the grinding tool so as to redistribute the paste evenly round the job. The width of the line which is produced after grinding indicates the seat width, and this width should not exceed 2 mm (0.08 in). If, after a moderate amount of grinding, it is apparent that the seating line is too wide, it probably means that the seat has already been cut back one or more times previously, or else the valve has been

ground several times. Here again, specialist advice is best sought.
14 Examine all the valve springs to make sure that they are in good condition and not distorted. If the engine has covered 30 000 miles (48 000 km) then fit new springs at reassembly. Renew the valve stem oil seals (photo).
15 At the same time renew the valve spring seating washers which sit directly on the cylinder head (photo). These wear fairly quickly.
16 Before reassembling the valves and springs to the cylinder head make a final check that everything is thoroughly clean and free from grit (photo), then lightly smear all the valve stems with engine oil prior to reassembly. The camshaft can now be refitted in the cylinder head and located with the retaining plate. This is then secured with its bolt and a new shakeproof washer

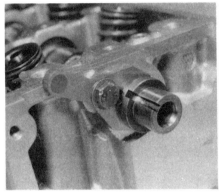
15.1A Remove the camshaft retaining plate ...

15.1B ... to allow camshaft withdrawal

15.2 Compress the valve spring and ...

15.3A ... remove the spring cup retainer ...

15.3B ... the spring and ...

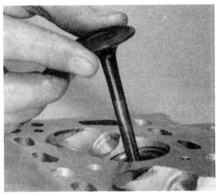
15.3C ... the valve

15.14 Valve stem oil seal

15.15 Valve spring seating washer

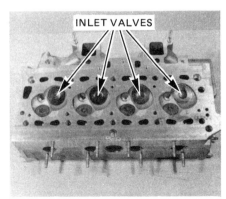
15.16 Cylinder head cleaned and reassembled

16 Examination and renovation of dismantled components

Crankshaft and main bearings

1   Carefully examine the crankpin and main journal surfaces for signs of scoring or scratches, and check the ovality and taper of each journal in turn. Use a dial gauge and V-blocks and check the main bearing journals for ovality. If any journals are found to be more than the specified amount out of round then they will have to be reground. If the crankpins are scored or scratched, don't bother measuring them as they will have to be reground.

2   If a bearing has failed after a short period of operation look for the cause and rectify before reassembly.

3   If the crankshaft is to be reground this will have to be done by your Citroën dealer or a competent automotive engineer. The regrinder will also be able to supply the new shell bearings to suit the undersize requirement. New thrust washers to control endfloat will also be supplied.

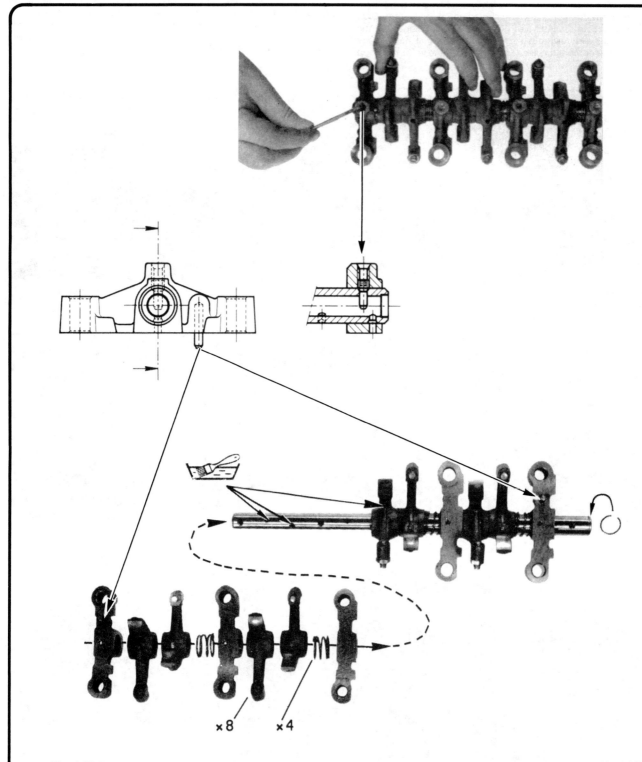

×8   ×4

Fig. 1.28 Rocker gear dismantling for inspection. Check that the lubrication ports in the shaft are clear (Sec 16)

Big-end bearings

4   The main bearing shells themselves are normally a matt grey in colour all over and should have no signs of pitting or ridging or discolouration as this usually indicates that the surface bearing metal has worn away and the backing material is showing through. It is worthwhile renewing the main bearing shells anyway if you have gone to the trouble of removing the crankshaft, but they *must,* of course, be renewed if there is any sign of damage to them or if the crankshaft has been reground.

5   If the crankshaft is not being reground, yet bearing shells are being renewed, make sure that you check whether or not the crankshaft has been reground before. This will be indicated by looking at the back of the bearing shells and will show whether it is undersize or not. The same type of shell bearing must be used when they are renewed.

6   The big-end bearings are subject to wear at a greater rate than the crankshaft journals. A sign that one or more big-end bearings are getting badly worn is a pronounced knocking noise from the engine, accompanied by a significant drop in oil pressure due to the increased clearance between the bearing and the journal permitting oil to flow more freely through the resultantly larger space. If this should happen quite suddenly and action is taken immediately, and immediately is meant within a few miles, then it is possible that the bearing shell may be renewed without any further work needing to be done.

7   If this happens in an engine which has been neglected, and oil changes and oil filter changes have not been carried out as they should have been, it is most likely that the rest of the engine is in a pretty terrible state anyway. If it occurs in an engine which has been recently overhauled, then it is almost certainly due to a piece of grit or swarf which has got into the oil circulation system and finally come to rest in the bearing shell and scored it. In these instances renewal of the shell alone accompanied by a thorough flushing of the lubrication system may be all that is required.

Cylinder liners, pistons and connecting rods

8   The liner bores may be examined for wear either in or out of the engine block; the cylinder head must, of course, be removed in each case.

9   First of all examine the top of the cylinder about a quarter of an inch below the top of the liner and with a finger feel if there is any ridge running round the circumference of the bore. In a worn cylinder bore a ridge will develop at the point where the top ring on the piston comes to the uppermost limit of its stroke. An excessive ridge indicates that the bore below the ridge is worn. If there is no ridge, it is reasonable to assume that the cylinder is not badly worn. Measurement of the diameter of the cylinder bore both in line with the piston gudgeon pin and at right angles to it, at the top and bottom of the cylinder, is another check to be made. A cylinder is expected to wear at the sides where the thrust of the piston presses against it. In time this causes the cylinder to assume an oval shape. Furthermore, the top of the cylinder is likely to wear more than the bottom of the cylinder. It will be necessary to use a proper bore measuring instrument in order to measure the differences in bore diameter across the cylinder, and variations between the top and bottom ends of the cylinder. As a general guide it may be assumed that any variation more than 0.25 mm indicates that the liners should be renewed. Provided all variations are less than 0.25 mm it is probable that the fitting of new piston rings will cure the problem of piston-to-cylinder bore clearances. Once again it is difficult to give a firm ruling on this as so much depends on the amount of time, effort and money which the individual owner is prepared, or wishes to spend, on the task. Certainly if the cylinder bores are obviously deeply grooved or scored, the liners must be renewed, regardless of any measurement differences in the cylinder diameter.

10   If new liners are to be fitted, new pistons will be required also, as they are supplied as matched sets.

11   With the pistons removed from the liners, carefully clean them and remove the old rings, keeping them in order and the correct way up. The ring grooves will have to be cleaned out, especially the top, which will contain a burnt carbon coating that may prevent the ring from seating correctly. A broken piston ring will assist in groove cleaning. Take care not to scratch the ring lands or piston surface in any way.

12   The top ring groove is likely to have worn the most. After the groove has been cleaned out, refit the top ring and any excessive wear will be obvious by a sloppy fit. The degree of wear may be checked by using a feeler gauge.

13   Examine the piston surface and look for signs of any hairline cracks especially round the gudgeon pin area. Check that the oil drain holes

below the oil control ring groove are clear, and, if not, carefully clean them out using a suitable size drill, but don't mark the piston.

14   If any of the pistons are obviously badly worn or defective they must be renewed. A badly worn top ring land may be machined to accept a wider, stepped ring, the stop on the outer face of this type of ring being necessary to avoid fouling the unworn ridge at the top of the cylinder bore.

15   Providing the engine has not seized up or suffered any other severe damage, the connecting rods should not require any attention other than cleaning. If damage has occurred or the piston(s) shows signs of irregular wear it is advisable to have the connecting rod alignment checked. This requires the use of specialised tools and should therefore be entrusted to a Citroën agent or a competent automotive engineer, who will be able to check and realign any defective rods.

16   New Citroën rings are supplied with their gaps already preset, but if you intend to use other makes the gaps should be checked and adjusted if necessary. Before fitting the new rings on the pistons, each should be inserted approximately 75 mm (3 in) down the cylinder bore and the gap measured with a feeler gauge. This should be between 0.38 and 0.97 mm. It is essential that the gap should be measured at the bottom of the ring travel, as if it is measured at the top of a worn bore and gives a perfect fit, it could easily seize at the bottom. If the ring gap is too small, rub down the ends of the ring with a very fine file until the gap, when fitted, is correct. To keep the rings square in the bore for measurement, line each up in turn by inserting an old piston in the bore upside down, and use the piston to push the ring down. Remove the piston and measure the piston ring gap.

Gudgeon pins

17   The gudgeon pins float in the piston and are an interference fit in the connecting rods. This interference fit between gudgeon pin and connecting rod means that heat is required (230 to 260°C/446 to 500°F) before a pin can be satisfactorily fitted in the connecting rod. If it is necessary to renew either the piston or connecting rod, we strongly recommend that the separation and assembly of the two be entrusted to someone with experience. Misapplied heat can ruin one, or all, of the components very easily.

18   Never re-use a piston if the original gudgeon pin has been removed from it.

Timing chain, sprocket and tensioner

19   Examine the teeth of both sprockets for wear. Each tooth on a sprocket is an inverted V-shape and wear is apparent when one side of the tooth becomes more concave in shape than the other. When badly worn, the teeth become hook-shaped and the sprockets must be renewed.

20   If the sprockets need to be renewed then the chain will have worn also and should also be renewed. If the sprockets are satisfactory, examine the chain and look for play between the links. When the chain is held out horizontally, it should not bend appreciably. Remember, a chain is only as strong as its weakest link and, being a relatively cheap item, it is worthwhile fitting a replacement anyway.

21   Check the condition of the tensioner slipper. If it is worn, renew it.

22   Inspect the oil pump drive gears for wear or damage and renew if necessary. Always fit a new timing cover oil seal (photo).

Camshaft and rocker gear

23   The camshaft lobes should be examined for signs of flats or scoring or any other form of wear or damage. At the same time the rocker arms should also be examined, particularly on the faces where they bear against the camshaft, for signs of wear. Very slight wear may be removed by rubbing with an oilstone but maintain the original contour.

24   The camshaft bearing journals should be in good condition and show no signs of pitting or scoring as they are relatively free from stress.

25   If the bearing surfaces are scored or discoloured it is possible that the shaft is not running true, and in this case it will have to be renewed. For an accurate check get your Citroën agent to inspect both the camshaft and cylinder head.

26   Worn camshaft bearings in the cylinder head can only be rectified by renewal of the head, an expensive business, as the bearings are machined directly in the head.

27   The rocker arms can be removed from the shaft after extracting the circlip (distributor end) and the Allen screw from the opposite end (see Fig.1.28) (photos).

28   When removing the various rocker components from the shaft take careful note of the sequence in which they are removed. In particular

16.22 Renew the timing cover oil seal   16.27A Rocker shaft retaining circlip   16.27B Rocker arms and spring
(arrowed)

note that the No 2 and No 4 rocker bearings are identical, keep the components in order as they are removed from the shaft for inspection.
29 Check the rocker shaft for signs of wear. Check it for straightness by rolling it on a flat surface. It is unlikely to be bent but if this is the case it must either be straightened or renewed. The shaft surface should be free of wear ridges caused by the rocker arms. Check the oil feed holes and clear them out if blocked or sludged-up.
30 Check each rocker arm for wear on an unworn part of the shaft. Check the end of the adjuster screw and the face of the rocker arm where it bears on the camshaft. Any signs of cracks or serious wear will necessitate renewal of the rocker arm.

Oil pump
31 The oil pump gears are exposed once the spacer plate is removed.
32 Side movement of the gear spindles will indicate wear in the bushes and the pump should be renewed complete.
33 Worn or chipped gear teeth must be rectified by renewal of the gear.
34 Check the clearance between the tip of the gear lobes and the oil pump body (photo).
35 If any of these clearances exceed the specified limit, renew the pump.
36 Remove the retaining pin from the relief valve housing and withdraw the cup, spring, guide and piston. Renew any worn components (photo).

Flywheel and starter ring gear
37 There are two areas in which the flywheel may have been worn or damaged.
38 The first is on the driving face where the clutch friction plate bears against it. Should the clutch plate have been permitted to wear down beyond the level of the rivets, it is possible that the flywheel will have been scored. If this scoring is severe it may be necessary to have it refaced or even renewed.
39 Evidence of tiny cracks on the flywheel driving face will indicate that overheating has occurred.
40 The other part to examine is the teeth of the starter ring gear around the periphery of the flywheel. If several of the teeth are broken or missing, or the front edges of all teeth are obviously very badly chewed up, then it would be advisable to fit a new ring gear.
41 The old ring gear can be removed by cutting a slot with a hacksaw down between two of the teeth as far as possible, without cutting into the flywheel itself. Once the cut is made a chisel will split the ring gear which can then be drawn off. To fit a new ring gear requires it to be heated first to a temperature of 220°C (435°F), no more. This is best done in a bath of oil or an oven, not with a naked flame. It is much more difficult to heat evenly and to the required temperature with a naked flame. Once the ring gear has attained the correct temperature it can be placed onto the flywheel; making sure that it beds down properly onto the register. It should then be allowed to cool down naturally. If by mischance, the ring gear is overheated, it should not be used. The temper will have been lost, thereby softening it, and it will wear out in a very short space of time.
42 Although not actually fitted into the flywheel itself, there is a bush in the centre of the crankshaft flange onto which the flywheel fits. Whilst more associated with gearbox and clutch, it should always be inspected when the clutch is removed. The main bearing oil seal is

revealed when the flywheel is removed. This can be prised out with a screwdriver but must always be renewed once removed. The spigot bush is best removed using a suitable extractor. Another method is to fill the recess with grease and then drive in a piece of close fitting steel bar. This should force the bush out. A new bush may be pressed in, together with a new seal. Make sure that the chamfered end of the bush abuts the seal. The bush is self-lubricating.

Transfer gears
43 The condition of the transfer gears, their bearings and the input and output shafts, is obviously critical as they transmit the power of the engine to the transmission unit, and are liable to be a source of noise if worn. Check the transfer gears, as described in Chapter 5.

17 Engine reassembly – general

1 It is during the process of engine reassembly that the job is either made a success or a failure. From the word go there are certain basic rules which it is folly to ignore, namely:

(a) *Absolute cleanliness. The working area, the components of the engine and the hands of those working on the engine must be completely free of grime and grit. One small piece of carborundum dust or swarf can ruin a big-end in no time, and nullify all the time and effort you have spent.*

(b) *Always, no matter what the circumstances may be, use new gaskets, locking tabs, seals, nyloc (self-locking) nuts and any other parts mentioned in the Sections in this Chapter. It is pointless to dismantle an engine, spend considerable money and time on it and then waste all this for the sake of something as small as a failed oil seal. Delay the rebuilding if necessary.*

(c) *Don't rush it. The most skilled and experienced mechanic can easily make a mistake if he is rushed.*

(d) *Check that all nuts and bolts are clean and in good condition and ideally renew all spring washers, lockwashers and tab washers as a matter of course. A supply of clean engine oil and clean cloths (to wipe excess oil off your hands) and a torque spanner are the only things which should be required in addition to all the tools used in dismantling the engine.*

(e) *The torque wrench is an essential requirement when reassembling the engine (and transmission) components. This is because the various housings are manufactured from aluminium alloy and whilst this gives the advantage of less weight, it also means that the various fastenings must be accurately tightened as specified to avoid distortion and/or damage to the components.*

18 Engine – preparation for reassembly

1 Assuming that the engine has been completely stripped for reconditioning and that the block is now bare, before any reassembly

16.34 Checking the oil pump lobe tip clearance

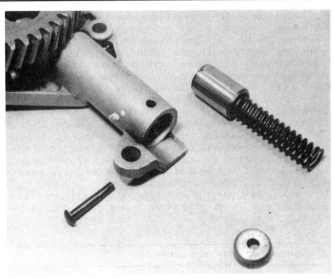
16.36 Oil pump relief valve components

19.4 One method of clamping cylinder liners

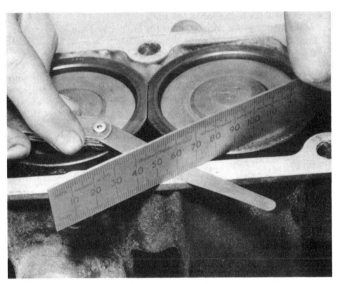
19.6 Measuring a cylinder liner projection

takes place it must be thoroughly cleaned both inside and out.

2   Clean out the oilways using a bottle brush, wire or other suitable implement, and blow through with compressed air. Squirt some clean engine oil through to check that the oilways are clear.

3   If the core plugs are defective and show signs of weeping, they must be renewed at this stage. To remove, carefully drive a punch through the centre of the plug and use the punch to lever the plug out. Clean the aperture thoroughly and prior to fitting the new plug, smear the orifice with sealant. Use a small-headed hammer and carefully drive the new core plug into position with the convex side outwards. Check that it is correctly seated on completion.

4   As the components are assembled, lubricate them with clean engine oil and use a suitable sealant where applicable.

5   Make sure that all blind tapped holes are clean, with any oil mopped out of them. This is because it is possible for a casting to fracture when a bolt is screwed in owing to hydraulic pressure.

19 Cylinder liner protrusion – checking

1   The protrusion of the cylinder liners when assembled to the block must be within prescribed limits so that a gastight seal can be achieved when the head is bolted on. One liner protruding too much or not enough will, despite the cylinder head gasket, make it impossible to secure a gas or watertight joint.

2   An O-ring seal is fitted between each liner mating flange and the cylinder block. These seals compress when the cylinder head is tightened down to effect a watertight seal.

3   Although the actual liner protrusion check method is the same, the procedure differs if the engine is assembled or dismantled.

4   If the cylinder head has been removed with the engine *in situ* the liners must be held under compression with the use of liner clamps (photo). Remove the dowels from the cylinder block top face to allow the clamps to be fitted, if necessary.

5   If the engine is dismantled, check that the seal mating surfaces of the liners and the cylinder block are clean then insert each liner into its respective position in the cylinder block without its seal.

6   Check each liner protrusion in turn measuring the distance between the top face of the liner and the top face of the cylinder block. Use a dial test indicator if available but, failing this, use a metal rule and feeler gauges to assess the protrusion.

7   As the protrusion of each liner in turn is checked, ensure that it is squarely located in the cylinder block. The protrusion of each liner should be within the limits specified (see Specifications at the start of this Chapter).

8   Finally check the difference in height between adjacent liners. Use the dial test indicators or rule and feeler gauges to measure the difference in height, if any, between adjacent liners at a point on each lying along the centre axis parallel with the crankshaft on the top face. Each difference in level must not exceed the maximum specified.

9   If the checks reveal a discrepancy on an installed engine it will be necessary to renew the liner O-rings or even one or more liners. In either case the engine/transmission unit will have to be removed for dismantling.

10   Once the checks have shown the liners to be within limits of protrusion and squareness reassembling can continue or, if appropriate, temporary retainer clamps/straps should be fitted to hold them in position. *Don't turn the crankshaft if the liners are not restrained from movement.* Cover the exposed engine internal parts if there is likely to be a delay before completing reassembly.

11   With new liners, once correctly located, mark their sequence in the block (see Fig. 1.27) and withdraw them so that their piston/rods can be fitted.

20 Engine – complete reassembly

Pistons and liners

1   Fit the piston rings to the pistons. Always fit the rings from the piston crown end. Use three old feeler blades equally spaced behind the ring so that it will slide down to the lower grooves without dropping into the higher ones (photo).

2   Make sure that the rings are correctly located and the right way up. If genuine Citroën piston rings are being used, refer to Fig. 1.30. If special proprietary rings are being fitted, follow the manufacturer's instructions.

3   Twist the piston rings so that the gap in the oil control ring expander aligns with the gudgeon pin and the gaps in the rails are offset from the gudgeon pin by between 20.0 and 50.0 mm. The caps in the top two compression rings should be equally spaced (120°) from the gap in the oil control expander around the piston.

4   If new piston/liner assemblies have been supplied, the identification marks on the piston and liner (photo) should be:

Piston	Liner
A	One file mark on rim
B	Two file marks on rim
C	Three file marks on rim

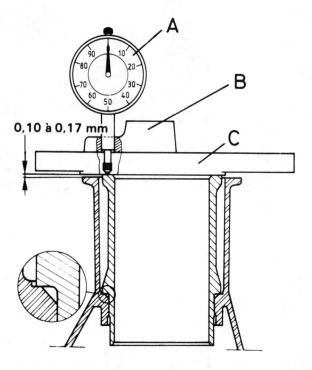

Fig. 1.29 Cylinder liner protrusion check using a dial gauge (Sec 19)

Gauge and mounting (A and B) and flat plate (C)

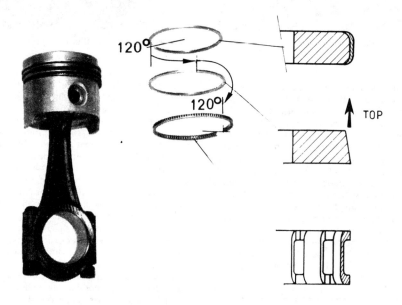

Fig. 1.30 Piston rings showing correct orientation (Sec 20)

5 All four pistons should be of the same grading.

6 Fit the liners to the piston/connecting rod assemblies so that when installed in the cylinder block, the rim mark on the liner will be towards the oil gallery side and the arrow on the piston crown facing towards the timing chain cover end of the engine (photo). Piston-to-rod relationship is not important.

7 Oil the piston rings liberally and fit a compressor to the piston and compress the rings fully. When fitted, the top edge of the ring compressor should be 4 to 5 mm below the crown of the piston.

8 Lubricate the bore of the liner and insert the piston. As this is done, the compressor will be pushed off (photo).

9 Push the liner down so that the piston crown is level with or just below the top edge of the liner.

10 With the pistons and liners reassembled, fit a new O-ring seal over the bottom end of each liner in turn, ensuring that the seals are not twisted as they are fitted (photo).

11 Remove the big-end caps, wipe the recesses in rod and cap absolutely clean and fit the bearing shells. If the original shells are being used again, make sure that they are being returned to their original locations.

12 Push the liner/rod assemblies into the block, without disturbing the seals and aligning the location marks (photo).

13 Fit clamps to hold the liners in the block.

Crankshaft

14 Place the block so that it rests on its top face, wipe out the recesses and fit the main bearing shells (photo).

15 Fit the semi-circular thrust washers which control crankshaft endfloat. The oil grooves of the thrust washers must be against the machined face of the crankshaft (photo).

16 Oil the shell bearings and lower the crankshaft into position (photo).

20.1 Method of fitting piston rings

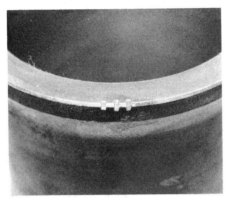
20.4 Piston/liner grading mark

20.6 Piston crown showing directional arrow

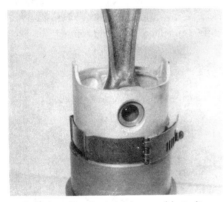
20.8 Fitting the piston/rod assembly to its cylinder liner

20.10 Cylinder liner O-ring seal

20.12 Installing piston/liner assembly

20.14 Shell bearings in position

20.15 Crankshaft thrust washers

20.16 Lowering the crankshaft into position

17 Now check the crankshaft endfloat. Do this by first pushing the crankshaft fully in one direction and then in the other. A dial gauge or feeler blades should be used to measure the endfloat (photo). If the endfloat is not within the specified limits, change the thrust washers and fit alternatives of suitable thickness. Thrust washers are available in a choice of four thicknesses.
18 Fit the big-end caps, complete with bearing shells, well lubricated. Make sure that the cap/rod matching marks are in alignment. This will ensure that both tongues of the shells are on the same side (photo).
19 Tighten the big-end nuts to the specified torque (photo).

Crankcase housing
20 Check that the three location dowels are in position in the cylinder block flange face and fit a new O-ring seal to each (photo).
21 Clean the recesses in the remaining crankcase housing section and fit the main bearing shells. Note that the grooved shells are located in positions 2 and 4. Lubricate the main bearing shells with clean engine oil.
22 Apply an even layer of jointing compound to the mating flange of the crankcase.
23 Locate the crankcase housing, taking care not to displace the bearing shells (photo).

24 Lubricate the bolt threads, then screw in the ten main bearing/casing bolts with flat washers; noting that the two longer bolts are at the flywheel housing end and the very long one at the crankshaft pulley end on the oil pump side.
25 Tighten the bolts in the sequence given in two stages to the specified torque (Fig. 1.31).
26 Now screw in and tighten the seven housing flange bolts with their spring washers (photo).
27 Grease the lips of a new crankshaft oil seal and drive it squarely into position (photo).

Cylinder head
28 Refit the cylinder head, as described in Section 8, paragraphs 28 to 33 (inclusive) and 37.

Timing chain and sprockets
29 Fit the timing chain tensioner oil filter and the crankshaft sprocket Woodruff key. Bolt the chain tensioner into position (photos).
30 Rotate the crankshaft by temporarily screwing in two flywheel bolts and placing a bar between them until the key is in alignment with the crankcase joint.

20.17 Checking the crankshaft endfloat

20.18 Fitting a big-end cap

20.19 Tightening a big-end cap nut

20.20 Crankcase flange O-ring seal in position on dowel

20.23 Fitting the crankcase housing

20.26 Crankcase housing flange bolts

20.27 Fitting the new crankshaft oil seal

20.29A Locate the chain tensioner filter ...

20.29B ... then fit the tensioner

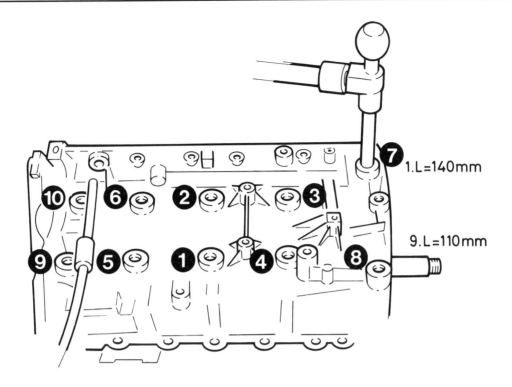

1.L=140mm

9.L=110mm

Fig. 1.31 Main bearing/casing bolt tightening sequence (Sec 20)

31 Temporarily fit the camshaft sprocket and rotate the camshaft until the keyway is positioned as shown in Fig. 1.32.
32 Fit the crankshaft sprocket (photo).
33 Loop the chain around the crankshaft sprocket so that the bright link on the chain is centred on the timing mark on the sprocket (photo).
34 Now loop the chain around the camshaft sprocket so that the two bright links are positioned one on each side of the sprocket timing mark. Push the sprocket with chain onto the camshaft, if necessary move the camshaft a fraction to align the keyway (photo).
35 Screw in the camshaft sprocket bolt with fuel pump eccentric and tighten to the specified torque (photos).
36 Where the first type chain tensioner is fitted, check that the tensioner shoe is locked in the retracted position and assemble the two retaining bolts and locking washers, the joint gasket and the spacer plate to the tensioner. Fit the tensioner to the block and tighten the two bolts to their specified torque. Arm the tensioner by turning the lock ratchet in a clockwise direction and allow the tensioner to automatically take up the chain tension; don't assist the action of the tensioner (photo).
37 Where the second type chain tensioner is fitted, fit the tensioner into position on the block and tighten the retaining bolts. Arm the tensioner by engaging the spring and prising it upwards (Fig. 1.33).
38 Refit the timing chain guide plate and tighten the two retaining bolts to the specified torque.

Oil pump
39 Check that the locating dowel is in position and fit the oil pump with spacer plate; no gasket is used. If the pump driven sprocket is hard to turn, release the pump mounting bolts and turn the pump slightly on its locating dowel. Re-tighten the bolts (photo).
40 Fit the oil pump drive sprocket and Woodruff key to the crankshaft (photo).

General
41 The engine is now ready for reconnection to the transmission unit. If required, certain engine ancillary items such as the oil filter, oil pressure sender and coolant pump can be fitted into position before reconnecting the engine and transmission (photo).

Fig. 1.32 Align the camshaft and crankshaft sprocket Woodruff key slots as shown (Sec 20)

20.32 Locate the crankshaft sprocket

20.33 Timing chain bright link at crankshaft sprocket

20.34 Timing chain bright links at camshaft sprocket timing mark

20.35A Fuel pump eccentric

20.35B Tightening the sprocket retaining bolt

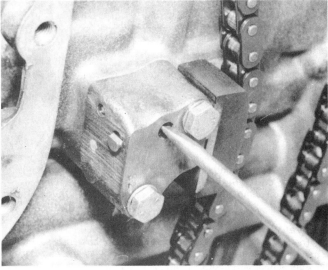

20.36 Releasing the timing chain tensioner (first type)

20.39 Fitting the oil pump with spacer plate

20.40 Oil pump drive sprocket

20.41 Oil pressure sender switch

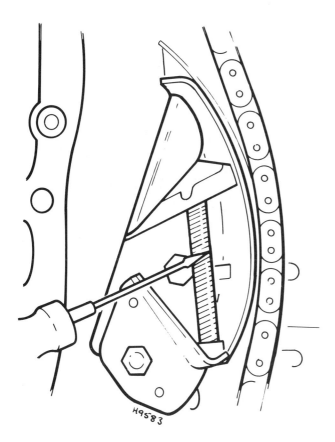

Fig. 1.33 Arming the second type chain tensioner (Sec 20)

21 Engine/transmission – reconnection

1   Check that the oil pick-up strainer is in position within the transmission casing.
2   Fit the sump cover using a new gasket.
3   Tighten the fixing bolts and drain plug to the specified torque.
4   Fit the cover plate.

5   Apply jointing compound to the mating surfaces on the engine and transmission. Ensure that an even layer of sealant is applied around the oil duct.
6   On the transmission, locate a new O-ring seal and check that the locating dowels and the studs are in position (photo).
7   Offer the transmission to the engine, screw in the connecting bolts and nuts and tighten to the specified torque (photo).
8   The timing cover can now be fitted (photo). The new timing cover gasket must be fitted dry and, prior to fitting the cover, check that the centering pin is in position and put the bolt nearest the coolant pump pulley into its cover hole, otherwise the pulley will prevent it from being fitted later (photo). Do not tighten the cover bolts yet.
9   Fit the coolant hose retainer under its cover bolts.
10 Use the crankshaft pulley to centralise the timing chain cover and then tighten the cover bolts to the specified torque.
11 Cut off the upper ends of the cover gasket flush. Lubricate the lips of the crankshaft pulley oil seal and locate it onto the crankshaft and into the timing cover. Drive the seal carefully into position using a suitable tube drift or mandrel.
12 Locate the Woodruff key into its groove in the crankshaft, refit the coolant pump drive pulley and tighten the retaining nut to the specified torque (photo). When tightening the pulley retaining nut, fit two bolts into the flywheel flange end of the crankshaft and jam a lever between them to prevent the crankshaft from turning. The nut threads should be treated with a suitable locking sealant prior to fitting.
13 Fit the alternator drivebelt pulley into position on the front end of the coolant pump drivebelt pulley and secure with the three bolts.
14 Fit the flywheel. Apply thread locking fluid to clean threads and screw in the flywheel bolts to the specified torque. The flywheel holes are offset so it will only go onto the crankshaft flange in one position (photos).
15 Fit the clutch and centralise the friction plate, as described in Chapter 5.
16 Fit a new gasket and the flywheel housing (Chapter 5) complete with transfer gears. Make sure that the engine lifting lug and earth strap are correctly located under their respective bolts.
17 If they were removed, bolt the engine mountings to the flywheel housing.
18 Fit the starter motor. Tighten the bolts and nuts in the following order:

   1   Starter drive end flange to flywheel housing
   2   Brush end bracket to engine crankcase
   3   Brush end bracket to starter motor

19 Adjust the valve clearances (Section 7). Use a new gasket and fit the rocker cover.
20 Refit the alternator and the remaining engine ancillary items still to be fitted; referring to Section 11. Reverse the removal sequence of the various items and refer to the relevant Chapter concerned for full fitting details.

21.6 O-ring seal on the transmission casing

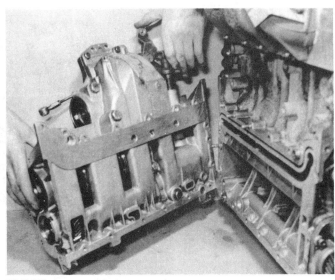

21.7 Offering transmission to engine

21.8A Refitting the timing cover with new gasket

21.8B Timing cover bolt nearest the coolant pump pulley

21.12 Tightening the crankshaft pulley nut

21.14A Insert the flywheel bolts ...

21.14B ... and tighten them to the specified torque

22 Engine – initial start-up after overhaul

1 Make sure that the battery is fully charged and that all lubricants, coolant and fuel are replenished. Top up the hydraulic system and prime the high pressure (HP) pump, as described in Section 5 (paragraph 10) of Chapter 8.
2 It will require several revolutions of the engine on the starter motor to pump the petrol up to the carburettor.
3 As soon as the engine fires and runs, keep it going at a fast tickover only (no faster), and bring it up to the normal working temperature.

4 With the engine running, repressurize the hydraulic system, as described in Section 5 (paragraph 11) of Chapter 8.
5 As the engine warms up there will be odd smells and some smoke from parts getting hot and burning off oil deposits. The signs to look for are leaks of water or oil which will be obvious if serious. Check also the exhaust pipe and manifold connections, as these do not always 'find' their exact gas tight position until the warmth and vibration have acted on them, and it is almost certain that they will need tightening further. This should be done of course, with the engine stopped.
6 When normal running temperature has been reached adjust the engine idling speed, as described in Chapter 3. Run the engine until the fan cuts in and then switch off. Check that no oil or coolant is leaking with the engine stationary.
7 Allow at least two hours for the engine to cool down and then retighten the cylinder head bolts after removing the rocker cover. Follow the bolt tightening sequence and, starting with the first, slacken the bolt and retighten it to the specified final tightening torque before loosening the second bolt. Repeat until all bolts have been retightened.
8 Check and adjust the valve clearances.
9 Check the ignition timing.
10 Road test the car to check that the timing is correct and that the engine is giving the necessary smoothness and power. Do not race the engine – if new bearings and/or pistons have been fitted it should be treated as a new engine and run in at a reduced speed.
11 Change the engine oil at 1000 miles (1600 km), if many of the engine internal components have been renewed. At the same mileage, check the tension of the drivebelt.

PART B: 171 and 159 ENGINES

23 General description

The 171 and 159 engine types fitted to the BX 16 and BX 19 models has four wet liner cylinders, a five bearing crankshaft and an overhead camshaft.

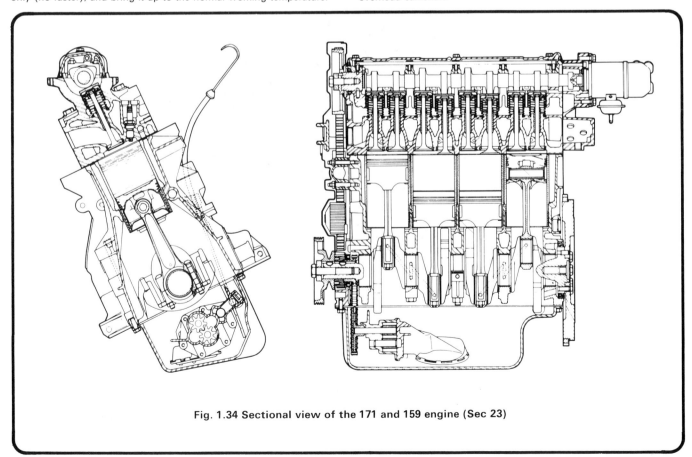

Fig. 1.34 Sectional view of the 171 and 159 engine (Sec 23)

Camshaft drive is by toothed belt. The belt is tensioned by a spring-loaded wheel and also drives the coolant pump. The camshaft operates directly on bucket tappets (cam followers); valve clearance adjustment is by shims inserted between the tappet and the valve stem. The distributor is driven directly from the tail of the camshaft.

The oil pump is located in the sump and is chain driven from the crankshaft.

The engine and transmission are mounted in line and located transversely in the engine compartment.

24 Routine maintenance

1 The routine maintenance procedures on the 171 and 159 engine types are, in general, the same as described for the smaller engine variants in Section 2, but the following differences apply.
2 The location of the engine oil level dipstick and the oil filter differ, as does the sump drain plug (photos).

25 Lubrication system – description

A pressure feed system of lubrication is fitted, with oil being circulated round the engine by a pump which draws oil from the sump below the engine unit.

The high output rotary pump is located in the bottom of the timing case and it is driven by a chain connected to a sprocket on the front of the crankshaft. Oil is drawn through a strainer in the sump and delivered to a filter cartridge mounted on the front of the crankcase. A relief valve operates to prevent excessive pressure when approximately 3.5 bar (50 lbf/in^2) is reached.

On leaving the cartridge filter, the oil is ducted by a gallery to the crankshaft main bearings. An internal duct conducts oil up to the camshaft and it is distributed to the camshaft bearings and rocker mechanism through the follow rocker shaft. The big-end bearings are supplied with oil through drillings in the crankshaft.

After lubricating the bearing surfaces to which it is ducted the oil leaks into the engine interior where, as spray or mist, it lubricates the other bearing surfaces such as cylinder walls, small-ends, gears and so on. The oil then drains down into the sump to repeat the cycle.

A pressure switch located directly above the oil filter in the crankcase will light the oil pressure warning light in the instrument panel if the pressure falls below 0.6 bar (8.7 lbf/in^2) with the ignition switched on. In the event of the cartridge filter becoming clogged a safety bypass valve located in the filter mounting will open to prevent oil starvation. Unfiltered oil is then supplied to the bearings.

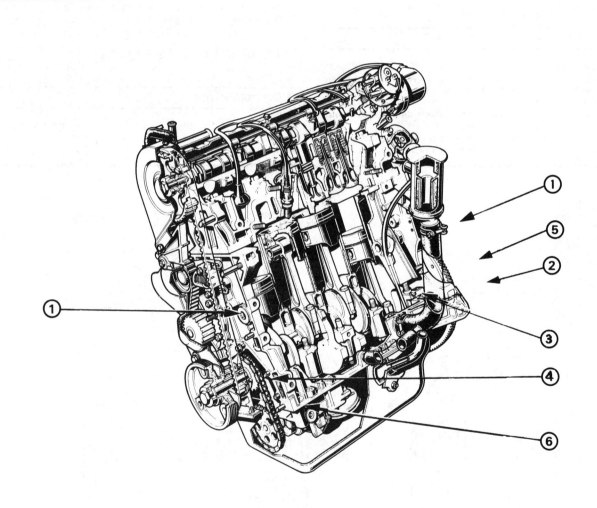

Fig. 1.35 Possible sources of oil leakage (171 and 159 engines) (Sec 24)

1 Lubrication groove plugs
2 Crankshaft seal at flywheel end
3 Bearing cap (No 1) at flywheel end
4 Lower crankcase front plate
5 Engine flywheel centering dowel
6 Lower crankcase

24.2A Oil filter (171 and 159 engines)

24.2B Sump drain plug (171 and 159 engines)

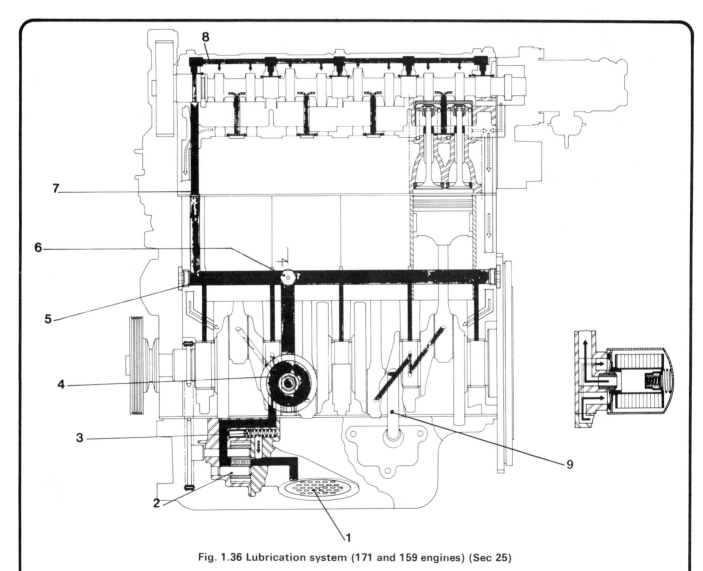

Fig. 1.36 Lubrication system (171 and 159 engines) (Sec 25)

1 Strainer
2 Oil pump
3 Relief valve
4 Filter cartridge (with bypass valve)
5 Crankshaft and connecting rod bearing lubrication groove
6 Oil pressure switch
7 Cylinder head lubricant filter
8 Bearings and cam oil gallery
9 Suction drainage well

26 Oil filter – removal and refitting

1   The oil filter is located on the inlet manifold side of the engine in the lower side face of the crankcase. The filter must be renewed at the specified intervals.
2   Removal and renewal of the oil filter is the same as that described for the smaller engine variants, therefore refer to Section 4 and proceed as described in paragraphs 2 to 5 inclusive.

27 Major operations possible with engine installed

The following items can be removed and refitted with the engine in the vehicle:

(a) *Cylinder head*
(b) *Camshaft and camshaft drivebelt*
(c) *Clutch and flywheel (after removal of transmission)*
(d) *Sump (after removal of the support member between the crossmember and the front cross panel. Disconnect the hydraulic line from the clip attached to the support member)*

28 Major operations requiring engine removal

The engine must be removed for the following operation.

(a) *Removal of the crankshaft and main bearings*

29 Valve clearances – checking and adjusting

1   The valve clearances must be checked and if necessary adjusted when the engine is cold, so allow it to cool down if recently run.
2   Remove the camshaft cover, trying not to damage the gasket.
3   Prepare to rotate the crankshaft, either by jacking up one front wheel and turning the wheel with 5th gear engaged, or with a spanner on the crankshaft pulley bolt. The crankshaft will be easier to rotate if the spark plugs are first removed.
4   Have ready a pencil and paper to record the measured clearances.
5   Turn the crankshaft until the cam lobe nearest the pulley end of the engine is pointing vertically upwards. Use feeler gauges to measure the clearance between the base of the cam and the tappet (photo). Record the clearance.
6   Repeat the measurement for the other seven valves, turning the crankshaft as necessary so that the cam lobe in question is always vertically upwards.
7   Calculate the difference between each measured clearance and the desired value (see Specifications). Note that the value for inlet valves is different from that for exhaust. Counting from either end of the engine, the valve sequence is:

Exhaust – Inlet – Inlet – Exhaust – Exhaust – Inlet – Inlet – Exhaust

8   If any clearance measured is outside the specified tolerance, adjustment must be carried out as described below.
9   If all clearances are within tolerance, refit the camshaft cover, using a new gasket if necessary. Note the copper washer under the bolt at the timing belt end (photo).

Valve clearances – adjustment
10   Remove the camshaft, as described in Section 31.
11   Lift off a tappet and its shim. Be careful that the shim does not fall out of the tappet. Clean the shim and measure its thickness with a micrometer (photos).
12   Refer to the clearance recorded for the valve concerned. If the clearance was larger than specified, a thicker shim must be fitted; if the clearance was too small, a thinner shim must be fitted.

Sample calculation – clearance too large:
   Desired clearance (A) 0.20 mm
   Measured clearance (B) 0.28 mm
   Difference (B–A) = +0.08 mm
   Original shim thickness 2.62 mm
   Required shim thickness 2.62 + 0.08 = 2.70 mm

Sample calculation – clearance too small:
   Desired clearance (A) 0.40 mm
   Measured clearance (B) 0.23 mm
   Difference (B–A) = –0.17 mm
   Original shim thickness 2.86 mm
   Required shim thickness 2.86 – 0.17 = 2.69 mm

13   Shims are available in thicknesses from 2.225 to 3.025 mm in steps of 0.025 mm and also from 3.100 to 3.550 mm in steps of 0.075 mm. Clean new shims before measuring or fitting them.
14   Repeat the operations on the other tappets and shims, keeping each tappet identified so that it can be refitted in the same position.
15   When reassembling, oil the shim and fit it on the valve stem, then oil the tappet and lower it smoothly into position. If the tappet is raised at any stage the shim may be dislodged.
16   When all the tappets are in position with their shims, refit the camshaft. Check the valve clearances before refitting the camshaft drivebelt in case a mistake has been made and the camshaft has to be removed again.

29.5 Measuring a valve clearance

29.9 Copper washer (arrowed) fits under bolt head

29.11A Lift off the tappet

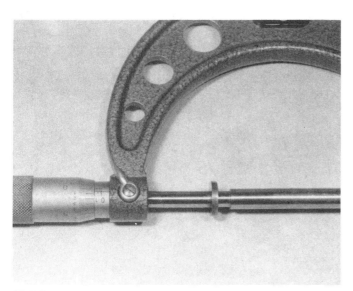

29.11B Measuring the thickness of a shim

30 Timing drivebelt – removal and refitting with engine installed

1 Disconnect the battery earth lead.
2 Remove the alternator drivebelt (Chapter 12) and the HP pump drivebelt (Chapter 8).
3 Unbolt and remove the camshaft timing sprocket cover (photo).
4 Turn the crankshaft until the dowel hole in the pulley is at about 12 o'clock and the hole in the camshaft sprocket is at about 7 o'clock. In this position a 10 mm dowel should pass through each hole and into the timing recess behind. Verify this and then remove the dowels (photo).
5 Remove the clutch/torque converter bottom shield. Have an assistant jam the starter ring gear while the crankshaft pulley bolt is undone. This bolt is very tight. **Do not** jam the pulley by means of the timing dowel: damage will result. Remove the bolts and washer.
6 Check that the 10 mm dowels will still enter the timing holes: adjust the crankshaft position if necessary by means of the starter ring gear. Remove the crankshaft pulley, retrieving the Woodruff key if it is loose.
7 Remove the timing covers from the front of the camshaft drivebelt. Note the location of the various bolts (photo).
8 Slacken the two nuts on the front of the drivebelt tensioner and the single nut at the rear. Use a spanner on the square end of the tensioner cam spindle to turn the cam to the horizontal position and so compress the tensioner spring. Tighten the cam locknut (photo).
9 Remove the camshaft drivebelt, taking care not to kink it or contaminate it with oil if it is to be re-used.
10 Commence refitting by positioning the belt on the crankshaft sprocket, then refitting the pulley and verifying the correct position of the crankshaft by means of the dowel. (Observe the arrows on the belt showing the direction of rotation, and the timing lines which align with marks on the crankshaft and camshaft sprockets) (photo).

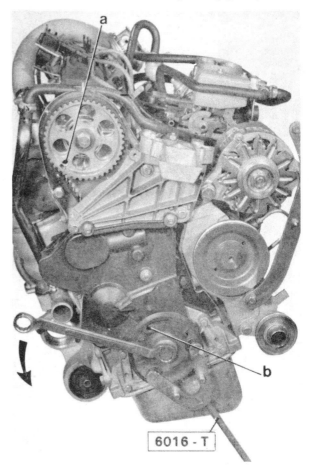

6016 - T

Fig. 1.38 Set the crankshaft pulley and camshaft sprocket dowel holes to the positions indicated at 'a' and 'b' (Sec 30)

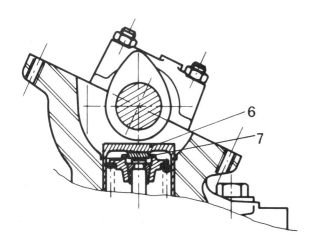

Fig. 1.37 Valve clearance is measured with the cam lobe vertically upwards. The tappet (6) and shim (7) are also indicated (Sec 29)

30.3 Camshaft timing sprocket cover removal

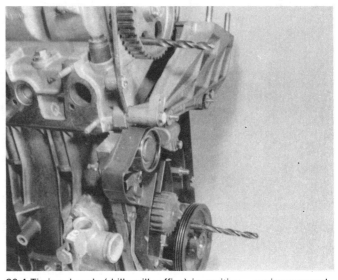

30.4 Timing dowels (drills will suffice) in position – engine removed for clarity

30.7 Central timing cover removed for access to tensioner

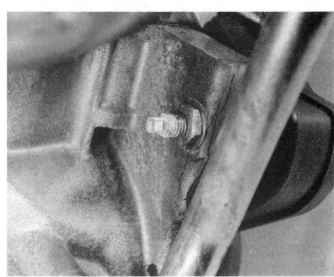

30.8 Tensioner cam spindle (square end) and locknut

30.10 Line on belt aligns with mark on camshaft sprocket

11 Fit the belt to the camshaft sprocket, round the tensioner and to the coolant pump sprocket.

12 Release the tensioner cam locknut and turn the cam downwards to release the spring. Tighten the locknut and the tensioner front nuts (photos).

13 Remove the timing dowels and turn the crankshaft through two full turns in the normal direction of rotation. Turn the crankshaft further to bring No 1 piston to TDC on the firing stroke (flywheel index mark aligned with the O-mark).

14 Slacken the tensioner front nuts and the cam locknut, then retighten them to the specified torque.

15 Turn the crankshaft further and make sure that the timing dowels can still be inserted. If not, remove the drivebelt and start again.

16 If a new belt has been fitted, it must be run in and retensioned as follows.

17 Tighten the crankshaft pulley bolt to the specified torque, then refit and tension the alternator drivebelt and the HP drivebelt. Temporarily refit the camshaft sprocket cover.

18 Run the engine up to operating temperature, indicated by the cooling fan operating, then stop it and allow it to cool for at least two hours.

19 Rotate the crankshaft to the TDC position, No 1 cylinder firing, then slacken and retighten the tensioner nuts once more.

20 Remove the alternator drivebelt, the HP drivebelt and the

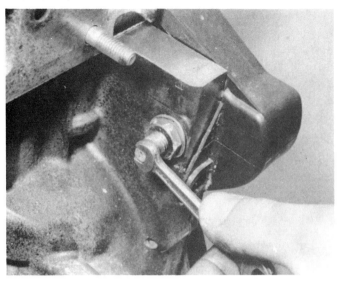

30.12A Turn the tensioner cam downwards ...

30.12B ... and tighten the drivebelt tensioner front nuts

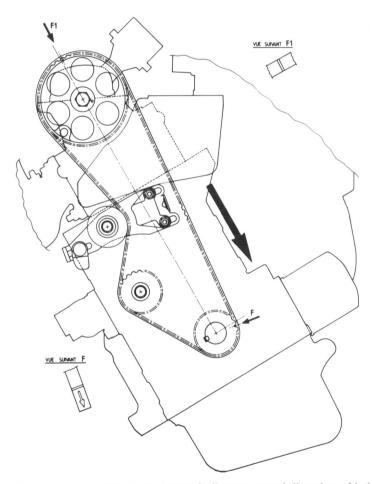

Fig. 1.39 Timing belt-to-sprockets alignment. Arrow indicates normal direction of belt rotation (Sec 30)

crankshaft pulley. Refit and secure the covers, then refit the pulley and tighten its bolt to the specified torque. Refit and tension the alternator drivebelt and the HP drivebelt.

21 Check the ignition timing and adjust if necessary.

31 Camshaft – removal and refitting with engine installed

1 Remove the camshaft drivebelt, as described in Section 30.

2 Remove the camshaft cover. For ease of access, remove the distributor cap and HT leads also.

3 Remove the distributor and the fuel pump from the thermostat housing.

4 Remove the camshaft lubrication manifold.

5 Lock the camshaft sprocket (eg with a timing dowel) and remove the sprocket retaining bolt. Remove the sprocket.

6 Unbolt and remove the camshaft sprocket inner cover plate from the cylinder head.

31.7A Undo the retaining screw ...

31.7B ... and remove the camshaft thrust plate

16 Refit the sprocket rear cover plate, locate it correctly with a 10 mm dowel and tighten its fastenings (photo). Fit the camshaft sprocket, dowel it and tighten its securing bolt to the specified torque.
17 Refit the fuel pump, the distributor and the lubrication manifold.
18 Refit the camshaft cover, the HT leads and the distributor cap.
19 Refit the camshaft drivebelt, referring to Section 30.

32 Cylinder head – removal and refitting with engine installed

1 Disconnect the battery earth lead.
2 Drain the cooling system, as described in Chapter 2.
3 Remove the air filter, as described in Chapter 3.
4 Disconnect and plug the feed and return hoses at the fuel pump.

31.16 Locating the cover plate with a 10 mm dowel

7 Unbolt and remove the camshaft thrust plate (photos).
8 The camshaft bearing caps can now be removed, starting with bearing number four at the distributor end. Make identifying marks if necessary then progressively loosen the bearing cap securing nuts. As the number four bearing is removed take care not to damage the seal between the distributor support and the bearing. Be prepared for the camshaft to spring upwards. Remove the camshaft.
9 Commence refitting by making sure that the crankshaft is in the correct (dowelled) position – if not, move it to this position to avoid possible piston/valve contact, (refer to the previous Section, paragraph 4).
10 Lubricate the camshaft bearings and lower the camshaft into position so that the fourth and sixth cams are resting on the tappets. Fit the centre bearing cap so that the oil hole is towards the front.
11 Refit the remaining bearing caps and tighten them to the specified torque in a progressive sequence. The seal bearing surface should have sealant applied. If the seal was damaged during dismantling, renew it and coat with a sealing compound.
12 If the oil seal at the camshaft sprocket end is being renewed (advisable), lubricate it with engine oil and drive it into position.
13 Refit and secure the camshaft stop (thrust) plate.
14 Check that the camshaft endfloat is as specified and if necessary renew the thrust plate.
15 Check that the valve clearances are as specified, referring to Section 29.

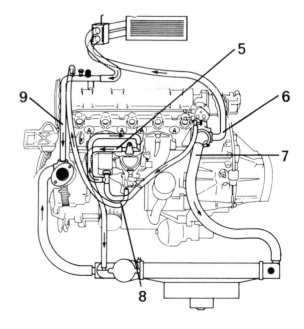

Fig. 1.40 Disconnect the hoses indicated for cylinder head removal (Sec 32)

5 Carburettor heating return hose
6 Water outlet duct hose
7 Water outlet duct hose
8 Inlet manifold hose
9 Heater coolant return pipe hose

5   Disconnect the coolant hoses from the thermostat housing, the inlet manifold and carburettor (heating return) – photo (Fig. 1.40).
6   Detach the heater coolant return hose from its securing clamp and support lug. Unbolt the dipstick tube support bracket (photos).
7   Remove the engine breather support screw.
8   Disconnect the accelerator cable at the carburettor.
9   Disconnect the coolant temperature leads and the lead from the carburettor idle cut-off solenoid.
10 Unclip and remove the distributor cap, detach the HT leads from the spark plugs and place them out of the way. Also disconnect the distributor LT leads. Remove the spark plugs.
11 Detach and remove the lining from the front right-hand wheel arch. This is best achieved with the vehicle raised at the front end and supported on safety stands. The roadwheel can then be removed to improve access under the wing for guard removal and subsequent operations.
12 Locate a spanner onto the crankshaft pulley bolt and turn the engine over to align the dowel hole in the pulley with the timing recess behind it. Insert a 10 mm dowel rod to lock the crankshaft in this position. The pistons must be at the half stroke position in their cylinders.
13 Unbolt and detach the exhaust downpipe.
14 Position a jack under the sump, interspace a piece of wood between the jack and sump to protect the sump, then raise the jack to support the weight of the engine (not lift it).

32.5 Coolant hose connections to carburettor auto-choke

32.6A Heater coolant hose and support clamp

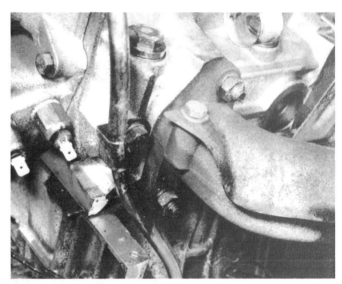

32.6B Dipstick guide tube support bracket

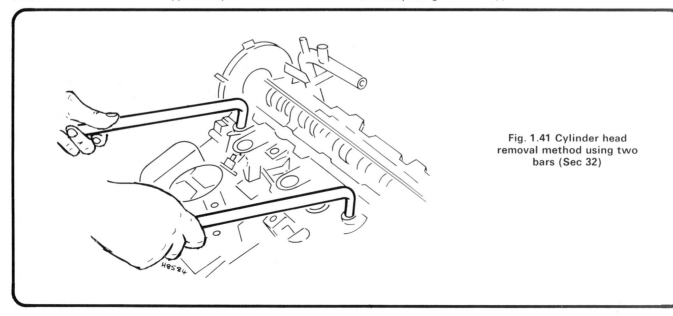

Fig. 1.41 Cylinder head removal method using two bars (Sec 32)

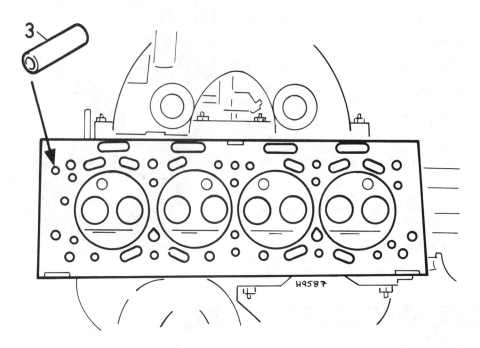

Fig. 1.42 Oil filter location in cylinder head (3) (Sec 32)

32.15 Right-hand engine mounting

15 Remove the alternator fan guard, then unbolt and remove the right-hand engine mounting (photo).
16 Unbolt and remove the upper and central timing covers.
17 Loosen the camshaft drivebelt tension, referring to paragraph 8 in Section 30, then disengage the belt from the camshaft sprocket.
18 Remove the camshaft cover. The cylinder head bolts can now be loosened half a turn at a time in the reverse order to that shown in Fig. 1.43 and removed. Discard the bolts – a new set should be obtained for refitting.
19 Remove the cylinder head, using a couple of bars through two of the bolt holes and 'rocking' it towards the front of the car. Remove the gasket and recover any loose dowels.
20 Fit cylinder liner clamps, or large washers secured with nuts and bolts, to keep the liners in position (photo). *If the liners are disturbed, the engine will have to be removed for new seals to be fitted.*
21 Before refitting the cylinder head, check that the mating faces are clean. Before removing the liner clamps, the liner protrusions should be

checked, as described in Section 43.
22 The oil filter in the cylinder head should be removed and renewed before refitting the cylinder head (Fig. 1.42).
23 Commence refitting by fitting the dowels to the cylinder block. Keep the flywheel end dowel raised by inserting a 5 mm punch or large nail through the hole in the front of the block (photo). Remove the liner clamps.
24 Fit the new gasket, dry, with the tab at the flywheel end. Lower the cylinder head into position, making sure that it mates with the dowels. Remove the punch or nail.
25 Fit the new cylinder head bolts, their threads clean and lightly oiled. Remember to fit the spacer to the bolt above the coolant pump.
26 Progressively tighten the bolts in the order shown in Fig. 1.43 to the Stage 1 specified torque.

32.20 Cylinder liners clamped with washers and bolts

27 Loosen cylinder head bolt number 1, then immediately retighten it to the Stage 2 specified torque, then tighten it further by the angle specified for Stage 3. Repeat for all the bolts, following the tightening sequence (photo).

28 Check the valve clearances and if necessary adjust them, referring to Section 29 for details. This is applicable even though the clearances may have been set when the cylinder head was removed.

29 Refit the timing belt and covers, as described in Section 30,

paragraph 10 on. Also refit the right-hand engine mountings. Tighten the securing bolts to the specified torque settings.

30 Refit the remaining components in the reverse order of removal. When reconnecting the exhaust balljoint connection smear the tube and bolts with Gripcott AF grease or similar.

31 Refill the cooling system, with reference to Chapter 2.

32 If hexagon headed cylinder head bolts are used, start the engine and warm it up until the cooling fan cuts in, then switch off and allow

32.23 Dowel is kept raised by inserting a rod or nail beneath it

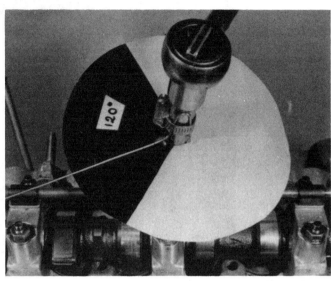

32.27 Home-made disc for measuring tightening angle. Disc is fixed and pointer rotates

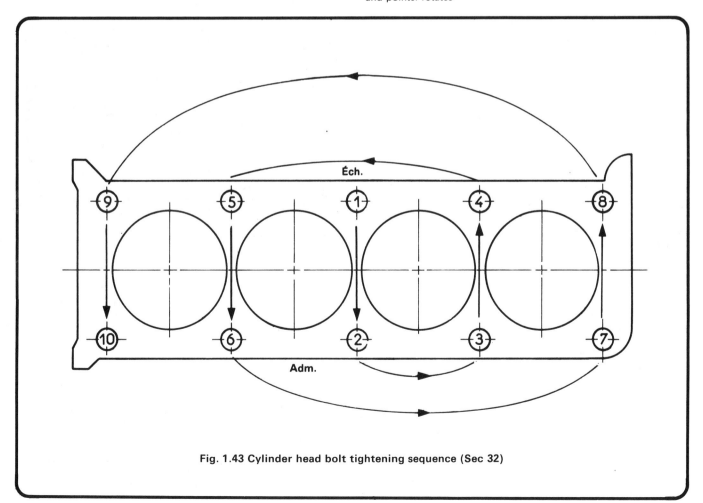

Fig. 1.43 Cylinder head bolt tightening sequence (Sec 32)

Fig. 1.44 Loosen the engine mounting bolt indicated (1) (Sec 32)

it to cool for at least two hours. Loosen the engine mounting bolt indicated in Fig. 1.44 then retighten the cylinder head bolts as described in paragraph 27. Retighten the mounting bolt then check the valve clearances. Note that if Torx type cylinder head bolts are fitted, retightening after warm-up is not required.

33 If a new belt has been fitted, retension it as described in Section 30.

33 Engine and transmission – removal

The engine and transmission removal, separation and refitting procedures described in this Chapter deal with the engine and manual transmission. If an automatic transmission is fitted, the procedures are similar except for the control linkages. Limited information only is available at the time of writing and the available details are given in Chapter 6.

If air conditioning is fitted, the system must be depressurized before disconnecting any system components – see Chapter 2.

1 The combined weight of the engine and transmission is not great due to the extensive use of aluminium alloy, but care must be taken not to damage components. An assistant will be required for some tasks.

2 Unbolt and remove the bonnet – see Chapter 11.

3 Detach the battery leads and remove the battery – see Chapter 12.

4 Chock the rear roadwheels, then raise the vehicle at the front so that the front roadwheels are clear of the ground. Unbolt and remove the front roadwheels.

5 The driveshafts must now be separated from the final drive housing. On the left-hand side unbolt and release the anti-roll bar connecting link, then separate the stub axle from the steering balljoint. Refer to Chapter 10 for details. Position a drain tray under the final drive housing then pull the left-hand driveshaft and wheel hub outwards to withdraw the inner end of the driveshaft from the final drive housing. About 1 litre of oil will drain from the final drive housing as the shaft is withdrawn.

6 Before removing the right-hand driveshaft, the differential sun gears must be supported in place, if possible using Citroën special tools 7101-TM and 7101-TN. If these special tools are not available it is possible to improvise using a suitable length of wooden dowel or tube approximately 24 mm in diameter, chamfered at the leading end to allow entry into the side gear splines.

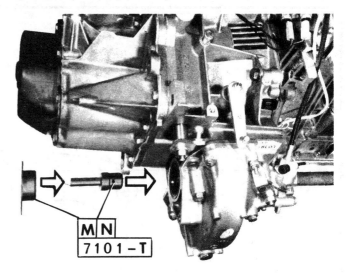

Fig. 1.45 Citroën special tool used to support the differential sun gears (Sec 33)

7 The right-hand driveshaft is disconnected from the differential housing by removing it completely. For details on its removal refer to Chapter 7, Section 4.

8 The hydraulic circuit must now be depressurized. Refer to Chapter 8, Section 2 for details.

9 Remove the air cleaner unit, as described in Chapter 3. Also unbolt and remove the air cleaner support bracket (photo).

10 Drain the cooling system and remove the radiator, referring to Chapter 2 for details.

11 Disconnect the throttle cable from the carburettor by releasing the inner cable nipple from the throttle quadrant then pulling the inner/outer cable from its support bracket. Place the cable out of the way.

33.9 Air cleaner support bracket

33.16 Reversing light switch and lead connections

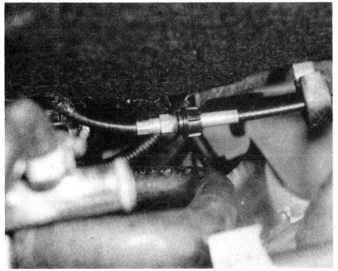

33.21 Speedometer drive cable connection between the engine and bulkhead

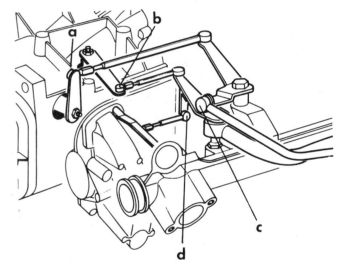

Fig. 1.46 Disconnect the gear linkages at the joints indicated (a, b, c and d) (Sec 33)

12 Disconnect the vent hose from the carburettor (this hose runs down to the radiator left-hand lower side).

13 Disconnect the fuel supply hose to the fuel pump and plug the hose.

14 Note the positions of the spark plug HT leads in the location clips on the top face of the cam cover and release them. Detach the HT leads from the spark plugs, and release the distributor cap. Disconnect the LT (low tension) leads from the distributor, then place the cap and leads out of the way.

15 Disconnect the wiring harness connection blocks under the battery support frame, also the wiring terminal block in line with the battery positive (+) lead.

16 Disconnect the reversing light switch leads from the gearbox (photo).

17 Undo the retaining nut and detach the battery earth (−) lead from the battery support tray. Remove the tray.

18 Disconnect the clutch cable from the lever by prising the lever rearwards.

19 Disconnect the battery earth lead and the braided earth strap from the gearbox.

20 Detach the diagnostic socket lead connector at the left-hand side under the ignition coil.

21 Disconnect the speedometer drive cable (photo).

22 Disconnect the heater coolant hoses at the bulkhead.

23 Disconnect the hydraulic suction pipe from the HP pump and the hydraulic pump from the pressure regulator outlet. Plug the pipes to prevent fluid loss and the ingress of dirt.

24 Detach the hydraulic pipe support clip from the alternator support strap.

25 Disconnect the rigid pipe from the pressure regulator unit and detach the pipe support clip. Position the pipe out of the way, but do not over-distort the pipe. Plug the end of the pipe.

26 Referring to Fig. 1.46, disconnect the gearchange linkages at the points indicated. The linkage rods have balljoints which are simply prised apart.

27 Working from underneath the vehicle, unbolt the exhaust downpipe and disconnect it from the manifold.

28 Unclip and detach the coolant bottom hose at connection on the right-hand rear lower corner of the engine. As the hose is pulled free from the connection allow for additional coolant spillage.

33.29 Engine lift support bracket – front right-hand side

33.30 Torque link and through-bolt (arrowed)

33.31 Left-hand side transmission mounting

33.34 Engine and transmission removal

29 Fit the lifting sling and hoist into position. Take the weight of the engine and transmission. Arrange the lifting sling so that when connected to the lifting eyes it will allow the gearbox to be tilted downwards at an angle of about 45° when the units are being lifted out (photo).

30 Working underneath the vehicle, detach the torque link by unscrewing and removing its through-bolt. If necessary position a jack under the engine to allow it to be raised and allow the bolt to be removed (photo).

31 Unbolt and detach the left-hand side transmission mounting (photo).

32 Unbolt and remove the right-hand upper engine mounting.

33 Check around the engine and transmission to ensure that all attachments are disconnected. Before lifting out the engine and transmission unit, it is advisable to position a protector plate of some description between the height corrector unit and the engine to prevent damage to the rubber dust cover during removal.

34 Carefully lift the engine and transmission unit upwards, tilting the transmission downwards as they are raised and manoeuvred from the engine compartment. There isn't much room to spare, so an assistant is necessary to guide the units clear of the surrounding fittings (photo).

35 Once clear of the car the engine and transmission can be removed for cleaning and repairs as necessary.

34 Engine dismantling – general

Refer to Section 10.

35 Engine dismantling – ancillary items

1 The extent of engine ancillary items to be removed is dependent on the extent to which the engine is to be dismantled and repaired. Refer to Section 11 of this Chapter and remove those items listed which are applicable, ignoring references to the coolant pump and, if the cylinder head is to be removed, the exhaust manifold. These two items are best removed later during the engine dismantling procedures.

2 Note that the clutch unit is removed after the engine and gearbox are separated (Section 36).

36 Engine and transmission – separation

1 If still in position, unbolt and remove the starter motor (photos). Refer to Chapter 12 for further details if necessary.

36.1A Starter motor is secured by three Allen bolts ...

36.1B ... and a mounting bracket

2   Unbolt and remove the remaining engine-to-transmission bolts.
3   Support the engine and pull the transmission away from it. Do not allow the weight of the transmission to hang on the primary shaft. Recover any loose dowels.

37 Engine – complete dismantling

1   Support the engine on the bench or a strong table. If such facilities are not available then it will have to be dismantled on the floor, but at least cover the floor with newspaper or a sheet of hardboard.
2   Remove any remaining ancillary components still attached to the engine (see Section 35).
3   The exhaust manifold may be removed now, or it can be left in place to serve as a handle until the head is removed.
4   Unbolt and remove the crankshaft pulley. Jam the flywheel teeth when undoing the pulley bolt to stop the crankshaft rotating.
5   Remove the camshaft drivebelt covers, noting the location of the various sizes of bolt.
6   Unbolt and remove the camshaft cover.
7   Rotate the crankshaft by means of the flywheel until a 10 mm diameter rod can be passed through the hole in the camshaft sprocket and into the timing recess. The pistons are now at mid-stroke so piston/valve contact cannot occur.
8   Release the camshaft drivebelt tensioner by slackening its nuts (two at the front and one behind the front plate) and using the square end of the cam spindle to bring the cam into a horizontal position.
9   Remove the camshaft drivebelt, taking care not to kink it and noting its direction of travel if it is to be re-used.
10 Unbolt and remove the camshaft drivebelt tensioner.
11 Remove the belt side covers and crankshaft sprocket. Recover the Woodruff key.
12 Unbolt and remove the camshaft sprocket. Restrain the sprocket from turning if necessary using the 10 mm diameter rod inserted through the timing hole in the sprocket (photo).
13 Unbolt and remove the engine mounting bracket, the camshaft sprocket backplate and the coolant pump.
14 Slacken the ten cylinder head bolts, working in the reverse sequence of that used when tightening (Fig. 1.43). Remove the bolts and washers.
15 Remove the cylinder head. If it seems to be stuck, use a couple of metal rods in two of the bolt holes to rock it free. Do not attempt to hammer or lever it off. Retrieve the two locating dowels if they are loose.
16 Fit liner clamps if it is not proposed to remove the pistons and liners. See Section 32, paragraph 20. Invert the engine.
17 Unbolt and remove the flywheel. It is dowelled so it can only be refitted one way.
18 Remove the suction drain pipe from the side of the sump.
19 Unbolt and remove the sump. Note the location of the three Allen-headed bolts (photo).

37.12 Lock the camshaft sprocket with a 10 mm rod

37.19 Location of the three Allen head bolts

20 Remove the bolts which secure the oil pump, noting the special centering bolt at the rear.

21 Unbolt and remove the oil seal carrier plate.

22 Lower the oil pump into the engine so that its chain can be removed. Withdraw the pump and recover the spacer, the dowel and the chain.

23 Pull the oil pump sprocket off the crankshaft and recover the Woodruff key.

24 Unscrew the connecting rod cap bolts. Before removing the caps check that they are marked in numerical order, also the connecting rods, liners and pistons. Mark them if they are not.

25 If the cylinder liners are being removed, then the pistons, rods and liners can be lifted out of the block as individual units, but mark their relative positions.

26 Remove the bolts from main bearing caps 1, 2, 4 and 5. Also remove the two nuts and the two side bolts from the centre cap. Make alignment marks on the bearing caps and remove them. Keep the bearing shells with their caps if they are to be re-used. Recover the thrust washer segments from either side of No 2 bearing cap.

27 Remove the oil seal from the flywheel end of the crankshaft.

28 Lift the crankshaft out of the crankcase. Recover the upper half main bearing shells and the other two thrust washer segments.

29 If the cylinder liners have been left clamped in position in the cylinder block, their protrusions above the cylinder block face must be checked, as described in Section 43, before reassembling the engine.

38 Engine components – examination and renovation (general)

Refer to Section 14.

39 Cylinder head – dismantling, decarbonising and reassembly

1 Unbolt and remove the inlet manifold (with carburettor) and the exhaust manifold. Remove their gaskets and note that these must be renewed when reassembling.

2 Remove the camshaft from the cylinder head, as described in Section 31, paragraphs 3 to 8 inclusive.

3 Remove the tappets and shims, identifying their locations if they are to be re-used.

4 Extract the oil filter gauze from the oilway.

5 Proceed as described in Section 15, paragraphs 2 to 15 inclusive, to remove the valves and clean and inspect the various components. Note, however, that the makers state that no machining of the cylinder head surface is permitted. A warped head must therefore be renewed.

6 Factory exchange cylinder heads may have had 0.2 mm machined off the mating face. These heads are identified by the letter R stamped on a boss at the distributor end of the head. A gasket 0.2 mm thicker than normal must be used with such a head; the thicker gasket is identified by a cut-out in the tab at the clutch end.

7 Commence reassembly of the cylinder head by fitting new valve stem oil seals into position, then locate the valves, the spring seat washers (lubricated with engine oil), the springs and collets. Oil the valve stems liberally; a smear of grease will hold the collets in position while the spring is compressed. The valve springs can be fitted either way up.

8 Lubricate the tappet bores. Secure each shim to its valve stem with a dab of grease and carefully fit the tappets. If new components have been fitted so that the valve clearances are unknown, fit the thinnest possible shims to all valves.

9 Fit the camshaft to the head and oil its lobes and journals (photo). Fit the bearing caps, making sure that the middle ones are the right way round. Progressively tighten the bearing cap nuts to the specified torque.

10 Fit the camshaft thrust plate and tighten its securing bolt.

11 Press the lubrication manifold into position (photo).

12 Fit a new filter gauze in the oilway (photo).

13 Fit the coolant outlet housing, using a new gasket. Fit the thermostat and its elbow to the housing, again with a new gasket.

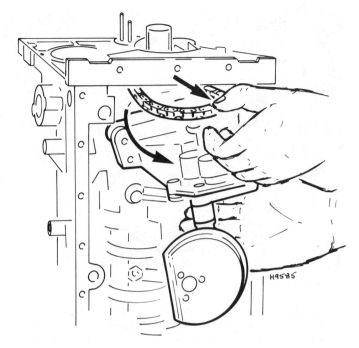

Fig. 1.47 Oil pump removal (Sec 37)

Fig. 1.48 The relative positions of the cylinder liners and block must be marked before removing them (Sec 37)

14 Fit the inlet and exhaust manifolds, using new gaskets, and tighten their fastenings to the specified torque.

15 Fit and secure the fuel pump (new gasket) and the distributor. If alignment marks were not made when dismantling, set the distributor in mid-slot. The drive is offset so it can only be fitted one way.

16 Fit the carburettor and its heat insulator.

17 Fit a new oil seal to the sprocket end of the camshaft, using a piece of tube to drive it home.

18 If valve clearance adjustment is to be carried out now, temporarily fit the camshaft sprocket and stand the cylinder head on wooden blocks so that open valves do not strike the work surface.

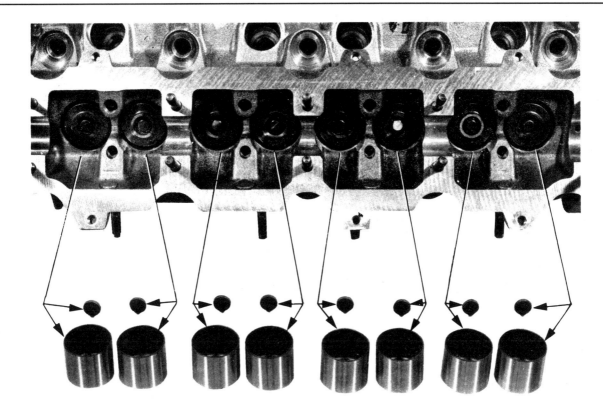

Fig. 1.49 Remove the tappets and shims and keep them in order (Sec 39)

39.9 Fit the camshaft into position

39.11 Refit the camshaft lubrication manifold

39.12 Insert the oil filter gauze in the cylinder head oilway

40 Examination and renovation of dismantled components

Crankshaft and main bearings

1   Refer to Section 16.
2   Later 171 (BX 16) engines (from 1984 on), in common with the 159 (BX 19) engines, have no spigot bush in the crankshaft tail; the diameter of the gearbox input shaft is correspondingly increased.
3   Therefore, on 171 type engines, if the later type crankshaft is being fitted and being mated to an earlier type input shaft, it will be necessary to obtain and insert a spigot bush.
4   If the reverse situation applies (new input shaft and old crankshaft), extract the spigot bush.

Big-end bearings

5   Refer to Section 16.

Cylinder liners, pistons, gudgeon pins and connecting rods

6   Refer to Section 16.

Timing drivebelt, sprockets and tensioner

7   Renew the drivebelt as a matter of course unless it is in perfect condition and is known to have covered only a nominal mileage. Renew the sprockets if they are damaged.

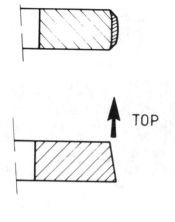

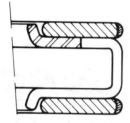

TOP

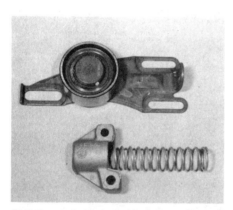

Fig. 1.50 Fitting direction for the standard piston rings (Sec 44)

8 The drivebelt tensioner should be examined for roughness of the wheel bearing and wear or distortion of the spring. Renew as necessary – the wheel, bearing and backplate must be renewed as an assembly (photo).

Oil pump

9 Remove the six bolts which hold the two halves of the oil pump together. Separate the halves, being prepared for the release of the relief valve spring and plunger (photo).
10 Inspect the rotors and their housing for wear and damage. No wear limits are published for this pump; any visible wear on the moving parts suggests that renewal is necessary. With the exception of the relief valve spring and plunger, individual components are not available (photos).
11 Lubricate the pump components well before reassembly. Bolt the two halves together, being careful not to trap the spring.
12 If the pump is to be renewed it is wise to renew the chain and the crankshaft sprocket also.

Camshaft and tappets

13 Inspect the camshaft lobes and bearing journals for wear and damage; if evident, renewal is probably necessary. Also inspect the bearing surfaces in the cylinder head and bearing caps.
14 Clean the camshaft lubrication manifold with solvent and then blow through it with compressed air. All the holes must be clear (photo).
15 Inspect the tappets for wear and scuffing; renew them as necessary. New tappets **must** be fitted if the camshaft is renewed; it is also advisable to renew the valve springs.

Flywheel and starter ring gear

16 Refer to Section 16, but ignore paragraph 42 as this is already dealt with in paragraphs 2 to 4 of this Section.

40.8 Camshaft (timing) drivebelt tensioner components

40.9 Separating the two halves of the oil pump

40.10A Inspect the pump gears for excessive wear

 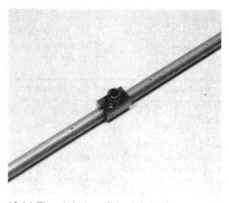

40.10B Oil pump relief valve spring and plunger

40.14 The pinholes of the lubrication manifold must be clear

41 Engine reassembly – general

Refer to Section 17.

42 Engine – preparation for reassembly

Refer to Section 18.

43 Cylinder liner protrusions – checking

Refer to Section 19.

44 Engine – complete reassembly

Pistons and liners

1 Reassemble the piston rings to the pistons and the pistons to the liners, as described in Section 20. Refer to Fig. 1.50 for the piston ring fitting orientation and arrange the oil control rings so that the rail gaps are offset to each other, and from the gudgeon pin hole by 20 to 30 mm (0.78 to 1.1 in).

2 the piston and liner assemblies can be fitted to the crankcase at this stage or, if preferred, after the crankshaft has been fitted. Again refer to Section 20 (paragraphs 10 to 13 inclusive).

Crankshaft

3 Position the block for access to the bottom end and fit the main bearing upper shells. Also fit the thrust washer segments to No 2 bearing, grooved sides outwards (photo); retain them with a smear of grease. It will be noted that the main bearing shells supplied comprise

plain and grooved type half shells. On early engine types there are two grooved half shells supplied, these being fitted to the number two and number four main bearings on the top (crankcase) side. On later engine types the bearing set contains seven grooved and three plain bearing shells, one plain bearing shell being located at the top (crankcase) side of number three main bearing and the other two are fitted to the number two and number four main bearing caps (Figs. 1.51 and 1.52).

44.3 Fitting the thrust washer upper segments

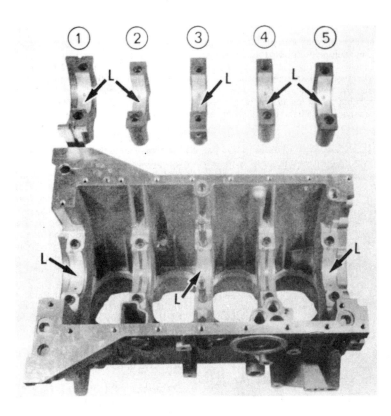

Fig. 1.51 Main bearing cap fitting positions – early type (Sec 44)

L   Plain bearing half shell positions

Fig. 1.52 Main bearing cap fitting positions – late type (Sec 44)

L   Plain bearing half shell positions

4   Oil the bearing shells and lower the crankshaft into position, taking
care not to dislodge the thrust washer segments (photo). Inject some
oil into the crankshaft oilways.
5   Check the crankshaft endfloat by pushing it in one direction then
the other along its length. A dial gauge or feeler gauges should be used
to measure the endfloat. If the endfloat measured is not within the
specified limits change the thrust washer segments and fit alternatives

44.4 Fitting the crankshaft

of suitable thickness. Thrust washers are available in a choice of five
thicknesses.
6   Fit new side seals to No 1 main bearing cap. Carefully fit the cap
with its bearing shell; lubricate the shell, the sides of the cap and the
locating surfaces in the block. There is a risk of displacing or distorting
the side seals as the cap is fitted, so protect them with a couple of feeler
blades or thin strips of tin which can be withdrawn rearwards after
fitting the cap (photos).
7   Fit the shells to the other main bearing caps, lubricate them and fit
the caps. Fit the thrust washer segments, grooved side outwards, to No
2 cap. Observe the mating marks made when dismantling; the lug on
each bearing cap points towards the timing sprockets. Ensure that the
thrust washer segment on each side of the number two main bearing
cap is of equal thickness to the corresponding upper segment washer
selected when setting the crankshaft endfloat.
8   Fit the main bearing cap nuts and bolts and tighten them to the
specified torque. Tighten the side bolts on No 3 cap last (photo).
9   Check the protrusion of No 1 cap side seals above the sump mating
face; it should be 2 mm. Trim off any excess.
10 Recheck the crankshaft endfloat (paragraph 5) and ensure that it
rotates freely.
11 Fit a new oil seal, lips inwards and lubricated, to the flywheel end
of the crankshaft. Drive it into place with a piece of tube (photo).
12 If not already fitted, fit new O-ring seals to the cylinder liners, then
fit the pistons and liners with reference to paragraphs 10 to 13
inclusive in Section 20 (photo).
13 Reconnect the connecting rod big-ends to the crankshaft as
described in paragraphs 18 and 19 in Section 20.

Oil pump
14 Fit the Woodruff key and oil pump drive sprocket to the crankshaft
nose. Fit the chain over the sprocket (photos).
15 Make sure that the locating dowel is in position, then engage the
oil pump sprocket in the chain and offer the pump to the block. Engage
the pump on the dowel, the lift it up far enough to slide the L-shaped
spacer in underneath it (photos).

44.6A Fitting a side seal to No 1 main bearing

44.6B Protect the side seals with feeler blades

44.8 Tightening the No 3 main bearing side bolt

44.11 Crankshaft oil seal – flywheel end

44.12 Arrow mark on piston crowns must point to the camshaft sprocket end (letter and number indicate liner and gudgeon pin grade)

44.14A Fitting the oil pump drive sprocket

44.14B Oil pump drive chain

44.15A Fitting the oil pump – chain must be engaged first

44.15B Locate the oil pump spacer

16 Fit the oil pump securing bolts, remembering that the special centering bolt is nearest the flywheel, and tighten them to the specified torque. Generously lubricate the pump and the chain (photo).

17 Refit the pulley oil seal carrier plate, using silicone jointing compound on the block mating faces. Fit a new oil seal, lubricated lips inwards, and drive it home with a piece of tube.

18 Fit the sump, using a new gasket, and tighten its securing bolts progressively to the specified torque. Remember the correct location of the three Allen-headed bolts.

19 Refit the suction drain pipe, using a new O-ring. Do not overtighten the securing nuts, refer to the Specifications for the correct torque setting.

Flywheel and clutch
20 Fit the flywheel to the crankshaft flange and secure with new bolts, using thread locking compound. Tighten the bolts progressively to the specified torque.

21 Fit the clutch friction plate and pressure plate, as described in Chapter 5.

Cylinder head
22 Position the engine for access to the cylinder head face. Rotate the crankshaft to bring the pistons to mid-stroke (none at TDC), then remove the liner clamps.

44.16 Special bolt fits here

23 Check that the head mating surface is clean and that the two locating dowels are present. Place a 5 mm diameter rod in the hole beneath the dowel at the flywheel end to stop the dowel being displaced downwards.
24 Fit a new cylinder head gasket, dry, with the protruding tab at the flywheel end (photo).
25 Lower the assembled cylinder head into position, making sure that it engages with the dowels.
26 Fit the cylinder head bolts, with their threads clean and lightly oiled. Remember to fit the spacer to the bolt above the coolant pump.
27 Tighten the cylinder head bolts progressively in the order shown in Fig. 1.43 to the Stage 1 specified torque.
28 Slacken cylinder head bolt number 1, then immediately retighten it to the Stage 2 specified torque, then tighten it further through the angle specified for Stage 3. Repeat this operation on the other bolts in sequence.

Timing drivebelt
29 Fit the camshaft sprocket backplate, using a 10 mm rod through the timing hole to locate it precisely before tightening its securing bolts.
30 Fit the camshaft sprocket, washer and bolt. Use the 10 mm rod to lock the sprocket in the correct position and tighten the bolt to the specified torque. Remove the rod.
31 Fit and secure the coolant pump, using a new gasket. Tighten the bolts to the specified torque (Chapter 2).
32 Fit the covers around the coolant pump, noting the locations of the various special bolts (Fig. 1.53). Smear the large bolt threads (E3) with sealant.
33 Fit the Woodruff key and the crankshaft sprocket.

34 Fit the camshaft drivebelt tensioner, but leave the nuts slack. Compress the spring by locking the cam in the horizontal position.
35 Temporarily fit the crankshaft pulley, its washer and bolt; lightly tighten the bolt. Carefully turn the crankshaft until a 10 mm rod will pass through the timing hole in the pulley and into the timing recess. If piston/valve contact occurs, back off and try again with the camshaft in a slightly different position. **Do not** try to force the crankshaft if a piston contacts a valve.
36 Use the 10 mm rod to position the camshaft sprocket, then remove the crankshaft pulley and fit the camshaft drivebelt. Be careful not to kink the belt as it is fitted, and observe the arrows showing the correct direction of rotation. The two white stripes on the belt should align with the timing marks on the sprockets.
37 Withdraw the timing rod. Tension the belt by turning the tensioner cam so that it points downwards; secure it with its locknut. Tighten the two nuts at the front of the tensioner.
38 Turn the crankshaft through two full turns in the normal direction of rotation; rotate it further to bring Nos 1 and 4 pistons to TDC with the valves on No 1 cylinder open.
39 Slacken the two nuts and the cam locknut on the drivebelt tensioner, then retighten them.
40 Temporarily refit the crankshaft pulley, rotate the crankshaft and check that the timing rods can be inserted simultaneously in the crankshaft pulley and camshaft sprocket holes. If not, remove the belt and try again. Remove the pulley.
41 Fit the engine mounting bracket and tighten its bolts.
42 Refit the drivebelt covers, but note that they will have to be removed later to retension the drivebelt if a new one has been fitted.
43 Fit the crankshaft pulley, washer and bolt, making sure that the Woodruff key is still in position. Jam the starter ring gear teeth and tighten the bolt to the specified torque.
44 Refit the camshaft cover, noting the copper washer at the sprocket end bolt, and using a new gasket.
45 Refit the ancillary components listed below; it may be preferable to leave delicate items such as the alternator and distributor until after the engine is refitted:

> (a) Oil filler/breather pipe
> (b) Oil pressure switch
> (c) Coolant inlet housing and pipe (photo)
> (d) Spark plugs, distributor and HT leads
> (e) HP pump and drivebelt (photo)
> (f) Alternator and drivebelt

46 Fit a new oil filter with its sealing ring well lubricated; tighten by hand only.

---

45 Engine and transmission – reconnection

1 Check that the clutch release components are correctly fitted in the gearbox and that the pressure plate and friction disc are fitted to the flywheel. (On automatic transmission models, check that the torque converter is properly located).
2 Smear a little anti-seize compound on the nose and splines of the transmission primary (input) shaft, then offer the transmission to the

44.24 Head gasket correctly fitted

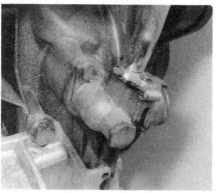

44.45A Securing the coolant pipe to the inlet housing

44.45B Refit the HP pump and drivebelt

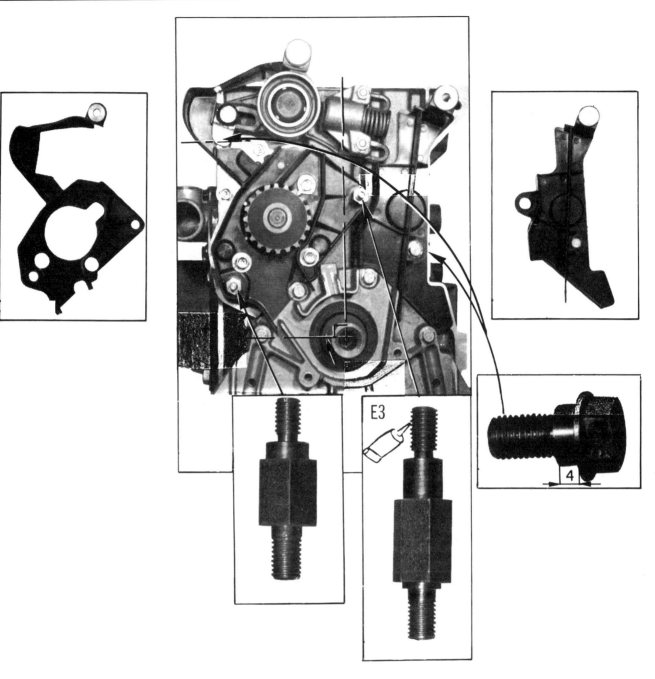

Fig. 1.53 Drivebelt cover special bolt locations (Sec 44)

E3 Use thread sealant

engine. Do not allow the weight of the transmission to hang on the input shaft. If the input shaft does not wish to pass the clutch, it is possible that the clutch disc is not centred. Check also that the transmission input shaft is compatible with the spigot recess in the crankshaft (Section 40, paragraphs 2 to 4).

3 Engage the engine-to-transmission dowels and loosely fit the bolts. Also fit the starter motor, which is secured by three Allen bolts and a bracket.

4 On manual transmission models, fit the clutch cable guide and pivot brackets.

46 Engine and transmission – refitting

1 Arrange the lift sling so that the gearbox tilts down at an angle of 45° when the engine and transmission are raised.

2 An assistant should be at hand to guide the engine and transmission into position as they are lowered and to take care not to damage any associated components within the engine compartment, the hydraulic lines in particular. The suspension height corrector control unit can be protected from possible damage by shielding it

78

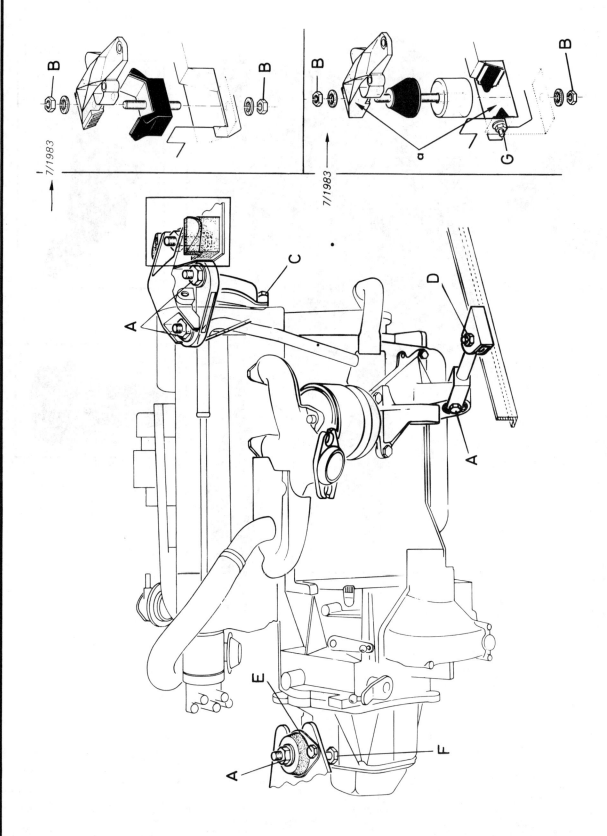

7/1983

7/1983

Fig. 1.54 Engine mountings and securing bolts. Refer to the Specifications for the tightening torques (Sec 46)

Inset top   Right-hand mounting up to July 1983   Inset bottom   Right-hand mounting from July 1983

with a suitable piece of sheet metal. Also, before lowering the combined units into position, check that the gearchange return levers are set parallel to the steering gear unit.

3 Carefully lower the engine and transmission into the engine compartment, guiding the gearbox down forwards of the battery tray support. When clear of the support, swivel the gearbox rearwards then raise it so that the mounting stud enters the mounting slot. Locate the mounting rubber (cone face upwards), then fit the flat washer and nut. Do not fully tighten it at this stage.

4 Further lower the lifting hoist to guide the engine down so that it engages with the right-hand mounting and its torque link (underneath towards the rear).

5 Locate a plain nut and washer to secure the right-hand mounting and insert the through-bolt and fit the self-locking nut to secure the torque link.

6 Tighten the mounting nuts and the torque link nut and bolt to their specified torque settings (Fig. 1.54).

7 Reconnect the following items referring, where necessary, to the relevant Section or Chapter for further details:

(a) The gearchange link rods
(b) The speedometer cable
(c) The coolant hoses to the 'coolant manifold' located between the cylinder head and the bulkhead
(d) Fuel feed and return hoses
(e) The HP pump unit hoses. Retighten the regulator bleed screw
(f) Accelerator cable to the carburettor
(g) Wiring harnesses
(h) Clutch cable to release arm. Lubricate the pushrod with grease at each end before assembling
(j) Exhaust downpipe
(k) Radiator and coolant hoses
(l) Braided earth straps to the gearbox, battery support tray and battery

8 When refitting the alternator guard, press the retaining grommet into the right-hand engine mounting bracket as shown using a rod and pliers (photo). Take care not to pierce the bottom end of the grommet – smear it with a little soapy solution to ease fitting.

9 The driveshafts and associated steering/suspension components should be refitted in accordance with the instructions described in Chapter 7 and 10 respectively. Refit the right-hand drive shaft first.

10 Before refitting the air filter and air ducts, check around the engine and gearbox to ensure that all fittings are securely and correctly made.

11 Top up and bleed the cooling system, as described in Chapter 2.

12 Top up the engine oil level, having checked that the sump plug is securely fitted (photo).

13 Top up the gearbox oil level with the specified quantity of oil. Note that the gearbox filler plug is **not** a level plug.

46.8 Method devised for securing the alternator guard retaining grommet

46.12 Topping up engine oil level

47 Engine – initial start-up after overhaul

1 Follow the check procedures described in paragraphs 1 to 5 inclusive in Section 22 of this Chapter.

2 If hexagon headed cylinder head bolts are fitted, allow the engine to cool for at least two hours. Loosen the bolt which secures the engine right-hand mounting bracket to the block, then retighten the cylinder head bolts as described in paragraph 33, of Section 32. Tighten the mounting bracket bolt on completion. No subsequent retightening is necessary. Note that where Torx type cylinder head bolts are fitted,

retightening after warm-up is not required.

3 Recheck the valve clearances (Section 29).

4 If a new camshaft drivebelt was fitted, retension it as described in Section 30, paragraphs 19 and 20.

PART C: ALL ENGINES

48 Fault diagnosis – engine

Symptom	Reason(s)
Engine will not turn over when starter switch is operated	Flat battery
	Bad battery connections
	Bad connections at solenoid switch and/or starter motor
	Starter motor jammed
	Defective solenoid
	Starter motor defective

Symptom	Reason(s)
Engine turns over normally but fails to fire and run	No sparks at plugs No fuel reaching engine Too much fuel reaching engine (flooding)
Engine starts but runs unevenly and misfires	Ignition and/or fuel system faults Incorrect valve clearance Burnt out valves Blown cylinder head gasket, dropped liners Worn out piston rings Worn cylinder bores
Lack of power	Ignition and/or fuel system faults Incorrect valve clearances Burnt out valves Blown cylinder head gasket Worn out piston rings Worn cylinder bores
Excessive oil consumption	Oil leaks from crankshaft oil seal, timing cover gasket and oil seal, rocker cover gasket, crankcase or gearbox joint Worn piston rings or cylinder bores resulting in oil being burnt by engine (smoky exhaust is an indication) Worn valve guides and/or defective valve stem Worn valve seals
Excessive mechanical noise from engine	Wrong valve-to-rocker clearance Worn crankshaft bearings Worn cylinders (piston slap) Slack or worn timing chain and sprockets (150 engine) Worn transfer gears and/or bearings (150 engine) Worn timing belt and/or sprockets (170 and 159 engines) Worn oil pump drive chain or sprockets (170 and 159 engines)

Chapter 2 Cooling system

For modifications, and information applicable to later models, see Supplement at end of manual

Contents

Specifications

General

System type	Pressurised, front mounted radiator (with integral header tank), coolant pump and thermostat. Electric cooling fan

Coolant capacity (including heater):
150 engines	6.5 litres (11.4 Imp pints)
171 and 159 engine	6.5 to 7.0 litres (11.4 to 12.3 Imp pints)

Antifreeze

Type/specification	Ethylene glycol based antifreeze (Duckhams Universal Antifreeze and Summer Coolant)

Mixture proportions:
Temperate climate	25% antifreeze, 75% water
Cold climate	50% antifreeze, 50% water

Degree of protection:
25% mixture	−15°C (+5°F)
50% mixture	−37°C (−35°F)

Thermostat

Travel (min)	7.5 mm (0.3 in)
Opening temperature (150 and 171 engines):	
Starts to open	82°C (180°F)
Fully open	93°C (200°F)
Opening temperature (159 engine):	
Starts to open	79°C (174°F)
Fully open	82°C (180°F)

Electric fan

Cut-in temperature:	
150 engine	91° to 96°C (196° to 205°F)
171 engine:	
1st speed	84° to 90°C (183° to 194°F)
2nd speed	90° to 96°C (194° to 205°F)
159 engine:	
1st speed	86° to 90°C (186° to 194°F)
2nd speed	90° to 94°C (194° to 201°F)

Engine coolant temperature switch

Operational temperatures:	
150 engine	110° to 113°C (230° to 235°F)
171 engine:	
Yellow connection	110° to 114°C (230° to 237°F)
Blue connection	103° to 107°C (217° to 224°F)
159 engine	105° to 112°C (221° to 233°F)

Radiator cap pressure
.... 1 bar (14.5 lbf/in²)

Torque wrench settings

	kgf m	lbf ft
Coolant pump:		
150 engine	1.75	12.6
171 and 159 engine	1.5	10.8
Coolant temperature switch:		
150 engine	4.5	32.6
171 and 159 engine	1.8	13.0
Coolant housing (171 and 159 engine)	1.6	11.6
Coolant housing plug (171 and 159 engine)	2.0	14.5
Thermostat housing cover	1.7	12.3

1 General description

The cooling system is of the pump-assisted thermal syphon type and is pressurised by means of a pressure valve filler cap. The main components of the system are the radiator, the coolant pump, the thermostat, the cooling fan, the heater and the connecting hoses. The system operates as follows.

Cold coolant from the bottom of the radiator is pumped into the coolant passages of the engine cylinder block and cylinder head. Heat from the combustion chambers and moving parts of the engine is absorbed by the coolant which is then directed to the upper section of the radiator. The passage of air through the radiator (due to the action of the cooling fan, when engaged, and to the forward movement of the car) cools the coolant as it passes down through the radiator matrix and the cycle is then repeated.

To accelerate the warming-up process when starting the engine, and thereafter to maintain the correct operating temperature, a thermostat is fitted in the coolant outlet from the engine to the radiator top hose. When the coolant is cold the thermostat is closed and circulation is limited to the engine coolant passages by means of a bypass route. As coolant temperature rises, the thermostat opens to allow coolant to flow through the radiator.

The system is pressurised to raise the boiling point of the coolant. This allows the engine to achieve its most efficient operating temperature as well as reducing the amount of coolant needed. It also brings the risk of scalding if the cap is removed whilst the system is pressurised.

Hot coolant is tapped from the system to supply the heater matrix for car interior heating and also to supply heat to the carburettor and inlet manifold to improve fuel vaporisation.

The cooling fan is driven by an electric motor and this only cuts in above a certain temperature when activated by a coolant temperature sensor switch. By this means the fan is only driven when it is really needed, with a consequent reduction in noise and power consumption.

On BX and BX 14 models, the coolant pump is driven in tandem with the alternator by a drivebelt driven from the crankshaft pulley. On BX 16 and BX 19 models the coolant pump is located in the front of the cylinder block at the timing case end and is driven by the timing belt.

Routine maintenance to the system is minimal but must not be ignored.

2 Routine maintenance

At the intervals given in the Routine Maintenance section at the start of this manual carry out the following.
1   Check the coolant level in the radiator, preferably when the engine is cold. If checking the level when the engine is hot, observe the cautionary notes given in paragraph 1 of Section 3.
2   On early models the coolant depth, when cold, must be 250 to 300 mm (9.8 to 11.8 in). The engine oil dipstick can be used for this, but wipe it off before and after use. Later models have a dipstick in the filler neck; the coolant must be between the MIN and MAX marks.
3   Where necessary, top up using a coolant mixture made up in similar proportions to the original antifreeze solution. The need for topping-up should arise only very infrequently. If regular topping-up is needed, check for a leaking hose or gasket.
4   Check the security and condition of the system hoses regularly.
5   Renew the coolant every two years.
6   On BX and BX 14 models check the condition and tension of the drivebelt, as described in Chapter 12, Section 9.

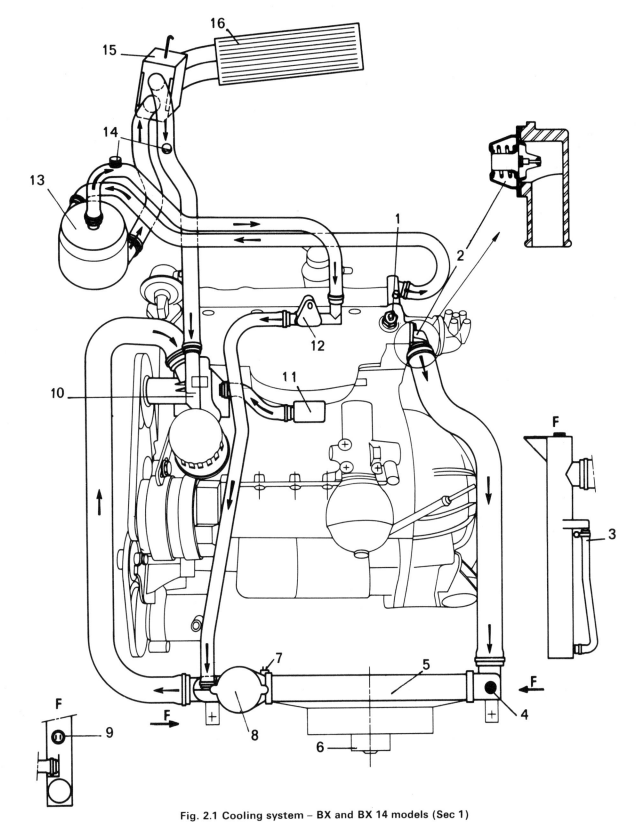

Fig. 2.1 Cooling system – BX and BX 14 models (Sec 1)

1	Coolant temperature switch	6	Electric fan
2	Thermostat	7	Fan thermal switch
3	Radiator drain pipe	8	Filler/pressure cap
4	Radiator bleed screw	9	Coolant minimum level switch
5	Radiator		

10	Coolant pump
11	Inlet manifold
12	Carburettor
13	De-aeration chamber

14	Bleed screw
15	Heater control
16	Heater matrix

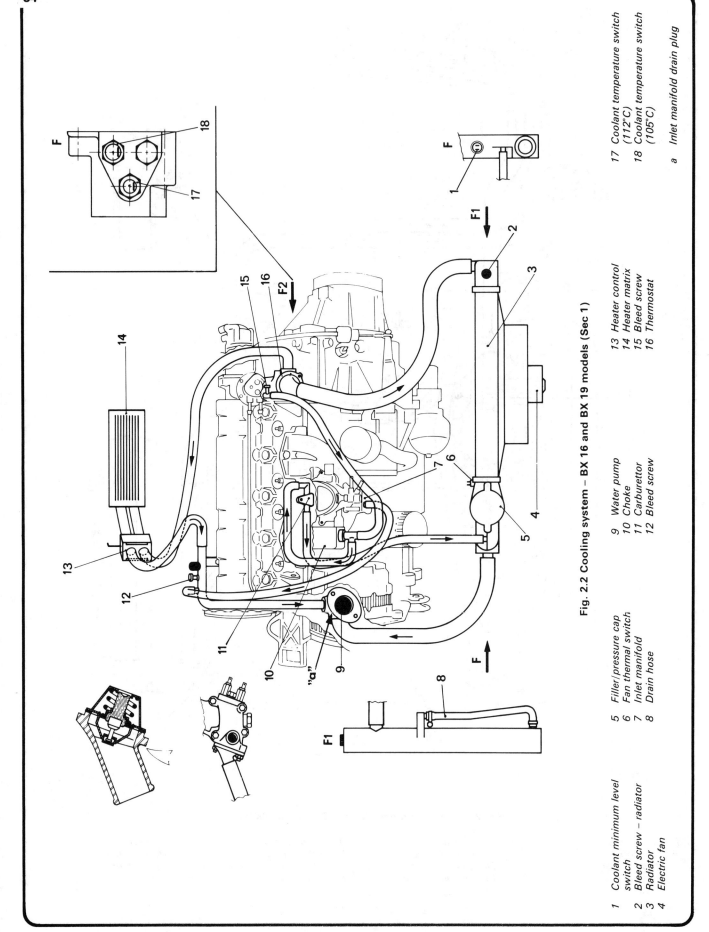

Fig. 2.2 Cooling system – BX 16 and BX 19 models (Sec 1)

1 Coolant minimum level
   switch
2 Bleed screw – radiator
3 Radiator
4 Electric fan

5 Filler/pressure cap
6 Fan thermal switch
7 Inlet manifold
8 Drain hose

9 Water pump
10 Choke
11 Carburettor
12 Bleed screw

13 Heater control
14 Heater matrix
15 Bleed screw
16 Thermostat

17 Coolant temperature switch
   (112°C)
18 Coolant temperature switch
   (105°C)

a Inlet manifold drain plug

3 Cooling system – draining

1   If the engine is cold, remove the filler cap from the radiator by turning the cap anti-clockwise. If the engine is hot, then turn the filler cap very slightly until pressure in the system has had time to be released. Use a rag over the cap to protect your hand from escaping steam. If, with the engine very hot, the cap is released suddenly the drop in pressure can result in the water boiling. With the pressure released the cap can be removed.

2   If antifreeze is used in the cooling system, drain into a bowl having a capacity of at least 13 pints (nearly 7.5 litres) for re-use if appropriate.

3   Position the bowl under the bottom hose connection to the radiator. Undo the retaining clip and pull the hose from the radiator (photo). To fully drain the system, the heater control knob on the facia must be moved to the full heat position.

4   When draining is complete, wipe any spillage from the body panels and surrounding components.

5   Remember that, without dismantling, it is impossible to drain the system dry as some coolant will be retained in the heater matrix. If there is no antifreeze in the system, frost damage is still possible in winter even though the system is 'drained'.

6   If you intend to re-use the coolant, cover it to prevent dust or other contaminants from affecting it.

7   Reconnect the bottom hose, unless the radiator is being removed or the bottom hose renewed.

4 Cooling system – flushing

1   If the coolant is maintained in good condition with a quality antifreeze or corrosion inhibitor, then the need for flushing is unlikely to arise. However, where the system has been neglected, efficiency can be restored in the following way.

2   First drain the system, as explained previously, and leave the bottom hose disconnected.

3   Protect the engine, in particular the ignition system components by covering them with a sheet of plastic.

4   To flush the radiator, direct a flow of water through the filler neck and allow the water to run through until it is seen to be clean when running out of the bottom hose connector. If the radiator is badly contaminated remove it (Section 6), invert it and reverse flush it; directing the water flow through the bottom hose connector. If, after a reasonable period, the water still does not run clear, the radiator should be flushed with a good proprietary cleaning system such as Holts Radflush or Holts Speedflush.

5   To flush the engine, leave the bottom hose disconnected. Remove the thermostat (Section 11) and refit the thermostat housing/hose.

6   Disconnect the radiator top hose and direct a flow of water into it. Flush through until clean water is seen to run from the bottom hose. Reverse the flow if badly contaminated.

7   On completion, refit the thermostat and connect the hoses. Refill the cooling system, as described in Section 5.

5 Cooling system – filling

1   Check the condition and security of all cooling system hoses and connections, and ensure that the drain tap is firmly closed and that the heater temperature control is in the 'hot' position.

2   Undo the system bleed screws from the points shown in Figs. 2.3 or 2.4 and photos (as applicable).

3   Fill the system slowly, using antifreeze mixture, until the level rises and overflows from the radiator filler neck (photo). As the level rises, the coolant will emerge from the bleed screws at which point the screws should be tightened.

3.3 Radiator bottom hose connection (BX 16 and BX 19 models)

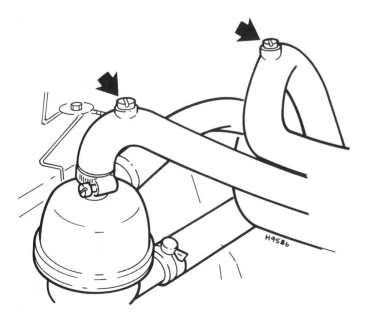

Fig. 2.3 Cooling system bleed screw locations (arrowed) – BX and BX 14 models (Sec 5)

Fig. 2.4 Radiator bleed screw location (arrowed) – all models (Sec 5)

5.2A Bleed screw – near thermostat housing (BX 16 and BX 19 models)

5.2B Bleed screw – heater hose connection (BX 16 and BX 19 models)

5.3 Topping-up the cooling system

3   Disconnect the wiring connections from the radiator temperature sensor unit (photo) and, where applicable, the coolant level indicator unit.
4   Pivot the bonnet stay out of the way, then unscrew and remove the five radiator front crosspanel securing bolts. Remove the cross panel (photo).
5   Carefully lift the radiator out of the engine compartment (photo).
6   Minor leaks from the radiator can be cured using Holts Radweld. Extensive damage should be repaired by a specialist or the unit exchanged for a new or reconditioned radiator. The radiator matrix, header and bottom tanks should be thoroughly examined for signs of damage, deterioration and leakage; very often a rusty sediment will have been deposited where a leak has occurred.
7   After inspection, the radiator should be flushed, as described in Section 4, and the matrix and exterior cleaned of dirt and dead flies with a strong jet of water.
8   Refitting the radiator is a reversal of the removal procedure, but the following additional points should be noted:

> (a) Examine and renew any clips, hoses and rubber mounting washers which have deteriorated
> (b) Refill the cooling system, as described in Section 5

4   Start the engine and run it at a fast idle speed so that the coolant is warmed up and the electric cooling fan cuts in and then out, at which point stop the engine.
5   With the engine stationary, carefully remove the radiator filler cap (see paragraph 1, in Section 3) and check the coolant level. If necessary top it up to the required level. On early models, the coolant height in the radiator header tank should be 250 to 300 mm (9.8 to 11.8 in) with the engine cold. This measurement can be checked with the engine oil dipstick – but wipe it clean before using (and after). Later models have an integral black plastic tube type dipstick. The level must be between the MIN and MAX marks.
6   If the original antifreeze is being re-used, remember that topping it up with plain water will dilute the mixture and weaken its properties; therefore it is best to use an antifreeze mixture for topping up.
7   Finally, run the engine again and check the system for any leaks.

6   Radiator – removal, inspection, cleaning and refitting

1   Drain the cooling system, as described in Section 3.
2   Unclip and disconnect the top hose and the smaller expansion return hose from the radiator.

6.3 Temperature sensor unit location in radiator

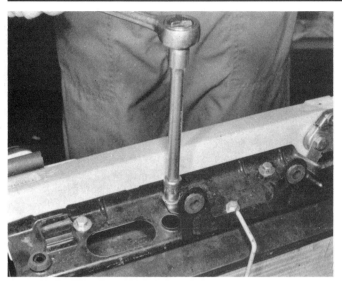

6.4 Undo the retaining bolts at the top ...

6.5 ... and lift the radiator out of the car

7 Cooling fan – removal and refitting

1   Raise and support the bonnet. Disconnect the battery earth lead.
2   Undo the retaining screws and detach the front grille panel.
3   Undo the fan unit retaining bolt (photo) at the top and lift out the fan unit sufficiently to detach the wiring connector, then fully remove the fan unit.
4   Refit in the reverse order of removal. Check for correct operation of the fan on completion.

8 Cooling fan thermal switch – removal and refitting

1   This switch unit is fitted into the rear face of the radiator bottom section and its purpose is to cut the cooling fan in and out in accordance with the coolant temperature.
2   To remove the switch, drain the coolant from the radiator, as described in Section 3.
3   Disconnect the switch wiring connector, then unscrew and remove the switch.

4   Refit the switch in the reverse order to removal. If the original switch is being refitted, check that the seal washer is in good condition.
5   Top up the coolant level on completion (Section 5) then run the engine and check that the cooling fan cuts in when the engine is warmed up.

9 Coolant low level warning switch – removal and refitting

1   If fitted, this unit is located in the radiator.
2   To remove the switch unit, partially drain the cooling system, disconnect the switch wiring connector then twist the switch anti-clockwise and withdraw it (photo).
3   Refit in the reverse order to removal, but ensure that its orientation is correct with the counterweight to the top, see Fig. 2.5.
4   Top up and bleed the cooling system on completion, as described in Section 5.

7.3 Fan retaining bolt

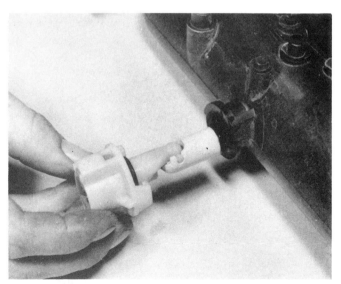

9.2 Coolant low level warning switch removal

Fig. 2.5 Coolant low level warning switch showing correct orientation when fitted, with mark 'a' at the top (Sec 9)

10.1 Coolant temperature switches (BX 16 and BX 19 models)

10 Coolant temperature switch – removal and refitting

1   The coolant temperature switch is screwed into the cylinder head adjacent to the thermostat housing. On BX 16 and 19 models there are two temperature switches fitted, both being screwed into the thermostat housing itself. The switch with the blue lead connector makes the warning lamp blink when the coolant temperature reaches 105°C (221°F). The switch with the yellow lead connector actuates the warning lamp when the coolant temperature reaches 112°C (233°F) (photo).
2   It is difficult to test a temperature switch without special equipment and the best method to use if a fault develops is to substitute a new switch, but only after the wiring to the gauge has been thoroughly checked.
3   To remove the coolant temperature switch, drain the coolant, as described in Section 3. Disconnect the wiring from the switch and unscrew the switch.
4   When refitting the switch, make sure that the seal is in good condition and do not overtighten it.
5   Refill the cooling system, referring to Section 5.
6   If the switch is changed and the gauge still does not register, then

the gauge should be checked by a competent auto-electrician. Access to the gauge is obtained after removing the instrument panel, as described in Chapter 12.

11 Thermostat – removal, testing and refitting

1   The function of the thermostat is to enable the engine to reach its most efficient operating temperature in the shortest time, and this is accomplished by restricting the circulation of coolant to the engine during warming up; after reaching the operating temperature the thermostat opens and allows the coolant to circulate through the radiator.
2   A faulty thermostat can cause overheating or slow engine warm-up as well as affecting performance of the heater.
3   The thermostat is located at the engine end of the radiator top hose under a cover secured to the cylinder head/adaptor.
4   To remove the thermostat, first partially drain the cooling system (Section 3) and then disconnect the top hose from the thermostat housing outlet (photo).
5   Unscrew and remove the two retaining bolts and carefully lift the coolant outlet away from the cylinder head/adaptor (photo).

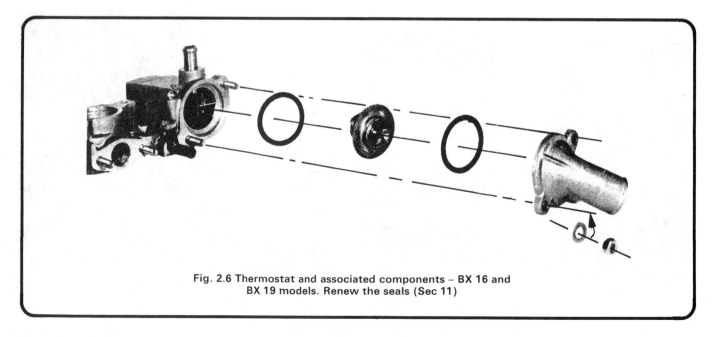

Fig. 2.6 Thermostat and associated components – BX 16 and BX 19 models. Renew the seals (Sec 11)

11.4 Thermostat housing cover
(BX and BX 14 models)

11.5 Thermostat housing cover (BX and
BX14 models)

11.6 Thermostat

6   Extract the thermostat from its recess and remove the old gasket (photo). Clean the faces of the cylinder head/adaptor and the mating thermostat cover free of all traces of gasket and sealant.
7   To test whether the thermostat is serviceable, suspend it by a piece of string in a pan of water, which is then heated – but make sure that it does not touch the pan. Use a similarly suspended thermometer to check the operating temperatures of the thermostat with reference to the information given in the Specifications. If the thermostat is faulty it must be renewed.
8   Refitting the thermostat is a reversal of the removal procedure, but it will be necessary to use a new gasket, and the cooling system must be refilled, as described in Section 5. To prevent leaks, the mating surfaces of the water outlet and head or manifold must be clean and free of excessive corrosion. When refitting the thermostat make sure that the vent pin is positioned upwards to allow air to escape from the system.

12 Coolant pump (BX and BX 14 models) – removal, inspection and refitting

1   Drain the engine coolant, as described in Section 3.
2   Loosen the drivebelt tension and disengage the belt from the pump pulley. Refer to Chapter 12, Section 9 for details.
3   Undo the retaining clips and detach the coolant hoses from the pump (photo). Unbolt the pump and remove it.

4   Any wear in the pump or leakage of coolant at the shaft gland will mean renewal of the pump, as repair is not possible.
5   Always renew the O-ring seal before fitting the pump to the cylinder block (photos).
6   Tighten the pump bolts to the specified torque.
7   Refit and adjust the drivebelt, referring to Section 9 in Chapter 12.
8   Refill the cooling system, referring to Section 5.

13 Coolant pump (BX 16 and BX 19 models) – removal, inspection and refitting

1   Drain the cooling system (Section 3).
2   Remove the camshaft drivebelt (Chapter 1).
3   Remove the camshaft drivebelt tensioner (three nuts).
4   Remove the plastic shield, noting the locations of the different types of bolt.
5   Remove the five bolts which secure the coolant pump. Remove the pump and recover the gasket (photo).
6   The pump cannot be repaired; if defective it must be renewed.
7   Refit in the reverse order of removal. Use a new gasket and tighten the securing bolts to the specified torque.
8   Refit and tension the camshaft timing belt, referring to Chapter 1 for full details.
9   Top up the cooling system, referring to Section 5 in this Chapter.

12.3 Coolant pump hoses (BX and BX 14 models)

12.5A Coolant pump O-ring seal (BX and BX 14 models)

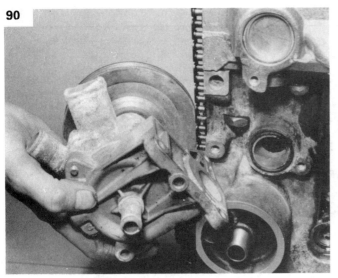

12.5B Fitting the coolant pump (BX and BX 14 models)

13.5 Coolant pump removal (BX 16 and BX 19 models)

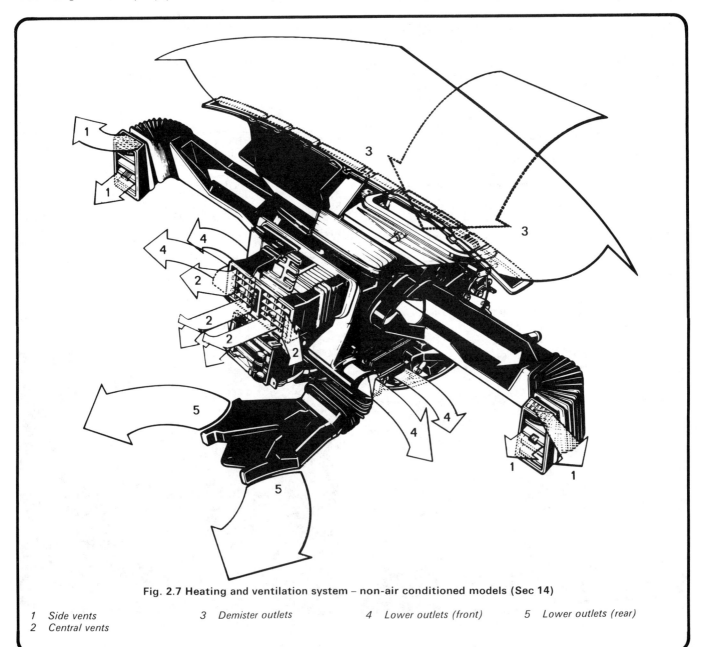

Fig. 2.7 Heating and ventilation system – non-air conditioned models (Sec 14)

1   Side vents
2   Central vents
3   Demister outlets
4   Lower outlets (front)
5   Lower outlets (rear)

14 Heating and ventilation system – description

1   The heater is located centrally under the facia and it supplies warm air for interior heating or windscreen demisting. Hot coolant is piped from the engine through a heater matrix and back to the engine when a manually operated valve is opened.
2   Stale air from the car interior is exhausted through slots in the tailgate closure recess.
3   Normally the heater components give very little trouble and require negligible maintenance. An occasional check of the hoses and connections for condition and leaks is all that is usually required.
4   Fresh air inlets are located at the ends of the facia.
5   Refer to Section 19 for details of the air conditioning system (if fitted).

15 Heater unit (non-air-conditioned models) – removal and refitting

1   Disconnect the battery earth lead.

2   Drain the engine coolant, as described in Section 3.
3   Detach the lower facia panel on the passenger side. It is secured by two screws on the outer end face and a single screw at the other end. Now undo the four screws securing the glovebox lid (Fig. 2.8) and remove the lid and lower facia panel.
4   Undo and remove the single screw retaining the heater unit from within the glovebox.
5   Remove the retaining screws and lower the speaker unit. Detach the wiring connector and remove the unit.
6   Withdraw the ashtray and pull free the heater/ventilation control knobs (photo).
7   Unscrew the two retaining screws and remove the ashtray support.
8   Remove the heater/ventilation control plate (photo).
9   Remove the radio and, where applicable, its housing unit – referring to Chapter 12.
10 Unscrew and remove the screws from the positions shown in Fig. 2.9.
11 Remove the upper and lower retaining screws from the opposite side of the heater/ventilation facia unit and withdraw the unit. As it is withdrawn detach the ashtray and heater control light lamps.
12 Remove the cigar lighter and its lamp (Chapter 12).
13 If applicable, remove the door lock electronic unit (Chapter 12).

15.6 Heater/ventilation control knob removal

15.8 Heater/ventilation control plate removal

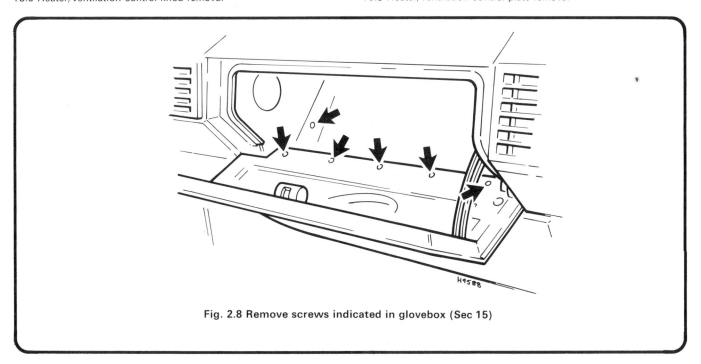

Fig. 2.8 Remove screws indicated in glovebox (Sec 15)

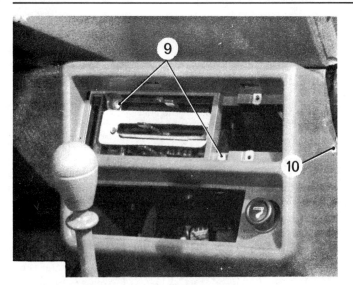

Fig. 2.9 Remove the screws indicated at 9 and 10 (Sec 15)

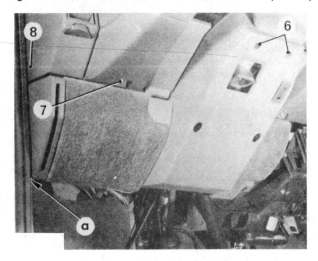

Fig. 2.10 Remove screws from positions 7, 8 and 'a'.
Steering column lower shroud upper retaining screw
positions also shown (6). Left-hand drive version shown
(Sec 15)

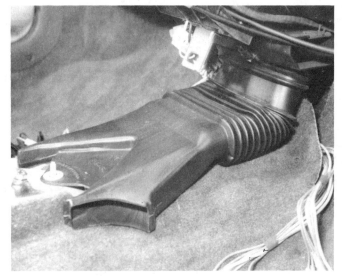

15.17 Rear passenger compartment heater nozzle

14 Unscrew and remove the driver's side lower finishing panel
retaining screw.
15 Prise free the blanking plugs (at the front and rear of the gear lever)
from the console, then undo the retaining nut (front) and bolt (rear).
16 Remove the two plastic dowels retaining the console to the heater
unit. Prise free the gear lever rubber gaiter, pull on the handbrake lever
and withdraw the front section of the console.
17 Detach the heater nozzle to the rear passenger compartment
(photo).
18 Undo the two screws from the top end of the underside of the
steering column and release the upper column shroud.
19 Undo and remove the three screws from the positions shown in
Fig. 2.10, then withdraw the lower driver's side facia, leaving the choke
control attached (manual choke models).
20 Detach the heater unit wiring harness connector and plug.
21 Loosen the feed and return coolant hose retaining clips and detach
the hoses from the heater unit (photo).
22 Carefully detach the bonnet seal rubber, then remove the plastic
cover from over the windscreen wiper motor.
23 Undo the two retaining screws and remove the heater air intake
grille.
24 Unscrew and remove the nuts from the positions shown in
Fig. 2.11.

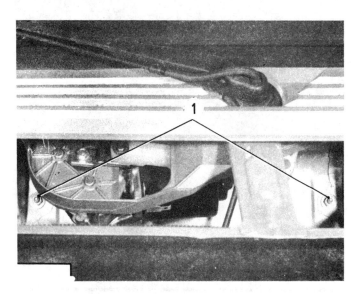

Fig. 2.11 Remove the heater retaining nuts (1) (Sec 15)

15.21 Heater flow and return hose connections at the
bulkhead/heater

25 Remove the central directional vent grilles. Insert a screwdriver between the grille and housing to release each grille and withdraw them (photo).

26 Using a screwdriver, prise out the vent grille housing by releasing the retaining clips. Remove the vent surround and grille (photo).

27 Detach the heater coolant drain pipe from its housing (photo).

28 Prise free and detach the heater coolant pipe (feed and return) scuttle seal, then withdraw the heater unit from the passenger side. As it is withdrawn disengage it from the side vent ducts.

29 Refitting is a direct reversal of the removal procedure. Ensure that the heater feed and return hoses are securely connected. Also make sure that all wiring connections are correctly and securely made.

30 On completion check the operations of all items which were disconnected and top up the cooling system with reference to Section 5.

16 Heater unit (air conditioned models) – removal and refitting

The removal and refitting procedures closely follow those given for the normal heater unit in Section 15, but the following differences apply.

1 Before starting the removal procedure have the air conditioning system depressurized and drained by your Citroën dealer or refrigeration specialist. **Do not** attempt this yourself.

2 Prise free and detach the wiring from the air recirculation switch mounted in the control console.

3 Referring to Fig. 2.12, loosen the retaining nuts and detach the two freon pipes from the heater unit (engine compartment side). Recover the O-ring seals.

15.25 Withdraw the vent grille ...

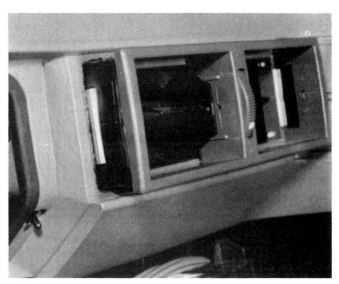

15.26 ... and grille housing

15.27 Heater coolant drain hose

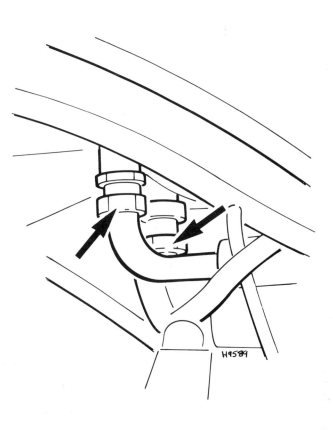

Fig. 2.12 Air conditioning freon pipe connections to the heater – arrowed (Sec 16)

4   Undo the retaining screws shown in Fig. 2.13 in addition to those shown in Fig. 2.11.

5   Remove the screws at positions 7 and 9, and the clips 6 and 8 in Fig. 2.14. Lift the two air intake pipes for access to the unit retaining screws.

6   Release both the coolant pipe and freon pipe seals at the bulkhead panel when removing the unit.

7   Refit in the reverse order of removal. Ensure that the freon pipe O-ring seals are located when attaching the pipes.

8   When reconnecting the heater unit wiring harness note the connections (Fig. 2.15).

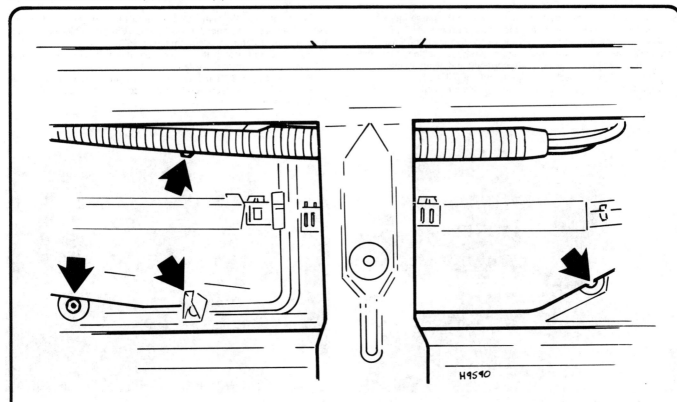

Fig. 2.13 Additional heater retaining screw locations (arrowed) – air conditioned models (Sec 16)

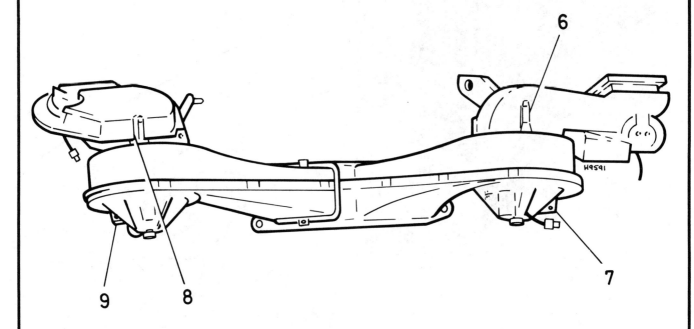

Fig. 2.14 Remove the screws from 7 and 9 and the clips from 6 and 8 (Sec 16)

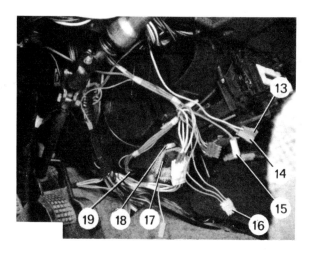

Fig. 2.15 Heater unit wiring harness connections – air conditioned models (Sec 16)

13 *Red plug – air blower control*
14 *Blue plug – compressor control*
15 *Yellow plug – air blower control*

16 *3-way orange connector*
17 *4-way brown connector*
18 *Green plug – heater unit control lighting*
19 *Relay (behind the heater unit)*

17 Heater blower motor – removal and refitting

1 Remove the heater unit, as described in Section 15 or 16.
2 Carefully prise free and remove the foam gaskets (Fig. 2.16).
3 Referring to Fig. 2.17, undo the five screws retaining the control bracket, drill out the rivet and retrieve its washer then release the eleven securing slips. Separate the housing.
4 Remove the five flaps.
5 Detach the wiring connectors from the blower motor and then pull the motor out of the housing.
6 To remove the grille from the blower motor undo the two retaining nuts.
7 Undo the two screws and withdraw the blower motor from the support.
8 Refitting is a reversal of the removal procedure. When refitting the flaps, you will need three 'end pieces' manufactured in 5 mm diameter steel wire, 50 mm in length. When the flaps are fitted to their pivot points, operate them to ensure correct fitting then fit the end pieces to the free end of flap numbers 6, 7 and 9 in Fig. 2.18.
9 When the half housings are reassembled and the clips are in position the end pieces can be removed.
10 When fitting the 4 mm rivet insert the plain washer.

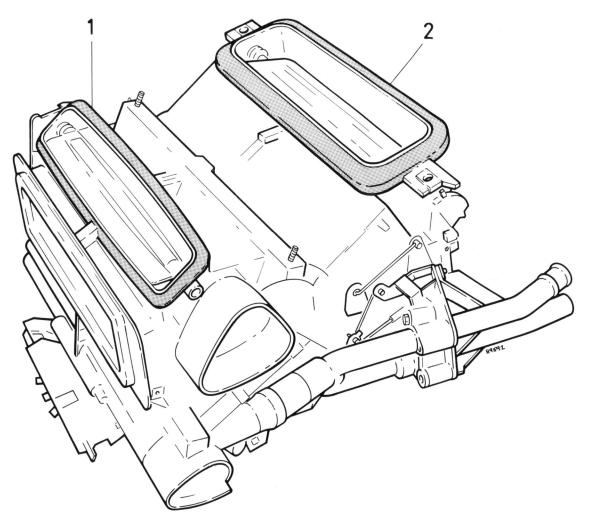

Fig. 2.16 Heater unit foam gaskets (1 and 2) (Sec 17)

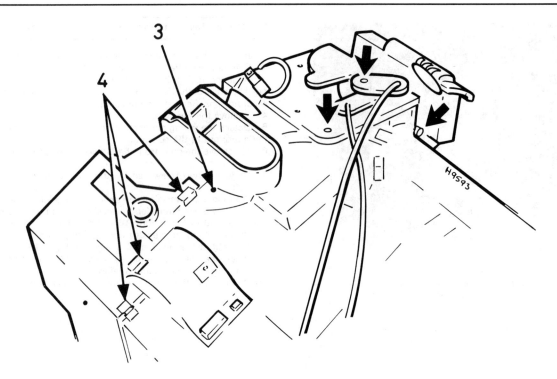

Fig. 2.17 Remove the rivets (3), clips (4) and screws (arrowed) (Sec 17)

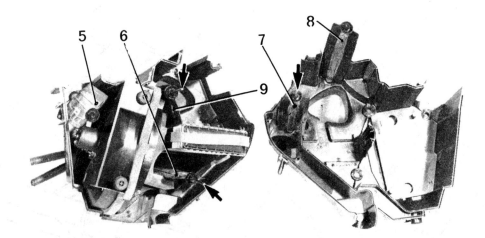

Fig. 2.18 Heater unit showing flaps (5, 6, 7, 8 and 9). End piece locations are arrowed (Sec 17)

18 Heater matrix – removal and refitting

1   Drain the cooling system, as described in Chapter 3.
2   Undo the retaining screws and remove the lower facia finishing panel on the driver's side.
3   Undo the four screws retaining the heater tap to the heater matrix (photo).
4   Undo the two screws retaining the matrix to the heater unit and the tap-to-heater unit screw. Reach up with a socket and extension from underneath for the tap-to-heater screw removal. As the tap is separated from the heater, allow for a certain amount of coolant spillage by positioning a rag and/or container underneath it (photo).
5   Prise apart the four locating clips and withdraw the matrix from the heater unit. Detach the control links as the matrix is withdrawn.
6   Loosen the hose retaining clips and detach the coolant pipes. Remove the gasket and the tap.
7   Loosen the cable clamp screw, disengage the location clip and then remove the control cable.
8   Refit in the reverse order to removal. During assembly, check that the heater control lever fully opens and closes the tap. Move the location clip position to adjust if necessary.
9   Prior to refitting the lower facia finishing panel, top up the cooling system, referring to Section 5, then check the heater hoses for any signs of leaks.

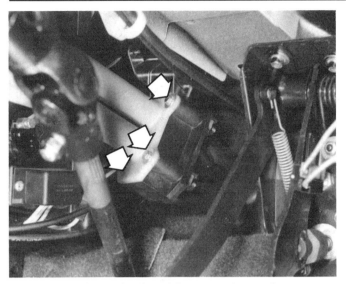

18.3 Heater tap (control) unit retaining screws (arrowed)

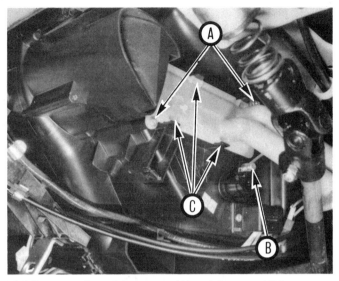

18.4 Heater matrix retaining screws (A) and the control link connection (B). Location clips (C) are also shown

19 Air conditioning system

1   An air conditioning system is available as an optional extra on some models. The system layout and the main components are shown in Figs. 2.19 and 2.20.

2   To allow for fitting of the system the engine crankcase was modified to suit and the Weber carburettor is fitted with a butterfly opener controlled by an 'Elbi' electrovalve (located underneath the battery tray). A battery of increased capacity is also fitted.

3   The heater system works on the normal principle in conjunction

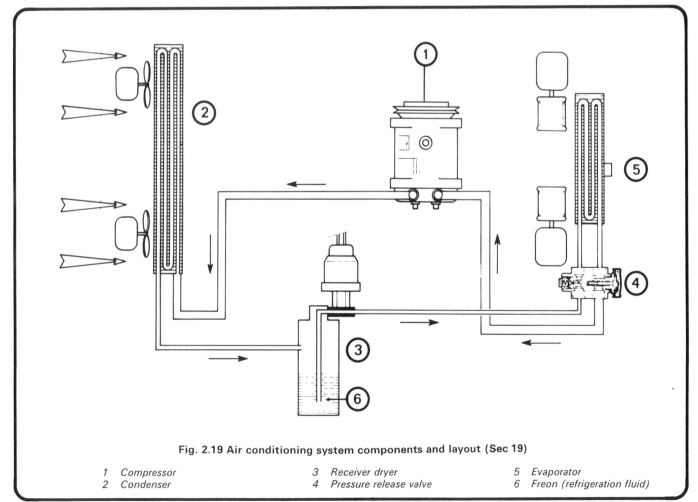

Fig. 2.19 Air conditioning system components and layout (Sec 19)

1 Compressor
2 Condenser
3 Receiver dryer
4 Pressure release valve
5 Evaporator
6 Freon (refrigeration fluid)

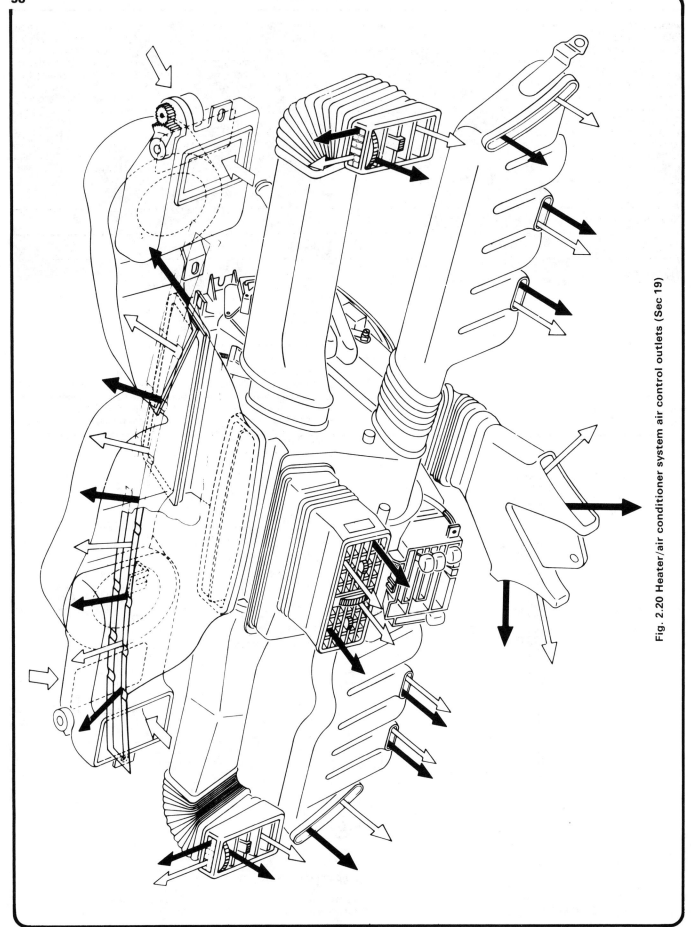

Fig. 2.20 Heater/air conditioner system air control outlets (Sec 19)

with the engine cooling system and incorporating its own booster (blower) motor.

4 If it is necessary to disconnect any part of the refrigeration system in order to undertake work on other components, it is most important that the circuit be discharged prior to commencing work by a Citroën dealer or refrigeration engineer having the necessary knowledge and equipment. On completion of the particular service or overhaul the refrigeration system must be recharged again requiring specialized equipment and knowledge.

5 Due to the nature of the refrigeration gases used in the system, no servicing other than a few basic inspection tasks can be undertaken by the home mechanic.

6 Check the condition and tension of the alternator/compressor drivebelt. Renew the belt if it shows signs of excessive wear.

7 Check the system components and hose for security and condition. Any hoses or components which are suspect must be renewed by your Citroën dealer or refrigeration engineer. The system contains freon R12 fluid and this is harmful to the eyes and skin; therefore, if the system develops a leak at any time, take care not to allow body contact with the fluid.

8 Should the system not be used regularly, the air conditioning must be run for a period of about ten minutes once monthly to keep it in good condition.

9 No maintenance is required for the electrical wiring part of the system, apart from the occasional check to ensure that the wiring and connections are in good condition and securely located. A line fuse is incorporated into the circuit and in the event of this 'blowing' the cause should be located and rectified before fitting a new fuse.

20 Fault diagnosis – cooling system

Symptom	Reason(s)
Overheating (check gauge for accuracy)	Low coolant level (due to leakage or neglect) Broken or slipping pump drivebelt (BX 14) Engine oil level low or incorrect grade Thermostat defective Fan not operating Coolant pump defective Internal or external clogging of radiator matrix Internal clogging of engine waterways Radiator pressure cap defective New engine not yet run-in Brakes binding (see Chapter 9) Ignition timing retarded or automatic advance defective (see Chapter 4) Mixture too weak (see Chapter 3) Cylinder head gasket blown Cylinder head or liner(s) distorted or cracked
Overcooling (check gauge for accuracy)	Defective thermostat
External leakage	Overfilling (loss due to expansion) Loose or perished hoses Leaking coolant pump or thermostat gaskets Defective pressure cap Coolant pump seals defective Radiator matrix damaged Heater matrix damaged
Internal leakage	Blown head gasket (steam in exhaust and/or combustion gases in coolant) Head or liner(s) cracked or warped Inlet manifold cracked

Chapter 3 Fuel and exhaust systems

For modifications, and information applicable to later models, see Supplement at end of manual

Contents

Specifications

General

Air cleaner	Dry type with replaceable cartridge. Manual or automatic air temperature controlled inlet system
Air cleaner element:	
BX 14	Champion V402
BX 16 and BX 19 (up to June 1987)	Champion W117
Fuel pump	Mechanical diaphragm driven by eccentric
Fuel tank:	
Type	High density polyethylene
Capacity:	
BX and BX 14	44 litres (9.7 gallons)
BX 16 and BX 19	52 litres (11.4 gallons)
Fuel filter:	
BX 14	Champion L101
BX 16 (up to June 1987)	Champion L101
BX 19 GTi	Champion L201
Fuel grade	Premium (super grade) 4-star, 97 RON

Carburettor

Type	Solex or Weber Twin choke
Application:	
150 A engine	Solex 30-30 Z 2 CIT 329
150 C engine	Solex 32-34 Z 2 CIT 348
171 engine:	
Up to June 1983	Weber 32-34 DRTC 100 W 121-50
	Solex 32-34 Z 1 CIT 319
From July 1983	Weber 32-34 DRTC 2/100 W 128-50
	Solex 32-34 Z 1 W 319
171 engine with automatic transmission	Weber 32-34 DRTC 4/100 W 130-50
	Weber 32-34 DRTC 8/100 W 136-50*
159 engine	Solex CISAC 34-34 Z1 381

* air conditioned models

Solex – 30-30 Z 2 CIT 329

	Primary	Secondary
Venturi	24	25
Main jet	112.5	125
Air corrector jet and emulsion tube	165 ZD	180 ZC
Idle jet	40	–
Bypass jet	–	50
Pneumatic enrichment device	50	–

Solex – 30-30 Z 2 CIT 329 (continued)

	Primary	Secondary
Pump injector	35	–
Econostat	–	80
Needle valve (mm)	1.6	
Float level setting (mm)	33 ± 1	
Primary choke valve opening (strangler valve fully shut) (mm)	0.9	
Strangler flap opening (by anti-flood capsule) under vacuum of 350 mbar (mm)	3.2 ± 0.5	
Idle speed	700 to 800 rpm	
CO percentage in exhaust gas	0.8 to 1.15	

Solex 32-34 Z 2 CIT 348

	Primary	Secondary
Venturi	24	25
Main jet	115	120
Air corrector jet and emulsion tube	155 ZE	160 ZC
Idle jet	40	–
Bypass jet	–	50
Pneumatic enrichment device	45	–
Pump injector	35	35
Econostat	–	80
Needle valve (mm)	1.6	
Float level setting (mm)	33 ± 1	
Primary choke valve opening (strangler valve fully shut) (mm)	0.75	
Strangler flap opening (by anti-flood capsule) under vacuum of 350 mbar (mm)	3.7 ± 0.5	
Idle speed	800 to 850 rpm	
CO percentage in exhaust gas	0.8 to 1.5	

Weber 32-34 DRTC 100 W 121-50

	Primary	Secondary
Venturi	24	26
Main jet	107	115
Air corrector jet	165	160
Emulsion tube	F27	F27
Idle jet	45	–
Bypass jet	–	70
Pump injector	55	–
Econostat	–	60
Needle valve	175	
Primary choke valve opening at 20°C (mm)	0.50	
Strangler flap opening (by anti-flood capsule) (mm)	4.5	
Float level setting (mm)	7.25 ± 0.25	
Idle speed	700 rpm	
CO percentage in exhaust gas	0.8 to 1.5	

Solex 32-34 Z 1 CIT 319

	Primary	Secondary
Venturi	24	26
Main jet	140	120
Air corrector jet	200	155
Emulsion tube	23	18
Idle jet	42	70
Accelerator pump injector	40	35
Needle valve diameter (mm)	1.8	
Float setting (mm)	33.0	
Primary choke valve opening (strangler flap fully shut) (mm)	0.45	
Strangler flap opening (by anti-flood capsule) (mm)	6.0	
Idle speed	650 to 700 rpm	
CO percentage in exhaust gas	1 to 2	

Solex 32-34 Z 1 CIT 319-1

This carburettor is fitted to the BX 16 models from March 1984. Its characteristics differ from the previous carburettor (Solex 32-34 Z 1 CIT 319) in the following ways:

	Primary	Secondary
Idling air correction jet	180	150
Enrichment device jet	55	–

Weber 32-34 DRTC 2/100 W 128-50

	Primary	Secondary
Venturi	24	26
Main jet	107	112
Air corrector jet	170	160
Emulsion tube	F27	F27
Idle jet	45	–
Bypass jet	–	50
Pump injector	50	–
Econostat	–	60

Weber 32-34 DRTC 2/100W 128-50 (continued)

	Primary	Secondary
Needle valve	175	
Float setting (mm)	7.5 ± 0.25	
Maximum difference between floats (mm)	1.0	
Primary choke valve opening (strangler flap fully shut) at 20°C (mm)	0.45	
Strangler flap opening (by anti-flood capsule) (mm)	4.5	
Idle speed	650 to 700 rpm	
CO percentage in exhaust gas	0.8 to 1.5	

Solex 32-34 Z1 W 319

	Primary	Secondary
Venturi	24	26
Main jet	140	120
Air corrector jet	200	155
Emulsion tube	23	18
Idle jet	42	–
Bypass jet	–	70
Pump injector	40	35
Enrichment device jet	55	–
Econostat	–	80
Needle valve diameter (mm)	1.8	
Primary choke valve opening (1st choke at 20°C) (mm)	0.45	
Strangler flap opening (by anti-flood capsule) under vacuum (mm)	6.0	
Idle speed	650 to 700 rpm	
CO percentage in exhaust gas	0.8 to 1.5	

Weber 32-34 DRTC 4 100 W 130-50

This carburettor is the same as the Weber 32-34 DRTC 2/100 W 128-50 with the following exceptions:
CO percentage in exhaust gas .... 1 to 2

Weber 32-34 DRTC 8/100 W 136-50

This carburettor is the same as the Weber 32-34 DRTC 4 100 W 130-50 with the following exceptions:
Idle speed .... 750 to 800 rpm

Solex CISAC 34-34 Z 1 381

	Primary	Secondary
Venturi	25	17
Main jet	115	125
Air corrector jet	150	160
Emulsion tube	18	20
Idle jet	43	90
Idle air correction jet	145	145
Enrichment device jet	50	–
Econostat	–	80
Pump injector	40	35
Needle valve (mm)	1.8	
Float adjustment (mm)	33	
Primary choke valve opening (strangler flap fully shut) at 20°C (mm)	0.45	
Strangler flap opening (by anti-flood capsule) (mm)	5 to 7	
Manual de-flooding (mm)	7 to 9	
Idle speed	650 to 750 rpm	
CO percentage in exhaust gas	1.5 ± 0.5	

Torque wrench settings

	kgf m	lbf ft
Carburettor to inlet manifold	1.5	10.8
Inlet manifold to cylinder head	2.2	16.0
Exhaust manifold to cylinder head	2.2	16.0

1 General description

The fuel system is conventional in layout and operation. The fuel tank is mounted on the underside of the vehicle directly beneath the rear passenger seats. Fuel is drawn from the tank by a mechanical diaphragm pump operated by an eccentric on the camshaft.

The carburettor is a twin choke downdraught type of Solex or Weber manufacture, the carburettor type being dependent on model. BX and BX 14 models are fitted with a manual choke while the other models in the range have an automatic choke.

The air cleaner is of the renewable element type. On BX and BX 14 models the temperature of the air entering the air cleaner unit has a manual control for seasonal setting. The other models in the range have an automatic temperature control fitted to the air cleaner.

All models are fitted with a basic emission control system which relies mainly on the correct setting of the carburettor and the ignition system to keep exhaust emission levels to a minimum.

The admission of warm air to the air cleaner on all models keeps the intake air at the carburettor at a constant temperature and this too makes for clean combustion.

The engine crankcase ventilation system transfers oil fumes and blow-by gases which get past the piston rings into the air cleaner where they are consumed during the normal combustion process.

2 Routine maintenance – fuel and exhaust system

The following routine maintenance procedures must be undertaken at the specified intervals given at the start of this manual. Note that, when making carburettor adjustments, the ignition system must be known to be in good condition and the timing adjustments correct, as described in Chapter 4. The engine valve clearances must also be correctly adjusted (Chapter 1).

1 **Air cleaner element:** Renew the air cleaner element at the specified intervals or sooner if the vehicle operates in a dusty or dirty environment. Refer to Section 3 for details.

2 **Engine idle speed:** With the engine warmed up to its normal operating temperature, connect up a tachometer and check the engine idle speed. If necessary adjust as described in Section 13.

3 **Fuel system general check:** Make periodic checks to ensure that all fuel line connections are secure, that fuel lines are in good condition and there are no signs of fuel leaks from the lines, connections or the carburettor.

4 **Exhaust system general checks:** Check the condition and security of the exhaust system at the specified intervals. A leaky or severely corroded system must be repaired or renewed, as described in Section 22.

5 On BX and BX 14 models, the **air cleaner air intake control** must be changed seasonally – see Section 5.

3.5 Air cleaner with cover removed – BX 16

3 Air cleaner – element renewal

BX and BX 14

1 Release the clip on the large hose at the air cleaner cover. Pull off the hose and twist it aside.
2 Unscrew the cover retaining knob.
3 Withdraw the cover/filter element.
4 Clean out the casing and fit the new filter cartridge, reversing the removal procedure.

BX 16 and BX 19

5 Unscrew the wing nut securing the air cleaner top cover and lift off the cover, complete with the intake duct; lifting the duct from the carburettor (photo).
6 Lift the old element out of the air cleaner case and discard it. Clean out the casing.
7 Insert the new element and check that it is correctly seated.
8 Relocate the top cover and inlet duct. Fasten the cover with the wing nut.

4 Air cleaner – removal and refitting

1 Detach the hoses/air ducts to the cleaner unit.
2 Unclip the retaining strap (BX and BX 14).
3 Undo the retaining bolt(s) and remove the unit.
4 Refit in the reverse order to removal.

5 Air intake heating system

1 To maintain engine performance in cold conditions, warm air is admitted to the air intake before entering the air cleaner. Air is preheated by a muff on the exhaust manifold and its intake is controlled manually by means of a lever on the top face of the intake ducting on BX and BX 14 models or automatically by an integral thermostat on BX 16 and BX 19 models.

2 The manual adjustment lever has three adjustment positions, these being shown in Fig. 3.2.

3 On automatic control models, the integral thermostat operates a valve which directs warm air from the exhaust manifold ducting or cool air through the normal air intake duct on the air cleaner unit.

4 The system calls for no special maintenance but, on manual control models, the adjustment lever must be set to the appropriate position as the season demands. Failure to make the seasonal adjustment will reduce efficiency, may cause the carburettor to ice up, and will certainly create emulsion in the engine breather pipes and rocker cover in very cold weather.

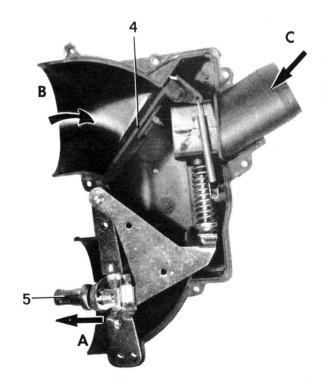

Fig. 3.1 Automatic air intake control (Sec 5)

4 *Air control flap*	B *Ambient air intake*
5 *Temperature sensor*	C *Heated air intake*
A *Air supply to filter*	

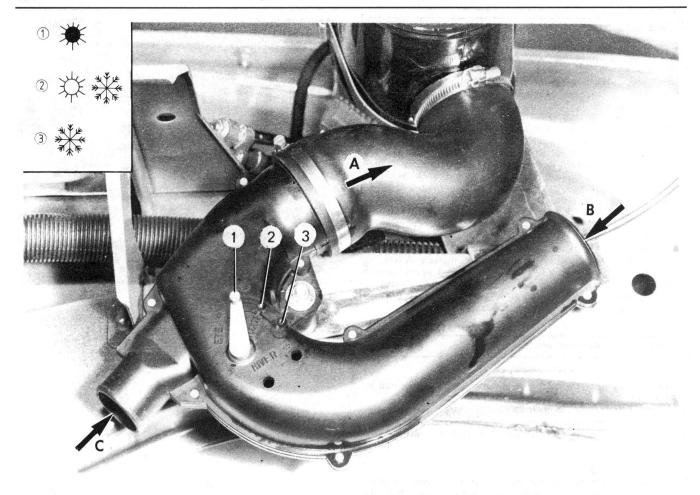

Fig. 3.2 Manual air intake control system (Sec 5)

1   ETE (Summer) setting   3   Hiver (Winter) setting   B   Ambient air intake
2   Mixte (Mixture) setting   A   Air supply to filter   C   Heated air intake

6   Fuel pump – testing

1   If the performance of the fuel pump is in doubt, first examine for fuel leaks and check that the fuel line connections are all sound.
2   Disconnect the fuel hose at the carburettor inlet connection and disconnect the high tension lead from the coil. Ensure that the tank contains fuel.
3   Direct the fuel feed hose into a suitable container and have an assistant operate the starter to crank the engine. A good spurt of fuel should be delivered on every second revolution of the engine. If not, check that the hose is not blocked. If that is clear the pump will need removal for examination or renewal.

7   Fuel pump – cleaning

1   The fuel pump may be one of several types. On one type, the filter cover is simply unbolted and removed. On another, the pump cover is removed (two screws), and with some pumps, the fuel outlet hose must be removed in order to be able to withdraw the pump cover. Inspection will determine which type of pump is fitted (photos).
2   With the cover removed, take out the filter screen and wash it in fuel until it is free from fluff and dirt (photo).
3   Mop out the fuel from the pump body and wipe out any sediment.

4   Refit the filter screen and cover making sure that the gasket is in good condition.

8   Fuel pump – removal, overhaul and refitting

1   Disconnect the fuel hoses from the pump (photo). Plug the inlet hose.
2   Unscrew the pump mounting bolts/nuts and lift the pump away (photos).
3   An insulator block with a gasket each side is fitted between the pump flange and the mounting flange on the engine. The gaskets must be renewed when refitting the fuel pump.
4   Where applicable, withdraw the pump operating pushrod (photo).
5   Further dismantling may not be possible on some types of pump. Even if it is, it should only be attempted if you have a repair kit. First mark the top and bottom halves of the pump for reassembly and then progressively loosen and remove the screws holding the two halves together. The diaphragm is connected to the operating mechanism beneath, and details will vary with different pumps. Note the sequence of assembly so that reassembly can be achieved in the same order.
6   Renew all defective parts; the kit will contain a variety of seals or gaskets which should automatically be fitted in place of the originals regardless of the fact that they may appear fit for further use.
7   Reassembly is the reverse of the dismantling sequence. Make sure that the upper and lower halves of the pump body are aligned and tighten the joint screws progressively and diagonally. Don't overtighten the top cover screws.

8   Before refitting the pump, check that the operating pushrod is in position (where applicable). Locate a new gasket each side of the insulator and refit the pump.
9   Tighten the securing bolts and make sure that the fuel hoses are reconnected to their correct pump connections.

9   Fuel level transmitter – removal and refitting

1   Disconnect the battery earth lead.
2   Fold the rear seat forwards and remove the insulator mat.
3   Prise free the circular plastic cover to expose the fuel level transmitter and disconnect the wiring from it (photo).
4   Before removing the transmitter from the fuel tank the safety precautions detailed in paragraph 2 in Section 10 should be observed.
5   Using a suitable tool, unscrew the transmitter mounting plate to release it from the securing tabs. Withdraw the transmitter unit.
6   Refitting is a reversal of removal, but use a new sealing ring if there is any doubt about the condition of the original one.

10   Fuel tank – removal and refitting

1   The fuel tank will normally only need removal from the vehicle if it is severely contaminated with sediment or other substance, or if it is to be renewed due to damage or for any repair work to the adjacent body or mechanical components.
2   As there is no drain plug incorporated in the tank, the best time to remove it is when it is nearly empty. If this is not possible, syphon as much as fuel as possible from the tank into a container which can be sealed, but before doing so, observe the following precautions:

(a) *Disconnect the battery*
(b) *Do not smoke or allow any naked lights near the working area*
(c) *Avoid placing the vehicle over an inspection pit as the fuel vapour is heavier than air; raise the vehicle at the rear and support it on safety stands*

3   From within the vehicle at the rear, disconnect the wiring from the fuel level transmitter (see previous Section).
4   Disconnect the fuel supply and return pipes from the fuel tank top

7.1A Fuel pump cover removal – non-removable filter type

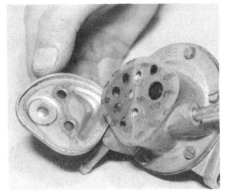
7.1B Fuel pump cover removal – removable filter type

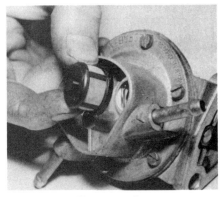
7.2 Fuel pump filter removal

8.1 Fuel supply hose removal from fuel pump

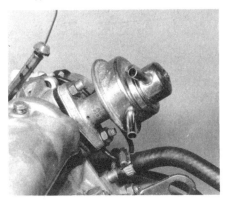
8.2A Fuel pump showing retaining nuts and black insulator block – BX 16

8.2B Fuel pump removal – BX 14

8.4 Fuel pump pushrod – BX 14

9.3 Fuel level transmitter

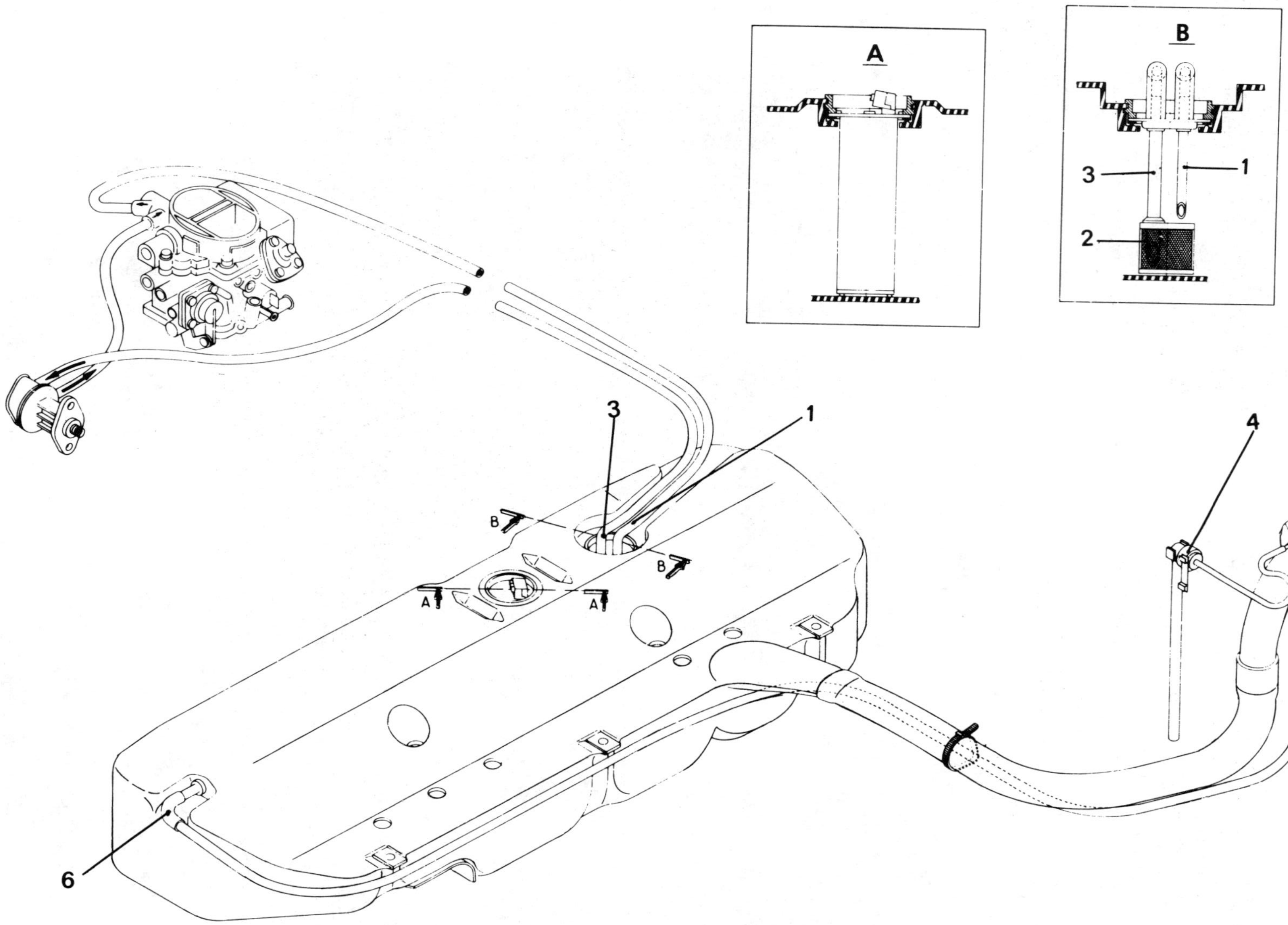

Fig. 3.3 Fuel tank and associated components (Sec 10)

1 Return hose
2 Suction pipe filter
3 Suction pipe (identified by yellow paint mark)

4 Vent unit with one-way valve
5 Filler pipe

6 Tank vent pipe
A Fuel level transmitter – note correct fitting orientation

B Fuel supply/return hose unit – note correct fitting orientation

face. Note that the fuel supply pipe is marked with yellow paint for identification. Plug the pipes to prevent fuel leakage and the ingress of dirt (photo).

5 Unbolt and remove the exhaust system (Section 22).
6 Unbolt and detach the height control linkage, complete with its intermediate bearing.
7 Unclip and detach the fuel filler pipe from the tank inlet nozzle.
8 Unfasten and peel back the carpet edging from the floor panel above the leading edge of the tank, then unscrew the two front tank retaining screws. Support the weight of the tank with a suitable jack or an assistant from underneath.
9 Unscrew and remove the three retaining bolts along the rear edge of the tank unit (from above), then lower the tank. As it is lowered, disconnect the ventilation pipe from the side of the tank. On BX and BX 14 models this pipe is connected to the right-hand side, whilst on BX 16 and 19 models the pipe connection is on the left-hand side.
10 If the tank is damaged, remove the fuel level transmitter unit (see previous Section) and renew the tank. It cannot be repaired.
11 If the tanks contains sediment, remove the fuel level transmitter and wash out the tank using paraffin, then rinse it out with clean fuel.
12 Refit in the reverse order of removal. Ensure that all hose connections are securely made.

10.4 Fuel tank supply and return hose connections

Fig. 3.4 Height control linkage (1) and intermediate bearing (2) (Sec 10)

11 Carburettors – description

1 A single Solex or Weber carburettor of twin choke downdraught design is fitted to all models in the range, the carburettor type being dependent on the engine capacity. Refer to the Specifications for application details.
2 A manual choke is fitted to the BX and BX 14 (150 A and 150 C models) variants whilst the BX 16 and BX 19 (171 and 159 engine) variants have an automatic choke.

3 Both types are conventional in operation and have a primary and main jet system and a mechanically operated acceleration pump. Both makes of carburettor incorporate exhaust emission control anti-pollution.
4 Reference to Fig. 3.5 and 3.6 will show cross-sectional views of the two carburettor types. The type identification number is stamped on a plate attached to the carburettor.
5 The Weber carburettor fitted to BX 16 models with automatic transmission is identical in design to the other Weber carburettor types fitted to manual transmission models, except that it also has a kickdown cam fitted.

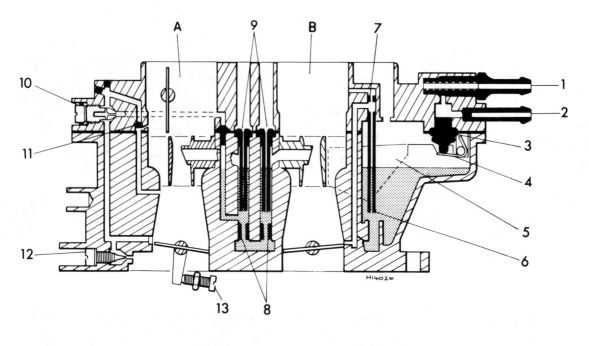

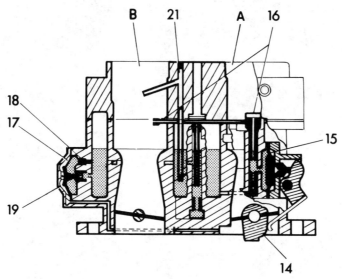

Fig. 3.5 Sectional view of the Solex carburettor fitted to the BX and BX 14 models (Sec 11)

1 Fuel inlet
2 Fuel return
3 Needle valve
4 Float level adjusting tab
5 Float
6 Progression fuel jet
7 Progression air jet
8 Main jets
9 Air correction jets

10 Idle jet
11 Idle air calibration
12 Idle mixture adjustment
    screw
13 Idle speed adjustment screw
14 Accelerator pump cam
15 Accelerator pump
16 Accelerator pump injectors

17 Power enrichener
18 Enrichener calibration
19 Enrichener valve
20 Enrichener fuel supply
21 Econostat
22 Econostat calibration
A Primary barrel
B Secondary barrel

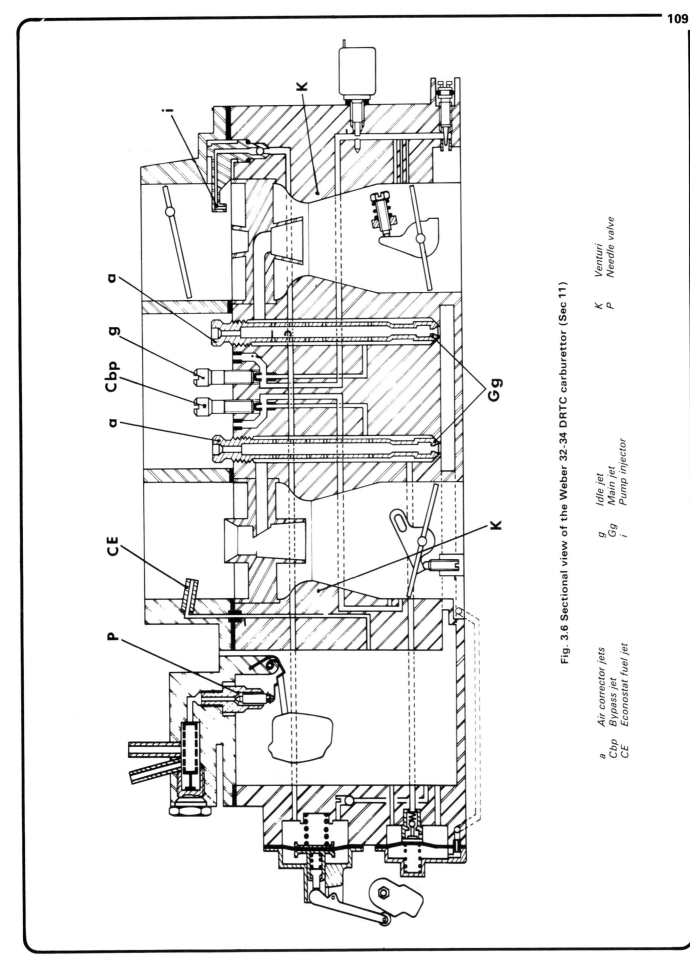

Fig. 3.6 Sectional view of the Weber 32-34 DRTC carburettor (Sec 11)

a   Air corrector jets
Cbp Bypass jet
CE   Econostat fuel jet

g   Idle jet
Gg   Main jet
i   Pump injector

K   Venturi
P   Needle valve

12 Carburettor – maintenance

1   Before blaming the carburettor for any shortcomings in engine performance, remember that there is no reason why the carburettor should lose tune, and in fact what usually happens is that, as the engine gets older and less efficient, more or less fruitless attempts are made to restore performance by interfering with the carburettor. In those parts of the world where exhaust emission is regulated by law it is inadvisable and may be illegal to alter carburettor settings without monitoring exhaust emission levels using special equipment.
2   The ultimate cause of most carburettor problems is wear in moving parts or dirt in the jets. The Solex and the Weber carburettors have no continuously moving parts, except for the float and the throttle spindle, which makes it a very reliable device so long as dirt does not get in. A drop of oil on the various linkages and flap spindle will ensure that they last for years without trouble; in consequence carburettor overhaul should be no more frequent than major engine overhaul.
3   Routine carburettor maintenance consists only of periodic cleaning of the float chamber and jets and (where applicable) an occasional look at the small gauze filters fitted in the fuel inlet connection and on the accelerator pump inlet valve. These tasks can be undertaken with the carburettor installed on the engine.
4   Before separating the top of the carburettor from the bottom, give the outside a good clean using paraffin or a proprietary cleaner and a stiff brush, afterwards drying with clean rag. It is well worth taking this extra trouble to reduce the risk of dirt getting into the carburettor.
5   After removing the jets, clean them by washing in clean fuel and blowing air through them. Never use a piece of wire as the jet calibration can be easily altered.
6   The float can be removed after taking out the hinge pin. The float needle valve can then be unscrewed and washed in fuel. Clean any dirt out of the float chamber using clean fuel but don't use rag for drying. The fuel inlet filter gauze and the accelerator pump valve gauze should both be washed in clean fuel and dried in air, again don't use rag to dry them. On refitting the float check, and if necessary adjust, the level setting, as explained in Section 16, 17 or 19, as applicable.
7   On completion check the carburettor idle speed (Section 13).

13 Carburettor – idle speed and mixture adjustments

1   Generally speaking, unless the carburettor is obviously out of tune or is malfunctioning it is not advisable to tamper with it. In any case the only running adjustment that can be made is to the idling.
2   Correct adjustment can only be achieved provided that the engine is in generally good condition. The valve clearances must be correct and the ignition system must be in good condition and adjusted correctly.
3   An independent tachometer is necessary to make accurate adjustment and it should be connected to the engine in accordance with the maker's instructions. The air filter must be fitted. Run the engine until warm, as indicated by the engagement of the cooling fan. On automatic transmission models, engage P. Allow the engine to run; when the cooling fan cuts out, adjustments can be made. During prolonged adjustments take care as the cooling fan will cut-in again periodically.
4   If local regulations preclude adjustment other than to the volume control screw, adjust the idling speed to that listed in the Specifications. The idle speed (volume control) setting screw and the mixture adjustment screw positions are shown in Fig. 3.7 and the photo.
5   After adjustment to the idle speed has been made on automatic transmission models, check that the handbrake is fully applied and place chocks against the roadwheels, then engage a gear and check that the idle speed drops to between 650 to 700 rpm. If required, further adjust the idle speed with the vehicle in gear to obtain this in-gear idle speed.
6   Where adjustment is to be made to the mixture control screw, it may first be necessary to prise free the tamperproof cap for access.
7   Turn the mixture screw to the position which provides the highest engine speed. Now reduce the engine speed to approximately 50 rpm above the specified idle speed for your model.
8   Repeat the procedures outlined in paragraph 7, then screw in the mixture control screw to reduce the engine speed by 30 to 50 rpm. Further minor adjustment to the idle speed may be necessary to bring the engine speed to within the idle speed range specified.

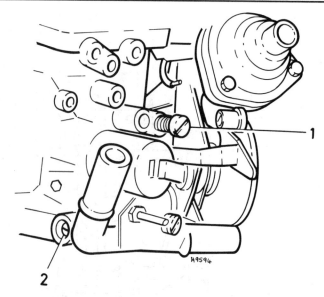

Fig. 3.7 Idle speed adjustment screw (1) and mixture adjustment screw (2) – Weber carburettor (Sec 13)

13.4 Idle speed adjustment screw (arrowed) – Solex 32-34

Fig. 3.8 Mixture adjustment screw location (6) – Solex 32-34 (Sec 13)

9   Whenever the mixture control screw setting has been reset it is advisable to have an exhaust CO reading taken by your Citroën dealer to ensure that the CO reading at the exhaust is within the specified limits. This is of particular importance in territories where strict emission controls are enforced.

14 Carburettor – removal and refitting

1   Disconnect the battery earth lead.
2   Unclip and detach the air ducting between the carburettor and the air cleaner unit.
3   Disconnect the wire from the idle cut-off solenoid.
4   Disconnect the fuel supply and return hoses from the carburettor. Plug the hoses (photo).
5   Detach the accelerator inner cable from the quadrant and the outer cable from its support at the carburettor and fold it back out of the way.
6   On manual choke models, detach the choke cable by loosening the inner cable clamp screw. Unscrew the outer cable location clamp bolt and move the cable out of the way.
7   On automatic choke models, clamp the coolant hoses each side of the choke unit, then loosen the securing clips and detach the hoses

from the choke unit (photo). If the hoses are not clamped, the cooling system will have to be partially drained to prevent coolant loss when the hoses are detached.
8   On BX 16 models fitted with the Solex 32-34 Z1 CIT 319-1 carburettor disconnect the ventilation hoses from the float chamber. Note that the upper hose is connected to the air filter at the other end (photo).
9   Where applicable, disconnect the vacuum hose from the carburettor (photo).
10   Unscrew and remove the space flange retaining screw and pull the flange away from the carburettor body.
11   Unscrew and remove the four nuts securing the carburettor to the inlet manifold, then lift the carburettor away from it for removal. Retrieve the old joint gasket and place a piece of clean cloth over the aperture in the manifold to prevent dirt or anything from accidentally falling into it while the carburettor is removed.
12   Refitting the carburettor is the reverse of the removal procedure. Remove all traces of the old gasket and use a new one on installation. After fitting the carburettor, reconnect the accelerator cable and, where applicable, the choke cable. When the choke control cable is fitted and the choke knob is pushed fully in, the flap should be fully open and there should be a small amount of possible additional movement on the control knob. Check that the flap closes when the control is pulled.

Fig. 3.9 Weber carburettor removal – items to be disconnected (Sec 14)

a and b	Coolant hoses to automatic choke
9	Air filter duct
10	Fuel inlet pipe
11	Fuel return pipe
12 and 13	Coolant hose retaining clips

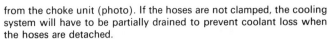
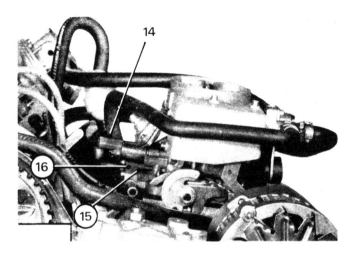

Fig. 3.10 Weber carburettor idle cut-off (14), spacer flange (15) and screws (16) (Sec 14)

14.4 Fuel supply and return hoses – Solex 32-34

14.7 Coolant hose connections – Solex 32-34

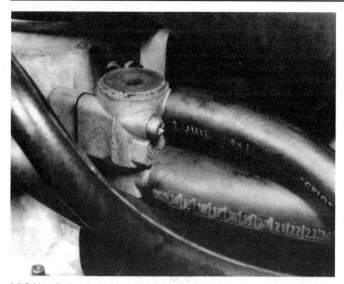

14.8 Ventilation hose connections – Solex 32-34

14.9 Vacuum hose connection (1) and spacer flange connection (2) – Solex 32-34

13 After reconnecting the two coolant hoses remove the clamps, if these were used, and in any case top up the cooling system.

14 Adjust the idle speed on completion, as described in Section 13.

15 Solex carburettor – dismantling, overhaul and assembly

1 The carburettor should not normally need to be dismantled except for cleaning and checking the float level.

2 If the carburettor is to be dismantled, remember that it is a relatively delicate instrument and therefore requires careful handling. Use the correct tools for the job and do not interchange jets or clean them out with wire or any similar item which could damage them and interfere with their calibration.

3 Before dismantling the carburettor, or any part of it, first clean the outside and prepare a clean work area. When taking anything mechanical apart, and this applies particularly to such components as carburettors, it is always sound policy to make sure that the individual parts are put back exactly where they came from, and even the same way round if it is possible to do otherwise, even though they may appear to be interchangeable. To help in this procedure mark or label items, put small parts in boxes or tins so that they don't get mixed up, and lay parts out in order of assembly on clean paper.

4 Identify the relevant illustrations for the carburettor being dismantled (Figs. 3.5, 3.11, 3.12A and 13.12B).

5 Undo the retaining screws and the choke link connecting screw, seen behind the arm of the spring in photo 17.5, and lift the carburettor top cover away from the main body (photo)

6 The float can be removed by pushing out the hinge pin and then the needle valve assembly can be unscrewed from the cover. Unscrew the fuel inlet connection and remove the gauze filter. Examine the filter for particles of foreign matter.

7 .Remove the accelerator pump operating rod and then remove the cover by progressively undoing the four retaining screws, restraining it against the action of the spring under the diaphragm. Examine the diaphragm for splits or damage.

8 Remove the accelerator pump inlet valve cover located in the bottom of the float chamber, taking care not to lose the ball valve. Examine the filter for contamination.

9 Unscrew and remove the jets, checking them for dirt or blockage. Observe the caution mentioned in paragraph 2.

10 It should not be necessary to interfere with any adjusting screws but, if this is necessary, count the number of turns required to remove the screw so that it can be refitted in approximately the same position.

11 Do not disturb the choke flap and throttle butterfly valve or spindles. Their actuating mechanisms are external and normally require

no attention unless excessively worn. If the spindles are worn in the carburettor body then serious consideration should be given to renewing the complete carburettor. Such wear is an indication that the carburettor is due for renewal and it would be false economy to refit the original instrument. Air leaks around worn spindles make it impossible to tune the carburettor correctly and poor performance and impaired economy will inevitably result.

12 The respective chambers, passages and jet seats can be brush cleaned using clean fuel and they should then be blown dry, if an air supply is available, or allowed to dry naturally. Don't use rag or cloth. Clean and blow through the jets in a similar manner.

13 Reassembly is the reverse of the dismantling procedure. Whenever possible use new washers, gaskets, or seals wherever fitted. During reassembly check and adjust the float level, as described in Section 16.

14 On refitting the carburettor, check the idle speed setting and adjust as necessary, as described in Section 13. Further 'on vehicle' carburettor adjustments may be necessary in which case refer to Section 16 or 17 as applicable.

15.5 Solex carburettor top cover screws (arrowed)

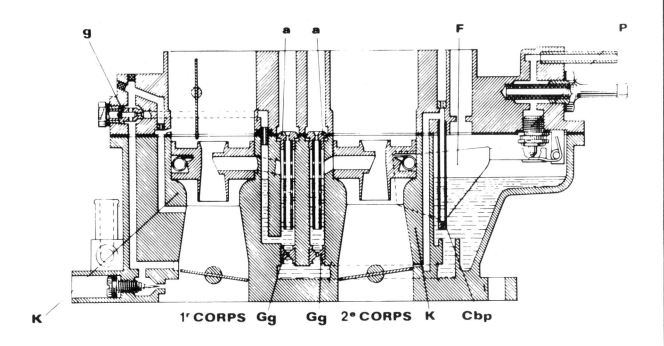

K   1ʳ CORPS   Gg   Gg   2ᵉ CORPS   K   Cbp

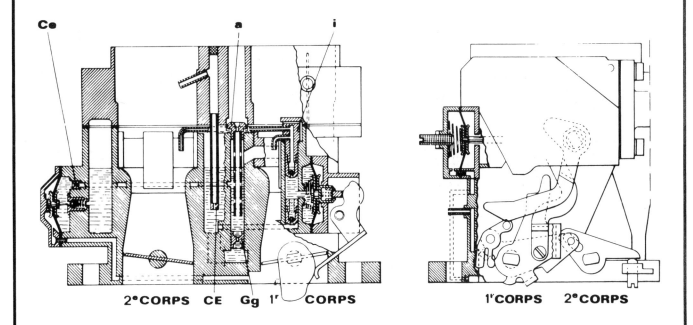

Fig. 3.11 Solex 32-34 carburettor with automatic choke fitted to BX 16 models (Sec 15)

a	Air corrector jet	CE	Econostat fuel jet	F	Float	K	Venturi
Cbp	Bypass jet	g	Idle jet	i	Pump injector	P	Needle valve
Ce	Enrichment device jet	Gg	Main jet				

Fig. 3.12A Solex 30-30 and 32-34 Z 2 carburettor, top view
with cover removed (Sec 15)

1   Main jet (primary)
2   Secondary venturi
3   Main jet/air corrector jet/emulsion tube (secondary)
4   Primary venturi
5   Pump injector

Fig. 3.12B Solex 32-34 and 34-34 Z 1 carburettor, top view
with cover removed (Sec 15)

1   Main jet
2   Primary venturi
3   Pump injector
4   Main jet/air corrector jet/emulsion tube (primary)
5   Secondary venturi

Fig. 3.13 Float level setting (A) – Solex 30-30 and 32-34 Z 2
carburettors (Sec 16)

Fig. 3.14 Float level setting gauge in position on a Solex
carburettor (Sec 16)

**16 Solex carburettors 30-30 Z 2 CIT 329 and 32-34 Z 2 CIT
348 – adjustments**

Float level setting
1   This check can be made with the carburettor in position in the car,
but the air cleaner duct will need to be detached and the carburettor
top cover disconnected and removed.
2   Check that the floats are not punctured, and also that the float arm
pivot pin and support holes are not excessively worn.
3   With the top cover inverted and the gasket in position, measure the
distance from the gasket to the tip of the float (A in Fig. 3.13). The
distance measured should be in accordance with the float level
specified for the carburettor type (see Specifications).
4   If adjustment is necessary, carefully bend the float tongue (which
bears on the needle) in the required direction and recheck the level
setting. Further adjustment may be necessary to achieve the correct
adjustment.

5   If the difference in height of each float exceeds 1 mm, bend the
float link arms so that they are level then recheck the float setting.
6   When refitting the top cover to the carburettor main body a new
gasket must be used.

Strangler (choke) flap setting
7   This check can be made with the carburettor in position, but the air
duct must be detached. Run the engine to provide the necessary
manifold vacuum.
8   Pull the choke lever to its full extent and retain it in this position.
This will subject the anti-flooding capsule to a vacuum of 350 mbar
and should open the strangler flap the specified amount. To check the
flap opening, insert a suitable gauge rod or twist drill down between
the flap and the inner wall of the venturi (B in Fig. 3.16).
9   If necessary, adjustment can be made to open or close the flap to
the specified clearance by turning the adjustment screw (3 in Fig.
3.17) in the required direction.

Fig. 3.15 Float level setting adjustment – Solex carburettors
(Sec 16)

1 Float arm link
2 Float tongue

Fig. 3.16 Strangler (choke) flap clearance B – Solex
carburettor (Sec 16)

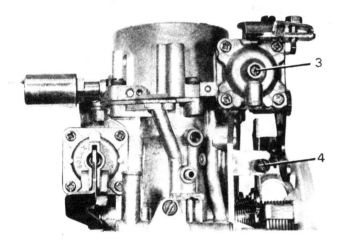

Fig. 3.17 Choke flap adjuster (3) and idle screw (4) – Solex
30-30 and 32-34 Z 2 carburettors (Sec 16)

Fig. 3.18 Primary choke (throttle) valve-to-venturi
clearance (C) (Sec 16)

Fig. 3.19 Primary choke valve adjuster screw location (5) –
Solex 30-30 and 32-34 Z 2 carburettors (Sec 16)

Primary choke valve (throttle) setting
10 The carburettor must be removed and inverted for this check.
11 Hold the strangler flap in the closed position and check the clearance between the outer edge of the butterfly valve and the venturi wall (C in Fig. 3.18). To check the clearance, insert a suitable gauge rod or twist drill of the same diameter as the specified clearance between the two.
12 If adjustment is necessary, prise free the tamperproof cap from the adjustment screw and turn the screw in the required direction to set the clearance (Fig. 3.19). On completion a new tamperproof cap should be fitted, but this must be entrusted to your Citroën dealer as a special tool is required.

17 Solex carburettor 32-34 Z 1 CIT 319, W 319 and 34-34 Z 1 381 – adjustments (on vehicle)

Float level setting
1 The float level setting check and adjustment procedure is similar to that described for other Solex carburettor models and reference should therefore be made to Section 16.

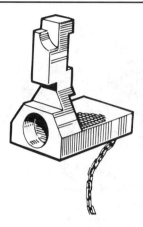

Fig. 3.20 Special automatic choke gauge (OUT 180 143-T)
for Solex carburettors (Sec 17)

Strangler (choke) flap setting

2   A special gauge is required to make this check, the Citroën reference number being OUT 180143-T. If this gauge is not available the check will have to be made by a Citroën dealer.

3   Start and run the engine up to its normal operating temperature when the cooling fan will cut-in and then out.

4   Remove the air intake duct from the carburettor.

5   Remove the cover from the automatic choke housing (photo).

6   Locate the special gauge into position and check that the mobile roller is correctly positioned between the two gauge slots; if not turn the adjustment screw of the heat-extensible capsule to meet this requirement (photo). Prevent the nut from turning using a 3 mm diameter drill (Fig. 3.21).

7   Now reposition the special tool so that it is as shown in Fig. 3.22 and, with the engine running at idle speed, check that the strangler flap is open to give a gap of 6 ± 1 mm between its outer edge and the wall of the carburettor. Use a gauge rod or twist drill of suitable diameter to assess the clearance. If adjustment is necessary, turn the adjustment screw A.

Fig. 3.21 Mobile roller adjustment – automatic choke control on the Solex 32-34 and 34-34 Z 1 carburettors (Sec 17)

4 Screwdriver	6 3 mm drill
5 Special gauge (OUT 180 143-T)	7 Nut
	8 Movable roller

Fig. 3.22 Strangler flap opening check – Solex 32-34 and 34-34 Z 1 carburettors (Sec 17)

A Adjuster screw	D Primary choke valve adjuster screw
B Gauge/twist drill	
C Actuator fork jaws	

17.5 Choke control unit shown with cover removed – Solex 32-34 Z1 W 319. Choke link screw (arrowed)

17.6 Access aperture for screwdriver to adjust the heat extensible capsule adjuster screw (arrowed) – Solex 32-34 Z1 W 319

8 Turn the engine off and leave the special tool in the previously set position. Open up the accelerator to its full extent, hold in this position and check the strangler flap-to-carburettor wall clearance which should be 8 mm. If this clearance is incorrect, prise open the actuating fork jaws (to increase the clearance) or pinch them together (to reduce the clearance) as necessary.

Primary choke valve (throttle) setting
9 Leave the special tool in the previously set position, connect up a tachometer to the maker's instructions and restart the engine. The engine speed should increase to between 2350 to 2450 rpm for models fitted with a shim on the choke cam or between 1700 and 1800 rpm for models without this shim. If the engine speed is not within these limits, adjust screw D in Fig. 3.22. **Note:** The above mentioned shim was fitted during manufacture to increase the engine speed during the choke phase when used during the first 600 miles. If still in position after this mileage has been covered, it can be removed by prising it free with a thin screwdriver (Fig. 3.23).
10 On completion of the above checks, remove the special tool and the tachometer, refit the choke cover and reconnect the air filter duct.

18 Weber carburettor – dismantling, overhaul and reassembly

1 The dismantling, overhaul and reassembly procedures for the Weber carburettor are similar to those described in Section 15 for the Solex carburettors.
2 Refer to Figs. 3.6 and 3.24 for guidance on component locations.
3 Before refitting the top cover, check the float level setting, as described in Section 19. Also make other checks and adjustments as necessary by referring to that Section.

19 Weber carburettor – adjustments

Float level setting
1 This check can be made with the carburettor in position in the car, but the air cleaner duct will need to be detached and the top cover disconnected and removed.

Fig. 3.23 Temporary shim fitted to the Solex 32-34 Z 1 CIT 319-1 carburettor (1) – remove after initial 600 miles (Sec 17)

2 Check that the floats are not punctured and also that the float arm pivot pin and support holes are not excessively worn.
3 Fit the gasket in position on the cover face and support the cover vertically so that the floats hang downwards. Check that the needle valve ball is not pushed in, then measure the clearance between the gasket and the float (a in Fig. 3.25).
4 Compare the distance measured with the specified float setting and, if necessary, adjust the float setting by bending the float arm tongue (which bears against the needle valve). Recheck the level setting. Further adjustment may be necessary.
5 If the difference in height between each float exceeds 1 mm, bend the float link arms so that they are level then recheck the float setting.
6 When refitting the top cover, a new gasket must be used.

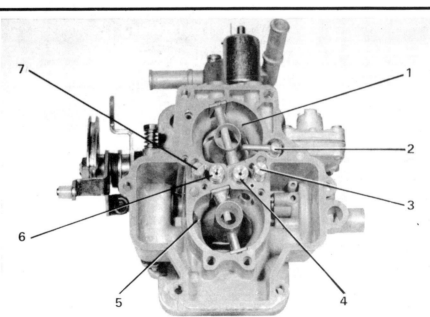

Fig. 3.24 Weber 32-34 DRTC carburettor, top view with the cover removed (Sec 18)

1 Primary venturi	5 Secondary venturi
2 Pump injector	6 Main jet (secondary)/air corrector jet/emulsion tube
3 Idle jet	7 Bypass jet
4 Main jet/air corrector jet/emulsion tube	

**Fig. 3.25 Float level check on the Weber carburettor
(Sec 19)**

a = float-to-gasket face clearance

**Fig. 3.26 Float level adjustment – Weber carburettors
(Sec 19)**

1   Float tongue   2   Float link arm

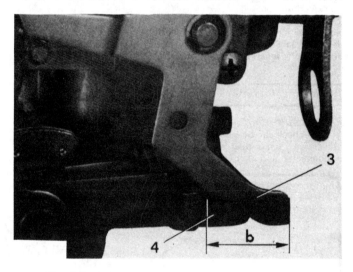

**Fig. 3.27 Strangler (choke) control check – Weber
carburettor (Sec 19)**

Measure distance (b) between lever endface (3) and roll (4)

Strangler (choke) control check

7   Before making this check, the engine must have been switched off for a minimum period of 30 minutes to allow the ambient temperature around the choke thermostatic capsule to have stabilized. You will need a thermometer to measure the air temperature when making the check.

8   Referring to Fig. 3.27, measure the distance between the lever end face and the roll (distance b). Measure the air temperature around the thermostatic capsule then refer to the temperature/distance tables shown in Fig. 3.28 and compare the readings taken. Where the temperature measured is not shown on the table an estimate can be made.

9   If adjustment is necessary, turn the adjuster screw shown in Fig. 3.29 in the required direction to the point where the correct distance is given.

Primary choke valve (throttle) setting

10 This check can only be made with the carburettor removed. When making the check the ambient temperature and the carburettor temperature should be 20°C.

11 Insert a gauge of the specified diameter between the venturi wall and the primary choke valve.

12 If the clearance is not as specified, adjust it by turning the adjustment screw shown in Fig. 3.30 in a clockwise direction to decrease the opening. To increase the opening turn the screw in an anti-clockwise direction. As with the strangler control check, the opening should be checked after the thermostatic capsule temperature has been allowed to stabilize for a minimum period of 30 minutes. If the ambient temperature around the capsule differs from that specified then the primary choke valve opening will differ also, and reference should then be made to the tables shown in Fig. 3.31. The valve opening should be in accordance with the ambient temperature shown.

13 Where the ambient temperature differs from those given an estimate can be made.

Strangler (choke) flap setting

14 Before checking the strangler flap opening, certain preliminary checks must be made. First remove the control spring by detaching the

retaining circlip at each end (Fig. 3.32). With the control spring removed, refer to Fig. 3.33 and check that the length measured between the end rings (a) is between 40.3 and 40.7 mm. If this measurement is not correct renew the control spring.

15 Remove the two anti-flooding capsule retaining screws (4 in Fig. 3.32) and unclip the capsule control rod retaining circlip. Remove the capsule unit and check that the port indicated in Fig. 3.34 is clear, also the gallery opening in the base of the carburettor.

16 Refit the anti-flood capsule and the control spring.

17 The strangler flap opening can now be checked. A clamp will need to be fabricated to hold the strangler in the low temperature position, and reference to Fig. 3.35 will show the clamp dimension requirement and fitting position. The clamp is fitted to ensure that the strangler flap is fully opened for the check. Position the clamp over the shaft and the thermostatic capsule heating pipe.

18 Push against the anti-flood capsule control rod and check the strangler flap opening at d in Fig. 3.36 using a gauge rod or twist drill of the same diameter as the specified clearance.

19 If the strangler flap opening is not as specified, adjust it by turning the screw within the anti-flood capsule in the appropriate direction. On completion remove the bracket.

Temperature in C degrees	Dimension « b » in mm
5	22.7
10	23.7
15	24.7
20	25.6
25	26.4
30	27.2
35	28
40	29.1
45	30.2

A

Temperature in C degress	Dimension ''b'' in mm
5	19
10	20.1
15	21.5
20	22.7
25	24.3
30	25.7
35	27.5
40	28.9
45	30.1

B

Fig. 3.28 Dimension b in Fig. 3.27 must be in accordance with temperature at thermostatic capsule (Sec 19)

A 32-34 DTRC 100 W 121-50   *B 32-34 DTRC 2/100 W 128-50*

Fig. 3.29 Automatic choke adjuster screw (5) – Weber carburettor (Sec 19)

Fig. 3.30 Weber carburettor – turn screw (6) to alter the primary choke valve opening. Thermostatic capsule (7) is also indicated (Sec 19)

Temperature in C degrees	Dimension « c » in mm
5	0.65
10	0.60
15	0.55
20	0.50
25	0.45
30	0.40
35	0.37
40	0.35
45	0.33

A

Temperature in C degrees	Dimension ''c'' in mm
5	0.60
10	0.55
15	0.50
20	0.45
25	0.40
30	0.37
35	0.30
40	0.25
45	0.20

B

Fig. 3.31 Primary choke valve opening to be in accordance with the temperature at the thermostatic capsule – Weber carburettor (Sec 19)

A   32-34 DTRC 100 W 121-50

B   32-34 DTRC 2/100 W 128-50

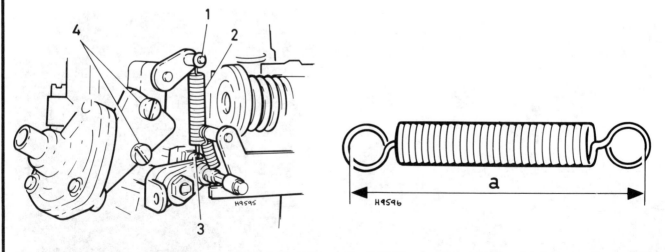

Fig. 3.32 Strangler flap opening check – Weber carburettor (Sec 19)

1   Circlip
2   Control spring
3   Circlip
4   Screws

Fig. 3.33 Measure the control spring between the end rings (Sec 19)

$a = 40.5 \pm 0.2$ mm

Fig. 3.34 Check that port (6) is clear – Weber carburettor
(Sec 19)

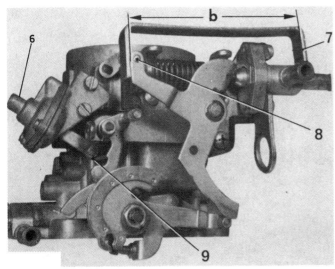

Fig. 3.35 Strangler flap opening adjustment – Weber
carburettor (Sec 19)

  6   Anti-flood capsule
  7   Clamp (dimension b to equal 103 mm)
  8   Shaft/heater pipe of thermal capsule
  9   Lever

Fig. 3.36 Strangler flap opening (d) – Weber carburettor
(Sec 19)

20 Accelerator cable – removal and refitting

1   Pivot the carburettor throttle control quadrant and hold it in the open throttle position. Release the accelerator inner cable from the quadrant groove.
2   Release the outer cable from the location bracket on the carburettor (photo).
3   Working inside the car, detach the cable end fitting from the end of the accelerator foot pedal. Withdraw the cable assembly from the car by pulling it into the passenger compartment, at the same time feeding it through the bulkhead grommet.
4   Before fitting a new cable assembly lubricate the inner cable with engine oil.
5   Refitting an accelerator cable assembly is the reverse of the removal procedure. On completion check cable operation is satisfactory through its range of travel and allows full throttle opening and closing on its return. If necessary adjust the outer cable at the location bracket as required and fit the securing clip.
6   On automatic transmission models the accelerator cable and kickdown cable adjustment checks are described in Chapter 6.

21 Choke cable – removal and refitting

1   Loosen the clamp bolt securing the inner cable to the choke flap operating link.
2   Loosen the bolt securing the clamp plate which holds the outer sheath on the carburettor bracket. Detach the inner cable and outer sheath from the carburettor.
3   Working inside the car, remove the knob from the choke control cable and undo the control retaining nut. Push the control through the facia and then disconnect the choke warning light cable from the switch on the control.
4   Pull the control assembly into the car, working it through the rubber grommet in the bulkhead.
5   Refitting the choke control is the reverse of the removal procedure. When fitted, with the air cleaner removed check that the choke is fully open when the control knob is pushed home and closed when the knob is pulled. Check that the warning light is on when the choke is pulled.

22 Manifolds and exhaust system

1   The inlet and exhaust manifolds are located on opposite sides of the cylinder head. They can be removed individually or together with the cylinder head. Removal of the exhaust manifold with the cylinder

20.2 Accelerator cable location bracket on the Solex carburettor. The adjustment/securing clip of the outer cable is indicated

head *in situ* is more difficult due to its close proximity to the bulkhead.

2   The inlet manifold can be removed, together with the carburettor, or after first removing the carburettor. Whichever method is to be employed the carburettor connections and associated coolant hoses must first be detached; refer to Section 14 for details.

3   When removing the exhaust manifold, first raise and support the vehicle at the front end to allow access to the manifold and exhaust downpipe flange connection nuts/bolts (photos).

4   If, on removal, the manifolds are found to be damaged in any way, they must be renewed.

5   Before refitting the manifolds, clean the mating flange faces of the manifold and the cylinder head. Always use new gaskets.

6   Tighten the retaining nuts and bolts to the specified torque setting.

7   Maintenance of the exhaust system is limited to checking for gas leaks and repair by renewal. Holts Flexiwrap and Holts Gun Gum exhaust repair systems can be used for effective repairs to exhaust pipes and silencer boxes, including ends and bends. Holts Flexiwrap is an MOT approved permanent exhaust repair. Holts Firegum is suitable for the assembly of all exhaust system joints.

8   When removing the old system don't waste a lot of time trying to undo rusted and seized nuts, bolts or clamps. Cut them off. New ones will be required in any case if they are that bad.

9   When fitting the new system, use an exhaust joint sealant when assembling pipe sections to ensure that the joints are free from leaks. Get the system into position, but don't tighten anything up until everything is properly located. After checking that all is well you can then tighten the securing bolts or nuts. If the flexible hangers are breaking up or otherwise deteriorated they must be renewed, otherwise the system will vibrate leading to leaks or even fractures (photo).

10 When reassembling the spring-loaded joint coupling, the joint and retaining screw heads must be lubricated with a special high temperature grease which can be obtained from a Citroën dealer. On BX and BX 14 models, tighten the joint bolts evenly to the point where the compressed spring length is 22 mm. On BX 16 and BX 19 models tighten the bolts evenly until the cup contacts the screw shoulder (Fig. 3.37) (photo).

22.3A Exhaust manifold with air filter hot air collector cowling fitted – BX 16

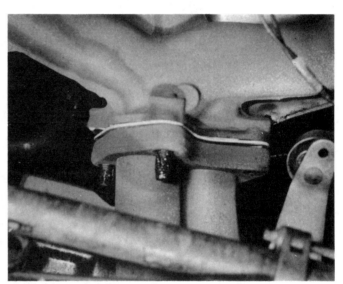

22.3B Exhaust manifold-to-downpipe connection – BX 16

22.9 Exhaust system flexible hanger (arrowed)

22.10 Exhaust system spring-loaded coupling – BX 16

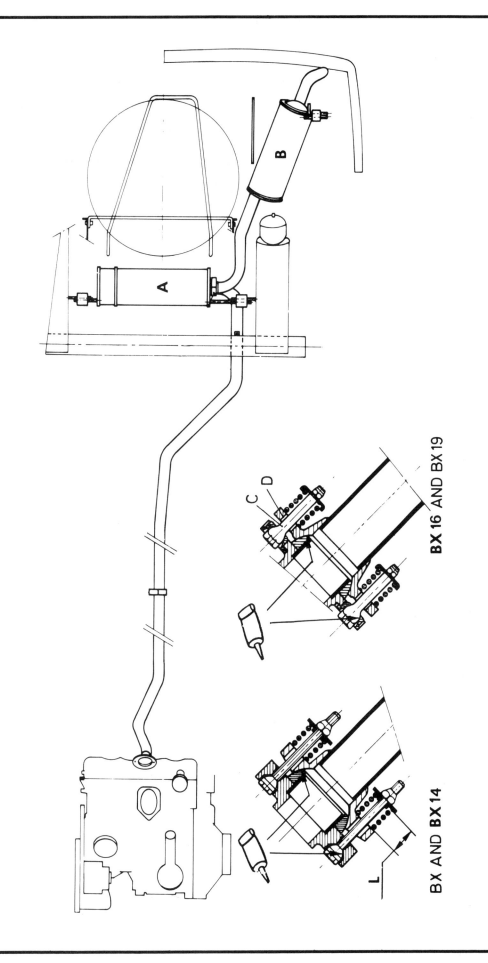

Fig. 3.37 Exhaust system layout. Lubricate as specified at points indicated, according to type (Sec 22)

L (BX and BX 14 models) = 22 mm   B Silencer   C Shoulder   D Cup

A Expansion chamber

BX 16 AND BX 19

BX AND BX 14

23 Fault diagnosis – fuel system

Unsatisfactory engine performance and excessive fuel consumption are not necessarily the fault of the fuel system or carburettor. In fact they more commonly occur as a result of ignition and timing faults. Before acting on the following it is necessary to check the ignition system first. Even though a fault may lie in the fuel system it will be difficult to trace unless the ignition is correct. The faults below, therefore, assume that this has been attended to first (where appropriate).

Symptom	Reason(s)
Smell of petrol when engine is stopped	Leaking fuel lines or unions Leaking fuel tank Float chamber vent blocked
Smell of petrol when engine is idling	Leaking fuel line unions between pump and carburettor Overflow of fuel from fuel chamber due to wrong level setting, ineffective needle valve
Excessive fuel consumption for reasons not covered by leaks or float chamber faults	Worn jets Over-rich setting Sticking mechanism Dirty air cleaner element
Difficult starting, uneven running, lack of power, cutting out	One or more jets blocked or restricted Float chamber fuel level too low or needle valve sticking Fuel pump not delivering sufficient fuel Induction leak
Difficult starting when cold	Choke control or automatic choke maladjusted Insufficient use of manual choke Automatic choke not cocked before starting Weak mixture
Difficult starting when hot	Excessive use of manual choke, or automatic choke malfunction Accelerator pedal pumped before starting Vapour lock (especially in hot weather or at high altitude) Over rich mixture
Engine does not respond properly to throttle	Faulty accelerator pump Blocked jet(s) Slack in accelerator cable
Engine idle speed drops when hot	Overheated fuel pump
Engine runs on	Weak mixture Idle speed too high

Chapter 4 Ignition system

For modifications, and information applicable to later models, see Supplement at end of manual

Contents

Specifications

Type .... Electronic (breakerless) system

Distributor
Make .... Ducellier or Bosch
Type number:
    150 A engine .... Ducellier 525 354
    150 C engine .... Ducellier 525 388
    171 A and 159 engine .... Ducellier 525 327 or Bosch 0237 009 013

HT leads (carburettor models) .... Champion CLS 9

Ignition coil
Make and type .... Bosch 0221 122 317 or Ducellier 520 015
Primary resistance:
    Bosch .... 0.82 ohm ± 10%
    Ducellier .... 0.8 ohm ± 5%
Secondary resistance:
    Bosch .... 8250 ohms ± 10%
    Ducellier .... 6000 ohms ± 5%

Ignition timing
Dynamic:
    BX (62 bhp) .... 8° BTDC at 850 rpm
    BX 14 (72 bhp) .... 10° BTDC at 850 rpm
    BX 16 (manual transmission) .... 10° BTDC at 900 rpm
    BX 16 (automatic transmission) and BX 19 .... 10° BTDC at 850 rpm

Spark plugs
Type .... Tapered seat
Application:
    BX and BX 14 (up to July 1988) .... Champion S9YCC or S281YC
    BX16 (up to September 1988) .... Champion S7YCC or S279YC
    BX 19 (up to July 1987) .... Champion S7YCC or S279YC
Electrode gap:
    S7YCC and S9YCC spark plugs .... 0.8 mm (0.032 in)
    S279YC and S281YC spark plugs .... 0.6 mm (0.025 in)

Torque wrench setting
	kgf m	lbf ft
Spark plugs	1.5 to 2.0	11 to 15

1 General description and precautions

The ignition system fitted to all models is of the electronic type and comprises a 12 volt battery, high output coil, a transistorised module, a distributor with a magnetic impulser generator and spark plugs.

The electronic ignition system relies on the distributor to produce an electrical pulse at each firing point; the pulse is produced by magnetic induction and is amplified by the ignition module which supplies LT current to the coil. HT voltage is generated and distributed in the traditional fashion.

Electronic ignition systems are normally very reliable; because the effects of contact breaker wear have been eliminated, the system does not go 'off tune'.

Take care not to damage the module or the distributor by applying wrong polarity or excessive voltage (eg, by using a 'boost' charger with the battery connected). *Take extra care to avoid receiving personal electric shocks from the system: considerably higher voltages may be present than in a conventional system.*

2 Routine maintenance – ignition system

Very little is required in the way of servicing for the electronic ignition system, but that is not to say that it should be ignored. The following items must be checked periodically and, where applicable, at the specified mileage intervals (see Routine Maintenance at the front of this manual).

1   Remove the distributor cap with the HT leads. Wipe the cap and leads clean and dry. Also wipe clean and dry the coil tower. Inspect the distributor cap, rotor arm and HT leads for signs of deterioration. If cracks or signs of arcing are visible renew the defective component. When refitting the distributor cap, ensure that the HT leads are securely fitted to the cap, plugs and coil. Also check that the carbon brush and the HT segments within the cap are not excessively worn.

2   At the specified mileage intervals remove and renew the spark plugs, as described in Section 9.

3   Dwell angle adjustment is not necessary with a breakerless ignition system and ignition timing, once set, should not require further attention.

3 Distributor – removal and refitting

1   Disconnect the HT leads from the spark plugs by pulling on the connectors (not the leads).

2   Unclip the distributor cap, release the HT leads from the location clips and position the leads and cap out of the way (photo).

3   Disconnect the LT wiring at the plug connector by releasing the spring retaining clip.

4   Clean the area around the distributor mounting flange and look for a timing alignment mark between the distributor and the cylinder head on BX and BX 14 models, or distributor and fuel pump/thermostat/distributor combined housing on BX 16 and BX 19 models (photo). If a timing alignment mark is not visible, scribe an alignment mark across the two faces.

5   Undo the retaining nuts and withdraw the distributor.

6   Refit in the reverse order of removal. The distributor drive is offset so there is no possibility of incorrect assembly (photo). Use the

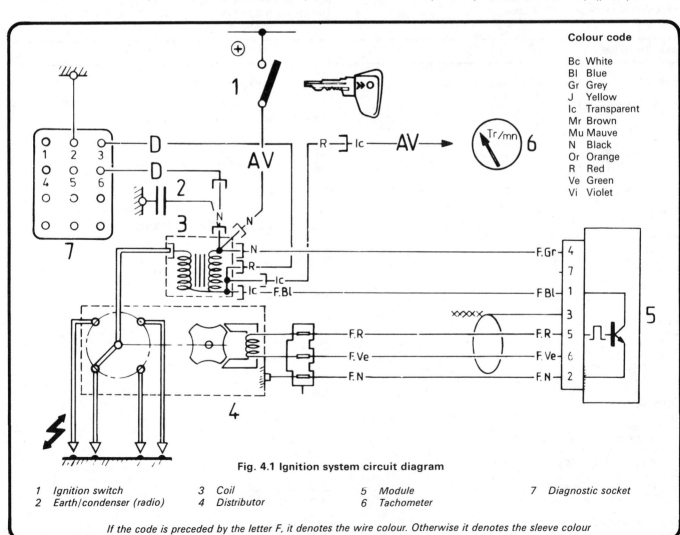

Fig. 4.1 Ignition system circuit diagram

1 Ignition switch	3 Coil	5 Module	7 Diagnostic socket
2 Earth/condenser (radio)	4 Distributor	6 Tachometer	

If the code is preceded by the letter F, it denotes the wire colour. Otherwise it denotes the sleeve colour

3.2 Removing the distributor cap (BX 16)

3.4 Distributor timing alignment mark (BX 16)

3.6 Distributor drive engagement dog is offset (BX 16)

alignment marks if refitting the old distributor; if fitting a new unit, set it to the middle of the travel allowed by the slotted holes.
7   Check the ignition timing and adjust if necessary (Section 5).

4 Distributor – dismantling and reassembly

1   Before commencing dismantling, check that spares are available. If the mechanical components of the distributor are worn it will be necessary to renew the complete distributor.

Ducellier
2   Commence dismantling by removing the screws which hold together the upper and lower halves of the body. The lugs are offset to guarantee correct reassembly. Separate the body sections.
3   The pick-up coil and vacuum unit can now be removed from the upper body section – note into which hole the vacuum unit link engages. The rotor and centrifugal advance weights can be removed after extracting the circlip from the shaft; the drive dog is secured to the shaft by a pin.
4   Reassemble in the reverse order to dismantling.

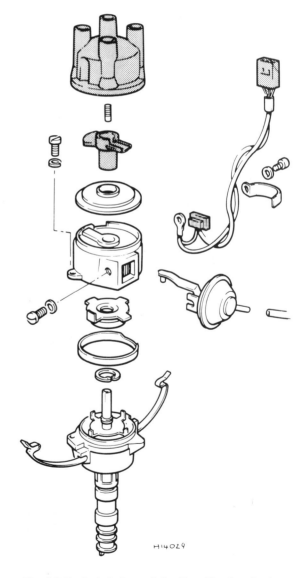
Fig. 4.2 Exploded view of the Ducellier breakerless distributor (Sec 4)

Bosch

5   The procedure is similar to that just described, but the distributor body is in one piece (photo).
6   Fit a new O-ring seal into the groove in the base of the distributor body before refitting it (photo).

5   Ignition timing

1   The ignition timing can only be checked dynamically and to do this you will need a stroboscopic timing light.
2   Start the engine and run it up to its normal operating temperature (cooling fan cuts in), then switch off the engine.
3   Turn the engine over slowly by hand so that the timing mark on the flywheel periphery can be seen through the aperture in the clutch housing. Highlight the timing mark by applying a white chalk mark or quick drying white paint to it (photo).
4   Disconnect the distributor vacuum advance hose.
5   Connect up a timing light (stroboscope) and a tachometer in accordance with the manufacturer's instructions. An HT type tachometer must be used.

6   Restart the engine and run it at the recommended idle speed. Point the timing light at the timing marks. They should appear stationary and in alignment. If they are not in alignment, loosen the distributor retaining nuts just enough to allow the distributor to be rotated by hand. Turn the distributor body in the required direction to bring the timing marks in alignment, then retighten the distributor retaining nuts.
7   Switch off the engine, remove the timing light and tachometer. Reconnect the ignition vacuum advance hose.
8   Once the timing has been reset, make a timing alignment mark across the faces of the distributor flange and the cylinder head or distributor housing on the engine. This will then act as a timing position guide when the distributor is next removed.

6   Diagnostic test socket

1   The Citroën BX range of models is fitted with a diagnostic test socket for electronic monitoring of engine performance and ignition system condition. Although this facility is of no use to the home mechanic it does enable a suitably equipped garage to make a quick assessment and with greater accuracy than the usual procedures (photo).

4.5 Remove the top plate for access to the rotor (Bosch distributor)

4.6 Bosch distributor drive dogs and O-ring seal (arrowed)

5.3 Flywheel timing mark aligned with the advance timing mark on the timing plate (BX 16)

6.1 Diagnostic test socket (BX 16)

2 With the appropriate equipment the following checks or adjustments can be made:

(a) Primary (LT) circuit condition
(b) Setting of initial advance
(c) Centrifugal and vacuum advance curves
(d) Engine speed

7 Ignition switch and steering lock

Removal and separation of the switch and lock is described in Chapter 10.

8 Ignition coil

1 The maintenance of the coil is minimal and is limited to periodically wiping its surfaces clean and dry and ensuring that the lead connectors are secure. High voltages generated by the coil can easily leak to earth over its surface and prevent the spark plugs from receiving the electrical pulses. Water repellent sprays are now available to prevent dampness causing this type of malfunction (photo).
2 Wipe clean and spray the HT leads and distributor cap also.
3 Special equipment is required to test a coil and is best left to an auto-electrician. Substitution of another coil is an alternative method of fault tracing.
4 The coils used in mechanical breaker and electric ignition systems are not interchangeable.

9 Spark plugs and HT leads

1 The correct functioning of the spark plugs is vital for the correct running and efficiency of the engine. It is essential that the plugs fitted are appropriate for the engine, and the suitable type is specified at the beginning of this chapter. If this type is used and the engine is in good condition, the spark plugs should not need attention between scheduled replacement intervals. Spark plug cleaning is rarely necessary and should not be attempted unless specialised equipment is available as damage can easily be caused to the firing ends.
2 To remove the plugs, first open the bonnet and pull the HT leads from them. Grip the rubber end fitting not the lead otherwise the lead connection may be fractured (photo).
3 The spark plugs are deeply recessed in the cylinder head and it is recommended that dirt is removed from the recesses using a vacuum cleaner or compressed air, before removing the plugs, to prevent dirt dropping into the cylinders.
4 Unscrew the plugs using the special box wrench supplied with the car and located in the engine compartment (photos).
5 Examination of the spark plugs will give a good indication of the condition of the engine.
6 . If the insulator nose of the spark plug is clean and white, with no deposits, this is indicative of a weak mixture, or too hot a plug (a hot plug transfers heat away from the electrode slowly, a cold plug transfers heat away quickly).
7 The plugs fitted should be as specified at the beginning of this Chapter. If the top and insulator nose are covered with hard black-looking deposits, then this is indicative that the mixture is too rich. Should the plug be black and oily, then it is likely that the engine is fairly worn, as well as the mixture being too rich.
8 If the insulator nose is covered with light tan to greyish brown deposits, then the mixture is correct and it is likely that the engine is in good condition.
9 The spark plug gap is of considerable importance as, if it is too large or too small, the size of the spark and its efficiency will be seriously impaired. For the best results the spark plug gap should be set in accordance with the Specifications at the beginning of this Chapter.
10 To set it, measure the gap with a feeler gauge, and then bend open, or close, the outer plug electrode until the correct gap is achieved. The centre electrode should never be bent as this may crack the insulation and cause plug failure if nothing worse.

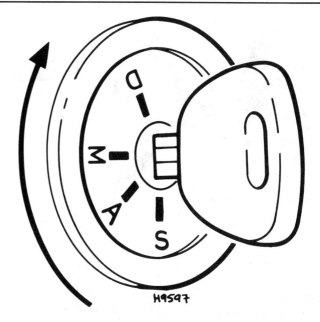

Fig. 4.3 Ignition switch positions

S   Off. Steering locked when   M   Ignition on
*   key removed   D   Starter motor energised*
A   Ignition off, accessories on

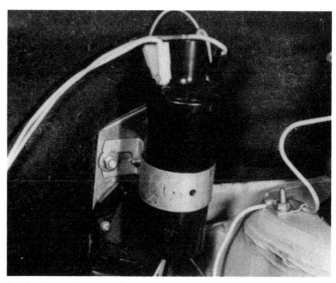

8.1 Ignition coil

11 Special spark plug electrode gap adjusting tools are available from most motor accessory stores.
12 Screw each plug in by hand. This will make sure that there is no chance of cross-threading.
13 Tighten to the specified torque. If a torque wrench is not available, just nip up each plug. It is better to slightly undertighten rather than overdo it and strip the threads from the light alloy cylinder head. The spark plugs have tapered seats without sealing washers. Overtightening this type of plug can make them extremely difficult to remove.
14 When reconnecting the spark plug leads, make sure that they are refitted in their correct order, 1 – 3 – 4 – 2. No 1 cylinder being at the flywheel end of the engine.
15 The plug leads require no attention other than being kept clean and wiped over regularly. When connecting the leads to the spark plugs, push on the rubber connectors, not on the leads themselves.

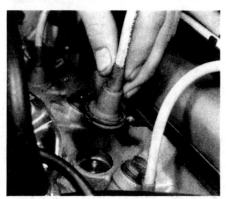

9.2 HT lead removal from the spark plug –
do not pull on the lead

9.4A Spark plug and special removal/fitting
spanner

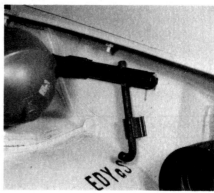

9.4B Spark plug spanner location

10 Fault diagnosis – ignition system

Symptom	Reason(s)
Starter turns but engine will not start	Faulty or disconnected leads Faulty spark plug Fault in ignition coil Fault in pick-up/starter unit
Engine starts but runs erratically	Incorrect timing Fouled spark plug Incorrectly connected HT leads Crack in distributor cap or rotor Poor battery, engine and earth connections

Chapter 5 Clutch

For modifications, and information applicable to later models, see Supplement at end of manual

Contents

Specifications

General

Type	Single dry plate with diaphragm spring. Cable operation
Driven (friction) plate diameter:	
BX and BX 14	180.3 mm (7.1 in)
BX 16 and BX 19	200.6 mm (7.9 in)
Lining thickness (under load)	7.7 mm (0.303 in)
Release bearing type	Sealed ball
Pedal free play	Nil
Pedal travel (minimum/maximum)	130 mm/150 mm (5.1/5.9 in)

Torque wrench settings

	kgf m	lbf ft
Clutch cover bolts	1.0	7.2
Transfer gear cover plate bolts	1.1	8.0
Lever pivot bolt	2.5	18.1
Clutch housing-to-engine mounting bolts	3.5	25.3

1 General description

On all models the clutch is of diaphragm spring, single dry plate with cable actuation.

The clutch pedal pivots in a bracket mounted under the facia and operates a cable to the clutch release arm. The release arm operates a thrust bearing (clutch release bearing) which bears on the diaphragm spring of the pressure plate. The diaphragm then releases or engages the clutch driven plate which floats on a splined shaft. On BX and BX 14 models this shaft (the engine output shaft) is part of the transfer gear assembly which is mounted on the clutch housing. The drive passes via an intermediate pinion to the gearbox primary (input) shaft.

The clutch release mechanism consists of a fork and bearing which are in permanent contact with release fingers on the pressure plate assembly. The fork pushes the release bearing forwards to bear against

the release fingers, so moving the centre of the diaphragm spring inwards. The spring is sandwiched between the two rings which act as fulcrum points. As the centre of the spring is pushed in, the outside of the spring is pushed out, so moving the press plate backwards and disengaging it from the clutch disc.

When the clutch pedal is released, the diaphragm spring forces the pressure plate into contact with the friction linings on the clutch friction plate and at the same time pushes the plate a fraction of an inch forwards on its splines, so engaging the plate with the flywheel. The plate is now firmly sandwiched between the pressure plate and the flywheel, so the drive is taken up.

A self-centering ball thrust bearing is employed and this is in permanent contact with the release mechanism. By using this type of thrust bearing no clutch pedal free play is required and wear in the linings of the friction plate is automatically compensated for.

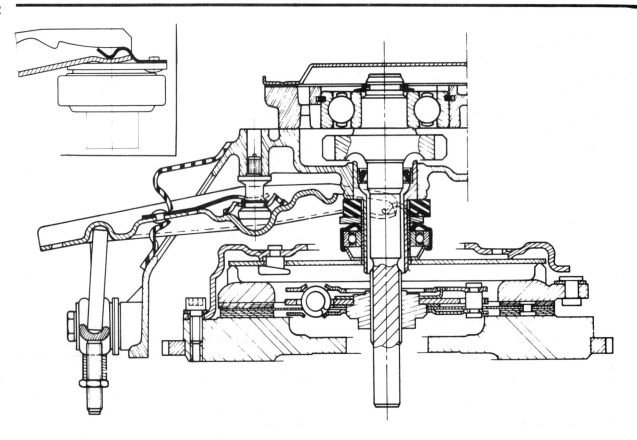

Fig. 5.1 Sectional view of the clutch unit – BX and BX 14 (Sec 1)

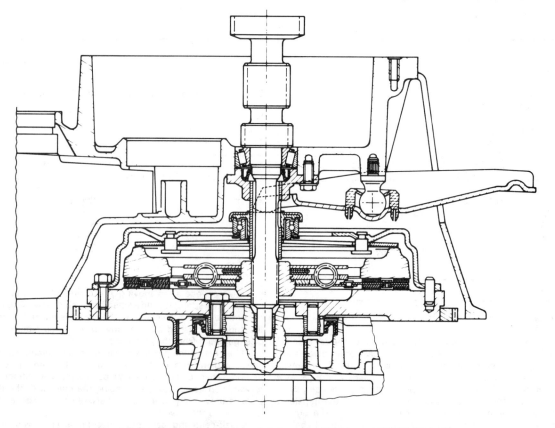

Fig. 5.2 Sectional view of the clutch unit – BX 16 and BX 19 (Sec 1)

2 Clutch – adjustment

1 The clutch must be checked for adjustment at the intervals specified in Routine Maintenance at the beginning of this manual.
2 First check the clutch pedal travel by measuring the total distance from the highest to the lowest point of its travel. The recommended travel distance is given in the Specifications at the start of this Chapter.
3 The clutch thrust bearing is of the self-centering ball type and it should be in permanent contact with the release mechanism. Check this by ensuring that there is no clutch pedal free play. Check the clearance between the pedal pin and the pedal unit support aperture lower limit (a in Fig. 5.3).
4 The clearance measured should be a minimum of 8 mm (0.31 in). If adjustment is necessary, raise and support the bonnet, then loosen the clutch pushrod locknut and take up any excessive play by turning the adjustment screw. When the adjustment is correct retighten the locknut (photo).

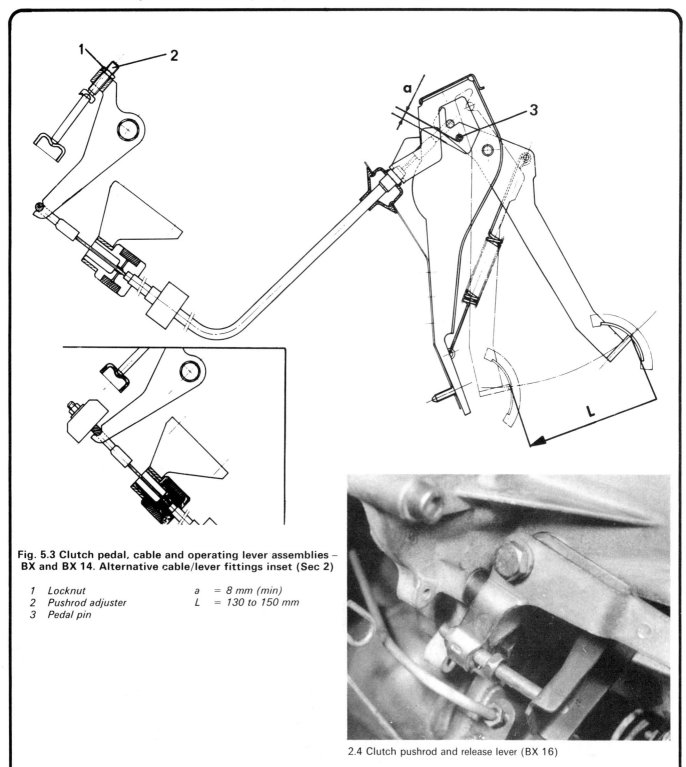

Fig. 5.3 Clutch pedal, cable and operating lever assemblies – BX and BX 14. Alternative cable/lever fittings inset (Sec 2)

1 Locknut
2 Pushrod adjuster
3 Pedal pin

a = 8 mm (min)
L = 130 to 150 mm

2.4 Clutch pushrod and release lever (BX 16)

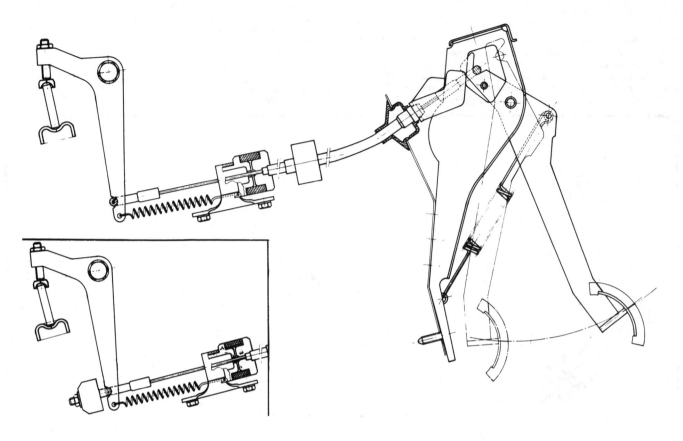

Fig. 5.4 Clutch pedal, cable and operating lever assemblies – BX 16 and BX 19. Alternative cable/lever fitting inset
(Sec 2)

3 Clutch cable – removal and refitting

1   The clutch cable connects the clutch pedal to the operating lever/rod.
2   Raise and support the bonnet. For improved access to the clutch cable in the engine compartment, remove the air cleaner unit, as described in Chapter 3.
3   Push the clutch operating lever towards the cable and disconnect the spring and inner cable from the lever, then remove the pushrod (photo).
4   Working from inside the vehicle, disconnect the brake stop-light switch wire connectors from the switch (photo).
5   Undo the two socket-head bolts and the two nuts securing the

brake and clutch pedal bracket. Withdraw the bracket from the bulkhead sufficiently to enable the clutch cable to be disconnected from the pedal.
6   Pull the cable through the bulkhead grommet into the engine compartment then withdraw the outer cable and location bush from the locating eye bracket on the transmission and remove the cable (photo).
7   The clutch cable fitted to later models has a steel weight fitted at the operating lever end. This is fitted to eliminate cable rattle. It does not affect cable adjustment or fitting and this later cable type is fully interchangeable with the earlier type.
8   Refit the clutch cable in the reverse order to removal. When refitting the pedal bracket, align the brake pedal with the pushrod. On completion, check the clutch adjustment as described in Section 2.

3.3 Clutch cable connection to the release lever (early type BX 16)

3.4 Clutch and brake pedal assemblies. Brake light switch and wires (arrowed)

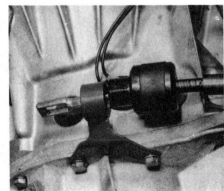

3.6 Withdraw the cable from the location eye bracket (BX 16)

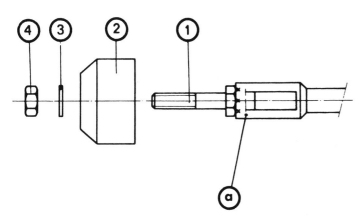

Fig. 5.5 Clutch cable end components on later models (Sec 3)

1 Bolt welded to yoke (a)   3 Washer
2 Steel weight   4 Nut

4 Clutch (BX and BX 14 models) – removal

1 The clutch unit can be removed from the BX and BX 14 models with the engine and gearbox in position in the vehicle. If the engine and gearbox have been removed, proceed from paragraph 17.
2 Drain the engine and gearbox oil.
3 Disconnect and remove the battery, as described in Chapter 12. With the battery removed, unbolt and remove the battery fixing clamp and support tray.

4 Unclip and detach the air intake duct between the carburettor and the air filter unit.
5 Disconnect the air intake pipe at the air filter heater pipe.
6 Disconnect the clutch cable at the operating lever and retrieve the pushrod.
7 Disconnect the wiring harness connectors where they join above the transfer casing.
8 Detach and remove the heater pipe and the air filter bracket.
9 Raise and support the vehicle at the front so that the roadwheel on the left-hand side can be unbolted and removed.
10 Prise free the retaining clips and remove the mud shield from the left-hand wheel arch.
11 Unbolt and remove the clutch cable bracket.
12 Unbolt the diagnostic socket with its support from the top of the clutch housing.
13 Position a jack underneath the engine and raise it to support the weight of the engine. To prevent possible damage to the engine, locate a suitable flat piece of wood between the engine and the jack saddle.
14 Unscrew the engine mounting nuts and washers from the points indicated in Fig. 5.6.
15 Raise the jack to lift the engine and free the mountings from the slotted holes.
16 Undo and remove the bolts from the points indicated, (1 in Fig. 5.6). Remove the engine mountings.
17 Undo and remove the clutch casing retaining bolts, noting that one bolt is hidden under the rib (arrowed in Fig. 5.7). Also unbolt and remove the lift sling bracket.
18 Check that all of the retaining bolts and fastenings have been disconnected then carefully withdraw the clutch/transfer gear case housing unit from the engine. The housing may need to be tapped free with a plastic-faced hammer applied to the casting bosses.
19 Unscrew the clutch fixing bolts. Jam the teeth of the flywheel ring gear to prevent rotation as the bolts are unscrewed.
20 Lift away the cover and friction plate.

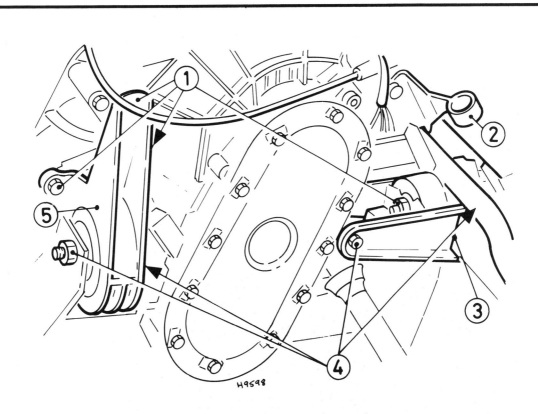

H9598

Fig. 5.6 Clutch removal (BX and BX 14). Disconnection points (Sec 4)

1 Bolts   3 Engine mounting   4 Mounting nuts and washers   5 Engine mounting
2 Cable bracket

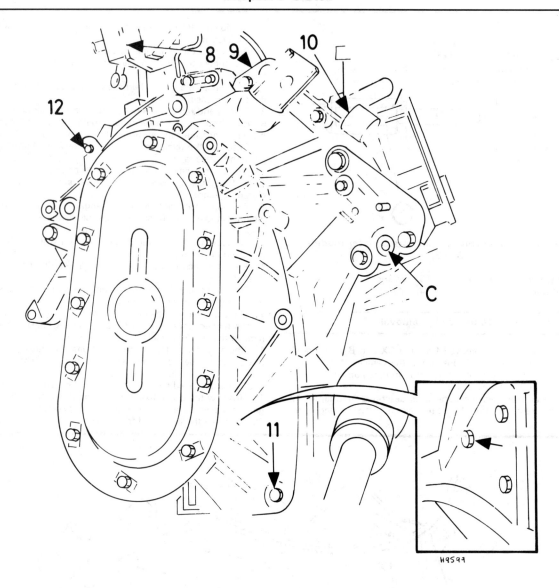

Fig. 5.7 Clutch removal (BX and BX 14). Disconnection points (Secs 4 and 6)

8 Diagnostic socket and support	9 Lift sling bracket	11 Retaining bolt	c Dowel
	10 Cable bracket	12 Extended head bolt	Inset shows hidden bolt

5   Clutch – inspection and repair

1   The clutch friction plate should be inspected for wear and for contamination by oil. Wear is gauged by the depth of the rivet heads below the surface of the friction material. If this is less than 0.6 mm (0.024 in) the linings are worn enough to justify renewal.

2   Examine the friction faces of the flywheel and clutch pressure plate. These should be bright and smooth. If the linings have worn too much it is possible that the metal surfaces may have been scored by the rivet heads. Dust and grit have the same effect. If the scoring is very severe it could mean that, even with a new clutch plate, slip and juddering and other malfunctions will recur. Deep scoring on the flywheel face is serious because the flywheel will have to be removed and machined by a specialist, or renewed. This can be costly. The same applies to the pressure plate in the cover although this is a less costly affair. If the friction linings seem unworn yet are blackened and shiny then the cause is almost certainly due to oil. Such a condition also requires renewal of the plate. The source of the oil must be traced also. It could be due to a leaking seal on the transmission primary shaft or from a leaking crankshaft oil seal (see Chapter 1 for details of renewal).

3   If the reason for removal of the clutch has been because of slip and the slip has been allowed to go on for any length of time, it is possible that the heat generated will have adversely affected the diaphragm spring in the cover with the result that the pressure is now uneven and/or insufficient to prevent slip, even with a new friction plate. It is recommended that under such circumstances a new assembly is fitted.

4   Do not attempt to reline the plate or dismantle the pressure plate cover, but obtain new or factory reconditioned units which are sometimes supplied on an exchange basis.

5   Clean away all old gasket from the housing mating flanges without scratching or scoring the surfaces of the metal. Obtain a new gasket.

6   Before refitting the clutch unit, check the clutch release mechanism components for wear, as described in Section 7. Renew any parts as necessary.

6   Clutch (BX and BX 14 models) – refitting

1   Support the friction plate between the flywheel and the clutch lever unit. Ensure that the greater projecting hub of the plate is facing towards the flywheel.

2 Locate the clutch cover unit into position on the flywheel, engaging with the three projecting dowels. Retain the cover in position on the flywheel with the bolts (hand tight only).

3 It is now necessary to align the centre of the friction plate with that of the flywheel. To do this use a special alignment tool or alternatively use a suitable diameter bar inserted through the plate into the flywheel spigot bearing, but take care not to damage the seal. It is possible to align the friction plate by eye, but difficulty will probably be experienced when refitting the output shaft. If the transfer gears have been separated from the clutch housing the friction plate can be aligned using the engine output shaft located in its normal running position (photo).

4 With the plate centralized the cover bolts should be tightened diagonally and evenly to the specified torque. Ideally new spring washers should be used each time a replacement clutch is fitted. When the bolts are tight remove the centralizing tool.

5 Before refitting the housing, check that the mating surfaces are clean and dry. Smear the bearing surface of the withdrawal pad on the diaphragm spring with medium grease.

6 To prevent the clutch release operating lever (fork) from becoming disengaged when refitting the clutch housing, retain it in position by looping a length of cord through the adjacent retaining bolt hole in the housing and tie the bracket so that it is secure.

7 Place a new gasket over the location dowels and then carefully offer the clutch housing/transfer pinion unit to the engine and insert the output and input shafts.

8 To assist the respective shaft splines to engage, rotate the flywheel and gearbox input shaft alternately until they slide home into position. Loosely locate bolts 11 and 12 in Fig. 5.7, then remove the cord retaining the operating lever to allow the housing to fit flush.

9 Insert the retaining bolts, remembering to replace any fittings retained by them. Tighten the bolts progressively to the specified torque.

10 Refit the engine mountings and tighten their retaining bolts to the specified torque settings (see Specifications in Chapter 1).

11 Release the jack and slowly lower the engine to rest in position on the bearers. Refit the retaining nuts with washers and tighten them to the specified torque setting (see Chapter 1).

12 Lubricate the clutch pushrod at each end with grease then reconnect the clutch cable and check/adjust the pedal height setting, as described in Section 2.

13 Refit the remaining items in the reverse order of removal.

14 On completion lower the vehicle at the front end and top up the engine and gearbox oil level to complete.

7 Clutch release mechanism (BX and BX 14 models) – removal and refitting

1 The clutch actuating rod can be removed by slackening the operating adjustment and unhooking the return spring.

2 To remove or overhaul the withdrawal bearing and fork the clutch flywheel housing must be removed. This is described in Section 4.

3 With the housing removed the withdrawal fork and bearing can be withdrawn from the output shaft for inspection.

4 Wipe clean and inspect the release bearing. If excessive wear is obvious, renew the bearing.

5 Inspect the fork retaining ball-stud and if obviously distorted or worn renew it. Drift the ball-stud from the housing using a suitable diameter drift. Fit the new one, together with a new rubber cup, by driving it carefully into position using a soft-faced hammer. Support the housing during this operation to prevent it from being damaged.

6 Before reassembly, check the clutch primary shaft oil seal. If it is leaking then the complete guide bush/seal assembly must be renewed as the seal is not supplied separately.

7 Press the guide bush out of the flywheel housing.

8 Press the new bush/seal assembly fully into its recess so that it seats firmly.

9 Any wear in the spigot bush which is located in the centre of the crankshaft rear flange (flywheel mounting) and supports the output shaft can be rectified by renewal of the bush, as described in Chapter 1.

10 To refit the fork, fit the spring blade so that it is located under the rubber cover as shown (photo).

11 Position the release bearing over the engine output shaft and

engage the retainers behind the fork fingers. The release bearing can be slid along the sleeve whilst holding the fork (photos).

12 Check the fork and bearing for correct operation and then refit the housing – see Section 6. Readjust the clutch operating clearance on completion – see Section 2.

6.3 Using transfer gear output shaft to centralise the clutch driven plate (BX and BX 14)

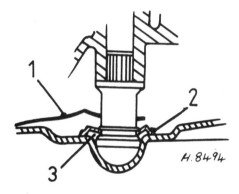

Fig. 5.8 Clutch release lever spring retaining clip (1) and rubber cover (2). Lubricate with grease (3) (Sec 7)

7.10 Release arm and bearing (BX and BX 14)

7.11A Release bearing retaining clips (BX and BX 14)

7.11B Release arm lever and bearing engaged on ball stud (BX and BX 14)

8 Transfer gears (BX and BX 14 models) – removal, overhaul and refitting

1   The transfer gears are located under a cover plate at the end of the clutch/flywheel housing. Their purpose is to transmit power from the engine crankshaft and clutch to the transmission primary (input) shaft which lies below the engine.

2   The gears are housed in the intermediate plate attached to the clutch/flywheel housing. Removal of the intermediate plate, complete with transfer gears, necessitates removal of the clutch/flywheel housing (see Section 4).

3   Unbolt and remove the cover plate and its gasket.

4   Remove the clutch release bearing and operating lever (Section 7).

5   Remove the transfer gear intermediate plate (photo). The plate will probably require tapping off with a plastic-faced hammer. Take care that the intermediate gear does not drop out as the plate is removed. Only tap the plate on the exposed lugs.

6   Remove the intermediate gear.

7   Clean away all old gasket material and obtain a new one.

8   To remove the input and output shaft units from the intermediate plate, expand the retaining clips and drive or press the shaft units from the plate.

9   Clean the input and output shaft ball-bearings and check them for excessive play and/or signs of damage. Inspect the intermediate shaft needle roller bearings. Renew any suspect or worn bearings. If a bearing has collapsed due to general wear and fatigue, then the chances are that the other bearings are close to failure and it is therefore advisable to renew all the bearings.

10   Carefully inspect the transfer gears. If excessive transmission noise has been experienced it may be reduced by changing the transfer gears. If the teeth are worn or damaged, then the gears should be renewed. Renew the gear set rather than a single gear; it is not good practice to mesh new gears with old as the wear rate of both is increased and they will be noisy in operation.

11   Check the input and output shafts, and inspect their splines for wear or damage. Renew them if necessary.

12   To remove the bearings, use circlip pliers and fully expand the circlip before pressing the shaft out of the bearing or the shaft/bearing out of the intermediate plate.

8.5 Transfer gears and intermediate plate removal (BX and BX 14)

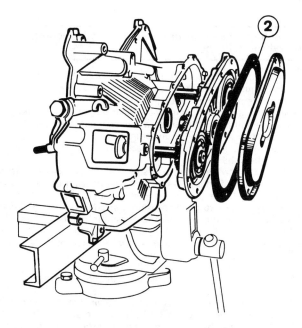

Fig. 5.9 Cover plate, gasket (2) and transfer gears removal – BX and BX 14 (Sec 8)

13 When reassembling, remember that the shorter shaft is located at the narrower end of the intermediate plate. Always use new circlips and support the plate adequately during the pressing operation.

14 Always use a new Belleville washer under the circlip so that its concave face is towards the bearing.

15 With the gears reassembled, check that the circlips are fully engaged by measuring their outside diameter which must not exceed 22.6 mm.

16 If the intermediate gear needle race is to be renewed in the intermediate plate, press the old one out and use the intermediate gear as an installation tool, but make sure that the gear teeth do not lock with those of the other gears during the pressing operation (photo).

17 Lubricate the bearings and fit the intermediate gear. It must be flush with the input and output gears when fitted.

18 Wind some plastic insulation tape around the output shaft splines to protect the seal during reassembly (photo).

19 Check that the dowels are in position in the clutch housing, apply sealant to the joint faces and locate the transfer gear housing over the dowels (photo).

20 Refit the cover plate using a new gasket and tighten the retaining bolts to the specified torque (photos).

21 Remove the protective tape from the output shaft splines (photo).

22 On completion, refit the clutch release bearing and operating lever, referring to Section 7 for details.

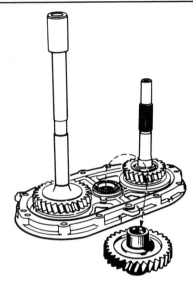

Fig. 5.10 Intermediate plate and gear removed (Sec 8)

8.16 Fitting a new intermediate gear roller bearing into its housing using the gear and a suitable draw bolt

8.18 Bind the output shaft splines with tape to protect the clutch housing seal

8.19A Apply sealant to the mating surface ...

8.19B ... assemble the clutch housing to the intermediate gear unit

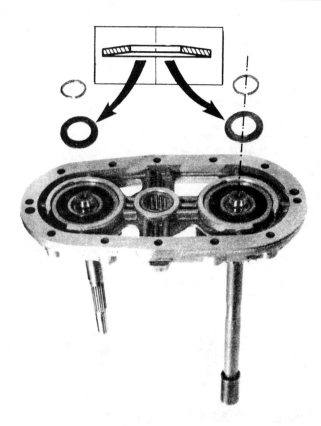

Fig. 5.11 Input and output shaft reassembly. Note orientation of Belleville washers (concave towards bearing) (Sec 8)

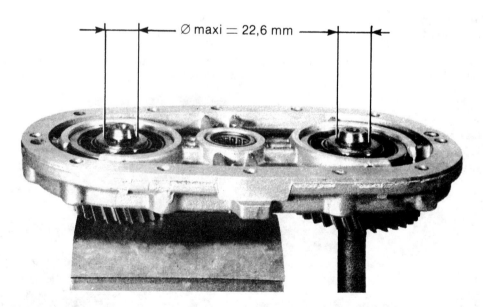

⌀ maxi = 22,6 mm

Fig. 5.12 Check that the outside diameter of the circlips does not exceed that specified (Sec 8)

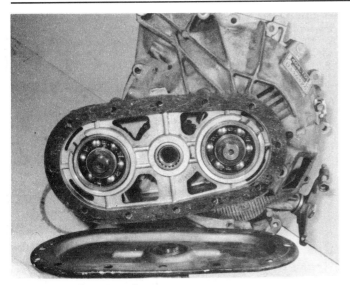

8.20A Locate the new gasket ...

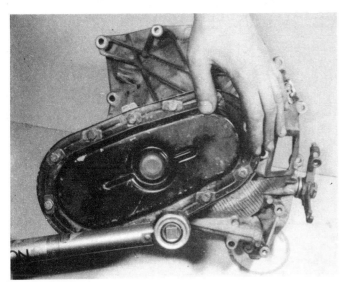

8.20B ... and refit the cover plate

9.2 Undo the clutch unit retaining bolts (BX 16)

9   Clutch (BX 16 and BX 19 models) – removal and refitting

1   The clutch unit can be removed from the BX 16 and BX 19 models after the gearbox has been removed from the vehicle or with the engine and gearbox removed and then separated. Refer to Chapters 1 and/or 6 as applicable for details.

2   Make alignment marks on the clutch pressure plate and the flywheel, then progressively slacken the six bolts which secure the pressure plate. Remove the bolts, the pressure plate and the clutch friction plate (photo).

3   Examine the clutch components, as described in Section 5, and renew any defective components as necessary.

4   Commence refitting by offering the clutch friction plate to the flywheel, making sure it is the right way round. It will only fit one way. Retain the disc in position by inserting a centering mandrel. Various proprietary centering tools are available, or alternatively one can be made from a piece of dowel or bar built up with tape (photo).

5   Fit the pressure plate, observing the alignment marks made when dismantling if the old plate is being refitted. Insert the six bolts and just nip them up so that the friction plate is lightly gripped.

6   Make sure that the friction plate is accurately centred, either by visual inspection or by inserting an old gearbox input (friction plate)

8.21 Remove the protective tape from the output shaft

9.4 Centering the clutch friction plate using a proprietary tool (BX 16)

shaft. If the disc is not centred it will not be possible to refit the gearbox.

7 With the centering mandrel in position, tighten the pressure plate securing bolts progressively to the specified torque. Remove the centering mandrel.

8 Refit the gearbox on completion.

10 Clutch release mechanism (BX 16 and BX 19 models) – removal and refitting

1 Access to the clutch release mechanism is gained after removing the gearbox, or the engine and gearbox from the vehicle. If the latter method is used, separate the engine from the gearbox after they are removed. Refer to Chapters 1 and 6 for details.

2 The clutch release bearing may be removed by freeing its spring clips from the release fork (photo).

3 The clutch release fork can be pulled or levered off its balljoint.

4 Renew the pivot bush if it is worn.

5 To remove the release fork balljoint use a slide hammer fitted with a suitable claw.

6 To refit the balljoint, apply thread locking compound to the splines and carefully drive it into position.

7 When refitting the clutch release fork to the balljoint, lubricate the joint with grease (photo).

8 Refit the release bearing and connect the release fork to it, reversing the removal procedure.

10.2 Detach the clutch release bearing from the release fork

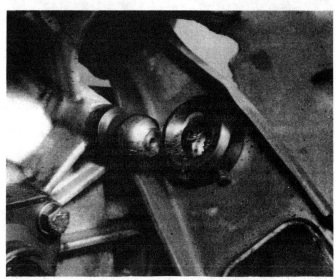

10.7 Refitting the clutch release fork assembly to the balljoint

11 Fault diagnosis – clutch

Symptom	Reason(s)
Judder when taking up drive	Loose engine or gearbox mountings Badly worn friction linings or contaminated with oil Worn splines on transfer shaft (BX and BX 14) or driven plate hub Worn spigot bush in crankshaft flange
*Clutch spin (failure to disengage) so that gears cannot be meshed	Incorrect release bearing-to-pressure plate clearance Rust on splines (may occur after vehicle standing idle for long periods) Damaged or misaligned pressure plate assembly Cable stretched or broken
Clutch slip (increase in engine speed does not result in increase in vehicle road speed – particularly on gradients)	Incorrect release bearing to pressure plate finger clearance Friction linings worn out or oil contaminated
Noise evident on depressing clutch pedal	Dry, worn or damaged release bearing Incorrect pedal adjustment Weak or broken return spring Excessive play between driven plate hub splines and shaft splines
Noise evident as clutch pedal released	Distorted driven plate Broken or weak driven plate cushion coil springs Incorrect pedal adjustment Weak or broken clutch pedal return spring Distorted or worn transfer gear shaft (BX and BX 14) Release bearing loose on retainer hub

*This condition may also be due to the driven plate being rusted to the flywheel or pressure plate. It is possible to free it by applying the handbrake, engaging top gear depressing the clutch pedal and operating the starter motor. If really badly corroded, then the engine will not turn over, but in the majority of cases the driven plate will free. Once the engine starts, rev it up and slip the clutch several times to clear the rust deposits.

Chapter 6 Transmission

For modifications, and information applicable to later models, see Supplement at end of manual

Contents

Specifications

Manual Transmission
General
Type .... Four or five forward speeds and one reverse syncromesh on all forward gears

Designation (Type BH3):
    BX .... 2 BT 52, BT 69, BT 78 (four-speed)
    BX 14 .... 2 BT 28, BT 73, BT 84 (five-speed)

Designation (Type BE1):
    BX 16 .... 2 BL 03, BL 64, BN 45 (five-speed)
    BX 19 .... BL 61, BL 68, BN 46 (five-speed)
       BL 62, BL 66, BN 44 (five-speed)

Gear Ratios:

	2 BT 52/ 69/78	2 BT 28/ 73/84	2 BL 03/ 64, BN 45	BL 61/ 68, BN 46	BL 62/ 66, BN 44
1st*	3.0833:1	3.0833:1	3.3077:1	3.3077:1	3.3077:1
2nd*	1.6471:1	1.8235:1	1.8824:1	1.8824:1	1.8824:1
3rd	1.0938:1	1.1923:1	1.2800:1	1.3600:1	1.2800:1
4th	0.7500:1	0.8929:1	0.9688:1	1.0690:1	0.9688:1
5th	—	0.7179:1	0.7568:1	0.8649:1	0.7568:1
Reverse	2.8333:1	2.8333:1	3.3333:1	3.3333:1	3.3333:1
Final drive	3.8666:1	3.8666:1	4.1875:1	3.6875:1	4.0625:1

*Note: *From January 1987 first and second gear ratios on BX 16 and BX 19 models have changed to:*
1st 3.2500:1
2nd 1.8500:1

Lubrication
Lubricant capacity:
    BX and BX 14 .... Integral with engine
    BX 16 and BX 19 .... 2.0 litres (3.5 Imp pints)
Lubricant type:
    BX and BX 14 .... Share engine oil
    BX 16 and BX 19 .... Gear oil, viscosity SAE 75W/80W (Duckhams Hypoid PT 75W/80)

Torque wrench settings
BX and BX 14 models

	kgf m	lbf ft
Drain plug	2.5	18.1
Sump cover	1.0	7.2
Oil pick-up screen	1.0	7.2

Detent plugs	1.2	8.6
Secondary shaft nut:		
Four-speed	2.5	18.1
Five-speed	9.5	68.8
Primary shaft nut	4.5	33.0
Speedometer drivegear	3.0	21.7
Reverse light switch	2.5	18.1
Reverse fork lock plate bolt	1.0	7.2
Crownwheel retaining bolts	6.0	43.5

BX 16 and BX 19

Engine-to-gearbox bolts	4.0	29.0
Starter motor bolts	4.0	29.0
Gearbox support shaft	3.5	25.3
Gearbox support nut	3.5	25.3
Gearbox support bolt	1.8	13.0
Clutch release bearing guide tube bolts	1.2	9.0
Fifth gear end cover bolts*	1.2	9.0
Primary and secondary shaft nuts	5.0	36.2
Selector rod lock plate bolt	1.5	10.8
Secondary shaft bearing retainer bolts	1.5	10.8
Reverse idler gear spindle bolt	2.0	14.5
Reversing light switch	2.5	18.1
Gearbox main casing-to-clutch housing bolts	1.2	9
Selector shaft spring bracket nut	1.5	10.8
Final drive extension bolts	1.0	7.2
Final drive half housing bolts:		
10 mm	4.0	29.0
7 mm	1.2	9
Crownwheel securing bolts	6.0	43.5
Drain plug:		
Final drive	3.0	21.7
Gearbox	1.0	7.2

* apply locking compound to the threads

Automatic transmission
General

Make	ZF
Type	7 HP 14
Number of speeds	Four forward and one reverse
Identification mark	2 GX 03
Ratios (overall):	
1st	0.564
2nd	0.321
3rd	0.234
4th	0.174
Reverse	0.663
Final drive ratio	51/59

Lubrication

Lubricant type	Dexron IID type ATF (Duckhams Uni-Matic or D-Matic)	
Lubricant capacity:		
From dry	6.5 litres	(11.4 Imp/pints)
Drain and refill	2.5 litres	(4.4 Imp/pints)
Final drive lubrication	Integral with transmission	

Torque wrench settings

	kgf m	lbf ft
Transmission-to-engine bolts	3.9	29
Starter motor bolts	3.9	29
Flexible mounting centre bolt	3.4	25
Flexible mounting plate screws	1.8	13
Driveplate-to-torque converter bolts	3.4	25
Torque converter housing screws	2.4	18
Fluid sump pan screws	1.0	7
Dipstick guide tube union nut	4.3	32
Fluid cooler centre fixing screw	4.9	36

1 General description – manual transmission

Gearbox types 2 BT 52 (four-speed) and 2 BT 28 (five-speed) – BX and BX 14 models

The transmission is mounted transversely below and to the rear of the engine with which it shares a common lubrication system.

The transmission casing is constructed in light alloy and incorporates the final drive and differential.

Power from the engine crankshaft is transmitted through the output shaft then the transfer gears to the transmission primary shaft.

Drive to the front roadwheels is transmitted through open driveshafts from the differential side gears.

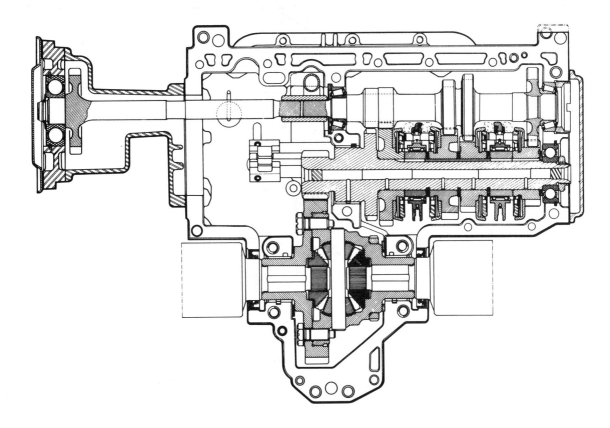

Fig. 6.1 Cross-sectional view of the four-speed (2 BT 52) gearbox (Sec 1)

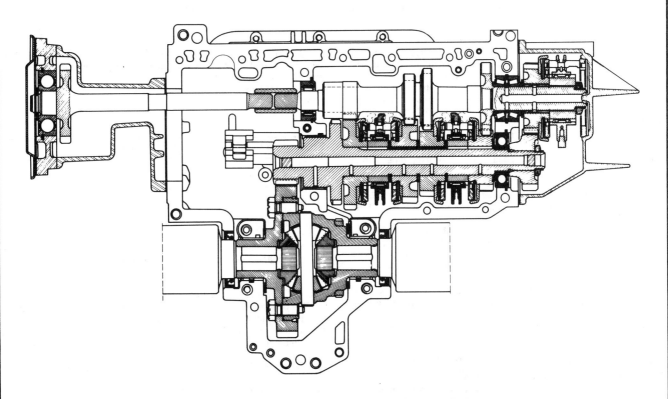

Fig. 6.2 Cross-sectional view of the five-speed (2 BT 28) gearbox (Sec 1)

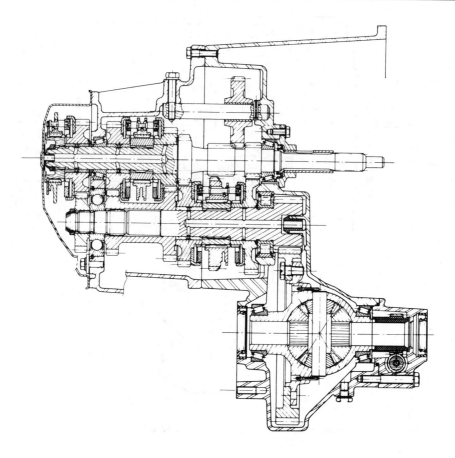

Fig. 6.3 Cross-sectional view of the five-speed (2 BL 03) gearbox (Sec 1)

The transmission may be of four or five-speed type, depending upon the vehicle model. Both types are similar except for the 5th gear located on the ends of the primary and secondary shafts.

The transmission is of conventional two shaft constant-mesh layout. There are four pairs of gears, one for each forward speed. The gears on the primary shaft are fixed to the shaft, while those on the secondary or pinion shaft float, each being locked to the shaft when engaged by the synchromesh unit. The reverse idler gear is on a third shaft.

On five-speed units, the 5th speed gears are of fixed type with an extra synchromesh assembly.

The gear selector forks engage in the synchromesh unit; these slide axially along the shaft to engage the appropriate gear. The forks are mounted on selector shafts which are located in the base of the gearbox.

The helical gear on the end of the pinion shaft drives directly onto the crownwheel mounted on the differential unit. The latter differs from normal practice in that it runs in shell bearings and the end thrust is taken up by thrust washers in a similar manner to the engine crankshaft.

Cautionary note: If it is necessary to have the vehicle towed for anything other than short distances, the front wheels **must** be lifted clear of the ground or the gearbox could seize due to lack of lubrication. This applies to models fitted with the B BT 52 or the BT 28 type gearbox.

Gearbox types 2 BL 03 (five-speed), BL 61 and BL 62 (five-speed) – BX 16 and BX 19 models

The transmission is mounted transversely in-line with the engine, the drive being taken direct from the crankshaft and not through transfer gears as on the smaller engine variants.

The gearbox has five forward gears, all with synchromesh, and one reverse. The 5th gear components are on the far side of an intermediate plate which carries one pair of shaft bearings.

The differential (final drive) unit is contained in its own housing which is bolted to the gearbox casing. The gearbox and differential share the same lubricant.

The transmission is conventional in operation and is as described above.

2   Routine maintenance – transmission

BX and BX 14 models
1   On these models the engine and transmission share the same lubrication system and therefore there is no separate transmission oil level check requirement, but the engine/transmission oil must be renewed at the intervals specified. Refer to Section 2 in Chapter 1 for oil draining and renewal details.
2   Periodic checks should be made around the transmission, differential and driveshaft joints to ensure that there are no serious oil leaks.

BX 16 (manual transmission) and BX 19 models
3   The only regular maintenance required is to change the lubricant at the specified intervals. There is no provision for checking the oil level in the gearbox or in the final drive unit. The oil must therefore be drained completely and the transmission be refilled with a known quantity of oil.
4   Apart from the regular oil change at the specified intervals, the oil should be changed in a new or reconditioned unit after the first 600 miles (1000 km), and in any unit after detection and rectification of an oil leak.
5   When draining the transmission oil, note that there are two drain plugs, one for the gearbox and one for the final drive. Both plugs must be removed (Fig. 6.4 and 6.5).
6   When refilling the transmission with oil, do so through the filler

Fig. 6.4 Rear view of the 2 BL 03 and BL 61/62 gearboxes (Sec 2)

1	Ventilation plug	2	Selector shaft showing selector positions	3	Drain plug – differential housing	4	Gear shift shaft showing shift positions

Fig. 6.5 Front view of the 2 BL 03 and BL 61/62 gearboxes (Sec 2)

5	Reversing light switch	6	Oil filler plug	7	Drain plug – gearbox	8	Reverse gear shaft clamp bolt – **do not remove**

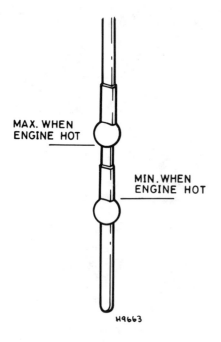

MAX. WHEN
ENGINE HOT

MIN. WHEN
ENGINE HOT

H9663

Fig. 6.6 Automatic transmission fluid level dipstick (Sec 2)

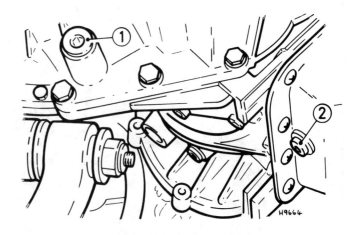

H9664

**Fig. 6.7 Automatic transmission drain plug locations
(1 and 2) (Sec 2)**

Scrupulous cleanliness is essential when dealing with the automatic transmission.

8   If topping-up is frequently necessary, inspect the transmission for leaks.

9   Also at the specified intervals, drain the transmission and final drive. **Caution:** *the transmission fluid may be very hot.* Refer to Section 25 for details (see Fig 6.7).

plug orifice. Remember to measure out the quantity of oil required beforehand (see Specifications). Do not overfill the transmission.

BX 16 (automatic transmission) models

7   At the specified intervals, or at the first sign of malfunction, the fluid level must be checked, as described in Section 25. Top up if necessary via the dipstick tube, using a clean funnel and a clean flexible tube.

3   Gearchange linkage (type 2 BT 52 and 2 BT 28) – adjustment

1   The gearchange linkage does not normally require adjustment. If new parts have been fitted, however, set the balljointed link rods so that the distance between the centres of the balljoints is as shown in Fig 6.8.

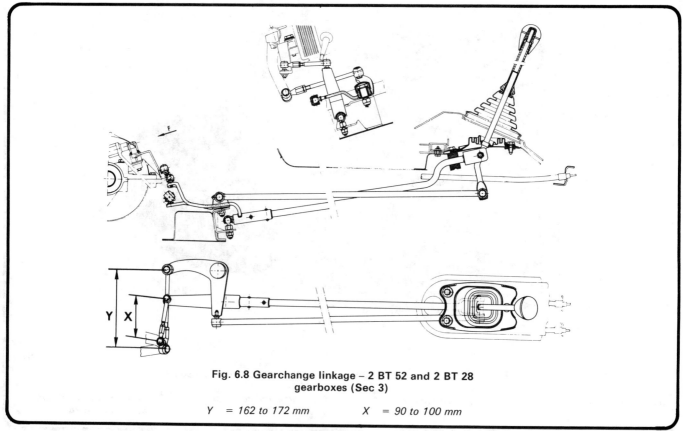

**Fig. 6.8 Gearchange linkage – 2 BT 52 and 2 BT 28
gearboxes (Sec 3)**

Y   = 162 to 172 mm   X   = 90 to 100 mm

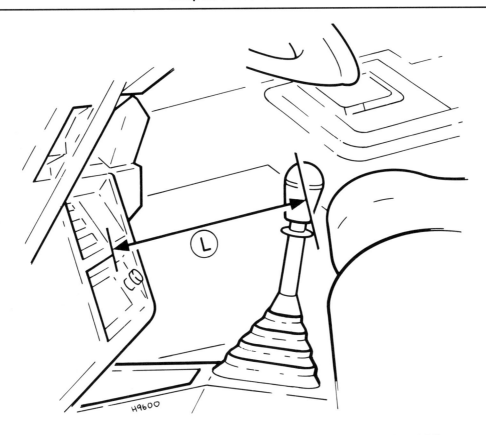

Fig. 6.9 Gear control lever set for longitudinal adjustment (Secs 3 and 14)

L = 235 mm (2 BT 52 and 2 BT 28)   *L = 215 mm (2 BL 03 and BL 61)*

2   When making a longitudinal adjustment of the control lever, position the gearlever in neutral so that the distance from the centre of the knob to the centre of the heater/fresh air control and radio facia panel is approximately 235 mm (Fig 6.9).

3   Referring to Fig 6.8, measure the distance between the centre of the gearchange link rod balljoints (Y). The distance should be between 162 and 172 mm. If adjustment is necessary, loosen the link rod balljoint locknut, separate the joint and turn it in the required direction to set it at the required distance. Decreasing the length Y will move the gearlever forward and vice versa. With distance Y correctly set, reconnect the balljoint and tighten the locknut.

4   Check the lateral adjustment of the control lever by first checking to see if, when in neutral, it is vertical when viewed in line with the vehicle. Now check the distance between the link rod balljoints (X). The correct distance requirement is between 90 and 100 mm.

5   If adjustment is necessary, proceed to adjust the link rod X in the same manner as that described for Y in paragraph 3, but note that decreasing the link rod length moves the gear control lever to the left and *vice versa* (when viewed from the front of the vehicle).

6   When making adjustment to the link rods the balljoints must be centralised when tightening the locknut.

4   Gearbox (Type 2BT 52 and 2 BT 28) – removal and refitting

The gearbox can only be removed with the engine and the two units then separated. Refer to Chapter 1, Sections 9 and 12 for details.

5   Manual transmission (all types) – preliminary overhaul notes

Although the transmission system employed is relatively simple, a

few words of warning must be stressed before any inexperienced dismantlers start work to make sure that they know what they are letting themselves in for.

First of all decide whether the fault you wish to repair is worth the time and effort involved. Secondly bear in mind that, if the transmission is well worn, then the cost of the necessary component parts could well exceed the cost of an exchange factory unit and, furthermore, you will get a guaranteed job without the bother of having to do it yourself. Thirdly, if you are intent on doing it yourself, make sure that you understand how the transmission works.

Special care must be taken during all dismantling and assembly operations to ensure that the housing is not overstressed or distorted in any way. When dismantled, check the cost and availability of the parts to be renewed and compare this against the cost of a replacement unit, which may not be much more expensive and therefore would be a better proposition.

On reassembly, take careful note of the tightening procedures and torque wrench settings of the relevant nuts and bolts. This is most important to prevent overtightening, distortion and oil leakage, and also to ensure smooth, trouble-free running of the unit.

6   Gearbox (Type 2 BT 52 and 2 BT 28) – dismantling into major assemblies

1   With the transmission on the bench, unbolt and remove the protective plate and sump cover (photo).

2   Unbolt and remove the oil pick-up screen (photo).

3   Remove the speedometer drivegear (photo).

4   Unscrew and remove the reverse lamp switch (photo).

5   Release, but do not remove, the nineteen bolts which hold the two transmission half casing sections together (Figs 6.10 and 6.11)

Four-speed unit

6   Unscrew and remove the primary shaft bearing ring nut by engaging a suitable tool in the nut cut-outs (photo)/

All units
7   Remove the casing bolts, separate the casing sections and lift out the primary shaft (photo).
8   Lift out the secondary shaft (photo).
9   Lift out the final drive/differential.
10 Remove the bearing shells, identifying them in respect of location if they are to be used again (photo).

11 Examine all components for wear or damage and carry out further dismantling as necessary and as described in the following Sections.
12 If it is intended to renew the casing sections then they must both be renewed at the same time as a pair.
13 Clean old gasket material from the original casings without scoring the metal and clean out the oilways.

Fig. 6.10 Remove bolts indicated from the top side – 2 BT 52 and 2 BT 28 gearboxes (Sec 6)

Fig. 6.11 Remove bolts indicated from the bottom side – 2 BT 52 and 2 BT 28 gearboxes (Sec 6)

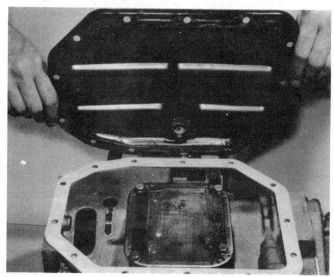

6.1 Sump cover and gasket

6.2 Oil pick-up screen

6.3 Speedometer drivegear

6.4 Reverse lamp switch

6.6 Primary shaft bearing ring nut cut-outs – arrowed (2 BT 52)

6.7 Primary shaft removal (2 BT 28)

6.8 Secondary shaft removal (2 BT 28)

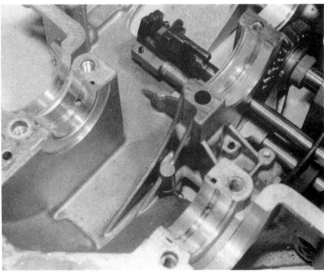

6.10 Transmission shaft bearing shells

7 Gearbox (Types 2 BT 52 and 2 BT 28) – inspection

1   Having removed and dismantled the transmission unit, the various components should be thoroughly washed with a suitable solvent or with petrol and paraffin, and then wiped dry. Take care not to mix components or to lose identification of where they fit and which way round they should be fitted. Don't use hard scrapers or emery cloth to clean the housing mating faces as the surface must be kept perfectly flat and undamaged.

2   Inspect the transmission housing and the differential unit housing for cracks or damage, particularly near bearings or bushes. The transmission housing, differential housing and the mainshaft centre bearing cap are all machined after assembly and none of these parts may be removed separately.

3   Components requiring special attention will have been noted as a result of the performance of the transmission when installed in the car or will have been noted during dismantling.

4   Examine the teeth of all gears for signs of uneven or excessive wear or chipping. If you find a gear in a bad state have a close look at the gear it engages with – this may have to be renewed as well. All gears should run smoothly on their bushes or in their bearings with no sign of rocking or sloppiness.

5   A not so obvious cause of noise and trouble is bearing wear. Wash and dry the bearings thoroughly and examine them closely for signs of scoring, pitted tracks or blueing. Rotate the races and feel for smooth movement with no grittiness or abnormal noise. A new ball-bearing will show no perceptible axial movement between the inner and outer races. As the bearing wears some play will be evident, but if this is excessive the bearing must be renewed. After examining bearings they should be lubricated with clean engine oil to prevent corrosion, and wrapped to avoid contamination with dust and dirt.

6   Carefully inspect the synchromesh units for excessive wear or damage. If weak or ineffective synchromesh action has been experienced, renew the units as complete assemblies.

7   Check the selector forks for wear in the areas which contact the synchromesh units. Any wear evident should be minimal; if in doubt renew the forks.

8   Inspect the selector shafts and detents for wear which can cause imprecise gear changing, and renew where necessary.

9   All remaining components such as the speedometer gears, locking plungers, springs, balls and so on, should be inspected for signs of wear or damage and, where necessary, renewed.

10   It is now worth reviewing the total requirements needed to restore the transmission unit to full serviceability, not forgetting the new lockwashers, circlips, roll pins, seals and gaskets. Compare the cost with that of an overhauled or good condition secondhand unit as it may be more economical to go for one of these alternatives.

11   Prise out the old oil seal from the clutch release bearing guide tube, but do not fit the new seal until so instructed during reassembly. The primary and secondary shaft nuts must be renewed during reassembly.

12   If a new primary shaft or differential bearings are to be fitted a selection of preload shims will be required. Read through the relevant procedures before starting work.

8 Primary shaft (Type 2 BT 52 and 2 BT 28) – overhaul

Four-speed unit

1   Either support the bearing and press the shaft from it or draw the bearing from the shaft using a two-legged puller.

2   Only the bearings can be renewed as the gears cannot be removed from the shaft.

3   When fitting the bearing, apply pressure to the inner track only.

Five-speed unit

4   Mark the position of the 5th speed synchro sleeve in relation to the hub.

5   Grip the shaft in a vice fitted with jaw protectors.

6   Unscrew the nut (photo).

7   Withdraw 5th speed synchro sleeve from the shaft (photo).

8   Support the gear and press the shaft out of the synchro-hub. Alternatively use a suitable puller (photo).

9   Remove 5th speed gear, bush and washer (photos).

10   Press the shaft out of the bearings or draw off the bearings using a suitable puller. Remove the washer (photo).

11   When refitting the bearings, apply pressure to the centre track only.

12   The bearings at the opposite end of the shaft are of single roller type.

13   If re-using the original 5th speed synchro sleeve and hub align them in accordance with the marks made during dismantling.

14   When refitting the synchro-hub use a **new** nut, tighten to the specified torque and stake the nut into the shaft groove to lock it.

Four and five-speed units

15   Never re-use a bearing which has been removed from a shaft.

16   Do not mix the components of one new bearing set with another and do not attempt to remove the original bearing grease.

8.6 Primary shaft nut (2 BT 28)

8.7 Removing 5th speed synchro sleeve ...

8.8 ... 5th speed synchro-hub ...

8.9A ... 5th speed gear ...

8.9B ... 5th speed gear bush ...

8.9C ... and 5th speed gear thrust washer (2 BT 28)

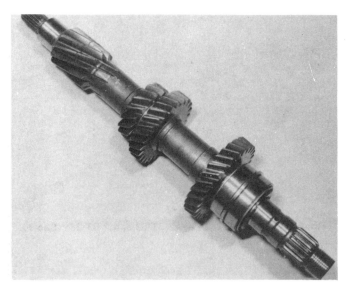

8.10 Primary shaft (2 BT 28)

9 Secondary shaft (Type 2 BT 52 and 2 BT 28) – overhaul

1 Secure the shaft in a vice fitted with jaw protectors and unscrew the nut.
2 Using a press or a suitable puller remove the bearing (four-speed) or bearing and 5th gear (five-speed) (photo).
3 Remove the spacer and 4th gear.
4 Mark the relationship of the hub to the sleeve of the 3rd/4th synchro unit and then remove the synchro unit.
5 Remove the key and spacer.
6 Take off 3rd gear.
7 Take off the spacer.
8 Remove 2nd gear and the spacer.
9 Mark the relationship of the hub to the sleeve of the 1st/2nd synchro unit.
10 Take off the 1st/2nd synchro unit.

Reassembly

11 As work progresses, dip each component in clean engine oil (photo).
12 To the shaft fit 1st gear (photo).
13 Fit the 1st/2nd synchro-hub (photo).

9.2 Removing the secondary shaft bearing and 5th gear (2 BT 28)

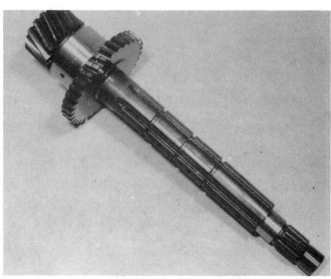

9.11 Secondary shaft

9.12 Fitting 1st gear to secondary shaft

9.13 Fitting 1st/2nd synchro-hub to secondary shaft

Fig. 6.12 Remove 3rd/4th synchro unit (2 BT 52 and 2 BT 28) having marked relative positions of hub and sleeve (Sec 9)

Fig. 6.13 Withdraw the key (2 BT 52 and 2 BT 28) (Sec 9)

14 Fit the spacer and align its splines so that the key can be fitted (photo).
15 Fit the 1st/2nd synchro sleeve so that its mark made at dismantling aligns with the one on the hub. The lines on the spacer pins are towards 1st gear (photos).
16 Fit 2nd gear (photo).
17 Fit the spacer and align the splines so that the key can be fitted (photo).
18 Fit 3rd gear (photo).
19 Fit the spacer, once more aligning the splines so that the key can be fitted (photo).
20 Push the key into the widest shaft groove so that the chamfered edge on the key is at the bottom of the groove. Push the key until it is

flush with the spacer (photo).
21 Fit the 3rd/4th synchro-hub (photo).
22 Fit the 3rd/4th synchro sleeve so that its mark made at dismantling aligns with the one on the hub. The line on the spacer pin must be towards 3rd gear (photo).
23 Fit 4th gear (photo).
24 Fit the spacer (photo).
25 Press the bearing (four-speed) or the bearing and 5th gear (five-speed) onto the shaft (photos).
26 Engage a new circlip in the bearing outer track groove.
27 Screw on a **new** shaft nut to the specified torque and stake the nut into the groove in the shaft (photo).

9.14 Fitting first spacer to secondary shaft

9.15A Fitting 1st/2nd synchro sleeve to secondary shaft

9.15B Lines on synchro spacer pins (arrowed)

9.16 Fit 2nd gear ...

9.17 ... and second spacer onto secondary shaft

9.18 Fit 3rd gear ...

9.19 ... and third spacer onto secondary shaft

9.20 Push key down into shaft groove

9.21 3rd/4th synchro-hub on secondary shaft

9.22 Fitting the 3rd/4th synchro sleeve onto the secondary shaft

9.23 Fit 4th gear ...

9.24 ... and 4th gear spacer onto the secondary shaft

9.25A Fit the secondary shaft bearing

9.25B Fitting 5th gear to the secondary shaft (2 BT 28)

9.27 Secondary shaft nut

10 Selector mechanism and reverse idler (Type 2BT 52 and 2 BT 28) – dismantling and reassembly

1　Unscrew and remove the three threaded detent plugs and extract the coil springs and balls. If the plugs are very tight, tap their end-face hard using a rod and hammer (Figs. 6.14 and 6.15).

Four-speed unit
2　Drive out the reverse fork roll pin.

Five-speed unit
3　Knock out the roll pin and unscrew the bolt and remove the reverse fork ball lock plate (Fig. 6.16). Extract the two balls (Fig. 6.17). Move the position of the selector shaft slightly to release the second ball.
4　Slide the 5th reverse selector shaft so that the dog contacts the housing web then drive out the roll pin which secures the dog.

All units
5　Withdraw the reverse selector shaft and retrieve the interlock disc.
6　Drive out the roll pin which secures the 3rd/4th fork to the selector shaft. Remove the fork from the shaft.
7　Drive out the roll pin which secures the fork to the 1st/2nd selector shaft.

Five-speed unit
8　Drive out the roll pin which secures the dog to the 1st/2nd selector shaft. Before doing this, slide the shaft so that the dog is in contact with the housing web.

All units
9　Withdraw the 1st/2nd selector shaft.
10　Withdraw the 3rd/4th selector shaft.
11　Remove the 1st/2nd and reverse selector forks.
12　Drive out the reverse idler shaft roll pin. On four-speed models it is

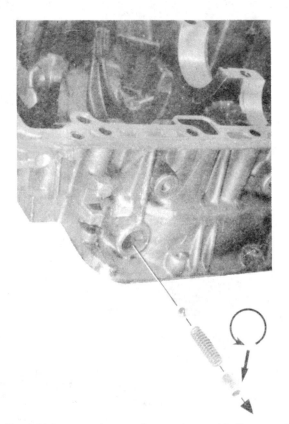

Fig. 6.14 Reverse detent plug, spring and ball removal (2 BT 52 and 2 BT 28) (Sec 10)

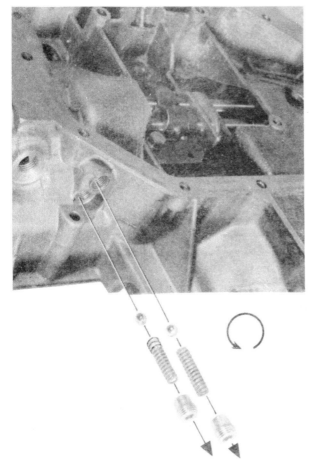

Fig. 6.16 Reverse fork ball lock plate (2 BT 28) (Sec 10)

Fig. 6.15 1st/2nd and 3rd/4th detent plugs, springs and balls removal (2 BT 52 and 2 BT 28) (Sec 10)

Fig. 6.17 Remove the two balls (2 BT 28) (Sec 10)

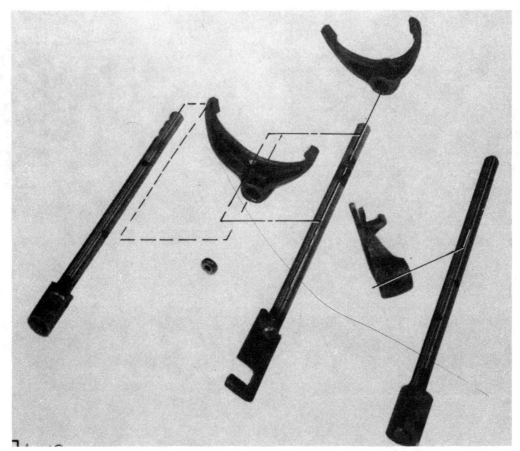

Fig. 6.18 Selector shaft and fork assemblies (2 BT 52) (Sec 10)

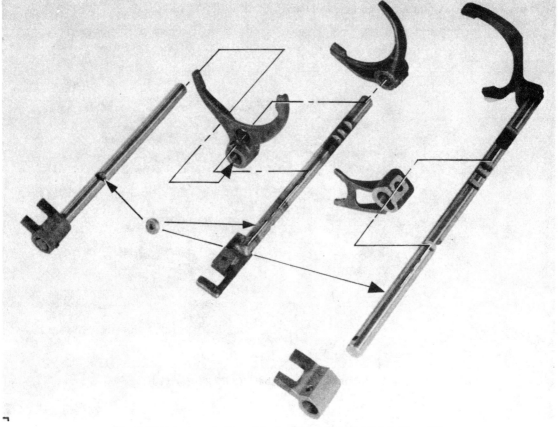

Fig. 6.19 Selector shaft and fork assemblies (2 BT 28) (Sec 10)

also necessary to remove the roll pin from the idler shaft over which the detent collar engages. Access to this roll pin is available after removing the shaft locating pin and sliding the shaft rearwards, (Fig. 6.20).

13 Remove the reverse idler shaft, the stop (or detent collar on four-speed models) and the reverse idler gear. Extract the detent ball (Fig. 6.21).

14 Remove the pivot bolt and withdraw the selector lever.

15 Drive out the dual roll pins at the selector finger and remove the finger.

16 Compress the coil spring using an open-ended spanner or forked tool and remove the cups.

17 Remove the remote control rod and extract the oil seal.

Reassembly

18 Lubricate all components with clean engine oil as work proceeds. Renew all roll pins and the remote control rod O-ring.

19 Fit the O-ring into its recess in the remote control rod housing.

20 Fit the remote control rod together with spacer, spring and stop.

21 Compress the coil spring and fit the half cups (Fig. 6.25).

22 Fit the selector finger, check for correct alignment and drive in the dual roll pins.

23 Using the pivot bolt, fit the gearchange rod lever. Tighten the pivot bolt.

24 On four-speed models refit the reverse idler gear, the detent collar and the idler shaft. Locate the detent ball. Slide the idler shaft beyond the inner location housing then drive the new detent collar location roll pins into position in the shaft so that they are set with an equal protrusion each side of the shaft. The roll pins must be fitted with their splits opposed and in-line with the shaft. Slide the idler shaft back so that the roll pins engage in the slot of the detent collar. Now align the shaft with the housing roll pin hole and insert the shaft securing roll pin. Check that the idler gear and detent collar can slide freely along the shaft then insert the detent spring and plug into the housing. Smear the plug threads with sealant and tighten to the specified torque settings.

25 On five-speed models, fit the reverse idler gear, the stop and the idler shaft. Drive in the shaft roll pin (photos).

26 Place reverse fork in position and then fit the 1st/2nd selector shaft with its fork. The shaft will pass through the reverse fork cut-out (photos).

Fig. 6.20 Removing the roll pin from the reverse idler shaft (2 BT 52) (Sec 10)

Four-speed unit
27 Pin the fork to the 1st/2nd selector shaft.

Five-speed unit
28 Pin the dog to the 1st/2nd selector shaft (photo).

All units
29 Fit the 3rd/4th selector shaft with its fork and drive in the securing pin.

Five-speed unit
30 Secure the fork to the 1st/2nd selector shaft by driving in the roll pin.

Fig. 6.21 Reverse idler shaft, gear, detent collar and ball (2 BT 52) (Sec 10)

160

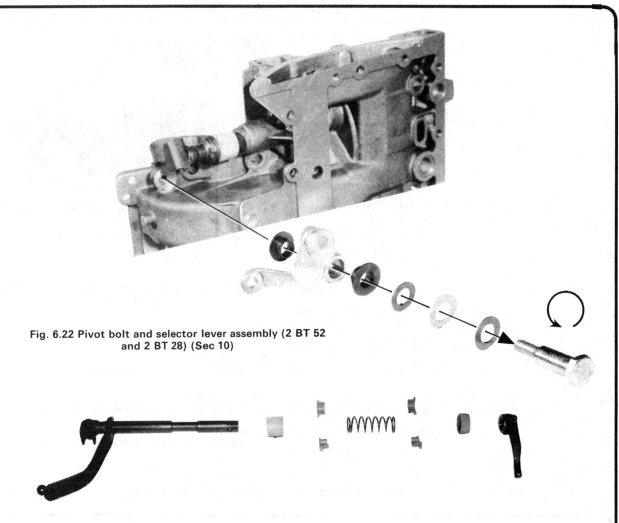

Fig. 6.22 Pivot bolt and selector lever assembly (2 BT 52 and 2 BT 28) (Sec 10)

Fig. 6.23 Remote control rod assembly (2 BT 52 and 2 BT 28) (Sec 10)

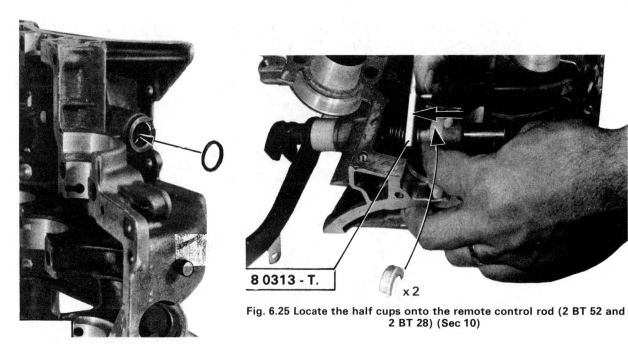

8 0313 - T.

x 2

Fig. 6.25 Locate the half cups onto the remote control rod (2 BT 52 and 2 BT 28) (Sec 10)

Fig. 6.24 Insert the new O-ring into the remote control rod housing (2 BT 52 and 2 BT 28) (Sec 10)

10.25A Reverse idler gear stop and shaft

10.25B Reverse idler shaft roll pin

10.26A 1st/2nd selector shaft with reverse fork (viewed from the oil pick-up screen side)

10.26B 1st/2nd selector shaft with reverse and 1st/2nd selector forks correctly located

10.28 1st/2nd selector shaft dog and roll pin

10.31 Interlock disc

10.33 Reverse fork roll pin (2 BT 52)

10.34A 5th/reverse selector dog roll pin

10.34B Selector shaft locations

10.35A Fitting first ball to reverse fork

10.35B Reverse fork second ball

10.35C Reverse fork lock plate

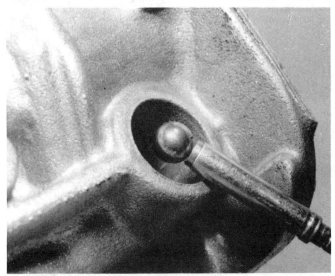

10.37A Using a pencil magnet to locate detent ball

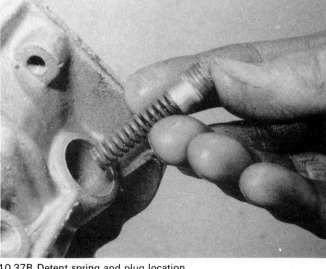

10.37B Detent spring and plug location

10.37C Location of remaining detent springs and plugs

10.37D Allen key used to tighten detent plug

All units
31 Insert the reverse interlock disc so that it engages positively in the slots in the selector shafts (photo).
32 Slide the reverse selector shaft without disturbing the interlock disc.

Four-speed unit
33 Secure the reverse fork to the selector shaft with a roll pin (photo).

Five-speed unit
34 Fit 5th/reverse dog to its selector shaft and secure it with a roll pin (photos).
35 Place one detent ball in the reverse fork then fit the plate with the second ball (photos).
36 Tighten the plate fixing bolt to the specified torque.

All units
37 Fit the three detent balls and their springs. Apply thread locking fluid to clean threads of the detent plugs and tighten the plugs to the specified torque. Do not apply too much fluid or it will run down and cause the balls to seize (photos).

11 Final drive/differential unit (Type 2 BT 52 and 2 BT 28) – overhaul

1   Unscrew the retaining bolts and remove the crownwheel from the differential unit casing.
2   Withdraw the differential shaft and remove the differential gears with their respective thrust washers (note their orientation). Keep them, together with the shaft, in their positions relative to the unit casing.
3   Remove the side gear and its thrust washer from the differential case. Remove the crownwheel side gear. This does not have a thrust washer.
4   If, on inspection, the gears are excessively worn or damaged, it is advisable to renew the differential as a unit rather than to replace individual gears. If the thrust washers show signs of excessive wear, renew them as a set.
5   Commence reassembly by fitting the differential side gear with its thrust washer ensuring that its orientation is correct as noted during removal
6   Fit the thrust washers to the differential gears, locate them in the differential casing and insert the differential shaft.
7   Locate the crownwheel with the differential case, insert the connecting bolts and tighten to the specified torque. Make sure that the pinion shaft is retained by two of the crownwheel bolts.

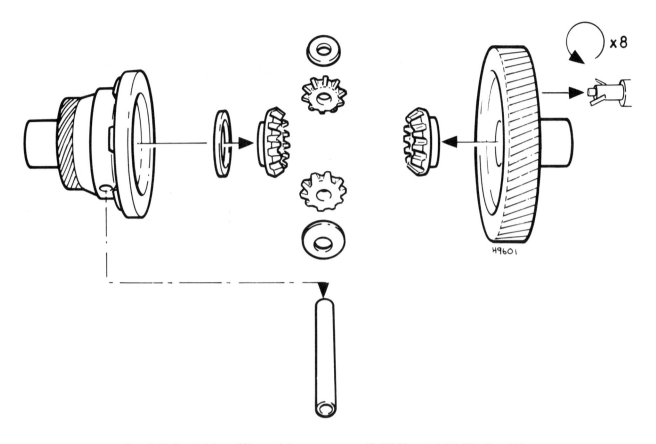

Fig. 6.26 Final drive differential components (2 BT 52 and 2 BT 28) (Sec 11)

12 Gearbox (Type 2 BT 52 and 2 BT 28) – reassembly

1 Renew all gaskets and oil seals, also the shaft nuts. As reassembly proceeds, apply clean engine oil to all components.
2 Check that the housing half casing positioning dowels are in place.
3 Make sure that new bearing shells are in their recesses in the casing. If the original shells are being used, check that they are returned to their original locations and their recesses and the shell backs are perfectly clean and free from grit.
4 The selector mechanism will already have been fitted, as described in Section 10.
5 Fit the final drive/differential, together with the thrust washers, into the selector shaft half casing. Make sure that the copper side of the thrust washer is towards the crownwheel and the tabs offset upwards (photo).
6 Fit the secondary shaft geartrain into the half casing, making sure that the selector forks engage in the synchro sleeve grooves and the bearing circlip fits into its casing groove.
7 Fit the primary shaft geartrain, remembering that on four-speed units the shaft must be fitted with bearing outer tracks and thrust washer. On five-speed units, the 5th/reverse synchro assembly must be positioned on the shaft with the longer spacer pins towards the end of the shaft (photo).
8 Make sure that the casing locating dowels are in positon and then apply jointing compound to the mating face of the half casings (photo).
9 Fit the casings together, making sure that the selector finger engages in the selector shaft dog cut-outs.
10 Use new lock washers and screw in the connecting bolts finger

12.5 Differential thrust washer with tabs offset

tight. Note the location of the various bolt sizes and lengths Fig. 6.28.
11 On four-speed transmissions, the primary shaft bearing preload must now be adjusted. Screw in the bearing ring nut finger tight and then tighten the casing internal bolts accessible through the sump plate aperture.

12.7 Gear trains and final drive (five-speed)

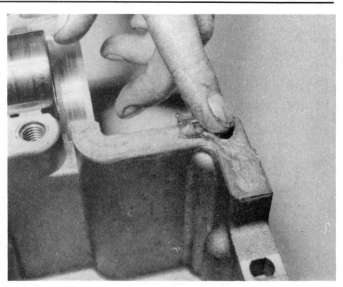

12.8 Apply jointing compound to casing flanges

Fig. 6.27 Primary shaft orientation and thrust washer location – arrowed (2 BT 52) (Sec 12)

12 Engage any gear and turn the nut on the end of the secondary shaft to settle the bearings.

13 Tighten the ring nut to 2.0 kgf m (15 lbf ft) then loosen it and retighten 0.9 kgf m (7 lbf ft).

14 Finally stake the nut into the shaft groove. In order to be able to turn the ring nut, make up an adaptor (to engage in the nut cut-outs) to which a torque wrench can be connected (Fig. 6.29).

15 Tighten the half casing retaining bolts to the Stage 1 then Stage 2 torque settings in the alphabetical sequence given in Figs. 6.30, 6.31, 6.32 and 6.33.

16 Fit the oil pick-up screen, tightening the bolts to the specified torque.

17 Refit the sump cover plate with a new gasket. Tighten the bolts to the specified torque (Chapter 1). Fit the reinforcement washer (photo).

18 Fit and tighten the drain plug (photo).

19 Refit the speedometer drive pinion with a new O-ring.

20 Screw in the reverse lamp switch.

21 If new driveshaft oil seals have not already been fitted drive them squarely into position now and fill their lips with grease.

Fig. 6.28 Gearbox half casing retaining bolts and locations (2 BT 52 and 2 BT 28) (Sec 12)

Fig. 6.29 Ring nut adaptor tool (2 BT 52) (Sec 12)

12.17 Sump cover bolt with reinforcement washer

12.18 Oil drain plug showing magnet

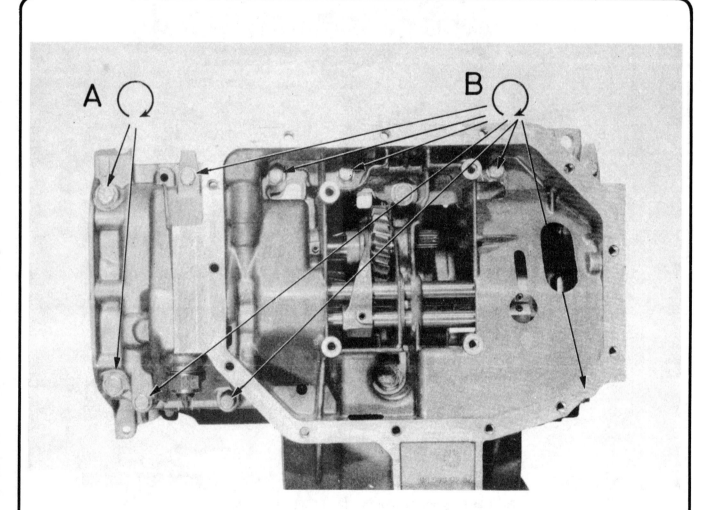

Fig. 6.30 Gearbox half case bolts shown must be tightened to Stage 1 as follows – A before B (2 BT 52 and 2 BT 28) (Sec 12)

A   1.0 kgf m (7.2 lbf ft)   B   1.25 kgf m (8.6 lbf ft)

Fig. 6.31 Gearbox half case bolts shown must be tightened to Stage 1 as follows – C before D (2 BT 52 and 2 BT 28) (Sec 12)

C   1.25 kgf m (8.6 lbf ft)   D   2.0 kgf m (14.5 lbf ft)

Fig. 6.32 Gearbox half casing bolts shown must be tightened to Stage 2 as follows (2 BT 52 and 2 BT 28) (Sec 12)

E   1.8 kgf m (13.0 lbf ft)

Fig. 6.33 Gearbox half casing bolts shown must be tightened to Stage 2 as follows – F before G – (2 BT 52 and 2 BT 28) (Sec 12)

F　1.8 kgf m (13.0 lbf ft)　　　　　　G　4.5 kgf m (33.0 lbf ft)

13 Differential/driveshaft oil seals (all models) – renewal

1 The differential oil seals can be removed and refitted with the engine/transmission unit in position in the car, but the driveshafts will obviously have to be removed. This operation is covered in Chapter 7.
2 With the driveshafts withdrawn the old oil seals can be extracted from the differential housing using a suitable screwdriver.
3 Clean out the seating before fitting a new seal. Lubricate the seal to assist assembly and drift carefully into position, with the lip facing inwards. Fill the seal lips with grease (photo).

13.3 Driveshaft oil seal at transmission

4 Always take care not to damage the oil seals when removing or refitting the driveshafts.

14 Gearchange linkage (Type 2 BL 03, BL 61 and BL 62) – adjustment

1 The gearbox linkage does not normally require adjustment. If new parts have been fitted, however, set the gearchange control lever to the neutral position.
2 First check the adjustment of the selector control. Refer to Fig. 6.34 and check that the selector control lever (a) is in the upright position. The reaction link rod length between the balljoint centres should be between 70 and 80 mm.
3 If necessary adjust the length of the reaction link rod by detaching at the balljoints, loosening the locknut and turning the balljoint in the required direction to the specified length. Retighten the locknut and reconnect the balljoint. Check that each joint is centralised over its ball when connected.
4 With the gear lever still in neutral, check the distance between the centre of the knob and the centre of the heater/fresh air control and radio facia panel (Fig. 6.9). This should be 215 mm. If adjustment is necessary, adjust the length of the gearchange link rod X (in Fig. 6.34) to between 245 to 255 mm in the same manner as that described in paragraph 3. When decreasing the length of the link rod the gearchange control lever moves forwards and *vice versa*.
5 Engage 2nd or 4th gear, prise free the rubber gaiter of the gear lever from the centre console and then check that the lever to the rear part of the box clearance is between 4 and 5 mm (minimum) – see b in Fig. 6.35.
6 To check the lateral adjustment of the gearchange control lever first check that, when in neutral, the lever is upright when viewed in line with the vehicle. If it isn't, change the length of link rod Y as described in paragraph 3 so that the length between the centre of the balljoints is between 122 and 132 mm. Decreasing the link rod length moves the control lever towards the left and *vice versa*.

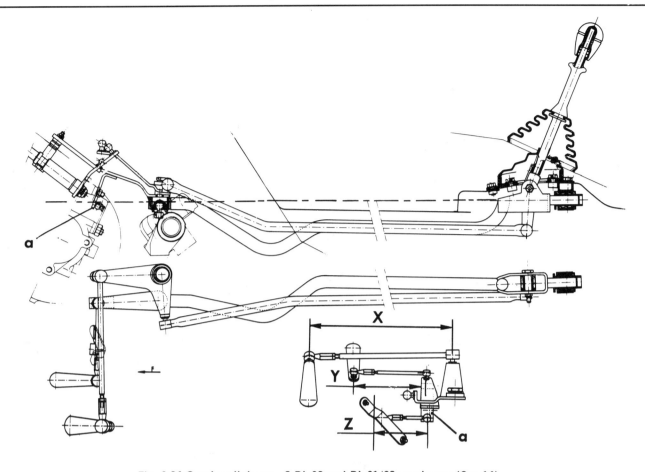

Fig. 6.34 Gearbox linkage – 2 BL 03 and BL 61/62 gearboxes (Sec 14)

a   *Selector control lever*   Y   = *122 to 132 mm*
X   = *245 to 255 mm*   Z   = *70 to 80 mm*

7   Adjustment to 1st and 2nd gear selection is possible by loosening the gearchange control box retaining bolts (1 in Fig. 6.35), then setting the gear lever into the 2nd gear position. Move the box to give a free play movement of 2 to 3 mm between the box and the lever guide block (J). Retighten the box retaining bolts.
8   Move the gear selector through all forward gears and the reverse gear position to check for satisfactory engagement. Also check the gears for satisfactory selection on a road test. Further minor adjustment of 1st and 2nd gear selection may be necessary.

15 Gearbox (Type 2 BL 03, BL 61 and BL 62) – removal and refitting

1   The gearbox can be removed separately or together with the engine. In the latter case refer to Chapter 1 for details.
2   Raise and support the vehicle so that the front and rear roadwheels are clear of the ground. When raised the vehicle must be level and securely supported.
3   Disconnect and remove the battery (see Chapter 12).
4   Disconnect and remove the air filter unit and its support (see Chapter 3).
5   Unbolt and disconnect the battery earth lead from the top of the gearbox.
6   Disconnect the clutch cable from the operating lever and retrieve the connecting rod (see Chapter 5).
7   Referring to the photo, disconnect the gearchange link rods at the balljoint connections indicated.
8   Detach the speedometer cable at the gearbox connection and position it out of the way.
9   Disconnect the reversing light wiring from the switch on top of the gearbox.

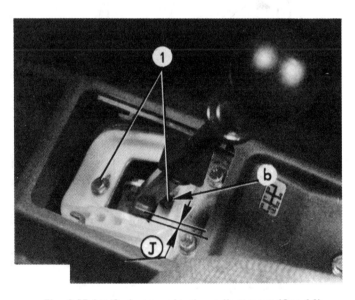

Fig. 6.35 1st/2nd gear selection adjustment (Sec 14)

1   *Gear control box retaining bolts*
b   = *at least 4 to 5 mm*
J   = *2 to 3 mm*

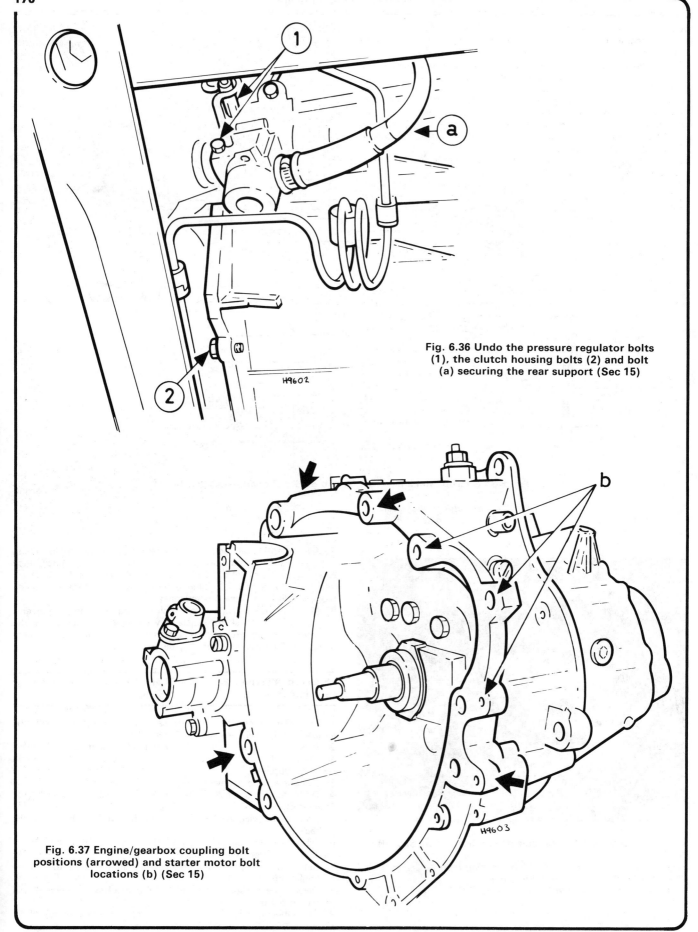

170

Fig. 6.36 Undo the pressure regulator bolts
(1), the clutch housing bolts (2) and bolt
(a) securing the rear support (Sec 15)

Fig. 6.37 Engine/gearbox coupling bolt
positions (arrowed) and starter motor bolt
locations (b) (Sec 15)

10 Remove the nearside front roadwheel then detach and remove the wing protector from the underside of the left-hand front wing by prising free the plastic retaining clips.

11 Disconnect the left and right-hand driveshaft, as described in Chapter 1, Section 33, paragraphs 5 to 7 inclusive.

12 Working underneath the vehicle at the front end, undo the three pressure regulator retaining bolts. There are two bolts positioned vertically in line to the left of the sphere and one bolt to the left of the unit body securing the rear support. When it is detached support the weight of the pressure regulator by tying it up to prevent distortion of the rigid pipes connected to it.

13 Undo the three clutch housing lower cover plate bolts and remove the cover.

14 The weight of the gearbox must now be supported. This is best achieved using a lifting sling and hoist and supporting it from above. Failing this, it may be possible to support it from underneath using a suitable trolley jack, but ensure that it is securely located.

15 Unbolt and remove the gearbox support and the support spindle.

16 Position a jack or blocks under the engine to support it.

17 Unbolt and remove the engine-to-gearbox coupling bolts and the starter motor bolts.

18 Check that gearbox associated fittings are detached and positioned out of the way, then withdraw the gearbox sideways from the engine. When the gearbox input shaft is clear of the clutch unit, carefully lower the gearbox and remove it from underneath the vehicle.

19 Refitting the gearbox is a reversal of the removal procedure, but note the following special points.

20 Prior to lifting the gearbox into position make a temporary provision to hold the clutch thrust bearing in position against the guide. This can be achieved by fitting two bolts into the clutch housing/engine bolt holes adjacent to the clutch release lever. Wind wire around the bolt heads and then twist the wire round the release lever to keep the thrust bearing against the guide (photo).

21 Apply a small amount of grease to the thrust bearing guide and the control shaft.

22 When assembling the gearbox to the engine, check that the two alignment dowels are in position on the engine flange face (one each side). Centering rods of suitable diameter fitted inside the dowels will assist in aligning the two assemblies as they are joined. Turn the flywheel to align the splines of the clutch friction plate with the gearbox input shaft.

23 When the gearbox is fitted flush to the engine insert the retaining bolts and tighten them evenly to the specified torque setting. If used, remove the alignment centering rods and remove the wire holding the clutch release lever in position.

24 When refitting the gearbox support shaft apply a locking sealant to the threads. Tighten the shaft, and the support nut and bolt to the specified torque settings.

25 When refitting the right-hand drive-shaft to the final drive unit an oil seal protector must be used to protect the oil seal as the shaft splines pass through it. Refer to Chapter 7 for further details on refitting the right and left-hand driveshafts.

26 When reconnecting the steering and suspension connections, use new nuts on the balljoints.

27 On completion, check that all connections are securely made and top up the gearbox oil level.

28 Check that the gear selection is satisfactory and if necessary adjust the linkage, as described in Section 14.

16 Gearbox (Types 2 BL 03, BL 61 and BL 62) – dismantling into major assemblies

1 Before deciding to dismantle the transmission, reference should be made to the precautionary notes outlined in Section 5.

2 Remove the eight bolts and washers which secure the end cover. Remove the cover.

3 Make alignment marks between the 5th gear synchro-hub and its sliding sleeves.

4 Engage 5th gear, then drive out the 5 mm roll pin which secures 5th gear selector fork to the selector rod (photo).

5 Hold 5th gear selector fork in the engaged positon and return the gear selector to neutral so that the selector rod moves through the fork.

6 Engage any other gear to lock up the shafts, then unscrew and remove the 28 mm nut from the end of the input shaft. If the nut is

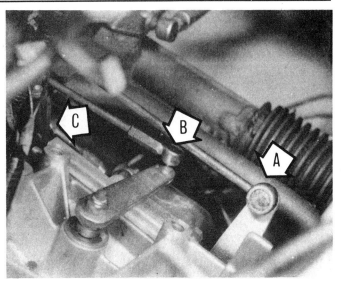

15.7 Disconnect the gearchange link rods at the joints indicated (A, B and C)

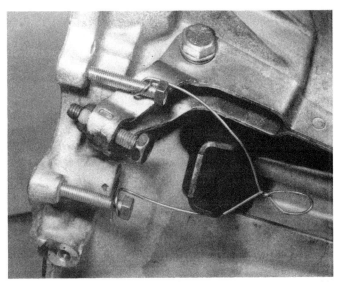

15.20 Retain the clutch release lever with two bolts and a length of wire

staked in position it will be necessary to relieve the staking (photo).

7 Remove 5th gear synchro-hub, sliding sleeve and selector fork from the primary shaft. Be prepared for the ejection of the detent ball from the selector fork.

8 Refit the 5th gear slidig sleeve and hub and engage 5th gear again. Relieve the staking from the secondary shaft nut and remove the nut. Remove the sliding sleeve and hub again (photo).

9 Remove from the primary shaft the 5th gear, its bush and the spacer.

10 Withdraw the 5th gear from the secondary shaft then remove the two bolts and washers which secure the secondary shaft rear bearing.

11 Remove the circlip from the secondary shaft rear bearing by prising up its ends. The circlip should be renewed anyway, so do not be afraid of breaking it. Raise the secondary shaft if the circlip is jammed in its groove.

12 Extract its securing bolt and remove the selector rod lockplate.

13 Remove the bolt which retains the reverse idler gear spindle (Fig. 6.38).

14 Remove the thirteen bolts and washers which secure the end casing to the main casing. Withdraw the end casing; it is located by dowels, and may need striking with a wooden or plastic mallet to free it. Do not use a metal hammer, nor lever in between the joint faces. Note the location of the clutch cable bracket.

16.4 5th gear selector fork showing roll pin (arrowed)

16.6 Undoing the primary shaft nut

16.8 Undoing the secondary shaft nut

15 Remove the selector arm and spring from the gear selector shaft. Remove the circlip and washer, push the shaft in and recover the O-ring (photo).

16 Drive out the roll pins which secure the selector finger and the interlock bracket to the selector shaft.

17 Pull the selector shaft out of the gearbox. From inside the gearbox recover, as they are freed from the shaft, the selector finger, the interlock bracket, the spring and its cup washers. Notice which way round the washers are fitted.

18 Screw the reverse idler spindle retaining bolt back into the spindle and use it as a lever to extract the spindle. Remove the reverse idler gear itself (photo).

19 Remove the swarf-collecting magnet from the casing (photo).

20 Carefully lift out the two gear trains with their shafts, the selector forks and the selector rods.

21 Remove the spring support bracket from inside the main casing.

22 If not already removed, drive out the selector shaft end cover, using a drift of diameter no greater than 14 mm.

23 Extract the lubrication jet, using a wire hook.

24 Unscrew and remove the reversing lamp switch.

25 Remove the nut and washer which secure the reverse selector fork spindle. Remove the spindle and the selector fork. Recover the detent plunger and spring (photos).

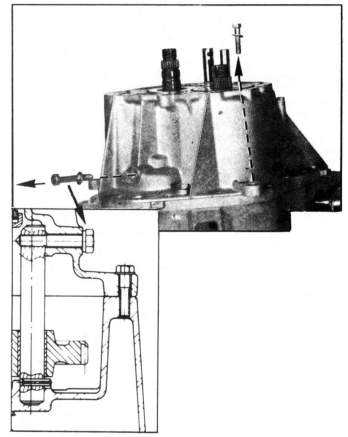

Fig. 6.38 Reverse idler gear spindle retaining bolt location (inset) and end casing bolts (Sec 16)

26 Unscrew and remove the breather from the main casing (photo).

27 Turning to the clutch housing, remove the clutch release bearing (if not already done). Pull off the release fork.

28 Unbolt and remove the release bearing guide tube.

29 From behind the tube, remove the preload shim and the outer track of the primary shaft front bearing.

16.15 Gear selector shaft is secured by a circlip

16.18 Removing the reverse idler spindle

16.19 Extract the swarf collecting magnet

16.25A Remove the reverse selector fork ...

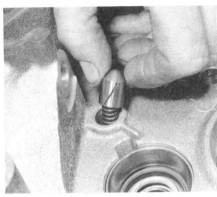
16.25B ... and detent plunger and spring

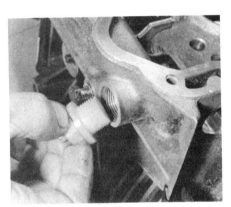
16.26 Remove the breather

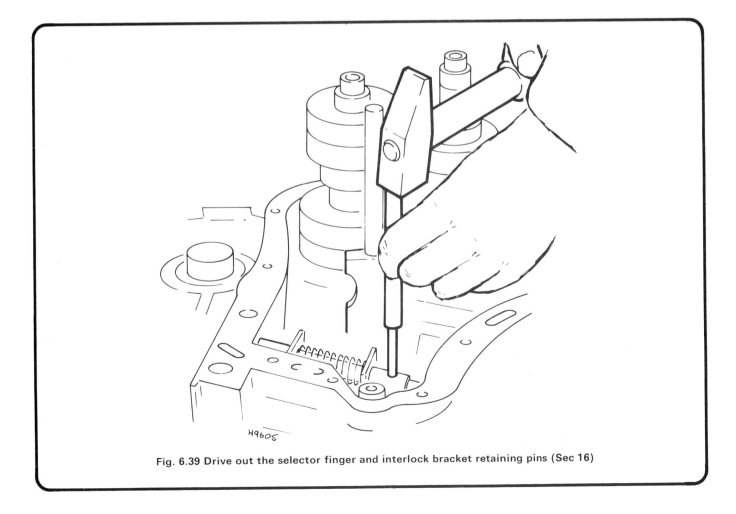
Fig. 6.39 Drive out the selector finger and interlock bracket retaining pins (Sec 16)

30 To remove the final drive unit, first unbolt and remove the speedometer pinion and its adaptor (photo).
31 Unbolt and remove the extension housing. Recover the speedometer driving gear and the bearing preload shim (photos).
32 Unbolt the final drive half housing. Remove the half housing and final drive unit. Note the location of the gearchange pivot bracket.
33 Identify the final drive bearing outer tracks: if they are to be re-used

they must be refitted on the same sides.
34 Remove the selector lever from the main casing. It is retained by a circlip and a washer.
35 If it is wished to remove the clutch release lever balljoint, do so with a slide hammer having a suitable claw. (A new gearbox will not necessarily be fitted with a balljoint).
36 The gearbox is now dismantled into its major assemblies.

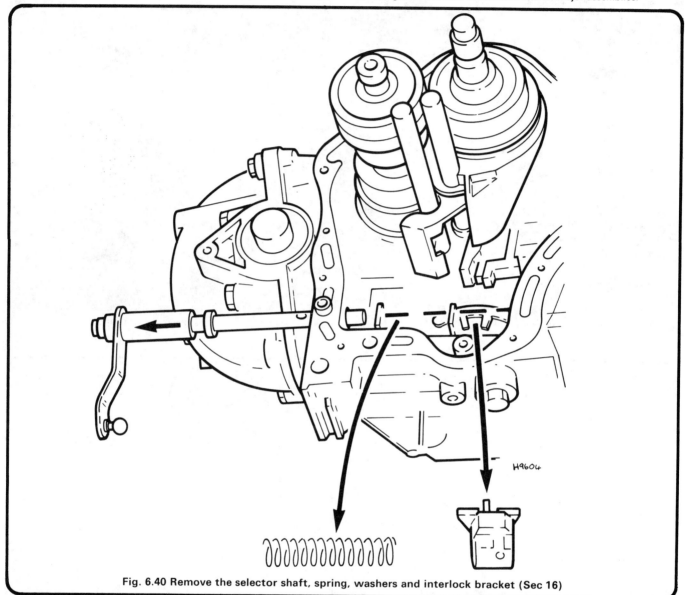

Fig. 6.40 Remove the selector shaft, spring, washers and interlock bracket (Sec 16)

16.30 Remove the speedometer pinion

16.31A Remove the final drive extension housing ...

16.31B ... and withdraw the speedometer drivegear

17 Gearbox (Type 2 BL 03, BL 61 and BL 62) – inspection

1   In general, the inspection procedures are similar to those described in Section 7 for the BT type gearboxes.
2   If new primary shaft or differential bearings are to be fitted, a selection of preload shims will be required. Read through the relevant procedures before starting work.

18 Primary shaft (Type 2 BL 03, BL 61 and BL 62) – overhaul

1   To remove the 3rd and 4th gear components from the primary shaft, support the assembly under the 3rd gear and press or drive the shaft through it. Protect the end of the shaft. Once the rear bearing cone is free, the other components can be removed from the shaft in order: 4th gear and its bush, 3rd/4th synchro sleeve and hub and 3rd gear (photos).
2   Mark the synchro sleeve and hub relative to each other and to show which side faces 4th gear.
3   Remove the front bearing from the shaft, preferably with a press or a bearing puller. As a last resort it may be possible to support the

bearing and drive the shaft through; be sure to protect the end of the shaft if this is done.
4   Once the primary shaft bearings have been removed, they must be renewed. Press the rear bearing outer track from the end casing and press in the new track, making sure it enters squarely.
5   If the primary shaft is to be renewed it should be noted that there are two primary shaft types available. On early models the front spigot bearing runs in a bush located in the rear end of the crankshaft. Later models do not have a spigot bush and the primary shaft journal diameter is increased to 15.5 mm. If fitting the later type primary shaft to replace an early type, the spigot bearing in the crankshaft must be removed to allow engagement.
6   Before commencing reassembly, make sure that the primary shaft is free from burrs and wear marks. Lubricate all parts as they are fitted.
7   Fit a new front bearing to the shaft, using a suitable tube to press or drive it home.
8   Fit 3rd gear, 3rd/4th synchro-hub and sleeve, 4th gear and its bush. Take care not to get 3rd and 4th gears mixed up, they are similar in appearance (4th gear has more teeth). If the original synchro components are being refitted, observe the mating marks made during dismantling.
9   Fit a new rear bearing to the shaft, again using a piece of tube.
10 The primary shaft is now reassembled.

18.1A Removing the primary shaft bearing cone ...

18.1B ... 4th gear ...

18.1C ... 4th gear bush ...

18.1D ... 3rd/4th synchro sleeve ...

18.1E ... synchro-hub ...

18.1F ... and 3rd gear

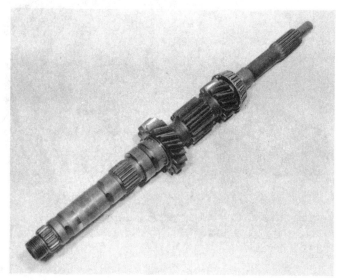

18.1G Primary shaft with everything removed except the front bearing

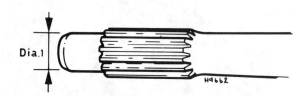

Fig. 6.41 Primary shaft modification (see text) (Sec 18)

Early type – diameter (1) = 12 mm
Later type – diameter (1) = 15.5 mm

19 Secondary shaft (Type 2 BL 03, BL 61 and BL 62 – overhaul

1   Remove 5th gear and the rear bearing from the secondary shaft. Use a puller or bearing extractor if they are a tight fit on the shaft (photo).
2   Remove 3rd/4th gear assembly, 2nd gear and its bush (photos).
3   Make alignment marks between the 1st/2nd synchro-hub and sleeve, then remove them from the shaft (photo).
4   Remove 1st gear and the half washers (early models) or needle thrust bearing and circlip (later models) (photos).
5   Press or drive the shaft out of the pinion end bearing, protecting the end of the shaft.
6   Before commencing reassembly, make sure that the shaft is free from burrs or wear marks. Lubricate all parts as they are fitted.
7   Fit the pinion end bearing to the shaft, using a piece of tube to drive or press it home. On later models, fit a new circlip.
8   Fit the half washers above the bearing, using a smear of grease to hold them in position. On later models, fit the needle thrust bearing instead.

19.1 Secondary shaft rear bearing

19.2A 3rd/4th gear assembly ...

19.2B ... 2nd gear ...

19.2C ... and 2nd gear bush

19.3 Remove 1st/2nd synchro sleeve

19.4A Remove 1st gear ...

19.4B ... the needle thrust bearing (later models) ...

Fig. 6.42 Secondary shaft and half thrust washers (early models) (Sec 19)

19.4C ... and the bearing circlips (later models)

9   Refit 1st gear, taking care not to dislodge the half washers (when fitted).

10   Refit the 1st/2nd synchro unit, observing the mating marks made when dismantling. The chamfer on the external teeth must face towards 1st gear.

11   Fit 2nd gear and its bush.

12   Fit the 3rd/4th gear assembly, making sure it is the right way round.

13   Fit the rear bearing, with the circlip groove nearest the tail of the shaft.

14   Fit the 5th gear, with its boss towards the bearing.

15   Fit a new nut to the secondary shaft but do not tighten it yet. Assembly of the secondary shaft is now complete.

20 Selector mechanism (Type 2 LB 03, BL 61 and BL 62) – dismantling and reassembly

1   One of the unusual features of this gearbox is that the detent springs and balls are located in the forks (photo). If a spring is weak, the whole fork must be renewed. (This does not apply to 5th gear fork).

2   Rotate the 1st/2nd and 3rd/4th selector rod to disengage the detent slots from the balls, then remove the rod from the forks.

3   Remove the 5th gear selector rod from the 1st/2nd fork.

4   Examine the forks and rods for wear and damage and renew as necessary.

5   Commence reassembly by inserting 5th gear selector rod into the 1st/2nd fork.

6   Offer the 3rd/4th fork to the 1st/2nd fork so that their holes and selector fingers align.

7   Insert the 1st/2nd and 3rd/4th selector rod, positioning the locking slot as shown (Fig. 6.44). Bring all the selector finger slots into line to position the selectors in neutral (photo).

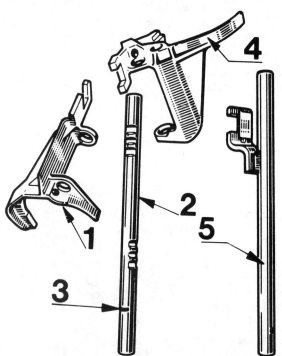

Fig. 6.43 Selector forks and rods (Sec 20)

1   3rd/4th fork   4   1st/2nd fork
2   1st/2nd and 3rd/4th rod   5   5th rod
3   Locking slot

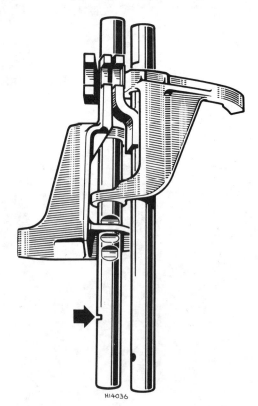

Fig. 6.44 Correct position of locking slot (arrowed) with forks and rods assembled (Sec 20)

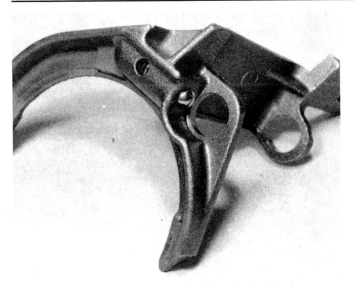

20.1 Gear selector fork showing captive detent ball and spring

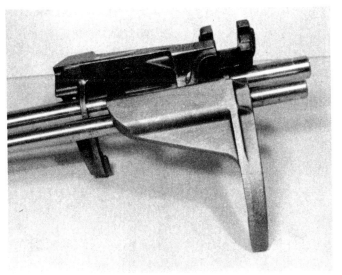

20.7 Selector forks and rods in neutral

21 Final drive/differential unit (Type 2 BL 03, BL 61 and BL 62) – overhaul

1   Unbolt the crownwheel from the differential housing.
until they can be removed (photo).
2   Remove the side gears by pushing them round inside the housing.
3   Drive out the roll pins which secure the differential gear spindle.
4   Remove the spindle, the differential gears and their washers (photo).
5   Use a press or bearing extractor to remove the bearings.
6   Examine all parts for wear and damage, and renew as necessary.

Lubricate all parts as they are assembled.
7   Fit the bearings, using a piece of tube to press or drive them home.
8   Fit the spindle with the differential gears and washers. Secure the spindle with new roll pins, which should be driven in until they are protruding between 9 and 10 mm (photo).
9   Fit the side gears, one at a time, and work them into their proper positions. Retain them in this position using tool 710-TM or equivalent (see Chapter 1, Section 33, paragraph 6), inserted from the crownwheel side (photo).
10   Fit the crownwheel with its chamfer towards the differential housing. Secure with the bolts, tightening them in diagonal sequence to the specified torque.

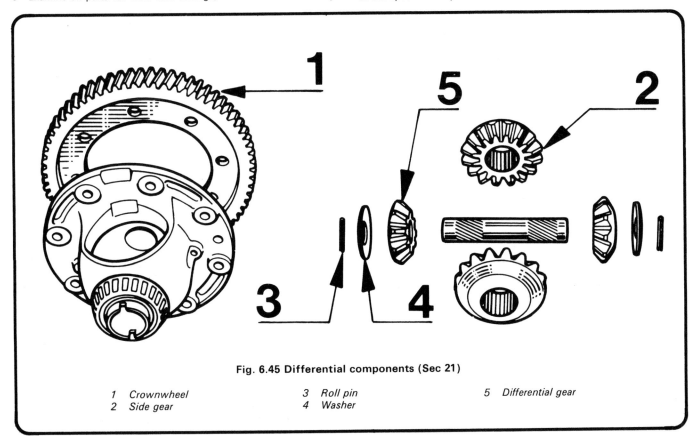

Fig. 6.45 Differential components (Sec 21)

1 Crownwheel	3 Roll pin	5 Differential gear
2 Side gear	4 Washer	

21.2 Removing a differential side gear

21.4 Removing the differential spindle, gears and washers

21.8 Roll pin location

21.9 Fabricated tool retaining the differential side gear

22 Gearbox (Type 2 BL 03 and BL 62) – reassembly

1   Commence reassembly by fitting the selector lever into the main casing. Make sure that the locating dowel is in position in the final drive housing mating face.

2   Apply jointing compound to the mating face, then fit the differential assembly with its bearing tracks (photo).

3   Fit the final drive half housing and the extension housing, but only tighten their securing bolts finger tight at this stage.

4   Fit a new oil seal, lips well greased, to the other side of the final drive housing from the extension.

5   Remove the extension housing, fit a preload shim 2.2 mm thick to the bearing outer track and refit the extension housing (without its 0-ring). Rotate the crownwheel while tightening the extension housing bolts until the crownwheel *just* starts to drag. This operation seats the bearings.

6   Remove the extension housing and the preload shim. With an accurate depth gauge, measure the distance from the final drive housing joint face to the bearing outer track. Call this dimension A. Similarly measure the protrusion of the spigot on the extension housing above the joint face. Call this dimension B (photos).

7   The thickness S of preload shim required is determined by the formula:

$$S = (A - B) + 0.10 \ mm$$

The extra 0.10 mm is the preload factor for the bearings. Shims are available in thicknesses of 1.1 to 2.2 mm in steps of 0.1 mm.

8   Tighten the final drive half housing securing bolts to the specified torque.

9   Fit the preload shim just determined, the speedometer driving gear and the extension housing with a new 0-ring. Tighten the securing bolts to the specified torque (photo). Make sure that the crownwheel is still free to rotate.

10 Fit and secure the speedometer pinion and its adaptor.

11 Fit a new oil seal, lips well greased, into the extension housing.

12 Fit a new gear selector shaft oil seal in the main casing.

13 From the clutch housing side, fit the clutch release bearing guide tube. Do not use a gasket under the guide tube flange, and only tighten the bolts finger tight. Invert the casing and fit a preload spacer (any size) and the primary shaft bearing outer track (photos).

14 Fit the gear selector shaft spring bracket and tighten its securing bolts to the specified torque.

22.2 Differential unit in position – note location dowel

22.6A Measure from the joint face to the bearing outer track ...

22.6B ... and measure the spigot protrusion

22.9 Fitting the preload shim

22.13A Input shaft preload shim ...

22.13B .. and front bearing outer track

15 If removed, fit the two locating dowels in the main casing mating face.

16 Fit and tighten the breather.

17 Refit the lubrication jet (photo).

18 Fit the reverse detent spring and plunger. Depress the plunger and fit the reverse selector fork and its spindle. Tighten the spindle securing nut. Note the modification shown in Fig. 6.46.

19 Fit the reversing lamp switch using a new copper washer. Tighten it to the specified torque (photo).

20 Assemble the geartrains and the selector forks and rods. Offer the whole assembly to the gearcase (photo).

21 Fit the reverse idler spindle and gear, with the chamfer towards the rear of the gearbox. Make sure the pin in the shaft is correctly located.

22 Refit the swarf-collecting magnet.

23 Insert the spring and washers into the bracket (photo).

24 Enter the selector shaft into the casing passing it through the compressed spring and washers inside the casing. Also engage the shaft with the selector finger and the interlock bracket. It may be helpful to keep the finger and the bracket together with a short length of rod (maximum diameter 14 mm) which can be withdrawn as the selector shaft enters (photo).

25 Make sure that the flat on the shaft and the roll pin hole are correctly orientated. Secure the selector finger and the interlock bracket with two new roll pins. The slots in the roll pins should be 180° away from each other and in line with the longitudinal axis of the shaft (photo).

26 On later models, fit the washer and a new circlip to the cover end of the shaft.

27 On all models, refit the selector shaft cover if it was removed.

28 To the lever end of the selector shaft fit a new 0-ring, a washer and a new circlip.

29 Apply jointing compound to the main casing/end casing mating face. Fit the end casing, making sure that the primary and secondary shafts and the selector rod pass through their respective holes. Fit the thirteen securing bolts and tighten them progressively to the specified torque; remember to fit the clutch cable bracket.

30 Fit the reverse idler spindle bolt, using a new washer. Tighten the bolt to the specified torque.

31 Fit the drain plugs, using new washers, and tighten them to the specified torque.

32 Fit the selector rod lockplate. Secure it with its bolt and washer, tightening the bolt to the specified torque (photo).

33 Fit the (secondary) shaft bearing circlip, making sure it is properly located in the groove.

34 Fit the secondary shaft rear bearing retaining washers and bolts. Tighten the bolts to the specified torque.

35 Fit the spacer (shoulder towards the bearing), 5th gear bush and 5th gear to the primary shaft. Also fit the sliding sleeve and hub, but not the selector fork (photos).

36 Lock up the gear trains by engaging 5th gear with the sliding sleeve and any other gear with the selector shaft. Fit the secondary shaft nut and tighten it to the specified torque, then lock it by staking its skirt into the groove.

37 Remove the 5th gear sliding sleeve and hub, then refit them with the selector fork. If the original components are being refitted, observe the mating marks made when dismantling. As the fork is being lowered into position, insert the detent ball into its hole. Alternatively, extract the roll pin and insert the detent ball and spring from the other end (photos).

38 Engage two gears agin, then fit the primary shaft nut and tighten it to the specified torque. Lock the nut by staking.

39 Secure 5th gear selector fork to its rod with a new roll pin.

40 Coat the mating faces with jointing compound, then refit the rear cover. Use thread locking compound on the securing bolts and tighten them to the specified torque.

41 Turn to the clutch housing and remove the release bearing guide tube. If new release lever balljoint is to be fitted, do so now: put thread locking compound on its splines and drive it in.

42 Refit the clutch release bearing guide tube with a preload spacer shim 2.4 mm thick and without a gasket. Insert the retaining bolts and tighten them progressively to a torque wrench setting of 1.0 kgf m (7.0 lbf ft). Rotate the primary shaft as the bolts are being tighten. As this torque setting is reached, the shaft should just start to drag as it is rotated: the bearings are then correctly seated.

43 Unbolt and remove the guide tube and shim. Using a depth gauge, accurately measure the distance from the bearing outer track to the

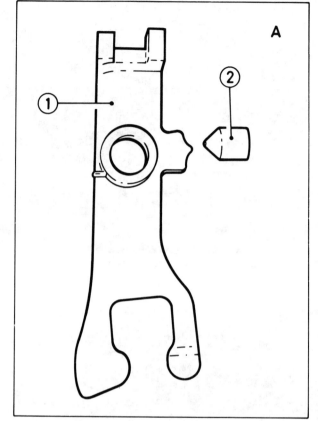

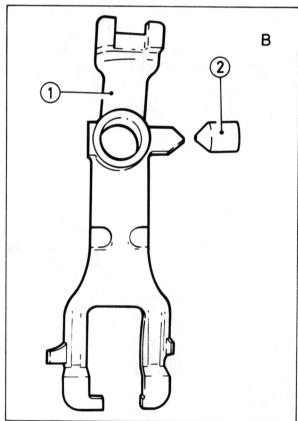

H9661

Fig. 6.46 Early (A) and late (B) reverse selector fork (1) and plunger (2) (Sec 22)

The two types are interchangeable

22.17 Refit the lubrication jet

22.19 The reversing lamp switch

22.20 Fitting the geartrains and selector mechanism

22.23 Spring and washers in the bracket

22.24 Fitting the selector shaft

22.25 Selector finger/interlock bracket roll pins

22.32 Selector rod lock plate bolt

22.35A 5th gear spacer ...

22.35B ... 5th gear bush ...

22.35C .. and primary shaft 5th gear

22.37A Insert the detent ball and spring ...

22.37B ... and secure with the roll pin

joint face on the casing. Call this dimension C. Similarly measure the protrusion of the spigot on the guide tube flange above the joint face. Call this dimension D (photos).

44 The thickness T of preload shim required is given by the formula:

$$T = (C - D) + 0.25$$

The extra (0.25 mm is to provide bearing preload, and allows for the thickness of the gasket which will be fitted. Shims are available in thicknesses from 0.7 to 2.4 mm in steps of 0.1 mm.

45 Fit a new oil seal, lips well greased, to the guide tube.

46 Fit the preload shim (of calculated thickness), a new gasket and the guide tube. Secure with the bolts and tighten them to the full torque setting given in the Specifications (photos).

47 Refit the clutch release fork and release bearing (see Chapter 5).

48 If not already done, refit the gearchange levers, making sure that they are in the correct position (photo). Also refit the clutch bellcrank (if removed) and the gearchange pivot bracket.

49 Reassembly of the transmission is now complete. Do not fill it with oil until the driveshafts have been engaged.

23 General description – automatic transmission

The automatic transmission is available on BX 16 models from July 1984 and BX 19 from September 1988. The transmission has four

22.43A Measure the distance from the joint face to the bearing outer track

22.43B Measure the spigot protrusion

22.46A Primary shaft preload shim

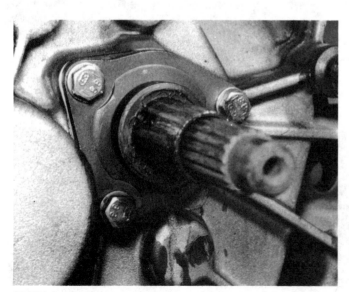
22.46B Guide tube in position

22.48 Gearchange levers in neutral position

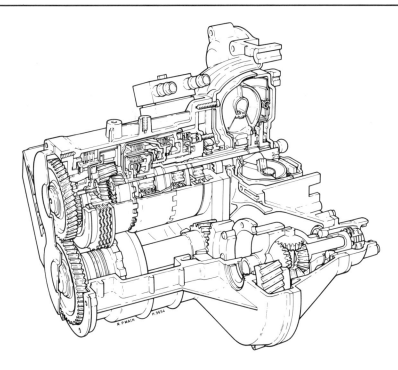

Fig. 6.47 Cutaway view of the ZF automatic transmission (Sec 23)

forward speeds and one reverse. In the interests of fuel economy the torque converter is completely bypassed in top (4th) gear and partially bypassed in 3rd; this reduces losses due to torque converter slip.

Gearchanging is automatic in use, the transmission responding to changes in speed and load. The usual kickdown facility is provided for enhanced acceleration when the throttle is depressed fully.

Instead of the customary oil cooler mounted in the radiator, cooling is by means of a coolant/oil heat exchanger mounted on the side of the transmission.

24 Automatic transmission – safety precautions

The following safety precautions must be adhered to where an automatic transmission is fitted.

Whenever the vehicle is parked, or is being serviced or repaired, ensure that the handbrake is fully applied and the selector lever is in P.

If it is necessary to tow a vehicle with automatic transmission, the towing speed must be restricted to 30 mph and the distance to 30 miles. If these conditions cannot be met, or if transmission damage is the reason for seeking a tow, the vehicle must be transported on a trailer.

25 Automatic transmission – fluid checking and renewal

Checking the fluid level

1   This check should be made directly after the vehicle has been used so that the transmission oil is at its normal operating temperatue.
2   With the vehicle parked on level ground and the engine running, move the selector lever through all positions a number of times then finally leave it in P. The handbrake must be fully applied throughout the check procedure.
3   With the engine still running, remove the transmission fluid level dipstick, wipe it clean, reinsert it fully then withdraw it again and check the fluid level. The fluid level must be between the Min and Max levels.
4   If required, top up the fluid level (but do not overfill) through the dipstick guide tube.
5   Stop the engine and refit the dipstick on completion.

Draining and fitting

6   Position a suitable container with a minimum capacity of three litres under the transmission. There are two drain plugs to be removed, these being shown in Fig 6.7. Remove the plugs and drain the fluid, then refit the plugs.
7   Refill, using 2.5 litres of the recommended fluid, through the dipstick guide tube.
8   Recheck the fluid level after a nominal mileage has been covered and, if necessary, top up the fluid, as described in paragraphs 1 to 5 inclusive.

26 Automatic transmission kickdown cable – checking and adjustment

1   The kickdown cable checks and adjustments must be made with the engine at its normal operating temperature, the electric cooling fan having cut in, then off.
2   Check and if necessary adjust the engine idle speed, as described in Chapter 3.
3   With the engine switched off, first check the accelerator cable for correct adjustment. Detach the kickdown cable from the cam on the carburettor. Pull the accelerator cable sheath stop pin out and reposition it to allow a small clearance at 'a' (Fig 6.48). Depress the accelerator pedal fully and simultaneously check that the throttle valves of the carburettor are fully opened. Reset the cable sheath stop pin on completion.
4   Reconnect the kickdown cable to the cam, then loosen the kickdown outer cable adjustment nuts at the bracket and check that the inner cable is free but not slack.
5   Pivot the kickdown cam and check that the crimped stop moves as soon as the cam is rotated.
6   Get an assistant to fully depress the accelerator pedal and check the crimped stop movement, which should be 50 mm (1.9 in) (Fig 6.50).
7   If necessary, adjust the outer cable at the bracket, but note that a clearance should always exist between the sleeve end fitting and the crimped stop. Tighten the outer cable adjustment locknuts on completion.
8   Kickdown cable renewal is a task that must be entrusted to your Citroën dealer.

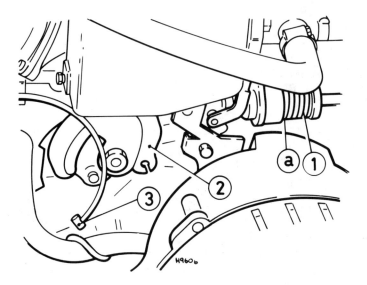

Fig. 6.48 Accelerator cable sheath stop pin (1) and
clearance point (a) with kickdown cable (3) detached from
cam (2) (Sec 26)

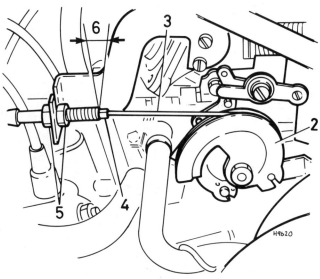

Fig. 6.49 Kickdown cable attachments (Sec 26)

2   Cam
3   Inner cable
4   Crimped stop

5   Sleeve end fitting nuts
6   Crimped stop-to-sleeve
    clearance (0.5 mm)

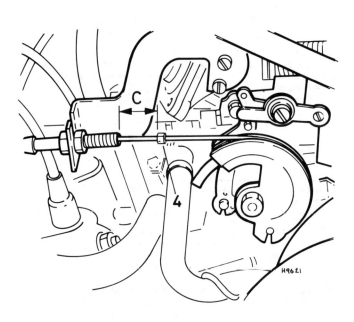

Fig. 6.50 Crimped stop (4) clearance from sleeve under full
acceleration (Sec 26)

C   = 50 mm (approximately)

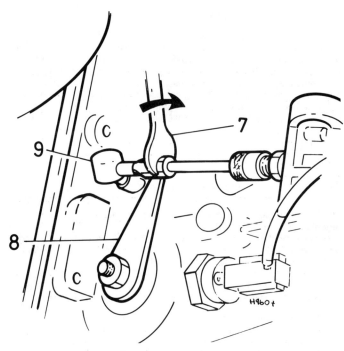

Fig. 6.51 Selector rod balljoint (9) detachment from the
selector lever (8) using spanner (7) (Sec 27)

27 Automatic transmission selector control – adjustment

1   Referring to Fig. 6.51, fit a spanner onto the flats of the selector rod
balljoint and twist it as indicated to disconnect the balljoint from the
selector lever.
2   Move the selector lever (within the vehicle) to N.
3   Move the gearbox selector lever into the N positon (Fig. 6.52).
4   The selector rod balljoint should align exactly with the coupling
ball on the selector lever so that when reconnected neither the selector

lever within the vehicle nor the selector lever on the gearbox move.
Adjust the position of the balljoint on the connecting rod if necessary.
5   If the selector control was adjusted, check the setting by starting
the engine and, when it has reached its normal operating temperature,
move the selector lever within the vehicle to P. The vehicle should be
stationary and the gearbox parking pawl fully engaged.
6   Now move the lever to R with the handbrake off. The vehicle
should move rearwards, the pawl having been released.
7   Turn the engine off and then check that the engine will only restart
when the lever is moved to P or N. The starter motor must not operate
in any other selected position.

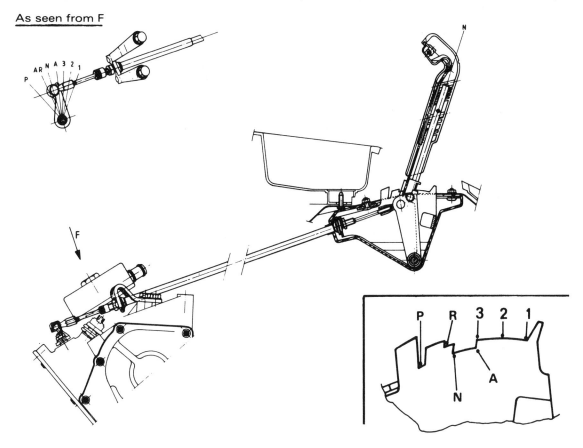

As seen from F

Fig. 6.52 Automatic transmission gear selector control (Sec 27)

28 Automatic transmission – removal and refitting

1 In general, the removal and refitting procedures are similar to those described for the Type 2 BL 03 manual transmission but ignoring references to the clutch mechanism (see Section 15).
2 With the torque converter lower shield removed, unscrew the three driveplate-to-torque converter connecting bolts. Turn the crankshaft by means of its pulley centre bolt to bring each of the connecting bolts into view.
3 Remove the brace from under the transmission then unscrew and remove the oil dipstick guide tube.
4 Disconnect the kickdown cable from the carburettor. Drain the cooling system (Chapter 2).
5 Disconnect the fluid cooler hoses.
6 Disconnect the gearchange cable.
7 Remove the starter and the engine-to-transmission connecting bolts.
8 Withdraw the transmission from the engine and bolt on a metal plate to prevent displacement of the torque converter.
9 Lower the transmission and remove it from under the car.
10 Refitting is a reversal of removal but observe the following points.

(a) *Check that the crankshaft centering ring is in position and well greased.*

(b) *Check that the transmission casing flange hollow dowels are correctly located.*
(c) *Refill with the specified quantity of transmission fluid. Refill the cooling system as described in Chapter 2.*

11 Note that, with automatic transmission, a centering tube is fitted through the side (sun) gears in the differential unit. This enables the driveshafts to be withdrawn without the need to insert a sleeve tube to locate the side gears as is the case on manual gearbox types.
12 If the transmission is removed for repairs, entrust the work to your Citroën dealer as specialised tools and knowledge are required to overhaul the transmission.
13 When the transmission is refitted check the adjustment of the kickdown cable and the selector control, as described in Section 26 and 28.

29 Fault diagnosis – automatic transmission

Faults not due to incorrect fluid level or wrong adjustment of the selector linkage must be diagnosed by a Citroën dealer or automatic transmission specialist.
Do not remove the transmission for specialist repair without allowing the specialist to test it *in situ.* Some faults cannot be diagnosed with the transmission removed.

30 Fault diagnosis – manual transmission

Symptom	Reason(s)
Weak or ineffective synchromesh	Synchromesh units worn, or damaged
Jumps out of gear	Gearchange mechanism worn Synchromesh units badly worn Selector fork badly worn

Symptom	Reason(s)
Excessive noise	Incorrect grade of oil or level too low
	Gear teeth excessively worn or damaged
	Intermediate gear thrust washers worn allowing excessive end play
	Worn bearings
Difficulty in engaging gears	Worn synchromesh
	Worn clutch
Noise when cornering	Wheel bearing or driveshaft fault
	Differential fault

Note: *It is sometimes difficult to decide whether it is worthwhile removing and dismantling the gearbox for a fault which may be nothing more than a minor irritant. Gearboxes which howl, or where the synchromesh can be beaten by a quick gearchange, may continue to perform for a long time in this state. A worn gearbox usually needs a complete rebuild to eliminate noise because the various gears, if re-aligned on new bearings, will continue to howl when different wearing surfaces are presented to each other. The decision to overhaul therefore, must be considered with regard to time and money available, relative to the degree of noise or malfunction that the driver has to suffer.*

Chapter 7 Driveshafts, hubs, wheels and tyres

For modifications, and information applicable to later models, see Supplement at end of manual

Contents

Specifications

Driveshafts

Driveshafts .... Front wheel driveshafts each having two tripod constant velocity joints; inner end splines permit axial movement

Wheel hub bearings

Front and rear .... Twin track ball-bearings

Wheels

Type .... Pressed steel or alloy

Size (steel):

BX and BX 14 .... 4.50 B 14 FH 4.30 or 120 TR 365 FH 4.30

BX 16 .... 120 TR 365 FH 4.30

BX 19 .... 5.00 B 14 FH 4.25

Estate .... 5.00 B 14 FH 4.25

Size (alloy):

BX 14 RE and BX 16 .... 120 TR 365 FH 4.30

BX 19 .... 5.00 B 14 CH 4.25

Tyres

Type .... Radial ply, tubeless

Sizes and pressures in bar (lbf/in²)*	Front	Rear
BX and BX 14:		
Michelin 145 SR MX or XZX	1.9 (27.5)	2.0 (29.0)
Alternatives 170/65 R 365 TRX AS	1.8 (26.0)	2.0 (29.0)
BX 16:		
Michelin 170/65 R 365 TRX AS	1.9 (27.5)	2.1 (30.5)
BX 19:		
Standard 165/70 R MXV	2.0 (29)	2.2 (32)
Alternative 165/70 R 14 MVX	2.0 (29)	2.2 (32)
Estate:		
165/70 R 14 MXL	2.3 (33)	2.5 (36)

* *Recommendations may vary. Consult owners handbook or a tyre specialist if in doubt*

Torque wrench settings

	kgf m	lbf ft
Roadwheel bolts:		
Steel wheels	8.0	57.8
Alloy wheels	9.0	65.1
Hub nut (front and rear)	27.0	195.3
Driveshaft intermediate bearing nuts (BX and BX 19)	1.0	7.2
Lower suspension arm/hub carrier balljoint nut	3.0	21.7

1 General description

The driveshafts fitted to the Citroën BX range of models are of conventional type with constant velocity joints and splined engagement with the wheel hubs and the differential/final drive unit. The driveshafts are of two distinct types, these being for the BX and BX 14 models or the BX 16 and BX 19 models. The right-hand driveshaft of the BX 16 and BX 19 type differs in that it has an intermediate support bearing.

The constant velocity universal joints are fitted near each end of the shafts to accommodate the steering and suspension angular movements. The inner ends of the shafts mate with the final drive using sliding splines which allow changes in length of the shafts resulting from suspension and steering movements.

The driveshafts are splined into the front wheel hubs. These run on double row ball-races located in the hub carrier at the bottom of each front shock absorber strut.

The rear wheel hubs run on twin track ball-bearings on stub axles.

Little maintenance is required to the driveshafts, but inspect the rubber bellows regularly for splits and grease leakage. To renew a bellows, refer to the Supplement.

The roadwheels are of pressed-steel type or, in some instances, alloy roadwheels are fitted to the higher performance models. For further details on roadwheels and tyres refer to Section 8.

190

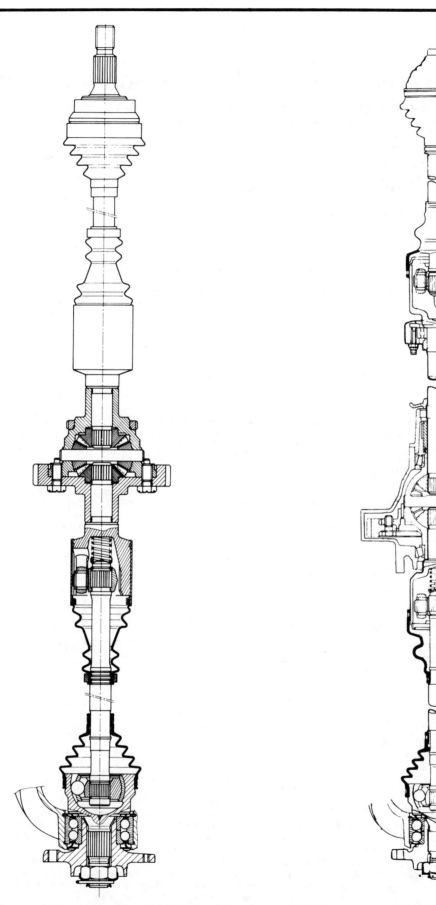

Fig. 7.1 Sectional view of the driveshaft fitted to BX and BX 14 models (Sec 1)

Fig. 7.2 Sectional view of the driveshaft fitted to BX 16 and BX 19 models (Sec 1)

2 Routine maintenance

Driveshafts

1   At the intervals specified in Routine Maintenance, check the driveshaft bellows for splits and leakage of grease, also the front and rear hub bearings for 'rock' or endfloat after having raised the roadwheels from the ground (photo).

2   Any leakage of grease from the joint protector or rubber boot must have immediate attention. Apart from the loss of the special lubricant, the risk of dirt contamination of the joint concerned demands prompt remedial action.

3   To renew the driveshaft bellows refer to Chapter 13.

Wheels

4   On cars with pressed-steel wheels, clean them (inner and outer surfaces) at regular intervals and keep them free from rust by repainting periodically if necessary.

5   Keep alloy wheels clean and free from corrosion using a proprietary product.

6   Check the wheel bolts for security. They should be tightened to their specified torque setting.

Tyres

7   Inspect the tyres for signs of excessive wear and damage. Check the tyre pressures and remove any embedded flints or stones from the tyre treads.

8   Renew the tyre when the tread has worn down to the legal limit or the tread wear indicator bars are visible.

9   When new tyres are fitted, have the wheels balanced and also whenever steering vibration or judder indicates the need for rebalancing.

3 Driveshafts (BX and BX 14 models) – removal and refitting

1   Check that the handbrake is fully applied and remove the roadwheel trim.

2   Extract the retaining clip and withdraw the hub nut retainer (photo).

3   Loosen the hub nut but do not remove it at this stage.

4   Loosen but do not remove the roadwheel bolts.

5   Place chocks against the rear roadwheels then raise and support the vehicle at the front end so that the front roadwheels are clear of the ground. Unbolt and remove the roadwheel at the front from the side concerned. Release the handbrake.

6   Loosen the lower arm balljoint nut then detach the joint using a balljoint separator. When the joint is free remove the separator and the retaining nut. Detach the lower arm.

7   Unscrew and remove the hub nut, then pull the hub carrier outwards and withdraw it from the outboard end of the driveshaft. Pivot the hub carrier as necessary as it is pulled outwards and take care not to strain the hydraulic line connection (photo).

8   Before withdrawing the driveshaft from the differential housing it is advisable to place a clean container under the differential housing to catch any oil leakage once the shaft is removed. Allow for about one litre of oil spillage.

9   Pull the driveshaft from the differential housing, taking care not to damage the housing oil seal. Grip the driveshaft joint cover, not the shaft, when pulling the driveshaft from the transmission, otherwise the CV joint may become dismantled due to displacement of the internal circlip.

10 It is emphasised that if any attempt is made to move the car on its wheels without the driveshafts fitted, there is a danger that the front wheel bearings will collapse.

11 The oil seal in the differential housing can be removed by prising it free using a suitable screwdriver, but take care not to damage the

2.1 Check the condition of the driveshaft bellows

3.2 Retaining clip and hub nut retainer

Fig. 7.3 Differential housing oil seal (6) (Sec 3)

3.7 Separating the driveshaft from the front hub (BX 16)

housing. Check that the housing is clean before fitting the new seal by driving it carefully into position using a tube of suitable diameter. This seal must not be damaged in any way as oil leakage past it could result in serious damage to both the transmission and the engine.

12 Refitting the driveshaft is a reversal of the removal procedure, but note the following special points.

13 Lubricate the differential hub seal lips and the corresponding hub of the driveshaft with grease prior to refitting to ease reassembly and to avoid damaging the oil seal.

14 Ensure that the balljoint cone on the hub carrier is clean before refitting the lower arm (but do not use a solvent to clean it). Tighten the locknut to the specified torque setting (Chapter 10).

15 When refitting the hub nut, lubricate the nut face and threads with grease and tighten the nut to the specified torque before refitting the roadwheel. To prevent the hub from turning get an assistant to fully apply the brakes. Once the nut is tightened locate the retainer and refit the retaining clip.

16 When the roadwheel is refitted release the handbrake and check that the hub rotates without excessive binding. A small amount of resistance will probably be present caused by transmission and brake pad drag.

17 On completion, lower the vehicle and tighten the roadwheel bolts to the specified torque settings. Replenish any loss of lubricant from the engine/transmission.

4 Driveshafts (BX 16 and BX 19 models) – removal and refitting

Manual transmission models

1 If both driveshafts are to be removed it is important that the left-hand driveshaft is removed first. This can be removed in the same manner as that described for the smaller engine variants in the previous Section.

2 With the left-hand driveshaft removed, it is necessary to insert a suitable tube or dowel rod into the left-hand side driveshaft aperture in the differential housing (photo). The diameter of the tube should be a fraction under the diameter of the driveshaft and its purpose when inserted is to retain the position of the sun gears when the right-hand driveshaft is removed. The tube must remain in position until the right-hand driveshaft is fully refitted.

3 Disconnect the outer end of the right-hand driveshaft as described for other models in the previous Section.

4 Undo the two intermediate bearing nuts and then turn the screws half a turn. The driveshaft can now be withdrawn from the differential housing and the intermediate bearing carrier then removed (photo).

5 Lever out the oil seal in the final drive/differential unit, and also the one in the wheel hub. Both seals must be renewed on refitting the driveshaft.

6 Lightly grease a new, double-lipped oil seal and carefully tap it into its recess in the final drive/differential unit with the side containing the spring facing into the unit. Make sure that the seal is abutting the internal shoulder in the unit case. Fill the space between the double lips with general-purpose grease. Similarly fit a new seal, of similar pattern, in the wheel hub; making sure that it abuts the bearing retaining ring. Again, fill the space between the lips with grease.

7 Check the driveshaft before fitting to make sure that it is free of obvious defects. Clean the splines at both ends and, at the wheel hub end only, give the splines a thin coat of Molykote 321R or a suitable alternative anti-friction agent.

8 Protective bushes will have been supplied with the new oil seals. The bushes are fitted to the driveshaft aperture in the differential housing to protect the oil seal from damage when refitting the driveshaft(s).

9 Refit the right-hand driveshaft first. Check that the two screws are located in the intermediate bearing and apply a small amount of lubricant to the bearing outer race prior to engagement of the driveshaft. When the driveshaft is in position tighten the bearing retaining nuts to the specified torque setting.

10 Reconnect the outer end of the right-hand driveshaft reversing the removal procedures and noting the special points described in the previous Section (paragraph 12 on).

11 Withdraw the locating tube from the left-hand driveshaft aperture in the differential housing. The oil seal in the differential housing and

4.2 Side (sun) gear on differential housing must be supported by inserting tube or rod into left side driveshaft aperture (manual gearbox models)

4.4 Intermediate bearing and retaining nuts

the wheel hub can now be removed and renewed on the left-hand side (as described in paragraphs 5 and 6).

12 Clean, check and prepare the left-hand driveshaft for refitting (paragraph 7) and locate the oil seal protector bush to the oil seal in the differential housing on the left-hand side.

13 Refit the left-hand driveshaft reversing the removal details and refer to the previous Section, paragraph 12 on for the special points to be noted during refitting.

Automatic transmission models

14 The differential sun gears on automatic transmission models are different from manual transmission models in that they are supported on a shaft. It is therefore not necessary to insert a tube or dowel through them when removing both driveshafts.

15 The removal and refitting procedures for both driveshafts, and also the renewal of the differential hub and outer wheel hub oil seals, are otherwise the same as those described for the manual transmission variants.

Fig. 7.4 Oil seal protector bush (3) (Sec 4)

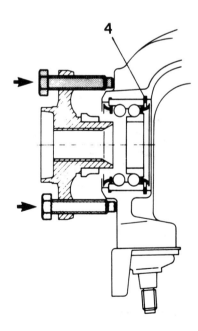

Fig. 7.5 Front hub removal method using bolts (arrowed). Note circlip location (4) (Sec 6)

5 Driveshaft intermediate bearing (BX 16 and BX 19) – renewal

1 Remove the right-hand driveshaft.

2 Unbolt and remove the engine mounting/intermediate bearing carrier (photo). If the bearing did not come away with the driveshaft, press it and its sealing ring out of the carrier.

3 Fit the new bearing and sealing ring, refit the carrier and the driveshaft. Tighten all fastenings to the specified torque, using new nuts on the steering and suspension balljoints.

6 Front wheel hub bearings – removal and refitting

1 Disconnect the driveshaft on the side concerned from the outer hub. This is described in Section 3, paragraphs 1 to 7 inclusive. Do not (unless necessary) withdraw the driveshaft from the differential housing, but leave it in position and supported so that the inner joint is not strained.

2 Set the height control to the 'low' position.

3 Remove the brake disc, referring to Chapter 9 for details.

4 Insert two bolts into the threaded holes in the flange face of the hub and tighten them evenly in a progressive sequence to withdraw the hub from the hub carrier (swivel unit).

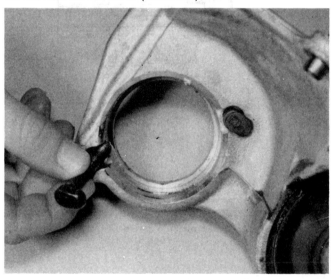

5.2 Driveshaft intermediate bearing carrier (removed) showing special bolts

Fig. 7.6 Bearing inner race removal using Citroën tool (Sec 6)

5 Remove the bearing inner race from the hub using Citroën tool 2405-T or a similar puller. Take care not to damage the hub.
6 Extract the bearing retaining circlip from the inboard side of the hub carrier.
7 To remove the bearing from the hub carrier the Citroën tool, kit number OUT 30 7104-T, should be used if available. Assemble the tool as shown in Fig. 7.7, and apply grease to the friction washer B. Tighten the centre bolt to push the bearing inwards. If this special tool is not available, fabricate a similar tool to that shown or try removing the bearing using a suitable tube drift to drive the bearing from the hub. The tube drift must locate on the outboard end of the bearing outer race and the bearing drifted inwards to remove it. Support the inboard side of the hub carrier during removal.
8 Clean and inspect the hub, hub carrier and bearings for signs of excessive wear or damage and renew as necessary. The inner and outer

seals are integral with the bearing and cannot be renewed individually.
9 If the circlip was damaged or distorted during removal it must be renewed.
10 Refitting is a reversal of the removal procedure.
11 Take care when fitting the circlip not to damage the inboard seal and ensure that the circlip is fully engaged in its groove in the hub carrier.
12 Lubricate the hub with grease prior to fitting. Also lubricate the seal lips with grease.
13 Refit the driveshaft, with reference to Section 3.
14 Refit the brake disc, with reference to Chapter 9. Take care not to get grease onto the disc.
15 When the roadwheel is refitted spin it to ensure that the bearings run freely without excessive play or drag. Apply the handbrake and lower the vehicle to the ground.

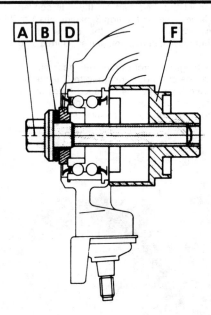

Fig. 7.7 Citroën tool OUT 30 7104-T (A, B, D and F) assembled for bearing removal from hub carrier. Tighten centre bolt (A) (Sec 6)

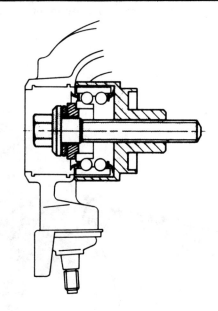

Fig. 7.8 Hub carrier bearing withdrawn into special tool (Sec 6)

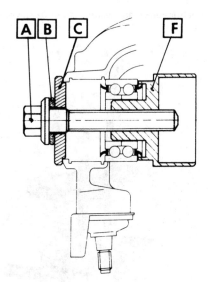

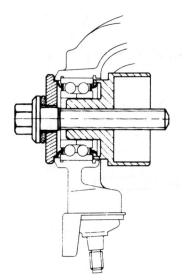

Fig. 7.9 Reverse the position of special tool item F to pull bearing into position in the hub carrier. Note support plate C (Sec 6)

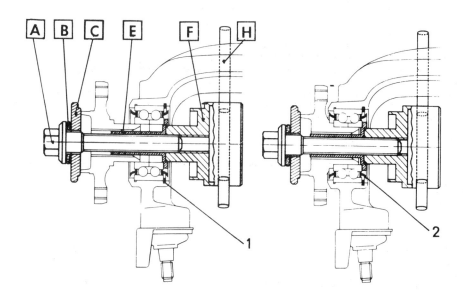

Fig. 7.10 Hub refitting method using items shown from Citroën special tool kit (Sec 6)

7 Rear wheel hub bearings – removal and refitting

1   Remove the rear wheel trim, prise free the hub cap, being careful not to distort it, then loosen, but do not remove at this stage, the hub nut and the roadwheel bolts (photo).
2   Raise and support the rear of the vehicle so that the rear roadwheels are clear of the ground. Remove the roadwheel from the side concerned.
3   Referring to Chapter 9, remove the rear brake pads and the brake caliper unit.
4   Undo the retaining screw and remove the brake disc.
5   Unscrew and remove the hub nut and the washer.
6   Withdraw the hub using a suitable puller or slide hammer.
7   Remove the bearing inner race using a suitable puller.
8   Remove the hub seal thrust cup.
9   Clean the components and inspect for excessive wear or damage. Renew as necessary.

10 Using a suitable tube drift, tap the thrust cup into position.
11 Refit the hub inner race by driving it home using the hub nut and a suitable bush. Clean and lubricate the race with grease.
12 Engage the hub onto the stub axle and drive it partially into position so that the thread of the stub axle protrudes a sufficient amount to allow the hub nut to be fitted onto it; complete the refitting of the hub by tightening the hub nut. Prevent the stub axle from turning by holding it with an Allen key from the rear (Fig. 7.14).
13 With the hub fitted, remove the nut. Clean and lubricate the hub/stub axle and bearing outer face with grease then locate the hub washer and fit a new hub nut. Tighten the nut to the specified torque and stake lock the nut to secure it (photo). Remove the Allen key used to hold the stub axle then check that the hub spins freely.
14 Tap the hub cap into position.
15 Refit the brake disc and the brake unit, as described in Chapter 9.
16 Refit the roadwheel and lower the vehicle to the ground.

7.1A Prise free the hub cap ...

7.1B ... and loosen the hub nut

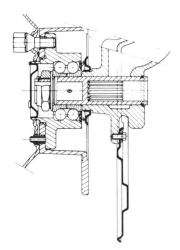

Fig. 7.11 Cross-sectional view of the rear hub (Sec 7)

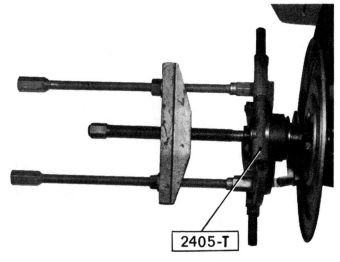

Fig. 7.12 Rear hub removal using Citroën tool 2405-T
(Sec 7)

Fig. 7.13 Rear hub thrust cup (5) fitting method with the
Citroën tool (Sec 7)

Fig. 7.14 Allen key location (arrowed) when tightening the
rear hub nut (Sec 7)

7.13 Stake lock the new hub nut to secure it

8   Wheels and tyres – general care and maintenance

Wheels and tyres should give no real problems in use provided that a close eye is kept on them with regard to excessive wear or damage. To this end, the following points should be noted.

Ensure that tyre pressures are checked regularly and maintained correctly. Checking should be carried out with the tyres cold and not immediately after the vehicle has been in use. If the pressures are checked with the tyres hot, an apparently high reading will be obtained owing to heat expansion. Under no circumstances should an attempt be made to reduce the pressures to the quoted cold reading in this instance, or effective underinflation will result.

Underinflation will cause overheating of the tyre owing to excessive flexing of the casing, and the tread will not sit correctly on the road surface. This will cause a consequent loss of adhesion and excessive wear, not to mention the danger of sudden tyre failure due to heat build-up.

Overinflation will cause rapid wear of the centre part of the tyre tread coupled with reduced adhesion, harsher ride, and the danger of shock damage occurring in the tyre casing.

Regularly check the tyres for damage in the form of cuts or bulges, especially in the sidewalls. Remove any nails or stones embedded in the tread before they penetrate the tyre to cause deflation. If removal of a nail *does* reveal that the tyre has been punctured, refit the nail so that its point of penetration is marked. Then immediately change the wheel and have the tyre repaired by a tyre dealer. Do *not* drive on a tyre in such a condition. If in any doubt as to the possible consequences of any damage found, consult your local tyre dealer for advice.

Periodically remove the wheels and clean any dirt or mud from the inside and outside surfaces. Examine the wheel rims for signs of rusting, corrosion or other damage. Light alloy wheels are easily damaged by 'kerbing' whilst parking, and similarly steel wheels may become dented or buckled. Renewal of the wheel is very often the only course of remedial action possible.

The balance of each wheel and tyre assembly should be maintained to avoid excessive wear, not only to the tyres but also to the steering and suspension components. Wheel imbalance is normally signified by vibration through the vehicle's bodyshell, although in many cases it is particularly noticeable through the steering wheel. Conversely, it should be noted that wear or damage in suspension or steering components may cause excessive tyre wear. Out-of-round or out-of-true tyres, damaged wheels and wheel bearing wear/maladjustment also fall into this category. Balancing will not usually cure vibration caused by such wear.

Wheel balancing may be carried out with the wheel either on or off the vehicle. If balanced on the vehicle, ensure that the wheel-to-hub relationship is marked in some way prior to subsequent wheel removal so that it may be refitted in its original position.

General tyre wear is influenced to a large degree by driving style – harsh braking and acceleration or fast cornering will all produce more rapid tyre wear. Interchanging of tyres may result in more even wear, but this should only be carried out where there is no mix of tyre types on the vehicle. However, it is worth bearing in mind that if this is completely effective, the added expense of replacing a complete set of tyres simultaneously is incurred, which may prove financially restrictive for many owners.

Front tyres may wear unevenly as a result of wheel misalignment. The front wheels should always be correctly aligned according to the settings specified by the vehicle manufacturer.

Legal restrictions apply to the mixing of tyre types on a vehicle. Basically this means that a vehicle must not have tyres of differing construction on the same axle. Although it is not recommended to mix tyre types between front axle and rear axle, the only legally permissible combination is crossply at the front and radial at the rear. When mixing radial ply tyres, textile braced radials must always go on the front axle, with steel braced radials at the rear. An obvious disadvantage of such mixing is the necessity to carry two spare tyres to avoid contravening the law in the event of a puncture.

In the UK, the Motor Vehicles Construction and Use Regulations apply to many aspects of tyre fitting and usage. It is suggested that a copy of these regulations is obtained from your local police if in doubt as to the current legal requirements with regard to tyre condition, minimum tread depth, etc.

9 Fault diagnosis – driveshafts

Symptom	Reason(s)
Knock or clunk when taking up drive	CV joints worn Splined couplings worn Front hub nuts loose or bearings worn
Vibration	Wheel nuts loose Wheels unbalanced (check for security of balance weights and accumulations of mud) CV joints or splined couplings worn
Metallic grating, varying with road speed	CV joints worn Wheel bearings worn
Abnormal noise when turning	Differential unit defective CV joints worn Wheel bearings worn

Chapter 8 Hydraulic system

Contents

Specifications

Hydraulic fluid
Type .... Green LHM fluid (Duckhams LHM Fluid)

High pressure pump
Type .... Five piston volumetric
Operating speed .... Half engine speed
Output (per pump cycle) .... 4 cc

Pressure regulator
Cut-out pressure .... 170 ± 5 bar (2465 ± 72 lbf/in²)
Cut-in pressure .... 145 ± 5 bar (2103 ± 72 lbf/in²)

Accumulator
Capacity .... 0.40 litre (0.70 Imp pint)
Calibration pressure .... $62\,^{+2}_{-32}$ bar ($899\,^{+29}_{-464}$ lbf/in²)

Security valve
Slide valve return spring calibration pressures:
   Isolation pressure (min) .... 80 bar (1160 lbf/in²)
   Suspension supply pressure (min) .... 100 bar (1450 lbf/in²)

Torque wrench settings
Hydraulic pipe unions:

	kgf m	lbf ft
3.5 and 4.5 mm diameter pipes	0.8 to 0.9	5.8 to 6.6
6.0 mm diameter pipes	0.9 to 1.1	6.6 to 8.0

1 General description

1 The hydropneumatic suspension and the braking system are pressurized by a common hydraulic system. The hydraulic system is illustrated diagrammatically in Figs. 8.1 and 8.2.

2 Hydraulic fluid is drawn from the hydraulic reservoir, mounted on the right-hand wing valance, and delivered under pressure to the hydraulic pressure regulator mounted on the engine crankcase. The hydraulic system is pressurised by a belt-driven pump, which is mounted onto the engine unit and is driven by the crankshaft pulley.

3 From the pressure regulator fluid passes to the security valve which has pipe connections running to the compensator control valve and the front and rear suspension height corrector units.

4 Fluid from the suspension height corrector units (one at the front and one at the rear) flows to the suspension unit cylinders. From the suspension cylinders the low pressure return fluid is returned through pipelines to the hydraulic reservoir.

5 The height correctors maintain the hydropneumatic suspension at the manually selected height by admitting fluid to, and releasing fluid from, the suspension cylinders according to the movement of the front and rear anti-roll bars to which they are connected.

6 The four height positions can be selected by the manual height control within the vehicle. The normal driving position is with the lever set at the second setting position from the front. The most forward setting position is the minimum height setting and is for use during repair and overhaul procedures on the vehicle. It should not be used for

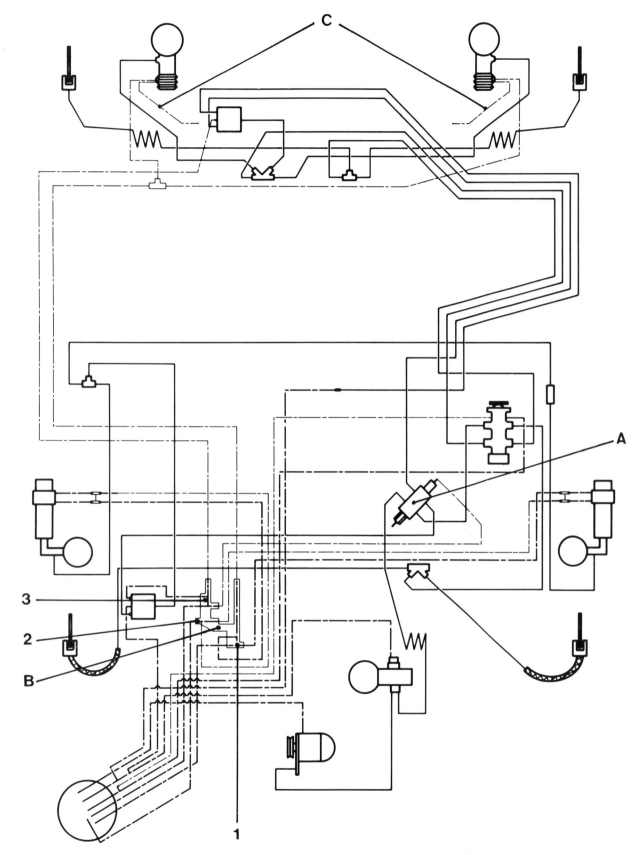

Fig. 8.1 Hydraulic system circuit diagram – manual steering models (Sec 1)

A   Security valve
B   Return pipes to reservoir (see 1 to 3)
C   Rear suspension vent line

1   Overflow return – front and rear suspension cylinders
2   Vent pipe – front suspension cylinders
3   Leakage from front and rear height correctors and security valve

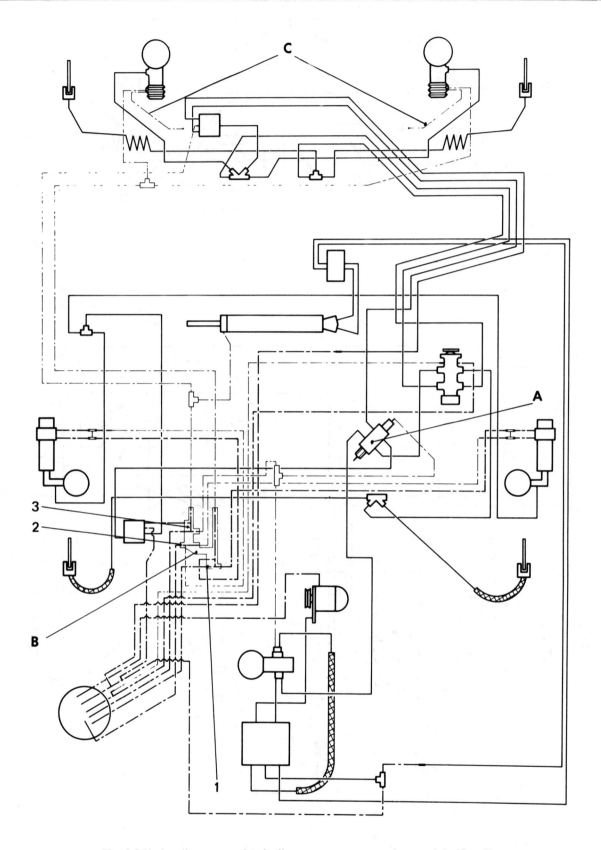

Fig. 8.2 Hydraulic system circuit diagram – power steering models (Sec 1)

A   Security valve
B   Return pipes to reservoir (see 1 to 3)
C   Rear suspension vent line

1   Overflow return – front and rear suspension cylinders
2   Vent pipe – front suspension cylinders
3   Leakage from front and rear height correctors and security valve

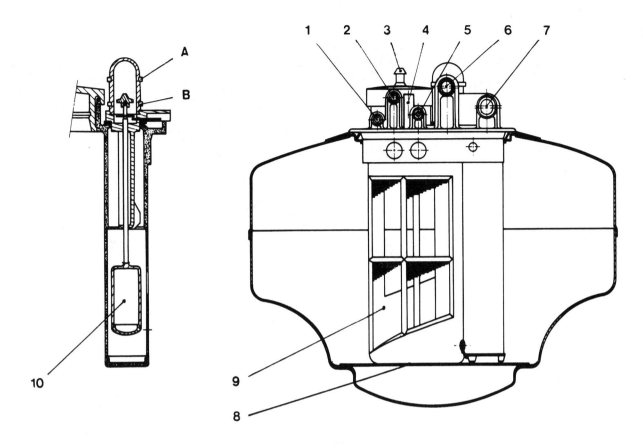

Fig. 8.3 Hydraulic system reservoir connections and components (Sec 1)

1   Front and rear suspension cylinders overflow return
2   Security valve and front/rear height correctors
3   Breather
4   Vent pipe – front suspension cylinders
5   Operational return/overflow return from brake control valve
6   Operational return from pressure regulator and height correctors

7   HP pump suction hose
8   Deflector
9   Filter
10 Fluid level indicator float with Maximum (A) and Minimum (B) marks

normal driving. The third setting position from the front raises the vehicle ride height to the intermediate setting. This is for use when traversing rough road conditions. The fourth setting position is when the lever is moved fully back and this raises the vehicle to its maximum height setting. Its primary use is to assist when changing the roadwheels and should not be selected when driving except under exceptional conditions such as negotiating undulating surfaces, but then only for short distances and at very low speeds.
7   Although the maximum height setting is a useful aid when undertaking inspection and repair tasks on the vehicle, it is essential that the vehicle is supported on safety stands when carrying out any service or repairs underneath the vehicle.
8   Hydraulic pressure for the braking system is supplied from the compensator control valve with separate front and rear circuits. The front circuit is supplied direct from the compensator control valve, whilst the rear brake circuits operate in conjunction with the hydraulic circuits to the rear suspension. This arrangement results in the braking effort being biased in favour of the front brakes, and at the same time regulates the braking effort on the rear wheels according to the load on the rear suspension – the heavier the load, the greater the pressure in the rear suspension, thus more braking effort.
9   Hydraulic pressure is released from the system by slackening the bleed screw on the pressure regulator. This allows the pressure fluid to bleed off to the reservoir (see Section 2, paragraph 5).
10 On power steering models a flow distributor is fitted between the HP pump and the pressure regulator unit. The purpose of the flow

distributor is to control the hydraulic pressure between the steering circuit and the suspension/brake circuits.

2   Hydraulic system and components – precautions

1   Cleanliness is of the utmost importance when working on the hydraulic system and its components. Clean all adjacent areas before disconnecting components, after removal blank off all orifices and ensure that components and pipes do not get contaminated.
2   Use only LHM mineral hydraulic fluid in the hydraulic system, the use of any other fluid will ruin the rubber rings and seals. LHM fluid is green in colour. Keep the fluid, carefully sealed, in its original container.
3   Use only genuine spare parts. Components are identified by painting or marking in green. All rubber parts are identified by their white or green colour and are of a special quality for use with LHM fluid.
4   Before starting work on the hydraulic system, the pressure must be released as follows:
5   With the engine switched off, place the manual height control lever in the 'low' (minimum) height position. Loosen the pressure regulator release screw one and a half turns, then wait for the vehicle to reach the low position. Only undo the regulator release screw by the specified amount, **do not** remove it (photo).

2.5 Pressure regulator unit (BX 16) showing the pressure release screw (arrowed)

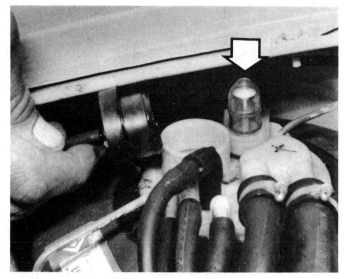

4.4 Filler cap removal from hydraulic fluid reservoir. Fluid level indicator location is arrowed

3 Routine maintenance – hydraulic system

Although relatively maintenance free the following checks and service procedures must be undertaken on the hydraulic system at the specified intervals.

1 **Hydraulic fluid level**: Check the fluid level in the hydraulic reservoir and if necessary top up the system, as described in Section 4.

2 **Fluid renewal and filter cleaning**: Renew the fluid and clean the filter at the specified intervals, as described in Section 5.

3 **General**: Periodically check the hydraulic system pipes and hoses for security and condition. Renew any that are defective, as described in Section 6.

4 Hydraulic fluid level – checking

1 With the engine idling, open the bonnet and locate the hydraulic fluid sight level indicator on the top of the reservoir located on the left-hand side of the bulkhead. The yellow indicator float must be between the two red rings with the ground clearance lever inside the vehicle fully rearwards in the maximum height position.

2 The difference between the maximum and minimum rings is approximately 0.45 litre (0.8 Imp pint).

3 Note that the fluid level indication is accurate only after the car has stabilised at the maximum height.

4 If topping-up is necessary, first clean the filler cap and the surrounding area, then remove the cap (photo).

5 Using genuine green LHM fluid, top-up the reservoir until the indicator reaches the upper red mark, then refit the cap and switch off the engine.

6 In an emergency, automatic transmission fluid (ATF), or SAE 10 or 20 engine oil, may be used *provided that the system is completely drained and fresh LHM fluid is substituted at the earliest opportunity.* However, care must be taken not to use an oil with any properties which would damage the rubber components of the system.

5 Hydraulic system – fluid renewal and filter cleaning

1 The LHM hydraulic fluid must be renewed at 36 000 mile (60 000 km) intervals. The reservoir and filters must be cleaned at the same time.

2 Move the ground clearance control lever inside the car fully to the minimum height position.

3 Loosen the pressure regulator bleed screw 1 to 1½ turns.

4 Spring back the reservoir cover retaining clip and release the cover and central block from the reservoir (photo).

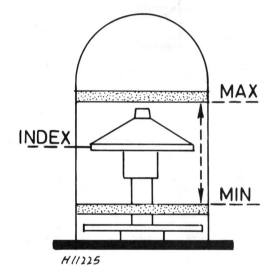

Fig. 8.4 LHM fluid level indicator located on the reservoir (Sec 4)

5 Remove the overflow and return filter and the supply filter from the central block.

6 Carefully lift the reservoir from the bulkhead and discard the fluid; also drain the high pressure pump supply pipe.

7 Remove the deflector plate from the bottom of the reservoir.

8 Clean the filters and reservoir with petrol and blow them dry with compressed air.

9 Refit the reservoir and deflector plate and fill it with 2.5 litres (4.4 Imp pints) of LHM hydraulic fluid. Reassemble the filters and clip the cover assembly onto the reservoir.

10 Disconnect the high pressure pump supply pipe from the reservoir cover central block and, using a small funnel, prime the pump with LHM hydraulic fluid.

11 Loosen the pressure regulator bleed screw 1 to 1½ turns (if it was retightened). Get an assistant to start the engine then, as it is started, quickly reconnect the high pressure pump supply pipe.

12 Grip the return pipe from the pressure regulator unit by hand and, as soon as it is felt to throb, retighten the bleed screw at the regulator.

13 When the vehicle height has stabilized, top up the fluid level in the reservoir so that the indicator is level with the upper (maximum) red ring level mark.

5.4 Hydraulic fluid level reservoir and central block retaining clip (arrowed)

6 Hydraulic pipes – removal and refitting

1 If at any time it is necessary to disconnect or remove any hydraulic pipeline in the suspension or braking circuits it is essential that the system pressure is first released. To release the pressure refer to Section 2, paragraph 5.

2 Before disconnecting the pipe concerned, thoroughly clean the union external surfaces.

3 If a complete pipe section is to be replaced, release the pipe from the retaining clips and/or clamps and bushings. Avoid distorting or damaging the pipe as it is withdrawn (photos).

4 If the pipe is not being replaced immediately, plug the union connections to prevent the ingress of dirt into the system.

5 To ensure that a perfect seal exists when hydraulic pipe joints are assembled, the following procedure must be carried out.

6 Clean the component port, hydraulic pipe, union nut and sealing rubber and lightly lubricate them with LHM fluid.

7 Slide the sealing rubber onto the end of the pipe until the pipe protrudes from it (photo).

8 Insert the pipe into the component so that the pipe end enters the central hole of the component port. The sealing rubber must enter its location hole fully. Check that the visible part of the pipe is located centrally in the component port.

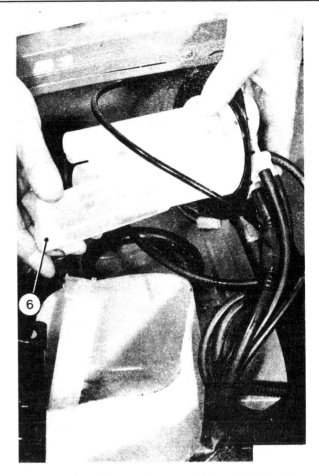

Fig. 8.5 Filter location in central block (6) (Sec 5)

9 Screw in the union nut by hand whilst keeping the hydraulic pipe stationary, then tighten it to the specified torque.

10 The pipe union is designed to provide increased sealing with increased fluid pressure. Tightening the nut more than the specified amount will not improve the seal, and may easily damage the pipe.

11 On completion, check that the hydraulic system pipes do not touch each other or any other component which may stress or chafe the pipes.

6.3A Hydraulic pipes and retaining clips which keep them correctly located

6.3B Hydraulic pipes and union connections – also secured by a clamp for security

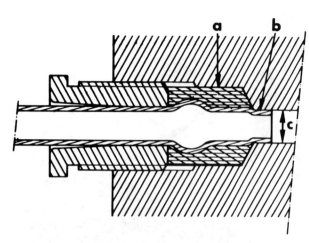

Fig. 8.6 Cross-section through a hydraulic pipe joint (Sec 6)

a   Sealing rubber   c   Union bore
b   Pipe

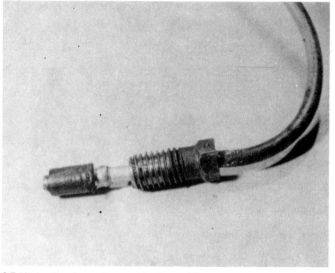

6.7 Hydraulic pipe union and sealing rubber

7   Hydraulic system – pressure checks

1   In order to carry out pressure checks on the hydraulic system a pressure gauge capable of measuring pressure from 0 to 250 bar (0 to 3625 lbf/in²) will be required. A suitable length of high pressure line will also be needed for attachment between the gauge and the operational pipe union on the pressure regulator; a gauge used to check injection pressure on diesel engines may be suitable.
2   Before making any checks, ensure that the hydraulic reservoir filters are clean (refer to Section 5) and also that the fluid level in the reservoir is correct.
3   Release the system pressure by loosening the bleed screw on the pressure regulator 1 to 1½ turns.
4   Disconnect the operational pipe from the pressure regulator by unscrewing the union nut. Move the pipe to one side and plug it to prevent the ingress of dirt.
5   Screw the pressure gauge pipe into the operational pipe port in the pressure regulator. Make the following checks in the order given.

Main accumulator pressure check

6   Tighten the pressure regulator bleed screw.
7   Disconnect the distributor-to-coil leads.
8   Get an assistant to spin the engine over on the starter motor. As the starter motor is operated check the pressure gauge needle reading; the pressure should gradually rise then stabilise within the calibration pressure readings given in the Specifications.
9   If the pressure is not within the specified limits the main accumulator is faulty.
10   Reconnect the ignition lead on completing this test.

Pressure regulator check

11   Loosen the bleed screw on the pressure regulator by 1 to 1½ turns.
12   Start the engine and run it at an increased idle speed, then retighten the pressure regulator bleed screw and observe the increase in pressure. When the pressure gauge needle stabilises, the cut-out pressure is reached and this should be within the pressure range specified.
13   Allow the engine to run at idle speed for a short period to allow the pressure to stabilise then switch off the engine and note the drop in pressure over a period of three minutes; if this exceeds 10 bar (14.5 lbf/in²) the regulator is faulty.
14   Start the engine again and run it at an increased idle speed then, when the cut-in occurs, loosen the pressure regulator bleed screw 1 to 1½ turns. The pressure reading should gradually fall then rise as the HP pump becomes operational. The minimum pressure reading taken should correspond to the cut-in pressure specified.
15   If the cut-out or cut-in pressure readings taken are incorrect then the regulator is faulty.

16   On completion, switch off the engine, release the system pressure and detach the pressure gauge. Remove the plug from the operational pipe and reconnect it to the pressure regulator unit.

8   Pressure regulator unit – removal and refitting

1   Release the system pressure by loosening the pressure bleed screw by 1 to 1½ turns on the pressure regulator unit. Allow the vehicle to drop to its fully lowered position.
2   Wipe clean the pressure regulator unit and the pipe connections in particular.
3   Loosen the retaining clip and detach the return pipe hose from the regulator. Plug the hose and position it out of the way.
4   Undo the union nuts and detach the two rigid pipes from the pressure regulator; plug them to prevent the ingress of dirt (photo).
5   Undo the two retaining bolts and the support bracket nut. Support the regulator unit as the bolts and nuts are removed and withdraw the regulator unit. Note the position of the hose location wire under the lower bolt head.
6   Refitting is a reversal of the removal procedure. Ensure that the connecting pipe connections are thoroughly clean before connecting them.

8.4 Disconnecting the rigid pipes from the pressure regulator. Note the plug inserted into the vacated port (arrow)

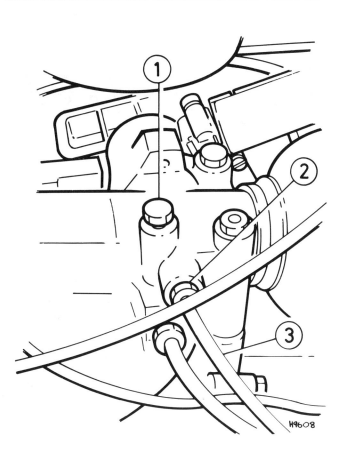

Fig. 8.7 Pressure regulator (Sec 8)

1   *Pressure release (bleed) screw*
2   *Union connector – operational pipe to pressure regulator*
3   *Operational pipe*

7   On completion top up the hydraulic fluid level in the reservoir and prise the HP pump with reference to Section 5, paragraph 10 on.

9 High pressure (HP) pump – removal and refitting

1   Release the pressure in the hydraulic system as described in Section 2, paragraph 5.
2   Wipe clean the pump and its pipe connections.
3   Disconnect the pump supply pipe from the inlet port and drain the fluid into a suitable container. If a roll type clip is fitted, remove it and obtain a screw type (worm drive) clip (photo).
4   Unscrew the high pressure output pipe from the pump (photo).
5   Loosen the drivebelt tension and disengage the drivebelt from the pump pulley.
6   Undo the two retaining bolts and withdraw the pump.
7   Refitting is a reversal of the removal procedure. Adjust the drivebelt tension, as described in Section 10.
8   When the pump is refitted and the hoses connected, prime the pump, as described in Section 5, paragraph 10 on.

10 High pressure (HP) pump drivebelt – removal, refitting and adjustment

1   On BX 16 and BX 19 models remove the alternator drivebelt, as described in Section 9 of Chapter 12.
2   Loosen the HP pump drivebelt jockey wheel mounting and adjuster bolts then pivot the jockey wheel inwards towards the engine to release the drivebelt tension (photo).

9.3 HP pump showing the supply and output pipe connections

9.4 Detach the output pipe. Pump retaining bolts arrowed

10.2 HP pump drivebelt jockey wheel mounting and adjuster bolts (arrowed) – BX 16 model

3   Remove the drivebelt from the HP pump and associate pulleys.
4   Refit in the reverse order to removal. When the belt is fitted onto the pulleys, set the tension by pivoting the jockey pulley outwards as much as possible by hand to take up any play in the belt on its longest run between pulleys. If any form of leverage is employed to achieve this tension great care must be taken not to damage any fittings. Tighten the jockey pulley mounting/adjuster bolt to set the tension. When the jockey wheel position is set, the belt tension must be felt to be taut under a reasonable thumb pressure at the midway point between the pulleys on its longest run. Note, however, that the belt tension must not be tightened excessively or the belt life will be short and damage to the pulleys and their drive bearings could result. Recheck the tension of a new belt after a nominal mileage has been covered.
5   Refit the alternator drivebelt and adjust its tension in a similar manner, as described in Chapter 12.

11 Security valve – removal and refitting

1   The security valve is located on the lower left-hand side of the front subframe, behind the steering gear (photo).
2   Loosen the pressure regulator bleed screw (Section 2, paragraph 5).
3   Disconnect the rubber overflow return pipe from the end of the valve.
4   Unscrew the union nuts securing the inlet and outlet pipes to the security valve, making a careful note of their location.
5   Disconnect the supply wire from the pressure switch terminal.

6   Unscrew and remove the mounting bolt and withdraw the valve. Where a brake limiter is fitted, this is also detached at the same time.
7   Refitting is a reversal of removal. Tighten the pressure regulator bleed screw when the pipes and wire are connected.

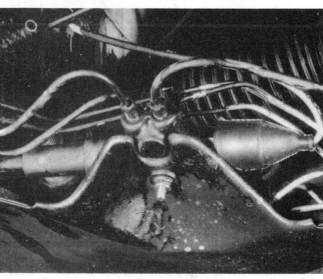

11.1 Security valve location

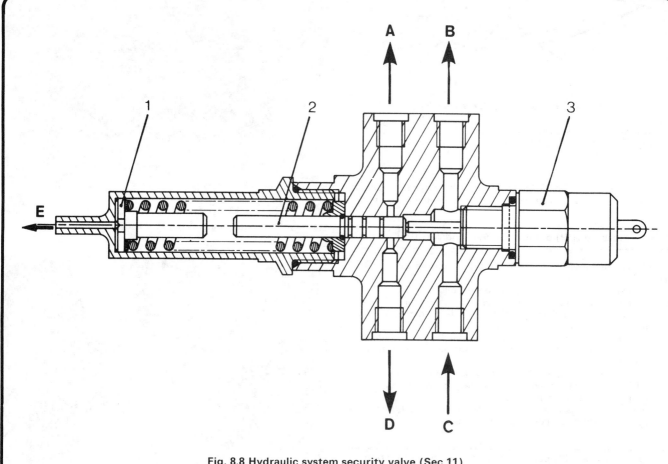

Fig. 8.8 Hydraulic system security valve (Sec 11)

A   Front height corrector supply pipe connection
B   Brake control valve supply pipe connection
C   Intake pipe connection from HP pump
D   Rear height corrector supply pipe connection
E   Security valve leakage return pipe connection

1   Adjustment shims
2   Slide valve
3   Fault detector (pressure) switch

12 Fault diagnosis – hydraulic system

Symptom	Reason(s)
Loss of hydraulic pressure	Reservoir filters blocked Pump supply pipe leaking Pressure regulator faulty Pump faulty or drivebelt broken Pressure regulator bleed screw loose
Excessive hydraulic pressure	Pressure regulator faulty
Loss of suspension pressure	Safety valve faulty Height corrector faulty Suspension cylinders faulty Height adjustment incorrect (see Chapter 10)
Loss of brake pressure	Brake valve faulty (see also Chapter 9)

Chapter 9 Braking system

For modifications, and information applicable to later models, see Supplement at end of manual

Contents

Specifications

System type

Main brakes	Discs all round, dual hydraulic circuit supplied by main hydraulic system, automatic rear brake limitation. Front pad wear warning system
Handbrake	Cable operation to front wheel discs

Front brakes

Disc diameter	266 mm (10.5 in)
Disc thickness:	
New	10 mm (0.39 in)
Wear limit	7 mm (0.28 in)
Maximum disc run-out	0.2 mm (0.008 in)
Minimum pad lining thickness..............................	Indicated by warning lamp

Rear brakes

Disc diameter	224 mm (8.8 in)
Disc thickness:	
New	7 mm (0.28 in)
Wear limit	4 mm (0.16 in)
Maximum disc run-out	0.2 mm (0.008 in)
Minimum pad lining thickness	2 mm (0.08 in) – suggested

Pedal

Brake pedal-to-compensator valve clearance:	
1st type	1.0 to 3.0 mm (0.04 to 0.12 in)
2nd type	0.1 to 1.0 mm (0.004 to 0.04 in)

Torque wrench settings

	kgf m	lbf ft
Compensator control valve	1.8	13.0
Rear brake disc screws	4.5	32.5
Rear caliper bolts	4.5	32.5
Front caliper bolt	11.0	79.5

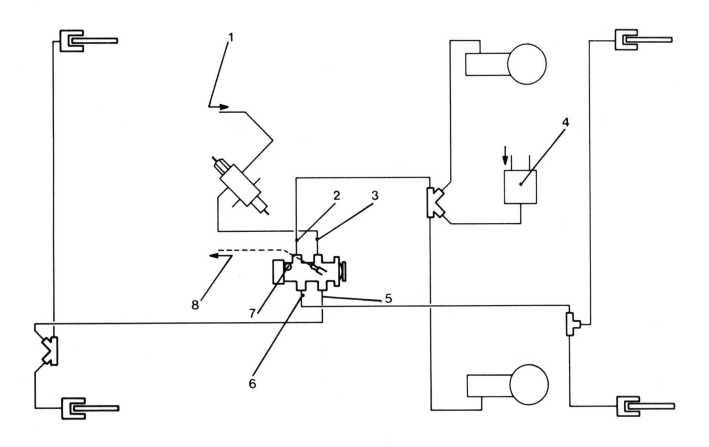

Fig. 9.1 Brake system circuit diagram (Sec 1)

1 High pressure source
2 Rear suspension pressure
3 High pressure to front brakes
4 Rear suspension height corrector
5 Front brakes pressure supply
6 Rear brakes pressure supply
7 Compensator bleed servo
8 Return to reservoir

1 General description

1 The dual circuit braking system, with disc brakes fitted to all four wheels, is hydraulically operated from the main hydraulic system. The front brakes are supplied from the hydraulic pressure regulator and the rear brakes are supplied from the rear suspension system. This arrangement favours the front brakes and imposes a braking effort limitation on the rear axle in relation to the load. The braking action is applied through the brake pedal operating a hydraulic control valve which allows pressure to the braking system.

2 The front disc pads are equipped with internal electric leads which operate a warning lamp on the instrument panel when the linings are due for renewal.

3 The front brake calipers comprise outer halves which are removable, and inner halves which are integral with the steering knuckles. The rear disc.pads and brake calipers are mounted on the rear suspension arms; these pads do not incorporate a warning system.

4 The handbrake is operated by a floor mounted lever and flexible cables run to and operate each front caliper to force the friction pads against the discs.

2 Routine maintenance

The following maintenance checks must be made to the brake system at the mileage intervals specified at the front of this manual.

1 Visually check the thickness of the brake friction pad linings. If worn down to or beyond the minimum allowable thickness they must be renewed without delay. When renewing the brake pads always fit new pads to both calipers on each axle (Sections 3 and 4).

2 Check and if necessary adjust the handbrake (Section 9).

3 Check the brake discs for signs of excessive wear, damage or deep scoring of the friction surfaces. Renew if necessary (Section 5).

4 Inspect the brake hydraulic system for signs of damage or corrosion and renew any sections which are suspect or defective (Section 13).

3 Disc pads (front) – renewal

1 The front disc pads must be renewed when they are worn down to the specified wear limit. The pad wear warning lamp will indicate that the front brake pads have worn down to this point. The pads must be renewed as a set.

2 Chock the rear roadwheels, jack up the front of the vehicle and support it on axle stands. Remove the front roadwheels.

3 Release the handbrake and turn the steering so that the brake caliper is facing out.

4 Disconnect the pad wear warning lamp wires from the wiring loom and the outer wire from the spring clip eyes (photos).

5 Using pliers, grip and extract the pin locating the lock plate then withdraw the lock plate (photos). Pressing down on the pad plates at the lower end will ease removal of the locking plate.

6 Each pad, together with its spring clip, can now be withdrawn from the caliper unit (photo).

7 The caliper piston must now be moved back into its cylinder to allow room for the new pads. To do this turn it in a clockwise direction

3.4A Disconnect the pad wear warning leads ...

3.4B ... and pull the wire from the spring clip eyes. Note pad wear indicator studs (arrowed)

3.5A Extract the lock plate pin ...

3.5B ... and withdraw the lock plate

3.6 Removing a front brake pad

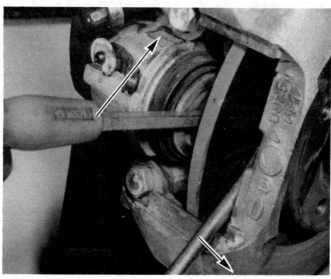

3.7 Method used to move the caliper piston back into its cylinder

whilst simultaneously applying pressure to it. To rotate the piston, engage a screwdriver with a 7 mm square shaft into the groove in the piston end face. Insert a second screwdriver or suitable lever between the disc outer face and the caliper frame and lever it outwards, but take care not to apply pressure on the disc friction surface (photo).

8   Remove any dust or dirt from the disc pad recesses in the caliper taking care not to inhale the dust.

9   As mentioned previously, if renewing the brake pads it is important that all four front pads are renewed at the same time.

10   Locate the springs onto each pad.

11   Set the piston position so that the pad engagement slot is aligned correctly as shown in Fig. 9.2.

12   Fit the brake pads into position, together with their springs (photo).

13   Slide the lock plate into position and insert the retaining pin.

14   If new brake pads have been fitted, check that a 1 mm clearance exists between the disc and pads. If required adjust the piston position accordingly (Fig. 9.4). Note that this clearance is to allow the handbrake self-adjusting mechanism to operate correctly, and is **not** the normal running clearance between the pads and disc.

15   Pass the outer pad wear indicator wire through the pad spring eyes, through the insulation sleeve, together with the inner pad wire, and reconnect them to the wiring loom connector (photo).

16   On completion, refit the roadwheel(s) and lower the vehicle to the ground.

17   Avoid harsh braking as far as possible for a few hundred miles to allow the new pads to bed in.

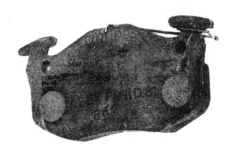

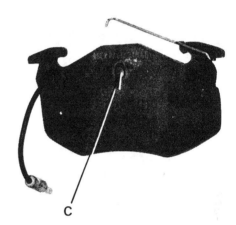

Fig. 9.2 Piston alignment position with identification mark (a) above (or below) the piston groove (b) (Sec 3)

Fig. 9.3 Pad peg (c) must engage in piston groove when fitted (Sec 3)

Pad springs correctly fitted

3.12 Brake pads and springs refitted

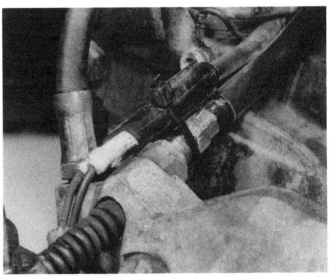

3.15 Reconnect the pad wear wiring and locate as shown

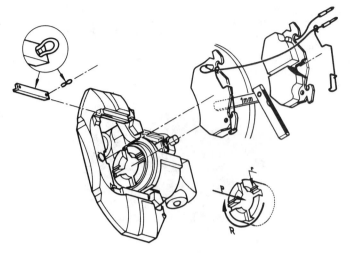

Fig. 9.4 Front brake pads reassembly – check clearance between the disc and pad with feeler gauges (Sec 3)

4 Disc pads (rear) – renewal

1   The rear disc pads must be inspected for wear at the intervals specified in Routine Maintenance.
2   Apply the handbrake, jack-up the rear of the car and support it on axle stands. Remove the roadwheel.
3   Unscrew and remove the retaining bolt and withdraw the disc pad cover from the caliper (photo).
4   Remove the spring clip and pull out the two disc pads with a pair of pliers (photos).
5   Brush any accumulated dust and dirt from the disc pads and caliper recesses, taking care not to inhale the dust.
6   Examine the disc pads for wear; if the friction material thickness is less than the specified minimum the pads must be renewed. Note that the rear disc pads must always be renewed in sets of four.
7   If new pads are to be fitted, the caliper pistons must be retracted to accommodate the extra friction material. To do this, partially insert the old pads, then lever them apart to depress the pistons.
8   Fit the new disc pads with the friction surfaces towards the disc.
9   Locate the spring clip with the crossbar at the bottom of the caliper and retain it in position with the through-bolt (photo).
10 Refit the disc pad cover and tighten the bolt.
11 Refit the roadwheel and lower the car to the ground.

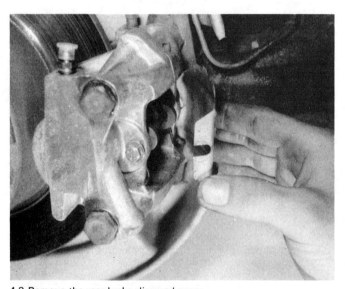

4.3 Remove the rear brake disc pad cover ...

4.4A ... withdraw the spring retainer clip ...

4.4B ... to extract the brake outer pad ...

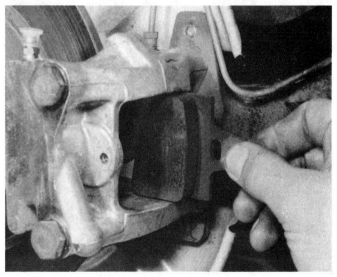

4.4C ... and inner pad

4.9 Locating the through-bolt

5 Brake disc – removal and refitting

Front disc

1   Remove the brake pads, as described in Section 3.
2   Unscrew and remove the disc-to-hub retaining screws and withdraw the disc.
3   Clean and examine the disc for deep scoring or grooving. Light scoring is normal, but if it is severe the disc must be refaced by a competent engineering works or, if worn to the specified wear limit, it must be renewed.
4   Check the disc for run-out to determine whether it is distorted or buckled. To do this accurately, a dial gauge will be necessary, but if this is not available, feeler blades can be used against a fixed block as the disc is rotated slowly. Do not confuse wear in the hub bearings with disc run-out. To check the disc run-out, refit it to the wheel hub and fully tighten the retaining screws. The mating surfaces of the hub and disc must be perfectly clean or a false reading could be given.
5   Refit in the reverse order to removal. Ensure that no oil or grease come into contact with the disc or pads during assembly.

Rear disc

6   Remove the brake pads, as described in Section 4.
7   Reinsert the pad/spring retaining bolt and tighten the securing nut to close the half calipers together.
8   Unscrew and remove the two caliper retaining bolts.
9   Undo the disc-to-hub retaining screw. Withdraw the disc and simultaneously raise the caliper unit a fraction to allow the disc to be renewed.
10 Clean and inspect the disc as described in paragraphs 3 and 4.
11 Prior to refitting the disc, check that the mating faces of both the disc and the hub are clean and smear the mating faces and the

Fig. 9.5 Front brake disc removal (Sec 5)

Fig. 9.6 Rear brake disc removal showing nut and pad/spring bolt (1 and 5), caliper bolts (4) and disc screw (7) (Sec 5)

Fig. 9.7 Rear brake disc removal (Sec 5)

retaining screw threads with grease. Do not allow any grease to contact the disc friction surfaces.

12 Refit in the reverse order to removal. Tighten the caliper retaining bolts and the disc retaining screw to the specified torque settings.

6 Front brake caliper unit – removal and refitting

1 Loosen the front roadwheel bolts on the side concerned, place chocks against the rear wheels, then raise and support the vehicle at the front so that the roadwheels are clear of the ground.

2 Remove the roadwheel bolts and withdraw the roadwheels.

3 Loosen the pressure release screw on the hydraulic pressure regulator unit by 1 to $^1/_2$ turns. Set the ground clearance height control lever to the 'low' position.

4 Unscrew and detach the rigid brake line from the bracket union on the inner wheel arch (photo). Plug the exposed pipe and union port to prevent fluid loss and the ingress of dirt.

5 Detach the flexible hose from the locating bracket by pulling the retaining plate free, then disconnect the hose from the support lug forward of the suspension strut.

6 Detach the brake pad wear leads from the main harness connector on the top face of the caliper unit.

7 Fully release the handbrake then disconnect the handbrake cable from the operating lever at the caliper.

8 Unbolt and remove the deflector plate.

9 Undo the two retaining bolts (on the inner face) and remove the caliper unit, together with the plate.

10 Refitting is a reversal of the removal procedure, but note the following special points:

  (a) Tighten the retaining bolts to the specified torque setting
  (b) Ensure that the brake hose is correctly located and secured in the location brackets. When reconnecting the rigid supply pipe use a new seal sleeve

  (c) On completion bleed the brakes, as described in Section 14, then refit the roadwheel and lower the vehicle
  (d) Remove the chocks from the rear roadwheels and check that the handbrake operates in a satisfactory manner

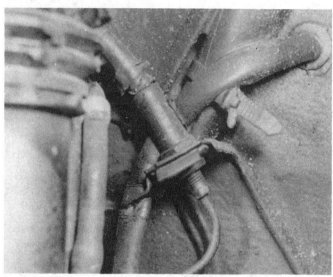

6.4 Rigid brake line connection under front wheel arch

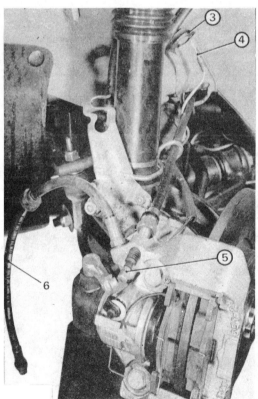

Fig. 9.8 Front caliper unit removal (Sec 6)

  3 Plate
  4 Hydraulic supply pipe (rigid)
  5 Handbrake cable
  6 Hydraulic supply hose (flexible)

Fig. 9.9 Front brake caliper deflector (1) and retaining bolt
(2) (Sec 6)

7 Front brake caliper unit – overhaul

1   Remove the caliper unit, as described in the previous Section, then clean it externally, but avoid breathing in any brake dust.
2   Remove the brake pads, as described in Section 3.
3   Before dismantling the brake unit, check that the following repair kits are available, depending on the extent of the overhaul:

   (a) *Piston seal replacement kit*
   (b) *Handbrake control repair kit*
   (c) *Caliper sliding mechanism repair kit*

4   A sectional view of the caliper is shown in Fig. 9.10. If the control mechanism is to be dismantled it will be necessary to obtain Citroën tool 228-T.
5   Prise free and remove the piston outer seal, then apply **low** air pressure (eg from a foot pump) through the fluid inlet pipe aperture to eject the piston. Catch the piston in a cloth to prevent damaging it as it is removed.
6   Prise free the inner seal from the cylinder.
7   Inspect the cylinder walls and the piston for signs of damage or excessively deep score marks. If such damage is apparent renew the caliper unit.
8   To remove the automatic handbrake control mechanism, prise free the rubber cover and withdraw it from the handbrake cable fork arm.
9   Unscrew and remove the brake bleed screw and remove the protective cover.
10 Extract the retaining circlip from the exposed end of the handbrake pivot arm.

11 Locate the compression tool 228-T as shown (Fig. 9.13) and compress the dished spring washers. Withdraw the handbrake cable pivot arm.
12 Remove the compression tool then withdraw the peg, spring, piston locater/adjuster dished spring washers and flat washer.
13 Withdraw the caliper sliding bushes and prise free the rubber gaiters.
14 Clean the caliper body thoroughly before reassembling. On the extent of the dismantling, new repair kits must always be used during reassembly.
15 Relocate the sliding mechanism gaiters (using the new ones from the kit) then lubricate the bushes with grease from the sachet supplied and push them into position. Check that they are correctly located.
16 Locate the new dished spring washers into position on the piston locater/adjuster, together with the flat washer. The washers must be orientated as shown in Fig. 9.17.
17 Lubricate the locater/adjuster with LHM fluid, then fit it into position in the caliper body, passing it through the lower washer. The end slot must be orientated as shown in Fig. 9.18. Locate the spring and peg, and fit the compression tool (228-T) into position as during dismantling.
18 Locate the new cover onto the handbrake pivot arm and invert it so that it is folded over the cable lever arm to allow fitting.
19 With the dished spring washers held under compression, insert the handbrake pivot arm and position it so that the peg engages with the ratchet, as shown in Fig. 9.19, and the spring end engages as shown in Fig. 9.20. Prise the spring down to engage it in the lip of the ratchet.
20 Locate the circlip into the groove in the exposed section of the pivot arm to secure it.

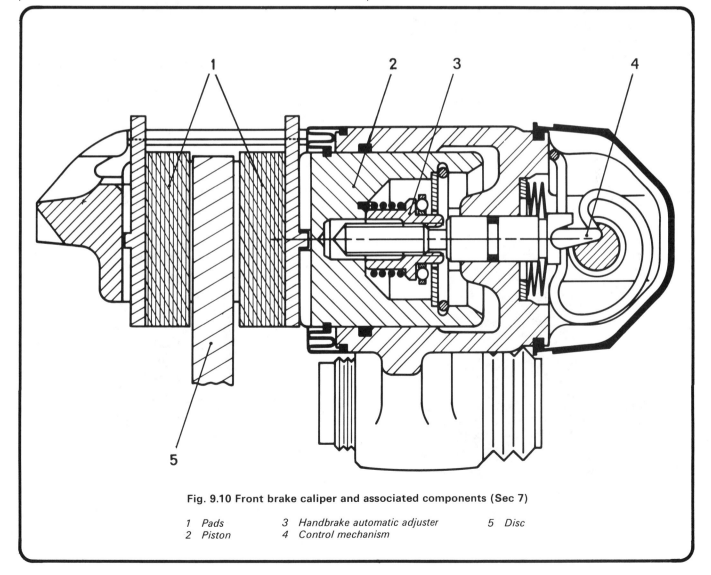

Fig. 9.10 Front brake caliper and associated components (Sec 7)

1 *Pads*   3 *Handbrake automatic adjuster*   5 *Disc*
2 *Piston*   4 *Control mechanism*

21 Lubricate the pivot arm and adjuster mechanism with grease from the sachet in the repair kit, then fold over the protective rubber cover and engage it in the caliper body groove.

22 Lubricate the cylinder wall and the piston with LHM fluid. Similarly lubricate and fit the inner piston seal into position in its groove in the cylinder wall. Check that when fitted it is not distorted.

23 Press and screw the piston into position so that, when fitted, the horizontal groove is in line with the bleed screw. To rotate the piston,

engage a scewdriver with a 7 mm square shaft into the piston groove in the end face.

24 Lubricate the outer seal with brake grease from the sachet and then fit it into position. When fitted check that it is fully engaged and not distorted.

25 Refit the bleed screw and protector.

26 Refit the brake pads, as described in Section 3, and the caliper unit, as described in Section 6.

Fig. 9.11 Piston removal from caliper (Sec 7)

Fig. 9.12 Prise free the cylinder inner seal (Sec 7)

Fig. 9.13 Using special tool to compress the dished
spring washers (Sec 7)

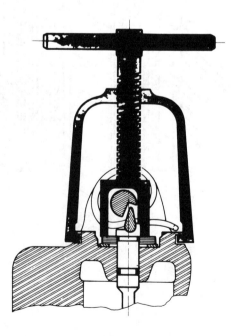

Fig. 9.14 Sectional view showing how the special tool
(228-T) is fitted (Sec 7)

217

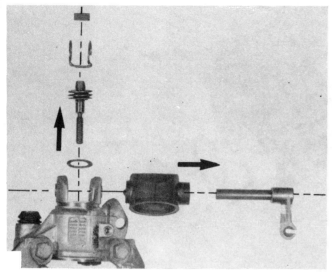

Fig. 9.15 Remove these handbrake components (Sec 7)

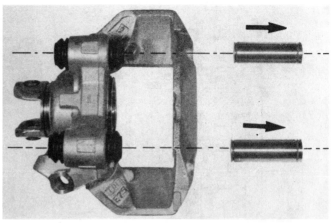

Fig. 9.16 Remove the caliper sliding bushes and gaiters (Sec 7)

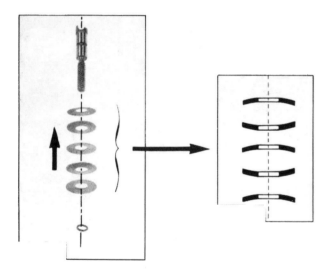

Fig. 9.17 Washer orientation (Sec 7)

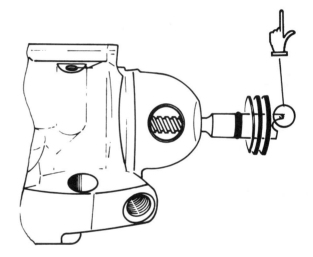

Fig. 9.18 Correct fitting position of the locator/adjuster in the caliper (Sec 7)

Fig. 9.19 Engage the peg with the ratchet (Sec 7)

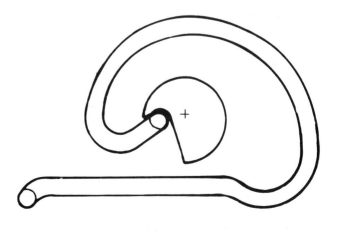

Fig. 9.20 Engage the spring end with the ratchet (Sec 7)

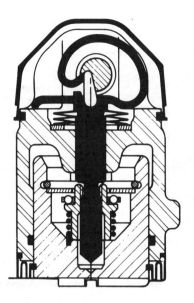

Fig. 9.21 Sectional view showing the caliper, piston and automatic handbrake adjustment components (Sec 7)

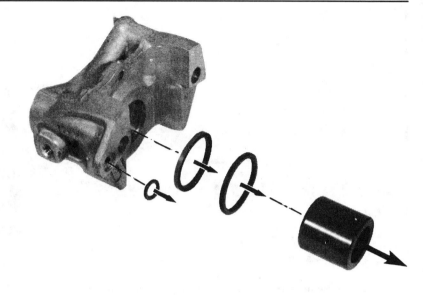

Fig. 9.22 Rear brake caliper piston and seals removal (Sec 8)

8 Rear brake caliper unit – removal, overhaul and refitting

1 Loosen the rear roadwheel bolts, check that the handbrake is fully applied, then place chocks against the front roadwheels.

2 Raise the rear of the vehicle and support it with safety stands. Remove the rear roadwheel(s).

3 Loosen the pressure release screw on the hydraulic pressure regulator unit by 1 to 1¹/₂ turns. Set the ground clearance height control to the 'low' position.

4 Clean the hydraulic pipe union to caliper connection then unscrew and detach the pipe at the union. Plug the pipe to prevent the ingress of dirt.

5 Undo the caliper retaining bolts and withdraw the caliper unit.

6 Remove the pads, as described in Section 4, and separate the two halves of the caliper unit.

7 To remove the pistons, apply **low** air pressure (eg from a foot pump) through the hydraulic pipe connection port whilst holding a piece of rag over the piston face to catch and cushion the piston in as it is ejected from its bore.

8 Clean the caliper and piston components. If, on inspection, the cylinder bore or piston is badly scored, damaged or corroded then the caliper unit must be renewed.

9 Note the position of the seals and their orientation before removing them. These must always be renewed.

10 Reassemble the caliper in the reverse order to removal. Lubricate each part as it is fitted with LHM fluid and ensure absolute cleanliness.

11 Compress the pistons back into their bores to ease fitting of the brake pads.

12 Tighten the retaining bolts to the specified torque and, on completion, bleed the brakes, as described in Section 14, before refitting the roadwheel and lowering the vehicle to the ground.

9 Handbrake cable – removal, refitting and adjustment

1 Position chocks against the rear roadwheels, loosen the front roadwheel bolts, raise the front of the vehicle and support on safety stands. Remove the front roadwheels.

2 Working inside the vehicle, prise free the rear cubby from the centre console. Reach through the cubby aperture and undo the console retaining bolt at the rear.

3 Remove the rubber bung and unscrew and remove the console retaining bolt at the front. Lift the console clear, disconnecting any switch wires as necessary.

4 Release the handbrake then, at the caliper end of the cable, unhook the cable from the link road.

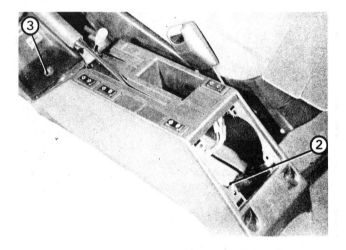

Fig. 9.23 Handbrake console retaining screw positions (2 and 3) (Sec 9)

5 Back inside the vehicle, pull the cable and disengage it from the compensator.

6 Withdraw the cable, passing it through the various location guides in the body.

7 Refit in the reverse order of removal. As the cable is fitted pass it through the guides in the following order.

    (a) Cable swivel guide
    (b) Cable wheel arch guide
    (c) Cable scuttle panel guide
    (d) Cable exhaust screen guide

8 When the cable is refitted and hooked onto the compensator, check that the sheath stop is correctly positioned in its housing.

9 Lubricate the link rod and compensator cable connections, but take care not to get grease onto the brake disc. Also lubricate the cable/wheel arch guide.

10 Check that the handbrake operates in a satisfactory manner and if required adjust as described below.

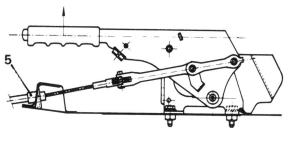

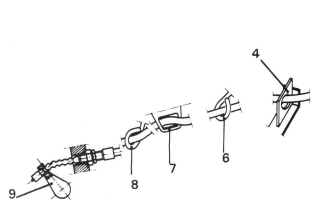

Fig. 9.24 Handbrake cable attachment and location points (Sec 9)

4 Cable guide on exhaust screen
5 Sheath stop
6 Scuttle panel guide
7 Wheel arch guide
8 Swivel arm guide
9 Connection to link rod

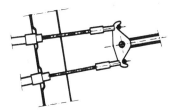

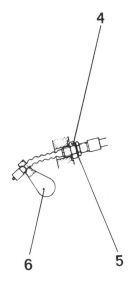

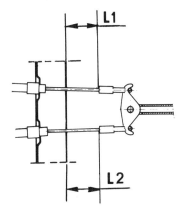

Fig. 9.26 Check cables at compensator for equal adjustment (Sec 9)

Distances at L1 and L2 to be equal (within 1.5 mm)

Fig. 9.25 Handbrake cable adjustment at the link rod end (Sec 9)

4 Adjuster nut   5 Locknut   6 Lever

Handbrake adjustment
11 Handbrake adjustment is automatic, being taken up when the handbrake travel reaches 12 to 15 notches.
12 Adjustment is possible after a new cable has been fitted by depressing the brake pedal and bringing the pads into contact with the discs. Release the pedal then move the handbrake lever to the 4th notch position.
13 Adjustment is now made at the link rod end of the cable. Loosen the locknut and turn the adjuster nut in the required direction to bring the lever (on the side being adjusted) into contact with the cam. Tighten the locknut.
14 Repeat the procedure with the cable to the other front wheel brake then check that the cable compensator is equalised, see Figs. 9.25 and 9.26.
15 Check that, when the handbrake is released, the pads do not contact the disc, irrespective of steering position. Tighten the locknuts then operate the handbrake several times to ensure that the handbrake is satisfactory. Refit the roadwheels and the console inside the car.
16 Lower the vehicle, apply the handbrake and remove the rear wheel chocks.

10 Brake compensator control valve – removal and refitting

1 Raise the vehicle at the front end and support it on safety stands. Chock the rear wheels.
2 Move the ground clearance control lever to the front ('low' position) then unscrew the hydraulic system pressure regulator bleed screw 1 to 1½ turns. Operate the brake pedal a few times to release the pressure.
3 Clean the control valve and the hydraulic pipe connections then identify each pipe before detachment from the valve to ensure correct reassembly (photo).
4 Unscrew the union nuts and pull the pipes clear of the brake compensator control valve.
5 Disconnect the overflow and return pipes from the brake compensator control valve.
6 Working from within the car, unscrew the retaining bolts at the bulkhead (directly in front of the brake/pedal assembly) then withdraw and remove the brake compensator control valve.
7 If the internal slide valves are worn, the brake valve must be renewed. If only the seals are worn, they can be removed separately. Check with a Citroën garage before removing the old seals. Dismantling is straightforward as can be seen from Fig. 9.27, but note that there are several different types of brake valve and identification is by various paint marks on the valve. The return outlet is located in different positions on the various types.

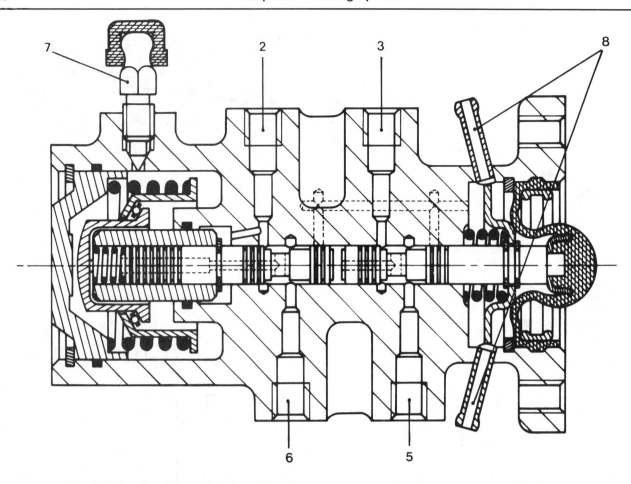

Fig. 9.27 Sectional view of the brake compensator control valve showing connections (Sec 10)

2   Rear suspension pressure line (from 4-way union)
3   High pressure connection to front brakes (from security valve)
5   Operating pressure to front brakes

6   Operating pressure to rear brakes
7   Bleed screw
8   Reservoir return

10.3 Brake compensator control valve and connections

8   Refitting is a reversal of removal, but bleed the braking system, as described in Section 14. Make sure that the pressure regulator bleed screw is tightened before using the car on the road.
9   On completion, check that the pedal-to-operating rod clearance is as specified according to type (Figs. 9.28 and 9.29). If adjustment is necessary proceed as described in Section 11.

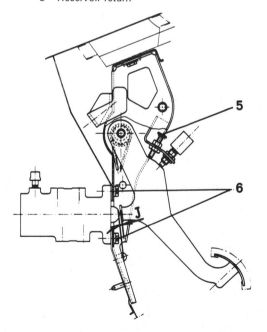

Fig. 9.28 Footbrake pedal adjustment – type 1 pedal (Secs 10 and 11)

5   Pedal adjustment stop screw
6   Brake compensator retaining bolts
J = 1.0 to 3.0 mm

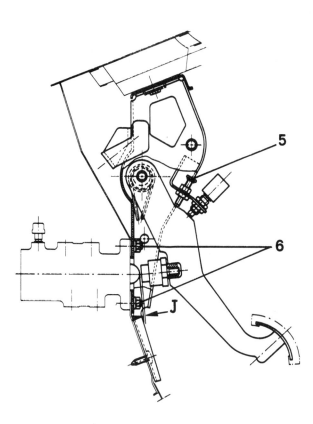

13 Hoses and brake lines – maintenance

1   Regularly inspect the condition of the flexible hydraulic hoses. If they are perished, chafed or swollen they must be renewed.
2   When fitting a flexible hose, make sure that it is not twisted, or touching any other components which may chafe or damage it.
3   The brake lines should be wiped clean regularly and examined for signs of corrosion or denting by flying stones. Examine the support clips to make sure that they are not causing wear to the line surface.
4   Check that the brake lines are not touching any adjacent components or rubbing against any part of the vehicle. Where this is observed, gently bend the line as necessary.
5   If a brake line is damaged or corroded it must be renewed immediately. Further details concerning hydraulic line replacements are given in Section 6 of Chapter 8.
6   After fitting a new hose or brake line, the braking system must be bled, as described in Section 14.

14 Brake hydraulic system – bleeding

1   The brake hydraulic system must be bled after renewing and refitting any components, brake line, or hose; if this procedure is not carried out, air will be trapped in the circuit and the brakes will not function correctly.
2   Before starting work, check all the brake lines, unions, hoses and connections for possible leakage.
3   If there is any possibility of fluid other than genuine LHM fluid being in the system, drain the complete hydraulic system, as described in Chapter 8, and fill it with the special rinsing solution obtainable from Citroën. Bleed the system and leave the solution in the circuit for approximately 600 miles (1000 km), then drain it out and fill with LHM fluid. If the rubber seals are damaged by the incorrect fluid, it will also be necessary to renew these items at the same time.
4   The brake bleeding procedure for the front and rear brakes differs, the procedures and requirements being given separately below.

Front brakes
5   When bleeding the front brakes there must be no pressure in the hydraulic system, therefore undo the release screw by 1 to $1^1/2$ turns on the pressure regulator (engine switched off).
6   You will now need two lengths of bleed tubing long enough to connect over the caliper bleed screws at one end, and to the reservoir at the other. The tubes must be transparent and clean.
7   Get an assistant to sit in the vehicle and depress the brake pedal.
8   Loosen the front brake bleed screws and restart the engine. Run the engine at idle speed and then, with the brake pedal still depressed, tighten the pressure regulator relief screw.
9   When the fluid flowing through each bleed hose to the reservoir shows no signs of air bubbles, retighten the bleed screws, and release the brake pedal.
10 Switch off the engine and detach the bleed tubes from the calipers.

Rear brakes
11 The rear brakes draw their hydraulic fluid from the rear suspension system circuit and therefore, when bleeding the rear brakes, the circuit must be under pressure.
12 Check that the handbrake is fully applied and chock the front roadwheels.
13 Loosen the rear roadwheel bolts then raise and support the rear of the vehicle using safety stands. Remove the rear roadwheels.
14 Clean each rear brake bleed nipple then attach a length of transparent and clean hose to the nipple on each side. Place the free end of each hose into a clean container.
15 Allow the pressure in the rear suspension to drop, then move the height control lever within the vehicle fully rearwards to the 'high' position.
16 Get an assistant to sit in the vehicle and depress the brake pedal. Restart the engine.
17 Loosen the bleed nipples approximately half a turn. The fluid will then flow through the bleed nipples into the jars.
18 When no more air bubbles are visible in the fluid, tighten the bleed nipples immediately, then release the brake pedal. The pressure should

Fig. 9.29 Footbrake pedal adjustment – type 2 pedal
(Secs 10 and 11)
5   Pedal adjustment stop screw
6   Brake compensator retaining bolts
J = 0.1 to 1.0 mm

11 Footbrake pedal – adjustment

1   The clearances between the footbrake pedal and the rubber damper of the brake compensator control valve must be as given in the Specifications. If not, loosen the locknut and adust the stop screw located over the pedal as necessary. Tighten the locknut when the adjustment is completed (Fig. 9.28 or 9.29 as applicable).
2   The pedal must now be checked for correct operation. First move the ground clearance lever fully to the minimum height position.
3   Loosen the pressure regulator bleed screw 1 to $1^1/2$ turns.
4   Depress the brake pedal several times to release the pressure.
5   Fully depress the pedal three or four times, making sure that it returns to its stop freely.
6   Check that the clearance adjusted in paragraph 1 has not altered. The pedal operation is correct if the clearance remains the same.
7   Tighten the pressure regulator bleed screw.

12 Stop-lamp switch – adjustment

1   Before adjusting the stop-lamp switch, the footbrake pedal must be adjusted, as described in Section 11.
2   The stop-lamp switch is located beneath the footbrake pedal, and the internal contacts should switch on the stop-lamps as soon as the pedal touches the brake valve.
3   If adjustment is necessary, loosen the switch locknut and turn the adjuster nut in the required direction. When the adjustment is correct retighten the locknut.

now build up in the hydraulic system, with the suspension arms assuming the 'high' position. If this fails to occur, increase the engine speed to approximately 3000 rpm, unscrew the pressure regulator bleed screw and leave it open for 30 seconds. Close the bleed screw, allow the engine to idle and recheck the position of the suspension arms.

Front and rear brakes
19 Remove the bleed tubes and locate the rubber caps over the bleed nipples.
20 Check the bleed nipples for leakage by fully depressing the brake pedal.

21 Switch off the engine, refit the roadwheels and lower the car to the ground (where applicable).
22 Check and top up the hydraulic fluid level in the reservoir, as described in Chapter 8.

Compensator control valve
23 If this valve unit is removed and refitted for any reason it will be necessary to bleed the compensator and the front and rear brakes. The compensator unit has a bleed nipple fitted into its top face towards the front.
24 When bleeding the compensator the hydraulic system must be under pressure (as for rear brake bleeding).

15 Fault diagnosis – braking system

Symptom	Reason(s)
Poor stopping ability	Brake pads and/or discs badly worn or scored
	Faulty brake valve
	Leak in brake hydraulic system
	Air in brake hydraulic system
	Low main hydraulic system pressure
	Brake pads contaminated with oil
Brake uneven and pulling to one side	Brake pads contaminated with oil
	Worn or distorted disc
	Caliper piston seized
	Different type of linings on disc pads
	Tyre pressures unequal
Inefficient handbrake operation	Worn pads
	Seized cable or levers
	Incorrect adjustments

Chapter 10 Suspension and steering

For modifications, and information applicable to later models, see Supplement at end of manual

Contents

Specifications

Suspension

Front .... Independent, with upper and lower arms and steering knuckle, hydropneumatic suspension cylinders supplied with fluid from main hydraulic system via front height corrector, anti-roll bar, bump and rebound stops

Rear .... Independent, with trailing arms, hydropneumatic suspension cylinders supplied with fluid from main hydraulic system via rear height corrector, anti-roll bar, bump and rebound stops

Suspension height – normal driving position (engine idling):

Front .... $166 \, {}^{+\,10}_{-\,7}$ mm $(6.54 \, {}^{+\,0.39}_{-\,0.28}$ in)

Rear .... $223 \, {}^{+\,10}_{-\,7}$ mm $(8.78 \, {}^{+\,0.39}_{-\,0.28}$ in)

Anti-roll bar diameter:
Front:
All models but Estate .... 22.5 mm (0.89 in)
Estate .... 23.0 mm (0.90 in)
Rear:
BX and BX 14 .... 16.5 mm (0.65 in)
BX 16 and BX 19 (not Estates) .... 17.0 mm (0.67 in)
BX 16 and BX 19 (Estates) .... 18.0 mm (0.71 in)

Steering

Type .... Rack-and-pinion with optional power steering, steering column with universal joint and coupling

Turning circle (between walls):
Manual steering .... 10.9 m (35.8 ft)
Power steering .... 11.2 m (36.7 ft)
Steering wheel turns (lock to lock):
Manual steering 3.76
Power steering 2.83
Steering shaft length:
Manual steering .... 384.5 mm (15.1 in)
Power steering .... 329.5 mm (12.9 in)

Wheel alignment

Front:

Toe-out	0 to 3 mm (0 to 0.118 in)
Camber angle	0° ± 30'
Castor angle	2° ± 35'
Wheel offset	−7.9 mm (−0.31 in)

Rear:

Toe-in	1.6 to 5 mm (0.06 to 0.2 in)
Camber angle	−1° ± 20'

Torque wrench settings

	kgf m	lbf ft
Front suspension		
Suspension strut unit upper mounting	2.0	14.4
Suspension strut to steering swivel	7.0	50.6
Suspension arm to steering swivel balljoint	3.0	21.6
Track rod balljoint	3.8	27.4
Suspension arm pivot (spindle) nut	16.0	115.7
Anti-roll bar connecting link	4.5	32.5
Anti-roll bar to subframe	2.7	19.5
Subframe bolts:		
BX and BX 14 (front, centre and rear)	5.7	41.2
BX 16 and BX 19 (front and centre)	5.7	41.2
BX 16 and BX 19 (rear)	9.5	68.7
Rear axle		
Suspension arm shaft	13.0	94.0
Anti-roll bar bearing flange	6.5	47.0
Axle mountings:		
Front	5.0	36.1
Rear	2.8	20.2
Steering		
Column upper mounting	1.2	8.6
Column upper joint clamp	2.0	14.4
Column lower flange joint	2.5	18.0
Rack mountings	5.7	41.2
Track rod inner to outer locknut	3.8	27.4
Track rod balljoint nut (outer)	3.8	27.4
Track rod balljoint nut (inner)	5.0	36.1

1 General description

1 The suspension used on all models in the range is of independent hydropneumatic type, similar to that used on other Citroën models.
2 At the front the suspension comprises a vertically mounted hydraulic suspension strut unit, a lower suspension arm and an anti-roll bar.
3 The suspension cylinders are supplied with hydraulic fluid from the main hydraulic system via the front height corrector which is actuated by the front anti-roll bar. The anti-roll bar is attached to the suspension arms with two links.
4 A trailing arm rear suspension system is used and the rear suspension cylinders are supplied with hydraulic fluid from the main system via the rear height corrector. As with the front, the height corrector is actuated by the rear anti-roll bar.
5 The ground height clearance may be adjusted with a lever mounted inside the car, the lever being connected by operating rods to the front and rear height correctors (photo). Automatic damping is incorporated in the suspension cylinders.
6 The steering is of rack-and-pinion type, mounted on a crossmember attached to the front subframe. The steering column incorporates a universal joint and a coupling. Power steering is fitted to some models and this system incorporates a self-centering action which varies according to the speed of the car.

2 Routine maintenance – suspension and steering

1 The following routine maintenance checks should be made at the intervals specified in the Routine Maintenance section at the front of this manual. The vehicle should be raised and supported at the front and rear on safety stands for most checks unless an inspection pit is available.
2 **Suspension hydraulic lines:** Check the suspension hydraulic

lines and hoses for condition and security. Renew damaged or corroded lines or hoses.
3 **Steering swivels and balljoints:** Check the swivels and balljoints for signs of excessive wear and renew if required. Check the balljoint rubbers and the steering rack/track rod gaiters for signs of damage.
4 **Suspension and steering system components:** Check the tightness of all nuts and bolts on the steering and suspension system components in accordance with the torque wrench figures in the Specifications.

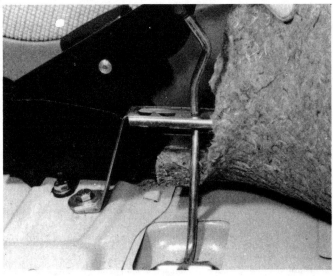

1.5 Height clearance adjustment lever

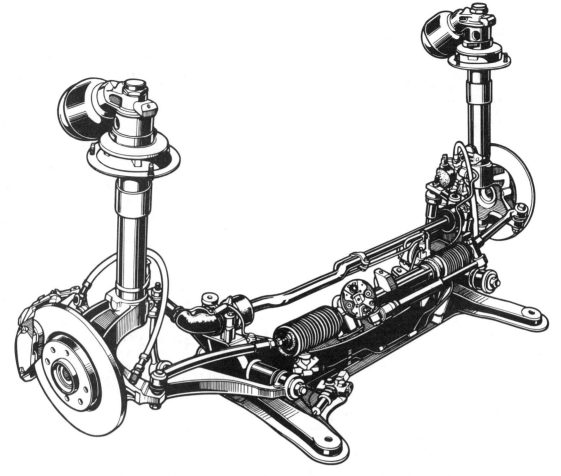

Fig. 10.1 Front axle, suspension and steering gear (LHD) (Sec 1)

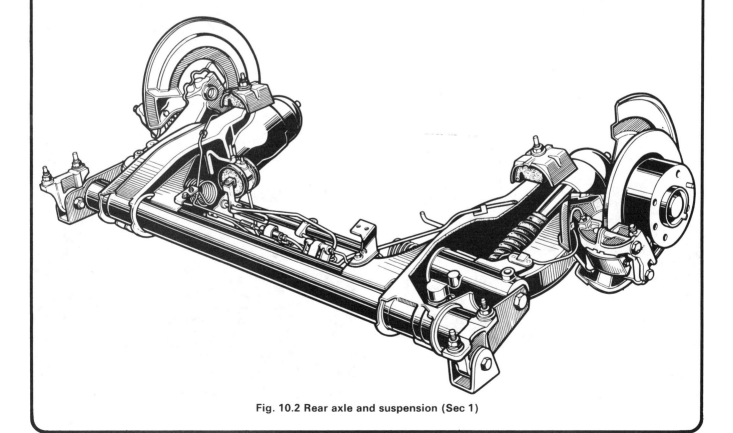

Fig. 10.2 Rear axle and suspension (Sec 1)

3 Front suspension arm – removal, servicing and refitting

1 Position chocks against the rear wheels, loosen the front roadwheel bolts then raise and support the vehicle at the front end on safety stands. Remove the front roadwheel(s).

2 Move the height control lever to the 'low' position.

3 Loosen the lower arm-to-steering swivel balljoint nut, locate a balljoint separator and detach the arm from the balljoint. Take care not to damage the balljoint rubber gaiter. When the joint is separated, remove the separator tool, unscrew the nut and detach the lower arm (photos).

4 Unscrew the retaining nut and detach the anti-roll bar connector track rod from the anti-roll bar (photo).

5 Unscrew and remove the suspension arm spindle nut at the rear end. Remove the cup washer (photo).

6 Unscrew and remove the suspension arm spindle nut at the front end (photo). Support the suspension arm and withdraw the spindle to the front. It may be necessary to attach a slide hammer to remove the spindle. As the spindle is withdrawn fom the suspension arm and subframe, make a note of the location of the cup washers and any shims or spacers used.

3.3A Steering swivel balljoint nut

3.3B Separate the swivel balljoint from the suspension arm

3.4 Anti-roll bar and connecting rod. Remove retaining nut (arrowed) to disconnect

3.5 Remove the suspension arm retaining nut at the rear (arrowed)

3.6 Remove the suspension arm retaining nut at the front (arrowed)

7 If the pivot bushes in the suspension arm are worn and in need of replacement then it is also probable that the pivot bearings in the subframe are also in need of renewal (see Section 4).

8 To remove the bushes from the suspension arm, first mount the arm in a soft jaw vice.

9 If possible use the Citroën special tool number 7104-T to remove the bushes and subsequently refit them. If this tool is not available you will need to fabricate a similar tool which comprises a length of threaded rod (14 mm diameter), some tube spacers, nuts and washers. The threaded rod should be of suitable length to pass through both suspension arm eyes and protrude enough at each end to enable the spacers and nuts to be fitted so that the bushes can be withdrawn.

10 Remove the rear bush first. Fit the tool through the arm and tighten the nut as indicated (at the front end of the rod) to draw the rear bush from its housing (Fig. 10.4).

11 Reverse the procedure to withdraw the front bush (Fig. 10.5). Care must be taken during the removal and refitting of the bushes not to distort the suspension arm by applying excessive force.

12 Clean out the bush bores in the suspension arm.

13 Commence refitting by drawing the front bush into position by reversing the withdrawal procedure. When fitted, the bush must be positioned as shown in Fig. 10.6.

14 Lubricate the rear bush before drawing it into position with a rubber lubricant or liquid soap. Check that the bush is correctly aligned

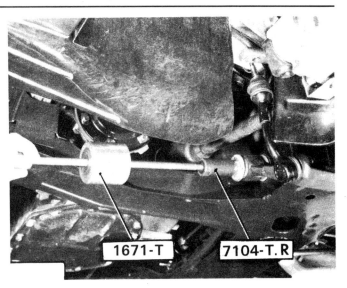

Fig. 10.3 Front suspension arm spindle removal method using Citroën special tools (Sec 3)

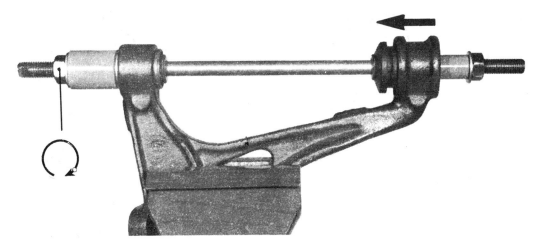

Fig. 10.4 Suspension arm rear bush removal using Citroën special tool. Note direction of removal (arrowed) (Sec 3)

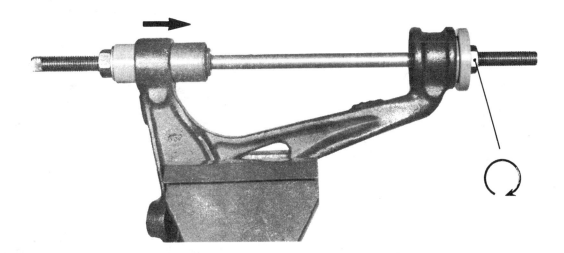

Fig. 10.5 Suspension arm front bush removal using Citroën special tool. Note direction of removal (arrowed) (Sec 3)

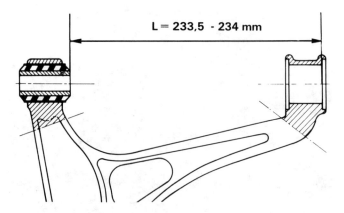

Fig. 10.6 Suspension arm front bush position (Sec 3)

when fitting and locate the index mark on the outer face to the rear (Figs. 10.7, 10.8 and 10.9).
15 Check the spindle for signs of excessive wear or damage before refitting and renew it if necessary.
16 Fit a new Nylstop nut onto the front end of the spindle and position it so that there is 7 mm (0.275 in) of thread exposed beyond the nut. Lubricate the spindle with grease. Slide a cup washer into position against the inner face of the nut, with the cupped side towards the nut.
17 Relocate the suspension arm and engage the spindle. As the spindle is pushed through (from the front), fit the cup washers so that they are facing the subframe (Fig. 10.10). If it was removed, ensure that the adjustment shim for the subframe bearings is refitted.
18 Fit the rear cup washer and the plain nut onto the rear end of the spindle and tighten the nuts hand tight.
19 Reconnect the balljoints, ensuring the joints are clean but do not lubricate them. New Nylstop nuts must be used and tightened to the specified torque settings.
20 Final tightening of the spindle (pivot) nuts to the specified torque must be carried out with the weight of the vehicle on its wheels and the suspension in the normal driving position.

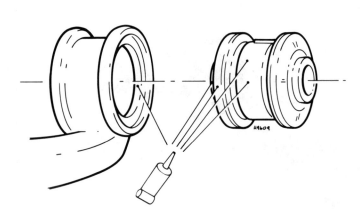

Fig. 10.7 Lubricate the suspension arm rear bush prior to fitting (Sec 3)

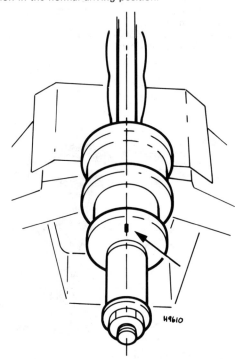

Fig. 10.8 Position the rear bush with the alignment mark as shown (Sec 3)

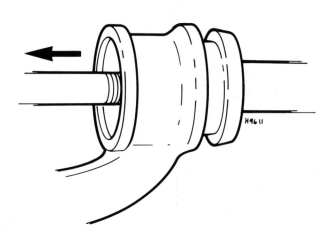

Fig. 10.9 Draw the rear bush into the suspension arm eye in the direction indicated (Sec 3)

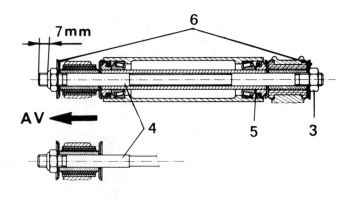

Fig. 10.10 Cross-section view of the suspension arm, spindle and subframe. Arrow indicates front (Sec 3)

3 Retaining nut – rear   5 Adjustment shim
4 Spindle   6 Cup washers

4 Subframe/front suspension arm bearings – removal and refitting

1 Remove the front suspension arm, as described in Section 3.
2 If the subframe unit or spacers are being renewed then the bearing

free play will need to be adjusted and, as this necessitates the use of special Citroën tools, the bearing renewal should be entrusted to your dealer.
3 Withdraw the spacer tube, washer, spacer and seal and the bearing inner race from the front end (Fig. 10.11).

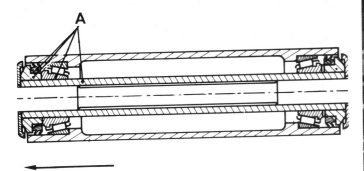

Fig. 10.11 Cross-section view of the subframe/suspension arm bearings (Sec 4)

Removal items A for access to remove the front bearing track
Arrow indicates front

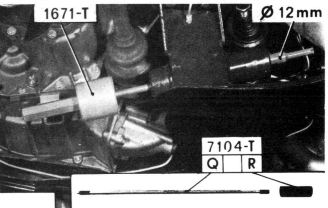

Fig. 10.12 Citroën special tools in position to remove the front bearing track (Sec 4)

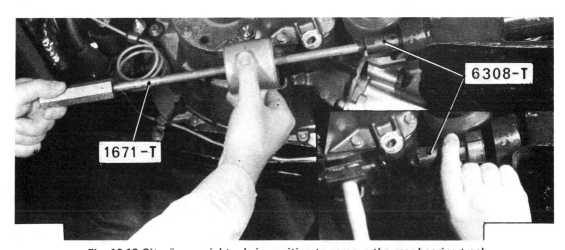

Fig. 10.13 Citroën special tools in position to remove the rear bearing track (Sec 4)

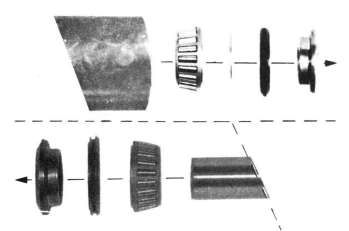

Fig. 10.14 Bearing, seal and spacer assemblies, rear (top) and front (lower). Note shim location for rear bearing (Sec 4)

4 To remove the front bearing track Citroën tool 1671-T will be required. This tool has an expanding end piece fitted which can be passed through the bearing track and expanded beyond the inside diameter of the bearing track. The tool can then be used as a slide hammer to withdraw the bearing track.
5 The rear bearing assembly is then removed in a similar manner to that described for the front bearing, but note that an adjustment shim is located between the bearing and spacer. When removing the rear outer bearing track, Citroën recommend that the bearing be driven out from the front end rearwards. This will entail fitting Citroën tool 6308-T onto the end of the special tool 1671-T (Fig. 10.13).
6 Refitting is a reversal of the removal procedures. Drive the new bearing tracks into position and ensure that they are fully fitted and flush against the inner shoulder.
7 Lubricate the new bearing races before fitting. Ensure that the adjustment shim is located between the rear bearing and the spacer (Fig. 10.14).
8 Fit new seals onto the spacer washers ensuring that they face the correct way (note this when removing the old seals).
9 Refit the suspension arm on completion and check that it pivots freely but without excessive play before reconnecting it to the steering swivel hub.

5 Front hydraulic suspension unit – removal and refitting

1   Loosen the front roadwheel bolts, chock the rear roadwheels and then raise and support the vehicle at the front end on safety stands. Remove the front roadwheel(s).

2   Undo the pressure release screw on the pressure regulator by 1 to 1^1/$_2$ turns and move the height control lever to the 'low' position (see Chapter 8, Section 2).

3   If a suitable spare jack is available, position it under the suspension unit on the side concerned and raise it to disperse as much oil as possible from the suspension unit being removed. This procedure is recommended rather than essential.

4   Unscrew and remove the sphere from the suspension unit at the top end (within the engine compartment). Grip the sphere with a chain or strap wrench to loosen it, then unscrew it by hand. It is important to note at this stage that the sphere support should not be removed (photo).

5   Unscrew and detach the rigid feed pipe union from the sphere support. Plug the union and port.

6   Undo the three top mounting nuts and unbolt and detach the rigid feed pipe location clips.

7   Working under the wheel arch, detach the hydraulic overflow and vent pipes (photo).

8   Unscrew and remove the swivel hub-to-suspension unit clamp bolt and nut (photo). Prise open the clamp using a suitable lever and separate the suspension unit from the hub. The suspension unit can then be withdrawn.

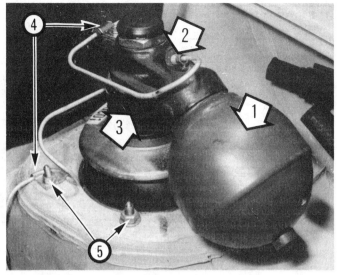

5.4 Front hydraulic suspension unit

1 Sphere	4 Pipe clamps
2 Rigid feed pipe union	5 Top mounting nuts (inboard side)
3 Sphere support	

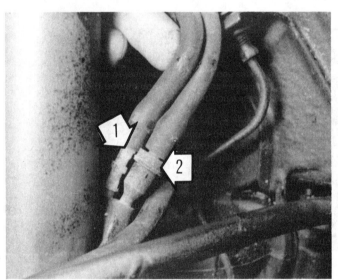

5.7 Hydraulic overflow (1) and vent (2) pipe connections under the wheel arch

9   Refitting is a direct reversal of the removal procedure, but note the following special points:

   (a) Tighten the retaining nuts and bolts to the specified torque settings

   (b) Ensure that the hydraulic pipe and hose connections are unplugged and clean before reconnecting them. When reconnecting the feed pipe union use a new seal

   (c) Ensure that the overflow return and vent pipe connections are correctly made

   (d) When refitting the sphere to the support, grease the mating face of the support

10   On completion, tighten the release screw on the pressure regulator unit, top up the fluid level as required and check that the height control system is satisfactory in operation.

6 Front anti-roll bar – removal and refitting

1   Jack-up the front of the car and support it on axle stands. Chock the rear wheels then remove the front wheels.

5.8 Swivel hub-to-suspension unit clamp bolt (arrowed)

2   Move the ground clearance lever fully to the minimum height position.

3   Loosen the hydraulic system pressure regulator bleed screw 1 to 1^1/$_2$ turns (Chapter 8, Section 2).

4   Undo the retaining nut and detach the anti-roll bar link rod on each side (photo 3.4).

5   Raise and support the steering swivels as high as possible then move the height control lever to the 'normal' height position.

6   Mark the anti-roll bar and height corrector clamp in relation to each other, then unscrew the clamp bolt and remove the clamp.

7   The procedures now differ according to model.

BX and BX 14

8   Loosen the front subframe securing bolts at the front and rear by approximately 10 mm (0.4 in) and leave them set at this position. Now unscrew and remove the subframe centre securing bolts (Fig. 10.15).

BX 16 and BX 19

9   Disconnect the gear control linkage rods and position the relay (3) to detach the balljoint (5) and locate the relay (4) at the rear of the anti-roll bar (Fig. 10.16).

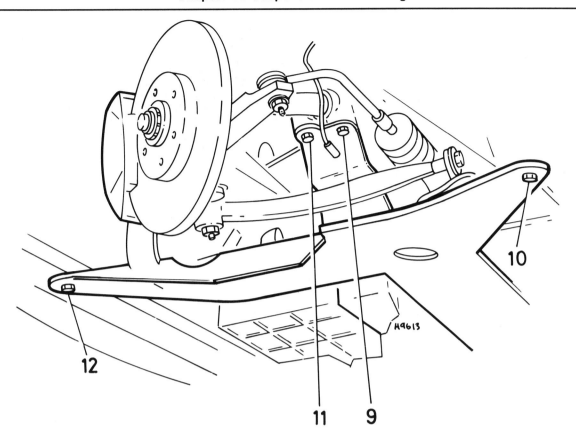

Fig. 10.15 Front anti-roll bar removal – BX and BX 14 models (Sec 6)

9 Anti-roll bar mounting to subframe

10 Subframe rear bolts (loosen)

11 Subframe centre bolts (remove)

12 Subframe front bolts (loosen)

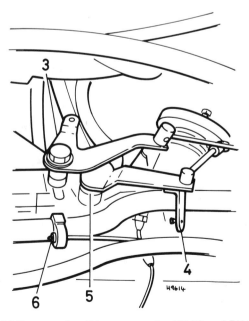

Fig. 10.16 Front anti-roll bar removal – BX 16 and BX 19 models (Sec 6)

3 Relay
4 Relay
5 Balljoint
6 Height control linkage collar

10 Referring to Fig. 10.17, move the protector back out of the way then loosen the collar securing bolts on the left-hand end of the anti-roll bar.

11 Follow the procedure described in paragraph 8 above.

All models

12 Unscrew and remove the anti-roll bar-to-subframe mounting bolt and nut on each side. Remove the anti-roll bar components, but leave collar and protector in position on the right-hand side.

13 Slacken the flange from the hydraulic return pipes.

14 Detach the hydraulic return pipes from the left-hand suspension cylinder.

15 To remove the anti-roll bar, move it towards the right-hand side, underneath the left-hand driveshaft, then back towards the left. Move the right-hand side of the bar towards the inner body. Now locate the left-hand end of the bar between left-hand lower suspension arm and the steering arm and remove it.

16 Before refitting the anti-roll bar, relocate the protector and collar so that they are in a straight position (Fig. 10.20).

17 Refitting is mostly a reversal of the removal procedure but note the following points of special note.

18 Lubricate the respective parts with grease prior to assembling then onto the anti-roll bar. Tighten the anti-roll bar bearing to sub-frame to the specified torque setting.

19 Refit the central subframe retaining screw then tighten the front, centre and rear subframe retaining bolts (in that order) to their specified torque settings.

20 The anti-roll bar will now need to be adjusted and to do this Citroën special tool number 7102-T is necessary. Referring to Fig. 10.21, locate the special tool so that it rests behind the collar, and tighten the nut so that the spring coils are touching. Loosen the nut 1 full turn and then tighten the collar.

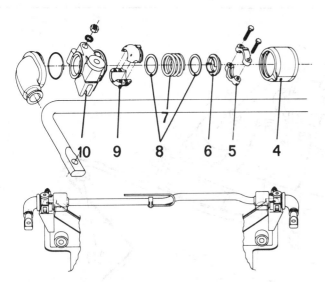

Fig. 10.17 Anti-roll bar and associated components (Sec 6)

4 Protector 8 Washer
5 Collar 9 Balljoint
6 Thrust cap 10 Bearing
7 Spring

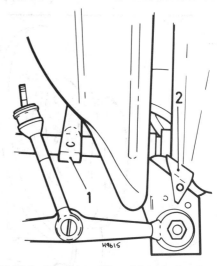

Fig. 10.18 Anti-roll bar (1) and hydraulic circuit return pipe flange (2) (Sec 6)

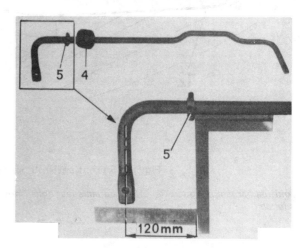

Fig. 10.20 Location for protector (4) and collar (5) on the anti-roll bar (Sec 6)

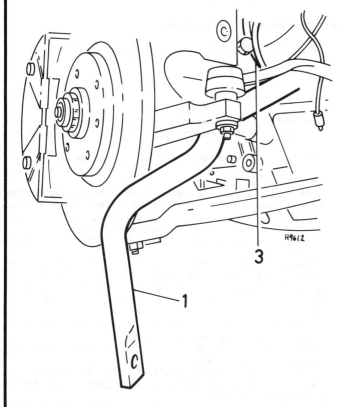

Fig. 10.19 Anti-roll bar (1) and hydraulic return pipes (3) on the left-hand side (Sec 6)

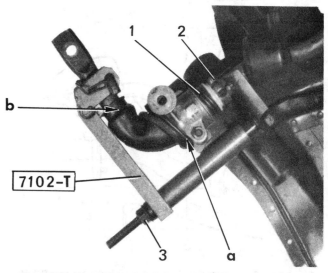

Fig. 10.21 Front anti-roll bar adjustment using special Citroën tool 710 2-T (Sec 6)

1 Spring a Protector clip
2 Collar b Collar clip
3 Nut

21 Lubricate the anti-roll bar bearings with Total Multis MS grease (about 30 grams), then refit the protectors and their circlips.
22 Reconnect the anti-roll bar to the link rods and tighten the nuts to the specifed torque setting.
25 On completion check the vehicle height settings, as described in Section 8.

7 Suspension height correctors – removal and refitting

1 Jack-up the front or rear of the car and support it on axle stands.
2 Move the ground clearance lever in the minimum height position. Unscrew the pressure regulator bleed screw 1 to 1^1/$_2$ turns (Chapter 8, Section 2).
3 Remove the right-hand side roadwheel.
4 Remove the plastic height corrector cover (where fitted).
5 Identify all the hydraulic pipes for location using masking tape, then disconnect them from the corrector (Fig. 10.22).
6 Unscrew the mounting bolts, disconnect the balljoint from the control lever, and withdraw the height corrector from the car (photo).
7 It is not possible to repair the height correctors; if faulty, they must be renewed.
8 Refitting is a reversal of removal, but the balljoint should be

lubricated with multi-purpose grease. Tighten the hydraulic pipe union screws to the specified torque (see Chapter 8). Check and adjust the suspension height, as described in Section 8; after tightening the pressure regulator bleed screw.

8 Suspension height – adjustment

1 Check that the tyre pressures are correct (Chapter 7). Ideally the vehicle should be parked over an inspection pit for this check, as access underneath the vehicle is required with it standing level and at its normal height.

Automatic height control
2 Set the ground clearance lever to the 'normal' position and start the engine. Allow the engine to run at idle speed.
3 Before making the height check, raise the vehicle by lifting it by hand as much as possible then release the weight and allow the vehicle to drop and rise, then stabilize. Before measuring the front height, move the vehicle back and forth slightly to relieve any stress in the suspension.
4 Refer to Figs. 10.23 and 10.24 then check that the front and rear

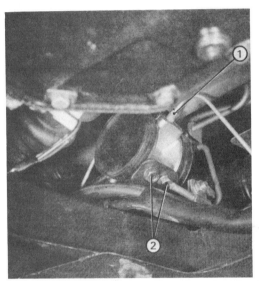

Fig. 10.22 Front height corrector location, showing feed pipe (1) and retaining bolts (2) (Sec 7)

7.6 Rear height corrector

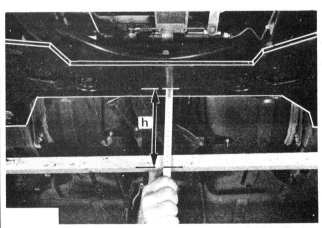

Fig. 10.23 Suspension height check – front (Sec 8)

h = ground to axle unit rear crossmember

Fig. 10.24 Suspension height check – rear (Sec 8)

h = ground to axle crossmember tube

suspension heights are as given in the Specifications. Measure the suspension height at each end twice and take the mean of the two as the height reading.

5 If adjustment is necessary it is made by rotating the automatic height control collar around the anti-roll bar (Figs. 10.25 and 10.26). When set, a clearance of 1.5 to 2.0 mm must exist between the balljoint and the bottom of its recess.

Manual height control
6 Set the automatic height control.
7 For adjustment at the front, refer to Fig. 10.27 and loosen the bracket clamp bolt then move the bracket along the control rod to

position the corrector control under the bracket pointer and meet the dimension requirements shown (a and b). Tighten the clamp bolt.
8 For adjustment at the rear also refer to Fig. 10.27 and set the reversing lever axis of rotation so that the corrector control is central in the reversing lever hole (L1 and L2).
9 With the engine still idling and the ground clearance lever still in the 'normal' position, check the front and rear suspension heights as follows. Lift the car by hand as far as possible, then release it and let it stabilise. Note the suspension height. Press the car down as far as possible, then release it and let it stabilise. Note the suspension height again. The average of the two measurements should be within the specified limits.

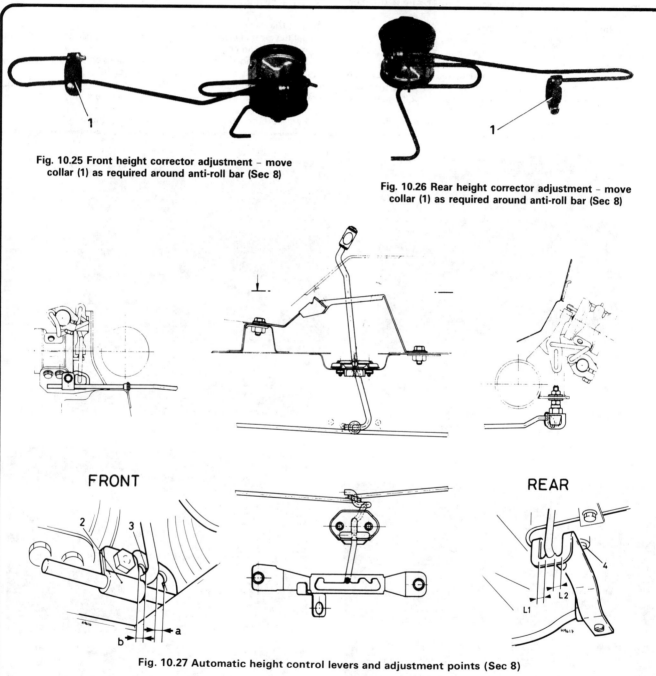

Fig. 10.25 Front height corrector adjustment – move collar (1) as required around anti-roll bar (Sec 8)

Fig. 10.26 Rear height corrector adjustment – move collar (1) as required around anti-roll bar (Sec 8)

Fig. 10.27 Automatic height control levers and adjustment points (Sec 8)

Front
2   Bracket
3   Bracket pointer
a = 7 to 7.5 mm
b = 4 to 4.5 mm

Rear
4   Reversing lever
L1 to equal L2

9   Rear suspension arm – removal, servicing and refitting

1   Jack-up the rear of the car and support it on axle stands. Apply the handbrake and remove the rear roadwheel.
2   Move the ground clearance lever fully to the rear in the minimum height position.
3   Loosen the hydraulic system pressure regulator bleed screw 1 to 1$^1/_2$ turns (Chapter 8, Section 2).
4   Unscrew the rear brake line union nut from the caliper and disconnect the brake line from the clip on the suspension arm top face.
5   Working underneath the vehicle, extract the pin and remove the anti-roll bar clamp on the side concerned.
6   Support the suspension arm with a jack then unscrew and remove the pivot shaft nut, withdraw the shaft then allow the suspension arm to drop to the vertical for removal.
7   The brake caliper and disc can be removed, as described in Chapter 9.
8   To remove the wheel hub and bearings from the stub axle refer to Chapter 7.
9   The brake backplate can be removed by undoing the three retaining bolts (Fig. 10.31).
10   To remove the pivot bearings from the suspension arm first mount the arm in a vice fitted with soft jaws, but do not grip the arm by the brake caliper lug.
11   To remove the bearings you will need Citroën tool numbers 1671-T and 7104-T, also expanding mandrels 12 mm and 35 mm in diameter.
12   Pass tool 1671-T through the pivot bore and locate the 12 mm diameter mandrel onto the tool. If this particular Citroën tool is not available a proprietary slide hammer and mandrel of suitable dimensions will do the job (Fig. 10.33).
13   Withdraw the bearing tube, bearing cone, seal and spacer.
14   Use a suitable tube drift to pass through the suspension arm and butt against the opposing bearing cone inner race and drive out the spacer, seal, shim and bearing.
15   Insert the 35 mm diameter mandrel into the bearing cone within the suspension arm and attach the mandrel to a slide hammer and draw the bearing out. Repeat the procedure on the opposing bearing cone and, if re-using the bearings, keep them with their respective assemblies.
16   If the suspension arm is being renewed then the bearing free play will need to be adjusted and, as this necessitates the use of specialised Citroën tools, this task should be entrusted to your dealer.
17   Reassembly of the bearings is a reversal of the removal procedure. Ensure that the bearing housings in the suspension arm are cleaned out thoroughly.

18   Drive the outer races (cups) into position so that they are flush against the inner shoulder.
19   Lubricate the bearing cones with bearing grease when refitting them.
20   Ensure that the adjustment shim is fitted between the bearing cone and the seal when reassembling the outer (wheel hub side) bearing assembly.
21   The brake backplate, caliper unit and wheel hub assemblies can be refitted to the suspension arm with references to Chapters 9 and 7.
22   When refitting the suspension arm to the vehicle, grease the pivot shaft along its entire length before inserting it. Ensure that the brake hose is positioned towards the rear of the arm. Use a new Nylstop nut to secure the pivot shaft and tighten it to the specified torque.
23   Check that the suspension arm pivots freely without excessive binding or free play then reconnect the anti-roll bar and tighten the mounting clamp bolts to the specified torque. Relocate the suspension cylinder rod pin.
24   Use a new seal when reconnecting the brake hose to the caliper and engage the brake line in the location clip on the location arm.
25   Bleed the brakes and refit the roadwheel to complete.

Fig. 10.28 Disconnect the brake line at the caliper (2) and the suspension arm (1) (Sec 9)

Fig. 10.29 Remove the pin (3) and clamp (4) from the anti-roll bar (Sec 9)

Fig. 10.30 Remove the suspension arm pivot bolt (6) (Sec 9)

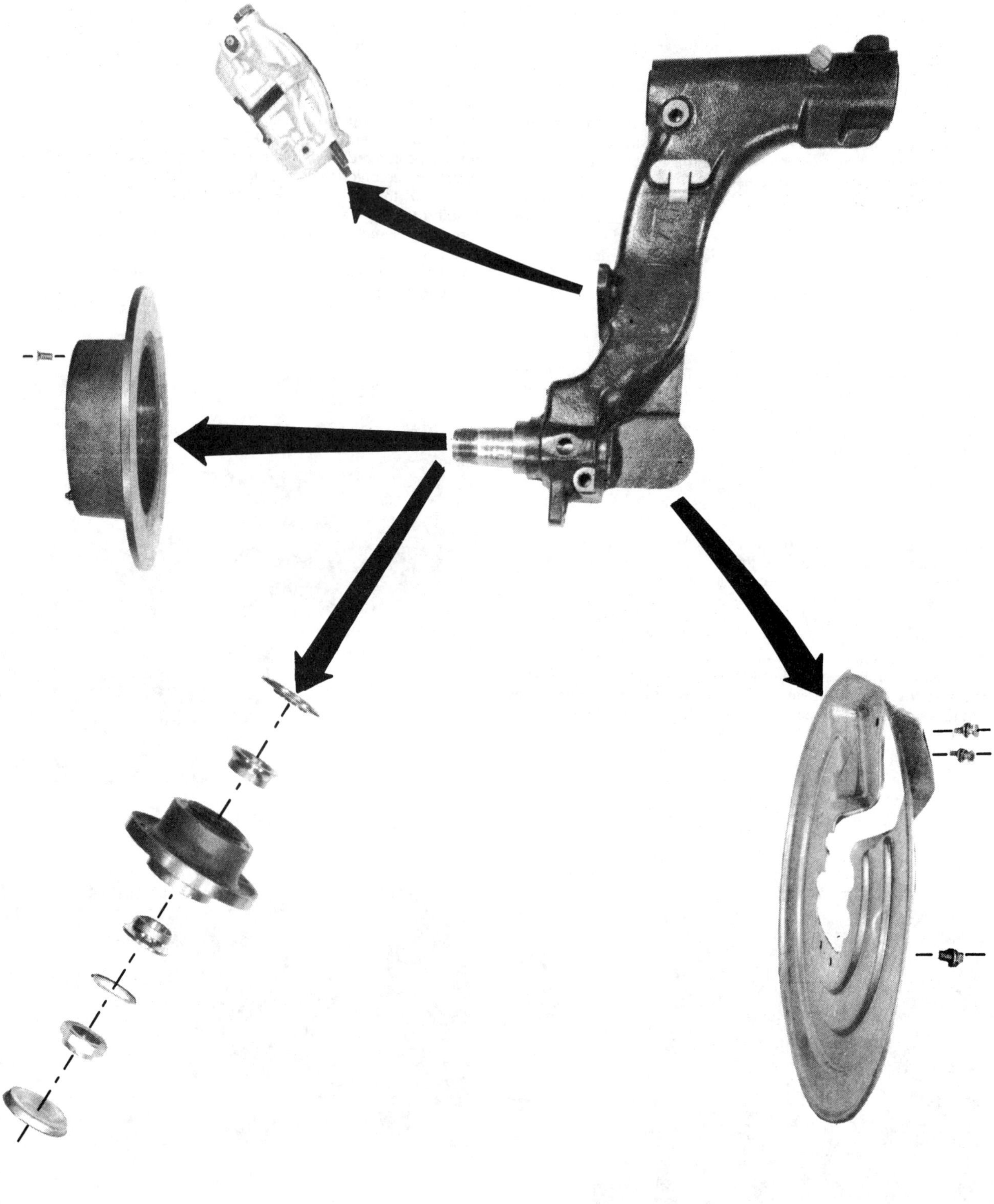

Fig. 10.31 Rear suspension arm and associated components (Sec 9)

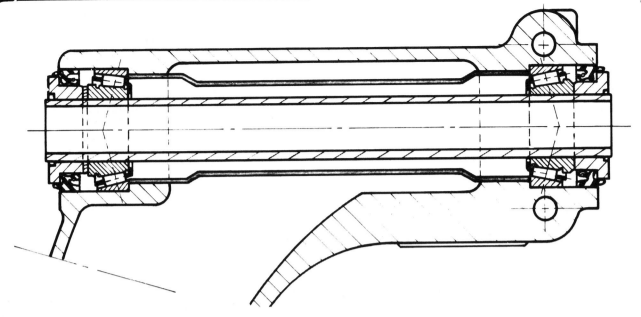

Fig. 10.32 Cross-section of the rear suspension arm pivot bearings assembly (Sec 9)

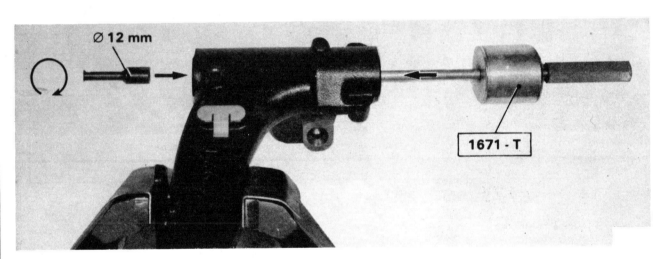

Fig. 10.33 Rear suspension arm bearing removal tools (Sec 9)

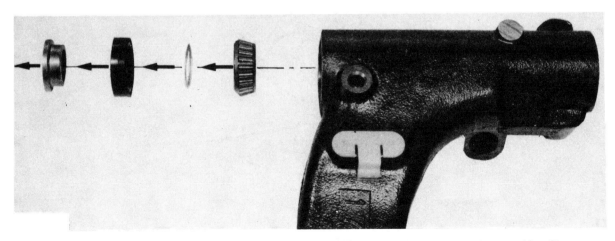

Fig. 10.34 Outer bearing cone, shim, seal and spacer fitted to the rear suspension arm (Sec 9)

10 Rear hydraulic suspension unit – removal and refitting

1   Loosen the rear roadwheel bolts, check that the handbrake is fully applied and check the front roadwheels. Raise the vehicle at the rear and support on safety stands. Remove the rear roadwheel(s).

2   Undo the pressure release screw on the pressure regulator by 1 to 1$\frac{1}{2}$ turns and move the height control lever to the 'low' position.

3   If a suitable spare jack is available, position it under the suspension unit and raise the rear suspension arm. This will disperse most of the fluid from the suspension cylinder.

4   Unscrew and remove the pneumatic sphere using a chain or strap wrench.

5   Unscrew and detach the rigid supply pipe at the union to the cylinder unit.

6   Disconnect the vent pipe and overflow return pipe from the cylinder (photo).

7   Withdraw the suspension rod clip (photo).

8   Allow the arm to hang free and pass the suspension rod between the subframe rear section and the stop. The suspension cylinder unit can then be withdrawn.

9   Refitting is a reversal of the removal procedure but note the following special points:

   (a) *When refitting the cylinder into position engage the suspension rod and locate the spring end part to the rear of the cylinder union (shown in Fig. 10.35)*

   (b) *Ensure that the supply pipe union is perfectly clean and use a new seal when reconnecting it*

   (c) *When refitting the pneumatic sphere, use a new seal and grease the support face of the cylinder*

10 On completion, tighten the release screw on the pressure regulator unit, top up the fluid level as required and check that the height control system is satisfactory in operation.

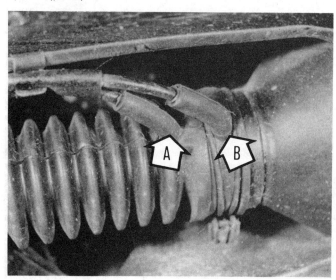

10.6 Rear suspension unit vent pipe (A) and return pipe (B)

10.7 Rear suspension unit rod clip

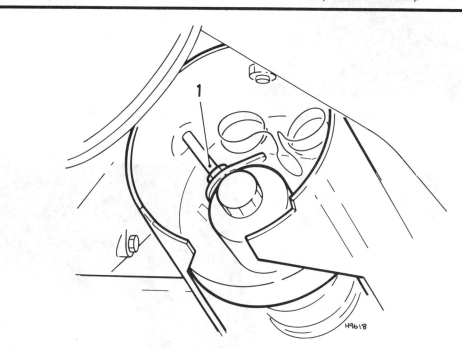

Fig. 10.35 Disconnect the supply pipe (1) at the rear suspension unit (shown with sphere removed) (Sec 10)

11 Rear anti-roll bar – removal and refitting

1   Check that the handbrake is fully applied and chock the front roadwheels. Loosen the rear roadwheel bolts.
2   Start the engine, allow it to idle and move the ground clearance lever to the fully raised position. Once fully raised, switch off the engine.
3   Jack up the rear of the vehicle so that the rear wheels are clear of the ground and support with safety stands. Remove the rear roadwheels.
4   Move the ground clearance lever back to the 'normal' height setting.
5   Mark the anti-roll bar and height corrector clamp in relation to each other, then unscrew and remove the clamp bolt (photo).
6   Unscrew and remove the anti-roll bar mounting flange each side, at the same time noting the location of the bearing flange blocks and thrust plates.
7   Move the anti-roll bar towards the right-hand side then withdraw it from the left-hand side.
8   To refit the anti-roll bar, reverse the removal procedure.
9   Locate the thrust plate between the bar and the arm before refitting the bearing flange block each side. Tighten the bearing flange block bolts to the specified torque.
10   Re-engage the height corrector automatic control with the manual control setting still in the 'normal' position. Align the clamp-to-anti-roll bar marks made during removal, semi-tighten the clamp bolt and

check that the control articulation point free play is between 1.5 to 2.0 mm (0.06 to 0.08 in). Adjust the clearance if necessary and then tighten the clamp bolt.
11   Refit the rear roadwheels and lower the vehicle to the ground.
12   Check and if necessary adjust the vehicle height, as described in Section 8.

12 Track rod/balljoint – renewal

1   Set the steering wheel and the front roadwheels in the straight-ahead position. Loosen the front roadwheel bolts then raise the vehicle at the front and support it on axle stands. Remove the roadwheel.
2   Loosen the track rod end balljoint nut then, using a suitable balljoint separator, detach the track rod from the steering arm on the swivel hub (photos).
3   At the inner end of the track rod, measure the amount of exposed thread and make a note of it. This will act as an adjustment guide when refitting the track rod (photo).
4   Grip the inboard end of the track rod hexagonal section and unscrew the outer rod from it after loosening the locknut a quarter of a turn.
5   Screw on the new track rod to the same position as the old one, tighten the locknut one quarter of a turn. The section of exposed thread should measure the same as that noted during removal.

11.5 Rear anti-roll bar and height corrector clamp

12.2A Loosen the balljoint nut ...

12.2B ... and use a separator to detach the joint

12.3 Track rod inner end showing the exposed thread

6   Ensure that the balljoint taper pin is clean and unlubricated, then insert it into the swivel arm and tighten the retaining nut to the specified torque.
7   Refit the roadwheel and lower the car to the ground.
8   Check the front wheel alignment, as described in Section 21.

13 Steering swivel (knuckle) – removal and refitting

1   Remove the roadwheel trim, extract the split pin from the driveshaft and withdraw the lockplate from the nut.
2   Have an assistant depress the footbrake (with the engine running), then loosen the nut; an extension bar will be necessary as the nut is very tight.
3   Jack-up the front of the car and support it on axle stands. Chock the rear wheels.
4   Remove the roadwheel and release the handbrake.
5   Move the ground clearance lever fully to the minimum height position.
6   Loosen the hydraulic system pressure regulator bleed screw 1 to 1$\frac{1}{2}$ turns.
7   Undo the brake hose bracket bolts, the deflector retaining bolts and the two caliper securing bolts. Remove the caliper and suspend it from a suitable point so that the hydraulic lines are not distorted or stretched.
8   Disconnect the track rod balljoint, as described in Section 12.
9   Loosen the suspension arm-to-swivel balljoint and separate the joint using a balljoint separator, then remove the nut and disconnect the joint.
10 Unscrew and remove the hub nut, then pull the hub outwards and disengage the driveshaft from it.
11 Unscrew and remove the suspension strut-to-swivel clamp bolt and nut. Prise apart the clamp and separate the swivel unit from the strut.
12 Removal and renewal of the hub seals and bearings is described in Chapter 7.
13 To remove the lower balljoint refer to Section 14.
14 Refitting is a reversal of removal, but note the following special points.

(a) Lubricate the hub seals with grease prior to refitting the driveshaft
(b) The bottom balljoint stem must be wiped clean and be assembled dry. Use a new Nylstop nut
(c) When reconnecting the suspension strut to the swivel engage the centre tenon with the slot in the swivel. Use a new Nylstop nut to fasten the clamp bolt
(d) Refit the brake caliper and deflector with reference to Chapter 9

(c) The track rod-to-steering arm balljoint must be assembled dry and a new Nylstop nut used to secure
(f) Wipe the driveshaft nut and threads with grease then tighten and secure, as described in Chapter 7

15 On completion check the steering and brakes for satisfactory operation. Check the wheel alignment, as described in Section 21.

14 Steering swivel (knuckle) bottom balljoint – renewal

1   Although the bottom balljoint can be removed with the swivel unit in position it will be necessary to use Citroën special tool 7103-T and a manual impact wrench Dynapact, Facom type. The manufacturers specify that no other should be used.
2   Raise the front of the vehicle and allow the front roadwheels to hang clear of the ground. Remove the roadwheel on the side concerned.
3   Move the height control lever to the low setting position.
4   Loosen the balljoint locknut, fit a balljoint separator to the joint and separate the lower suspension arm from the taper pin. Remove the separator and nut then detach the suspension arm from the balljoint.

Fig. 10.36 Detaching the steering swivel/suspension arm balljoint using a Citroën separator (Sec 13)

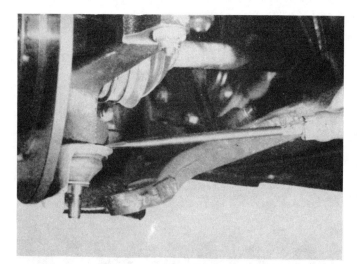

Fig. 10.37 Prise free the protector plate (Sec 14)

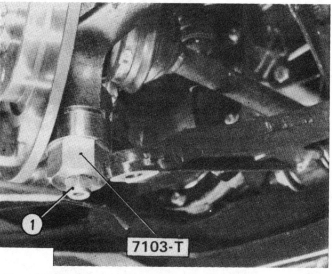

Fig. 10.38 Citroën tool 7103-T in position on lower balljoint (Sec 14)

1 Nut

5   Prise the protector plate from the balljoint rubber.
6   Locate special tool 7103-T into position on the balljoint and fasten with a nut.
7   Unscrew the balljoint unit from the swivel hub unit using the recommended impact wrench.
8   Refit in the reverse order to removal noting the following special points.

(a)   *When refitting the balljoint use the special tools recommended and take care not to damage the rubber gaiter*

(b)   *When tightening the balljoint, stop the swivel from rotating. If available, bolt Citroën special tool 6310-T into position on the hub using the wheel bolts as shown in Fig. 10.40. Tighten the joint to the specified torque setting, then lock in position by peening into the notches at the points shown in Fig. 10.41*

(c)   *Relocate the protector plate over the joint before refitting the suspension arm to it. Assemble the joint to arm dry and use a new Nylstop nut. Tighten it to the specified torque setting*

Fig. 10.39 Balljoint unit removal using the recommended impact wrench (Sec 14)

Fig. 10.40 Type of tool used to prevent the swivel hub from turning (Sec 14)

1   Wheel bolts

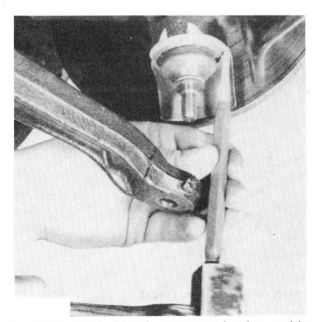

Fig. 10.42 Carefully drive the protector plate into position (Sec 14)

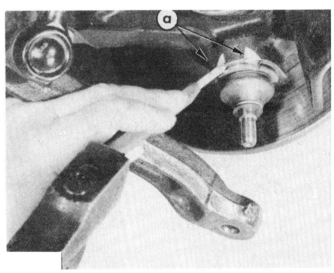

Fig. 10.41 Lock the lower joint by stake punching at the points indicated (a) (Sec 14)

15 Steering wheel – removal and refitting

1   The steering wheel and upper column shaft are removed together. First disconnect the battery earth leads.
2   Remove the steering column lower shroud and facia by unscrewing the screws from the points indicated in Fig. 10.43.
3   Unscrew and remove the column universal joint upper bolt and loosen the lower bolt.
4   The universal joint can now be slid downwards to free the shaft splines.
5   Use a suitable pair of circlip pliers and release the circlip retaining the cup washer and spring, then withdraw the steering wheel and upper shaft.
6   If required, the ball-bearing units at the top and bottom ends of the column housing can now be withdrawn. Use a suitable puller if necessary.
7   Two distinct upper steering column and wheel/shaft assembly types have been used and these are shown in Fig. 10.44.

242

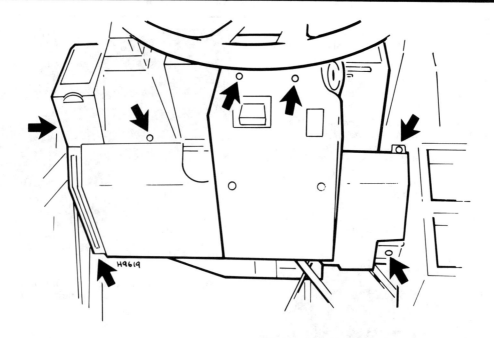

Fig. 10.43 Steering column lower shroud/finishing panel retaining screw positions – left-hand drive shown (Sec 15)

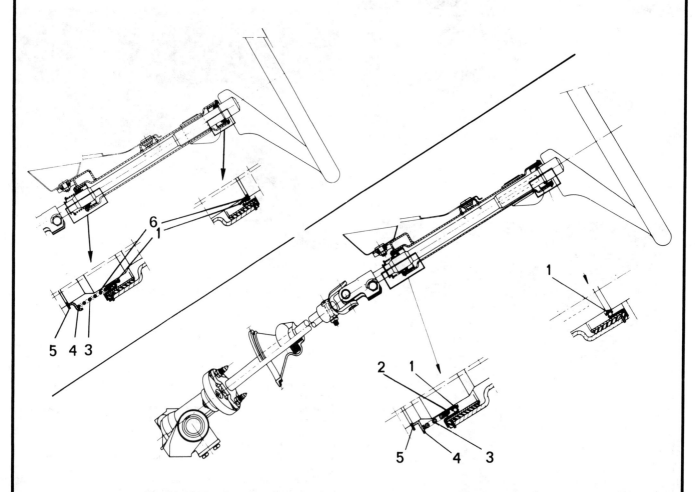

Fig. 10.44 The first (lower) and second (top) steering column types (Sec 15)

1   Ball-bearings
2   Centre cup – first type (chamfer to bearing)
3   Spring
4   Thrust cup
5   Circlip
6   Split rings

8 To refit the first type, locate the bearings into the column housing, insert the steering wheel/shaft. The centering cup must face towards the upper bearing. At the lower end engage the spring, cup washer and circlip over the lower end of the shaft.

9 To refit the second type upper column, the bearings must be in position in the column. Fit the upper split ring to the steering wheel then insert the upper shaft and steering wheel. Locate the second split ring at the base of the lower bearing then engage the coil springs, cup washer and circlip over the shaft lower end.

10 To engage the circlip in the shaft groove you will need to compress the coil spring and cup washer. In the workshop we engaged an open jaw spanner over the shaft and pulled the spanner upwards against the cup washer and spring so that the spanner cleared the spring. An assistant simultaneously moved the circlip into position in its groove and once engaged, the spanner was withdrawn (photos).

11 Align the upper steering shaft and refit it to the universal joint. When the front roadwheels are in the straight-ahead position the steering wheel spoke should point vertically down, and the pinion flange be parallel to the steering rack housing.

12 Refit the upper retaining bolt and tighten it and the lower bolt.

13 Refit the column lower shroud to complete.

16 Steering column housing – removal and refitting

1 Remove the steering wheel and upper shaft, as described in Section 15.

2 Disconnect the steering lock/ignition switch wiring harness at the connector.

3 Raise and support the bonnet. Remove the air deflector grille in front of the radiator then detach the bonnet release cable from the lock unit. Retain the cable clamp and sheath stop.

4 Unscrew the four column housing mounting nuts and lower the column.

5 To remove the bonnet opening cable squeeze the two tabs together behind the mounting bracket and withdraw the cable through the bracket (photo).

6 To remove the steering lock/ignition switch unit refer to Section 17.

7 Refitting is a reversal of the removal procedure. Ensure that the steering lock/ignition switch wiring harness passes over the steering column. Tighten the housing mounting nuts.

15.10A Use a spanner to compress the spring and washer ...

15.10B ... then locate the circlip

15.10C The circlip located in its groove

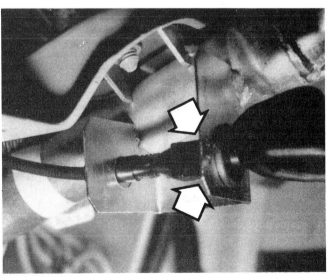

16.5 Bonnet release cable securing tabs (arrowed)

17.4 Remove the bolt (arrowed) ...

17.5 ... and press pin to withdraw the lock/switch unit

17 Steering lock/ignition switch – removal and refitting

1   Disconnect the battery earth lead.
2   Undo the retaining screws and remove the steering column lower shroud.
3   Detach the ignition switch wiring from the multi-connector.
4   Unscrew the small bolt with shakeproof washer from the switch unit housing (photo).
5   Set the ignition switch so that the key slot aligns with the arrow mark between the 'A' and 'S' positions then press in the pin and withdraw the lock/switch unit (photo).
6   Refitting is a reversal of the removal procedure. Check the operation of the steering lock and ignition switch functions to ensure that they are satisfactory on completion.

18 Manual steering gear unit – removal and refitting

1   Chock the rear roadwheels and loosen the front roadwheel bolts. Raise the vehicle at the front end and support on safety stands. Remove the front roadwheels.
2   Remove the lower steering column shroud, then loosen the column universal joint bolt on the lower left side.
3   Loosen the track rod outer balljoint nut then, using a balljoint separator, detach the joint. Remove the separator and nut then repeat the procedure on the opposing side track rod outer joint. Take care not to damage the balljoint rubber during separation.
4   Unscrew and remove the lower column flexible coupling retaining nuts.
5   Detach and remove the heat shield from the steering gear unit. It is

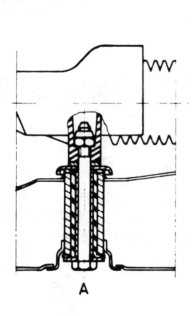

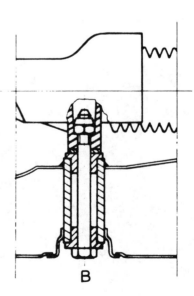

Fig. 10.45 Steering gear mountings on early models (pre 1984) (Sec 18)

A   BX and BX 14   *B   BX 16 and BX 17*

secured by a screw on the topside and a wire clip underneath (photo).
6 On BX and BX 14 models loosen the bolt retaining the
speedometer cable support and rotate the support towards the rack
housing to disengage the speedometer cable.
7 On BX 16 and 19 models undo the bolt and disconnect the
gearchange control pivot from its balljoint (photo).
8 Unscrew the two steering gear retaining bolts and withdraw them
from the underside of the subframe (photo). The steering gear can now
be withdrawn from the side of the vehicle. As it is withdrawn, collect
the thrust washers and shims from the mounting points and mark them
for identification. Keep them separate, as they must be refitted to their
original positions or the steering geometry will be upset.
9 Refitting is a reverse of the removal procedure, but note the
following special points.

   (a) Locate the mounting thrust washers and shims in their
        original positions
   (b) Where fitted, always use new Nylstop nuts
   (c) Tighten all nuts and bolts to their specified torque settings
   (d) When reconnecting the steering column joints, ensure that
        the alignment is correct (see Section 15, paragraph 11)

10 On completion check the front wheel alignment, as described in
Section 21.

18.4 Flexible coupling retaining nuts (arrowed)

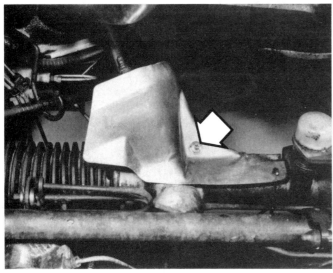
18.5A Undo the heat shield retaining screw (arrowed) ...

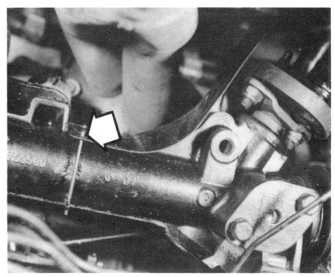
18.5B ... and release the retaining clip on the underside (arrowed)

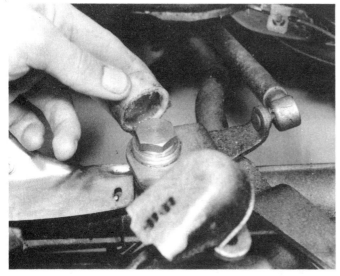
18.7 Gearchange control pivot bolt and cover – BX 16 and BX 19
models

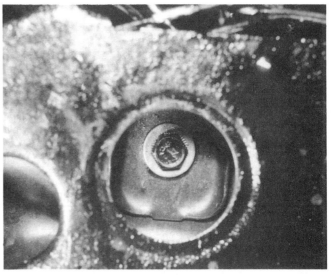
18.8 Steering gear retaining bolt location through the subframe (all
later models)

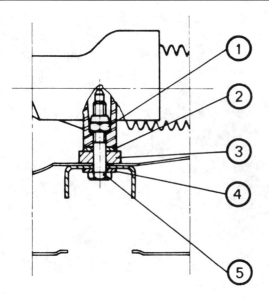

Fig. 10.46 Steering gear mountings on all 1984 on models (Sec 18)

1 *Locknut*   4 *Flexible washer*
2 *Adjustment shim*   5 *Bolt*
3 *Spacer (11 mm thick)*

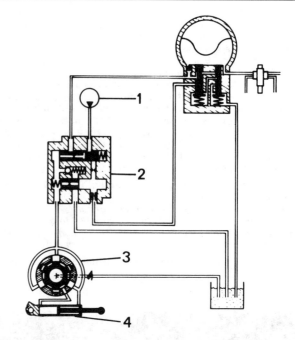

Fig. 10.47 Power steering components and hydraulic circuit (Sec 19)

1 *HP pump*   3 *Control valve (integral with*
2 *Flow distributor*   *steering gear pinion)*
                           4 *Power operating ram*

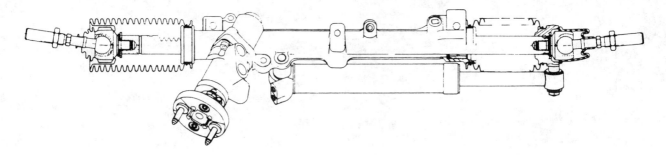

Fig. 10.48 Power steering gear unit (Sec 19)

19 Power-assisted steering – general

Power-assisted steering is available on certain models. The power assistance is derived from a power-operated hydraulic ram cylinder mounted on the steering rack. The hydraulic pressure to the ram is supplied by the main suspension and braking system hydraulic circuit; the pressure being controlled by a flow distributor unit and a control valve. The system layout and hydraulic circuit diagrams are shown in Figs. 10.47 and 10.48.

20 Power steering gear unit – removal and refitting

1   Chock the rear roadwheels and loosen the front roadwheel bolts. Raise the vehicle at the front end and support on safety stands. Remove the front roadwheels.
2   Release the hydraulic system pressure by loosening the pressure regulator release screw 1 to 1$\frac{1}{2}$ turns.
3   Rotate the steering wheel from lock to lock to remove as much hydraulic fluid as possible from the steering ram cylinder.

4   Working inside the vehicle, detach and remove the lower steering column shroud then loosen the upper steering column universal joint bolt and the joint-to-steering wheel shaft clamp bolt (1 in Fig. 10.49). Prise free the lower column-to-bulkhead gaiter.
5   Undo the two lower column-to-flexible flange coupling nuts to disengage the coupling.
6   Loosen the track rod outer balljoint nut then, using a balljoint separator, detach the joint. Remove the separator and the nut and repeat the procedure on the opposite track rod outer balljoint. Take care not to damage the balljoint rubber during separation.
7   Unscrew the bolt and disconnect the gearchange control pivot from its balljoint.
8   Clean the hydraulic supply and return pipe unions at the steering ram connections, also the overflow pipe, then disconnect them from the ram. Plug them to prevent leakage and the ingress of dirt (Figs. 10.50 and 10.51).
9   Detach and remove the heat shield from the steering gear unit.
10 Undo the steering ram retaining bolt at each end and detach the ram from the steering gear unit.
11 Unscrew the two steering gear retaining bolts and withdraw them from the underside of the subframe.
12 The steering gear is now ready to be withdrawn. As it is withdrawn, collect the shims from each mounting, mark them for identification and

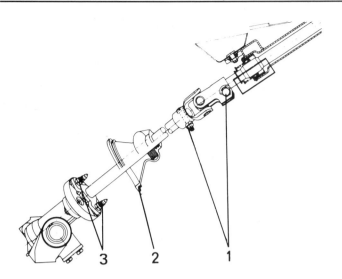

Fig. 10.49 Steering column joints (Sec 20)

1 Upper coupling bolts   3 Lower coupling nuts
2 Rubber gaiter

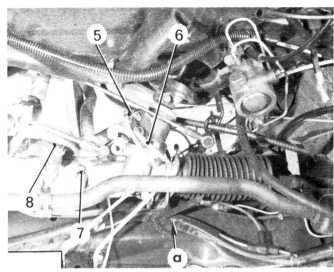

Fig. 10.50 Power steering gear removal – LH drive shown
(Sec 20)

5 Supply pipe   8 Pivot bolt (gearchange)
6 Return pipe   a Return pipes retaining collar
7 Gearchange balljoint

Fig. 10.51 Power steering gear unit attachments and
mountings – LH drive shown (Sec 20)

9   Hydraulic pipe union (feed)   13 Overflow return pipe
10 Hydraulic pipe union (feed)   14 Hydraulic ram retaining bolt
11 Heat shield   15 Steering gear mounting
12 Hydraulic ram retaining bolt   bolts

Fig. 10.52 Power steering gear unit removal (Sec 20)

keep them separate. The shims must be refitted to their original positions or the steering geometry will be upset. As the steering gear is removed, turn it fully on to the right-hand lock, engage the steering to the right and withdraw the steering gear from the underside of the vehicle.
13 Refitting is a reversal of the removal procedure, but note the following special points.

(a) Observe the special points outlined in Section 18, paragraphs 9 and 10
(b) Use a new seal when reconnecting the high pressure supply pipe. The return pipe and the ram supply pipes do not have seals fitted
(c) When reconnecting and securing the steering column universal joint ensure that the steering is in the straight-ahead position and the steering wheel spoke is downwards

14 Check the front wheel alignment on completion and top up the hydraulic fluid system if required, as described in Chapter 8. Turn the steering from lock-to-lock with the engine running to ensure satisfactory action and road test the car.

21 Wheel alignment – checking and adjusting

1 Accurate wheel alignment is essential for good steering and slow tyre wear. Before checking it, make sure that the suspension heights are correct and that the tyres are correctly inflated.
2 Place the car on level ground with the wheels in the straight-ahead position.
3 With the ground clearance lever in the 'normal' position and the

engine idling, measure the toe of the front wheels using a wheel alignment gauge. The amount of toe must be as given in the Specifications.

4 If adjustment is necessary, proceed as follows to adjust the front wheel alignment.

5 Hold the track rod inner end stationary by fitting a spanner onto its hexagonal section and loosen the outer rod locknut (photo). Repeat this procedure on the opposing track rod.

6 Adjustment is now made by turning the track rod inner end each side by an equal amount. It may also be necessary to release the steering gaiters to prevent them from distorting as the inner track rods are turned. Turn the track rod inner ends by an equal amount each side until the alignment is correct, then retighten the locknut on each side.

7 A further steering geometry check can be made by checking for any variation of the wheel alignment each side then set between the normal (intermediate) and high position. The variation per wheel should be between 0.5 mm toe-out and 1.0 mm toe-in.

8 Any adjustment necessary in this instance is made by fitting an alternative shim between the steering gear rack housing and the axle. Shims are available in thicknesses of 0.5, 1.0 and 1.5 mm. A 1.0 mm thick shim gives an equivalent toe-out variation. Refer to Section 18 for the shim location and fitting details according to model.

9 Castor and camber angles can only be checked with special equipment and this work is best entrusted to a Citroën garage. These angles are set in production and cannot be adjusted. Any deviation from specification must therefore be due to damage or gross wear in the suspension components.

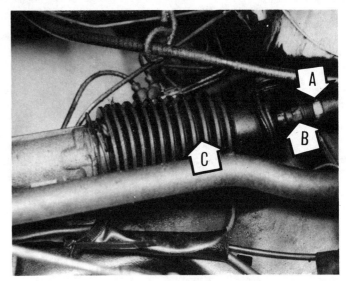

21.5 Track rod locknut (A), inner end (B) and rack gaiter (C)

22 Fault diagnosis – suspension and steering

Symptom	Reason(s)
Excessive free movement in steering wheel	Worn steering gear Worn track rod end balljoints Worn flexible coupling
Wander	Incorrect wheel alignment Worn steering knuckle balljoints Uneven tyre pressures Faulty suspension cylinder Worn or seized suspension arm bearings
Heavy or stiff steering	Incorrect wheel alignment Tyre pressures incorrect (see Chapter 7) Seized balljoint Faulty steering gear Faulty control valve or flow distributor (power steering)
Wheel wobble and vibration	Roadwheels out of balance Incorrect wheel alignment Worn wheel bearings
Low suspension height	Fault in hydraulic system Incorrect adjustment of height correctors Seized height corrector balljoints Faulty suspension cylinder Damaged hydraulic pipe
Excessive tyre wear	Incorrect wheel alignment Incorrect tyre pressures (see Chapter 7)

Chapter 11 Bodywork and fittings

For modifications, and information applicable to later models, see Supplement at end of manual

Contents

1 General description

The bodywork on all current BX models is of the five-door Hatchback type, although at the time of writing a five-door Estate variant was being introduced.

The main bodyshell and underframe are of all-steel monocoque construction, but certain panels, such as the bonnet, tailgate and rear quarter panels, are manufactured in synthetic material. Apart from their rust-free qualities, these panels reduce the total weight of the vehicle (Fig. 11.1).

The laminated windscreen is bonded in position and provides a considerable increase in the torsional rigidity of the bodyshell.

The bumpers are of EPDM polypropylene construction and have the combined advantages of being both light in structure and resistant to low speed impact.

Certain body panels are detachable to reduce the cost of repair and, where necessary, replacement.

2 Maintenance – bodywork and underframe

1 The general condition of a vehicle's bodywork is the one thing that significantly affects its value. Maintenance is easy but needs to be regular. Neglect, particularly after minor damage, can lead quickly to further deterioration and costly repair bills. It is important also to keep watch on those parts of the vehicle not immediately visible, for instance the underside, inside all the wheel arches and the lower part of the engine compartment.

2 The basic maintenance routine for the bodywork is washing – preferably with a lot of water, from a hose. This will remove all the loose solids which may have stuck to the vehicle. It is important to flush these off in such a way as to prevent grit from scratching the finish. The wheel arches and underframe need washing in the same way to remove any accumulated mud which will retain moisture and tend to encourage rust. Paradoxically enough, the best time to clean the underframe and wheel arches is in wet weather when the mud

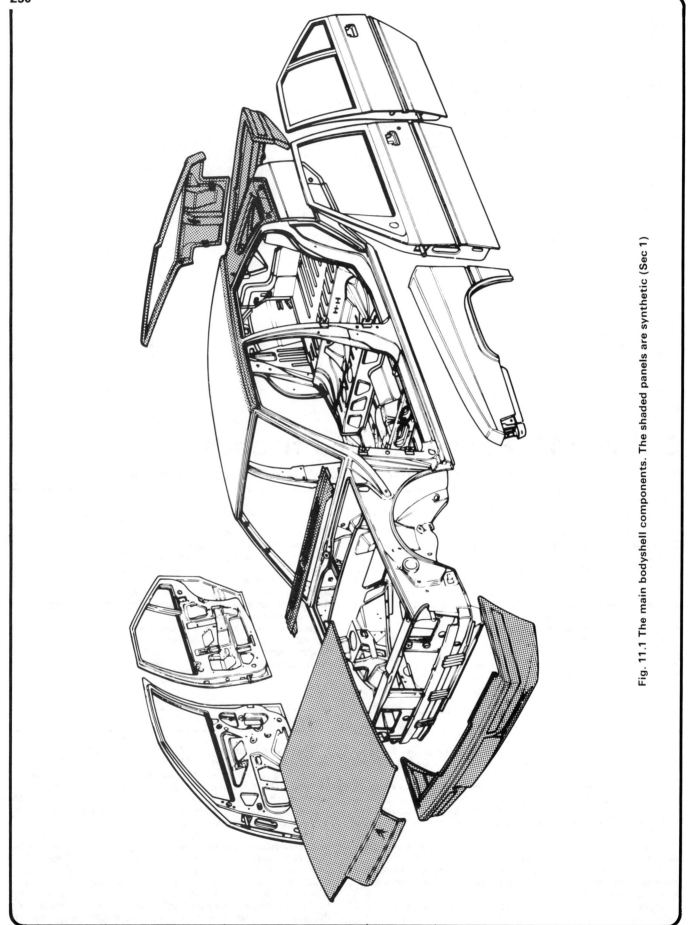

Fig. 11.1 The main bodyshell components. The shaded panels are synthetic (Sec 1)

is thoroughly wet and soft. In very wet weather the underframe is usually cleaned of large accumulations automatically and this is a good time for inspection.

3 Periodically, except on vehicles with a wax-based underbody protective coating, it is a good idea to have the whole of the underframe of the vehicle steam cleaned, engine compartment included, so that a thorough inspection can be carried out to see what minor repairs and renovations are necessary. Steam cleaning is available at many garages and is necessary for removal of the accumulation of oily grime which sometimes is allowed to become thick in certain areas. If steam cleaning facilities are not available, there are one or two excellent grease solvents available, such as Holts Engine Cleaner or Holts Foambrite, which can be brush applied. The dirt can then be simply hosed off. Note that these methods should not be used on vehicles with wax-based underbody protective coating or the coating will be removed. Such vehicles should be inspected annually, preferably just prior to winter, when the underbody should be washed down and any damage to the wax coating repaired using Holts Undershield. Ideally, a completely fresh coat should be applied. It would also be worth considering the use of such wax-based protection for injection into door panels, sills, box sections, etc, as an additional safeguard against rust damage where such protection is not provided by the vehicle manufacturer.

4 After washing paintwork, wipe off with a chamois leather to give an unspotted clear finish. A coat of clear protective wax polish, like the many excellent Turtle Wax polishes, will give added protection against chemical pollutants in the air. If the paintwork sheen has dulled or oxidised, use a cleaner/polisher combination such as Turtle Extra to restore the brilliance of the shine. This requires a little effort, but such dulling is usually caused because regular washing has been neglected. Care needs to be taken with metallic paintwork, as special non-abrasive cleaner/polisher is required to avoid damage to the finish. Always check that the door and ventilator opening drain holes and pipes are completely clear so that water can be drained out (photos). Bright work should be treated in the same way as paint work. Windscreens and windows can be kept clear of the smeary film which often appears by the use of a proprietary glass cleaner like Holts Mixra. Never use any form of wax or other body or chromium polish on glass.

3 Maintenance – upholstery and carpets

Mats and carpets should be brushed or vacuum cleaned regularly to keep them free of grit. If they are badly stained remove them from the vehicle for scrubbing or sponging and make quite sure they are dry before refitting. Seats and interior trim panels can be kept clean by wiping with a damp cloth and Turtle Wax Carisma. If they do become stained (which can be more apparent on light coloured upholstery) use a little liquid detergent and a soft nail brush to scour the grime out of the grain of the material. Do not forget to keep the headlining clean in the same way as the upholstery. When using liquid cleaners inside the vehicle do not over-wet the surfaces being cleaned. Excessive damp could get into the seams and padded interior causing stains, offensive odours or even rot. If the inside of the vehicle gets wet accidentally it is worthwhile taking some trouble to dry it out properly, particularly where carpets are involved. *Do not leave oil or electric heaters inside the vehicle for this purpose.*

4 Synthetic body panels – repair notes

Certain body panels on the BX range are manufactured in synthetic materials to reduce body weight and to give the added advantage of being non-corrosive. The synthetic panels used differ in their composite properties and any repairs to be made will differ in technique according to type. The various panels and their material type are shown in Figs. 11.2 and 11.3. To increase the strength of some panels (such as the bonnet and tailgate) the material is reinforced with glass-fibre.

Repair methods and the materials used differ according to the panel type and the extent of the repair required. The use of the correct repair materials and their application is therefore critical to the success and lasting qualities of any repairs. In view of this, repairs to damaged panels are not generally recommended to be undertaken by the

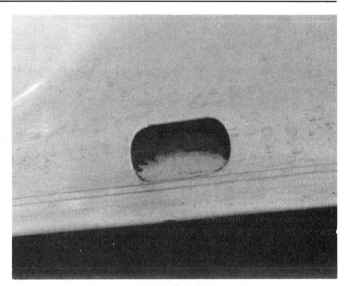

2.4A Drain/ventilation holes in the base of the doors must be kept clear

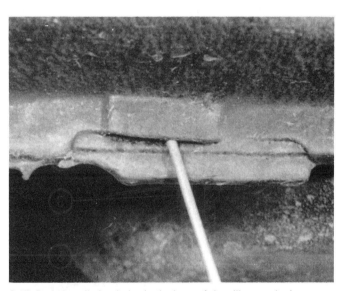

2.4B Drain/ventilation holes in the base of the sills must be kept clear. Use a suitable rod to clear them

average home mechanic due to the specialised tools, material requirements and skills required to effect satisfactory repairs.

If, however, you have had experience in repairing synthetic panels and are confident enough to undertake a competent repair, first consult your Citroën dealer for advice on the material requirements and any special procedures which may be necessary for the panel concerned.

Where extensive repairs are required, it will pay to obtain a repair quote from your Citroën dealer or qualified motor body repair shop and compare the cost against fitting a replacement panel. The cost of a new panel may be comparable, if not cheaper, in which case panel renewal would be the easier and more satisfactory solution.

5 Minor body damage – repair

The colour bodywork repair photographic sequences between pages 32 and 33 illustrate the operations detailed in the following sub-sections.

Note: *For more detailed information about bodywork repair, the Haynes Publishing Group publish a book by Lindsay Porter called The Car Bodywork Repair Manual. This incorporates information on such aspects as rust treatment, painting and glass fibre repairs, as well as details on more ambitious repairs involving welding and panel beating.*

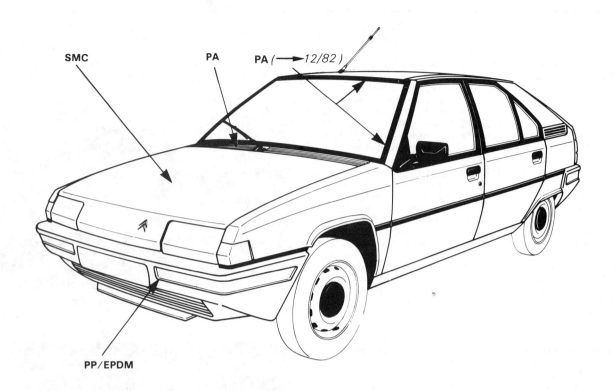

Fig. 11.2 Three quarter front view showing synthetic panel locations and composition types (Sec 2)

Symbol	Material	Components
PA	Polyamide	Front and rear vent grilles
PC	Polycarbonate	Quarter panel centre section (BX 16)
PP/EPDM	Polypropylene	Front and rear bumpers
SMC	Sheet moulding compound	Bonnet, roof panel side edges. Rear quarter panels (BX 14). Rear quarter panel upper section (BX 16)
BMC	Bulk moulding compound	Tailgate

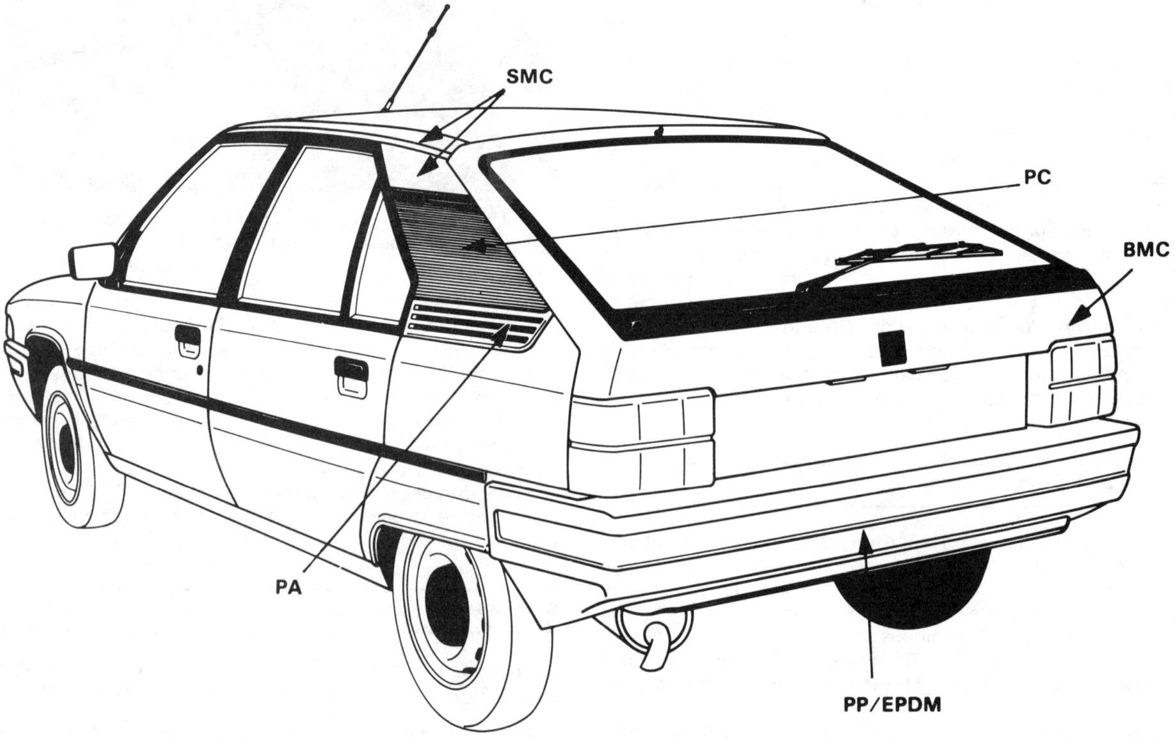

Fig. 11.3 Three quarter rear view (BX 16), showing synthetic panel locations and composition types (Sec 2)

Repair of minor scratches in bodywork

If the scratch is very superficial, and does not penetrate to the metal of the bodywork, repair is very simple. Lightly rub the area of the scratch with a paintwork renovator like Turtle Wax New Color Back, or a very fine cutting paste like Holts Body + Plus Rubbing Compound to remove loose paint from the scratch and to clear the surrounding bodywork of wax polish. Rinse the area with clean water.

Apply touch-up paint, such as Holts Dupli-Color Color Touch or a paint film like Holts Autofilm, to the scratch using a fine paint brush; continue to apply fine layers of paint until the surface of the paint in the scratch is level with the surrounding paintwork. Allow the new paint at least two weeks to harden: then blend it into the surrounding paintwork by rubbing the scratch area with a paintwork renovator or a very fine cutting paste, such as Holts Body + Plus Rubbing Compound or Turtle Wax New Color Back. Finally, apply wax polish from one of the Turtle Wax range of wax polishes.

Where the scratch has penetrated right through to the metal of the bodywork, causing the metal to rust, a different repair technique is required. Remove any loose rust from the bottom of the scratch with a penknife, then apply rust inhibiting paint, such as Turtle Wax Rust Master, to prevent the formation of rust in the future. Using a rubber or nylon applicator fill the scratch with bodystopper paste like Holts Body + Plus Knifing Putty. If required, this paste can be mixed with cellulose thinners, such as Holts Body + Plus Cellulose Thinners, to provide a very thin paste which is ideal for filling narrow scratches. Before the stopper-paste in the scratch hardens, wrap a piece of smooth cotton rag around the top of a finger. Dip the finger in cellulose thinners, such as Holts Body + Plus Cellulose Thinners, and then quickly sweep it across the surface of the stopper-paste in the scratch; this will ensure that the surface of the stopper-paste is slightly hollowed. The scratch can now be painted over as described earlier in this Section.

Repair of dents in bodywork

When deep denting of the vehicle's bodywork has taken place, the first task is to pull the dent out, until the affected bodywork almost attains its original shape. There is little point in trying to restore the original shape completely, as the metal in the damaged area will have stretched on impact and cannot be reshaped fully to its original contour. It is better to bring the level of the dent up to a point which is about ⅛ in (3 mm) below the level of the surrounding bodywork. In cases where the dent is very shallow anyway, it is not worth trying to pull it out at all. If the underside of the dent is accessible, it can be hammered out gently from behind, using a mallet with a wooden or plastic head. Whilst doing this, hold a suitable block of wood firmly against the outside of the panel to absorb the impact from the hammer blows and thus prevent a large area of the bodywork from being 'belled-out'.

Should the dent be in a section of the bodywork which has a double skin or some other factor making it inaccessible from behind, a different technique is called for. Drill several small holes through the metal inside the area – particulary in the deeper section. Then screw long self-tapping screws into the holes just sufficiently for them to gain a good purchase in the metal. Now the dent can be pulled out by pulling on the protruding heads of the screws with a pair of pliers.

The next stage of the repair is the removal of the paint from the damaged area, and from an inch or so of the surrounding 'sound' bodywork. This is accomplished most easily by using a wire brush or abrasive pad on a power drill, although it can be done just as effectively by hand using sheets of abrasive paper. To complete the preparation for filling, score the surface of the bare metal with a screwdriver or the tang of a file, or alternatively, drill small holes in the affected area. This will provide a really good 'key' for the filler paste.

To complete the repair see the Section on filling and re-spraying.

Repair of rust holes or gashes in bodywork

Remove all paint from the affected area and from an inch or so of the surrounding 'sound' bodywork, using an abrasive pad or a wire brush on a power drill. If these are not available a few sheets of abrasive paper will do the job just as effectively. With the paint removed you will be able to gauge the severity of the corrosion and therefore decide whether to renew the whole panel (if this is possible) or to repair the affected area. New body panels are not as expensive as most people think and it is often quicker and more satisfactory to fit a new panel than to attempt to repair large areas of corrosion.

Remove all fittings from the affected area except those which will act as a guide to the original shape of the damaged bodywork (eg headlamp shells etc). Then, using tin snips or a hacksaw blade, remove all loose metal and any other metal badly affected by corrosion. Hammer the edges of the hole inwards in order to create a slight depression for the filler paste.

Wire brush the affected area to remove the powdery rust from the surface of the remaining metal. Paint the affected area with rust inhibiting paint like Turtle Wax Rust Master; if the back of the rusted area is accessible treat this also.

Before filling can take place it will be necessary to block the hole in some way. This can be achieved by the use of aluminium or plastic mesh, or aluminium tape.

Aluminium or plastic mesh or glass fibre matting, such as the Holts Body + Plus Glass Fibre Matting, is probably the best material to use for a large hole. Cut a piece to the approximate size and shape of the hole to be filled, then position it in the hole so that its edges are below the level of the surrounding bodywork. It can be retained in position by several blobs of filler paste around its periphery.

Aluminium tape should be used for small or very narrow holes. Pull a piece off the roll and trim it to the approximate size and shape required, then pull off the backing paper (if used) and stick the tape over the hole; it can be overlapped if the thickness of one piece is insufficient. Burnish down the edges of the tape with the handle of a screwdriver or similar, to ensure that the tape is securely attached to the metal underneath.

Bodywork repairs – filling and re-spraying

Before using this Section, see the Sections on dent, deep scratch, rust holes and gash repairs.

Many types of bodyfiller are available, but generally speaking those proprietary kits which contain a tin of filler paste and a tube of resin hardener are best for this type of repair, like Holts Body + Plus or Holts No Mix which can be used directly from the tube. A wide, flexible plastic or nylon applicator will be found invaluable for imparting a smooth and well contoured finish to the surface of the filler.

Mix up a little filler on a clean piece of card or board – measure the hardener carefully (follow the maker's instructions on the pack) otherwise the filler will set too rapidly or too slowly. Alternatively, Holts No Mix can be used straight from the tube without mixing, but daylight is required to cure it. Using the applicator apply the filler paste to the prepared area; draw the applicator across the surface of the filler to achieve the correct contour and to level the filler surface. As soon as a contour that approximates to the correct one is achieved, stop working the paste – if you carry on too long the paste will become sticky and begin to 'pick up' on the applicator. Continue to add thin layers of filler paste at twenty-minute intervals until the level of the filler is just proud of the surrounding bodywork.

Once the filler has hardened, excess can be removed using a metal plane or file. From then on, progressively finer grades of abrasive paper should be used, starting with a 40 grade production paper and finishing with 400 grade wet-and-dry paper. Always wrap the abrasive paper around a flat rubber, cork, or wooden block – otherwise the surface of the filler will not be completely flat. During the smoothing of the filler surface the wet-and-dry paper should be periodically rinsed in water. This will ensure that a very smooth finish is imparted to the filler at the final stage.

At this stage the 'dent' should be surrounded by a ring of bare metal, which in turn should be encircled by the finely 'feathered' edge of the good paintwork. Rinse the repair area with clean water, until all of the dust produced by the rubbing-down operation has gone.

Spray the whole repair area with a light coat of primer, either Holts Body + Plus Grey or Red Oxide Primer – this will show up any imperfections in the surface of the filler. Repair these imperfections with fresh filler paste or bodystopper, and once more smooth the surface with abrasive paper. If bodystopper is used, it can be mixed with cellulose thinners to form a really thin paste which is ideal for filling small holes. Repeat this spray and repair procedure until you are satisfied that the surface of the filler, and the feathered edge of the paintwork are perfect. Clean the repair area with clean water and allow to dry fully.

The repair area is now ready for final spraying. Paint spraying must be carried out in a warm, dry, windless and dust free atmosphere. This condition can be created artificially if you have access to a large indoor working area, but if you are forced to work in the open, you will have to pick your day very carefully. If you are working indoors, dousing the floor in the work area with water will help to settle the dust which would otherwise be in the atmosphere. If the repair area is confined to one body panel, mask off the surrounding panels; this will help to minimise the effects of a slight mis-match in paint colours. Bodywork fittings (eg chrome strips, door handles etc) will also need to be masked off. Use genuine masking tape and several thicknesses of newspaper for the masking operations.

Before commencing to spray, agitate the aerosol can thoroughly, then spray a test area (an old tin, or similar) until the technique is mastered. Cover the repair area with a thick coat of primer; the thickness should be built up using several thin layers of paint rather than one thick one. Using 400 grade wet-and-dry paper, rub down the surface of the primer until it is really smooth. While doing this, the work area should be thoroughly doused with water, and the wet-and-dry paper periodically rinsed in water. Allow to dry before spraying on more paint.

Spray on the top coat using Holts Dupli-Color Autospray, again building up the thickness by using several thin layers of paint. Start spraying in the centre of the repair area and then, with a single side-to-side motion, work outwards until the whole repair area and about 2 inches of the surrounding original paintwork is covered. Remove all masking material 10 to 15 minutes after spraying on the final coat of paint.

Allow the new paint at least two weeks to harden, then, using a paintwork renovator or a very fine cutting paste such as Turtle Wax New Color Back or Holts Body + Plus Rubbing Compound, blend the edges of the paint into the existing paintwork. Finally, apply wax polish.

6 Major body damage – repair

Where serious damage has occurred or large areas need renewal due to neglect, it means certainly that complete sections or panels will need to be renewed and this is best left to professionals. If the damage is due to impact it will also be necessary to completely check the alignment of the bodyshell structure. Due to the principle of construction the strength and shape of the whole car can be affected by damage to a part. In such instances the services of a Citroën agent with specialist checking jigs are essential. If a body is left misaligned it is first of all dangerous as the car will not handle properly and secondly uneven stresses will be imposed on the steering, engine and transmission, causing abnormal wear or complete failure. Tyre wear may also be excessive.

7 Maintenance – hinges and locks

1 Oil the hinges of the bonnet, doors and boot or tailgate with a drop or two of light oil periodically. A good time is after the car has been washed.
2 Oil the bonnet release catch mechanism and striker pin periodically.
3 Do not over lubricate door latches and strikers. Normally a little oil on the lock spindle is sufficient.

8 Door rattles – tracing and rectification

1 Check that the door is not loose at the hinges and that the latch is holding it firmly in position. Check also that the door lines up with the aperture in the body.
2 If the door is out of alignment, adjust it as described in Section 19.
3 If the latch is holding the door in the correct position but the latch still rattles, the lock mechanism is worn out and requires renewal.
4 Other rattles from the door could be caused by wear in the window operating mechanism or electric motors, interior lock mechanism, or loose glass channels.

9 Bonnet – removal, refitting and adjustment

1 Support the bonnet in its open position, and place some cardboard or rags beneath the corners by the hinges.
2 The bonnet is not adjustable at the hinges for position so there is no need to mark their relative positions.

9.3 Bonnet hinge retaining nuts. Note earth strap under lower nut and washer

3 With the help of an assistant, unscrew the four retaining nuts, noting that an earth strap is located on the rear ones (photo). Lift the bonnet from the car.
4 Refitting of the bonnet is a reversal of the removal procedure. When fitted, close the bonnet and check it for correct alignment. An even clearance should exist around the bonnet at the wings, the bulkhead grille and the headlights, and the front bumper at the leading edge.
5 When fully closed, there should be a 10 mm (0.4 in) clearance between the bonnet leading edge and the headlamp unit each side, the bonnet top face being flush to the top edge of the wing panels.
6 Check that, when fully closed, the bonnet is fully locked then release the lock and check that the safety catch is satisfactory.
7 If necessary the bonnet lock and safety catch can be adjusted by loosening the retaining bolts or nuts as applicable, repositioning the lock unit or safety catch and retightening the bolts/nuts. Recheck the operation of the lock and safety catch on completion.

10 Bonnet lock – removal and refitting

1 Open the bonnet and support it. If a malfunction of the bonnet lock or cable does not allow the bonnet to open by normal means, it can be released by inserting a suitable length of wire rod hooked over at its end between the headlamp unit and the underside of the bonnet. Hook the end of the rod onto the release lever and pull it towards the left to release the lock (Fig. 11.4).
2 Loosen the cable clamp screw and disconnect the cable from the lock operating lever (photo).
3 Mark the location of the lock with a pencil, then loosen the two retaining bolts and withdraw the lock.
4 Refit the lock reversing the removal procedure. Align it with the pencil marks made during removal before tightening the bolts. Adjust the release cable to remove almost all slackness from it. This can be judged by allowing a fraction of free movement at the release knob end.
5 Closure of the bonnet should now be checked and adjusted, if necessary, as described in the previous Section.

11 Front wing – removal and refitting

1 Disconnect the battery earth lead.
2 Referring to Chapter 12, remove the headlight unit and front indicator unit from the side concerned.
3 Where possible, make pencilled alignment marks of the wing fitting position against corresponding body panels to assist with correct realignment when refitting.

Fig. 11.4 Alternative method of releasing the bonnet catch (Sec 10)

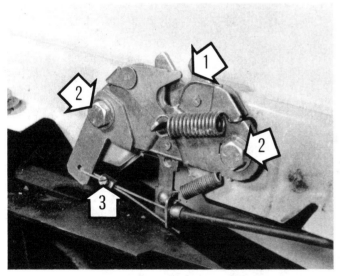

10.2 Bonnet lock (1), retaining bolts (2) and cable clamp (3)

Fig. 11.5 Remove the retaining bolts and washers (arrowed) from the front wing leading edge (Sec 11)

4 Undo and remove the bolts and nuts along the top edge of the wing (five in all).
5 Disconnect the wing at the front leading edge by undoing the two retaining bolts (Fig. 11.5).
6 Undo and remove the single retaining bolt and washer shown in Fig. 11.6.
7 Open the front door fully then undo the two rear edge retaining bolts shown in Fig. 11.7.
8 The wing panel can now be lifted away after prising it free from the mastic at the flange joints.

9 Before refitting the wing panel clean away all traces of the old mastic sealant and apply a new bead of sealant. Check that the three captive nuts are in the positions shown in Fig. 11.8.
10 When refitting the wing, do not fully tighten the retaining bolts until they are all in position and the wing is correctly aligned with the adjacent panels.
11 When the headlight and indicator units are refitted, reconnect the battery and check for satisfactory operation of the lights and the headlamp alignment (see Chapter 12).

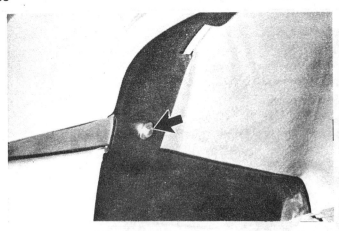

Fig. 11.6 Remove single retaining bolt and washer (arrowed) from the front wing (Sec 11)

Fig. 11.7 Front wing rear edge retaining bolt locations (arrowed) (Sec 11)

Fig. 11.8 Captive nut locations (arrowed) for attachment of front wing (Sec 11)

12.2 Door mirror adjuster knob and gaiter

12.4 Countersunk screw retaining the inner plate (arrowed)

12.5A Door mirror retaining nuts (arrowed)

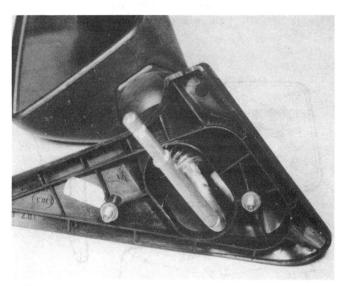

12.5B Door mirror unit removed

12 Door mirror – removal and refitting

1   If the mirror glass has broken, this can be renewed without removing the mirror from the door by referring to Section 13.
2   Prise back the rubber gaiter from the trim panel and pull free the adjuster knob and gaiter (photo).
3   Undo the inset screw and remove the trim plate.
4   Undo the countersunk screw and remove the inner retaining plate (photo).
5   Support the mirror unit and undo the two retaining nuts using a suitable socket or box spanner and remove the mirror unit (photos).
6   Refit in the reverse order of removal.

13 Door mirror glass – renewal

1   This can be achieved with the mirror unit in position on the door, but to protect the door paintwork wind down the door window and cover the panel with a suitable cloth.
2   One of two types of mirror will be fitted, being either of Britax or Hohe manufacture (see Fig. 11.9). The glass replacement for each differs as given below.

Britax mirror

3   With this type, the glass is bonded in position in each corner at the points indicated in Fig. 11.10. Break the glass (using care) and remove the remaining fragments.
4   Clean the bonding adhesive from the four points indicated in the mirror unit.
5   Carefully peel off the backing paper from the adhesive squares on the rear of the new glass then carefully locate and press the glass into position in the mirror unit.

Hohe type mirror

6   Carefully prise free the retaining ring from the perimeter of the glass using a flat-bladed screwdriver and extract the glass.
7   A new retaining ring will be supplied with the mirror glass and it will be necessary to cut the ring securing lugs down by half before the mirror and ring can be fitted.
8   Clean the perimeter area of the mirror unit to which the retaining ring is to fit. Apply a thin bead of sealant (epoxy glue Ref ZC 9 865 105 U, polyurethene sealant Ref Zc 9 867 433 U or equivalent) around the perimeter area of the mirror unit to which the sealing ring will fit (Fig. 11.12).
9   Carefully locate the glass and the retaining ring into position. Secure them in this position using adhesive tape for the period specified by the glue/sealant manufacture to allow full adhesion of the ring and glass to the mirror, then remove the tape.

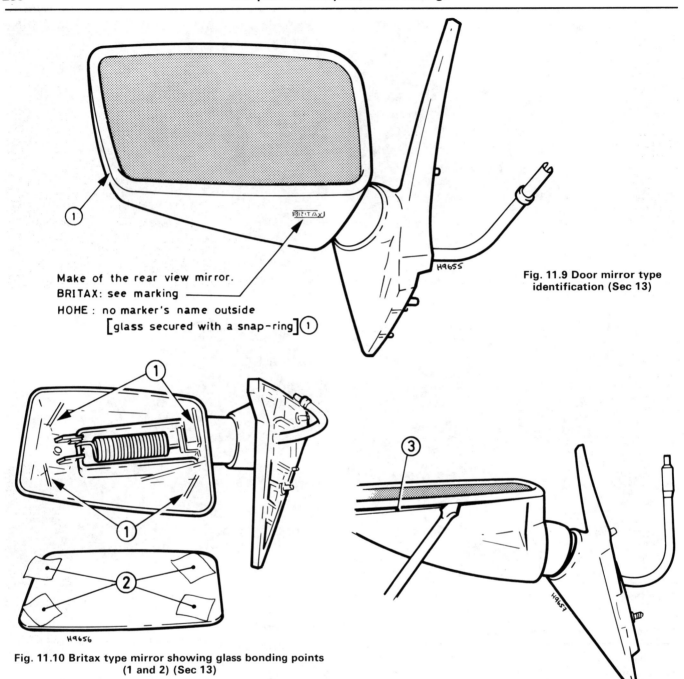

Make of the rear view mirror.
BRITAX: see marking
HOHE : no marker's name outside
    [glass secured with a snap-ring]①

Fig. 11.9 Door mirror type
identification (Sec 13)

Fig. 11.10 Britax type mirror showing glass bonding points
(1 and 2) (Sec 13)

Fig. 11.11 Prise free the retaining ring (3) to remove the glass
– Hohe type mirror (Sec 13)

Fig. 11.12 Apply sealant around perimeter (a) – Hohe type
mirror (Sec 13)

14 Door trim panel – removal and refitting

1   On models fitted with a manual window regulator, insert a piece of wire, having a small hook at its end, between the window winder handle and the boss on the door inner panel. Engage the hook with the handle securing spring clip and extract the clip. Remove the handle (photo).

2   Unscrew and remove the door lock knob.

3   Undo the three retaining screws and remove the door pull/armrest. Unclip and remove the door pull/armrest bezel.

4   Remove the door mirror adjuster knob, gaiter and trim plate, as described in Section 12.

5   Using a wide-bladed tool (or the fingers) inserted between the door inner trim panel and the door, release the panel securing clips.
6   Remove the trim panel and, on models fitted with a manual window winder regulator, take off the winder handle coil spring.
7   For access to the inner door components, carefully peel back the plastic insulation sheet.
8   Refitting is a reversal of the removal procedure.

15 Front door window regulator and glass – removal and refitting

1   Remove the door inner trim panel, as described in Section 14.
2   To remove the electric type window regulator unit refer to Chapter 12. Unbolt the roller runner channel (photo).
3   To remove the manual window regulator unit, unscrew the regulator retaining nuts and push the regulator into the door cavity.
4   Support the glass and release the rollers from the runner channel.
5   Withdraw the regulator from the door.
6   To remove the door glass, carefully detach and remove the waistline seal by prising it free from the retaining clips. Renew this seal if it is excessively worn or damaged.
7   Tilt the glass upwards at the rear and carefully withdraw it from the door.
8   Refitting is a reversal of the removal procedure. Lubricate the regulator guide channels with light grease.

16 Rear door window regulator and glass – removal and refitting

1   The procedures for removal and refitting are the same as those given for the front doors. However, before removing the door glass it is also necessary to remove the channel weatherstrip from the window aperture at its upper, lower and rear edges.
2   When refitting the glass, lower it into position and locate it into its guide channels in the lower door section then refit the weatherstrip.

17 Rear door quarter window – removal and refitting

1   Lower the door window then remove the inner door trim panel, as described in Section 14. Peel back the insulation sheet from the rear quarter section of the door.
2   Detach the main window weatherstrip from the rear separator and partially along its upper and lower aperture fixings (Fig. 11.13).
3   Detach and remove the rear separator and the lower inner strip from the bottom edge of the quarter window.
4   Press the quarter window downwards and forwards and carefully lever it away inwards at the top corner. Remove the quarter window, complete with its weatherstrip.
5   If re-using the weatherstrip clean it of mastic sealant.
6   Refitting is a reversal of the removal procedure. Apply a thin bead of mastic sealant around the outer periphery of the quarter window weatherstrip prior to fitting it into position.

18 Door lock, lock cylinder and handles – removal and refitting

1   Fully raise the door window then, referring to Section 14, remove the inner trim from the door.

Door lock

2   Prise free the nylon grommet from the rear edge of the door (photo).
3   Disconnect the control rods from the lock unit, taking care not to damage the nylon fasteners (photo). As they are disconnected, note their respective connecting points.
4   Undo the three retaining screws and withdraw the lock unit.
5   Refitting is a reversal of the removal procedure.

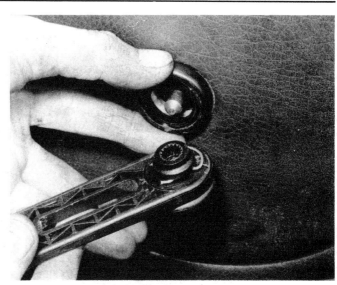

14.1 Window winder handle (manual)

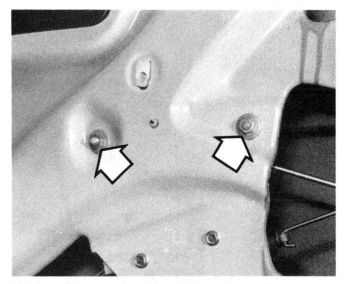

15.2 Door glass runner channel retaining nuts (arrowed)

Lock cylinder

6   Detach the connecting rod, then prise free the retaining clip (photo). Withdraw the cylinder.
7   Refit in the reverse order of removal.

Outer handle

8   Detach the connecting rod from the lock unit then undo the two retaining nuts and remove the handle (photo).
9   Refit in the reverse order of removal.

Inner handle

10   Detach the connecting rod to the lock unit, undo the two retaining bolts and remove the handle (photo).
11   Refit in the reverse order of removal.

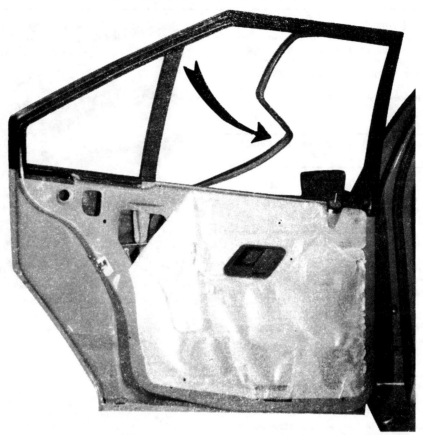

Fig. 11.13 Fold back the weatherstrip from the rear door window/quarter window (Sec 17)

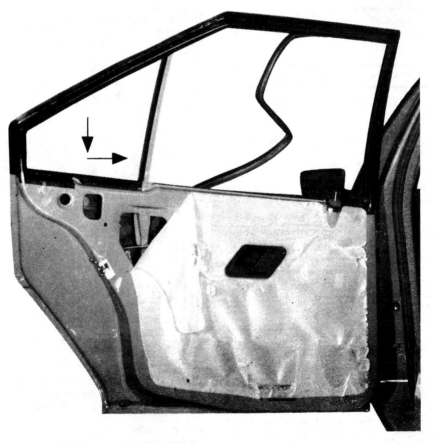

Fig. 11.14 Rear door quarter window removal (Sec 17)

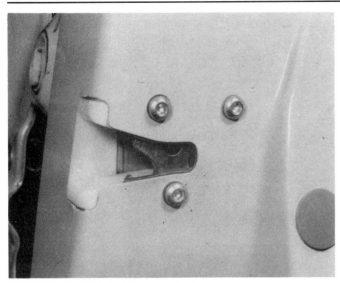
18.2 Door lock retaining screws and nylon grommet

18.3 Door lock control rods and nylon fasteners

18.6 Door lock cylinder and retaining clip (arrowed)

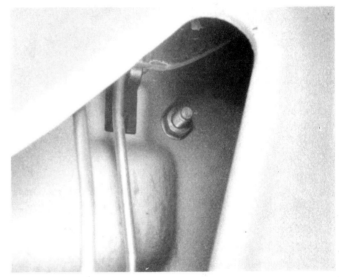
18.8 Door outer handle retaining nut

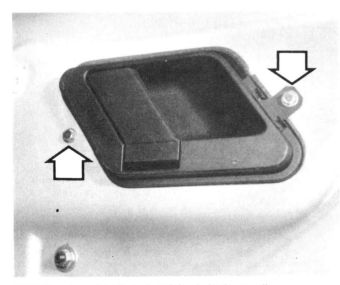
18.10 Door inner handle and retaining bolts (arrowed)

19 Doors – removal and refitting

1 Remove the door trim as described in Section 14.
2 Disconnect the wiring from the lock solenoid and the window regulator units, as applicable, and pull the wiring harness from the leading edge of the door.
3 Open the door fully and support it with blocks or a suitable jack. Use a newspaper or rag to protect the paintwork from bring scratched by the support.
4 Use a suitable diameter punch and drive out the roll pins from the door check strap and hinges. Get an assistant to support the door during this operation. Take care not to distort the hinges when removing the pins. Lift the door from the vehicle.
5 Refitting is a reversal of removal. On completion, check the door for alignment, as follows.
6 Close the door gently. If it will not close or if, when it is closed, the door exterior panel is not flush or in correct alignment with the adjacent body panels, adjust the door in the following way.
7 Open the door and using a suitably cranked bar, prise the relevant hinge. The hinges are welded to the door and the body pillar, and bending the hinges is the only means of adjustment. Do not overdo this, or it will be virtually impossible to rectify matters and the hinges will have to be renewed using a welding torch.

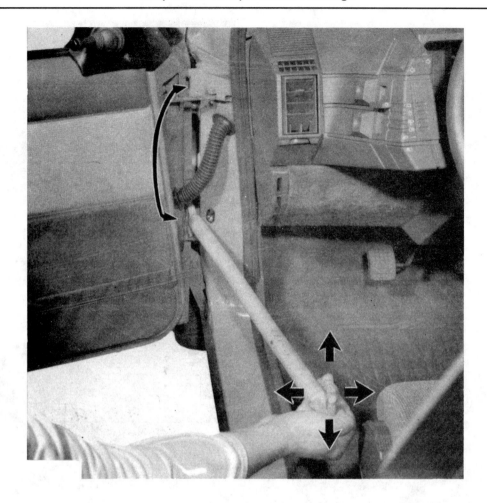

Fig. 11.15 Door adjustment is made with a cranked bar (Sec 19)

Fig. 11.16 Door adjustment tool (Sec 19)

8   Once the adjustment is correct, release the door striker and adjust its position to engage smoothly in the lock tongue.

20 Tailgate – removal and refitting

1   Disconnect the battery earth lead.
2   Prise free the retaining clips and remove the rear trim panels from the tailgate.
3   Detach the wiring connections to the rear number plate lamps, the rear window demister, the rear wiper motor and the lock solenoid unit (as applicable). Also disconnect the earth wires – noting their connections.

4   Disconnect the hose from the rear washer nozzle.
5   Withdraw the wires and the rear washer hose from the tailgate.
6   Get an assistant to support the tailgate or securely prop it, then disconnect the gas-filled struts by extracting the retaining clip at their top or bottom ends (photos).
7   Carefully prise free the hinge retaining clip each side and remove the tailgate (photo). If renewing the hinge pin and retaining clips note that there are three types used (see Fig. 11.17).
8   Refitting is a reversal of the removal procedure. On completion check the operation of the tailgate functions prior to refitting the trim panels. Check the tailgate for alignment and satisfactory locking action.

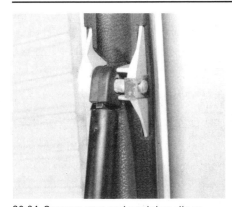

20.6A Support strut and retaining clip to tailgate

20.6B Tailgate support strut and retaining clip to body

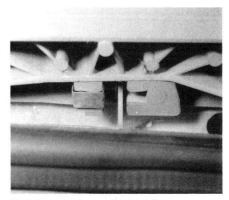

20.7 Tailgate hinge retaining clip

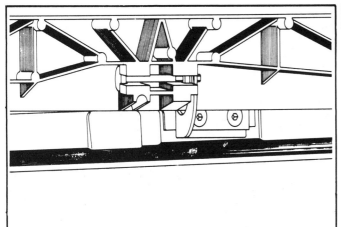

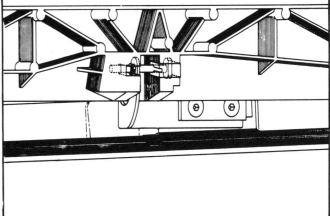

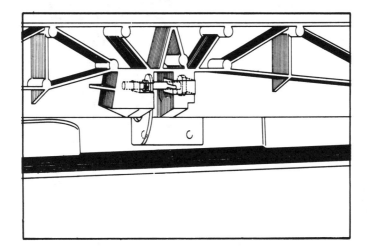

Fig. 11.17 Tailgate hinge types used (Sec 20)

21 Bumpers – removal and refitting

Front bumper

1 Raise and support the bonnet. Detach and remove the flexible panel between the headlamp units.

2 Unscrew and remove the three bumper retaining bolts from the top face of the bumper (between the headlamp units).

3 From underneath, unscrew and remove the five bolts indicated in Fig. 11.18.

4 With the aid of an assistant, simultaneously pull the bumper outwards at each corner and withdraw the bumper forwards from the vehicle.

5 Refit in the reverse order of removal, ensuring that the captive nuts are in position before fitting the bumper into position.

Rear bumper

6 Open the tailgate and remove the rear combination light units (see Chapter 12).

Fig. 11.18 Front bumper retaining bolts (arrowed) – underneath (Sec 21)

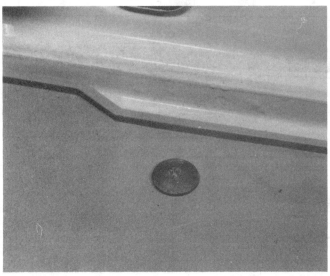

21.7 Bumper retaining bolt

21.8 Rear bumper retaining bolts – underneath

7   Unscrew and remove the three retaining bolts from the top face of the bumper (photo).
8   From underneath, unscrew and remove the three retaining bolts at the rear (photo), then remove the bumper in the same manner as that described for the front bumper (paragraph 4).
9   Refit in the reverse order of removal, ensuring that the captive nuts are in position before fitting the bumper into position.

22 Dashboard – removal and refitting

1   Disconnect the battery earth lead.
2   Prise free the glovebox light lens, withdraw the switch/light unit and detach the wiring connections from it.
3   Remove the retaining screws and remove the steering column lower shroud and lower trim panel on the driver's side, and the lower trim panel on the passenger side.
4   Remove the instrument panel, referring to Chapter 12 for details.
5   Disconnect the wiring connector at the point indicated in Fig. 11.19.

6   Remove the screw from the side of the corner vent trim (open the door for access).
7   Referring to Chapter 12, detach the fuse/relay box unit and disconnect from it the wiring loom connections from the steering column switches.
8   Undo the four retaining bolts and lower the steering column from the upper mounting bracket.
9   Remove the upper facia-mounted speaker units from each side (see Chapter 12).
10 Working from the engine compartment, undo the dashboard retaining bolt from each side of the bulkhead (Fig. 11.20).
11 The dashboard can now be carefully withdrawn. As it is removed check that all wiring connections to it are disconnected, and withdraw the left-hand column switch wiring harness (to the fusebox) through with it – noting its route location on the underside of the dashboard.
12 Refitting is a reversal of the removal procedure. Ensure that all wiring connections are securely and correctly made and that the loom routing is made as noted during removal.
13 On completion check the operations of the various switch and instrument functions.

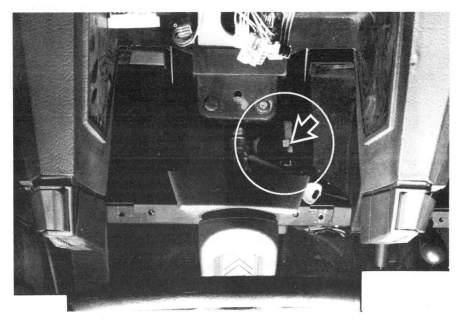

Fig. 11.19 Detach the wiring connector (arrowed) (Sec 22)

Fig. 11.20 Undo the two retaining bolts from the positions arrowed (Sec 22)

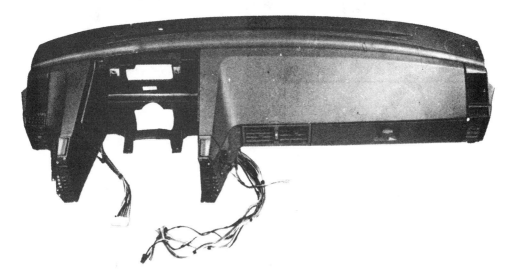

Fig. 11.21 The dashboard unit (LHD) (Sec 22)

23 Sunroof – manual operation

1   In the event of a malfunction of the sunroof electric motor, the roof panel can be closed manually.
2   Check that the sunroof operating switch is in the off position, then undo the four screws retaining the roof console in position and lower the console from the roof.
3   A manual crank handle is contained within the roof console, secured by spring clips. Remove the crank handle and engage it into the manual crank hole in the winder mechanism and turn it to shut the roof panel (Fig. 11.22).

24 Sunroof – removal, refitting and adjustments

1   With the roof panel in the closed position, raise it at its rear edge so that it is in the airflow to the passenger compartment position.
2   If required, undo the three retaining screws and remove them from the mobile frame at the front edge.
3   Unscrew and remove the three retaining screws each side and then lift out the sunroof from its tilt frame.
4   Refitting is a reversal of the removal procedure. Check that the tilt pivots are engaged each side before refitting the panel.
5   On completion, check the roof panel for correct alignment when in the closed position, referring to Fig. 11.24. The panel should be parallel at its forward and rear edges with the vehicle roof within the tolerances indicated.
6   If the alignment is not within the limits specified, lower the roof console and check to see if the alignment marks of the motor reduction gears correspond (Fig. 11.25). If they do not then proceed as follows.
7   Insert the emergency manual crank handle, check that the roof panel is fully closed and move the reducer lever clockwise to the angle shown in Fig. 11.26 to disengage the reducer.
8   Undo the two retaining screws and uncouple the motor/reducer unit from the operating cables. Check that the roof alignment is now correct.

9   To adjust the reducer gears, turn the small cam anti-clockwise to the point where the large gear cam stops meshing with it. It is important that the microswitch is located on the rear of the large cam and not in the cam recess (Fig. 11.27). Holding the cam firmly in this position, turn the small cam clockwise to the point where the gears start to mesh then move the reducer lever back to its original position. Turn the cams to align the gear alignment marks (Fig. 11.25).
10   Reconnect the operating cables, relocate the motor reducer unit and refit the two retaining screws.
11   Refit the roof console and check that the sunroof operates in a satisfactory manner. Recheck the sunroof alignment and free play when closed. If excessive distortion (more than 3 mm) still exists proceed as follows.
12   Remove the roof console and turn the reducer lever clockwise to the angle shown in Fig. 11.26.
13   Engage the emergency manual handle with the small reduction cam and wind it to fully open the roof panel.
14   Undo the two retaining screws and uncouple the motor reducer unit from the operating cables, then push the two cables with cams towards the front by pressing the frame pivots each side (Fig. 11.28).
15   Refit the motor/reducer and engage the cables.
16   Manually close the sunroof and recheck the roof alignment and free play. If necessary, adjust the reducer gear alignment marks as described previously, paragraphs 8 to 11 inclusive. Reset the reducer lever to its original setting before refitting the roof console.

25 Windscreen and tailgate glass – renewal

If you are unfortunate enough to have a windscreen or tailgate glass breakage, the removal and fitting of a replacement is one of the few jobs that the average owner is advised to leave to a Citroën dealer or body repair specialist. Body specialists are familiar with the procedures involved and have the necessary equipment for renewal. Specific sealant products are also required and unless these are used the rigidity of the assembly and its sealing capabilities will be impaired.

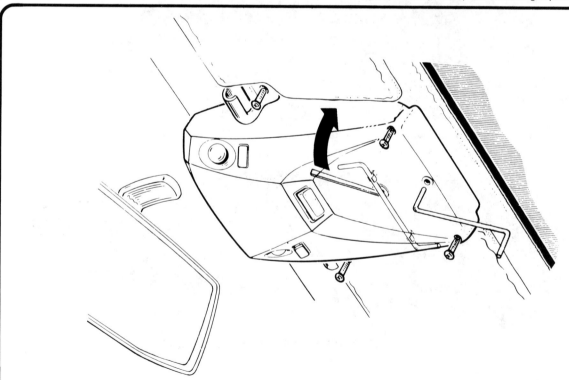

Fig. 11.22 Crank handle for the sunroof manual adjustment is located within the roof console (Sec 23)

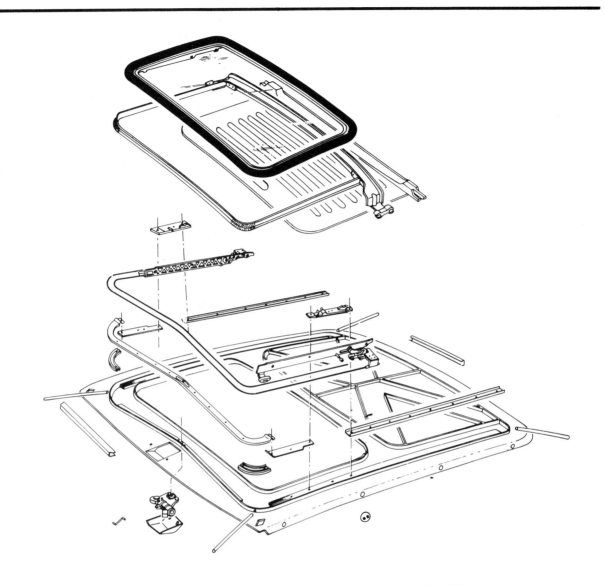

Fig. 11.23 Exploded view of the sunroof components (Sec 24)

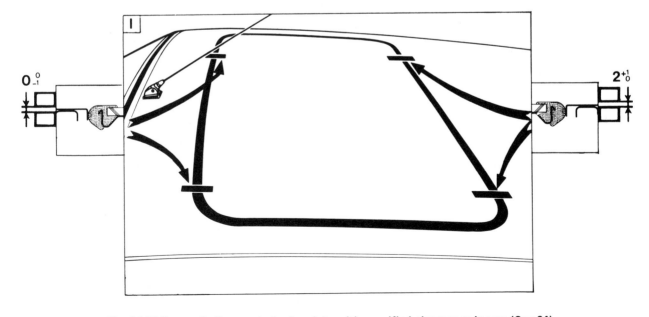

$0\,_{-1}^{\,0}$

$2\,_{\,0}^{+1}$

Fig. 11.24 Sunroof alignment check points with specified clearances in mm (Sec 24)

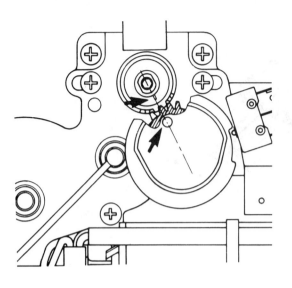

Fig. 11.25 Sunroof motor reduction gears in alignment (Sec 24)

Fig. 11.26 Reducer lever set to disengage the reducer (b) (Sec 24)

Retaining screws (2) are also shown

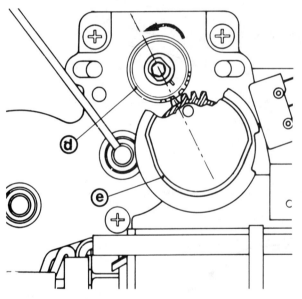

Fig. 11.27 Reducer gears adjustment: turn small cam (d) anti-clockwise to disengage from large cam (e) (Sec 24)

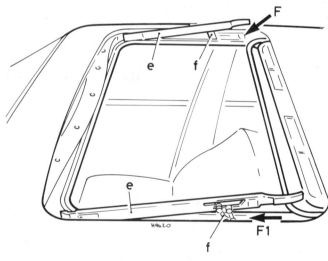

Fig. 11.28 Sunroof side channels (e) and cams (f) – shown with glass panel removed for clarity (Sec 24)

F and F1 are the frame pivots

Chapter 12 Electrical system

For modifications, and information applicable to later models, see Supplement at end of manual

Contents

Specifications

General

System type	12 volt, negative earth
Battery rating:	
BX and BX 14	29 or 35 amp hour
BX 16 and BX 19	33, 45 or 50 amp hour
BX 16 and BX 19 with air conditioning	50 or 60 amp hour
Wiper blades	Champion X-5103

Alternator

Make .... Bosch, Ducellier, Paris-Rhone or Melco
Type application:
  BX and BX 14 (up to February 1984) .... Bosch 0120 489 163 164
                                                   Ducellier 516 039
                                                   Paris-Rhone A 13 N 43
    Regulator .... Bosch 1 197 311 100
                                                   Ducellier 511 020
                                                   Paris-Rhone YH 1639
  BX and BX 14 (from February 1984) .... Bosch B 120 427 315
                                                   Paris-Rhone A 13 N 38
    Regulator .... Bosch 1 1973 11008
                                                   Paris-Rhone YH 1925
  BX 16 and BX 19 (up to February 1984) .... Melco A 002 T 26 391
                                                   Bosch A 120 427 141
    Regulator .... Melco A 866 T 03 870
                                                   Bosch 1 1973 311 100
  BX 16 and BX 19 (from February 1984) .... Bosch 0 120 489 258 259
                                                   Paris-Rhone A 13 N 95
    Regulator .... Bosch 1 197 311 008
                                                   Paris-Rhone YH 1925
  BX 16 – air conditioned models (80A/1120W) .... Melco A 3 T 45 191 G
                                                   Melco A 003 T 45 291
    Regulator .... Melco 03870 RS 3809
Alternator output (minimum) at 13.5 volts:
  BX, BX 14, BX 16 and BX 19:
    At 900 rpm engine speed .... 32 amps (at 2000 rpm alternator speed)
    At 1800 rpm engine speed .... 47 amps (at 4000 rpm alternator speed)
  BX 16 – air conditioned models:
    At 900 rpm engine speed .... 54 amps (at 2000 rpm alternator speed)
    At 1800 rpm engine speed .... 75 amps (at 4000 rpm alternator speed)

Starter motor

Type and make .... Pre-engaged, 12 volt, Ducellier, Paris-Rhone or Bosch
Type application:
  BX and BX 14 .... Ducellier 532 014
                                                   Paris-Rhone D 8 E 151
                                                   Bosch 9 000 142 002
  BX 16 and BX 19 .... Ducellier 534 039
                                                   Paris-Rhone D 9 E 48
                                                   Bosch A 001 208 316 F
                                                   Bosch 0 001 208 516 E

Fuses

Mark/rating (amp)/colour

BX and BX 14 models:

Protected circuits

F1/10A/Red .... Alternator. Reverse lamp. Idle cut-off and cooling fan relay coil

F2/25A/White .... Econoscope. Indicators. Air blower. Engine oil level. Clock. The following warning lamps:
        Engine oil pressure
        Fuel minimum level
        Hydraulic fluid pressure and level
        Coolant temperature
        Coolant level
        Choke
        Battery charge
        Emergency STOP
        Brake pad wear indicator and handbrake

F3/25A/White .... Windscreen wiper motor and washer pump. Rear window wiper motor and washer pump. Relay coil and indicator lamp for heated rear window. Stop-lamps. Rheostat and dashboard lighting. Ashtray light, cigar lighter and heating control panel lighting. Front/rear window winder relay coil. Horn

F4/25A/White .... Door locking device (unit and motors)
F5/25A/White .... Electric cooling fan
F6/10A/Red .... Hazard warning lamps
F7/25A/White .... Rear door window winder
F8/20A/Yellow .... Side interior lights. Glove compartment and boot lights. Cigar lighter, clock, radio and ashtray lighting
F9/25A/White .... Front door window winder
F10/20A/Yellow .... Heated rear window
F11/5A/Brown .... Rear foglamps and warning lamp
F12/5A/Brown .... Side and tail lamps. Number plate lamps. Side and tail warning lamp. Clock attenuated lighting. Attenuated lighting for heated rear window and hazard warning switches

Fuses

BX 16 and BX 19:

		Protected circuits
F1/10A/Red	....	Coolant temperature flasher unit. Alternator. Reverse lamp. Oil gauge unit. Cooling fan relay coil. Idle cut-off
F2/25A/White	....	Indicator. Air blower. Fuel gauge. Tachometer. Clock lighting. The following warning lamps: Fuel minimum level, Engine oil pressure, Hydraulic fluid level and pressure, Coolant temperature, Coolant level, Emergency STOP, Door locking device, Battery charge, Brake pad wear indicator and handbrake
F3/25A/White	....	Windscreen wiper motor and washer pump. Rear window wiper motor and washer pump. Heated rear window relay coil and indicator lamp. Stop-lamps. Rheostat and lighting for dashboard, ashtray, cigar lighter and heater control. Front and rear window winder relay coil. Horn
F4/25A/White	....	Door locking device (unit and motors)
F5/30A/White	....	Electric cooling fan
F6/10A/Red	....	Hazard warning lamps
F7/30A/White	....	Rear door window winders
F8/20A/Yellow	....	Map reading (swivel) lamp. Side interior lamps. Boot and glove compartment lights. Cigar lighter and lighting. Clock. Radio. Ashtray light
F9/30A/White	....	Front door window winder
F10/20A/Yellow	....	Heated rear window
F11/5A/Brown	....	Rear foglamps. Rear foglamp warning light
F12/5A/Brown	....	Side, tail and number plate lamps. Side and tail warning lamp. Clock attenuated lighting. Attenuated lighting for hazard warning and heated rear window

Bulbs

		Wattage
Headlamps (main/dip)	....	60/55
Direction indicators	....	21
Stop-lamps	....	21
Reverse lamps	....	21
Rear foglamps	....	21
Tail lamps	....	5
Number plate lamps	....	5
Sidelamps	....	4
Speedometer lamps	....	4
Interior lamps	....	7
Boot lamp	....	5
Heater control	....	1.2
Ashtray	....	1.2
Cigar lighter	....	1.2
Dashboard warning lamps	....	1.2
Switch warning lamps	....	1.2

1 General description

The electrical system is of the 12 volt negative earth type. The major components comprise a 12 volt battery of which the negative terminal is earthed, an alternator which is driven from the crankshaft pulley, and a starter motor.

The battery supplies a steady amount of current for the ignition, lighting and other electrical circuits and provides a reserve of electricity when the current consumed by the electrical equipment exceeds that being produced by the alternator.

The alternator is controlled by a regulator which ensures a high output if the battery is in a low state of charge or the demand from the electrical equipment is high, and a low output if the battery is fully charged and there is little demand for the electrical equipment.

When fitting electrical accessories it is important, if they contain silicone diodes or transistors, that they are connected correctly, otherwise serious damage may result to the components concerned. Items such as radios, tape recorders, electronic ignition systems, electronic tachometer, automatic dipping etc, should all be checked for correct polarity.

It is important that the battery is always disconnected if the battery is to be charged; also, if body repairs are to be carried out using electric arc welding equipment, the alternator must be disconnected, otherwise serious damage can be caused to it. Whenever the battery has to be disconnected it must always be reconnected with the negative terminal earthed.

2 Routine maintenance – electrical system

Routine maintenance of the electrical system is minimal, and mainly visual. The following items should be checked.

Battery: Check the battery terminals and lead connections for signs of corrosion, also check the electrolyte level – see Sections 3 and 4.

Alternator: Check the condition and adjustment of the alternator drivebelt – see Section 9.

Lights and horn: Check that the front and rear lights, also the horn, operate in a satisfactory manner. Check the headlights for correct alignment.

3 Battery – maintenance and inspection

1 The modern battery seldom requires topping-up but, nevertheless, the electrolyte level should be inspected weekly as a means of providing the first indication that the alternator is overcharging or that the battery casing has developed a leak. The battery plates should always be covered to a depth of 6.0 mm (0.25 in) with electrolyte.
2 When topping-up is required, use only distilled water or melted ice from a refrigerator (frosting, not ice cubes).
3 Acid should never be required if the battery has been correctly filled from new, unless spillage has occurred.
4 Inspect the battery terminals and mounting tray for corrosion. This is the white fluffy deposit which grows at these areas. If evident, clean it away and neutralise it with ammonia or baking soda. Apply petroleum jelly to the terminals and paint the battery tray with anti-corrosive paint.
5 Keep the top surface of the battery casing dry.
6 Inspect the battery for cracks. If a crack is found, clean and plug it with one of the proprietary components marketed for this purpose. If leakage through the crack has been excessive then it will be necessary to refill the appropriate cell with fresh electrolyte, as detailed in Section 4. Cracks are frequently caused in the top of the battery cases by topping-up with distilled water in the middle of winter after instead of before a run. This gives the water no chance to mix with the electrolyte and so the former freezes and splits the battery case.
7 If topping-up the battery becomes excessive and the case has been inspected for cracks that could cause leakage, but none are found, the battery is being over-charged and the voltage regulator will have to be checked.
8 Measure the specific gravity with a hydrometer to determine the state of charge and condition of the electrolyte. There should be very little variation between the different cells and if a variation in excess of 0.025 is present it will be due to either:

(a) Loss of electrolyte from the battery at some time caused by spillage or a leak, resulting in a drop in the specific gravity of the electrolyte when the deficiency was replaced with distilled water instead of fresh electrolyte
(b) An internal short-circuit caused by buckling of the plates or a similar malady pointing to the likelihood of total battery failure in the near future

9 The specific gravity of the electrolyte at different states of charge is given in the following table:

	Ambient temperature over 32°C (90°F)	Ambient temperature under 32°C (90°F)
Fully charged	1.210 to 1.230	1.270 to 1.290
Half discharged	1.130 to 1.150	1.190 to 1.210
Fully discharged	1.050 to 1.070	1.110 to 1.130

10 Some models are fitted with a low maintenance battery. Refer to Chapter 13 for maintenance guidelines.

4 Battery electrolyte – replenishment

1 If the battery is in a fully charged state and one of the cells maintains a specific gravity reading which is 0.025 or more lower than the others, and a check of each cell has been made with a voltage meter to check for short circuits (a four to seven seconds test should give a steady reading of between 1.2 and 1.8 volts), then it is likely that electrolyte has been lost from the cell with the low reading.
2 If a significant quantity of electrolyte has been lost through spillage it will not suffice merely to refill with distilled water. Top-up the cell(s) with electrolyte which is a mixture of sulphuric acid and water in the ratio of 2 parts acid to 5 parts water.
3 When mixing the sulphuric acid and water, never add water to sulphuric acid – always pour the acid slowly onto the water in a glass container. If water is added to sulphuric acid, it will explode.
4 Top-up the cell(s) with freshly made electrolyte, then recharge the battery and check the hydrometer readings.

5 Battery – charging

Note: Some low maintenance batteries require special conditions when charging – see Supplement.
1 In winter when a heavy demand is placed on the battery, such as when starting from cold, and much electrical equipment is continually in use, it is a good idea to occasionally have the battery fully charged from an external source at a rate of 3.5 to 4 amps.
2 Continue to charge the battery at this rate until no further rise in specific gravity is noted over a four hour period.
3 Alternatively, a trickle charger, charging at the rate of 1.5 amps can be safely used overnight.
4 Special rapid 'boost' charges which are claimed to restore the power of the battery in 1 to 2 hours are most dangerous unless they are thermostatically controlled as they can cause serious damage to the battery plates through overheating.
5 While charging the battery ensure that the temperature of the electrolyte never exceeds 37.8°C (100°F).
Caution: If the battery is being charged from an external power source whilst the battery is fitted in the car, both battery leads must be disconnected to prevent damage to the electrical circuits.

6 Battery – removal and refitting

1 The battery is on a carrier fitted to the wing valance of the engine compartment. It should be removed once every three months for cleaning and testing. Disconnect the negative and then the positive leads from the battery terminals by undoing and removing the terminal nuts and bolts. Note that two cables are attached to the positive terminal.
2 Release the battery clamp and carefully lift the battery from its carrier. Hold it vertically to ensure that none of the electrolyte is spilled. Note the earth strap attached to the clamp stud.
3 Refitting is a direct reversal of this procedure. Reconnect the positive lead before the negative lead and smear the terminals with petroleum jelly to prevent corrosion. Never use ordinary grease

7 Alternator – maintenance and special precautions

1 Periodically wipe away any dirt or grease which has accumulated on the outside of the unit and also check the security of the leads. At the same time check the tension of the drivebelt and adjust it, if necessary, as described in Section 9.
2 Take extreme care when making electrical circuit connections on the car, otherwise damage may occur to the alternator. Always make sure that the battery leads are connected to the correct terminals. Before using electric-arc welding equipment to repair any part of the car, disconnect the battery leads and the alternator output lead. Disconnect the battery leads before using a mains charger. Never run the alternator with the output wire disconnected.

8 Alternator – removal and refitting

1 Open the bonnet and disconnect the negative battery terminal followed by the positive battery terminal.
2 Note the location of the alternator supply wires, then disconnect them from the rear cover.
3 On BX and BX 14 engines remove the HP pump drivebelt, as described in Chapter 8 (Section 10).
4 Loosen the adjustment and pivot bolts, swivel the alternator towards the engine and remove the drivebelt from the pulley (photo).
5 Support the alternator and unscrew and remove the adjustment and pivot bolts; the alternator can then be carefully lifted from the vehicle.
6 Refitting the alternator is a reversal of the removal procedure but the alternator wiring should be connected and the nuts tightened before the battery is reconnected.
7 Refer to Section 9 to adjust the alternator drivebelt tension. On BX and BX 14 models refer to Chapter 8 (Section 10) to refit and adjust the HP pump drivebelt.

8.4 Alternator, drivebelt and adjustment strap (BX 16)

9 Alternator drivebelt – removal, refitting and adjustment

1   To remove the alternator drivebelt, refer to the previous Section and follow the procedures given in paragraphs 3 and 4. Refitting is a reversal of removal but the adjustment must be made before fully tightening the mounting/adjustment strap bolts.

2   Correct tensioning of the alternator drivebelt will ensure that it has a long and useful life. If the belt is loose, alternator performance will be affected and possibly the battery could be discharged. If the belt is too tight it will cause unnecessary alternator bearing wear. In either case the belt itself will suffer and its life will be shortened.

3   The drivebelt is tensioned by pivoting the alternator out and securing it when the belt is correctly tensioned.

4   To adjust the drivebelt tension, first check that it is correctly located in both pulleys then, with the mounting and adjustment strap bolts loosened, pivot the alternator outwards to tighten the drivebelt. You can use a lever to help achieve this but it must be a wooden one and it must be used only at the pulley end of the alternator. Levering on the case or at the end opposite to the drive pulley can easily cause expensive damage.

5   Tighten the belt as much as possible (but without over stretching it) to take up any play in the belt at its mid point on the longest run between the pulleys. Whilst a taut tension is required the belt must not

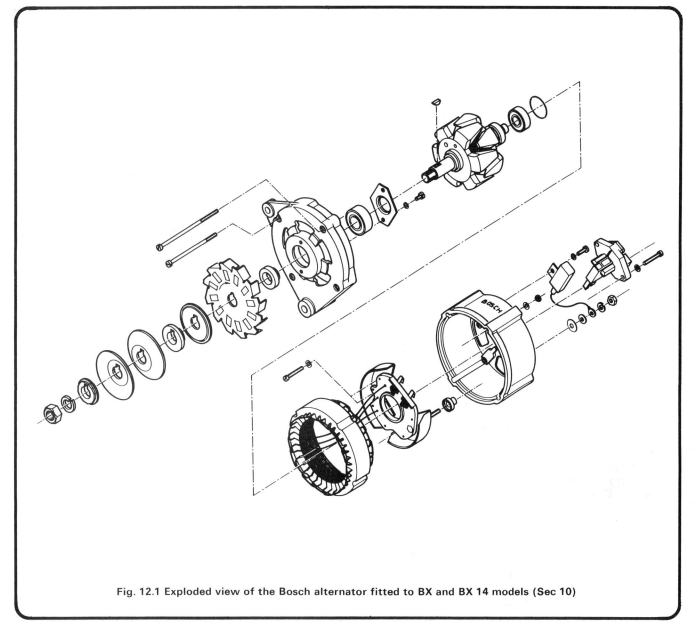

Fig. 12.1 Exploded view of the Bosch alternator fitted to BX and BX 14 models (Sec 10)

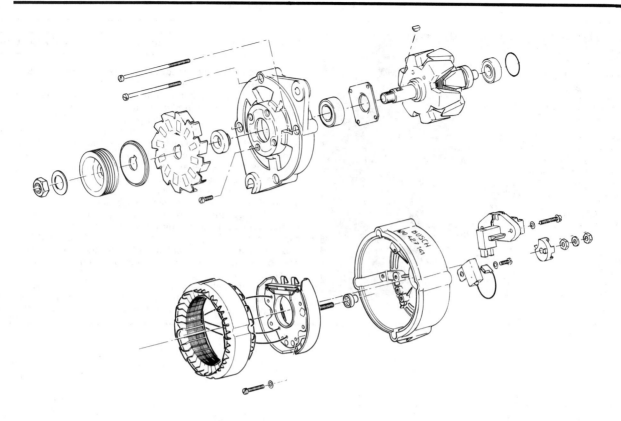

Fig. 12.2 Exploded view of the Bosch alternator fitted to BX 16 models (Sec 10)

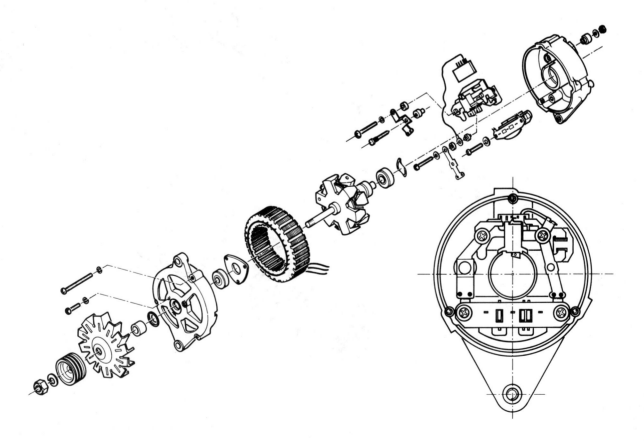

Fig. 12.3 Exploded view of the Melco alternator fitted to BX 16 models (Sec 10)

be overtightened. Tighten the alternator mounting and adjuster strap bolts to set the tension.

6 If a new belt has been fitted recheck its tension after a nominal mileage has been covered.

10 Alternator – fault diagnosis and repair

1 Due to the specialist knowledge and equipment required to test or service an alternator it is recommended that if the performance is suspect, the car be taken to an automobile electrician who will have the facilities for such work.

2 Should the alternator fail to charge, or the system be suspect, the following points may be checked before seeking further assistance:

    (a) Check the drivebelt tension, as described in Section 9
    (b) Check the battery, as described in Section 3
    (c) Check the condition of the brushes and renew, if necessary, as described in the following Section

11 Alternator – brush renewal

1 Because of the different types of alternator fitted, it is not practical to describe the procedure for each one in detail. This procedure applies to the Paris-Rhone 750W alternator; detail difference will be found with other makes.

2 Remove the alternator from the vehicle.

3 Remove the rear shield; some force may be needed to prise it off (photo).

4 Remove the two screws which secure the regulator/brush holder assembly. Disconnect the regulator lead from the spade terminal and slide the assembly out (photos).

5 Unsolder the old brushes and solder in the new ones. Have this done professionally if you lack skill in soldering.

12 Starter motor – general description

    The starter motor is of the pre-engaged type, ie the drive pinion is brought into mesh with the starter ring gear on the flywheel before the main current is applied.

    When the starter switch is operated, current flows from the battery to the solenoid, which is mounted on the top of the starter motor body. The plunger in the solenoid moves inwards, so causing a centrally pivoted lever to push the drive pinion into mesh with the starter ring gear. When the solenoid plunger reaches the end of its travel, it closes an internal contact and full starting current flows to the starter field coils. The armature is then able to rotate the crankshaft, so starting the engine.

    A special freewheel clutch is fitted to the starter drive pinion so that as soon as the engine fires and starts to operate on its own it does not drive the starter motor.

    When the starter switch is released, the solenoid is de-energised and a spring moves the plunger back to its rest position. This operates the pivoted lever to withdraw the drive pinion from engagement with the starter ring gear.

13 Starter motor – testing in the car

1 If the starter motor fails to operate, first check the condition of the battery by switching on the headlamps. If they glow brightly, then gradually dim after a few seconds, the battery is in an uncharged condition.

2 If the battery is in good condition, check the terminal connections for security. Also check that the earth lead is making good contact with the bodyframe. Check the security of the main cable and solenoid cable connections on the starter motor.

3 If the starter motor still fails to turn, check that the solenoid is being energised. To do this, connect a 12 volt test lamp and leads between the large solenoid terminal and earth. When the ignition key is turned to the starting position the lamp should glow. If not, either the supply circuit is open due to a broken wire or a faulty ignition switch, or the solenoid is defective. If the solenoid is supplying current to the starter motor, the fault must be in the starter motor.

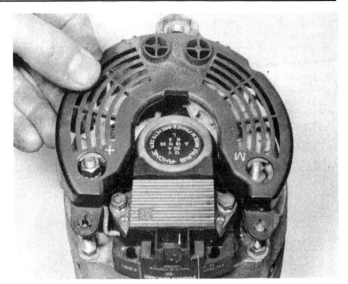

11.3 Brush renewal – Paris-Rhone alternator. Remove the rear shield ...

11.4A ... disconnect the regulator lead ...

11.4B ... regulator and brush holder unit

14 Starter motor (BX and BX 14 models) – removal and refitting

1   Disconnect the earth lead from the battery terminal.
2   Disconnect the leads from the starter motor and the red identification plug from the solenoid unit.
3   Support the engine and gearbox using a jack underneath or a hoist and sling from above.
4   Referring to Fig. 12.4, unscrew and remove the two starter motor retaining bolts indicated.
5   Referring to Fig. 12.5, unscrew and remove the engine mounting nuts indicated.
6   Raise the engine/gearbox unit just enough to provide access to the starter motor retaining bolt beyond the mounting (see Fig. 12.6).
7   Unscrew and remove the two bolts securing the starter motor rear bearing then withdraw the starter motor.
8   Refitting is a reversal of the removal procedure.

Fig. 12.4 Remove the starter motor bolts 1 and 2 (BX 14) (Sec 14)

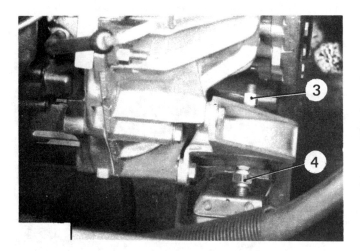

Fig. 12.5 Remove the engine mounting nuts 3 and 4 (BX 14) (Sec 14)

Fig. 12.6 Starter motor retaining bolt (5) beyond the mounting (BX 14) (Sec 14)

15 Starter motor (BX 16 and BX 19 models) – removal and refitting

1   Disconnect the battery earth lead from the battery terminal.
2   To improve access to the starter motor, disconnect and remove the air filter duct.
3   Disconnect wiring from the starter motor, taking note the connecting positions.
4   Undo the two bolts securing the starter motor mounting bracket to the engine and note that the lower bolt secures the hydraulic line location clip.
5   Unscrew and remove the three socket-head bolts on the transmission side then withdraw the starter motor, complete with its mounting bracket.
6   Refitting is a reversal of the removal procedure.

16 Starter motor – dismantling and reassembly

1   Such is the inherent reliability and strength of the starter motor fitted that it is very unlikely that a motor will ever need dismantling until it is totally worn out and in need of replacement. It is not a task for the home mechanic because, although reasonably easy to undertake, the reassembly and adjustment before refitting is beyond his scope because of the need of specialist equipment. It is usually more satisfactory to fit an exchange motor or have an overhaul done by a specialist auto-electrician. However, the more ambitious DIY proce-

dure is as follows for a Ducellier starter; other makes are similar.
2   Unscrew the two nuts securing the engine mounting bracket to the motor and remove the bracket. Remove the locknuts and retaining nuts and take off the endplate.
3   Hold the shaft from turning by jamming the drive pinion, and undo the end bearing seal retaining bolt. Remove the seal assembly with its spring (photo).
4   To gain access to the brushes, lever the bearing plate from the body. The brushes are mounted on the underside of the plate (photo).
5   Lift the positive brush spring and remove the brush from its housing to enable the bearing plate to be removed (photo). Note the arrangement of washers on the armature shaft.
6   Disconnect the terminal from the solenoid and carefully slide the body from the armature.
7   To separate the armature from the pinion end bracket, tap out the pivot pin and loosen the solenoid retaining nuts. The armature assembly can be removed by disconnecting the solenoid-operated lever, and withdrawing the assembly at the same time (photos).
8   To withdraw the pinion from the armature, drive the special collar washer down the shaft, using a suitable piece of tubing, to expose the snap-ring. After extracting the snap-ring from the groove in the shaft, the pinion assembly can be slid from the shaft.
9   With the starter motor dismantled the various components can be cleaned and inspected for general wear and/or signs of damage. The components likely to need attention will be the brushes, the solenoid or possibly the drive pinion unit.
10 The brushes can be removed by unsoldering the connecting wires to the holder and to the field coil unit. Take care not to damage the latter during removal and assembly of the brushes (photo).

16.3 Removing the seal assembly and spring

16.4 Removing the bearing plate

16.5 Bearing plate and brushes

16.7A Removing the lever pivot pin (arrowed)

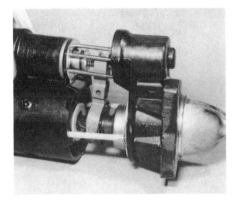

16.7B Separating the pinion end bracket

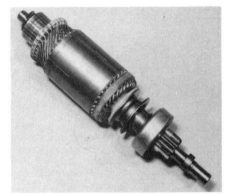

16.7C Armature/pinion assembly

16.7D Starter solenoid and lever

16.10 Brush connections to field coil

16.16 Using a puller to locate the snap-ring collar washer

11 If the starter motor has shown a tendency to jam or a possible reluctance to disengage then the starter pinion is almost certainly the culprit. Dirt around the pinion and shaft could cause this. When cleaned, check that the pinion can move freely in a spiral movement along the shaft. If the pinion tends to bind or is defective in any way renew it.

12 Undercut the separators of the commutator using an old hacksaw blade to a depth of about 0.5 to 0.8 mm (0.02 to 0.03 in). The commutator may be further surface cleaned using a strip of very fine glass paper. Do not use emery cloth for this purpose, as the carborundum particles will become embedded in the copper surfaces.

13 Testing of the armature is best left to an auto-electrician, but if an ohmmeter is available it can be done by placing one probe on the armature shaft and the other on each of the commutator segments in turn. If there is a reading indicated at any time during the test, then the armature is defective and must be renewed.

14 The field coil can also be tested using an ohmmeter. Connect one probe to the field coil positive terminal and the other to the positive brush holder. If there is no indication of a reading then the field coil circuit has a break in it.

15 Connect one lead of the meter to the field coil positive lead and the other one to the yoke. If there is a low resistance then the field coil is earthed due to a breakdown in the insulation. If this proves to be the cause the field coils must be renewed. As field coil replacement requires special tools and equipment it is a job that should be entrusted to your auto-electrician. In fact it will probably prove more economical and beneficial to exchange the starter motor for a reconditioned unit.

16 Reassembly of the starter motor is a reversal of the dismantling procedure, but note the following:

(a) The snap-ring and collar can be difficult to relocate. To assist in this, a suitable puller can be used
(b) Reassemble the correct number of thrust washers and in the correct sequence, namely, fibre, steel, spring, steel fibre
(c) Align the key and slot when assembling the body
(d) Make sure that the brushes slide freely in their holders
(e) Sparingly lubricate the armature shaft with a general purpose grease. Do not lubricate the pinion and splines

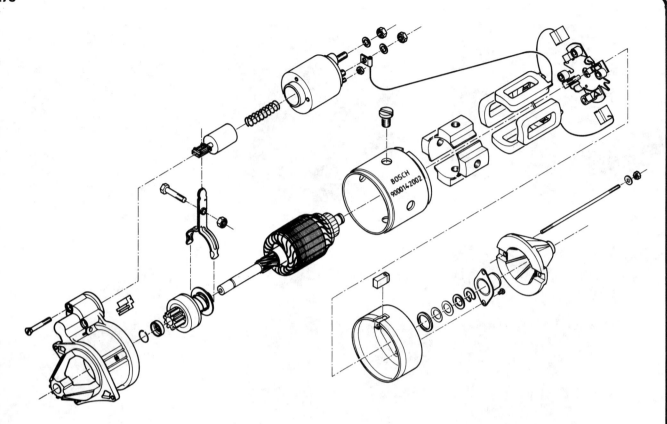

Fig. 12.7 Exploded view of the Bosch starter motor fitted to BX 14 models (Sec 16)

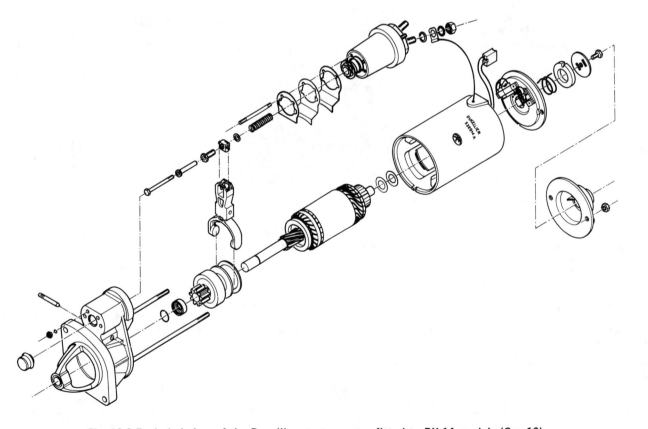

Fig. 12.8 Exploded view of the Ducellier starter motor fitted to BX 14 models (Sec 16)

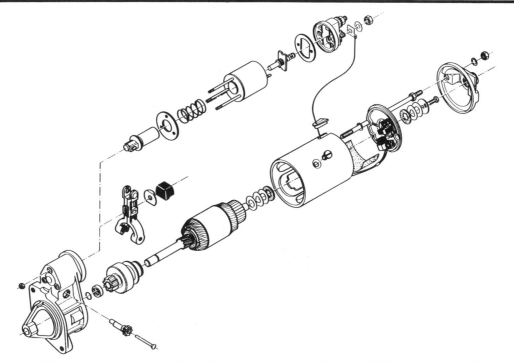

Fig. 12.9 Exploded view of the Paris-Rhone starter motor fitted to BX 14 models (Sec 16)

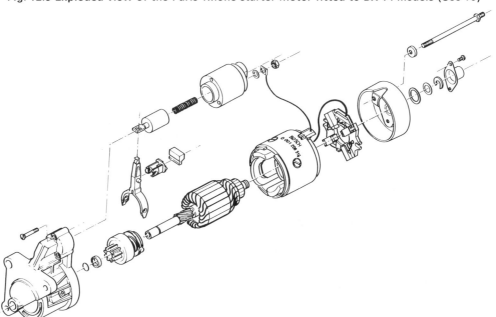

Fig. 12.10 Exploded view of the Bosch starter motor fitted to BX 16 models (Sec 16)

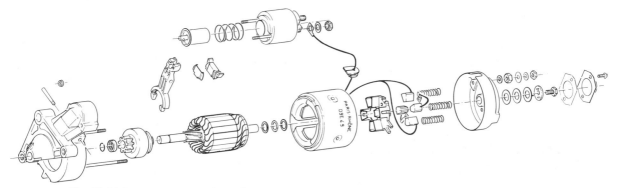

Fig. 12.11 Exploded view of the Paris-Rhone starter motor fitted to BX 16 models (Sec 16)

17 Fuses and relays

1   The fuse/relay box is located under the lower trim panel on the passenger side.
2   The circuits protected by the fuses, together with their colour and rating, are given in the Specifications at the start of this Chapter.
3   Access to the fuses is gained by pulling the release handle and swinging the box down (photo).
4   Always renew a fuse with one of similar rating and never renew it more than once without finding the source of trouble. If necessary, refer to the wiring diagrams at the end of this Chapter.
5   Relay units rarely give problems, but they can easily be renewed by pulling them from their location in the box. The relay units and their functions are also shown in the wiring diagrams at the end of this Chapter. Some relay units are connected in-line and are separate from the main fuse/relay box unit.

18 Lights (exterior) – removal, refitting and bulb renewal

Headlight
Bulb renewal
1   The bulbs are renewed from the rear of the headlamp unit, access being from the engine compartment.
2   Pull free the wiring connector, release the bulb retaining clip and withdraw the bulb (photos).
3   Where halogen bulbs are fitted, do not touch the glass with your fingers or with a fluffy cloth and, if necessary, allow the bulb to cool before removing it. If the glass is inadvertently touched, clean it with methylated spirit.
4   Refitting is a reversal of the removal procedure. When inserting the bulb into position it must be correctly aligned with the location notches (photo). Check the headlights for satisfactory operation and alignment on completion.

Removal and refitting
5   Raise the bonnet, and pull free the headlamp wiring connector and the sidelight bulbholder.
6   The headlamp unit can then be carefully prised from its ball and socket adjustable mountings (photo).
7   Refitting is a reversal of removal. Check lamp operation and alignment on completion.

Sidelight
8   This bulb is located in the rear of the headlight unit, directly underneath the headlight bulb. Pull free the bulbholder, complete with wiring connections, from the headlamp unit then withdraw the bulb from its holder (photo).
9   Refit in the reverse order to removal and check the operation of the sidelights.

Front indicator
10   Reach down within the engine compartment and press the front indicator unit retaining tabs to release the unit from the front wing panel (photo).
11   Withdraw the bulb holder from the indicator unit and withdraw the bulb (photo).
12   Refit in the reverse order of removal. Press the indicator unit fully into position, ensuring that the retaining tabs clip home fully. Check the operation of the indicators.

Rear combination lights (Hatchback)
13   Press the lens forwards with one hand and simultaneously reach within the luggage compartment and release the unit retaining clip by pinching it firmly. The lens, complete with the combination bulbholder unit, can then be withdrawn from the vehicle and separated from access to the bulbs by pressing the retaining catch (photos).
14   Withdraw the defective bulb and renew it.
15   Refit in the reverse order of removal. Ensure that the retaining catch and clip are securely engaged and check the operation of the respective lights in the unit.

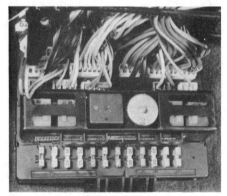

17.3 The fuse and relay box

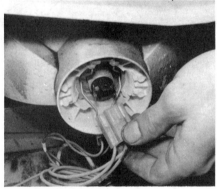

18.2A Disconnecting the wiring connector

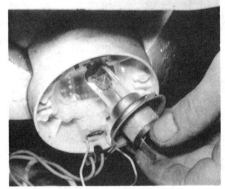

18.2B Headlight bulb removal

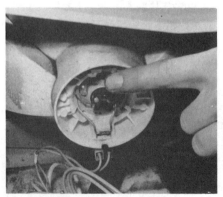

18.4 Correct headlamp bulb alignment

18.6 Headlamp ball and socket mounting

18.8 Sidelight bulb removal

Rear combination lights (Estate)
Bulb renewal
16 Raise the tailgate and remove the lens securing screws. Lower the lens slightly and pull it away from the bulbs.
17 To refit the lens, engage the lower lug at the bottom and secure with the retaining screws.
Removal and refitting
18 No information was available at the time of writing, but this task should be relatively straightforward.

Number plate light (Hatchback)
19 Raise the tailgate and prise free the square cover from the trim panel adjacent to the light unit.
20 Reach through the trim aperture and withdraw the bulb (photo).
21 Refit in the reverse order of remova and check the light for satisfactory operation.

Number plate light (Estate)
22 Unscrew the fixing screw and pull the assembly from the tailgate.
23 The lens is clipped to the bulbholder, and must be removed to renew the bulb.
24 Refitting is a reversal of removal.

18.10 Withdraw the front indicator unit ...

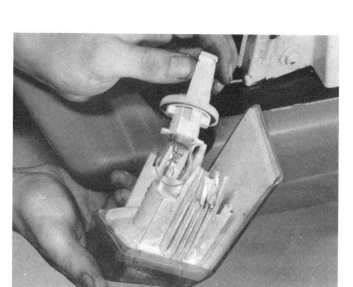
18.11 ... and extract the bulb holder

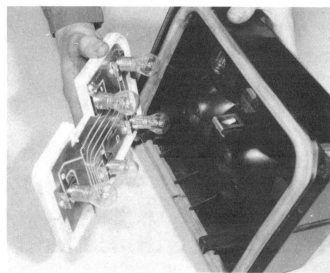
18.13A Removing the bulb holder assembly from the lens unit

18.13B Rear combination light bulb holder assembly

18.20 Number plate light unit shown with access cover removed from the trim panel

19 Light (interior) – bulb renewal

Interior light (dome type)
1   Prise free the lens unit from its aperture and withdraw the light unit.
2   Ease the festoon bulb free from the terminal springs (photo).
3   Refitting is a reversal of removal.

Interior light (map lamp type)
4   Undo the four retaining screws and remove the roof console. On some types the light unit is secured by spring clips, and in this case prise free the unit (photo).
5   Ease the festoon bulb free from the terminal springs.
6   Refit in the reverse order of removal.

Glovebox light
7   Prise free the lens then ease the festoon bulb from the terminal springs.
8   Refit in the reverse order of removal.

Luggage compartment light
9   Prise free the light unit then ease the festoon bulb from its terminal springs (photo).
10   Refit in the reverse order of removal.

Heater control panel and ashtray lights
11   Remove the ashtray and pull free the heater control knobs from their levers.
12   Undo the two screws and remove the ashtray support and heater control panel.
13   The bulbs are now accessible and can be withdrawn from their holders as required (photo).
14   Refit in the reverse order of removal.

Instrument panel lights
15   Refer to Section 22 and remove the instrument panel unit. The bulb(s) can then be withdrawn and inspected/renewed as required.

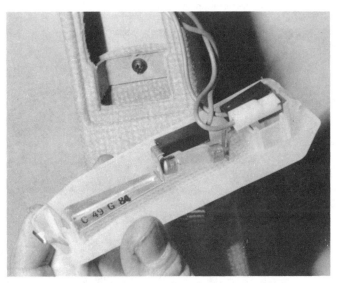

19.2 Interior dome lamp festoon bulb and wiring connections

19.4 Interior map lamp bulb – festoon type

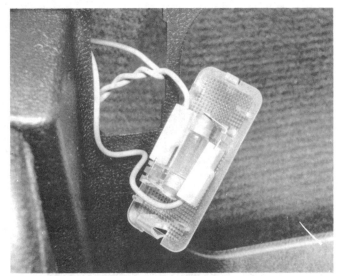

19.9 Luggage compartment light

19.13 Heater control panel bulb

20 Headlamps – alignment

1   Accurate headlamp alignment should be carried out by a Citroën garage. However, in an emergency the following procedure will provide an acceptable light pattern.
2   Position the car on a level surface with tyres correctly inflated. Start the engine and allow it to idle, then check that the ground clearance lever is in the normal running position. The car should be positioned approximately 10 metres (33 feet) in front of a wall or garage door.
3   Mark the headlamp bulb centres on the wall.
4   Switch on the main beam and check that the areas of maximum illumination coincide with the marks on the wall. If not, turn the plastic knobs located on the rear of the headlamps as required (Fig. 12.12).
5   Switch off the engine when the adjustment is completed.

21 Horn – general

1   The horn, which is located near the air intake grille above the front bumper, should not require any attention or adjustment thoughout its life.
2   Provided the circuit fuse and operating switch are in good order, any fault must be in the wiring, the earth bond or the unit itself.
3   A weak or intermittent horn signal may be due to a corroded support bracket connection. Unbolt the horn and scrape the bracket and body contact faces clean.

22 Instrument panel – removal and refitting

1   Disconnect the battery earth lead.
2   Prise free and lift clear the inspection panel above the instrument panel (photo).
3   Unscrew and remove the upper fixing screws (photo).
4   Referring to Fig. 12.13, undo the two centre screws indicated on the underside of the steering column and remove the top cover (1).

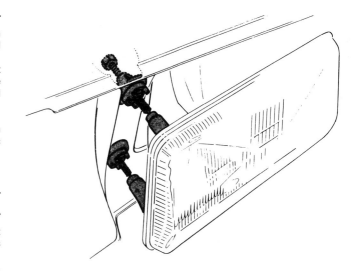

Fig. 12.12 Headlamp adjustment screws (Sec 20)

5   Unscrew and remove the lower panel fixing bolts from the positions marked by the outer arrows.
6   Disconnect the wiring multi-connectors and the speedometer cable from the instrument panel and carefully withdraw the panel unit (photo).
7   To renew the instrument panel bulbs, untwist and withdraw the bulb holders and extract the bulb (photo).
8   The instrument panel main body can be detached from the front section by undoing the four retaining screws; but take care not to damage the printed circuits.

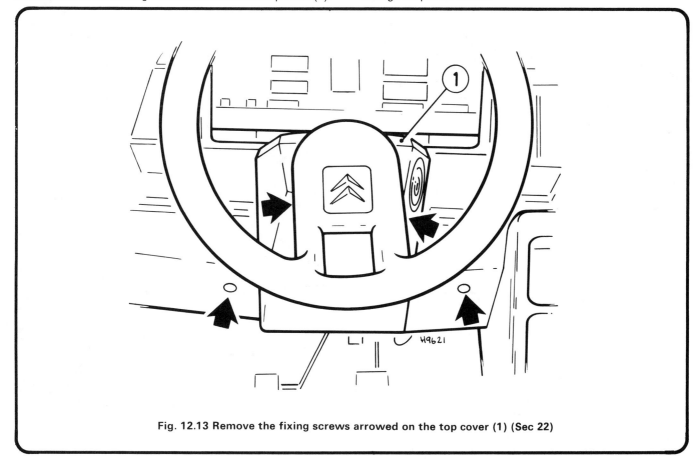

Fig. 12.13 Remove the fixing screws arrowed on the top cover (1) (Sec 22)

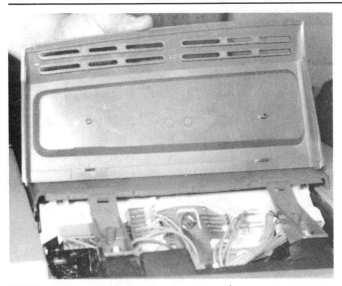

22.2 Instrument panel inspection cover removal

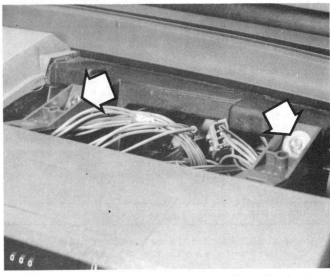

22.3 Remove the instrument panel upper fixing screws (arrowed)

22.6 Instrument panel removed

22.7 Bulb holder removal from the instrument panel

9   Further dismantling of the instrument panel is not recommended. If any item in the instrument cluster is malfunctioning, have the unit checked by your Citroën dealer.
10 Refitting is a direct reversal of the removal procedure. If a new vent is being fitted check that the captive nuts are in position for the lower retaining bolts. Ensure that all wiring connectors are securely made. On completion check the operating of the various instrument panel functions.

23 Steering column switches – removal and refitting

1   Disconnect the battery earth lead.
2   Although their functions differ, the switch controls on each side of the steering column are identical. The accompanying photographs illustrate the removal of the right-hand switch unit, but the instructions apply to both the right and left-hand switch units.

Windscreen wiper/washer and horn control switches

3   Carefully prise free the centre panels and remove them (photo).
4   Unscrew the two retaining screws and withdraw the three control switches (photos).
5   If required the switch multi-connector panel can be withdrawn,

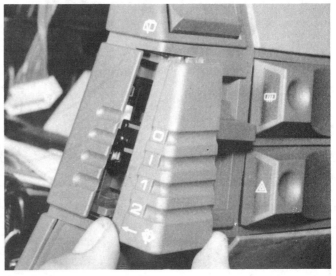

23.3 Removing the central panel

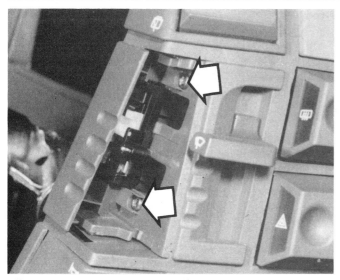

23.4A Remove the two retaining screws (arrowed) and ...

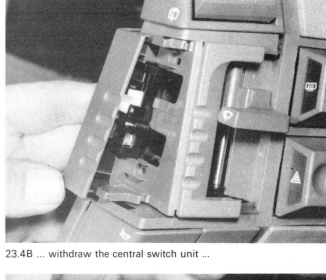

23.4B ... withdraw the central switch unit ...

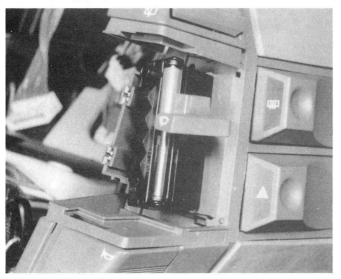

23.4C ... and selector control unit

23.4D Remove the upper ...

together with the wires, after detaching the wiring connectors from the main loom (photo).

6   Any switch that is defective must be renewed.

7   Refitting is a reversal of the removal procedure. Check the various switch functions on completion for satisfactory operation.

Rear window demister and hazard switches

8   Use a thin-bladed screwdriver to prise free the switch from its leading edge (the pivot end), then withdraw the switch (photo).

9   If the switch warning bulb is to be renewed, carefully prise the outer section away from the inner section and then withdraw the bulb (photo).

10 Refitting is a reversal of the removal procedure. Check the switch(es) for satisfactory operation on completion.

---

24 Door courtesy and boot light switches – removal and refitting

Courtesy switch

1   Disconnect the battery earth lead.

2   Open the door then undo the switch retaining screw. Pull the switch from the pillar and detach the wires (photo).

3   Refit in the reverse order of removal.

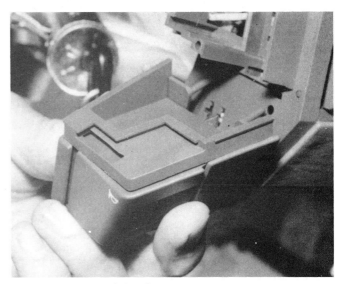

23.4E ... and lower switch units

23.5 Withdrawing the multi-connector panel

23.8 Removing the rear window demister switch

23.9 Switch warning bulb location

24.2 Door courtesy light switch

24.5 Boot light switch unit removal

25.2 Electric window operating switch removal

26.2 Handbrake console retaining nut at the rear (arrowed)

26.3 Console retaining bolt at the front

26.5 Handbrake warning light switch

Boot light switch

4 Disconnect the battery earth lead and open the tailgate.
5 Reaching up from the underside of the switch, compress the retaining clips and push the switch upwards through its location aperture (photo).
6 Detach the wiring connector and remove the switch.
7 Refit in the reverse order of removal.

25 Electric window switches – removal and refitting

1 Disconnect the battery earth lead.
2 Carefully prise free the switch from the handbrake console. Withdraw the switch and disconnect the wiring (photo).
3 Refit in the reverse order to removal.

26 Handbrake warning switch – removal and refitting

1 Disconnect the battery earth lead.
2 Prise free the cubby from the rear end of the handbrake lever console. Reach through the cubby aperture and undo the console retaining nut at the rear (photo).
3 Remove the rubber grommet and undo the console retaining bolt at the front (photo). Lift the console clear, disconnecting the wires to any console mounted switches (where applicable) and note their connections.
4 Withdraw the handbrake lever console.
5 Detach the wiring connector from the handbrake warning light switch, compress the retaining clips and withdraw the switch from its mounting bracket (photo).
6 Refitting is a reversal of the removal procedure. Check the operation of the switch on completion.

27 Cigar lighter – removal and refitting

1 Disconnect the battery earth lead.
2 Remove the radio, as described in Section 36.
3 The cigar lighter bulb is contained in a shuttle housing on the side of the cigar lighter unit. Withdraw the bulb holder. Extract the bulb if this is to be renewed.
4 Disconnect the wiring connector from the cigar lighter then compress the retaining clips and withdraw the lighter unit (photo).
5 Refit in the reverse order of removal.

28 Wiper blade – renewal

1 Lift the wiper arm away from the windscreen.
2 With a small screwdriver, release the plastic lug and withdraw the wiper blade from the arm (photo).
3 Refitting is a reversal of removal.

29 Wiper arm – removal and refitting

1 Make sure that the wiper motor is stopped in the parked position. Using a felt tipped pen, make an alignment mark of the wiper blade position on the screen when in the parked position.
2 Disconnect the cleaning fluid hose from the nipple on the pivot by pulling it free (photo).
3 Lift the cover from the securing nut then unscrew the nut (photo) and prise the arm from the spindle with a wide-bladed screwdriver. Take care not to damage the paintwork.
4 Refitting is a reversal of removal. Align the wiper arm and blade with the temporary alignment marking on the windscreen/rear window. On completion wipe the alignment mark clean with a dampened cloth and check the operation of the wiper.

30 Windscreen wiper motor – removal and refitting

1 Disconnect the battery earth lead.
2 Remove the wiper arm, as described in the previous Section.

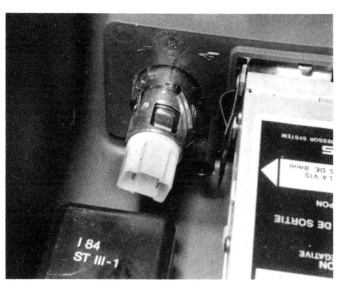
27.4 Cigar lighter with bulb and wiring connector detached

28.2 Wiper blade removal from arm

29.2 Detach the washer hose ...

29.3 ... and unscrew the wiper arm retaining nut

3   Raise and support the bonnet. The wiper motor is located in the body cavity above the engine compartment bulkhead (directly in front of the windscreen) under a plastic cover. Remove the plastic cover by peeling back the rubber seal along its leading edge and prising free the retaining clips (photos).
4   Disconnect the wiring connector from the wiper motor (photo).
5   Unscrew and remove the wiper arm pivot nut (photo).
6   Unscrew the wiper motor mounting bracket retaining bolts and the linkage nut (photo). Alternatively prise free the spring clip and release the linkage arm from the cranked connecting arm pivot, but take care not to lose the spring clip (photo). Withdraw the wiper motor.
7   Refit in the reverse order to removal. On completion check the windscreen wiper for satisfactory operation.

31 Rear window wiper motor – removal and refitting

1   Disconnect the battery earth lead.
2   Remove the rear wiper arm and blade as described in Section 29.
3   Raise the tailgate and remove the trim panel from it by carefully prising free the plastic retaining clips.
4   Unscrew and remove the wiper motor mounting bracket bolts and note the earth lead located under the head of one of the bolts (photo).
5   Undo the wiper arm pivot nut and lower the motor and mounting bracket away from the tailgate.
6   Disconnect the wiring from the wiper motor and the wiring location clip from the mounting bracket.
7   Unbolt and remove the motor from the mounting bracket.
8   Refitting is a reversal of the removal procedure. Check the wiper for satisfactory operation on completion.

32 Rear window heater element – maintenance and repair

1   The heating elements applied to the glass interior surface should be treated with respect.
2   Clean the glass only with warm water and detergent, and wipe in the direction of the element lines. Take care not to scratch the elements with rings on the fingers or by careless stowage of luggage.
3   Do not stick labels over the elements.
4   To repair a break in the element, use one of the conductive paints which are now readily available from motor accessory stores. Follow the manufacturer's instructions very carefully.

33 Windscreen and rear window washer units – removal and refitting

1   These are located each side at the rear of the engine bulkhead.
2   The pump unit is integral with the filler cap (photo).
3   Should the pump fail to operate, check there is sufficient fluid in the reservoir and that the suction and supply hoses are securely connected and clear.
4   Check that the wiring connections are secure. A test light can be used to check the wiring continuity at the pump terminals.
5   If the pump is defective, renew it by detaching the wiring and the suction and supply pipes.
6   The reservoir can be removed by withdrawing the cap/pump unit, releasing the retaining clip and lifting the unit out.
7   Refit in the reverse order of removal and check for satisfactory operation.

34 Electrically-operated window regulator units – removal and refitting

1   Disconnect the battery earth lead.
2   Remove the door trim panel, as described in Chapter 11.
3   Detach the wiring connectors from the regulator wiring, and release the regulator wires from the nylon retaining clip (photo).
4   Support the door window, then unscrew the five regulator-to-door retaining nuts and the two nuts securing the lower channel to the door.
5   Slide the regulator rearwards and disengage it from the window channels then remove it through the inner door panel aperture.

30.3A Peel back the cover seal ...

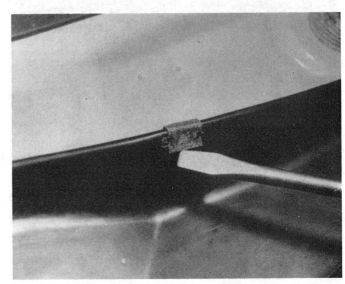
30.3B ... and prise free the cover clips

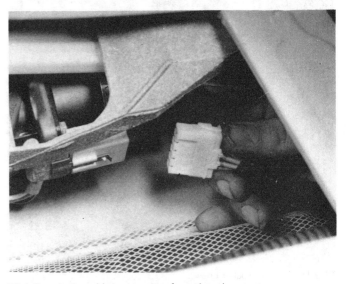
30.4 Detach the wiring connector from the wiper motor

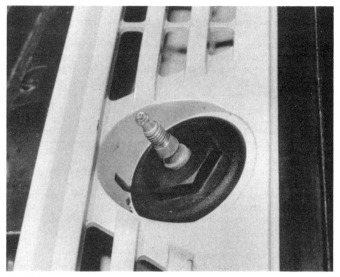

30.5 Wiper arm pivot nut

30.6A Wiper motor retaining bolt (arrowed)

30.6B Wiper motor linkage arm spring clip (arrowed)

31.4 Rear window wiper motor

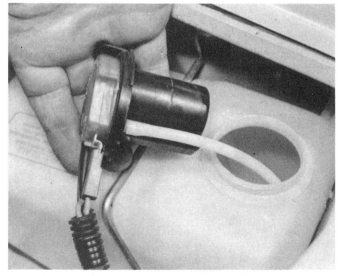

33.2 Washer unit filler cap/pump unit

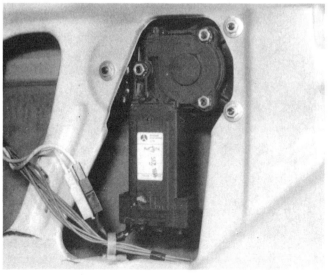

34.3 Electric window regulator unit and wiring connections

6 Refit in the reverse order of removal. Check that the wiring is correctly located and routed so that it will not interfere with the window movement. Check that the window regulator action is satisfactory before refitting the door trim panel.

35 Central locking door solenoid unit – removal and refitting

Side door
1 Disconnect the battery earth lead.
2 Remove the door trim, as described in Chapter 11.
3 Disconnect the wiring connectors from the end of the solenoid unit (photo).
4 Undo the solenoid retaining bolts, detach the solenoid unit from the inner door panel then disengage it from the lock control rod. Withdraw the solenoid unit through the inner door aperture.
5 Refit in the reverse order of removal. Check the operation of the lock on completion.

Tailgate
6 Disconnect the battery earth lead.

7 Raise the tailgate and remove the trim panel from it by carefully prising free the retaining clips.
8 Detach the wiring connector from the solenoid unit (photo).
9 Prise the retaining clip free from the lock barrel (photo).
10 Undo the retaining bolts and remove the lock solenoid unit (photo).
11 Refit in the reverse order to removal.

36 Radio/cassette – removal and refitting

1 Disconnect the battery earth lead.
2 Remove the ashtray from its holder and pull free the heater control lever knobs.
3 Undo the two screws from the ashtray holder, remove the holder plate and heater control mounting plate (Fig. 12.14).
4 Undo the two diagonally opposed screws securing the centre facia at the heater control (photo).
5 Remove the retaining screws and remove the lower trim panel on the passenger side.
6 Remove the retaining screws and remove the steering column lower shroud.

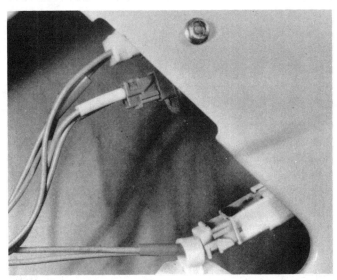
35.3 Wiring connections to door lock solenoid (central locking)

35.8 Wiring connector to the tailgate solenoid (central locking)

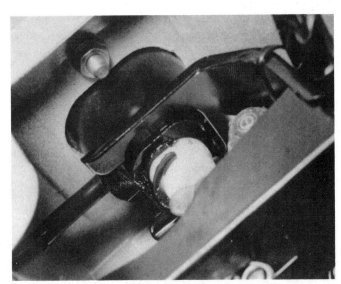
35.9 Lock barrel and retaining clip (central locking)

35.10 Tailgate central locking solenoid and lock unit

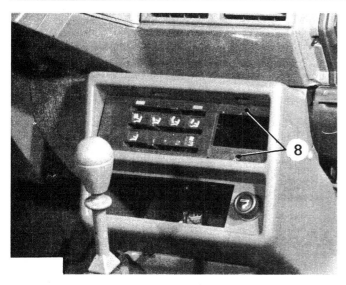

Fig. 12.14 Ashtray holder/heater control plate retaining screws (8) (Sec 36)

36.4 Remove the panel screws indicated

36.8 Rear side of the radio unit

7 Undo the single retaining screw on the passenger side and the two retaining screws on the driver's side which secure the centre facia unit. Withdraw the facia unit and disconnect the wiring to the heater control lights, the cigar lighter and the radio/cassette. Disconnect the radio aerial.
8 The facia unit can now be removed and the radio/cassette retainers (depending on type) released from the rear side to allow the unit to be withdrawn (photo).
9 Refit in the reverse order of removal. Ensure that the wiring and aerial connections are securely made.
10 If fitting a new radio/cassette unit, the aperture in the facia will take any standard-sized equipment.
11 The radio must be connected to a power source, the aerial and loudspeaker leads must be plugged in and a good earth bond made between the receiver and a metal part of the car.
12 Once installed, the aerial will have to be trimmed using the small screw provided in the receiver. Tune in to a weak station on the medium wave band and turn the screw until the reception is at its loudest and clearest.

37 Speakers (standard) – removal and refitting

Facia mounted – upper
1 Carefully prise free the grille panel from the top of the facia on the side concerned.
2 Undo the two retaining screws and withdraw the speaker unit. Disconnect the leads.
3 Refit in the reverse order of removal.

Facia mounted – lower
4 Unscrew the retaining screws from the positions shown in Figs. 12.15 and 2.8 (Chapter 2), and withdraw the lower trim panel and the glove compartment.
5 Undo the retaining screws and lower the speaker unit. Detach the wiring connector.
6 Refit in the reverse order of removal.

38 On-board computer system

1 This device is fitted to the BX 19 model and is located in the floor console forward of the gear lever.
2 The system has fifteen possible functions; the main ones being to log petrol consumption, average speed, journey time elapsed and the estimated time of arrival, plus the range possible on the remaining fuel.

37.2 Facia-mounted speaker (upper) shown with grille panel removed

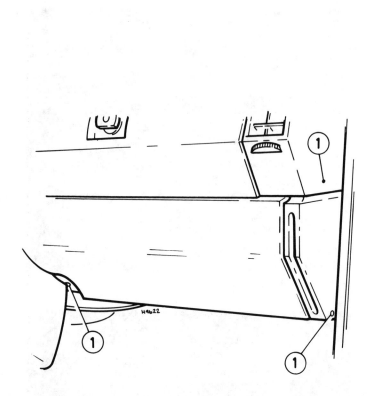

Fig. 12.15 Remove the lower trim panel screws indicated
(Sec 37)

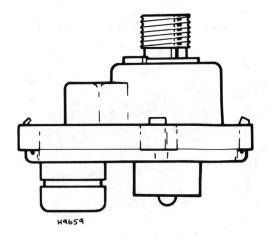

Fig.12.16 On-board computer system distance sensor (Sec 38)

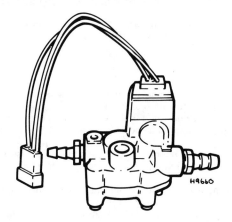

Fig. 12.17 On-board computer system fuel output sensor
(Sec 38)

3   The main components of the system, in addition to the computer unit, are the distance sensor and the fuel output sensor.
4   The distance sensor, which is driven by the speedometer cable, provides electric impulses to the computer at a frequency relative to the vehicle speed.
5   The fuel output sensor is a photo-electric cell and turbine. This relays electric pulses to the computer, each pulse relating to a given quantity of fuel passing through the fuel supply lines.
6   The computer maximum memory storage for mileage is 6000 miles (10 000 km). The maximum memory storage for time is 256 hours and for fuel consumption the storage capacity is 1000 litres (220 gallons).
7   In the event of a malfunction in the computer system, have it checked by your Citroën dealer.

39 Electrically-operated sunroof motor – removal and refitting

1   Disconnect the battery earth lead.
2   Undo the four retaining screws and lower the roof console.
3   Disconnect the wiring from the motor/reducer unit, noting their connections.
4   Undo the retaining screws and partially withdraw the motor/reducer unit so that the operating cables can be detached, then fully remove the motor unit.

5   Refitting is a reversal of the removal procedure. Before refitting the roof console, check the operation of the sunroof and make any adjustments necessary, as described in Chapter 11.

40 Wiring diagrams

The wiring diagrams in this manual represent typical examples of those available. Unfortunately, lack of space has forced the use of only a selected sample.
To assist you in using the diagrams, here is an explanation of the various letters and their use in conjunction with the wiring diagram keys.

(a) **Large numbers** – identify the various components.
(b) **Capital letters printed in the middle of a wire** – indicate which harness the wire is located in.
(c) **Small letters located at the connection points** – indicate colour; either of the wires (which have an 'F.' prefix), of the end fitting, of the marking on the wire, or a combination of any two. For example, F.Bl is a blue wire, Mv is a mauve marking, and F.J.Ve is a yellow wire with a green marking.
(d) **Connecting blocks** – the first number and the letters inside the boxes indicate the size and colour of the connecting block. Note that, due to lack of space, 0 is used to denote 10. The last number gives the relative location of the relevant wire in that connecting block.

41 Fault diagnosis – electrical system

Symptom	Reason(s)
Starter fails to turn engine	Battery discharged Battery defective internally Battery terminal leads loose or earth lead not securely attached to body Loose or broken connections in starter motor circuit Starter motor switch or solenoid faulty Starter brushes badly worn, sticking, or brush wires loose Commutator dirty, worn or burnt Starter motor armature faulty Field coils earthed
Starter turns engine very slowly	Battery in discharged condition • Starter brushes badly worn, sticking or brush wires loose Loose wires in starter motor circuit
Starter spins does not turn engine	Pinion or flywheel gear teeth broken or worn
Starter motor noisy or excessively rough engagement	Pinion or flywheel gear teeth broken or worn Starter motor retaining bolts loose
Battery will not hold charge for more than a few days	Battery defective internally Electrolyte level too low or electrolyte too weak due to leakage Plate separators no longer fully effective Battery plates severely sulphated Drivebelt slipping Battery terminal connections loose or corroded Alternator not charging Short-circuit causing continual battery drain Regulator unit not working correctly
Ignition light fails to go out, battery runs flat in a few days	Drivebelt loose and slipping or broken Alternator brushes worn, sticking, broken or dirty Alternator brush springs weak or broken Internal fault in alternator Regulator faulty
Horn operates all the time	Horn push either earthed or stuck down Horn cable to horn push earthed
Horn fails to operate	Cable or cable connection loose, broken or disconnected Horn has an internal fault Blown fuse Horn button contact fault
Horn emits intermittent or unsatisfactory noise	Cable connections loose
Lights do not come on	If engine not running, battery discharged Wire connections loose, disconnected or broken Light switch shorting or otherwise faulty
Lights come on but fade out	If engine not running, battery discharged
Lights work erratically – flashing on and off, especially over bumps	Battery terminals or earth connections loose Lights not earthing properly Contacts in light switch faulty
Wiper motor fails to work	Blown fuse Wire connections loose, disconnected or broken Brushes badly worn Armature worn or faulty
Wiper motor works very slowly and takes excessive current	Commutator dirty, greasy or burnt Armature bearings dirty or unaligned Armature badly worn or faulty
Wiper motor works slowly and takes little current	Brushes badly worn Commutator dirty, greasy or burnt Armature badly worn or faulty
Wiper motor works but wiper blades remain static	Wiper motor gearbox parts badly worn

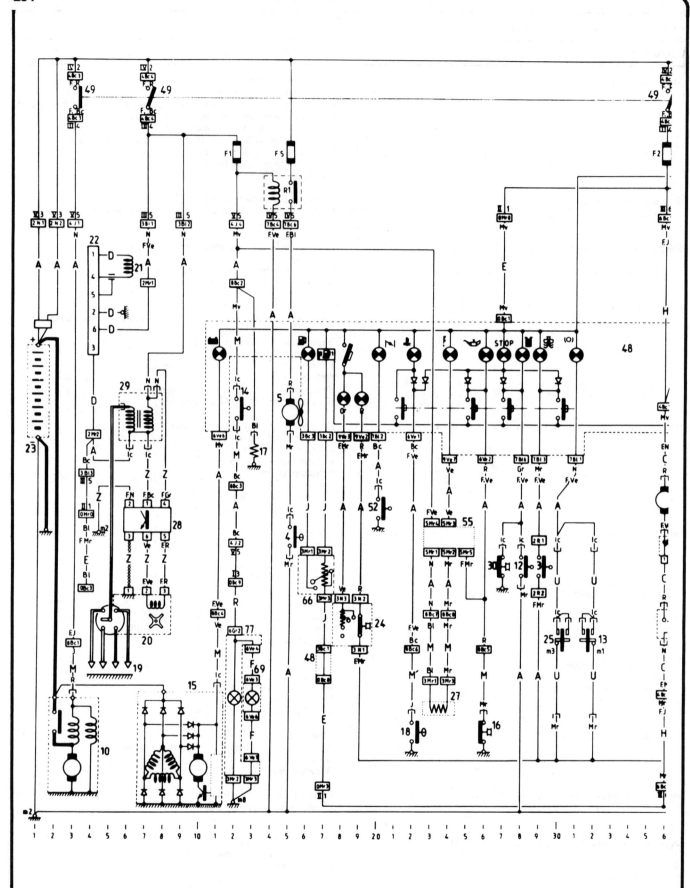

Fig. 12.18 Typical wiring diagram – BX and BX 14 models from July 1983

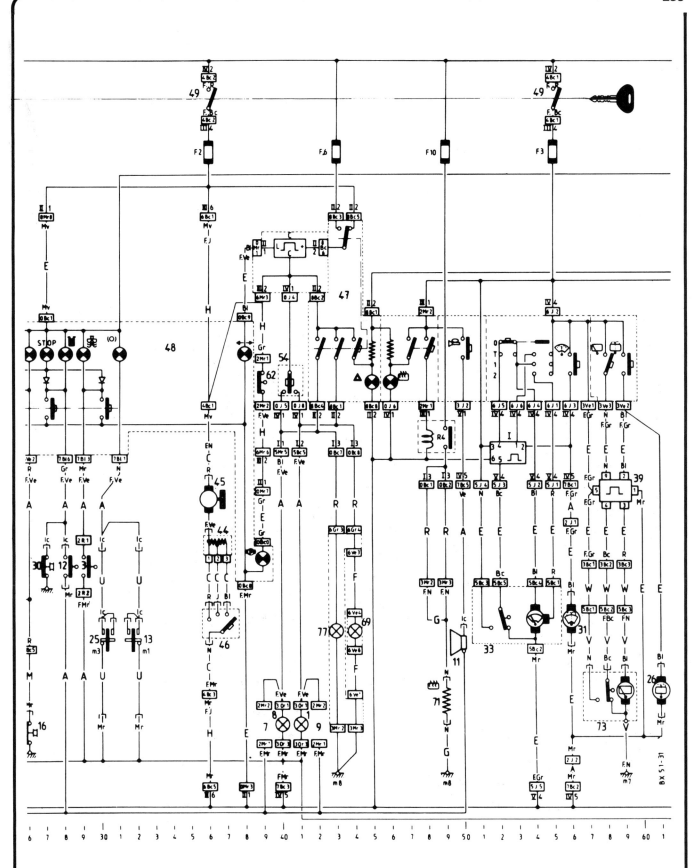

Fig. 12.18 (continued) Typical wiring diagram – BX and BX 14 models from July 1983

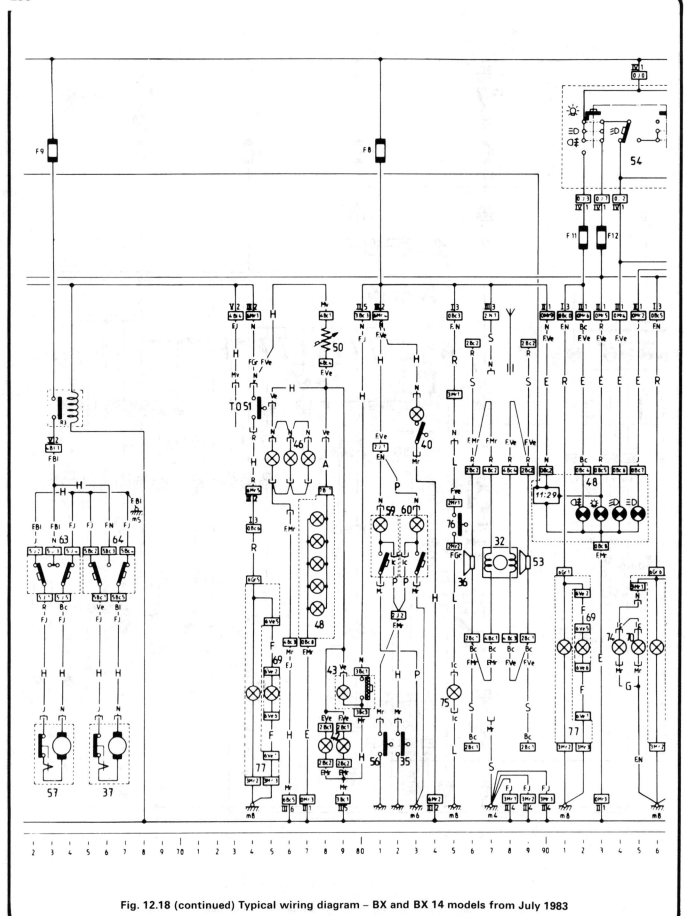

Fig. 12.18 (continued) Typical wiring diagram – BX and BX 14 models from July 1983

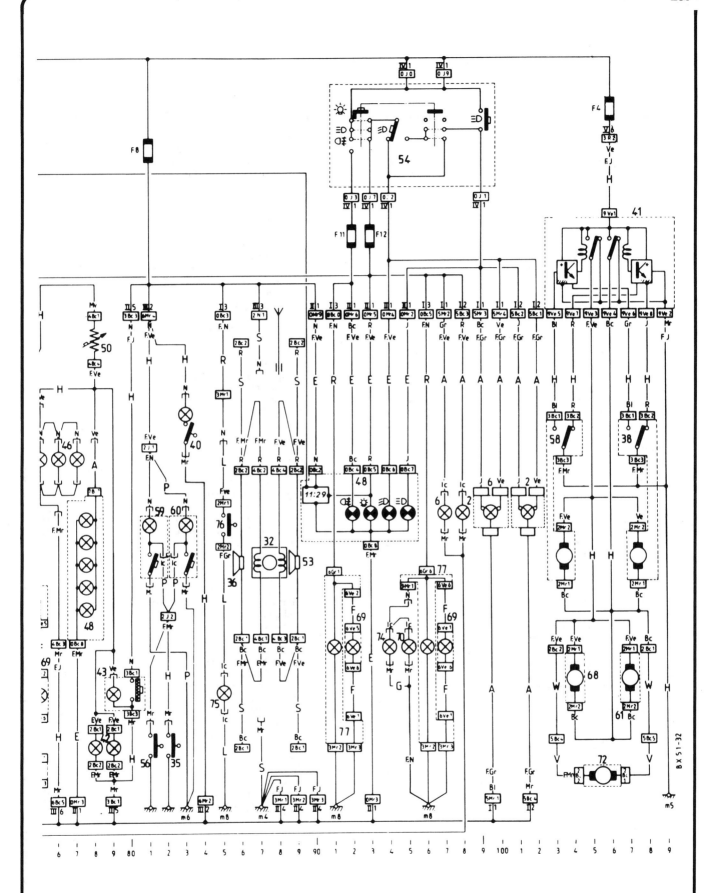

Fig. 12.18 (continued) Typical wiring diagram – BX and BX 14 models from July 1983

Key to Fig 12.18

Number	Description	Location
1	Front direction indicator RH side	41
2	Headlamp:	
	Sidelamp	98
	Main and dipped beams	101,102
3	Water level switch	29
4	Electrical fan thermal switch	15
5	Electric cooling fan	15
6	LH headlamp:	
	Sidelamp	97
	Main and dipped beams	99,100
7	Connection block for LH side repeater	39
8	Front direction indicator LH side	40
9	Connection for RH side repeater	42
10	Starter motor	2 to 4
11	Horn	50
12	Hydraulic fluid level switch	28
13	Front brake unit RH side (wear)	32
14	Reversing lamp switch	12
15	Alternator (with integrated regulator)	7 to 11
16	Engine oil pressure switch	26
17	Idle cut-off	13
18	Coolant temperature switch	22
19	Sparking plugs	4 to 6
20	Distributor	4 to 8
21	TDC sensor (diagnosis)	6
22	Diagnostic plug	4
23	Battery	1
24	Econoscope sensor	18,19
25	Front brake unit LH side (wear)	30
26	Rear window washer pump	61
27	Engine oil level sensor	23,24
28	Electronic ignition unit (module)	6 to 8
29	Ignition coil	6,7
30	Hydraulic pressure switch	27
31	Windscreen washer pump	56
32	Double channel "Boomer"	87,88
33	Windscreen wiper motor	51 to 55
34	Connection box	
35	Front door switch	82
36	LH loudspeaker	86
37	Front door window winder RH	65 to 67
38	Front door locking device unit, RH	107,108
39	Rear window wiper timer unit	58,59
40	Glove compartment lighting	83
41	Door locking device electronic unit	103 to 109
42	Ashtray lighting	78,79
43	Cigar lighter and lighting	79,80
44	Air blower resistor	36, 37
45	Air blower	36
46	Air blower control and lighting	36,37,75 to 77
47	RH control unit:	
	Windscreen wiper and washer	52 to 56
	Heated rear window	46 to 48
	Horn	50
	Hazard warning device	42 to 45

Number	Description	Location
48	Dashboard:	
	Main beam warning lamp	95
	Dipped beam warning lamp	94
	Sidelamp warning lamp	93
	Direction indicator warning lamp	38
	Rear foglamp warning lamps	92
	Clock	90
	Dashboard lighting	77,78
	Fuel gauge indicator	17
	Econoscope warning lamp and switch	18,19
	Handbrake warning lamp	39
	Emergency STOP warning lamp	27
	Warning lamp test buttom	22,25,27,30
	Battery charge warning lamp	11
	Fuel min. level warning lamp	16
	Water temperature warning lamp	22
	Front brake pad wear warning lamp	31
	Choke warning lamp	20
	Hydraulic fluid warning lamp (pressure and level)	28
	Engine oil pressure warning lamp	26
	Coolant level warning lamp	29
	Oil level warning lamp	24
49	Anti-theft switch	3,7,36,55
50	Lighting rheostat	78
51	Stoplamp switch	74
52	Choke control	20
53	Loudspeaker	89
54	LH control unit: Lighting	92 to 99
	Direction indicators	40,41
55	Engine oil level electronic unit	23 to 25
56	LH door switch	81
57	LH front window wiper motor	62 to 64
58	Front door locking device unit, LH	103,104
59	LH interior lamp	81
60	RH interior lamp	83
61	Rear door locking device motor RH	107
62	Handbrake switch	39
63	Front window winder switch, LH	62 to 64
64	Front window winder switch, RH	65 to 67
66	Fuel gauge rheostat	16,17
68	Rear door locking device motor LH	104
69	Rear lamp cluster:	
	RH tail lamp	97
	Stop-lamp – Foglamp	75,92
	Reversing lamp – Direction indicator	13,44
70	Number plate lighting RH	95
71	Heated rear window	49
72	Tailgate locking device motor	105
73	Rear window wiper motor	57 to 59
74	Number plate lighting, LH	94
75	Boot lighting	85
76	Boot lighting switch	85
77	Rear lamp cluster:	
	LH tail lamp	90
	Stop-lamp – Foglamp	74,51
	Reversing lamp – Direction indicator	12,43

Wiring colour code

Bc	White
Bl	Blue
Gr	Grey
Ic	Transparent
J	Yellow
Mr	Brown
Mv	Mauve
N	Black
Or	Orange
R	Red
Ve	Green
Vi	Violet

If the code is preceded by the letter F, it denotes the wire colour. Otherwise it denotes the sleeve colour

Earthing points

m1	Earthing point for RH front brake pad wear	32
m2	Battery earthing point on bodyshell	1,4
m3	Earthing point for LH front brake pad wear	30
m4	Connection box earthing point	87
m5	Earthing point on centre console	67,109
m6	Earthing point on windscreen frame upper part	83
m7	RH rear earthing point (rear window wiper and locking device)	59
m8	LH rear earthing point (rear window, lighting LH and RH rear lamps)	12,43,49,74,85,91,96

Harness code

A	Front
AB	Front foglamp socket
B	Boot locking – intermediate
C	Heater
D	Diagnostic
E	Windscreen wiper and dashboard
F	Ribbon-type – between rear lamps
G	Tailgate – LH
H	Passenger compartment
J	Petrol gauge
L	Boot lighting
M	Engine
P	Interior lamp
R	Ribbon-type – rear
S	Radio
U	Front brakes (pad wear)
V	Tailgate – RH (rear window wiper)
W	Tailgate – RH intermediate
X	Starting safety device
Z	Transistorised ignition

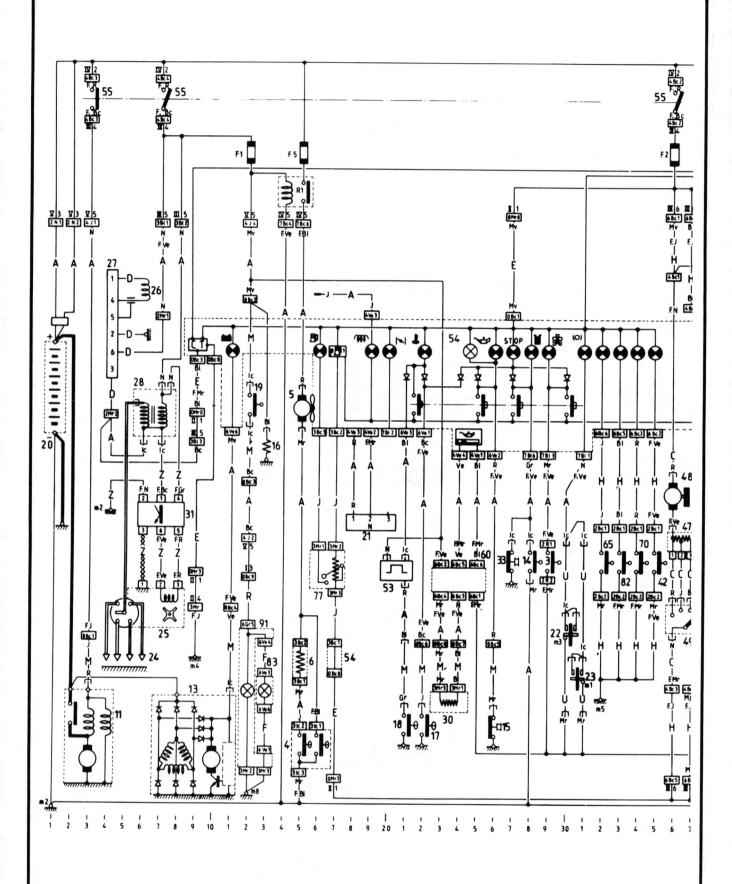

Fig. 12.19 Typical wiring diagram – BX 16 models from July 1983

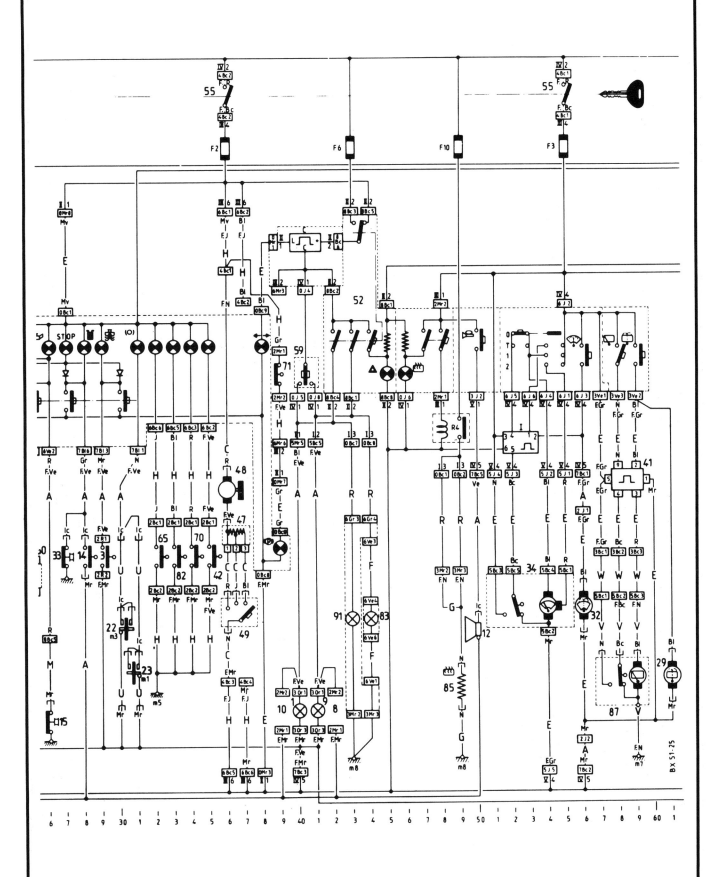

Fig. 12.19 (continued) Typical wiring diagram – BX 16 models from July 1983

Fig. 12.19 (continued) Typical wiring diagram – BX 16 models from July 1983

303

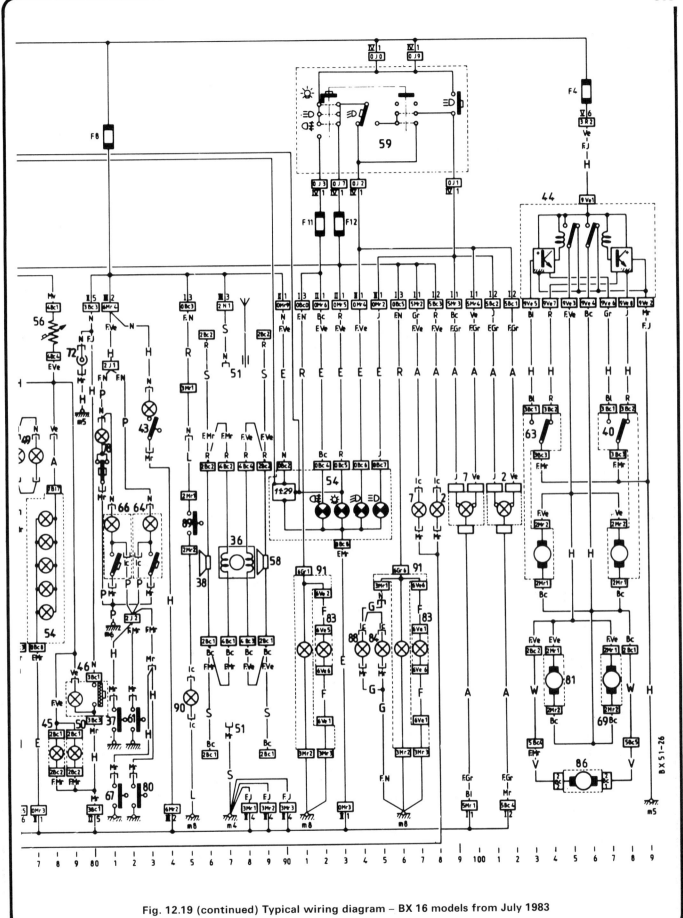

Fig. 12.19 (continued) Typical wiring diagram – BX 16 models from July 1983

Key to Fig 12.19

Number	Description	Location
1	Front direction indicator RH	40
2	RH headlamp:	
	Sidelamp	98
	Main and dipped beams	101,102
3	Water level switch	29
4	Electric fan double thermal switch	15,16
5	Electric cooling fan	15
6	Electric fan resistor	15
7	LH headlamp:	
	Sidelamp	97
	Main and dipped beams	99,100
8	Connector for LH side repeater	42
9	Front direction indicator LH side	41
10	Connector for RH side repeater	39
11	Starter motor	2 to 4
12	Horn	50
13	Alternator with incorporated regulator	7 to 11
14	Hydraulic fluid level switch	28
15	Engine oil pressure switch	26
16	Idle cut-off	13
17	Water temperature warning switch	22
18	Water temperature switch (flasher)	21
19	Reversing lamp switch	12
20	Battery	1
21	Connection block for diesel tachometer sensor	18 to 20
22	LH front brake unit (wear)	30
23	RH front brake unit (wear)	31
24	Ignition sparking plugs	4 to 6
25	Distributor	4 to 8
26	TDC sensor (diagnostic)	6
27	Diagnostic socket	4
28	Ignition coil	6 to 8
29	Rear window washer pump	61
30	Engine oil level sensor	23,24
31	Ignition electronic unit (module)	6 to 8
32	Windscreen washer pump	56
33	Hydraulic fluid pressure switch	27
34	Windscreen wiper motor	51 to 55
35	Connection box	
36	Double-channel "Boomer"	87,88
37	RH front door switch	81
38	RH loudspeaker	86
39	RH front window winder motor	65 to 67
40	RH front door locking device unit	107,108
41	Rear window wiper timer unit	58,59
42	RH front door locking device switch	35
43	Glove compartment lighting	83
44	Electronic unit for door locking device	103,109
45	Ashtray lighting	78
46	Cigar lighter and lighting	79,80
47	Air blower resistors	36,37
48	Air blower	36
49	Air blower control and lighting	36,37,75 to 77
50	Ashtray lighting	79
51	Radio connections	86 to 89
52	RH control unit:	
	Horn	50
	Windscreen wiper and washer	53 to 56
	Heated rear window	46 to 48
	Hazard warning device	42 to 45
53	Water temperature flasher	20,21
54	Dashboard:	
	Lighting	77,78
	Main beam warning lamp	95

Number	Description	Location
	Dipped beam warning lamp	94
	Side and tail lamp warning lamp	93
	Direction indicator warning lamp	38
	Rear foglamp warning lamp	92
	Door locking device warning lamp	32 to 35
	Handbrake warning lamp	39
	Clock	90
	Engine oil level indicator	24,25
	Fuel gauge indicator	17
	Tachometer	9
	Battery charge warning lamp	11
	Fuel min. level warning lamp	16
	Water temperature warning lamp	22
	Front brake pad wear warning lamp	31
	Emergency STOP warning lamp and STOP test button	22,25,27,30
	Hydraulic fluid warning lamp (pressure and level)	28
	Engine oil pressure warning lamp	26
	Coolant level warning lamp	29
55	Anti-theft switch	3,7,36,55
56	Lighting rheostat (via anti-theft switch)	78
57	Stop-lamp switch (braking)	74
58	LH loudspeaker	89
59	LH control unit:	
	Lighting	92 to 99
	Direction indicator	40,41
60	Electronic unit for engine oil level	23 to 25
61	LH front door switch	82
62	LH front window winder motor	62 to 64
63	LH front door locking device unit	103,104
64	LH interior lamp	83
65	LH front door locking device switch	32
66	RH interior lamp	81
67	RH rear door switch	81
68	RH rear window winder motor	71 to 73
69	RH rear door locking device motor	107
70	RH rear door locking device switch	34
71	Handbrake switch	39
72	Accessory plug	79
73	RH rear window winder switch	71 to 73
74	LH front window winder switch	62 to 64
75	RH front window winder switch	65 to 68
76	LH rear window winder switch	68 to 70
77	Fuel gauge rheostat	16,17
78	Map reading lamp	81
79	LH rear window winder motor	68 to 70
80	LH rear door switch	82
81	LH rear door locking device motor	104
82	LH rear door locking device switch	33
83	RH rear lamp cluster:	
	Tail lamp	97
	Stop-lamp – Foglamp	75,92
	Reversing lamp – Direction indicator	13,44
84	Number plate lamp RH	95
85	Heated rear window	49
86	Tailgate locking device motor	105
87	Rear window wiper motor	57 to 59
88	Number plate lamp, LH	94
89	Boot lighting switch	85
90	Boot lighting	85
91	LH rear lamp cluster:	
	Tail lamp	96
	Stop-lamp – Foglamp	74,91
	Reversing lamp – Direction indicator	12,43

Not all items are fitted to all models

Wiring colour code

Bc	White
Bl	Blue
Gr	Grey
Ic	Transparent
J	Yellow
Mr	Brown
Mv	Mauve
N	Black
Or	Orange
R	Red
Ve	Green
Vi	Violet

If the code is preceded by the letter F, it denotes the wire colour. Otherwise it denotes the sleeve colour

Earthing points

m1	Earthing point for RH front brake pad wear	31
m2	Battery earthing point on bodyshell	1,4
m3	Earthing point for LH front brake pad wear	30
m4	Earthing point for connection box and dashboard	9,69,87
m5	Earthing point on console	67,79,109
m6	Earthing point on windscreen frame upper part	81
m7	RH rear earthing point (rear window wiper)	59
m8	LH rear earthing point (heated rear window boot)	49,85
	LH and RH rear lamps	12,43,74,91,96

Harness code

A	Front
AB	Front foglamp socket
B	Boot locking – intermediate
C	Heater
D	Diagnostic
E	Windscreen wiper and dashboard
F	Ribbon-type – between rear lamps
G	Tailgate – LH
H	Passenger compartment
J	Petrol gauge
L	Boot lighting
M	Engine
P	Interior lamp
R	Ribbon-type – rear
S	Radio
U	Front brakes (pad wear)
V	Tailgate – RH (rear window wiper)
W	Tailgate – RH intermediate
X	Starting safety device
Z	Transistorised ignition

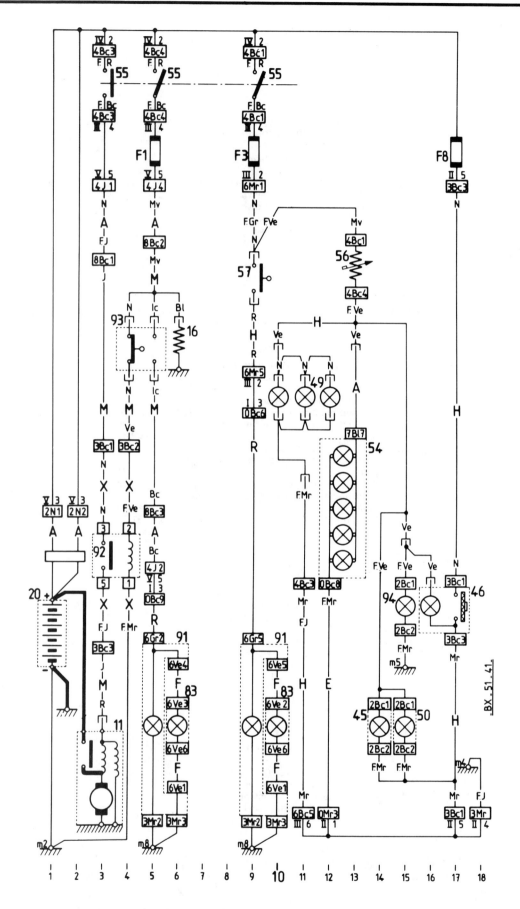

Fig. 12.20 Wiring diagram – BX 16 models automatic transmission

Key to Fig. 12.20

Number	Description	Location
11	Starter	2 to 4
16	Float chamber electric ventilation	6
20	Battery	1
45	Ashtray lighting	14
46	Cigar lighter and lighting	16,17
49	Air blower control lighting	10 to 12
50	Ashtray lighting	15
54	Dashboard lighting	12,13
55	Anti-theft switch	3,5,9
56	Lighting rheostat	13
57	Stop-lamp switch	9
83	RH rear lamp cluster	6,10
91	LH rear lamp cluster	5,9
92	Starter motor relay, starter motor	3,4
93	Switch for starter motor, reversing lamps	4,5
94	Gearchange diagram lighting	15

Harness code

A	Front
AB	Front foglamp socket
B	Boot locking – intermediate
C	Heater
D	Diagnostic
E	Windscreen wiper and dashboard
F	Ribbon-type – between rear lamps
G	Tailgate – LH
H	Passenger compartment
J	Petrol gauge
L	Boot lighting
M	Engine
P	Interior lamp
R	Ribbon-type – rear
S	Radio
U	Front brakes (pad wear)
V	Tailgate – RH (rear window wiper)
W	Tailgate – RH intermediate
X	Starting safety device
Z	Transistorised ignition

Wiring colour code

Bc	White
Bl	Blue
Gr	Grey
Ic	Transparent
J	Yellow
Mr	Brown
Mv	Mauve
N	Black
Or	Orange
R	Red
Ve	Green
Vi	Violet

If the code is preceded by the letter F, it denotes the wire colour. Otherwise it denotes the sleeve colour.

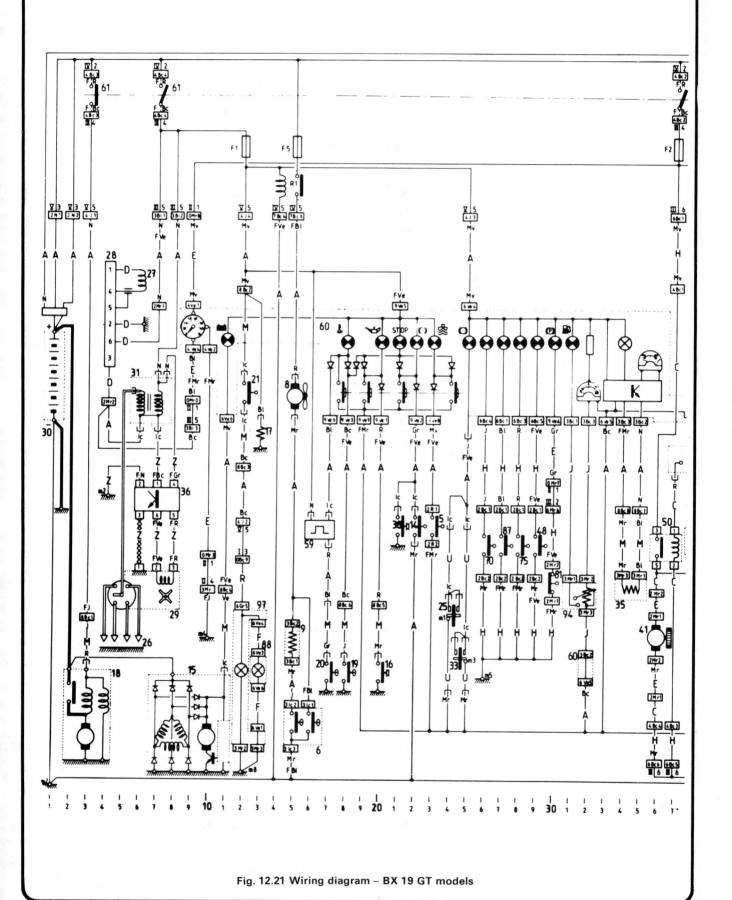

Fig. 12.21 Wiring diagram – BX 19 GT models

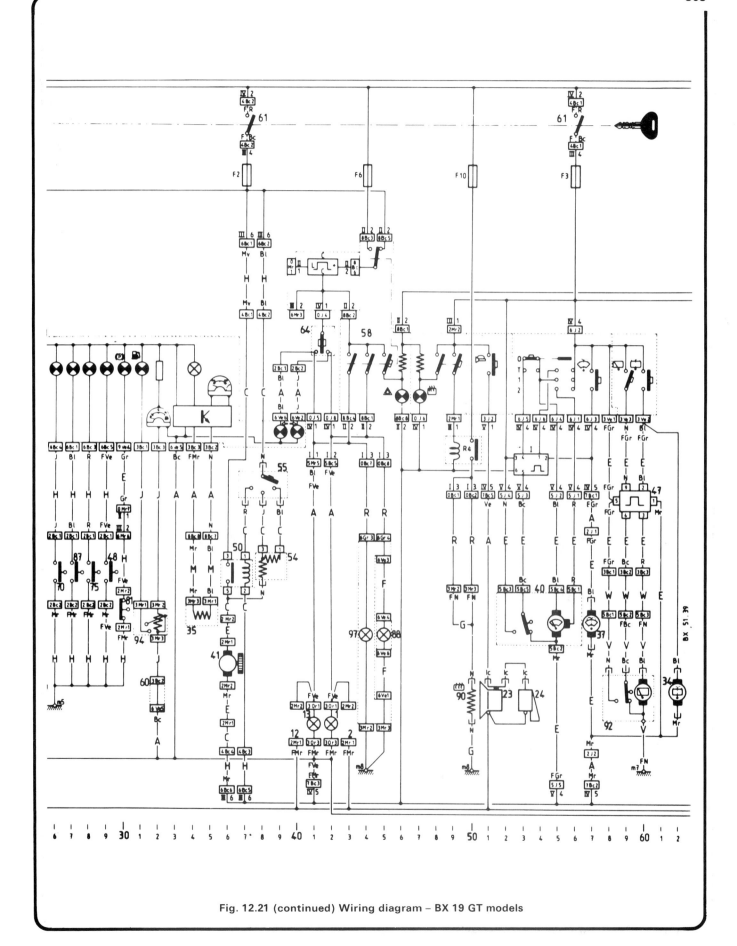

Fig. 12.21 (continued) Wiring diagram – BX 19 GT models

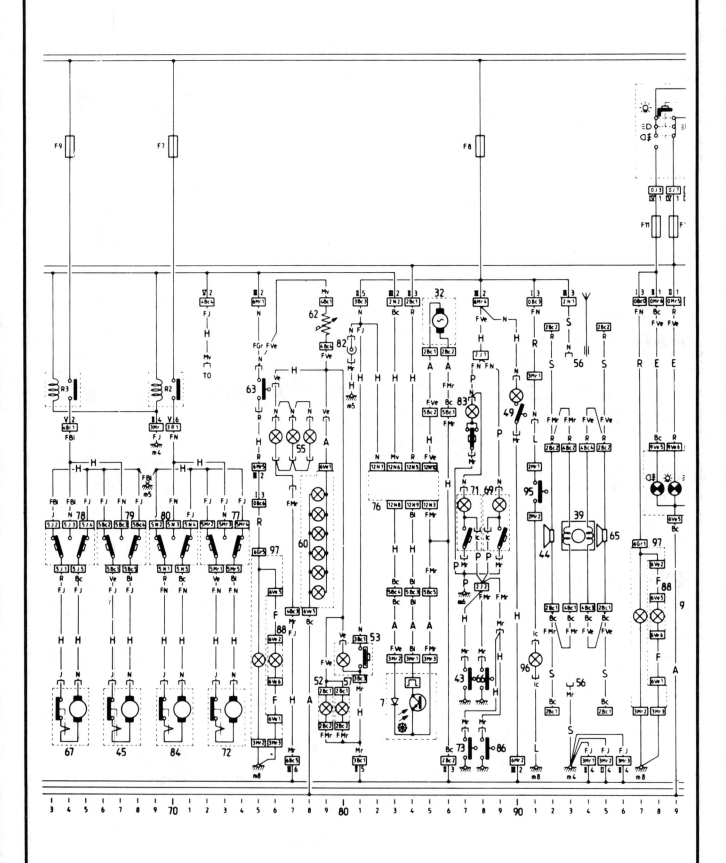

Fig. 12.21 (continued) Wiring diagram – BX 19 GT models

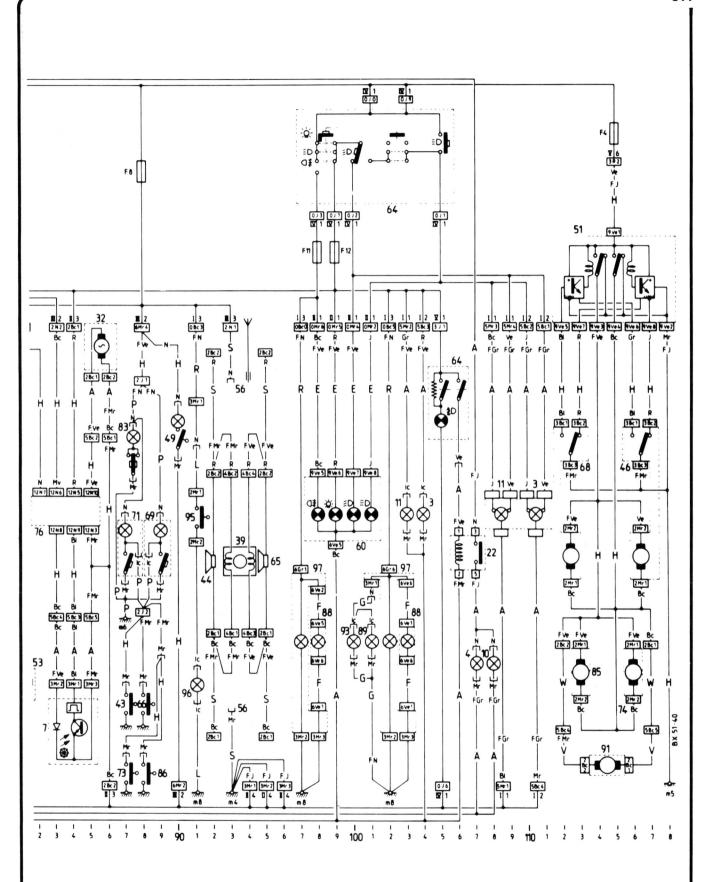

Fig. 12.21 (continued) Wiring diagram – BX 19 GT models

Key to Fig. 12.21

Number	Description	Location
1	RH front direction indicator	42
2	Connector for RH side repeater	43
3	RH headlamp:	
	Sidelamp	104
	Main and dipped beams	110,111
4	RH foglamp	102
5	Water level switch	23
6	Electric fan double thermal switch	15,16
7	Flowmeter	83,85
8	Electric cooling fan	15
9	Electric fan resistor	15
10	LH foglamp	107
11	LH headlamp:	
	Sidelamp	103
	Main and dipped beams	108,109
12	Connector for LH side repeater	40
13	LH front direction indicator	41
14	Hydraulic fluid level switch	21
15	Alternator with integrated regulator	7 to 11
16	Engine oil pressure switch	20
17	Idle cut-off	13
18	Starter motor	2 to 4
19	Emergency coolant temperature switch	18
20	Water temperature warning switch	17
21	Reversing lamp switch	12
22	Foglamp relay	106,107
23	Low-pitched tone horn	51
24	High-pitched tone horn	53
25	RH front brake unit	23,24
26	Sparking plug	4 to 6
27	TDC sensor	6
28	Diagnostic socket	4
29	Distributor	4 to 8
30	Battery	1
31	Ignition coil	6 to 7
32	Speed sensor	85,86
33	LH front brake unit	24,25
34	Rear screen washer pump	62
35	Engine oil level sensor	34,35
36	Electronic ignition module	6 to 8
37	Windscreen washer pump	57
38	Hydraulic fluid pressure switch	21
39	Double channel "Boomer"	93,94
40	Windscreen wiper motor	52 to 56
41	Air blower	36
42	Connection box	–
43	RH front door switch	87
44	RH front loudspeaker	92
45	RH front window winder motor	67
46	RH front door locking device motor	103
47	Rear window wiper timer unit	59,60
48	RH front door closing switch	29
49	Glove compartment lighting	90
50	Air blower relay	36,37
51	Electronic unit for door locking device	112,118
52	Ashtray lighting	79
53	Cigar lighter and lighting	80,81
54	Air blower resistor	38,39
55	Air blower control and lighting	37 to 39, 76 to 78
56	Radio connectors	92 to 95
57	Ashtray lighting	80
58	RH control box:	
	Front windscreen wiper	53,55
	Rear screen wiper	59,60
	Heated rear window	47,49
	Hazard warning device	43,46
	Horn	51
59	Water temperature flasher unit	16,17
60	Dashboard:	
	Coolant level	23
	Water temperature warning lamp	17
	Emergency STOP warning lamp	21
	Engine oil pressure warning lamp	19
	Warning lamp for hydraulic fluid pressure and level	22
	Battery charge warning lamp	11
	Side and tail lamps warning lamp	99
	Dipped beam warning lamp	100
	Main beam warning lamp	101
	Rear foglamp warning lamp	98
	Warning lamp for opened doors and tailgate	26 to 30
	LH flasher warning lamp	39
	RH flasher warning lamp	40
	Front brakes pad wear warning lamp	25
	Handbrake warning lamp	30
	Fuel min level warning lamp	31
	Fuel level indicator	32
	Engine oil level indicator, electronic unit and lighting	33,36
	Dashboard lighting	78,79
	Rev. counter	9
61	Anti-theft switch	2,6,37,56
62	Rheostat for dashboard lighting	79
63	Stop-light switch	75
64	LH control box:	
	Direction indicators	41,42
	Lighting	98,105
	Foglamp	105,106
65	LH loudspeaker	95
66	LH front door switch	88
67	LH front window winder motor	63,64
68	LH front door locking device motor	112,113
69	LH interior lamp	86,87
70	LH front door closing switch	26
71	RH interior lamp	88,89
72	RH rear window winder motor	73
73	RH rear door contact switch	87
74	RH rear door locking device motor	76
75	RH rear door closing switch	28
76	On-board computer	82 to 85
77	RH rear window winder selector switch	72 to 74
78	LH front window winder selector switch	63 to 65
79	RH front window winder selector switch	66 to 68
80	LH rear window winder selector switch	69 to 71
81	Handbrake contact switch	30
82	Plug for accessories (12 volts)	80
83	Map reading lamp	87
84	LH rear window winder motor	70
85	LH rear door locking device motor	113
86	LH rear door contact switch	88
87	LH rear door closing switch	27
88	RH rear signals unit:	
	Side and foglamps	103,98
	STOP lamp, reversing lamp	76,13
	Direction indicator	45
89	Number plate RH lighting	101
90	Heated rear window	50
91	Boot locking device motor	115
92	Rear window wiper motor	58 to 60
93	Number plate LH lighting	100
94	Fuel gauge rheostat	31,32
95	Boot lighting switch	91
96	Boot lighting	91
97	LH rear signals unit:	
	Tail and foglamp	102,97
	STOP lamp, reversing lamp	75,12
	Direction indicator	44

Wiring colour code

Bc	White
Bl	Blue
Gr	Grey
Ic	Transparent
J	Yellow
Mr	Brown
Mv	Mauve
N	Black
Or	Orange
R	Red
Ve	Green
Vi	Violet

If the code is preceded by the letter F, it denotes the wire colour. Otherwise it denotes the sleeve colour

Harness code

A	Front
AB	Front foglamp socket
B	Boot locking – intermediate
C	Heater
D	Diagnostic
E	Windscreen wiper and dashboard
F	Ribbon-type – between rear lamps
G	Tailgate – LH
H	Passenger compartment
J	Petrol gauge
L	Boot lighting
M	Engine
P	Interior lamp
R	Ribbon-type – rear
S	Radio
U	Front brakes (pad wear)
V	Tailgate – RH (rear window wiper)
W	Tailgate – RH intermediate
X	Starting safety device
Z	Transistorised ignition

Chapter 13 Supplement:
Revisions and information on later models

Contents

Citroën BX 19 GTi 16 valve

1 Introduction

This Supplement contains information which is additional to, or a revision of, the material given in the first twelve Chapters. The Sections in this Supplement follow the same order as the Chapters to which they relate. The Specifications are all grouped together for convenience, but follow Chapter order.

Before any work is undertaken, it is recommended that reference is made to the relevant Section(s) in this Supplement, and any changes to the procedures in the main Chapter noted.

Generally speaking, the main changes relate to model updates, which are as follows.

August 1986: the BX 19 GTi was introduced, having the same engine and gearbox as the BX 19, but fitted with a Bosch electronic fuel injection system for added performance. At the same time, the BX 19 TRS model replaced the BX 19 GT, and a BX 19 TRS Estate fitted with automatic transmission became available. The facia and instruments were modified on all models, with round instruments being used. Other aesthetic improvements were made to improve the external appearance of certain models.

March 1987: The BX 19 GTi models were fitted with anti-lock ABS braking. The BX 16 RE Saloon version was added to the range, fitted with the 1.6 litre engine and a five-speed gearbox.

July 1987: The BX 19 GTi 16 valve, with 16 valve engine and Motronic fuel injection/ignition system, was introduced.

August 1988: 1360 cc K1G engine with 2CA type four- or five-speed transmission introduced on all BX 14 models.

April 1989: BE3/5 gearbox introduced for BX 16 and BX 19 models, replacing BE1/5 gearbox.

March 1990: BX 19 TZi catalytic converter-equipped Saloon and Estate models added to range.

Late 1992: BX 16 TXi catalytic converter-equipped Saloon and Estate models added to the range.

Although, as stated previously, most of the information in this Supplement relates to the new models, in the course of modification and rationalisation, some of the design changes are incorporated into earlier models by the fitting of modified parts. It is therefore necessary, when replacing parts, to pay close attention to interchangeability, and to note any specification changes which may occur when fitting modified parts. Where any doubt exists about interchangeability, the advice of your local Citroën dealer should be sought.

Underbonnet view of BX 14 (K1G engine) model

1	Front suspension sphere	7	Fuel pump	13	Air intake tube
2	Heater hose bleed screw	8	Hydraulic system fluid reservoir	14	Radiator filler cap
3	Air cleaner	9	Alternator	15	Radiator bleed screw
4	Battery	10	Engine oil filler cap	16	Air cleaner Winter/Summer lever
5	Right-hand engine mounting	11	Ignition coil	17	Bonnet lock
6	Carburettor	12	Hot air intake hose		

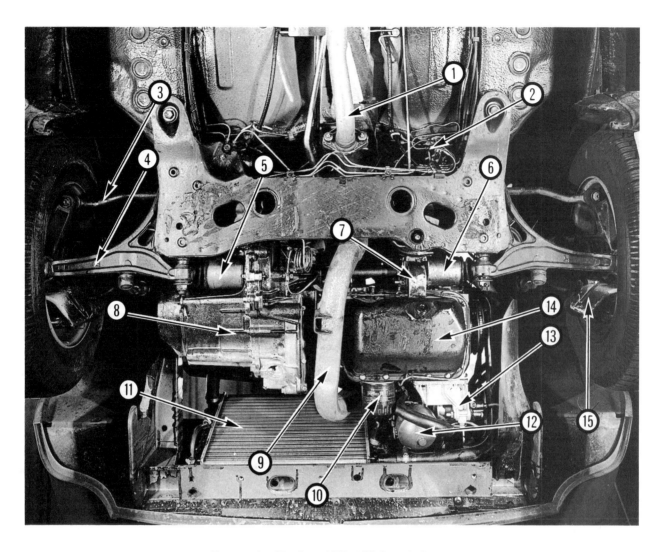

Front underside view of BX 14 (K1G engine) model

1	Exhaust front section	7	Driveshaft intermediate bearing	12	Hydraulic system fluid pressure regulator
2	Hydraulic system pipes and union	8	Transmission		
3	Steering track-rod	9	Exhaust downpipe	13	Hydraulic system fluid pump
4	Front suspension arm	10	Oil filter	14	Sump
5	Driveshaft inboard joint	11	Radiator	15	Brake disc air deflector
6	Driveshaft inboard joint				

Underbonnet view of BX 19 GTi

1	Battery	8	Hydraulic system fluid reservoir	14	Fuel rail
2	ABS hydraulic control unit	9	Alternator	15	Engine oil filler cap
3	Airflow meter	10	Right-hand engine mounting	16	Thermostat housing
4	Air cleaner	11	Front suspension unit	17	Distributor
5	Throttle butterfly housing	12	Rear window washer reservoir	18	Heater blower motor
6	Inlet manifold	13	Fuel pressure regulator	19	Windscreen washer reservoir
7	Radiator filler cap				

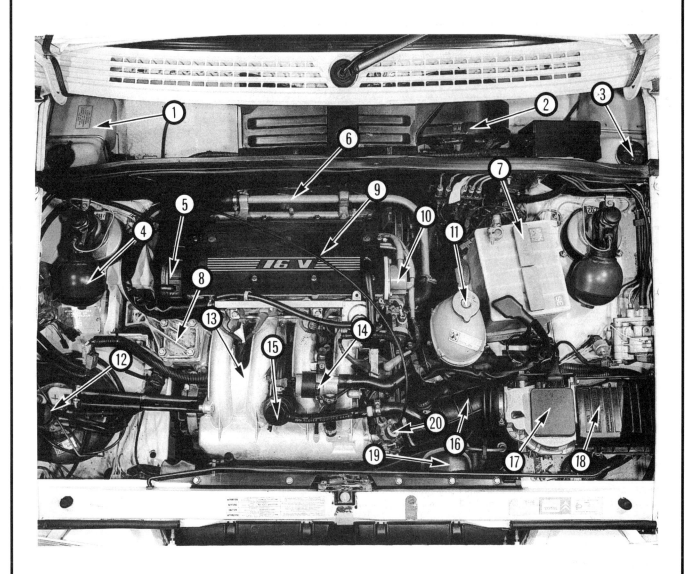

Underbonnet view of BX 19 GTi 16 valve

1	Rear window washer reservoir	8	Right-hand engine mounting	15	Engine oil filler cap
2	Heater blower motor	9	Camshaft cover	16	Air intake hose
3	Windscreen washer reservoir	10	Distributor	17	Airflow meter
4	Front suspension sphere	11	Coolant expansion tank	18	Air cleaner
5	Timing belt cover	12	Hydraulic system fluid reservoir	19	Radiator
6	Coolant distribution pipe	13	Inlet manifold	20	Throttle butterfly housing
7	Battery	14	Idle actuator		

Engine - BX 14 models (from August 1988)
Specifications as for the type 150 engine, but with the following differences:

General

Engine type reference..	K1G
Maximum power DIN (BHP)...	72 at 5600 rpm
Maximum torque DIN (lbf ft)	78 at 3400 rpm

Camshaft

Drive...	Toothed belt

Crankshaft

Endfloat..	0.052 to 0.452 mm

Cylinder liners

Protrusion from block (without seal)...	0.03 to 0.10 mm
Protrusion difference between liners	0.05 mm

Valves

Seat combined angle:	
Inlet..	120°
Exhaust...	90°
Valve clearances (cold):	
Inlet..	0.20 mm
Exhaust...	0.40 mm
Valve timing (nominal valve clearance of 0.7 mm):	
Inlet opens..	7° 14' BTDC
Inlet closes	39° 45' ABDC
Exhaust opens...	54° 30' BBDC
Exhaust closes	0° 45' BTDC

Lubrication

Oil pump drive	Chain from crankshaft
Oil capacity, with filter change	3.5 litres (6.2 pints)
Oil filter..	Champion F104
Difference between Min and Max marks on the dipstick	1.4 litres (2.5 pints)
Oil pressure at 90°C (194°F):	
650 rpm	1.5 bars (22 lbf/in^2)
4000 rpm	4.0 bars (58 lbf/in^2)

Torque wrench settings

	kgf m	lbf ft
Crankshaft pulley...	10.2	74
Camshaft sprocket	8.2	59
Big-end bearing cap	3.9	28
Flywheel	6.6	48
Clutch pressure plate bolts..	1.5	11
Distributor/fuel pump housing..	0.8	6
Camshaft thrust fork	1.7	13
Thermostat housing...	0.8	6
Main bearing cap casting main bearing bolts:		
Stage 1	2.1	15
Stage 2	Angle-tighten a further 45°	Angle-tighten a further 45°
Oil pump	0.8	6
Sump	0.8	6
Main bearing cap casting to block	0.8	6
Water pump housing:		
8 mm bolt..	3.1	22
6 mm bolts..	5.1	37
Cylinder head bolts:		
Stage 1	2.1	15
Stage 2	Angle-tighten a further 240°	Angle-tighten a further 240°
Timing belt tensioner	2.1	15
Timing cover	0.6	4
Valve cover	0.5	4
Dipstick tube...	1.5	11
Oil pressure switch	2.9	21
Oil filter..	1.5	11

Engine - BX 16 RE models
Specifications as for the type 171 engine, but with the following differences:

General
Engine type reference	B1A/A
Compression ratio	9.35 to 1
Maximum power DIN (BHP)	80 at 5600 rpm
Maximum torque DIN (lbf ft)	97.6 at 2800 rpm

Valves
Valve timing:	
Inlet opens	5° 6' BTDC
Inlet closes	23° 7' ABDC
Exhaust opens	35° 8' BBDC
Exhaust closes	0° 8' BTDC
Valve clearances (cold):	
Inlet	0.15 to 0.20 mm
Exhaust	0.35 to 0.40 mm

Engine - BX 16 models (except TXi model - from September 1988)
Specifications as for the type 171C engine, but with the following differences:

General
Engine type reference	B2C (XU52C)
Compression ratio	8.95:1
Maximum power DIN (BHP)	94 at 6000 rpm
Maximum torque DIN (lbf ft)	97 at 3200 rpm

Valves
Length	108.0 mm
Exhaust valve head diameter	34.5 mm
Inlet valve head diameter	41.5 mm

Engine - fuel-injected BX 16 models
Specifications as for the type 171C engine, but with the following differences:

General
Engine type reference	BDY (XU5M 3Z)
Compression ratio	8.95:1
Maximum power DIN (BHP)	89 at 6400 rpm
Maximum torque DIN (lbf ft)	97 at 3000 rpm

Engine - BX 19 TRS models (from July 1986)
Specifications as for the type 159A engine, but with the following differences:

General
Engine type reference	D2A (XU92C)
Maximum power DIN (BHP)	105 at 5600 rpm
Maximum torque DIN (lbf ft)	119 at 3000 rpm

Engine - BX 19 TRS/TZS models (for 1990 model year)
Specifications as for the type 159A engine, but with the following differences:

General
Engine type reference	D2E (XU92C+)
Maximum power DIN (BHP)	105 at 6000 rpm
Maximum torque DIN (lbf ft)	118 at 3000 rpm

Engine - BX 19 TZS models (from 1991 model year)
Specifications as for the type 159A engine, but with the following differences:

General
Engine type reference	D2F (XU92C+)
Maximum power DIN (BHP)	107 at 6000 rpm
Maximum torque DIN (lbf ft)	122.5 at 3000 rpm

Engine - BX 19 GTi models (up to 1991 model year)
Specifications as for the type 159A engine, but with the following differences:

General
Engine type reference	D6A (XU9J2)
Maximum power DIN (BHP)	125 at 5500 rpm
Maximum torque DIN (lbf ft)	129 at 4500 rpm
Compression ratio	9.3:1

Valves
Valve head diameter:
Inlet	40.6 mm
Exhaust	33.0 mm
Valve length	105 mm
Valve lift (inlet and exhaust)	11.5 mm

Valve timing (nominal valve clearance of 0.7 mm):
Inlet opens	5° 9' BTDC
Inlet closes	48° ABDC
Exhaust opens	43° 4' BBDC
Exhaust closes	1° 10' ABDC

Valve clearances (cold):
Inlet	0.10 to 0.15 mm
Exhaust	0.20 to 0.30 mm

Engine - BX 19 GTi models (from 1991 model year)
Specifications as for the type D6A engine, but with the following differences:

General
Engine type reference	D6D (XU9J2)
Maximum power DIN (BHP)	123 at 5500 rpm
Maximum torque DIN (lbf ft)	127 at 2750 rpm

Engine - BX 19 GTi 16 valve (dohc)
Specifications as for the type 159A engine, but with the following differences:

General
Engine type reference	D6C (XU9J4)
Compression ratio	10.4:1
Maximum power DIN (BHP)	160 at 6500 rpm
Maximum torque DIN (lbf ft)	133 at 5000 rpm

Crankshaft
Crankshaft journal diameter	59.7 to 60.0 mm
Crankpin diameter	49.7 to 50.0 mm
Crankshaft endfloat thrustwasher thicknesses	2.33 to 2.53 mm, available in 0.05 mm increments

Valves
Head diameter:
Inlet	34.7 mm
Exhaust	29.7 mm
Valve lift	9.2 mm

Valve timing (theoretical valve clearance 1.0 mm):
Inlet valve opens	1° 35' BTDC
Inlet valve closes	45° 50' ABDC
Exhaust valve opens	47° 0' BBDC
Exhaust valve closes	0° 30' ATDC
Cam followers	Hydraulic (valve clearance adjustment not required)

Lubrication
Capacity (with filter change)	5.3 litres (9.3 pints)
Difference between Min and Max marks on the dipstick	1.5 litres (2.6 pints)

Oil pressure:
At 850 rpm	2.0 bars (29 lbf/in^2)
At 3000 rpm	4.8 bars (60 lbf/in^2)

Torque wrench settings
	kgf m	lbf ft
Camshaft bearing cap Allen screws	1.0	7.4
Main bearing cap bolts and nuts	5.0	37

Centre main bearing cap side bolts	2.5	18
Sump pan bolts	2.0	15
Big-end bearing cap nuts:		
Stage 1	4.0	30
Stage 2: slacken, then tighten to	2.0	15
Stage 3: then immediately	Angle-tighten a further 70°	Angle-tighten a further 70°
Oil pump bolts	2.0	15
Flywheel bolts	5.0	37
Clutch cover bolts	2.5	18
Crankshaft sprocket bolt	11.0	82
Coolant pump bolts	1.5	11
Camshaft sprocket bolts	4.5	33
Timing belt tensioner locking screw	2.0	15
Engine mounting bracket at timing cover end:		
Larger bolts	7.2	53
Smaller bolts	4.5	33
Crankshaft damper bolts	2.5	18
Camshaft rear pulley bolt	4.5	33
Inlet manifold bolts	2.0	15
Exhaust manifold bolts	2.5	18
Cylinder head bolts:		
Stage 1	6.0	43
Stage 2: slacken, and then tighten each bolt in turn to	2.0	15
Stage 3: then immediately	Angle-tighten a further 300°	Angle-tighten a further 300°

Engine - BX 19 TZi models with catalytic converter
Specifications as for the type D6A engine, but with the following differences:

General

Engine type reference	DKZ (XU9JAZ)
Compression ratio	9.18:1
Maximum power DIN (BHP)	122 at 6000 rpm
Maximum torque DIN (lbf ft)	115 at 3000 rpm

Valves

Valve head diameter:	
Inlet	34.5 mm
Exhaust	41.5 mm
Valve length	108.0 mm

Cooling system - BX 14 with K1G engine
General

Coolant capacity	6.5 litres (11.5 pints)
Warning light switch operating temperature	110°C (230°F)
Electric cooling fan operating temperature	90°C (194°F)
Thermostat:	
Starts to open	88°C (190°F)
Fully open	102°C (216°F)

Torque wrench settings

	kgf m	lbf ft
Water pump upper stud	1.6	12
Water pump lower bolt	0.8	6
Housing inlet elbow	0.8	6
Housing to block:		
8 mm bolts	3.1	22
10 mm bolts	5.1	37

Cooling system - BX 19 GTi and BX 19 GTi 16 valve
General

Coolant capacity	7.1 litres (12.5 pints)
System pressure	1 bar (14.5 lbf/in²)
Thermostat opening temperature	79 to 82°C (174 to 180°F)
Electric fan cut-in temperature:	
1st speed	86 to 90°C (186 to 194°F)
2nd speed	90 to 94°C (194 to 201°F)
Engine coolant switch temperature	105 to 112°C (221 to 233°F)

Fuel and exhaust systems - carburettor models

BX 14 from July 1988

Carburettor type	Solex 34 PBISA 17
Venturi bore (mm)	26
Main jet	132
Air correction jet	155
Emulsion tube	EC
Idle jet	42 to 46
Enrichment jet	55
Accelerator pump jet	40
Float chamber needle valve (mm)	1.6
Idle speed	750 ± 50 rpm
CO percentage in exhaust gas	0.8 to 1.2

BX 16 RE

Carburettor type	Weber 36 TLP 1/100
Venturi bore (mm)	28
Main jet	142
Air correction jet	150
Emulsion tube	F80
Idle jet	47 to 51
Enrichment jet	50
Accelerator pump injector	50
Float chamber needle valve (mm)	1.5
Idle speed	700 ± 50 rpm
CO percentage in exhaust gas	1 to 2

BX 16 from September 1988 to 1991 model year

Air cleaner element	Champion U543	
Carburettor type	Solex 32-34 Z1 PSA	
	Primary	**Secondary**
Venturi bore (mm)	24	26
Main jet	112.5	125
Air correction jet	145	140
Emulsion tube	ZD	ZC
Idling jet	44	50
Air correction jet	180	150
Enrichment jet	55	-
Econostat jet	-	80
Accelerator pump jet	40	40
Fuel inlet needle valve	1.8	
Idle speed:		
Manual gearbox	800 ± 100 rpm	
Automatic transmission	750 ± 50 rpm	
CO percentage in exhaust gas	0.8 to 1.5	

BX 19 from July 1986 to 1991 model year

Air cleaner element (from July 1987)	Champion U543	
Carburettor type:		
Manual gearbox	Solex 34-34 Z1 CIT 391	
Manual gearbox (with air conditioning)	Solex 34-34 Z1 CIT 291-1	
Automatic transmission	Weber 34-34 DRTC 14/100	
Automatic transmission (with air conditioning)	Weber 34-34 DRTC 15/100	
Solex carburettors:	**Primary**	**Secondary**
Venturi bore (mm)	25	27
Main jet	115	115
Air correction jet	150	160
Emulsion tube	ZD	ZC
Idling jet	43	90
Idling air correction jet	145	145
Enrichment device jet	50	-
Econostat calibration	-	70
Pump injector	40	56
Needle valve diameter (mm)	1.8	
Float adjustment (mm)	33	
Positive opening of primary valve (at 20°C) (mm)	0.45	
Strangler flap opening by anti-flood capsule (mm)	5 to 7	
Manual anti-flooding (mm)	7 to 9	
Idle speed	700 ± 50 rpm	
Fast idling (air conditioning)	900 ± 50 rpm	
CO percentage in exhaust gas	1.0 to 2.0	

Weber carburettors:	Primary	Secondary
Venturi bore (mm)	25	27
Main jet	110	125
Air correction jet	160	150
Emulsion tube	F45	F27
Idling jet	52	50
Idling air correction jet	150	70
Enrichment device jet	55	-
Econostat calibration	-	85
Pump injector	50	-
Float adjustment (mm)	7	
Positive opening of primary valve (at 20°C) (mm)	0 ± 1	
Strangler flap opening by anti-flood capsule (mm)	4.5 ± 1	
Manual anti-flooding (mm)	8.5	
Idle speed	800 ± 50 rpm	
Fast idling (air conditioning)	900 ± 50 rpm	
CO percentage in exhaust gas	1.0 to 2.0	

BX 19 from 1991 model year

Air cleaner element	Champion U543	
Carburettor type	Solex 34-34 Z1	
	Primary	Secondary
Venturi bore (mm)	26	27
Main jet	115 ± 5	122 ± 5
Air correction jet	140 ± 20	160 ± 20
Emulsion tube	3Z	ZC
Idling jet:		
Manual	45 ± 5	110 ± 10
Automatic	44 ± 3	110 ± 10
Idling air correction jet:		
Manual	145 ± 20	145 ± 20
Automatic	145 ± 20	140 ± 20
Enrichment jet	50 ± 20	-
Econostat jet	-	50 ± 20
Accelerator pump jet	45	40
Fuel inlet needle valve	1.8	
Idle speed	750 ± 50 rpm	
CO percentage in exhaust gas	0.8 to 1.2	

Fuel and exhaust systems - fuel-injected models
BX 19 GTi up to July 1990

System type	Bosch LE3 Jetronic electronic injection, with integral electronic control unit
Air filter element	Champion U543
System fuel pressure (at idle speed)	2 bars
Idle speed:	
Manual gearbox	825 ± 25 rpm
Automatic transmission	900 ± 50 rpm
Idle speed - with air conditioning on (where applicable)	975 ± 25 rpm
CO percentage in exhaust gas (maximum)	2.0
Fuel filter	Champion L201
Fuel tank capacity	66 litres (14.5 gallons)

BX 19 GTi from July 1990, BX 19 GTi 16 valve and BX 19 TZi

System type:	
BX 19 GTi 16 valve models up to 1991 model year	Motronic ML4.1
BX 19 GTi 16 valve models from 1991 model year, and BX 19 TZi models with catalytic converter	Motronic M1.3
BX 19 GTi models from July 1990	Motronic MP3.1
Idle speed:	
Motronic ML4.1	850 rpm (not adjustable)
Motronic M1.3:	
BX 19 GTi 16 valve models	850 rpm (not adjustable)
BX 19 TZi models	850 to 950 rpm
Motronic MP3.1	850 to 900 rpm
CO percentage in exhaust gas:	
Motronic ML4.1	0.8 to 1.5
Motronic M1.3:	
BX 19 GTi 16 valve models	0.8 to 1.5
BX 19 TZi models	Controlled by ECU
Motronic MP3.1	1.0 to 2.0

BX 19 GTi from July 1990, BX 19 GTi 16 valve and BX 19 TZi (continued)

Air cleaner element	Champion U543
Fuel filter	Champion L201

BX 16 TXi

System type	Magneti Marelli G6.10
Idle speed	Controlled by ECU*
CO percentage in exhaust gas	Controlled by ECU*
Fuel system regulated operating pressure	0.8 bars
Air cleaner element	Champion type not available
Fuel filter	Champion type not available

The idle speed and mixture are constantly monitored and adjusted by the ECU, and can only be checked and adjusted using special electronic diagnostic equipment - see text for further information.

Ignition system

Ignition timing

Dynamic (vacuum hose detached):

BX 14 (from July 1988)	6 to 10° BTDC at 750 rpm
BX 16 RE	10° BTDC at 700 rpm
BX 16 (from 1988)	10° BTDC at 850 rpm
BX 19 GTi (up to July 1990)	5° BTDC at 900 rpm

Spark plugs

Application:

BX 14 (from July 1988 on)	Champion RC9YCC or C9YCX
BX 16 carburettor models - from September 1988	Champion RC7YCC or C7YCX
Fuel-injected BX 16 models	Champion C9YCX
BX 19, carburettor (from July 1987)	Champion RC7YCC or C7YCX
BX 19, fuel injection (except GTi 16 valve)	Champion RC7YCC or C7YCX
BX 19 GTi 16 valve	Champion RC7BMC

Electrode gap:

Fuel-injected BX 16 models	0.9 mm (0.036 in)
BX 19 GTi 16 valve	1.6 mm (0.063 in)
All other models	0.8 mm (0.032 in)

Torque wrench settings

	kgf m	lbf ft
Spark plugs:		
Taper seat type	1.2	9
Flat seat type (with washer)	2.5	18

Clutch

BX 19 GTi 16 valve

Friction plate diameter	215.0 mm (8.5 in)

Manual transmission - BX 14 (from August 1988)

General

Type	Four or five forward gears and one reverse, synchromesh on all forward gears

Designation (type MA):

Four-speed gearbox:

Pre-October 1989	2 CA 16
October 1989 to September 1990	2 CA 51
September 1990 to September 1991	2 CA 77
From September 1991	2 CB 35

Five-speed gearbox:

Pre-October 1989	2 CA 14
October 1989 to September 1990	2 CA 49
September 1990 to September 1991	2 CA 91
From September 1991	2 CB 48

Gear ratios	Four-speed	Five-speed
1st	3.417:1	3.417:1
2nd	1.810:1	1.810:1
3rd	1.130:1	1.276:1
4th	0.814:1	0.975:1
5th	-	0.757:1
Reverse	3.583:1	3.583:1
Final drive	4.286:1	4.538:1

Lubrication
Oil type/specification .... Gear oil, viscosity SAE 75W/80W (Duckhams Hypoid PT 75W/80)
Oil capacity .... 2.0 litres (3.5 pints)

Torque wrench settings (type 2CA transmission)

	kgf m	lbf ft
Gearbox housing to clutch/final drive housing	1.8	13
Intermediate plate to clutch/final drive housing	5.1	37
Pressed-steel housing	1.8	13
Bearing half-rings	1.8	13
Output shaft nut (2CA 14)	14.3	103
Drain and filler plugs	2.6	19
Gearbox to engine	4.6	33

Manual transmission - BX 19 GTi and BX 19 GTi 16 valve

General
Type.. Five forward speeds and one reverse, synchromesh on all forward gears

Designation (type BE1):
    BX 19 GTi BN10, BN47
    BX 19 GTi 16 valve BN48

Gear ratios ....

	BN10 (up to Jan 1987)	**BN10, BN47** (from Jan 1987)	**BN48**
1st	3.31:1	3.25:1	2.92:1
2nd	1.88:1	1.85:1	1.85:1
3rd	1.36:1	1.36:1	1.28:1
4th	1.07:1	1.07:1	0.97:1
5th	0.86:1	0.86:1	0.76:1
Reverse	3.33:1	3.33:1	3.33:1
Final drive	3.59:1	3.59:1	4.43:1

Lubrication
Oil type/specification .... Gear oil, viscosity SAE 75W/80W (Duckhams Hypoid PT 75W/80)
Oil capacity .... 2.0 litres (3.5 pints)

Manual transmission - BX 16 and BX 19 from April 1989
Specifications as for the BE1/5 gearboxes, but with the following differences:

General
Designation.. BE3/5

Gear ratios
    1st 3.45:1

Lubrication
Oil capacity:
    Up to serial number 2445106.. 2.2 litres (3.8 pints)
    From serial number 2445106 .... 1.8 litres (3.2 pints)

Automatic transmission

General
Type.. 4 HP 14, four forward speeds, one reverse
Application (from September 1988)... BX 16, BX 19 GTi and 19 TRi

Gear ratios
    1st 2.42:1
    2nd 1.37:1
    3rd 1.00:1
    4th 0.74:1
    Reverse 2.83:1
    Final drive 3.82:1

Wheels and tyres

BX 14 Estate
Wheel size (standard) .... 4.50 B 14 FH 4.30
Tyre size (standard) - tubeless.. 145 R 14

BX 14 Estate (continued)

Tyre pressures - bars (lbf/in^2):

Front	2.2 (32)
Rear	2.5 (36)

BX 16 RE

Wheel size	5.00 B 14 FH 4.25
Tyre size (standard)	165/70 R 14

Tyre pressures - bars (lbf/in^2):

Front	2.0 (29)
Rear	2.0 (29)

BX 16 with automatic transmission (from 1987)

Tyre size	155 R 14

Tyre pressures - bars (lbf/in^2):

Front	2.2 (32)
Rear	2.2 (32)

BX 19 GTi

Wheel size (standard)	5 1/2 J 14 FH 4.18
Tyre size (standard)	185/60 (H)R 14

Tyre pressures - bars (lbf/in^2):

Without ABS:

Front	2.2 (32)
Rear	2.2 (32)

With ABS:

Front	2.0 (29)
Rear	2.2 (32)

BX 19 GTi 16 valve

Wheel size (standard)	6 J 14 CH 4.15 (alloy)
Tyre size (standard)	195/60 VR 14

Tyre pressures - bars (lbf/in^2):

Up to March 1989:

Front	2.2 (32)
Rear	2.1 (30)

From March 1989:

Front	2.1 (30)
Rear	2.0 (28)

Anti-lock braking system (ABS)

General

Description	Electro-hydraulic controlled anti-lock brake system, complementary to the normal brake system

Wheel sensor air gap (non-adjustable):

Front	0.30 to 1.0 mm (0.012 to 0.04 in)
Rear	0.50 to 1.10 mm (0.020 to 0.043 in)

Electronic control unit:

Make	Teves
Reference number	ATE 100901-0014-4

Front discs:

Type	Ventilated
Disc thickness	20.4 mm (0.80 in)

Torque wrench setting	**kgf m**	**lbf ft**
Wheel sensor (front)	1.0	7.2

Suspension and steering

Anti-roll bar

Diameter - BX 19 GTi and BX 19 GTi 16 valve up to March 1989:

Front	23 mm (0.90 in)
Rear	19 mm (0.75 in)

Diameter - BX 19 GTi 16 valve from March 1989:

Front	23 mm (0.90 in)
Rear	21 mm (0.83 in)

Electrical system

Fuses (all models)

	Protected circuits
F1 10A Red	Engine cooling fan relay coil, water level indicator unit, oil level control unit, tachometer, reversing lights, water temperature control unit
F2 25A White	Air blower (and ventilation system), instrument panel
F3 25A White	Heater fan speed control lighting, instrument panel lighting, stop-lights, cigar lighter, on-board computer, heated rear screen relay coil, rear wash/wipe, windscreen wash/wipe (and timer), "door not locked" symbol lighting (and warning lights), electric window relay coil, rear view mirror, sunroof, front seat spotlight, interior light timer unit
F4 30A Green	Engine cooling fan
F5 10A Red	Hazard warning lights
F6 30A Green	Electric rear windows
F7 30A Green	Glovebox lighting, on-board computer (+ direct supply), cigar lighter, supply socket, door locking, roof light and timer unit, boot lighting, radio electrical supply
F8 20A White	Horn, heated rear screen
F9 30A Green	Electric window control unit
F10 5A Brown	Rear foglights and warning light
F11 5A Brown	RH tail light
F12 5A Brown	LH tail light, rear number plate lights
F13 5A Brown	Side and tail warning lights, sidelights, switch lighting, on board computer lighting, front foglight switch (and warning light, relay coil)
F14 10A Red*	Hydraulic unit for ABS

*May be 25A White on later models

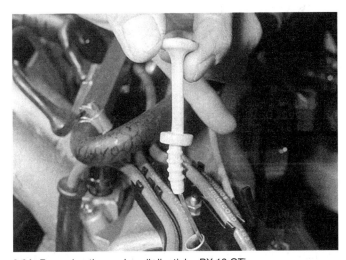

3.2A Removing the engine oil dipstick - BX 19 GTi

3.2B Removing the engine oil filler cap - BX 19 GTi

---

3   Routine maintenance

1   The routine maintenance procedures for later models are in general the same as those described for earlier models in the previous Chapters of this manual. However, for the BX 19 GTi model, the renewal procedures for the fuel filter and the air cleaner element differ from those for the carburettor models, and the relevant details concerning these items are described in the *"Routine maintenance"* Section at the front of the manual.

2   The engine oil level dipstick and oil filler for BX 19 GTi models are shown in the accompanying photographs (photos).

3   It is advisable to renew the camshaft drivebelt on all BX models (except those with the type 150 engine) every 36 000 miles. Although this task is not specifically required by the manufacturers, if the belt breaks in service, the consequences for the engine are potentially disastrous.

---

4   Engine modifications

BX and BX 14 (type 150 engines) - from December 1985

Main bearing shells

1   From the above date, the main bearing shell location tags and their slots in the crankcase upper and lower half-sections have been changed, and are now as shown in Figs. 13.1 and 13.2.

Cylinder head-to-cylinder block dowels

2   The cylinder head location dowels are now reduced in diameter from 16 mm to 14 mm. The cylinder head gasket is modified to suit. In certain instances (e.g. fitting a new-type head to an old-type block) the use of stepped dowels will be necessary; these are available from Citroën dealers.

Cylinder head and rocker assembly

3   The rocker assembly on later models has a location dowel on

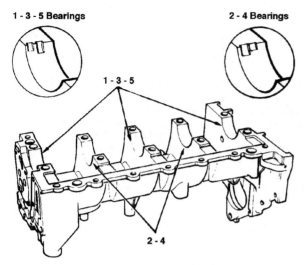

Fig. 13.1 Main bearing shell location tags - later BX and BX 14 engines (crankcase lower half shown) (Sec 4)

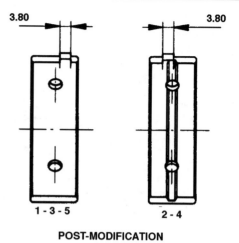

POST-MODIFICATION

Fig. 13.2 Main bearing shell identification - later BX and BX 14 engines (Sec 4)

each pedestal, instead of one at each end as on earlier models. The dowel locations are shown in Fig. 13.3. The cylinder head also has corresponding dowel holes.

4   At the same time, the rocker cover retaining screw holes are increased in diameter, and are now 8.5 mm (previously 7.5 mm). The location holes in the rocker assembly are correspondingly increased, and larger bolts used.

Minimum oil level indicator

5   This item is no longer fitted to the BX, BX 14 and BX 16 RS models.

BX 16 and BX 19 (type 171 and 159 engines) - from March 1986

6   The crankcase breather circuit is modified, and shown in Fig. 13.4. The oil separator unit fitted to earlier models is no longer fitted, and the other main difference is that the rocker cover now has a breather pipe connection ("P" in Fig. 13.4).

BX 16 and BX 19 (type 171 and 159 engines) - from July 1986

Main bearing shells

7   A further arrangement for the location and fitting of the crankshaft main bearing shells became available from the above date. The plain bearing shells are fitted to the main bearing caps of bearings 2 to 5 inclusive. The number 1 bearing cap and upper half-shells are all grooved, as shown in Fig. 13.5.

8   The bearing shell location lug recesses in the crankcase are changed to suit the new bearings; earlier- and later-type shell bearings are thus not compatible. When ordering replacement bearing shells, it is therefore important to be specific on which type is required, by quoting the engine number.

Minimum oil level indicator - BX 16 RS

9   Refer to paragraph 5 in this Section.

Rocker arms and shaft (BX and BX 14 type 150 engines) - from February 1987

10   From February 1987, the rocker arms, shaft and rocker cover have been modified.

11   The new components can be fitted to earlier engines, provided all the arms, shaft and cover are fitted at the same time.

Cylinder head bolts (BX 16 type 171 and BX 19 type 159 engines) - from February 1987

12   From February 1987, new cylinder head bolts are fitted to these engines. The new bolts are of the Torx type, and replace the original

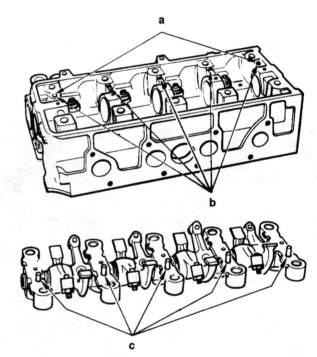

Fig. 13.3 Rocker assembly positioning dowels on later BX and BX 14 engines (Sec 4)

a   Early models
b   Later models
c   Dowel locations on later rocker assembly

hex-head bolts. The revised tightening procedure is given in the Specifications for Chapter 1. Note that the revised tightening procedure means that the Torx-type bolts require no further tightening; it is not necessary to retighten the bolts once the engine has been warmed up to normal operating temperature. However, the Torx-type cylinder head bolts **must** be renewed whenever they are disturbed.

Timing belt covers (BX 16 type 171 and BX 19 type 159 engines) - from May 1987

13   As from May 1987, a simplified three-piece timing belt cover has been fitted.

14   The later-type cover can be fitted to earlier vehicles, but will require the purchase of an additional nut and screw.

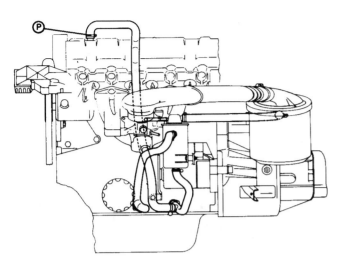

Fig. 13.4 Modified crankcase breather circuit on later BX 16 and BX 19 carburettor models (Sec 4)

P   Rocker cover connection

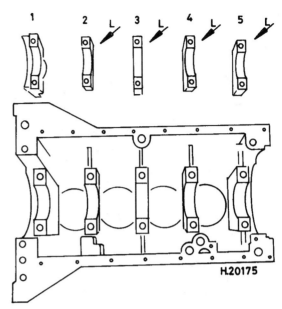

H.20175

Fig. 13.5 Main bearing shell locations on BX 16 and BX 19 engines from July 1986 (Sec 4)

L   Plain shells in caps

Main bearing shells (type 171 and 159 engines) - from July 1987

15   As from this date, grooved shells are used in the crankcase seats, and plain shells in the main bearing caps.

Modified timing belt arrangement (B2C, BDY, D2F, D6D and DKZ type engines) from January 1992 - general information, removal and refitting

General information

16   On the above engines, from January 1992, the timing belt spring tensioner mechanism is superseded by an eccentric roller tensioner mechanism.

17   To accommodate the revised components, a number of the surrounding engine components are modified, as follows. The modified components are shown in the accompanying illustration (Fig. 13.6).

    Tensioner assembly
    Camshaft drivebelt
    Front crankshaft oil seal carrier plate
    Water pump
    Right-hand engine mounting
    Cylinder block (has an extra threaded hole for tensioner centre bolt)
    Camshaft drivebelt covers

18   Note that the modified camshaft drivebelt has 114 teeth and yellow/orange markings. The drivebelt used with the spring belt tensioner mechanism has 113 teeth and white markings. If the drivebelt is to be renewed, ensure that the correct type of replacement drivebelt is obtained.

Removal and refitting

Note: *Citroën specify the use of a special tool (SEEM belt tension measuring equipment) to correctly set the belt tension. If this equipment cannot be obtained, an approximate setting can be achieved using the method described below. If the method described here is used, the tension must be checked using the special equipment at the earliest opportunity. Do not drive the vehicle over large distances, or use high engine speeds, until the belt tension is known to be correct. Refer to a Citroën dealer for advice.*

19   Proceed as described in Chapter 1, Section 30, paragraphs 1 to 7, noting that the crankshaft pulley timing dowel must be of 10 mm diameter, stepped down to 8 mm at one end to engage with the smaller hole in the timing recess.

20   With the camshaft timing belt covers removed, slacken the tensioner roller bolt to relieve the belt tension, then withdraw the belt, noting the direction of fitting and the markings.

21   Commence refitting by slipping the belt over the camshaft sprocket, followed by the crankshaft sprocket, the water pump sprocket, and finally over the tensioner roller. Observe the arrows on the belt indicating the direction of rotation, and the timing lines which align with corresponding marks on the crankshaft and camshaft sprockets.

22   With the camshaft timing dowel fitted, rotate the tensioner roller anti-clockwise by hand as far as possible to take up any slack in the belt, then tighten the tensioner roller bolt sufficiently to hold the roller in position. If the special belt tension measuring equipment is available, it should be fitted to the front run of the belt, and the tensioner roller should be moved to give a reading of 30 SEEM units. Tighten the roller bolt to the specified torque, taking care not to move the roller as the bolt is tightened.

23   Check that the crankshaft and camshaft are still positioned correctly by temporarily refitting the crankshaft pulley and reinserting the timing dowel.

24   Remove the timing dowels, temporarily refit the crankshaft pulley, and turn the crankshaft through two full turns in the normal direction of rotation. Check that both timing dowels can still be inserted. If not, remove the drivebelt and start again. **Never** turn the crankshaft backwards during this procedure.

25   If all is well, remove the dowels, and turn the crankshaft through two further turns in the normal direction of rotation.

26   Refit the camshaft timing dowel, and check that the belt can just be twisted through 90° (using moderate pressure from the forefinger and thumb) at the midpoint of the longest belt run between the camshaft and crankshaft sprockets. If in doubt about this setting, it is better to err on the tight side until the tension can be checked by a Citroën dealer, as if the belt is too slack, it may jump on the sprockets; this could result in serious engine damage. If the special belt tension measuring equipment is available, it should be refitted to the front run of the belt. The reading should now be between 42 and 46 units.

27   If the tension is not as specified, repeat the tensioning operation.

28   On completion, refit all disturbed components, tightening the crankshaft pulley bolt to the specified torque, and tension the alternator drivebelt and HP pump drivebelt, as described in the relevant Sections of Chapters 8 and 12.

B1A/A and B2C type engines - description

29   The B1A/A and B2C type engines are used in later BX 16 models, and are a development of the type 171 engine described in Chapter 1. All modifications are of a minor nature, mainly concerning the fuel and exhaust systems, details of which appear later in this Supplement.

EARLIER ASSEMBLY   LATER ASSEMBLY

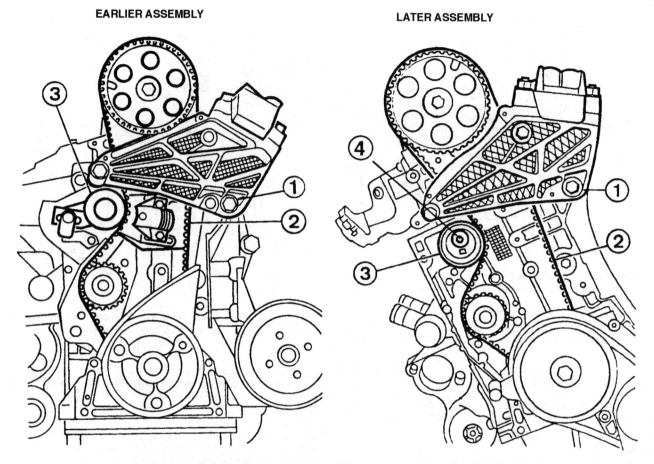

Fig. 13.6 Modified timing belt and tensioner arrangement - B2C, BDY, D2F, D6D and DKZ engines (Sec 4)

1   *Right-hand engine mounting*   3   *Tensioner assembly*
2   *Timing belt*   4   *Tensioner roller bolt*

30   All procedures for the later engine are as described for the type 171 engine in Chapter 1, but refer to the preceding paragraphs of this Section for details of applicable modifications.

BDY type engine - description

31   The BDY type engine is used in the fuel-injected BX 16 models which were first introduced in late 1992. The engine is fed by a Magneti Marelli single-point injection engine management system, which incorporates a closed-loop catalytic converter.
32   The engine is a development of the type 171 engine described in Chapter 1, and all procedures are as described in Chapter 1, referring to the preceding paragraphs of this Section for details of applicable modifications.

D2A, D2E and D2F type engines - description

33   The D2A engine superseded the type 159A engine used in BX 19 models for the 1987 model year, and the D2A engine was itself superseded by the D2E for the 1990 model year. As part of a process of continual development, the D2E engine was replaced by the D2F engine for the 1991 model year. All modifications are of a minor nature, mainly concerning the fuel and ignition systems, details of which appear later in this Supplement.
34   All procedures for the later engines are as described for the type 159A engine in Chapter 1, but refer to the preceding paragraphs of this Section for details of applicable modifications.

D6A and D6D type engines - description

35   The D6A engine was introduced to power the BX 19 GTi model. The engine is a development of the type 159A engine described in

Chapter 1. All modifications are of a minor nature, mainly concerned with the cylinder head, and the fuel injection system components which replace the carburettor used on other BX 19 models.
36   The D6D engine superseded the D6A engine for the 1991 model year, and uses a Motronic engine management system.
37   All procedures for these engines are as described for the type 159A engine in Chapter 1, but refer to the preceding paragraphs of this Section for details of applicable modifications.

DKZ type engine - description

38   The DKZ engine was introduced in the BX 19 TZi models in March 1990, and operates in conjunction with a catalytic converter.
39   The engine is a development of the 159A engine described in Chapter 1, and all procedures are as described for this engine in Chapter 1, but refer to the preceding paragraphs of this Section for details of applicable modifications.

---

5   Engine - BX 14 (type K1G)

PART A: GENERAL

K1G type engine - description

1   This engine is fitted to all BX 14 models after August 1988.
2   It is an all-alloy unit, and although the dimensions, clearances and tolerances are similar to those of the type 150C (XY6D) engine (see Chapter 1), there are several major differences.
3   These include the camshaft drive, which is of toothed belt type, and the oil pump, which is chain-driven from the crankshaft.

Fig. 13.7 Cutaway view of the K1G engine (Sec 5A)

Operations possible with engine in car

4   The following components can be removed and refitted with the engine in the car.

   (a) Timing belt and camshaft.
   (b) Cylinder head.
   (c) Sump and oil pump.
   (d) Clutch and flywheel (after removal of gearbox - see Section 13).

5   Since the sump and cylinder head can be removed *in situ*, it is possible to renew the pistons, liners and big-end bearings without re-moving the engine. However, this work is not recommended, since it can be performed more easily with the engine on the bench.

Timing belt - renewal *in situ*

6   The removal operations are described in paragraphs 62 to 68 of Section 5B, but as the engine is in the car, carry out the following pre-liminary work.

7   Disconnect the battery.

8   Release the tension and remove the drivebelts for the hydraulic pump (outer) and the alternator (inner).

9   Refitting is a reversal of removal, with reference to paragraphs 43 to 50, Section 5C.

Cylinder head - removal and refitting

10   The removal operations are described in paragraphs 44 to 58 and 62 to 74 of Section 5B, but as the engine is in the car, the following preliminary work must be carried out with reference to the appropriate Chapter.

11   Disconnect the battery.

12   Drain the cooling system.

13   Remove the air cleaner.

14   Disconnect the choke and throttle cables from the carburettor.

15   Unbolt the exhaust downpipe.

16   Refitting is a reversal of removal, with reference to paragraphs 34 to 50 and 54 to 71 of Section 5C.

Sump pan and oil pump - removal and refitting

17   The operations are described in paragraphs 82 and 83 of Section 5B, but as the engine is in the car, carry out the following preliminary work.

18   Drain the engine oil.

19   Unbolt the engine rear mounting and yoke.

20   Disconnect the hydraulic system pipeline from its clip on the sump pan, and tie it away from the sump pan.

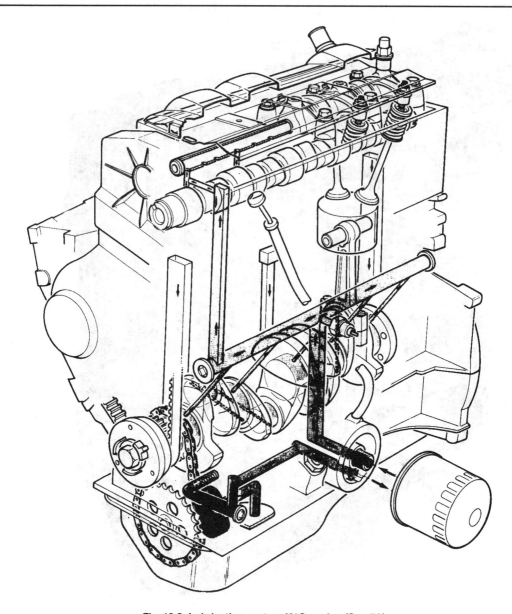

Fig. 13.8 Lubrication system K1G engine (Sec 5A)

21 Refitting is a reversal of removal, with reference to the Specifications for the torque wrench settings.

PART B: ENGINE REMOVAL AND DISMANTLING

Engine - removal and refitting

Removal

1   The engine and transmission assembly is removed as a unit by lifting it upwards from the engine compartment.
2   Remove the bonnet as described in Chapter 11 (photo).
3   Remove the battery as described in Chapter 12 (photo).
4   Raise the front of the car, and support it securely on axle stands placed under the body sill jacking points.
5   Drain the cooling system as described in Section 7 (photo).
6   Drain the engine oil.
7   Drain the transmission oil.
8   Disconnect the choke and throttle cables from the carburettor (photo).
9   Remove the air cleaner (see Section 8).
10 Disconnect the fuel supply hose from the fuel pump, and the return hose from the "tee" union.
11 Refer to Chapter 2 and remove the radiator.
12 Refer to Chapter 7 and remove both driveshafts.

13 Unbolt and remove the front downpipe from the exhaust manifold, and also the front section of the exhaust system, noting the support bracket on the transmission.
14 Pull out the rubber cotter pin, and disconnect the speedometer cable from the transmission (photo).
15 Disconnect the gearchange control rods by prising the sockets off the balljoints with an open-ended spanner (photo).
16 Remove the bolt from the engine rear mounting (photo).
17 Unbolt the rear mounting yoke and the driveshaft support bearing bracket, and remove them.
18 Release the clips which hold the suspension levelling pipeline to the underside of the engine and transmission.
19 Loosen the mounting and belt adjuster link bolts on the hydraulic pump, and remove the drivebelt.
20 Set the suspension height control lever in the "low" position, and then gently release the screw on the hydraulic pressure regulator through one turn (photo).
21 Disconnect the small pipe union on the hydraulic pressure regulator, and the one on the security valve (Chapter 8, Section 11). Release the fixing clips and withdraw the disconnected section of pipeline from below the car, noting carefully its routing.
22 Unbolt the hydraulic pump/regulator assembly from the cylinder

5B.2 Removing the bonnet

5B.3 Loosen the retaining clamp (arrowed) and remove the battery

5B.5 Cylinder block drain plug (arrowed)

5B.8 Carburettor connections

A Choke cable
B Throttle cable
C Distributor vacuum hose

5B.14 Speedometer cable rubber cotter pin (arrowed)

5B.15 Using an open-ended spanner (arrowed) to disconnect a gearchange rod balljoint

5B.16 Engine rear mounting and yoke

5B.20 Hydraulic pressure regulator

A Pipe union
B Pressure relief screw

5B.22 Unbolting the hydraulic pump/regulator assembly

block bracket (photo).

23 Raise the assembly, and rest it on the crossmember with the hydraulic flexible hose still connected (photo).

24 Disconnect the clutch cable from the release lever on the transmission (photo).

25 Disconnect the heater hoses from the engine.

26 Disconnect the heater hose from the carburettor (photo).

27 Disconnect the earth cables from the transmission casing (photo).

28 Disconnect the wiring from the alternator and the plug which serves the temperature switch, oil pressure switch and reversing light switch (photo).

29 Connect a suitable hoist to the engine lifting eyes, and take the weight of the engine and transmission.

30 Unscrew the through-bolt of the left-hand mounting, then unbolt and remove the mounting bracket (photos).

31 Unscrew the through-bolt from the right-hand engine mounting (photo).

32 Swivel the engine/transmission so that the transmission is to-

wards the left-hand front corner of the engine compartment.

33 Raise the hoist slowly, and lift the engine/transmission out of the engine compartment (photo).

34 The transmission can be separated from the engine after removing the starter motor, the TDC sensor, and the flywheel cover plate, and disconnecting the reversing light switch leads.

35 Undo and remove the clutch bellhousing-to-engine bolts.

Refitting

36 Refitting is a reversal of removal, but observe the following points.

37 Use a plastic protective sleeve to prevent damage to the oil seal lips when fitting the right-hand driveshaft.

38 Adjust the clutch cable as described in Chapter 5, Section 2.

39 Refill the engine and transmission with oil (photo).

40 Refill the cooling system as described in Section 7 (photo).

41 Tension the drivebelts.

42 Top-up the hydraulic system.

43 The use of self-locking pliers will facilitate reconnection of the gearchange rod balljoints (photo).

5B.23 Hydraulic pump/pressure regulator resting on crossmember

5B.24 Clutch cable connection at release lever

5B.26 Heater hose connection at carburettor (arrowed)

5B.27 Earth cables at transmission (arrowed)

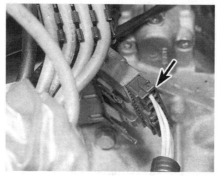

5B.28 Temperature switch/oil pressure switch/reversing light switch wiring connector (arrowed)

5B.30A Left-hand engine mounting through-bolt (arrowed)

5B.30B Removing the left-hand engine mounting bracket

5B.31 Right-hand engine mounting through-bolt (arrowed)

5B.33 Lifting the engine/transmission from the engine compartment

5B.39 Filling the engine with oil

5B.40 Filling the cooling system

5B.43 Reconnecting a gearchange rod balljoint

5B.44 Unbolting the HT lead support

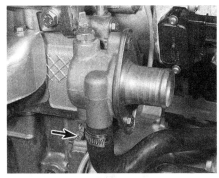

5B.46 Water pump hose (arrowed) at thermostat housing

5B.47 Removing the inlet manifold complete with carburettor

5B.49 Alternator pivot (A), adjustment (B) and tensioner (C) bolts

5B.50 Unbolting the crankshaft pulley

5B.51 Ignition coil (arrowed) located above distributor

5B.55 Removing the thermostat housing

5B.56 Distributor mounting flange retaining bolts (arrowed)

5B.57 TDC sensor mounting bolt (arrowed)

Engine - complete dismantling

44   Disconnect the HT leads from the spark plugs, unbolt the lead support (photo), disconnect the HT lead from the coil, and remove the distributor cap. Remove the spark plugs.
45   Disconnect the vacuum hose between the distributor and carburettor.
46   Disconnect the hoses between the fuel pump and carburettor (be prepared for fuel spillage, and take adequate fire precautions), and between the water pump and thermostat housing (photo).
47   Unscrew the nuts, and remove the inlet manifold complete with carburettor from the studs on the cylinder head (photo). Note that there is no gasket.
48   Unbolt and remove the fuel pump, and remove the gasket.
49   Loosen the alternator pivot and adjustment bolts, then unscrew the tension bolt and slip the drivebelt from the pulleys. Remove the pivot and adjustment bolts, and remove the alternator (photo).
50   Unbolt the pulley from the front of the crankshaft (photo).

51   Unbolt and remove the coil (photo), after unclipping the TDC sensor connector.
52   Unbolt the exhaust manifold hot air shroud.
53   Unscrew the brass nuts, remove the washers, and remove the exhaust manifold from the studs on the cylinder head. Remove the gaskets.
54   Remove the distributor with reference to Chapter 4.
55   Remove the thermostat as described in Section 7, then unbolt the thermostat housing from the cylinder head (photo).
56   Unbolt the distributor mounting flange from the cylinder head (photo).
57   Unbolt the TDC sensor from the flywheel end of the cylinder block, and unclip the lead from the timing plate (photo).
58   Unbolt and remove the timing plate (photo).
59   Unscrew and remove the oil filter, using a strap wrench if necessary (photo).
60   Unscrew and remove the oil pressure switch.

5B.58 Timing plate (arrowed)

5B.59 Removing the oil filter

5B.61 Unbolting the dipstick holder upper mounting

5B.62A Removing a rocker cover nut

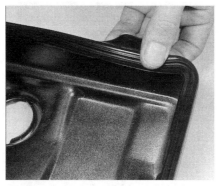

5B.62B Removing the rocker cover gasket

5B.63A Remove the rocker cover spacers (arrowed) . . .

5B.63B . . . and the baffle plate

5B.64A Unbolting the upper timing cover

5B.64B Removing the upper timing cover

5B.64C Removing the intermediate timing cover

5B.64D Removing the lower timing cover

5B.65 Camshaft sprocket held at TDC

5B.66 Using a long bolt (arrowed) to align the TDC holes in the flywheel and cylinder block

5B.67 Loosening the timing belt tensioner roller nut

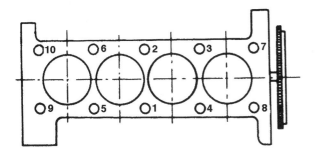

Fig. 13.9 Cylinder head bolt tightening sequence - K1G engine (Sec 5B)

61   Unscrew the mounting bolt, and pull the engine oil dipstick holder from the main bearing cap casting. Remove the dipstick from the holder (photo).
62   Unscrew the nuts and remove the rocker cover. Remove the rubber gasket from the cover (photos).
63   Remove the two spacers and baffle plate from the studs (photos).
64   Unbolt the upper timing cover, followed by the intermediate cover and lower cover (photos).
65   Turn the engine clockwise, using a socket on the crankshaft sprocket bolt, until the small hole in the camshaft sprocket is aligned with the corresponding hole in the cylinder head. Insert the shank of a close-fitting twist drill (e.g. a 10 mm drill) into the holes (photo).
66   Align the TDC holes in the flywheel and cylinder block rear flange, and insert a further twist drill or long bolt (photo).
67   Loosen the timing belt tensioner roller nut (photo), turn the tensioner clockwise using a screwdriver or square drive in the special hole, then re-tighten the nut.
68   Mark the normal direction of rotation on the timing belt, then remove it from the camshaft, water pump, and crankshaft sprockets.
69   Unscrew the tensioner nut, and remove the tensioner roller.
70   Progressively loosen the cylinder head bolts using the reverse sequence to that shown in Fig. 13.9, then remove all the bolts.
71   Lift off the rocker arm assembly (photo).
72   Rock the cylinder head to free it from the block, then lift it from the location dowels (photo). Two angled metal rods (shown in Fig. 13.10) may be used for this purpose.
73   Remove the cylinder head gasket from the block.
74   Fit liner clamps (see Chapter 1, Section 19) if it is not proposed to remove the pistons and liners.
75   Progressively loosen the clutch pressure plate bolts, and remove the pressure plate and friction disc from the flywheel (photo).
76   Unbolt the water pump housing from the side of the block, and

5B.71 Removing the rocker arm assembly

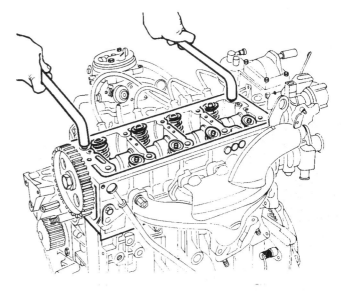

Fig. 13.10 Using two metal rods to free the cylinder head from the block (Sec 5B)

5B.72 Lifting the cylinder head from the cylinder block

5B.75 Removing the clutch pressure plate and friction disc

5B.77A Removing the crankshaft sprocket bolt . . .

5B.77B . . . the hub/sprocket . . .

5B.77C . . . and the timing belt guide plate

5B.78 Prising out the crankshaft front oil seal

5B.82A Unscrew the sump nuts and bolts. . .

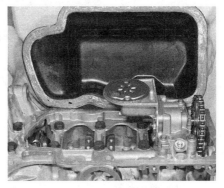

5B.82B . . . then remove the sump

5B.83A Unscrew the retaining bolts . . .

prise out the O-ring.

77   Have an assistant hold the flywheel stationary with a wide-bladed screwdriver inserted between the starter ring gear teeth, then unscrew the crankshaft sprocket bolt and remove the hub/sprocket and timing belt guide plate (photos).

78   Using a screwdriver, prise the front oil seal from the block and main bearing casting (photo).

79   Hold the flywheel stationary as described in paragraph 77, and unscrew the flywheel bolts. Lift the flywheel from the dowel on the crankshaft rear flange.

80   Prise out the crankshaft rear oil seal using a screwdriver.

81   Invert the engine, and support it on blocks of wood.

82   Unscrew the nuts and bolts securing the sump to the main bearing casting, and remove it by carefully prising it free of the jointing compound (photos).

83   Unbolt the oil pump, and tilt it to release the drive sprocket from the chain (photos).

84   Support the block on its flywheel end.

85   Mark the liners for position, starting with No 1 (at the flywheel end). Similarly mark the big-end bearing caps.

86   Temporarily refit the crankshaft sprocket bolt, and turn the crankshaft so that Nos 1 and 4 pistons (No 1 at flywheel end) are at bottom dead centre (BDC).

87   Unscrew the nuts and remove the big-end bearing caps (photo). Remove the lower big-end shells, keeping them identified for position.

88   Remove the clamps and withdraw the liners, complete with pistons, from the block (photo).

89   Remove the liner bottom O-rings.

90   Repeat the procedure for Nos 2 and 3 pistons and liners.

91   Invert the engine again, and unscrew the bolts securing the main bearing cap casting to the block (photos).

92   Progressively unscrew the main bearing bolts, and lift the main bearing cap casting from the block. Gently tap it with a wooden or soft-headed mallet to release it. Prise out the main bearing shells, keeping them identified for location.

93   Remove the oil pump sprocket and chain from the crankshaft (photo).

94   Lift the crankshaft from the block, and remove the main bearing shells, keeping them identified for location. Also remove the endfloat thrustwashers from No 2 main bearing location (photos).

5B.83B . . . and remove the oil pump

5B.87 Removing a big-end bearing cap

5B.88 Removing a liner/piston assembly

5B.91A Unscrew the main bearing cap casting front bolts . . .

5B.91B . . . and the side bolts (arrowed)

5B.93 Removing the oil pump chain from the crankshaft

5B.94A Removing a main bearing shell . . .

5B.94B . . . and endfloat thrustwasher

5B.95A Unscrew the camshaft sprocket bolt . . .

Cylinder head - dismantling, decarbonising and reassembly
95   Remove the twistdrill from the camshaft sprocket, then hold the sprocket stationary using an oil filter strap wrench or tool as shown in photo 5B.102. Unscrew the bolt and remove the sprocket (photos).
96   Unbolt and remove the camshaft thrust fork (photo).
97   Prise out the oil seal, and carefully withdraw the camshaft from the cylinder head (photos).
98   Remove the valves and springs, clean and check the cylinder head, and refit the valves and springs with reference to Chapter 1, Section 15 (photos).
99   Oil the camshaft bearings, and insert the camshaft into the cylinder head.
100 Refit the camshaft thrust fork, and tighten the bolt (photo).
101 Dip the new oil seal in oil, then press it into the cylinder head until flush, using a metal tube or large socket and hammer (photo).
102 Refit the camshaft sprocket so that the location peg enters the cut-out. Insert and tighten the bolt while holding the sprocket stationary, using either the method described in paragraph 95, or make up a tool as shown (photo).

5B.95B . . . and remove the camshaft sprocket bolt - note location peg and cut-out (arrowed)

5B.96 Camshaft thrust fork (arrowed)

5B.97A Prise out the camshaft oil seal . . .

5B.97B . . . and withdraw the camshaft

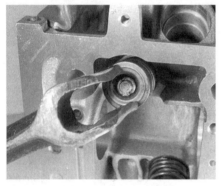

5B.98A Compress the valve spring and remove the split collets . . .

5B.98B . . . the retainer . . .

5B.98C . . . the spring . . .

5B.98D . . . the spring seat . . .

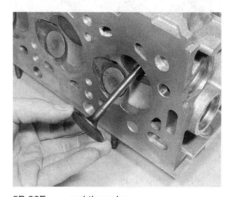

5B.98E . . . and the valve

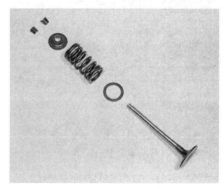

5B.98F Valve components

5B.100 Fitting the camshaft thrust fork

5B.101 Fitting a new camshaft oil seal

5B.102 Using a home-made tool to hold the camshaft sprocket stationary

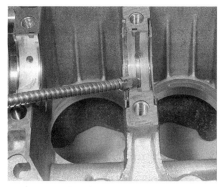
5C.4 Oiling the main bearing shells

5C.8A Apply jointing compound to the crankcase mating face . . .

5C.8B . . . then lower the main bearing cap casting into position

5C.9A Tighten the main bearing cap bolts to the initial torque . . .

5C.9B . . . then angle-tighten by a further 45°

5C.15A Fitting a piston ring compressor

Engine components - examination and renovation (general)
103 Refer to Chapter 1, Section 14.

Examination and renovation of dismantled components
104 Refer to Chapter 1, Section 16, but note that there is no camshaft lubrication manifold, as the camshaft runs in an oil bath. Also note that, although the timing belt should be renewed when the engine is overhauled, or if the belt is contaminated with oil, there is no specified renewal mileage. When handling the timing belt, do not bend it sharply, as this may damage the internal fibres.

PART C: ENGINE REASSEMBLY AND REFITTING

Engine reassembly - general
1   Refer to Chapter 1, Section 17.

Engine - complete reassembly
2   With the block upside-down on the bench, press the main bearing upper shells into position. Note that the grooved bearings are fitted to positions No 2 and 4.
3   Smear a little grease on the thrustwashers, and locate them each side of No 2 bearing with their grooves facing outwards.
4   Oil the bearings and lower the crankshaft into position (photo).
5   Check that the crankshaft endfloat is as given in the Specifications, using a feeler blade between a thrustwasher and the crankshaft web. The thrustwashers are available in four thicknesses.
6   Fit the oil pump sprocket and chain to the front of the crankshaft, locating the sprocket on the Woodruff key.
7   Press the main bearing lower shells into position in the main bearing cap casting, noting that the grooved bearings are fitted to positions No 2 and 4.
8   Apply jointing compound to the mating face, then lower the main bearing cap casting into position over the crankshaft (photos). At the same time, feed the oil pump chain through the aperture.
9   Insert the main bearing bolts dry, then tighten them evenly to the

5C.15B Using a hammer handle to push a piston into its liner

initial torque wrench setting. Angle-tighten the bolts by a further 45° (photos).
10   Refit the bolts securing the main bearing cap casting to the block, and tighten them to the specified torque.
11   Support the block on its flywheel end.
12   Check that the lower big-end bearing shells are fitted to the big-end caps and the upper shells to the connecting rods.
13   Oil the liner bores and piston rings.
14   Position the piston ring end gaps at 120° from each other, so that none is in line with another.
15   Fit a piston ring compressor to each piston in turn, and push the pistons in their respective liners using a hammer handle (photos). Make sure that the arrows on the piston crowns face the front (timing belt end) of the liners.
16   Fit the bottom O-rings to the liners, taking care not to twist them.
17   Check that the crankshaft rotates freely, then position Nos 1 and 4 crankpins at bottom dead centre (BDC). Oil the crankpins.

5C.18 Tightening a big-end bearing cap nut

5C.24 Crankshaft rear oil seal located over rear of crankshaft

5C.26A Applying locking fluid to a flywheel bolt

5C.26B Tightening a flywheel bolt

5C.28 Crankshaft front oil seal located over front of crankshaft

5C.29 Tightening the crankshaft sprocket bolt

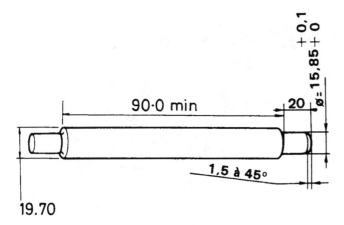

Fig. 13.11 Clutch centralising tool dimensions for the K1G engine (Sec 5C)

Dimensions in mm

18   Insert No 1 liner/piston into the block, and guide the connecting rod big-end onto the crankpin. Refit the big-end bearing cap, and tighten the nuts evenly to the specified torque (photo).
19   Check that the crankshaft rotates freely, while holding the liner in position with a clamp. Temporarily refit the crankshaft sprocket bolt to turn the crankshaft.
20   Repeat the procedure to fit the remaining pistons and liners.
21   Support the block upside-down on the bench.
22   Check that the oil pump location pin is fitted to the main bearing casting, then refit the oil pump, tilting it to engage the drive sprocket with the chain. Insert and tighten the bolts.
23   Apply jointing compound to the mating faces of the sump and main bearing casting. Refit the sump, insert the bolts and tighten them to the specified torque.
24   Dip the new crankshaft rear oil seal in oil, and locate it over the rear of the crankshaft (photo).

25   Franchised garages use their special tool (0132U) to fit the oil seal, but it can be fitted by using the flywheel. Temporarily locate the flywheel on the crankshaft using four bolts, then tighten the bolts evenly until the flywheel contacts the rear flange. Remove the flywheel and use a metal tube or block of wood to drive the oil seal fully into position.
26   Apply locking fluid to the threads of the flywheel bolts, locate the flywheel on the crankshaft dowel, then insert the bolts and tighten them to the specified torque while holding the flywheel as described in Section 5B, paragraph 77 (photos).
27   Support the engine upright on the bench.
28   Dip the crankshaft front oil seal in oil, locate it over the front of the crankshaft, and drive it in flush with the front of the block using a metal tube or socket (photo). There is no seating, so take care not to drive it in too far.
29   Fit the oil seal flange, followed by the hub/sprocket. Insert the sprocket bolt and spacer, and tighten the bolt to the specified torque while holding the flywheel stationary (photo).
30   Refit the water pump housing together with a new O-ring, and tighten the bolts to the specified torque.
31   Locate the clutch friction disc and pressure plate on the flywheel with the dowels engaged. Insert the bolts finger-tight.
32   Centralise the friction disc using a universal tool, or by making a wooden adapter to the dimensions shown in Fig. 13.11 (photo).
33   Tighten the pressure plate bolts evenly to the specified torque (photo).
34   Clean the cylinder head and block joint faces thoroughly. Also clean the cylinder head bolt holes.
35   Locate the new cylinder head gasket on the block dowels, with the manufacturer's name uppermost (photo).
36   Align the TDC holes in the flywheel and block rear flange, and insert a twist drill or long bolt.
37   Align the small hole in the camshaft sprocket with the hole in the cylinder head, and insert a twist drill or bolt (photo).
38   Lower the cylinder head onto the block so that it engages the two dowels.
39   Refit the rocker arm assembly.

5C.32 Centralising the clutch friction disc using a universal tool

5C.33 Tightening a clutch pressure plate bolt

5C.35 Cylinder head gasket correctly located

5C.37 Camshaft sprocket held at TDC using twist drill

5C.40 Tighten the cylinder head bolts to the initial torque . . .

5C.41 . . . then angle-tighten through the specified angle

Fig. 13.12 Using special tool (0132X) to tension the timing belt (Sec 5C)

40 Lubricate the cylinder head bolt threads and heads with molybdenum disulphide grease. Insert them and tighten to the initial torque using the sequence in Fig. 13.9 (photo).
41 Using the same sequence, angle-tighten the bolts through the specified angle (photo).
42 Refit the timing belt tensioner roller, turn it clockwise, and tighten the nut.
43 Engage the timing belt with the crankshaft sprocket then, keeping it taut, feed it onto the camshaft sprocket, around the tensioner pulley, and onto the water pump sprocket.
44 Loosen the nut and turn the tensioner roller anti-clockwise by hand. Tighten the nut.
45 Franchised garages use the special tool shown in Fig. 13.12 to tension the timing belt. A similar tool may be fabricated using an 8.0 cm (3.2 in) long arm and a 1.5 kg (3.3 lb) weight. The torque applied to the roller will approximate 12 kgf cm (10.5 lbf in). Pre-tension the timing belt with the tool and tighten the nut, then remove the timing pins and rotate the crankshaft through two complete turns. Loosen the nut and allow the roller to re-position itself. Tighten the nut.
46 If the special tool is not available, an approximate setting may be achieved by turning the roller hub anti-clockwise, until it is just possible to turn the timing belt through 90° by finger and thumb midway between the crankshaft and camshaft sprockets. The square in the roller hub should then be directly below the adjustment nut, and the deflection of the belt in the midway position should be approximately 6.0 mm (0.24 in). If using this method, the tension should be re-checked by a Citroën dealer at the earliest opportunity.
47 Refit the lower, intermediate, and upper timing covers, and tighten the bolts (photo).
48 Adjust the valve clearances as described in paragraphs 72 to 81.
49 Refit the baffle plate with its edges pointing downwards, followed by the two spacers.
50 Fit the rubber gasket to the rocker cover, locate the cover in position and tighten the nuts.
51 Apply a little sealant to the end of the engine oil dipstick holder, and insert it in the main bearing cap casting. Insert and tighten the mounting bolt.

5C.47 Timing covers correctly refitted

5C.77 Adjusting a valve clearance

52   Insert and tighten the oil pressure switch.
53   Smear a little oil on the sealing ring, and tighten the oil filter into position by hand only.
54   Refit the timing plate and tighten the bolts.
55   Refit the TDC sensor and tighten the bolt. Fix the lead in the plastic clip on the timing plate. Note that the main body of the TDC sensor should be 1.0 mm (0.04 in) from the flywheel.
56   Apply jointing compound to the distributor mounting flange, then refit it to the cylinder head, and tighten the bolts.
57   Apply jointing compound to the thermostat housing, then refit it to the cylinder head, and tighten the bolts to the specified torque.
58   Refit the thermostat.
59   Refit the distributor as described in Chapter 4.
60   Refit the exhaust manifold together with new gaskets. Refit the nuts and washers, and tighten securely.
61   Refit the exhaust manifold hot air shroud and tighten the bolts.
62   Locate the coil and bracket over the distributor, and tighten the bolts.
63   Position the pulley on the front of the crankshaft. Insert and tighten the bolts.
64   Refit the alternator, and insert the pivot and adjustment bolts. Slip the drivebelt onto the pulleys, and tighten the tension bolt until the deflection of the belt midway between the pulleys is approximately 6.0 mm (0.24 in) under firm thumb pressure. Tighten the pivot and adjustment bolts.
65   Refit the fuel pump with a new gasket, and tighten the bolts.
66   Thoroughly clean the mating faces of the inlet manifold and cylinder head, and apply jointing compound.
67   Refit the inlet manifold complete with carburettor, and tighten the nuts.
68   Reconnect the hose between the fuel pump and carburettor, and tighten the clips.
69   Reconnect the vacuum hose between the distributor and carburettor.
70   Refit and tighten the spark plugs.
71   Refit the HT leads and distributor cap.

Valve clearances - checking and adjustment
72   Disconnect the crankcase ventilation hose from the rocker cover.
73   Unscrew the nuts and remove the rocker cover.
74   Remove the two spacers and baffle plate from the studs.
75   Prepare to rotate the crankshaft, either by jacking up one front wheel and turning the wheel with 4th or 5th gear engaged, or by using a spanner on the crankshaft sprocket bolt. Rotation will be easier if the spark plugs are first removed.
76   Rotate the crankshaft until No 1 exhaust valve (flywheel end) is fully open. No 3 inlet valve and No 4 exhaust valve clearances may now be checked and adjusted.
77   Insert a feeler blade of the correct thickness between the rocker arm and valve stem. It should be a firm, sliding fit if the clearance is

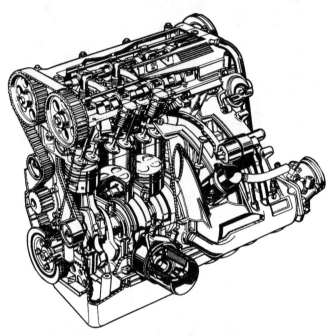

Fig. 13.13 Cutaway view of BX 19 GTi 16 valve engine (Sec 6A)

correct. If adjustment is necessary, loosen the adjuster nut with a ring spanner, turn the adjuster as required with a screwdriver, then retighten the nut (photo).
78   Adjust the valve clearances in the following sequence.

Valve fully open	Adjust valves
No 1 Exhaust	*No 3 Inlet and No 4 Exhaust*
No 3 Exhaust	*No 4 Inlet and No 2 Exhaust*
No 4 Exhaust	*No 2 Inlet and No 1 Exhaust*
No 2 Exhaust	*No 1 Inlet and No 3 Exhaust*

79   When all the valve clearances have been adjusted, refit the baffle plate with its edges pointing downwards, followed by the two spacers.
80   Check that the rubber gasket is re-usable (renew if necessary), then refit the rocker cover and tighten the nuts.
81   Reconnect the crankcase ventilation hose.

Engine - initial start-up after overhaul
82   Refer to Chapter 1, Section 22.
83   The cylinder head bolts do not require re-tightening on the K1G engine, and the timing belt does not require re-tensioning.
84   If new bearings and/or pistons have been fitted, treat the engine as new, and run it in at reduced speeds. Also change the engine oil at 1000 miles (1500 km).

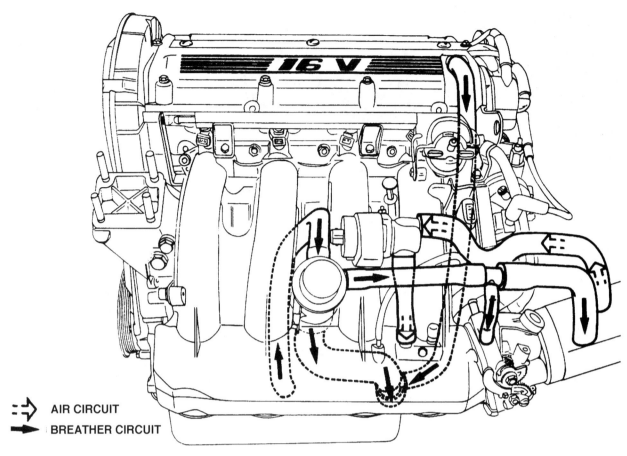

AIR CIRCUIT

BREATHER CIRCUIT

Fig. 13.14 Crankcase ventilation system - BX 19 GTi 16 valve engine (Sec 6A)

6 Engine - BX 19 GTi 16 valve

PART A: GENERAL

D6C type engine - description

1   The engine is a development of the BX 19 GTi (D6A-XU9J2) engine, which itself is based upon the type 159A engine (refer to Chapter 1).
2   Introduced in July 1987, the essential difference is the 16 valve double overhead camshaft cylinder head, the camshafts being driven by a toothed belt tensioned by two idler rollers.
3   Hydraulic tappets (cam followers) are used, eliminating the need for valve clearance adjustment.
4   The pistons have been re-designed, with valve head recesses machined in the piston crown.
5   The gudgeon pins are of the "floating" type, secured by circlips in the piston.
6   The crankshaft has lighter balancing counterweights, and a damper fitted to the sprocket end.
7   The oil capacity has increased because an oil cooler has been fitted.

Lubrication system - description and maintenance

8   A conventional dipstick is fitted to check the engine oil level.
9   The oil filter is of disposable screw-on canister type, mounted on the oil cooler housing.
10   Pressurised oil is supplied by an oil pump located within the sump pan, the pump being driven by chain from the crankshaft.
11   The undersides of the pistons are cooled by oil jets located in lubrication pipes within the crankcase.
12   The oil filler pipe is an independent assembly, remote from the engine, in order to provide a reasonable position for pouring oil into the steeply-canted engine.
13   Always drain the oil hot by unscrewing the sump drain plug, taking precautions against scalding. An oil filter wrench may be needed to unscrew the disposable-type filter cartridge.
14   Oil the sealing ring of the new filter, and screw it on using hand pressure only.
15   Fill the engine with the specified quantity and grade of oil, start the engine, and allow it to run for a few minutes. The oil warning light will take a few seconds to go out, due to the filling of the empty oil filter.
16   Switch off the engine and wait a few minutes; check the oil level, and top-up if necessary.

Crankcase ventilation system - general

17   The layout of the system is shown in Fig. 13.14.
18   Periodically check the condition and security of the system hoses; otherwise, no maintenance is required.

Operations possible with engine in car

19   The following components can be removed and refitted with the engine in the vehicle.
   (a) Timing belt and camshafts.
   (b) Cylinder head.
   (c) Sump pan
   (d) Oil pump.
   (e) Engine mountings.

Timing belt - renewal
Note: *Accurate adjustment of the timing belt entails the use of Citroën special tools. An approximate setting can be achieved using the method described in this Section, but is essential that the tension is checked by a dealer on completion.*
20   Disconnect the battery.

6A.21 Removing the front right-hand wheel arch blanking panel

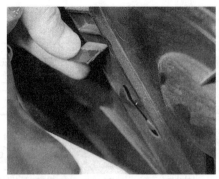

6A.23 Removing a timing belt cover spring clip

6A.30 Camshaft sprocket stepped locking pin

6A.31A Crankshaft sprocket locking rod in position

6A.31B Camshaft sprocket locking pins in position

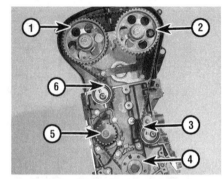

6A.32 Fit the timing belt in a clockwise direction, starting at No 1

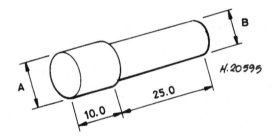

Fig. 13.15 Stepped pin fabrication diagram (Sec 6A)

    a   *8.43 mm diameter*
    b   *6.38 mm diameter*

21   Remove the front right-hand roadwheel, then unclip and remove the wheel arch blanking panel to provide access to the timing cover, the crankshaft sprocket and damper (photo).
22   Loosen the alternator mounting bolts and the belt adjuster link, and remove the alternator drivebelt.
23   Pull out the keyhole slot-type spring clips from the front face of the timing belt cover (photo).
24   Extract the screws and remove the timing belt cover.
25   Using the centre bolt in the crankshaft damper, turn the crankshaft until the slot in the crankshaft sprocket is aligned with the one on the oil pump cover, and the pin holes in the camshaft sprockets are aligned with the holes in the cylinder head.
26   Unscrew the bolts and take off the damper from the front end of the crankshaft.
27   Remove the timing belt lower cover.
28   Using an Allen key, release the belt tensioner locking screws.
29   Remove the timing belt.
30   Setting tools will be required when fitting the new belt. In the absence of the Citroën special tools (0153M and 0153G), make up two stepped pins as shown in Fig. 13.15, and a short length of rod which

will be a snug fit in the cut-outs of the crankshaft sprocket and the oil pump cover (photo).
31   Insert the camshaft sprocket stepped pins and the crankshaft rod (photos).
32   Fit the new timing belt in a clockwise direction, following the numerical sequence shown (photo), and adjust the tensioning pulleys on both sides to make the belt taut. Check that the longest run of the belt can be twisted through 45° when gripped between the finger and thumb. Tighten the tensioner screws to the specified torque. **Note:** *In this application, the tensioners serve two purposes; to tension the belt and to provide fine adjustment of the valve timing.*
33   Remove the two stepped pins and the rod.
34   Turn the crankshaft through two complete revolutions. Fit the crankshaft sprocket locking rod.
35   The two stepped pins should now slide smoothly through the holes of the camshaft sprockets into the holes in the cylinder head. Even the slightest misalignment will require re-adjustment of the tensioner pulleys to provide perfect alignment.
36   Remove the pins and rod, and recheck after turning the crankshaft through two more complete revolutions. It is strongly recommended that the belt tension should be checked by your Citroën dealer using the special tensioner device (Seemtronic 87).
37   Fit the timing belt lower cover, the crankshaft damper and the belt main cover (photos).
38   Refit and reconnect all the other components in reverse order of removal, referring to the Specifications for the appropriate torque wrench settings.

Cylinder head - removal, overhaul and refitting
39   Drain the cooling system as described in Section 7, and disconnect the battery.
40   Release the screws and remove the cover plate from the centre of the camshaft cover (photo).
41   Disconnect the spark plug leads from the spark plugs, and disconnect the coolant temperature sender lead.
42   Extract the screws and remove the distributor cap, complete with leads.
43   Disconnect the fuel hose from the fuel rail.

6A.37A Timing belt lower cover refitted

6A.37B Fitting a crankshaft damper bolt

6A.40 Removing camshaft centre cover plate

6A.46A Extracting a camshaft cover screw

6A.46B Extracting a timing belt cover screw

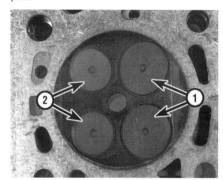

6A.61A View of combustion chamber showing inlet valves (1) and exhaust valves (2)

6A.61B Valve components

44   Disconnect the fuel injector wiring plugs, and then unbolt the fuel rail and remove complete with injectors.

45   Disconnect the coolant hoses from their cylinder head connections.

46   Extract the screws and take off the camshaft cover and the timing belt cover (photos).

47   Using the centre bolt in the crankshaft damper, turn the crankshaft until the slot in the crankshaft is aligned with the one on the oil pump cover, and the pin holes in the camshaft sprockets are aligned with the holes in the cylinder head, using two stepped pins to lock the sprockets in this position as shown in photo 6A.31B.

48   Release the tension of the timing belt by slackening the Allen screws in the two tensioner rollers, then slip the belt from the camshaft sprockets, having marked the direction of rotation on the belt.

49   Pull the lubrication pipes from the camshaft bearing caps. The camshafts can be removed independently of the cylinder head if re-

quired, or the complete cylinder head can be removed and then dismantled.

50   Assuming that the cylinder head is to be removed complete, release and remove the high pressure pump drivebelt from the end of the exhaust valve camshaft.

51   Note that the camshaft bearing caps are numbered 1 to 5 from the flywheel end of the engine, and are dowelled so that they can only be fitted one way.

52   Progressively unscrew the Allen screws in reverse order to that shown in Fig. 13.17, and remove the camshaft bearing caps in the following order - No 4 first, then Nos 2, 3, 1 and 5.

53   Lift out the camshafts, labelling them "exhaust" and "inlet".

54   Disconnect the air intake duct from the air cleaner, and the hoses, control cables and leads from the inlet manifold and throttle housing.

55   Unscrew the inlet manifold nuts, and lift the manifold from the cylinder head.

56   Unscrew the exhaust manifold nuts and pull it away from the cylinder head. The lower nuts are more accessible from underneath.

57   Using a TX55 Torx bit, unscrew and remove the cylinder head bolts in the reverse order to that shown in Fig. 13.16.

58   Remove the cylinder head. If it is stuck, rock it using pieces of wood inserted in the inlet ports. Discard the cylinder head gasket.

59   As soon as the head is removed, fit liner clamps to prevent the liner base seals being disturbed.

60   Remove the hydraulic tappets (cam followers), keeping them in order of installation.

61   Removal of the valves and decarbonising are as described in Chapter 1, Section 15, but the valves must be identified as to original location (photos).

62   When refitting a valve, some difficulty may be experienced in inserting the split collets, and the use of a pencil magnet or a dab of thick grease will help.

63   The valve stem oil seals can be removed with a pair of long-nosed pliers. Fit the new ones using a piece of tubing of suitable bore.

64   With everything clean and new gaskets to hand, remember that as refitting proceeds, all nuts and bolts must be tightened to the torque wrench settings given in the Specifications at the beginning of this Supplement. Remove the liner clamps.

6A.66 Fitting a new cylinder head gasket

6A.68A Inserting a cylinder head bolt

6A.68B Torx bit for tightening cylinder head bolt

6A.68C Tightening a cylinder head bolt

6A.68D Angle-tightening a cylinder head bolt

6A.70 Fitting a camshaft bearing cap

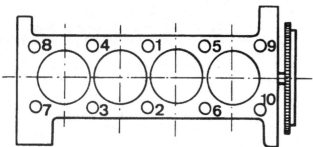

Fig. 13.16 Cylinder head bolt tightening sequence - BX 19 GTi 16 valve engine (Sec 6A)

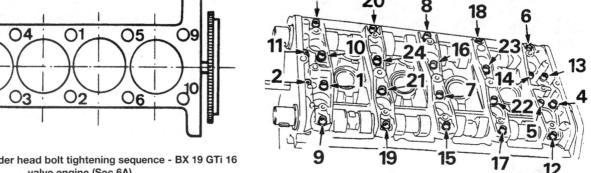

Fig. 13.17 Camshaft bearing cap screw tightening sequence (Sec 6A)

65   Smear the hydraulic tappets (cam followers) with grease, then re-fit them in their original locations.

66   Place a new cylinder head gasket on the top of the cylinder block (photo).

67   Lower the cylinder head onto the positioning dowels.

68   Lightly oil the cylinder head bolts, then insert and tighten them in the order shown in Fig. 13.16, to the torque wrench settings given in the Specifications (photos).

69   Locate the camshafts with new oil seals. Assuming that the crankshaft has not been moved from its position aligned with the oil pump housing, the camshafts should be set with the keyways at the three o'clock position. This is so that when the camshaft sprockets are fitted, the pin holes will be in alignment with the corresponding holes in the cylinder head.

70   Fit the camshaft bearing caps, and tighten the bolts to the specified torque in the sequence shown in Fig. 13.17 (photo).

71   Fit the camshaft lubrication pipes (photo).

72   Fit the timing belt rear cover and the camshaft sprockets, ensuring the alignment is correct by using the stepped pins described earlier. Use an open-ended spanner on the flats of the camshaft to hold it whilst tightening the sprocket bolt to the specified torque (photos).

73   Refit the timing belt as described earlier in this Section.

74   Fit the timing belt cover. Check that the spark plug hole oil seals are in position (photo), and then fit the cam cover.

75   Fit the distributor cap, and connect the spark plug leads.

76   Using new gaskets, reconnect the inlet and exhaust manifolds to the cylinder head (photos).

77   Reconnect and tension the drivebelts, and connect the air cleaner intake.

78   Reconnect the electrical leads to the cylinder head switches, and reconnect the coolant hoses and control cables.

79   Reconnect the fuel hoses, fuel rail and injectors (photo).

80   Reconnect the battery.

81   Refill the cooling system as described in Section 7.

Sump pan - removal and refitting

82   Disconnect the battery, and drain the engine oil.

83   Disconnect the lead from the engine oil temperature switch.

84   Unbolt and remove the member which runs under the sump pan.

85   Remove the bolts and the sump pan.

6A.71 Camshaft lubrication pipe - note seal on spigot

6A.72A Timing belt rear cover correctly refitted

6A.72B Fitting a camshaft sprocket bolt

6A 74 Spark plug hole oil seal

6A.76A Exhaust manifold gasket correctly located

6A.76B Exhaust manifold fitted

6A.76C Inlet manifold fitted

6A.79 Fitting the fuel rail and injectors

6A.90 Removing the crankshaft sprocket bolt and spacer

86   With the mating surfaces clean and using a new gasket, refit the sump pan, ensuring that the gasket does not move.

87   Refitting is a reversal of removal. Tighten the bolts to the specified torque wrench settings.

Oil pump - removal and refitting

Note: *As removal of the oil pump requires the timing belt to be removed, it is advisable to read the procedure for timing belt removal and refitting before starting work.*

88   Remove the sump pan as described earlier in this Section.

89   Remove the timing belt as described earlier in this Section.

90   Undo the centre bolt from the front end of the crankshaft. The crankshaft must not turn from its set position while the bolt is undone, so either remove the starter motor (see Chapter 12) and lock the flywheel ring gear with a suitable screwdriver, or jam one of the crankshaft counterweights with a block of wood. Remove the bolt and the spacer (photo).

91   Pull off the crankshaft sprocket and timing belt guide (photo), then remove the Woodruff key from the crankshaft.

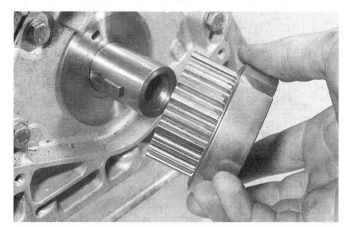

6A.91 Removing the crankshaft sprocket

6A.92A Extract the Allen screws (arrowed) . . .

6A.92B . . . and remove the sump spacer plate

6A.94A Oil pump in position

6A.94B Removing the oil pump with drivechain and sprocket

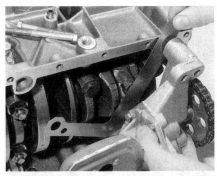

6A.94C Removing the oil pump drivechain tension adjustment shim

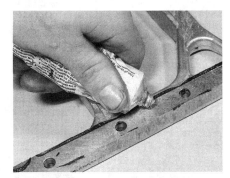

6A.98 Applying instant gasket to the sump spacer plate

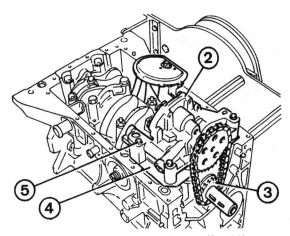

Fig. 13.18 Fitting the oil pump (Sec 6A)

2   Pump body   4   L-shaped shim
3   Chain and sprocket   5   Centralising bolt

6A.99A Refitting the sump pan and gasket

6A.99B Tightening a sump pan securing bolt

92   Extract the Allen screws and remove the sump spacer plate (photos).
93   Extract the bolts and remove the front oil seal carrier plate.
94   Extract the bolts and withdraw the oil pump, at the same time sliding the drivechain and sprocket off the crankshaft. Note the adjustment shim used to tension the drivechain during production (photos).
95   Before refitting the oil pump, fit a new oil seal. A new pump should be primed with oil.
96   Refitting is a reversal of removal, but observe the following points.
97   Use a new oil pump gasket. Note that bolt "5" in Fig. 13.18 centralises the pump, and should be fitted first.
98   Use silicone-type instant gasket (applied to clean surfaces) to seal the sump spacer plate to the crankcase (photo).
99   Refit the sump pan and timing belt as described earlier in this Section (photos).

Engine mountings - renewal
100   The engine mountings can be renewed with the engine/transmission supported from below on a trolley jack, or from above using an engine crossbar-type hoist.
101   Only disconnect and renew one flexible mounting at a time.

6B.3A Hydraulic pump drive pulley (arrowed)

6B.3B Hydraulic pump (arrowed)

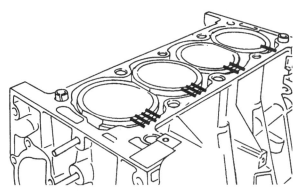

Fig. 13.19 Method of marking cylinder liner numbering from flywheel end (Sec 6B)

PART B: ENGINE REMOVAL AND DISMANTLING

Engine - removal and refitting

1   The operations are essentially as described in Chapter 1, Section 33. The connections for the Motronic engine management system (described in Section 11 of this Supplement) must be taken into account, and references to a carburettor ignored.

2   The pressure regulator for the hydraulic system, which is located on the forward-facing side of the crankcase, must be withdrawn and tied aside.

3   The hydraulic pump, which is driven by the exhaust camshaft pulley, must be removed from its drivebelt and mounting, and tied to one side (photos).

Engine - complete dismantling

Note: *As dismantling of the engine requires the timing belt to be removed, it is advisable to read the procedure for timing belt removal and refitting before starting work.*

4   Refer to Chapter 1, Section 35.

5   Clean away all external dirt using water-soluble solvent or paraffin and a stiff brush.

6   Unbolt the ignition coil from the inlet manifold.

7   Withdraw the engine oil dipstick.

8   Remove the oil filler pipe assembly.

9   Unplug the fuel injectors, release the fuel rail (two screws) and withdraw the rail/injector assembly.

10   Remove the cover plate from the centre of the cam cover, the cam cover itself, then disconnect and withdraw the spark plug HT leads.

11   Unscrew and remove the spark plugs.

12   Disconnect the hoses and remove the coolant distribution pipe.

13   Unbolt and remove the inlet manifold complete with throttle housing. Discard the gasket.

14   Unbolt and remove the thermostat housing.

15   Unbolt the exhaust manifold, and discard the gasket.

16   Unbolt and remove the coolant multi-union from the exhaust side of the crankcase.

17   Unbolt and remove the mounting bracket from the front of the cylinder block.

18   Remove the distributor and drive flange as described in Section 11 of this Supplement.

19   Remove the pulley and plastic guard from the rear end of the exhaust camshaft. The camshaft may be held against rotation using the spanner flats on the camshaft.

20   Unscrew and remove the oil pressure, temperature and level switches.

21   Remove the oil filter, using an oil filter removal wrench.

22   If necessary, remove the oil cooler by disconnecting the hoses and then unscrewing the large fixing nut.

23   Extract the Allen screws, slide the timing belt cover upwards, and remove it.

24   Remove the timing belt as described earlier in Section 6A.

25   Hold the flats on the camshafts with an open-ended spanner, unscrew the bolts which secure the camshaft sprockets, then remove the sprockets.

26   Unbolt and remove the crankshaft sprocket. Take out the Woodruff key.

27   Remove the timing belt guide plate from the crankshaft.

28   Remove the timing belt upper cover backplate.

29   Remove the coolant pump with reference to Section 7.

30   Pull off the camshaft lubrication pipes.

31   Remove the cylinder head as described earlier in Section 6A.

32   Unbolt and remove the clutch assembly.

33   Unbolt and remove the flywheel.

34   Remove the sump pan, spacer plate and the oil pump as described earlier in Section 6A.

35   Mark the adjacent surfaces of the connecting rods and their caps by centre-punching 1 to 4 from the flywheel end on the inlet manifold side.

36   Unbolt the big-end cap nuts and remove the caps, keeping the shell bearings with their respective rods or caps if they are to be used again.

37   Mark the upper rims of the cylinder liners 1 to 4 from the flywheel end, using paint marks as shown in Fig. 13.19. Make the marks on the inlet side if the original liners are to be used again.

38   Discard the liner base seals after the piston, connecting rod and liner assemblies have been withdrawn.

39   If the piston rings are to be removed, push the piston and connecting rod out of the liner, and insert three old feeler blades at equidistant points behind the top ring. Remove the ring off the top of

6B.49 Removing a hydraulic tappet

6C.1 Fitting a crankcase lubrication pipe

6C.2 Fitting a grooved bearing shell to the crankcase

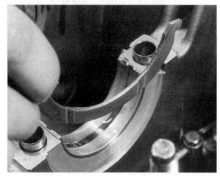

6C.3A Fitting a crankshaft thrustwasher

6C.3B Crankshaft thrustwashers correctly located

6C.4 Lowering the crankshaft into the crankcase

6C.5A Main bearing cap with plain shell fitted

6C.5B Fitting a main bearing cap

6C.6 Flywheel end main bearing cap showing side sealing strip

the piston using a twisting motion.

40 Extract the circlips and push the gudgeon pin out of the piston and connecting rod. If the pin is tight, immerse the piston in very hot water.

41 Note the marking of the main bearing caps; N at the flywheel end and then 2, 3, 4 and 5, read from the flywheel end.

42 Unscrew the main bearing cap bolts or the nuts on the centre cap. The centre cap is also secured by bolts entered from each side of the crankcase.

43 Remove the main bearing caps, keeping the bearing shells with their respective caps if the shells are to be used again.

44 Semi-circular thrustwashers are located at No. 2 main bearing cap.

45 Lift out the crankshaft. Retrieve the thrustwashers from their crankcase seats at No. 2 main bearing.

46 If necessary, remove the lubrication pipes.

Engine components - examination and renovation

47 Refer to Chapter 1, Sections 14 and 16, ignoring references to rocker gear and timing chain.

48 The rubber toothed timing belt and the oil pump drive chain

should be renewed at time of major overhaul.

49 The hydraulic tappets (cam followers) cannot be dismantled, and noisy operation will indicate the need for renewal (photo).

PART C: ENGINE REASSEMBLY AND REFITTING

Engine - complete reassembly

1 With the crankcase clean and oil galleries probed clean, commence reassembly by fitting the lubrication pipes. Note that the pipes are offset towards the crankcase webs (photo).

2 Wipe out the main bearing shell seats in the crankcase, and fit the grooved shells (photo).

3 Using thick grease, place the thrustwashers (oil grooves visible) on each side of No 2 web (photos).

4 Oil the shells and lower the crankshaft into the crankcase (photo).

5 Fit the plain shells in the main bearing caps and fit the caps in numbered sequence, making sure that the thrustwashers are located in No 2 cap (photos).

6 Fit the crankshaft rear oil seal before tightening down the main bearing cap at the flywheel end, and make sure that new cap side sealing strips are correctly located (photo).

6C.7 Tightening a main bearing cap bolt

6C.8 Centre main bearing cap side bolt

6C.9A Refit the piston to the connecting rod . . .

6C.9B . . . and insert the gudgeon pin circlips

6C.12A Fitting a piston/connecting rod/liner assembly

6C.12B Typical cylinder liner clamps fitted

7   Tighten the main bearing cap bolts and nuts to the specified torque (photo). Using a dial gauge or feeler blades, check the crankshaft endfloat as described in Chapter 1. If necessary, change the thrustwashers to bring the endfloat within tolerance.

8   Fit and tighten the centre main bearing cap side bolts to the specified torque (photo).

9   Assemble the pistons to the connecting rods. The gudgeon pin should be a sliding fit in the piston and connecting rod small end. Immerse the piston in hot water if necessary to ease gudgeon pin installation. The gudgeon pin is retained by circlips which have the gaps facing the rings when fitted. Make sure that the piston-to-rod alignment is correct as shown in Fig. 13.20 (photos).

10   Fit the piston rings as shown in Fig. 13.21, and space the ring gaps at 120° either side of the scraper (bottom) ring gap.

11   Using a piston ring compressor and plenty of oil, slide the piston assemblies into their liners.

12   Fit a new O-ring seal to the base of each cylinder liner, and install each piston/connecting rod/liner assembly into the block. If old assemblies are being fitted, ensure that they are located in their original positions. Check that the pistons are correctly aligned, with the arrow on the piston crown towards the timing belt. Fit cylinder liner retaining clamps (photos).

13   Push the pistons down their bores, and connect the connecting rod big-end (complete with shell bearing) to the crankshaft.

14   Fit the big-end caps (complete with shell bearings) to their respective connecting rods.

Fig. 13.20 Piston-to-connecting rod alignment (Sec 6C)

a   Bearing shell notch

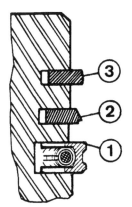

Fig. 13.21 Piston ring fitting diagram (Sec 6C)

1   Oil control ring (scraper)   3   Top compression ring
2   Second compression ring

6C.15A Tightening a big-end cap nut

6C.15B Angle-tightening a big-end cap nut

6C.17 Tightening a flywheel bolt

6C.18 Fitting the clutch components

6C.29 Fitting the oil cooler retaining tube and nut

6C.31 Oil temperature switch in sump pan

6C.32A Refitting the oil pressure switch

6C.32B Refitting the oil level sensor

6C.33 Camshaft plastic guard and pulley correctly refitted

15 Screw on the nuts and tighten to the specified torque. The crankshaft may have to be turned to facilitate fitting the main bearing caps, and to tighten the nuts (photos).
16 Fit the oil pump, spacer plate and sump pan as described earlier in Section 6A.
17 Bolt the flywheel to the end of the crankshaft (the flywheel has a positioning dowel). Apply thread-locking fluid to clean bolt threads, and tighten to the specified torque (photo).
18 Fit the clutch driven plate with the longer projecting hub facing the clutch cover (photo). Remember to align the driven plate as described in Chapter 5.
19 Fit the cylinder head and camshafts as described earlier in Section 6A.
20 Fit the camshaft lubrication pipes.
21 Fit the coolant pump as described in Section 7 of this Supplement.
22 Fit the timing belt upper cover backplate.
23 Fit the Woodruff key to the crankshaft, then push on the timing belt guide and the sprocket. Apply thread-locking fluid to the bolt threads, then fit the bolt and spacer. Tighten the bolt to the specified torque.
24 Fit the two camshaft sprockets, tighten the securing bolts to the

specified torque.
25 Fit and tension the timing belt as described earlier in Section 6A.
26 Fit the timing belt lower cover, then bolt on the crankshaft damper, tightening the bolts to the specified torque.
27 Locate the spark plug hole seals and fit the camshaft cover, tightening the bolts to the specified torque.
28 Fit the main timing belt cover.
29 Fit the oil cooler using a new gasket, and tighten the fixing nut (photo).
30 Apply a smear of engine oil to the rubber seal of a new oil filter, and screw it on, using hand pressure only.
31 Screw the oil temperature switch into the sump pan (photo).
32 Screw the oil pressure switch into the crankcase. Refit the oil level sensor (photos).
33 Fit the plastic guard and the pulley to the rear end of the exhaust camshaft (photo).
34 Fit the distributor components to the end of the inlet camshaft (see Section 11).
35 Bolt the engine mounting bracket to the front of the cylinder block.
36 Bolt the coolant multi-hose union to the exhaust side of the crankcase (photo).

6C.36 Coolant multi-hose union correctly refitted

6C.40A Coolant distribution pipe (arrowed)

6C.40B Coolant distribution pipe fixing clip (arrowed)

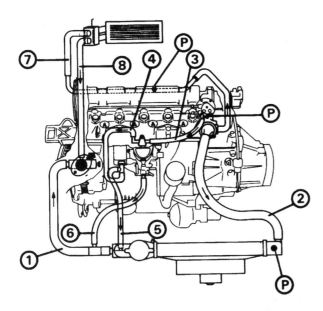

Fig. 13.22 Modified cooling system - BX 16 and BX 19 carburettor models from July 1985 (Sec 7)

1	Bottom hose	6	Inlet manifold-to-radiator hose
2	Top hose	7	Inlet manifold-to-heater hose
3	Coolant outlet hose from carburettor	8	Coolant inlet housing-to-heater hose
4	Choke control-to-carburettor heating hose	P	Bleed screws
5	Choke control-to-radiator hose		

37   Fit the exhaust manifold with new gaskets.

38   Bolt on the thermostat housing.

39   Bolt on the inlet manifold using new gaskets. Note the support strut at the front of the manifold.

40   Connect and secure the coolant distribution pipe (photos).

41   Fit the fuel rail and injectors.

42   Fit the oil filler pipe assembly.

43   Insert the oil dipstick.

44   Bolt the ignition coil to its bracket.

45   Screw in the spark plugs using a suitable plug spanner.

46   Connect and route the HT leads, and then fit the cover plate to the centre of the cam cover. Do not overtighten the two fixing screws.

Initial start-up after major overhaul

47   Make sure that the battery is fully charged, and that all lubricants, coolant and fuel are replenished. Top-up the hydraulic system and prime the high pressure (HP) pump, as described in Section 5 (paragraph 10) of Chapter 8.

48   As soon as the engine fires and runs, keep it going at a fast tickover only (no faster), and bring it up to the normal working temperature.

49   With the engine running, repressurise the hydraulic system, as described in Section 5 of Chapter 8.

50   As the engine warms up, there will be odd smells and some smoke from parts getting hot and burning off oil deposits. Look for oil and water leaks, which will be obvious if serious. Check also the exhaust pipe and manifold connections, as these do not always "find" their exact gas-tight position until the warmth and vibration have acted on them, and it is almost certain that they will need tightening further. This should be done of course, with the engine stopped. Check all fuel system connections for any sign of leakage.

51   Road test the car to check that the ignition timing is correct, and that the engine is giving the necessary smoothness and power. Do not race the engine - if new bearings and/or pistons have been fitted, it should be treated as a new engine, and run-in at a reduced speed.

52   Change the engine oil at 1000 miles (1600 km), if many of the engine internal components have been renewed.

---

7   Cooling system

BX 16 and BX 19 models - modifications from July 1985

1   The cooling system circuit is modified, the main differences being the revised carburettor heating circuit and the water inlet casing. The revised system is shown in Figs. 13.22 and 13.23.

2   The opening temperatures for the thermostat, and the temperature switch operating temperatures are both revised (see Specifications).

3   The cooling system capacity and pressure remain the same.

Radiator (GTi models) - removal and refitting

4   The removal and refitting details for the GTi model radiator are the same as those described for other models in Chapter 2, but note that the crosspanel has the fuel system air inlet duct attached. The inlet duct hose will need to be detached from the panel and moved out of the way, then subsequently reconnected during refitting (photo).

Heating and ventilation system - later models

5   Although the operating principles remain the same, the heating and ventilation system on later models has been revised, and the removal and refitting of some system components differs to the earlier variants described in Chapter 2.

6   The removal and refitting details of the items concerned are given below.

Heater unit (later models) - removal and refitting

7   Although the heater unit is much the same as the earlier type described in Chapter 2, the controls and the blower motor differ.

8   The blower motor will need to be removed to gain access to the heater unit retaining bolts. Access to the heater motor unit differs, in that the later-type facia panel and assemblies will have to be removed

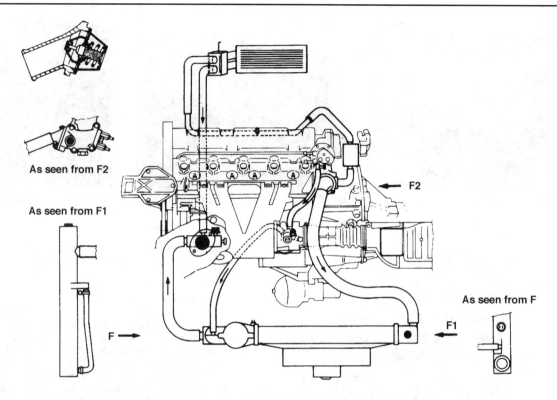

As seen from F2

As seen from F1

F →

F1 ←

As seen from F

Fig. 13.23 Modified cooling system - BX 19 GTi from July 1985 (Sec 7)

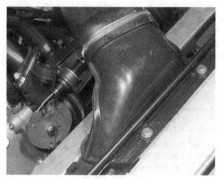

7.4 Air inlet duct attached to crosspanel - GTi

7.16 Removing the plastic cover from the heater blower motor

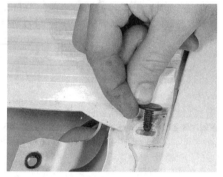

7.17 Removing an air intake grille securing clip

for access. Refer to Section 18 in this Chapter for details of their removal.

9   The heater unit retaining bolt positions are as shown in Fig. 2.11 (Chapter 2).

10   Disconnect the fresh air/heater ducts from the heater unit, and remove the main facia unit.

11   The heater unit can now be removed in a similar manner to that described for earlier models (Chapter 2).

12   Refitting of the heater unit and the associated fittings is a reversal of the removal procedure. Ensure that the heater feed and return hoses are securely connected, also the wiring connections.

13   On completion, check the operation of all items which were disconnected, and top-up the cooling system with reference to Chapter 2.

Heater blower motor (later models) - removal and refitting

14   Disconnect the battery earth lead.

15   Remove the windscreen wiper arm and spindle nut (refer to Chapter 12 for details).

16   The heater blower motor is located in the bulkhead cavity just forward of the windscreen, beneath a plastic cover. Remove the plastic cover by prising free the rubber seal along its front edge and releasing

the retaining clips at the rear edge (photo).

17   Removal of the air intake grille at the base of the windscreen is advisable - this is secured by plastic clips. Carefully prise free the clips and remove the grille (photo).

18   Remove the single retaining bolt and the support bracket screws, and disconnect the wiring connectors from the blower motor unit. Carefully lift out and remove the blower motor unit (photo).

19   To remove the motor from its housing unit, unclip and separate the half-housings and undo the retaining screws.

20   Refit in the reverse order of removal and check for satisfactory operation.

Heater matrix (later models) - removal and refitting

21   Drain the cooling system with reference to Section 7 or Chapter 2.

22   Remove the upper and lower steering column shrouds. These are secured by screws recessed into the lower shroud.

23   Unbolt the upper and lower steering column mountings.

24   Unbolt and separate the upper-to-lower column universal joint, then withdraw the upper steering column unit so that it clears the matrix unit. Complete removal of the upper steering column will necessitate detaching the column switch wiring at the harness connectors.

25   The heater matrix is now accessible for withdrawal, and can be

7.18 Blower motor unit support bracket screws (arrowed)

7.29 Removing a heater/ventilation control panel retaining screw

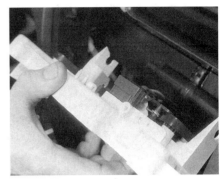

7.32 Withdrawing the heater control unit

7.35 Radiator filler cap

7.48 Heater hose bleed screw

removed in the same manner described for the earlier variants in Chapter 2.

26   Refit in the reverse order of removal.

Heater control panel (later models) - removal and refitting

27   Disconnect the battery earth lead.

28   Pull free the heater/ventilation control knobs.

29   Undo the two retaining screws (photo).

30   Remove the two ventilation grilles from their apertures above the heater control panel. Pull to release the retaining clips each side, and withdraw the outer control panel.

31   Disconnect the wiring from the rear face of the cigar lighter.

32   The inner control unit is secured by four screws, but it cannot be removed on its own. Either remove it together with the heater unit, or detach the controls at the heater and withdraw the control unit (photo).

33   Refit in the reverse order of removal, and check for satisfactory operation.

Fan control module for air conditioning - from January 1987

34   The fan control module on later models is located on the fan motor casing within the scuttle plenum chamber, instead of being mounted on the steering column support bracket.

Cooling system (BX 14 - K1G engine) - draining, flushing and refilling

35   With the engine cold, unscrew the filler caps from the expansion bottle and radiator (photo).

36   Place a suitable container beneath the left-hand side of the radiator, then unscrew the drain plug and drain the coolant.

37   Drain the cylinder block by removing the plug located on the front left-hand side of the block.

38   To flush the radiator, disconnect the top and bottom hoses and insert a garden hose in the top inlet. Flush with cold water until there are no traces of sediment.

39   With the system clean, refit the hoses and tighten the drain plugs.

40   Release the rubber ring and tie the expansion bottle to the bonnet as high as possible.

41   Loosen the bleed screws on the thermostat housing and heater hose.

42   Fill the radiator with coolant. Tighten the thermostat housing bleed screw when the water flows free of air bubbles.

43   Fill the radiator to overflowing, then refit and tighten the radiator filler cap.

44   Fill the expansion bottle to the maximum level mark, then tighten the heater hose bleed screw when the water flows free of air bubbles.

45   Add more coolant to the expansion bottle until the level is about 30.0 mm (1.2 in) above the maximum mark. Refit and tighten the filler cap.

46   Start the engine and run it at 1500 rpm until the electric cooling fan starts.

47   Let the engine idle, then when the cooling fan stops, unscrew the expansion bottle filler cap (using a thick cloth as a precaution against scalding).

48   Slowly loosen the radiator bleed screw until coolant flows, then re-tighten it. Similarly purge any air from the bleed screws on the thermostat housing and heater hose (photo).

Coolant pump (BX 14 - K1G engine) - removal and refitting

49   Drain the cooling system as previously described.

50   Unbolt and remove the upper and intermediate timing covers, leaving the lower cover in position.

51   Turn the engine clockwise using a socket on the crankshaft pulley bolt until the small hole in the camshaft sprocket is aligned with the

7.58A Bypass hose connection to water pump housing (arrowed)

7.58B Water pump housing securing bolts (arrowed)

7.58C Water pump housing O-ring seal (arrowed)

7.59A Removing the water pump from the housing

7.59B Water pump O-ring (arrowed)

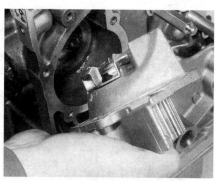

7.69 Withdrawing the coolant pump

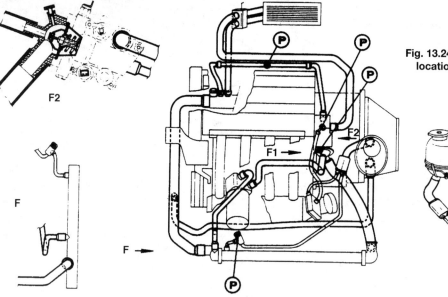

Fig. 13.24 Cooling system bleed screw locations (P) on BX 19 GTi 16 valve engine (Sec 7)

corresponding hole in the cylinder head. Insert a close-fitting twist drill or bolt into the holes.

52   Align the TDC holes in the flywheel and cylinder block rear flange, and insert a further twist drill or long bolt.

53   Loosen the timing belt tensioner roller nut, turn the tensioner clockwise using a screwdriver or square drive in the special hole, then re-tighten the nut.

54   Release the timing belt from the water pump sprocket.

55   Unscrew the nut from the right-hand engine mounting.

56   Using a trolley jack and block of wood, lift the right-hand side of the engine as far as possible.

57   Unscrew the nuts and remove the mounting bracket from the water pump housing.

58   Disconnect the hoses from the housing, then unbolt the housing

from the block. Remove the housing O-ring seal (photos).

59   Unbolt the water pump from the housing, and remove the pump O-ring (photos). If necessary, similarly remove the inlet elbow.

60   Refitting is a reversal of removal, but note the following points.

(a) Renew the pump and housing O-rings.
(b) Make sure that the housing-to-block location dowels are in position.
(c) Tighten all nuts and bolts to the specified torque.
(d) Refit and tension the timing belt with reference to Section 5A.
(e) Refill the cooling system.

Thermostat (BX 14 - K1G engine) - removal and refitting

61   The procedure is as given in Chapter 2, but note the different housing on the K1G engine.

7.73A Thermostat housing in position

7.73B Thermostat housing dismantled

7.73C Thermostat housing bleed screw (arrowed)

Cooling system (BX 19 GTi 16 valve) - draining, flushing and refilling

62   The operations are similar to those described earlier for the K1G engine, but note that a radiator cap is not fitted, and filling is carried out through the expansion bottle.
63   Refer to Fig. 13.24 for locations of the bleed screws.

Coolant pump (BX 19 GTi 16 valve) - removal and refitting

Note: *As removal of the coolant pump requires the timing belt to be removed, it is advisable to read the procedure for timing belt removal and refitting before starting work.* •
64   Drain the cooling system as described earlier.
65   Remove the alternator drivebelt.
66   Refer to Section 6A and release the tension on the timing belt. Slip the belt from the two camshaft pulleys.
67   Remove the camshaft cover, then holding each camshaft using an open-ended spanner on the camshaft flats, undo and remove the bolts and the camshaft sprockets.
68   Remove the timing cover upper backplate.
69   Unscrew the coolant pump fixing bolts and withdraw the pump (photo).
70   Refitting is a reversal of removal, but use a new gasket.
71   Tension the timing belt and drivebelts (see Section 6A).

Thermostat housing (BX 19 GTi 16 valve) - removal and refitting

72   This is located at the flywheel end of the cylinder block.
73   The housing incorporates the coolant temperature switch, a sensor for the Motronic engine management system and a bleed screw (photos).
74   Removal and testing of the thermostat is described in Chapter 2, but note the different housing on the GTi 16 valve engine.
75   Use new seals and a new gasket when reassembling.

8   Fuel and exhaust systems - carburettor models

BX 16 and BX 19 models - modifications from November 1985

1   The fuel line pipes have reduced inside diameter connections, and are now 6 mm in diameter instead of 8 mm as on earlier models. All connections to the fuel pump, fuel filter, carburettor and fuel flow meter are now of the same diameter. When renewing any of these items, ensure that the correct type is obtained, as the early- and later-type connections are not directly interchangeable. The only exception to this is if a later-type Solex carburettor is fitted. In this instance, it will be necessary to renew the fuel feed connection to suit. Note also that the later-type fuel lines are secured with clips.
2   A new type of carburettor, the Weber 36 TLP, is fitted to BX 16 RE models. This is covered later in the Section.
3   A bench adjustment procedure is given for the Solex Z1 carburet-

Fig. 13.25 Strangler (choke) flap setting - Solex 32-34 Z1 and 34-34 Z1 carburettors (Sec 8)

a   Refer to Fig. 13.26   4   Primary choke flap
3   Roller   adjustment screw

Temperature in C degrees	Dimension "a" in mm
5	29.5
10	28.8
15	28.4
20	27.6
25	27
30	26.3

Fig. 13.26 Table relating distance "a" in Fig. 13.25 to temperature (Sec 8)

tors. This is an alternative to the on-vehicle procedure (Chapter 3, Section 17) and needs no special tools.

Solex 32-34 Z1 and 34-34 Z1 - adjustments after overhaul

4   The carburettor must be removed from the vehicle for these adjustments.
Strangler (choke) flap setting
5   Remove the cover from the automatic choke housing. Measure the distance from the top of the choke housing to the roller (Fig. 13.25)

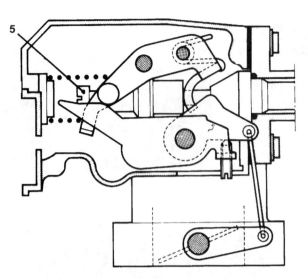

Fig. 13.27 Strangler (choke) flap adjustment screw (5) -
Solex 32-34 Z1 and 34-34 Z1 carburettors (Sec 8)

Fig. 13.28 Anti-flood capsule adjustment - Solex 32-34 Z1
and 34-34 Z1 carburettors (Sec 8)

| 1 | Link rod (arrow indicates rest position) | 2 | Locknut |
| | | 3 | Adjustment screw |

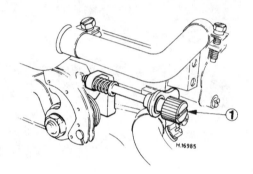

Fig. 13.29 Idle speed adjustment screw (1) -
Weber 36 TLP carburettor (Sec 8)

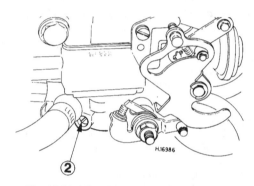

Fig. 13.30 Idle mixture adjustment screw (2) -
Weber 36 TLP carburettor (Sec 8)

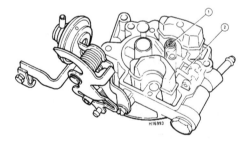

Fig. 13.31 Top cover of Weber 36 TLP carburettor (Sec 8)

| 1 | Main jet | 2 | Fuel inlet needle valve |

and compare it with the value in Fig. 13.26. Adjust if necessary using a screwdriver inserted through the hole just above the deflooding capsule - see Chapter 3, photo 17.6.

Primary choke valve (throttle) setting

6   With the ambient temperature at a steady 20°C (68°F), insert a gauge rod or drill shank to establish the opening of the primary choke throttle valve (see Chapter 3, Fig. 3.19). The opening should be as given in Chapter 3 Specifications. If not, adjust the appropriate screw (Fig. 13.25).

Anti-flood capsule setting

7   Using pliers, push the anti-flood capsule link rod back into the capsule as far as it will go. Measure the strangler (choke) flap opening with the link rod in this position. If the opening does not correspond to

that given in Chapter 3 Specifications, adjust by means of the locknut and screw on the outside of the anti-flood capsule. Release the link rod.

Mechanical (forced) deflooding

8   Fully open the primary throttle valve, and measure the strangler flap opening in this position. It should be 8 mm (0.32 in). Adjust if necessary by bending the actuator fork jaws (see Chapter 3, Fig. 3.22).

9   Refit the choke housing cover when adjustments are complete.

BX 16 models with Solex 34-34 Z1 carburettor - modification

10   On BX 16 models with the Solex 34-34 Z1 carburettor, a modification has been introduced to prevent engine hesitation at high temperatures when driving in heavy traffic; this is due to percolation of the principal and enrichment circuits of the carburettor. The modification consists of the fitting of a different primary main jet and idling jet, and the drilling of a small hole in the carburettor body behind the enrichment device cover. Refer to your Citroën dealer for further information.

Weber 36 TLP carburettor - description

11   This carburettor is fitted to the B1A/A engine found on BX 16 RE models. It is a single choke downdraught type, with a manual choke.

Weber 36 TLP carburettor - adjustment and overhaul

12   Idle adjustments are essentially as described in Chapter 3, Section 13. Refer to Figs. 13.29 and 13.30 for the location of the idle speed and mixture adjustment screws.

13   For overhaul refer to Chapter 3, Section 15 for general principles, and to Figs. 13.31 and 13.32 for jet locations.

14   For float level setting, make up a gauge as shown in Fig. 13.33. Remove the float chamber cover and hold it vertically. With the gasket in position, the gauge should just contact the floats. Bend the float tongue and connecting bars if necessary.

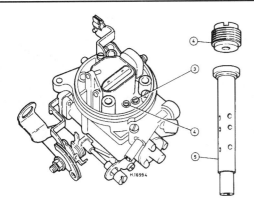

Fig. 13.32 Jet locations on the Weber 36 TLP carburettor (Sec 8)

3   Idle jet   5   Emulsion tube
4   Air correction jet

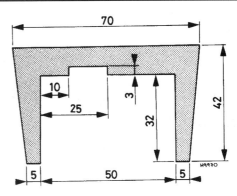

**Fig. 13.33 Float level setting gauge - Weber 36 TLP carburettor
(Sec 8)**

Dimensions in mm

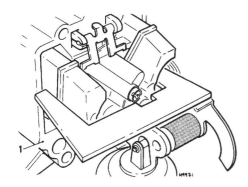

**Fig. 13.34 Checking the float level - Weber 36 TLP carburettor
(Sec 8)**

1   Gasket

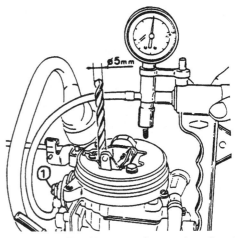

**Fig. 13.35 Checking strangler opening after starting -
Weber 36 TLP carburettor (Sec 8)**

1   Anti-flood capsule adjustment screw

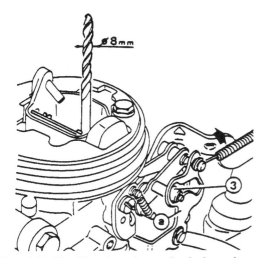

**Fig. 13.36 Checking strangler mechanical opening -
Weber 36 TLP carburettor (Sec 8)**

a   Cam   3   Roller

Weber 36 TLP carburettor - cold start (choke) adjustments

15   These are not routine adjustments, but should be performed if difficult cold starting is experienced.

Strangler opening after starting

16   Remove the air inlet from the top of the carburettor. Pull the choke control knob out fully to close the strangler flap.

17   Disconnect the vacuum pipe from the anti-flood capsule. Connect a hand vacuum pump (or a modified bicycle pump) to the capsule.

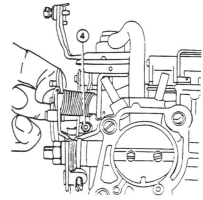

**Fig. 13.37 Strangler mechanical opening adjustment nut (4) -
Weber 36 TLP carburettor (Sec 8)**

18   Apply vacuum (400 mm Hg approx.) to the capsule. The strangler flap should open far enough to admit a drill shank or rod 5 mm in diameter.

19   Adjust if necessary by means of the screw on the anti-flood capsule.

20   Disconnect the vacuum pump, remake the original vacuum connection, and close the strangler flap.

Mechanical opening

21   Having adjusted the anti-flood capsule as just described, move the strangler opening roller into the recess of the cam as shown in Fig. 13.36.

8.31A Prise down the toggle clips . . .

8.31B . . . and withdraw the lid/element assembly

8.34A Air intake disconnected from air cleaner casing

8.34B Removing the insulated hose from the exhaust manifold hot air collector plate

8.35A Disconnecting a crankcase vent hose from the air cleaner

8.35B Removing the air intake duct from the carburettor and air cleaner

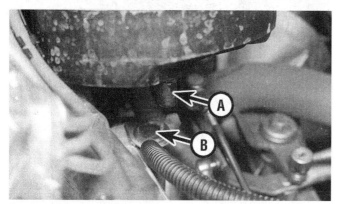
8.35C Air cleaner casing

    A   Base locating spigot   B   Spigot grommet

8.36 Air cleaner Winter/Summer lever

22 Check that the strangler flap opening just admits a drill shank or rod 8 mm in diameter.
23 Adjustment is carried out by turning the nut shown (Fig. 13.37) after removing the carburettor.
24 When adjustment is complete, refit the carburettor (if removed) and the air inlet.

Tamperproof adjustment screws (all models) - caution
25 Certain adjustment points in the fuel system (and elsewhere) are protected by "tamperproof" caps, plugs or seals. The purpose of such tamperproofing is to discourage, and to detect, adjustment by unqualified operators.
26 In some EEC countries (though not yet in the UK), it is an offence to drive a vehicle with missing or broken tamperproof seals.
27 Before disturbing a tamperproof seal, satisfy yourself that you will not be breaking local or national anti-pollution regulations by doing so. Fit a new seal when adjustment is complete, when this is required by law.
28 Do not break tamperproof seals on a vehicle which is still under warranty.

In-line fuel filter (BX 16 RE) - general
29 From November 1987, an in-line fuel filter is fitted between the fuel pump and the carburettor.
30 Renew the filter at the specified intervals, making sure that the directional arrow on the filter points towards the carburettor.

Air cleaner (BX 14 - K1G engine) - element renewal
31 Prise down the toggle clips and withdraw the lid/element assembly (photos).
32 Wipe out the casing, and fit the new element.

Air cleaner (BX 14 - K1G engine) - removal and refitting
33 Remove the element as previously described.
34 Release the large clip, then separate and remove the air intake from the air cleaner casing. Note the insulated hose connecting with the exhaust manifold hot air collector plate (photos).
35 Disconnect the air intake duct from the carburettor and the crankcase vent hoses, and withdraw the air cleaner casing upwards. Note the locating spigot at the base of the casing (photos).
36 Refitting is a reversal of removal. On completion, set the Winter/Summer lever to the appropriate position (photo).

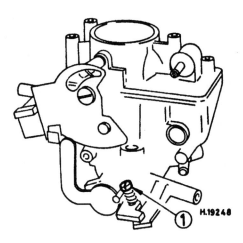

Fig. 13.38 Throttle stop screw (1) on Solex 34 PBISA carburettor (Sec 8)

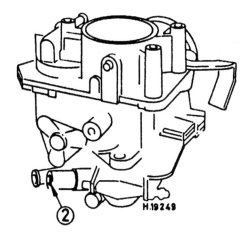

Fig. 13.39 Mixture adjustment screw (2) on Solex PBISA carburettor (Sec 8)

Solex 34 PBISA 17 carburettor - removal and refitting

37   Refer to Chapter 3, Section 14 for the removal procedure, having removed the air cleaner as described earlier.

Solex 34 PBISA 17 carburettor - adjustment

38   The following adjustments must be made with the ignition timing correctly adjusted, the air cleaner and filter element fitted, and the engine at normal operating temperature.

39   Connect a tachometer to the engine and, where necessary, remove the tamperproof cap from the mixture adjustment screw.

Without an exhaust gas analyser

40   Turn the throttle stop screw to adjust the engine speed to 750 ± 50 rpm.

41   Turn the mixture adjustment screw to obtain the highest idling speed.

42   Repeat the procedure given in paragraphs 40 and 41 until the engine speed is 750 ± 50 rpm (i.e. after adjusting the mixture screw).

43   Screw in the mixture adjustment screw slightly until the engine speed starts to decrease.

With an exhaust gas analyser

44   Turn the throttle stop screw to adjust the engine speed to 750 ± 50 rpm.

45   Turn the mixture adjustment screw to obtain the specified CO reading.

46   Repeat the procedure in paragraphs 44 and 45 until the idle speed is 750 ± 50 rpm.

Unleaded petrol - general information and usage

47   As a general rule, all pre-1988 carburettor models are not suitable for running on unleaded petrol, and must be run on 97 RON leaded fuel only. Models manufactured between 1988 and 1991 should also only be run an 97 RON leaded fuel, but most models produced between these dates are suitable for running on 95 RON unleaded fuel if the suitable adjustments are first carried out. For full information on the use of unleaded petrol, consult your Citroën dealer - he will be able to inform you if your vehicle is capable of running on unleaded fuel and, where possible, of the necessary adjustments required. The use of unleaded fuel in a vehicle not designed, or suitably adjusted, to run on unleaded fuel will lead to serious damage of the valve seats.

---

9   Fuel injection system

Note: *The following procedures are applicable to the Bosch LE3 Jetronic system. For procedures applicable to the Motronic/Magneti Marelli integrated engine management (fuel injection/ignition) systems used on certain models, refer to Section 11.*

Warning: *Many of the procedures in this Section require the removal of fuel lines and connections, which may result in some fuel spillage. Before carrying out any operation on the fuel system, refer to the precautions given in "Safety first!" at the beginning of this manual, and follow them implicitly. Petrol is a highly-dangerous and volatile liquid, and the precautions necessary when handling it cannot be overstressed.*

Note: *Residual pressure will remain in the fuel lines long after the vehicle was last used; before disconnecting any fuel line, depressurise the fuel system as described in paragraphs 12 to 15.*

Fuel injection system - general description and precautions

1   The fuel injection system components and their locations are shown in Fig. 13.40. A roller-type electric fuel pump draws the fuel from the fuel tank, and pumps the fuel through the filter to the injectors via a distribution pipe. The electronic control unit, which is triggered by the ignition circuit, sends impulses to the injectors, which operate simultaneously and inject fuel in the vicinity of the inlet valves. The electronic control unit is provided with sensors to determine engine temperature, speed and load, and the quantity of air entering the engine. This information is computed to determine the period of injection. A diagram of the system's electrical circuit is shown in Fig. 13.41, and the main control units are shown in Fig. 13.42.

2   For cold starting, additional air is provided by a supplementary air device; this excess air "tricks" the system into providing more fuel.

3   A fuel vapour recirculation system is integrated into the fuel system, the layout of which is shown in Fig. 13.43. The fuel tank is vented via the charcoal filter canister. When the engine is started, any fuel vapour in the de-aerating reservoir and charcoal canister is drawn through the airflow meter and into the throttle housing by the normal induction method, and is burnt in the engine.

4   The following sub-Sections describe procedures which can be carried out by the home mechanic. Work involving the use of pressure gauges is not included.

5   In order to prevent damage to the electrical components of the system, the battery must **never** be disconnected with the engine running, the electronic control unit **must not** be disconnected with the ignition on, and a test light **must not** be used for checking the circuits.

Routine maintenance - fuel injection system

6   Refer to the *"Routine maintenance"* Section at the start of this manual for fuel injection system maintenance.

Air cleaner - element renewal

7   Raise and support the bonnet.

8   Undo the air cleaner/airflow meter unit intake hose clip, and detach the hose.

9   Release the retaining clips and lift the air cleaner/airflow meter unit away from the lower cleaner housing.

9.10 Removing the air cleaner element

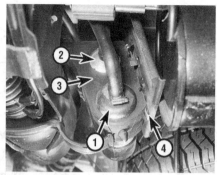

9.18 Fuel pump (1), fuel filter (2), insulator (3) and heat shield (4) pivoted towards the centre for removal

9.19 Fuel pump wiring connections

9.27 Idle speed adjustment screw (arrowed)

10   Lift out the old air cleaner element from the housing, and discard it (photo).
11   Wipe clean the air cleaner housing, then fit the new air cleaner element into position. Refit the air cleaner/airflow meter unit and intake hose, reversing the removal procedures.

Fuel system - depressurisation

Note: *Refer to the warning note at the start of this Section before proceeding.*
Warning: *The following procedure will merely relieve the pressure in the fuel system - remember that fuel will still be present in the system components and take precautions accordingly before disconnecting any of them.*
12   The fuel system referred to in this Section is defined as the fuel pump, the fuel filter, the fuel injectors and the pressure regulator, and the metal pipes and flexible hoses of the fuel lines between these components. All these contain fuel which will be under pressure while the engine is running and/or while the ignition is switched on. The pressure will remain for some time after the ignition has been switched off, and must be relieved before any of these components are disturbed for servicing work.
13   Disconnect the battery negative terminal.
14   Place a suitable container beneath the relevant connection/union to be disconnected, and have a large rag ready to soak up any escaping fuel not being caught by the container.
15   Slowly loosen the connection or union nut (as applicable) to avoid a sudden release of pressure, and position the rag around the connection to catch any fuel spray which may be expelled. Once the pressure is released, disconnect the fuel line, and insert plugs to minimise fuel loss and prevent the entry of dirt into the fuel system.

Fuel pump - removal and refitting

Note: *Refer to the warning note at the start of this Section before proceeding.*
16   The fuel pump is located on the underside of the vehicle, at the

rear on the right-hand side, just to the rear of the fuel tank. The pump unit is housed in a rubber insulator, together with the fuel filter unit which is located directly above it.
17   For access to the pump (and/or filter), raise and support the vehicle at the rear. Disconnect the battery earth lead.
18   Unclip and swing the heat shield, insulator, pump and filter units towards the centre (photo).
19   Pull back the rubber protective gaiter from the end of the fuel pump, and then detach the wiring connectors. Note that, whilst both wires are yellow, one has a white connector sleeve for identification. Note which has the sleeve and its connection (photo).
20   Bearing in mind the information given above on depressurising the fuel system, loosen the clips and remove the fuel lines from the front and rear of the pump unit.
21   Carefully pull and withdraw the pump unit from the insulator.
22   Refitting is a reversal of the removal procedure. Ensure that all connections are correctly and securely made. On completion, check for satisfactory operation, and for any signs of fuel leaks from the pump connections.

Fuel filter - removal and refitting

Note: *Refer to the warning note at the start of this Section before proceeding.*
23   The fuel filter is located on the underside of the vehicle, at the right-hand side, just to the rear of the fuel tank. The filter is located in a rubber holder, in tandem with the fuel pump unit which is directly beneath it.
24   To remove the fuel filter, proceed as described for fuel pump removal (paragraphs 16 to 21). Note that it may not be necessary to completely detach and remove the pump unit in order to remove the filter, but this would improve access. As it is removed, note which way round the filter is fitted, to ensure correct orientation when refitting.
25   Refit in the reverse order of removal. On completion, check for satisfactory operation, and for any sign of fuel leaks from the pump and filter connections.

Idle speed and mixture - adjustment

26   Before making any adjustments to the fuel system, the following conditions must be met.
  (a) The ignition system must be in good condition and correctly adjusted (see Chapter 4).
  (b) The fuel system air filter element must be clean.
  (c) The throttle initial position must be correctly set, as must the throttle butterfly spindle switch. These adjustments are described at the end of this Section.
  (d) The engine must be at its normal operating temperature, the cooling fan having cut in and out.
27   Connect a tachometer and an exhaust gas analyser to the engine. If the idle speed is incorrect, turn the adjustment screw in the required direction to set the speed to that specified (photo).
28   To adjust the idle mixture setting, you will need to punch a hole in the tamperproof plug over the mixture screw, and prise out the plug (**Caution:** *See paragraphs 25 to 28 in the previous Section*). Turn the

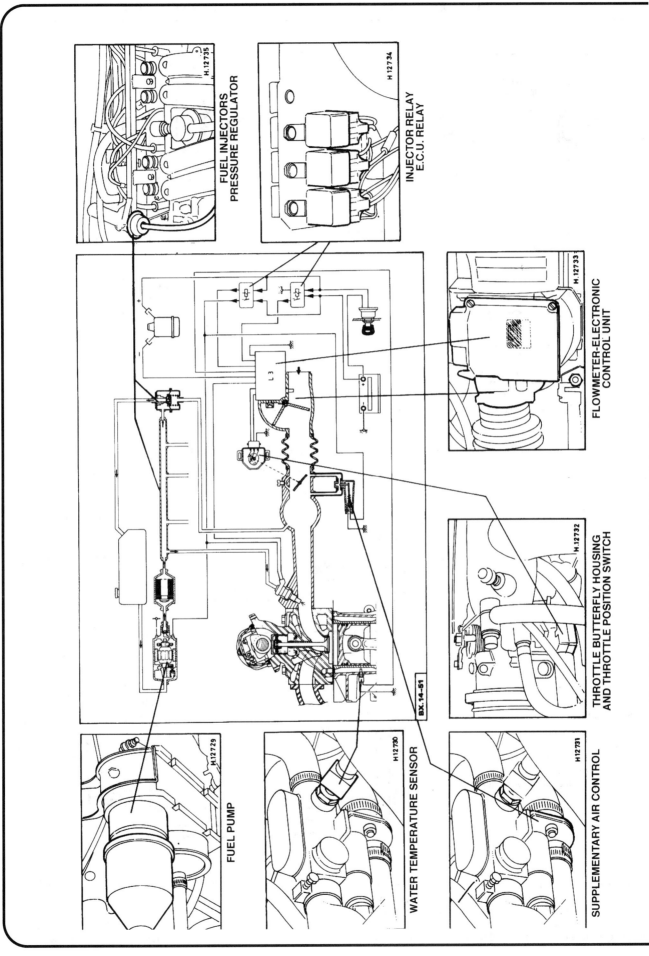

FUEL INJECTORS
PRESSURE REGULATOR

INJECTOR RELAY
E.C.U. RELAY

FLOWMETER-ELECTRONIC
CONTROL UNIT

THROTTLE BUTTERFLY HOUSING
AND THROTTLE POSITION SWITCH

FUEL PUMP

WATER TEMPERATURE SENSOR

SUPPLEMENTARY AIR CONTROL

Fig. 13.40 Bosch LE3 Jetronic fuel injection system principal components (Sec 9)

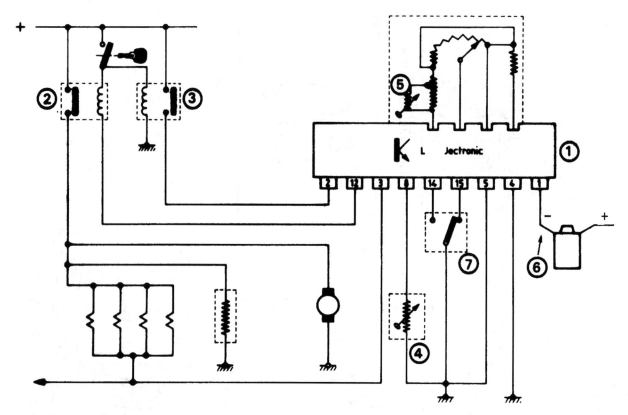

Fig. 13.41 Wiring diagram for the Bosch LE3 Jetronic fuel injection system (Sec 9)

1   Electronic control unit (ECU)   3   ECU feed relay   5   Air temperature sensor   7   Throttle position switch
2   Injector relay   4   Coolant temperature sensor   6   Distributor

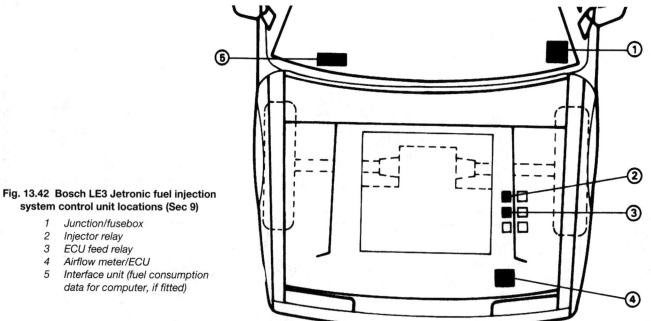

**Fig. 13.42 Bosch LE3 Jetronic fuel injection
system control unit locations (Sec 9)**

1   Junction/fusebox
2   Injector relay
3   ECU feed relay
4   Airflow meter/ECU
5   Interface unit (fuel consumption
    data for computer, if fitted)

mixture adjustment screw to give a maximum CO reading of 2.0%. If required, readjust the idle speed as described previously (photo).
29   Recheck the CO reading, and readjust the mixture setting and idle speed settings as necessary.
30   On completion, a new tamperproof plug should be fitted over the

mixture screw. Disconnect the tachometer and the exhaust gas analyser to complete.

Accelerator cable - removal and refitting

31   The procedure is much the same as that described for the carburettor models in Section 20 of Chapter 3. The cable connection to the

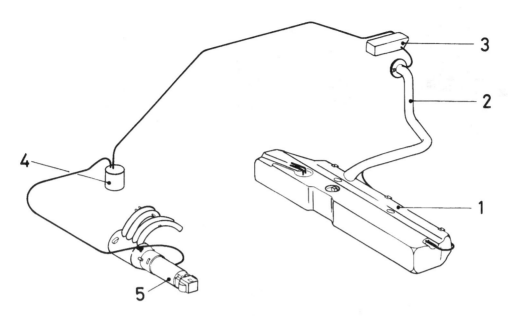

Fig. 13.43 Fuel vapour recirculation system - GTi with Bosch LE3 Jetronic fuel injection system (Sec 9)

1 Fuel tank	3 De-aeration reservoir	5 Airflow meter (throttle butterfly
2 Fuel tank filler	4 Charcoal canister	housing)

9.28 Idle mixture adjustment screw (arrowed)

9.31 Accelerator cable adjustment ferrule (arrowed)

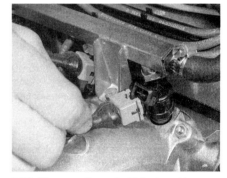

9.34 Disconnecting a fuel injector wiring connector

9.35A Prising the fuel rail free from the injectors

9.35B Fuel rail/injector clip

9.36A Fuel supply rail retaining bolt (arrowed)

throttle housing on fuel injection models is shown in the accompanying photograph (photo).

32   The cable adjustment is the same as the carburettor type. Whenever the cable has been removed and refitted, or adjusted, check the idle speed as described elsewhere in this Section.

Injectors - removal and refitting
Note: *Refer to the warning note at the start of this Section before proceeding.*

33   Disconnect the battery earth lead.

34   Detach the wiring connections from the injectors by prising open the wire retaining clip in the connector (photo).

35   Prise free the injector-to-fuel supply rail (tube) retaining clip, using a screwdriver as a lever (photos).

36   Bearing in mind the information given earlier in this Section on depressurising the fuel system, undo the retaining bolts and remove the fuel supply rail. The hoses and pressure regulator can be left attached (photos).

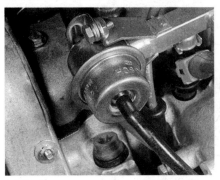

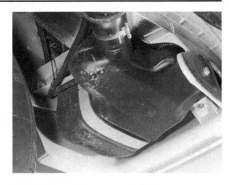

9.36B Pressure regulator attached to fuel rail

9.39 Fuel tank supply and return hoses (GTi)

9.40 De-aeration reservoir (GTi)

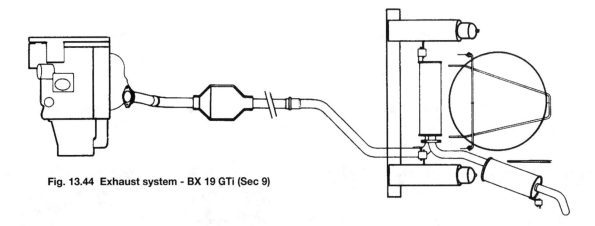

Fig. 13.44 Exhaust system - BX 19 GTi (Sec 9)

37 Withdraw the injectors. Ensure that no dirt is allowed to enter the fuel system whilst disconnected.
38 Refitting is a reversal of the removal procedure. Use new injector seals. To ease fitting of the injectors to their cylinder head ports, lubricate the seals with a small amount of soapy solution. Check for signs of fuel leakage on completion.

Fuel tank and de-aeration reservoir

Note: *Refer to the warning note at the start of this Section before proceeding.*
39 The fuel tank and its connections are basically the same on the BX 19 GTi as the fuel tank fitted to the carburettor models. Bear in mind the information given earlier in this Section on depressurising the fuel system when disconnecting the tank fuel lines (photo). If removing the fuel level transmitter or the tank, reference should therefore be made to Chapter 3, Section 9 or 10 as applicable.
40 The de-aeration reservoir is located at the rear of the car, under the right-hand rear wheel arch (photo). It is connected to the fuel filler pipe and the charcoal filter canister, their function being to vent the fuel tank. Any petrol vapour stored in them is drawn into the throttle housing when the engine is started.
41 If removing the de-aeration reservoir, take the same precautions as those mentioned for fuel tank removal. Detach the hoses from the reservoir, undo the retaining strap and mounting bolts, then lower and remove it (photo).
42 A vent valve is also fitted, and is located near the de-aeration reservoir. This can be removed by detaching the hoses and unclipping the valve (photo).
43 Refitting is a reversal of the removal procedure. Renew any hoses or clips as necessary, and check for leakage and security on completion.

Manifolds and exhaust system

44 The basic procedures are much the same as those given for carburettor models in Chapter 3.

45 When removing the air intake manifold, items such as the injectors and the ignition coil will need to be detached (see elsewhere in this Chapter). The manifold can either be removed together with, or separate from, the throttle housing. Disconnect as appropriate, but note the hose connections.
46 As with carburettor models, always use new gaskets where applicable when refitting.
47 The exhaust system on the fuel injection model differs to that fitted to carburettor models, the main difference being that the front pipe section incorporates an expansion chamber. All other components in the system are also specific to the model, and this must be considered when ordering any parts of the system (refer to Fig. 13.44).

Throttle initial position setting

48 This is not a routine adjustment. It should only be necessary if new components have been fitted, or if the setting has been accidentally disturbed.
49 Remove the tamperproof plug from the throttle butterfly stop screw (on the other side of the throttle housing from the idle speed adjuster screw).
50 Unscrew the throttle butterfly stop screw until it is no longer in contact with its stop, and the butterfly is fully closed. Screw it in again until it just contacts the stop. From this position, screw it in exactly one quarter of a turn.
51 Fit a new tamperproof plug, when required.
52 Check the throttle butterfly switch setting.

Throttle position switch setting

53 Disconnect the multi-plug from the throttle position switch. Connect an ohmmeter or continuity tester between switch terminals 2 and 18.
54 Insert a feeler blade, 0.30 mm (0.012 in) thick, between the butterfly stop screw and its stop.
55 Slacken the switch mounting screws. Turn the switch in either direction until the contacts are just closed (continuity or zero resistance).

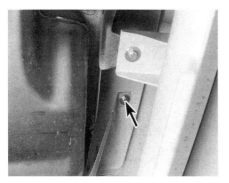

9.41 De-aeration reservoir retaining strap and mounting bolt (arrowed)

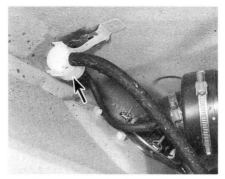

9.42 Vent valve location (arrowed) - GTi

10.2 Ignition coil location (GTi with Bosch LE3 Jetronic fuel injection system)

Tighten the screws in this position.
56   Remove this feeler blade and insert another, 0.70 mm (0.028 in) thick. With this blade inserted, the contacts must be open (no continuity, or infinite resistance). If not, repeat the adjustment. Remove the feeler blade.
57   Transfer the ohmmeter to terminals 3 and 18. Have an assistant depress the throttle pedal to the floor. At full-throttle, the contacts must be closed.
58   Disconnect the test equipment and reconnect the multi-plug.

Unleaded petrol - general information and usage
59   Models equipped with the Bosch LE3 Jetronic fuel injection system should be run on 97 RON leaded petrol only. However, they are suitable for running on 95 RON unleaded fuel if the suitable adjustments are first carried out. Consult your Citroën dealer for further information. Note that the use of unleaded fuel in a vehicle not suitably adjusted will lead to serious damage of the valve seats.

10   Ignition system

Ignition coil - BX 19 GTi
1   The ignition coil type and location on the BX 19 GTi differs to that on other models in the range.
2   The coil is mounted on the underside of the air intake manifold (photo).
3   To remove the coil, detach the wiring connectors and unbolt the unit, complete with its retaining bracket.
4   Refitting is a reversal of the removal procedure.

Spark plug spanner - general
5   From 1986, the special spanner shown in photo 9.4A in Chapter 4 is no longer provided as standard equipment.
6   On later models, it will therefore be necessary to obtain a suitable box spanner or socket.

Spark plug types - general
7   From July 1987, the engines of BX 19 carburettor models are fitted with conventional flat-seat spark plugs with washers, instead of the taper-seat type plugs without a washer used previously. BX 14 and BX 16 models followed suit in July and September of 1988 respectively.
8   The flat-seat spark plug with washer is also used on the BX 19 GTi and BX GTi 16 valve engines.
9   Always use the correct type of spark plug and tightening torque according to type of spark plug seat (see Specifications).

Distributor - BX 14 (K1G engine)
10   The distributor fitted to this engine is of Ducellier type, similar to that described in Chapter 4. The cap is secured however by two screws, not spring clips.
11   Refer to Chapter 4 for the procedures to remove and dismantle the distributor, referring to the Specifications for ignition timing.

11   Engine management systems

Warning: *Many of the procedures in this Section require the removal of fuel lines and connections which may result in some fuel spillage. Before carrying out any operation on the fuel system, refer to the precautions given in "Safety first!" at the beginning of this manual, and follow them implicitly. Petrol is a highly-dangerous and volatile liquid, and the precautions necessary when handling it cannot be overstressed.*
Note: *Residual pressure will remain in the fuel lines long after the vehicle was last used; before disconnecting any fuel line, depressurise the fuel system.*

PART A: MOTRONIC SYSTEM - BX 19 TZI, GTI AND GTI 16 VALVE

Description
1   Three types of Motronic engine management systems have been fitted to the Citroën BX range, as follows.
Motronic ML4.1 - fitted to BX 19 GTi 16 valve until the 1991 model year.
Motronic M1.3 - fitted to BX 19 GTi 16 valve from the 1991 model year (supersedes Motronic ML4.1 system), and BX 19 TZi models equipped with a catalytic converter (note that catalyst-equipped models **must always** be operated on unleaded petrol).
Motronic MP3.1 - fitted to BX 19 GTi from July 1990 (supersedes Bosch LE3 Jetronic fuel injection system).
2   The Motronic system controls the functions of both the fuel injection and ignition systems, to provide fine control of the engine to suit the prevailing operating conditions.
3   The Motronic Electronic Control Unit (ECU) receives signals from various sensors, and computes the optimum volume of fuel to be injected, and the optimum ignition advance setting to suit the prevailing conditions.
4   In the event of the failure of a system component, the ECU has the capability to permit the engine to operate, albeit at reduced power and efficiency, until the fault can be investigated by a Citroën dealer or a suitably-qualified specialist who will have access to the necessary specialist test equipment.
5   The following sensors supply the ECU with information.
Airflow meter - measures the volume of air entering the engine.
Air temperature sensor - measures the temperature of the air entering the engine (integral with the airflow meter).
Throttle position switch - senses the position of the throttle valve.
Coolant temperature sensor.
TDC sensor - measures engine speed and crankshaft position.
Knock sensor (only fitted to BX 19 GTi 16 valve with Motronic M1.3 system) - senses the engine vibrations associated with pre-ignition ("pinking"), which may cause engine damage unless the ignition timing is retarded as a preventative measure.
Lambda (oxygen) sensor (only fitted to models equipped with Motronic M1.3 system and catalytic converter) - measures the oxygen content of the exhaust gases.

11A.6A Fuel pump location (GTi 16 valve with Motronic ML4.1)

11A.6B Idle actuator (arrowed) - GTi 16 valve with Motronic ML4.1

11A.6C Injector and fuel pump relays protected by plastic cover (GTi 16 valve with Motronic ML4.1)

6   Additionally, the Motronic systems comprise the following components (photos).

Air cleaner - located on the left-hand front wing valance, the air cleaner casing incorporates the airflow meter.

Fuel pump and filter - as described in Section 9 of this Supplement.

Fuel pulsation damper - located in the fuel line close to the filter, reduces fuel pump noise.

Fuel pressure regulator - located on the end of the fuel rail within the engine compartment, maintains a constant fuel pressure.

Fuel injectors - as described in Section 9 of this Supplement.

Idle actuator - (BX 19 GTi 16 valve with Motronic M1.3 system, and Motronic ML4.1 system) - controls the volume of air bypassing the throttle valve at idle, thus maintaining a suitable idle speed during warm-up, and a constant speed when the engine is warm.

Supplementary air device (models with Motronic M1.3 system and catalytic converter, and Motronic MP3.1 system) - provides supplementary air to the idling circuit as an aid to starting and warm-up.

Throttle butterfly housing - two throttle valves open simultaneously, and the housing is coolant-heated to improve fuel atomization.

Electronic control unit (ECU) - located under the driver's seat, the ECU controls the components of the system.

HT distributor (all except Motronic MP3.1 system) - the distributor simply distributes HT current to the spark plugs, and consists of a rotor arm on the end of the camshaft (inlet camshaft on 16 valve models) and a conventional distributor cap.

Ignition coil - for the Motronic ML4.1 and M1.3 systems, a conventional ignition coil is used, but it is triggered by signals from the ECU. The Motronic MP3.1 system uses a distributorless ignition system with a double coil which operates on the "wasted-spark" principle, supplying current directly to the spark plugs when triggered by signals from the ECU.

Relays - injector and fuel pump relays are fitted, and both are controlled by the ECU.

Idle mixture (CO) adjustment potentiometer - for the Motronic ML4.1 and M1.3 (non-catalyst) systems, the idle mixture adjustment potentiometer is incorporated in the airflow meter casing. The Motronic MP3.1 system uses a remotely-mounted potentiometer located in the engine compartment on the inner right-hand wing panel. Note that on models equipped with the M1.3 system and a catalytic converter, no adjustment of idle mixture is possible.

7   All the Motronic systems function in a similar manner, the differences between systems being of a minor nature, mainly associated with system sensors and the programming of the ECU.

Motronic systems - adjustments

Motronic ML4.1

8   The idle speed and the ignition timing are controlled by the ECU, and no adjustment is possible. To adjust the idle mixture, proceed as follows.

9   Run the engine until it reaches normal operating temperature (the cooling fan should have cut in and out), then stop the engine and connect an exhaust gas analyser in accordance with the equipment manu-

facturer's instructions.

10   Where applicable, remove the tamperproof cap from the mixture (CO) adjustment screw on the airflow meter (**Caution:** *Refer to Section 8, paragraphs 25 to 28*) (photo).

11   With the engine idling, turn the adjustment screw as necessary to obtain the specified CO content.

12   On completion, stop the engine, then disconnect the exhaust gas analyser, and where necessary, fit a new tamperproof cap to the mixture adjustment screw.

Motronic M1.3 without catalyst

13   On non-catalyst equipped models with Motronic M1.3, the idle speed and ignition timing are controlled by the ECU, and no adjustment is possible, but the idle mixture can be adjusted as described in the preceding paragraphs for the Motronic ML4.1 system.

Motronic M1.3 with catalyst

14   On models equipped with the Motronic M1.3 system and a catalytic converter, the idle mixture and the ignition timing are controlled by the ECU, and no adjustment is possible, but the idle speed can be adjusted as follows.

15   Run the engine until it reaches normal operating temperature (the cooling fan should have cut in and out), then stop the engine and connect a tachometer in accordance with the equipment manufacturer's instructions.

16   Clamp the fuel vapour recycling hose which connects to the inlet manifold.

17   Where applicable, remove the tamperproof cap from the idle speed adjustment screw on the throttle butterfly housing (**Caution:** *Refer to Section 8, paragraphs 25 to 28*).

18   With the engine idling, turn the adjustment screw to obtain the specified idle speed.

19   On completion, stop the engine, then disconnect the tachometer, and where necessary, fit a new tamperproof cap to the idle speed adjustment screw.

Motronic MP3.1

20   Both idle speed and mixture can be adjusted on the Motronic MP3.1 system, but the ignition timing is controlled by the ECU. Proceed as follows.

21   Run the engine until it reaches normal operating temperature (the cooling fan should have cut in and out), then stop the engine and connect a tachometer and an exhaust gas analyser in accordance with the equipment manufacturer's instructions.

22   Remove the tamperproof cap from the idle speed adjustment screw on the throttle butterfly housing (**Caution:** *Refer to Section 8, paragraphs 25 to 28*).

23   With the engine idling, turn the adjustment screw as necessary to obtain the specified idle speed.

24   Remove the tamperproof plug from the idle mixture adjustment potentiometer (located on the right-hand inner wing panel), again noting the caution referred to previously.

25   Turn the adjustment screw as necessary to obtain the specified CO reading.

26   If necessary readjust the idle speed, then recheck the CO reading.

11A.10 Idle mixture adjustment screw tamperproof cap (arrowed)

11A.33 Removing a fuel injector from the fuel rail

11A.36 ECU location (GTi 16 valve with Motronic ML4.1)

Fig. 13.45 Idle speed adjustment screw (arrowed) - models with Motronic M1.3 and catalyst (Sec 11A)

Fig. 13.46 Idle speed adjustment screw (1) - GTi with Motronic MP3.1 (Sec 11A)

Fig. 13.47 Idle mixture adjustment potentiometer location (2) - GTi with Motronic MP3.1 (Sec 11A)

27   If necessary, repeat the procedure given in paragraph 26 until the idle speed and CO values are as specified.

28   On completion, stop the engine, then disconnect the tachometer and exhaust gas analyser, and where necessary, fit new tamperproof caps to the idle speed adjustment screw and the idle mixture adjustment potentiometer.

Fuel system - depressurisation
29   Refer to the information given for the LE3 Jetronic fuel injection system in paragraphs 12 to 15 of Section 9 of this Chapter.

Motronic system components - removal and refitting
Note: *Little information was available regarding removal and refitting of the Motronic system components at the time of writing.*

Air cleaner element
30   To renew the air cleaner element, follow the procedure described in Section 9 of this Supplement.

Fuel pump and filter
31   Proceed as described in Section 9 of this Supplement.

Accelerator cable
32   Proceed as described in Section 9 of this Supplement, but note that there is no need to check the idle speed after refitting. Instead, check that the throttle butterfly is fully closed with the accelerator pedal in the rest position.

Fuel injectors
33   Proceed as described in Section 9 of this Supplement (photo).

Fuel tank and de-aeration reservoir
34   Where applicable, proceed as described in Section 9 of this Supplement.

Manifolds and exhaust system
35   Proceed as described in Section 9 of this Supplement, but note that on models fitted with a catalytic converter, it will be necessary to disconnect the wiring from the lambda sensor before removing the exhaust front section. It may also be necessary to remove the heat shield from the underbody area around the catalytic converter, to allow sufficient clearance to remove the exhaust system.

Electronic Control Unit (ECU)
36   The ECU is located under the driver's seat (photo).
37   To remove the unit, first disconnect the battery negative lead.
38   To gain access to the unit, unclip the front seat cushion from the seat frame, then release it from the upholstery retaining hooks and remove the seat cushion.
39   Unscrew the bolt securing the unit to its mounting bracket, then disconnect the ECU wiring plug and withdraw the unit.
40   Refitting is a reversal of removal.

HT distributor
41   Disconnect the battery negative lead, then disconnect the HT

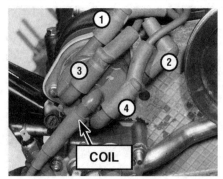

11A.41 Distributor cap and HT leads (GTi 16 valve with Motronic ML4.1)

11A.43 Removing a rotor arm securing screw (GTi 16 valve with Motronic ML4.1)

11A.44 Rotor drive flange (GTi 16 valve with Motronic ML4.1)

leads from the spark plugs (photo).

42 Loosen the securing screws, and withdraw the distributor cap complete with HT leads.

43 Where applicable, remove the three securing screws, then pull the rotor arm from the end of the camshaft (photo).

44 On BX 19 GTi 16 valve models, the rotor drive flange can be removed after removing the single Torx retaining screw, and the plastic baseplate can then be removed (photo).

45 Refitting is a reversal of removal, but where applicable on BX 19 GTi 16 valve models, clean the threads of the rotor drive flange retaining screw, and apply locking fluid before refitting. Note that the components will only fit in one position.

TDC sensor

46 The TDC sensor is mounted in the gearbox bellhousing.

47 Disconnect the wiring plug, then disconnect the wiring from the sensor.

48 Remove the sensor securing screw, and withdraw the sensor from the bellhousing. Where applicable, recover the shim which may be fitted between the sensor and the bellhousing.

49 Refitting is a reversal of removal, noting the following.

50 On BX 19 GTi 16 valve models, using a depth gauge, measure the distance between the sensor mounting face and the top of one of the teeth on the flywheel.

51 If the reading obtained is 25.0 mm, refit the sensor without a shim. If the reading is 24.1 mm, a suitable shim (available from Citroën dealers) must be fitted between the sensor and the bellhousing.

Airflow meter

52 The airflow meter is integral with the air cleaner casing.

53 To remove the assembly, disconnect the battery negative lead and the sensor wiring plug, then release the retaining clips and lift the assembly away from the air cleaner body.

54 Refitting is a reversal of removal.

Motronic systems - fault diagnosis

55 Complete and accurate fault diagnosis is only possible using special test equipment available to a Citroën dealer, and it is strongly recommended that any fault occurring with a Motronic system is referred to a suitably-equipped dealer.

56 Where a component is obviously defective, it can be removed and a new component fitted in its place.

57 Although certain electrical checks can be carried out to establish continuity or resistance, this is not recommended; the incorrect use of test probes between component connector pins can cause damage to the internal circuitry of some components.

Unleaded petrol - general information and usage

58 Pre-1991 GTi 16 valve models are suitable for running on 97 RON leaded petrol only, and cannot be run on unleaded petrol. All other models **not** equipped with a catalytic converter can be run on either 97 RON leaded fuel or 95 RON unleaded fuel without adjustment.

59 Models equipped with a catalytic converter **must** be run on 95 RON unleaded fuel **only**. The use of leaded fuel will seriously damage the catalytic converter (see below).

Catalytic converter - general information and precautions

60 The catalytic converter is a reliable and simple device, which needs no maintenance in itself, but there are some facts of which an owner should be aware if the converter is to function properly for its full service life.

(a) DO NOT use leaded petrol in a car equipped with a catalytic converter - the lead will coat the precious metals, reducing their converting efficiency, and will eventually destroy the converter.

(b) Always keep the ignition and fuel systems well-maintained, in accordance with the manufacturer's schedule - particularly, ensure that the air cleaner filter element, the fuel filter (where fitted) and the spark plugs are renewed at the correct interval - if the intake air/fuel mixture is allowed to become too rich due to neglect, the unburned surplus will enter and burn in the catalytic converter, overheating the element and eventually destroying the converter.

(c) If the engine develops a misfire, do not drive the car at all (or at least as little as possible) until the fault is cured - the misfire will allow unburned fuel to enter the converter, which will result in its overheating, as noted above.

(d) DO NOT push- or tow-start the car - this will soak the catalytic converter in unburned fuel, causing it to overheat when the engine does start - see (b) above.

(e) DO NOT switch off the ignition at high engine speeds - in particular, do not "blip" the throttle before switching off. If the ignition is switched off at anything above idle speed, unburned fuel will enter the (very hot) catalytic converter, with the possible risk of its igniting on the element and damaging the converter.

(f) DO NOT use fuel or engine oil additives - these may contain substances harmful to the catalytic converter.

(g) DO NOT continue to use the car if the engine burns oil to the extent of leaving a visible trail of blue smoke - the unburned carbon deposits will clog the converter passages and reduce its efficiency; in severe cases, the element will overheat.

(h) Remember that the catalytic converter operates at very high temperatures - hence the heat shields on the car's underbody - and the casing will become hot enough to ignite combustible materials which brush against it. DO NOT, therefore, park the car in dry undergrowth, or over long grass or piles of dead leaves.

(i) Remember that the catalytic converter is FRAGILE - do not strike it with tools during servicing work, and take great care when working on the exhaust system. Ensure that the converter is well clear of any jacks or other lifting gear used to raise the car, and do not drive the car over rough ground, road humps etc in such a way as to "ground" the exhaust system.

(j) In some cases, particularly when the car is new and/or is used for stop/start driving, a sulphurous smell (like that of rotten eggs) may be noticed from the exhaust. This is common to many catalytic converter-equipped cars, and seems to be due to the small amount of sulphur found in some petrols reacting with hydrogen in the exhaust to produce hydrogen sulphide

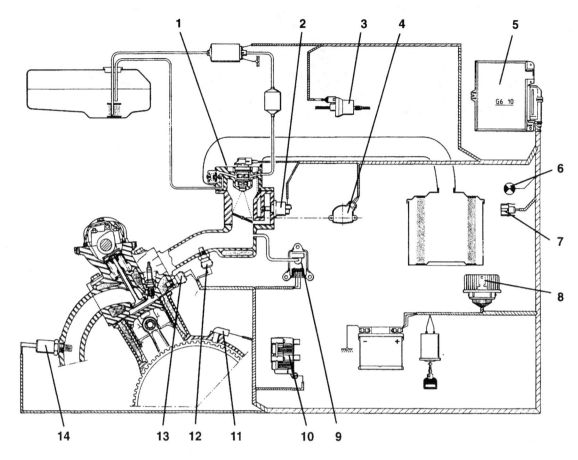

Fig. 13.48 Components of the Magneti Marelli engine management system (Sec 11B)

1 Throttle body injector housing	8 Relay unit
2 Idle speed stepper motor	9 Manifold absolute pressure (MAP) sensor
3 Charcoal canister purge valve	10 Ignition HT coil
4 Throttle potentiometer	11 Crankshaft sensor
5 ECU	12 Fuel/air mixture temperature sensor
6 Instrument panel warning light	13 Coolant temperature sensor
7 Diagnostic wiring connector	14 Lambda (oxygen) sensor

(H2S) gas; while this gas is toxic, it is not produced in sufficient amounts to be a problem. Once the car has covered a few thousand miles, the problem should disappear - in the meanwhile, a change of driving style or of the brand of petrol used may effect a solution.

(k) The catalytic converter, used on a well-maintained and well-driven car, should last for between 50 000 and 100 000 miles - from this point on, careful checks should be made at all specified service intervals of the CO level, to ensure that the converter is still operating efficiently - if the converter is no longer effective, it must be renewed.

PART B: MAGNETI MARELLI SYSTEM - FUEL-INJECTED BX 16 MODELS

Description

1   On fuel-injected BX 16 models, a fully-integrated Magneti Marelli G6.10 engine management system is used to control both the single-point fuel injection and ignition systems. The engine management system also incorporates a closed-loop catalytic converter and an evaporative emission control system, and complies to the very latest emission control standards. The system operates as follows.

2   The fuel pump, mounted on the rear of the subframe, pumps fuel from the fuel tank to the fuel injector, via a filter. Fuel supply pressure is controlled by the pressure regulator in the throttle body assembly,

which lifts to allow excess fuel to return to the tank when the optimum operating pressure of the fuel system is exceeded.

3   The electrical control system consists of the ECU, along with the following sensors.

(a) Manifold absolute pressure (MAP) sensor - informs the ECU of load on engine.

(b) Crankshaft sensor - informs the ECU of crankshaft position and engine speed.

(c) Throttle potentiometer - informs the ECU of the throttle valve position and the rate of throttle opening/closing.

(d) Coolant temperature sensor - informs the ECU of engine temperature.

(e) Fuel/air mixture temperature sensor - informs the ECU of the temperature of the fuel/air mixture charge entering the cylinders.

(f) Lambda (oxygen) sensor - informs the ECU of the oxygen content of the exhaust gases (explained in greater detail later in this Section).

In addition, the ECU senses battery voltage (adjusting the injector pulse width to suit, and using the stepper motor to increase the idle speed and, therefore, the alternator output if the voltage is too low). Short-circuit protection and diagnostic capabilities are incorporated. The ECU can both receive and transmit information via the engine management circuit diagnostic connector, thus permitting engine diagnosis and tuning by special diagnostic equipment.

11B.10 Magneti Marelli engine management system diagnostic connector

11B.14A Release the retaining clips . . .

11B.14B . . . then lift up the lid and withdraw the air cleaner element

4   All the above signals are compared by the ECU, using digital techniques, with set values pre-programmed (mapped) into its memory. Based on this information, the ECU selects the response appropriate to those values, and controls the ignition HT coil (varying the ignition timing as required), and the fuel injector (varying its pulse width - the length of time the injector is held open - to provide a richer or weaker mixture, as appropriate). The mixture, idle speed and ignition timing are constantly varied by the ECU, to provide the best settings for cranking, starting and engine warm-up (with either a hot or cold engine), idle, cruising and acceleration.

5   The ECU also regulates the engine idle speed, via a stepper motor which is fitted to the throttle body. The motor has a pushrod which controls the opening of an air passage which bypasses the throttle valve. When the throttle valve is closed, the ECU controls the movement of the motor pushrod, which in turn regulates the amount of air which flows through the throttle body, and so controls the idle speed. The bypass passage is also used as an additional air supply during cold starting. **Note:** *There is no provision for the adjustment or alteration of the idle speed, except by reprogramming the ECU using special diagnostic equipment; if checking the idle speed, remember that it will vary constantly under ECU control.*

6   On the ignition side of the engine management system, the ECU also has full control. The ignition system is of the static, distributorless type, and consists solely of an ignition HT coil with four outputs. The ignition coil actually consists of two separate HT coils which supply two cylinders each (one coil supplies cylinders 1 and 4, and the other cylinders 2 and 3). Under control of the ECU, the ignition coil operates on the "wasted-spark" principle, ie. each spark plug sparks twice for every cycle of the engine, once on the compression stroke and once on the exhaust stroke. The ECU uses its inputs from the various sensors to calculate the required ignition advance setting and coil charging time.

7   The ECU also controls the exhaust and evaporative emission control systems, which are described in detail later in this Section.

8   If there is an abnormality in any of the readings obtained from any of engine management circuit sensors, the ECU has a back-up facility; it ignores any abnormal sensor signals, and assumes a pre-programmed value which will allow the engine to continue running at reduced efficiency. On entering the back-up facility, the ECU will illuminate the engine management warning light in the instrument panel, informing the driver of the fault, and stores the relevant fault code in the ECU memory. If the warning light is illuminated, the vehicle should be taken to a Citroën dealer at the earliest opportunity. There, a complete test of the engine management system can be carried out, using a special electronic diagnostic test unit which is simply plugged into the system's diagnostic connector. This process allows the fault to be quickly traced and rectified, alleviating the need to test the system components individually.

Magneti Marelli system - testing

9   If a fault appears in the engine management (ignition/fuel injection) system, first ensure that all the system wiring connectors are securely connected and free of corrosion. Then ensure that the fault is not due to poor maintenance; ie. check that the air cleaner filter ele-

ment is clean, the spark plugs are in good condition and correctly gapped, that the valve clearances are correctly adjusted, and that the engine breather hoses are clear and undamaged, referring to Chapters 1 and 4 for further information.

10   If these checks fail to reveal the cause of the problem, the vehicle should be taken to a suitably-equipped Citroën dealer for testing. A wiring block connector is incorporated in the engine management circuit, into which a special electronic diagnostic tester can be plugged (photo). The tester will locate the fault quickly and simply, alleviating the need to test all the system components individually, which is a time-consuming operation that carries a high risk of damaging the ECU.

Magneti Marelli system - adjustments

11   As mentioned above, the idle speed, mixture adjustment and ignition timing are all monitored and controlled by the ECU, and do not normally require adjustment. While experienced home mechanics with a considerable amount of skill and equipment (including a good-quality tachometer and a good-quality, carefully-calibrated exhaust gas analyser) may be able to check the exhaust CO level and the idle speed, if these are found to be in need of adjustment, the car **must** be taken to a suitably-equipped Citroën dealer. Adjustments can be made only by re-programming the ECU, using special diagnostic equipment connected to the system via the diagnostic connector.

Fuel system - depressurisation

12   Refer to the information given for the LE3 Jetronic fuel injection system in paragraphs 12 to 15 of Section 9 of this Chapter.

Magneti Marelli system components - removal and refitting

Air cleaner element

13   The air cleaner housing is situated in the left-hand front corner of the engine compartment.

14   To remove the filter element, release the five housing lid retaining clips, then lift the lid until there is sufficient clearance to withdraw the element from the air cleaner housing (photo).

15   On refitting, ensure the new element is correctly seated in the housing, then refit the lid and secure it in position with the retaining clips.

Fuel pump and filter

16   Refer to the information given in Section 9 of this Chapter (photo).

Accelerator cable

17   Proceed as described in Section 9 of this Supplement, but note that there is no need to check the idle speed after refitting. Adjust the cable until there is only a small amount of freeplay present at the throttle body end of the cable.

Throttle body assembly

Note: *Refer to the warning note at the start of this Section before proceeding.*

18   Undo the two nuts securing the intake trunking to the throttle body, and position the trunking clear of the body along with its rubber sealing ring (photos).

19   Depress the retaining tabs and disconnect the wiring connectors

11B.16 Fuel pump and filter (plastic cover unclipped for clarity)

11B.18A Undo the two nuts . . .

11B.18B . . . then disconnect the intake trunking and remove the rubber sealing ring

11B.19A Disconnect the wiring connectors from the throttle potentiometer . . .

11B.19B . . . the idle control stepper motor . . .

11B.19C . . . and the injector wiring loom

from the throttle potentiometer, the stepper motor, and the injector wiring loom connector which is situated on the front of the throttle body (photos).

20   Bearing in mind the information given earlier in this Section about depressurising the fuel system, release the retaining clips and disconnect the fuel feed and return hoses from the throttle body assembly (photo).

21   Disconnect the accelerator inner cable from the throttle cam, then free the outer cable from its retaining bracket and position it clear of the throttle body (photo).

22   Disconnect the purge valve hose from the front of the throttle body assembly, and the breather hose from the rear of the throttle body.

23   Working quickly to minimise coolant loss, disconnect the two coolant hoses from the rear of the throttle body assembly, and plug the hose ends with a suitable bolt or screw.

24   Undo the two retaining bolts, and remove the throttle body assembly from the manifold along with its sealing gasket (photo).

25   If necessary, with the throttle body removed, undo the two retaining screws and separate the upper and lower sections, noting the gasket which is fitted between the two.

26   Refitting is a reverse of the removal procedure, bearing in mind the following points.

(a) Where necessary, ensure the mating surfaces of the upper and lower throttle body sections are clean and dry, then fit a new gasket and reassemble the two, tightening the retaining screws securely.

(b) Ensure the mating surfaces of the manifold and throttle body are clean and dry, then fit a new gasket. Securely tighten the throttle body retaining bolts.

(c) Ensure all hoses are correctly reconnected and, where necessary, that their retaining clips are securely tightened.

(d) Adjust the accelerator cable so that only a small amount of freeplay is present at the throttle body end of the cable.

(e) If necessary, top-up the cooling system as described in Section 7 or Chapter 2.

Fuel injector

Note: Refer to the warning note at the start of this Section before pro-

ceeding. If a faulty injector is suspected, before condemning the injector, it is worth trying the effect of one of the proprietary injector-cleaning treatments, such as Holt's Redex Injector Treatment. If this fails, the vehicle should be taken to a Citroën dealer for testing using the appropriate specialist equipment. At the time of writing, it appears that the fuel injector is not available separately and, if faulty, the complete upper throttle body assembly must be renewed.

27   Undo the two nuts securing the intake trunking to the throttle body, and position the trunking clear of the body along with its rubber sealing ring.

28   Release the retaining tangs and disconnect the injector wiring connector (photo).

29   Undo the retaining screw, then remove the retaining clip and lift the injector out of the housing, noting its sealing ring. As the screw is slackened, place a rag over the injector to catch any fuel spray which may be released.

30   Refitting is a reverse of the removal procedure, ensuring that the injector sealing ring is in good condition.

Fuel pressure regulator

Note: Refer to the warning note at the start of this Section before proceeding. At the time of writing, it appears that the fuel pressure regulator is not available separately. If the fuel pressure regulator assembly is faulty, the complete upper throttle body assembly must be renewed; refer to a Citroën dealer for further information. Although the unit can be dismantled for cleaning if required, it should not be disturbed unless absolutely necessary.

31   Undo the two nuts securing the intake trunking to the throttle body, and position the trunking clear of the body along with its rubber sealing ring.

32   Using a suitable marker pen, make alignment marks between the regulator cover and throttle body, then undo the four retaining screws (photo). As the screws are slackened, place a rag over the cover to catch any fuel spray which may be released.

33   Lift off the cover, then remove the spring and withdraw the diaphragm, noting its correct fitted orientation. Remove all traces of dirt, and examine the diaphragm for signs of splitting. If damage is found, it will be necessary to renew the complete upper throttle body assembly as described earlier in this Section.

11B.20 Slacken the throttle body fuel feed hose retaining clip

11B.21 Disconnecting the accelerator inner cable from the throttle cam

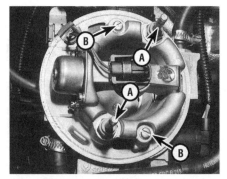

11B.24 Throttle body retaining bolts (A) and housing retaining screws (B)

11B.28 Disconnecting the injector wiring connector - injector retaining screw arrowed

11B.32 Fuel pressure regulator retaining screws (arrowed)

11B.35 Idle control stepper motor location

11B.38 Throttle potentiometer retaining screws (arrowed)

11B.40 Fuel/air mixture temperature sensor location

11B.45A Slacken and remove the three retaining nuts and bolts . . .

34   Refitting is a reverse of the removal procedure, ensuring that the diaphragm and cover are fitted the correct way around and the retaining screws are securely tightened.

Idle control stepper motor
Note: *If a faulty stepper motor is suspected, the vehicle should be taken to a Citroën dealer for testing using the appropriate specialist equipment. At the time of writing, it appears that the stepper motor is not available separately and, if faulty, the complete lower throttle body assembly must be renewed as described earlier in this Section.*

35   To remove the stepper motor, depress the retaining tabs and disconnect the wiring connector. Undo the two retaining screws, and withdraw the motor from the rear of the throttle body assembly (photo).
36   Refitting is a reverse of removal.

Throttle potentiometer
37   Disconnect the battery negative terminal, then depress the retaining tabs and disconnect the wiring connector from the throttle potentiometer.
38   Undo the two retaining screws, and remove the throttle potentiometer from the right-hand side of the throttle body assembly (photo).
39   Refitting is a reversal of the removal procedure, ensuring that the throttle potentiometer tang is correctly engaged with the throttle spindle.

Fuel/air mixture temperature sensor
40   The fuel/air mixture temperature sensor is screwed into the right-hand side of the inlet manifold, and is removed as follows (photo).
41   Disconnect the battery negative terminal.
42   Disconnect the wiring connector, then unscrew the fuel/air mixture temperature sensor from the inlet manifold.
43   Refitting is a reverse of the removal procedure, ensuring the switch is securely tightened.

Manifold absolute pressure (MAP) sensor
44   The MAP sensor is mounted onto a bracket which is situated just behind the alternator. To remove the sensor, first disconnect the battery negative terminal.
45   Slacken and remove the three retaining nuts and bolts, then free the MAP sensor from the bracket. Disconnect the wiring connector and vacuum hose, and remove the sensor from the engine compartment (photos).
46   Refitting is a reverse of the removal procedure.

Coolant temperature sensor
47   The coolant temperature sensor is located on the left-hand end of the rear face of the cylinder head, and access to the sender is strictly limited. Either drain the cooling system, or be prepared for some coolant loss as the sensor is removed.

11B.45B . . . then free the MAP sensor from the bracket, and disconnect the vacuum hose and wiring connector

11B.53 Crankshaft sensor wiring connector situated behind the ignition coil

11B.54 Crankshaft sensor location (retaining screw arrowed)

11B.56 ECU is located under the driver's seat

11B.59 Disconnect the ignition HT coil wiring connector

11B.60 Disconnect the HT leads, noting the cylinder number markings on the HT leads and coil (arrowed)

48   To improve access to the sensor, remove the coil as described later in this Section.

49   Disconnect the wiring connector from the coolant temperature sensor.

50   Unscrew the sensor, then remove it from the cylinder head and plug the sensor aperture to prevent the entry of dirt; if the cooling system has not been drained, work quickly to minimise coolant loss.

51   Refitting is a reverse of removal, noting that if a sealing washer is fitted, renew it. If no sealing washer is fitted, apply a smear of sealant to the sensor threads to prevent leakage.

Crankshaft sensor

52   The crankshaft sensor is fitted to the top of the transmission housing, beside the left-hand end of the cylinder block. To remove the sensor, first disconnect the battery negative terminal.

53   Trace the wiring back from the sensor to its wiring connector, then depress the retaining tabs and disconnect it from the main wiring harness (photo).

54   Undo the bolt securing the sensor to the transmission housing, and remove the sensor from the vehicle (photo).

55   Refitting is a reverse of removal.

Electronic Control Unit (ECU)

56   Refer to the information given for the Motronic system in Part A of this Section (photo).

Ignition coil

57   The ignition coil is mounted onto the left-hand end of the cylinder head, and can be removed as follows.

58   Disconnect the battery negative terminal.

59   Disconnect the wiring connector from the base of the coil (photo).

60   Make a note of the correct fitted positions of the HT leads, then disconnect them from the coil terminals. Note that on genuine Citroën leads, each HT lead is marked with its cylinder number, indicated by red blocks printed near the end of the lead; the coil terminals are also numbered for identification (photo).

61   Undo the four Torx retaining screws, and remove the coil from the end of the cylinder head.

62   Refitting is a reverse of the removal procedure, ensuring the HT leads are correctly reconnected.

Engine management system relay assembly

63   The engine management relay assembly is situated in the engine compartment, mounted onto the right-hand wing valance (photo).

64   To remove the relay, first disconnect the battery negative terminal.

65   Disconnect the wiring connector, then undo the retaining screw and remove the relay assembly from the engine compartment.

66   Refitting is a reverse of removal.

Fuel tank and de-aeration reservoir

67   Refer to the information given in Section 9 of this Chapter.

Inlet manifold

68   Remove the throttle body assembly as described earlier in this Section.

69   Drain the cooling system as described in Section 7 or Chapter 2.

70   Disconnect the wiring connector from the fuel/air mixture temperature sensor, located on the right-hand side of the manifold.

71   Undo the nut securing the oil filler cap/breather to the side of the manifold, then release the assembly from its retaining stud and position it clear of the manifold (photo).

72   Undo the bolt securing the wiring/hose support bracket to the top of the manifold, and position the bracket clear of the manifold.

73   Disconnect the coolant hose and the MAP sensor vacuum hose from the front of the manifold (photo).

74   Undo the six manifold retaining nuts, and remove the manifold from the engine unit. Remove the gasket and discard it; a new one should be used on refitting.

75   Refitting is a reverse of the removal procedure, noting the following points:

(a) Ensure that the manifold and cylinder head mating surfaces are clean and dry, and fit a new manifold gasket. Refit the manifold and securely tighten its retaining nuts.

(b) Ensure all relevant hoses are reconnected to their original positions, and are securely held (where necessary) by the retaining clips.

11B.63 Engine management relay assembly location

11B.71 Oil filler/breather cap retaining nut (arrowed)

11B.73 Slackening the coolant hose retaining clip from the front of the inlet manifold - note MAP sensor hose (arrowed)

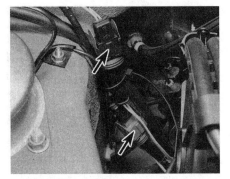

11B.80 Lambda sensor wiring connectors (arrowed) are situated in the right-hand corner of the engine compartment

11B.82 Lambda sensor location

11B.96 Disconnecting the purge valve wiring connector

(c) *Refit the throttle body assembly as described earlier in this Section.*

(d) *On completion, refill the cooling system as described in Section 7 or Chapter 2.*

Exhaust system and manifold

76 Refer to the information given for the Motronic system in Part A of this Section.

Exhaust emission control system - general information and component renewal

General information

77 To minimise the amount of pollutants which escape into the atmosphere, these models are fitted with a catalytic converter in the exhaust system. The system is a "closed-loop" system; the lambda sensor in the exhaust system provides the engine management system ECU with constant feedback (which enables it to adjust the mixture, to provide the best possible conditions for the converter to operate).

78 The lambda sensor has a built-in heating element, controlled by the ECU through the relay assembly to quickly bring the sensor's tip to an efficient operating temperature. The sensor's tip is sensitive to oxygen, and sends the ECU a varying voltage depending on the amount of oxygen in the exhaust gases. If the intake air/fuel mixture is too rich, the exhaust gases are low in oxygen, so the sensor sends a low-voltage signal; the voltage rises as the mixture weakens and the amount of oxygen in the exhaust gases rises. Peak conversion efficiency of all major pollutants occurs if the intake air/fuel mixture is maintained at the chemically-correct ratio for the complete combustion of petrol of 14.7 parts (by weight) of air to 1 part of fuel (the "stoichiometric" ratio). The sensor output voltage alters in a large step at this point, the ECU using the signal change as a reference point, and correcting the intake air/fuel mixture accordingly by altering the fuel injector pulse width.

79 Regular checks of the lambda sensor's operation should be performed. This can be done only by attaching Citroën diagnostic equipment to the sensor wiring, and checking that the voltage varies from low to high values when the engine is running. **Do not** attempt to "test"

any part of the system with anything other than the correct test equipment.

Lambda sensor - removal and refitting

Note: *The lambda sensor is delicate, and will not work if it is dropped or knocked, if its power supply is disrupted, or if any cleaning materials are used on it.*

80 Open up the bonnet and locate the lambda sensor wiring connectors, which are clipped to the right-hand end of the engine compartment bulkhead (photo). Disconnect the battery negative terminal, then disconnect both the wiring connectors and free the wiring harness from any relevant retaining clips.

81 Chock the rear wheels, then jack up the front of the car and support it on axle stands.

82 Free the lower end of the lambda sensor wiring from any relevant retaining clips, then unscrew the sensor from the front pipe and remove it along with its sealing washer (photo).

83 Prior to refitting, examine the sealing washer for signs of damage, and renew as necessary.

84 Ensure the sensor and manifold threads are clean, then apply a smear of high-temperature anti-seize compound to the sensor's threads.

85 Fit the sealing washer to the sensor, then refit the sensor to the front pipe and tighten it securely.

86 Ensure the sensor wiring is correctly routed up the bulkhead, and secure the wiring in position with any relevant clips or ties.

87 Return to the engine compartment, then reconnect the sensor wiring connectors and secure the wiring to the bulkhead with any remaining clips or ties. Reconnect the battery, and lower the vehicle to the ground.

Evaporative emission control system - general information and component renewal

General information

88 To minimise the escape of unburned hydrocarbons into the atmosphere, an evaporative emissions control system is incorporated in the

Magneti Marelli engine management system. The fuel tank filler cap is sealed, and a charcoal canister is mounted underneath the right-hand wing to collect the petrol vapours generated in the tank when the car is parked. It stores them until they can be cleared from the canister (under the control of the engine management system ECU, via the purge control valve) into the inlet tract, to be burned by the engine during normal combustion.

89   To ensure that the engine runs correctly when it is cold and/or idling, and to protect the catalytic converter from the effects of an over-rich mixture, the purge control valve is not opened by the ECU until the engine has warmed up. The valve solenoid is then modulated on and off, to allow the stored vapour to pass into the inlet tract.

90   If the system is thought to be faulty, disconnect the hoses from the charcoal canister and purge control valve, and check that they are clear by blowing through them. If the purge control valve or charcoal canister are thought to be faulty, they must be renewed.

Charcoal canister - removal and refitting
91   Disconnect the battery negative terminal.
92   Chock the rear wheels, then jack up the front of the vehicle and support it on axle stands. Remove the right-hand front roadwheel.
93   Release the retaining clip(s) and disconnect the hoses from the canister.
94   Undo the retaining screw(s) and/or release the retaining clips (as applicable), then free the canister assembly from its retaining bracket and remove it from underneath the wheel arch.
95   Refitting is a reverse of the removal procedure, ensuring the hoses are correctly routed and securely reconnected.

Purge valve - removal and refitting
96   Disconnect the battery negative terminal, then disconnect the wiring connector from the purge valve, situated just behind the alternator (photo).
97   Disconnect the inlet and outlet hoses, then remove the valve from the engine compartment.
98   Refitting is a reverse of the removal procedure, ensuring the inlet and outlet hoses are securely reconnected.

Unleaded petrol - general information and usage
99   As with all models equipped with a catalytic converter, these models **must** be run on 95 RON unleaded fuel **only**. The use of leaded fuel will seriously damage the catalytic converter.

Catalytic converter - general information and precautions
100 Refer to the information given in Part A of this Section for the Motronic system.

12   Clutch

Clutch release mechanism (BX 19 GTi 16 valve, and all models with BE3/5 gearbox) - removal and refitting
1   On BX 19 GTi 16 valve models, the mechanism consists of a release fork supported on a pivot shaft instead of on a ball stud as on other models in the BX range. Certain models with the BE3/5 gearbox may be fitted with a similar arrangement.
2   To gain access to the release components, the gearbox (or the engine and the gearbox) must be removed from the vehicle. If the latter method is used, separate the engine from the gearbox after they are removed.
3   Pull the clutch release bearing from the guide sleeve, and (where applicable) release the spring clips from the fork ends.
4   Using a suitable punch, drive out the roll pin securing the release lever to the pivot shaft, then withdraw the release lever, noting its orientation.
5   Prise the upper pivot shaft bush from the bellhousing.
6   Lift the lower end of the release lever pivot shaft from the lower bush in the bellhousing, then lower the pivot shaft into the bellhousing, and manipulate it as necessary to enable removal.
7   If desired, the lower pivot bush can be prised from the bellhousing.

Fig. 13.49 Clutch release mechanism - BX 19 GTi 16 valve (Sec 12)

8   Reassembly is a reversal of dismantling, but ensure that the pivot bushes are correctly located in the bellhousing, and ensure that the release lever is correctly orientated as noted before removal.
9   Note that there have been some reported cases of the release lever breaking away from its pivot shaft. To resolve this problem, new release lever assemblies are reinforced by fitting a 5 mm thick washer onto the top of the release lever and welding it to the lever and pivot shaft. Refer to your Citroën dealer for further information.

13   Transmission

Transmission oil level (BX 16 and BX 19)
1   From October 1986, a filler/level plug is fitted in the transmission end cover. The oil level can be checked and if necessary topped-up at routine service intervals; the oil level should be up to the lower edge of the hole.
2   Routine oil changes are not specified for BX or BX 14 models, only for BX 16 and BX 19.

Gearbox bellhousing (BX 19 GTi 16 valve) - modifications
3   From approximately June 1988, the gearbox bellhousing was modified to allow for the fitting of a modified flywheel and TDC sensor.
4   An early-type bellhousing cannot be used with a new-type flywheel, although the new-type bellhousing (the early type is no longer available) can be fitted to a vehicle with the early flywheel.
5   Refer to Section 11 when removing and refitting the TDC sensor from the bellhousing.

Type 2CA transmission (BX 14 models from August 1988) - description
6   The 2CA gearbox is mounted on the left-hand side of the engine, and may be removed separately, leaving the engine in the car. It has either four or five forward gears depending on the model (all with synchromesh), and one reverse gear. All the synchromesh units are located on the output shaft, and the differential unit is located in the main gearbox casing.

Type 2CA transmission - removal and refitting
7   The transmission may be removed independently, or together with the engine.
8   The operations for removal and refitting are essentially as described in Chapter 6, except for minor differences in mounting, and gearchange linkage design (see Section 5B of this Supplement).

384

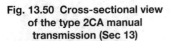

Fig. 13.50 Cross-sectional view of the type 2CA manual transmission (Sec 13)

1 Gearbox housing
2 Intermediate plate
3 Clutch and final drive housing
4 Clutch fork (on shaft)
5 Release bearing
6 Release bearing guide sleeve
7 Input shaft
8 Output shaft
9 1st speed driven gear
10 1st/2nd speed synchro (and reverse driven gear)
11 2nd speed driven gear
12 3rd speed driven gear
13 3rd/4th speed synchro
14 4th speed driven gear
15 5th speed drive gear
16 5th speed driven gear
17 5th speed synchro
18 Differential housing
19 Differential pinions
20 Differential gears
21 Speedometer drive worm
22 Speedometer drive pinion
Inset shows 4-speed gearbox

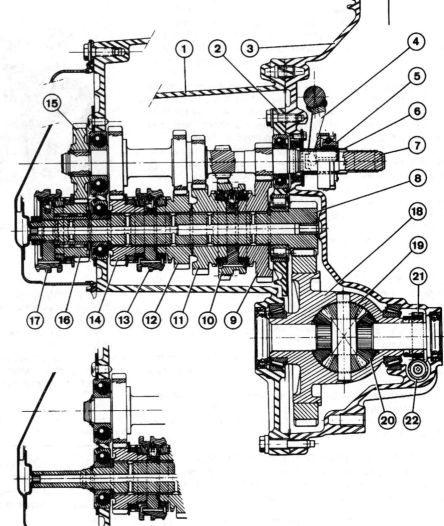

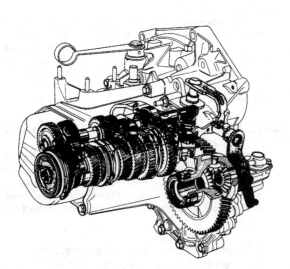

Fig. 13.51 Internal components of the type 2CA manual transmission (Sec 13)

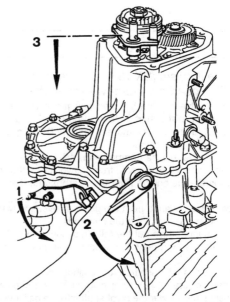

Fig. 13.52 Sequence to select reverse and 5th speed gears - type 2CA transmission (Sec 13)

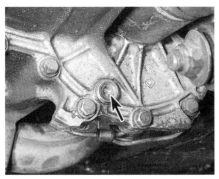

13.9A Transmission oil drain plug (arrowed)

13.9B Transmission oil filler/level plug

13.10 Removing the clutch release bearing

13.12A Unscrewing the speedometer drive pinion locking bolt

13.12B Removing the speedometer drive pinion

13.13A Remove the securing bolt . . .

13.13B . . . and withdraw the pressed-steel housing

13.16A Removing the output shaft nut . . .

13.16B . . . and the lockwasher

13.17 Removing the 5th synchro unit and selector fork

Type 2CA transmission - dismantling into major assemblies

9   With the unit removed from the car, clean all exterior surfaces and wipe dry. If not already done, drain the oil (photos).

10   Pull the clutch release bearing from the guide sleeve, and release the spring clips from the fork ends (photo).

11   Position the gearbox with the clutch end downwards.

12   Unbolt and remove the speedometer drive pinion (photos).

13   Unbolt the pressed-steel housing. Remove the rubber gasket (photos).

5-speed gearbox only

14   Drive the pin from the 5th speed selector fork.

15   Engage both reverse and 5th gears with reference to Fig. 13.52, then loosen the nut on the end of the output shaft. Return the gears to neutral.

16   Remove the nut and lockwasher (photos).

17   Remove the 5th synchro unit together with its selector fork, making sure that the sleeve remains central on the hub, to avoid loss of the internal balls and springs (photo).

13.18A Removing the 5th synchro ring . . .

13.18B . . . 5th speed driven gear . . .

13.18C . . . needle bearing . . .

13.18D . . . sleeve . . .

13.18E . . . and thrustwasher

13.19 Removing the special washer from the input shaft

13.20 Removing the 5th speed drive gear

13.21A Unscrewing a bearing half-ring Torx screw

13.21B Removing the bearing half-rings

13.22 Unscrewing a gearbox housing securing bolt

13.23 Lifting the gearbox housing from the clutch/final drive housing

13.24A Removing the plastic ring . . .

18   Remove the output shaft, the 5th synchro ring, followed by the 5th speed driven gear, needle bearing, sleeve, and thrustwasher (photos).

19   Extract the circlip from the end of the input shaft, followed by the special washer, noting that the convex side is uppermost (photo).

20   Using a suitable puller if necessary, pull the 5th speed drive gear from the splines on the input shaft (photo).

4- and 5-speed gearboxes

21   Unscrew the Torx screws and extract the half-rings from the grooves in the shaft bearings, noting their locations (photos).

13.24B . . . the reverse idler gear shaft . . .

13.24C . . . and reverse idler gear

13.25A Removing the reverse selector shaft . . .

13.25B . . . and selector arm

13.28 Removing the selector shaft

13.29 Removing the neutral return spring and plastic cups

13.30A Interlocking key and selector finger assembly

13.30B Interlocking key and selector finger separated

13.32 Lifting the geartrains and the selector fork shafts from the clutch/final drive housing

22   Unscrew the bolts securing the gearbox housing to the clutch/final drive housing, noting the location of the bolts (photo).

23   Lift the gearbox housing from the clutch/final drive housing (photo), at the same time guiding the selector fork shafts through the housing. Do not prise the housings apart with a screwdriver - use a wooden or hide mallet to release them from the sealant.

24   Remove the plastic ring from the reverse idler shaft, then remove the shaft from the clutch/final drive housing and remove the idler gear (photos).

25   Press down on the reverse selector arm directly over the shaft, and at the same time extract the shaft from the intermediate plate. Remove the reverse selector arm (photos).

26   Lift the gate lever to the 1st/2nd position, and support with a block of wood.

27   Using a suitable pin punch, drive out the pin securing the selector finger to the selector shaft. Recover the pin, and return the gate lever to neutral.

28   Pull out the selector shaft, and remove the rubber boot from it (photo).

29   Prise out the neutral return spring, together with the two plastic cups (photo).

30   Lift the gate lever, and at the same time remove the interlocking keys and selector finger (photos).

31   Tie the two selector fork shafts together as an aid to reassembly.

32   Using both hands, lift the input and output shafts, together with the selector fork shafts, directly from the clutch/final drive housing (photo). Separate the input shaft from the output shaft, and disengage the selector forks from the synchro units on the output shaft.

33   Unscrew the bolts and remove the intermediate plate from the clutch/final drive housing (photo). Adhesive is used on assembly, so some difficulty may be experienced; do not, however, lever directly on the mating faces.

34   Remove the reverse locking plunger and spring, using a magnet if available (photos).

35   Lift out the differential unit (photo).

36   The gearbox is now dismantled into its major assemblies.

Type 2CA transmission - examination and renovation

37   Clean all components, and examine them thoroughly for wear and damage. Circlips, locking pins, gaskets and oil seals should all be renewed as a matter of course. Read through the reassembly sub-Section, and obtain the necessary adhesive and sealants required.

13.33 Removing the intermediate plate

13.34A Removing the reverse locking plunger . . .

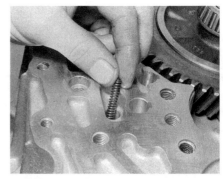

13.34B . . . and spring

13.35 Removing the differential unit

13.38 Removing the gate lever

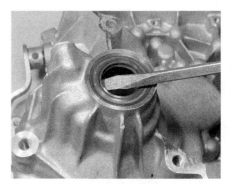

13.40A Prising out a driveshaft oil seal

13.40B Prising out an input shaft oil seal

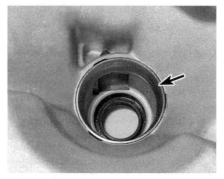

13.42 Right-hand final drive bearing outer track (arrowed)

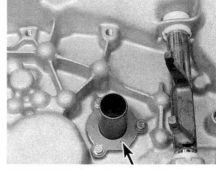

13.43 Clutch release bearing guide sleeve (arrowed)

Clutch/final drive housing (type 2CA transmission) - overhaul

38   Using a suitable punch, drive out the locking pin and remove the gate lever from the shaft (photo).
39   Withdraw the shaft, and prise the oil seal from the housing.
40   Prise out the driveshaft and input shaft oil seals (photos).
41   If necessary, drive out the location dowels.
42   If necessary, drive out the right-hand final drive bearing outer track, using a punch through the cut-outs provided (photo).
43   Unbolt the clutch release bearing guide sleeve (photo).
44   Clean all the components.
45   Commence reassembly by refitting the clutch release bearing guide sleeve, together with a new input shaft seal. Apply locking compound to the threads, then insert and tighten the bolts. Smear a little oil on the seal.
46   Using a metal tube, drive the right-hand final drive bearing outer track fully into the housing.
47   Drive in the location dowels.
48   Oil the new driveshaft oil seal, and drive it into the housing using a block of wood.
49   Oil the new gate lever shaft oil seal, and drive it into the housing.

Oil the shaft and refit it.
50   Locate the gate lever on the shaft towards the final drive, align the holes, and drive in the new locking pin.

Transmission housing (type 2CA transmission) - overhaul

51   Prise out the driveshaft oil seal.
52   If necessary, drive out the left-hand final drive bearing outer track, using a punch through the cut-outs provided (photo).
53   Using a metal tube, drive the new outer track fully into the housing.
54   Oil the new driveshaft oil seal, and drive it into the housing using a block of wood.

Input shaft (type 2CA transmission) - dismantling and reassembly

55   On the 4-speed gearbox, extract the circlip with circlip pliers, and remove the washer.
56   On 4- and 5-speed gearboxes, pull the bearing from the 4th speed end of the input shaft using a suitable puller. Similarly pull the bearing from the 1st speed end. Note that the re-use of removed bearings is not recommended.

13.52 Left-hand final drive bearing outer track (arrowed)

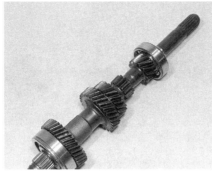

13.57 Input shaft and bearings assembled

13.60 Output shaft bearing (arrowed)

13.61A Removing the thrustwasher . . .

13.61B . . . 4th gear . . .

13.61C . . . 4th synchro ring . . .

13.61D . . . 3rd/4th synchro unit . . .

13.61E . . . and the 3rd synchro ring

13.62 Removing the C-clip . . .

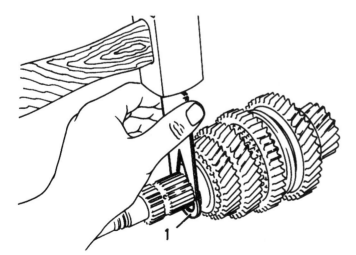

Fig. 13.53 Using a forked tool to remove the C-clip (1) from the output shaft (Sec 13)

57   To reassemble, drive the bearing on the 1st speed end of the shaft, using a length of metal tube on the inner track. Similarly drive the bearing on the 4th speed end, but note that the groove in the outer track must be towards the end of the shaft (photo).

58   Locate the washer over the end of the shaft on the 4-speed gearbox. Rest the circlip on the tapered end of the shaft, and use a socket to drive it into the groove. Check that the circlip is seated correctly by squeezing it with pliers.

Output shaft (type 2CA transmission) - dismantling and reassembly

59   On the 4-speed gearbox, extract the circlip with circlip pliers, and remove the washer.

60   On 4- and 5-speed gearboxes, pull the bearing from the shaft using a suitable puller if necessary (photo).

61   Remove the thrustwasher, followed by 4th gear, the 4th synchro ring, the 3rd/4th synchro unit, and the 3rd synchro ring (photos). Keep the synchro unit sleeve central on the hub.

62   Tap out the C-clip using a screwdriver, or a forked tool made with reference to Fig. 13.53 (photo).

63   Remove the 3rd gear, the C-clip, the 2nd gear, 2nd synchro ring,

13.63A . . . 3rd gear . . .

13.63B . . . C-clip . . .

13.63C . . . 2nd gear . . .

13.63D . . . 2nd synchro ring . . .

13.63E . . . 1st/2nd synchro unit . . .

13.63F . . . 1st synchro ring . . .

13.63G . . . C-clip . . .

13.63H . . . 1st gear . . .

13.63I . . . and the final C-clip (arrowed)

13.66 Pressing the C-clip into its groove

13.72 Driving the bearing onto the output shaft

13.74 Speedometer drive worm (arrowed)

1st/2nd synchro unit, 1st synchro ring, the C-clip, 1st gear, and the final C-clip (photos). Keep the synchro unit sleeve central on the hub.

64   Remove the final bearing using a suitable puller, or by supporting the bearing in a vice and driving the output shaft through it. Note that the re-use of removed bearings is not recommended.

65   To reassemble, drive the bearing onto the output shaft using a length of metal tube on the inner track. Do not support the shaft on the plastic lubrication disc.

66   Press the C-clip into its groove, followed by 1st gear and the next C-clip (photo).

67   Fit the 1st synchro ring, then lower the 1st/2nd synchro unit onto the splines with the selector groove downwards, at the same time

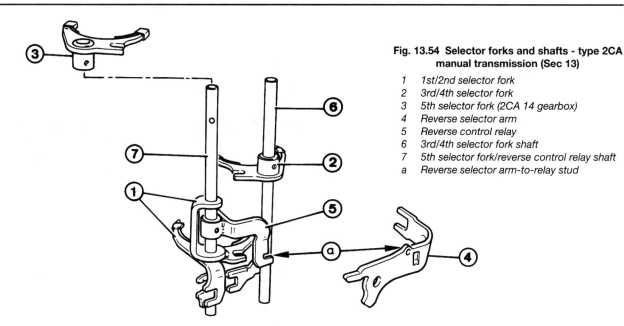

Fig. 13.54 Selector forks and shafts - type 2CA manual transmission (Sec 13)

1   1st/2nd selector fork
2   3rd/4th selector fork
3   5th selector fork (2CA 14 gearbox)
4   Reverse selector arm
5   Reverse control relay
6   3rd/4th selector fork shaft
7   5th selector fork/reverse control relay shaft
a   Reverse selector arm-to-relay stud

aligning the projections on the 1st synchro ring with the rockers on the synchro unit.

68   Fit the 2nd synchro ring, aligning the projections as described in paragraph 67.

69   Fit the 2nd gear, the C-clip, 3rd gear, and the C-clip.

70   Fit the 3rd synchro ring, 3rd/4th synchro unit, and the 4th synchro ring as described in paragraph 67.

71   Fit the 4th gear and thrustwasher.

72   Locate the bearing on the shaft, with the groove towards the end of the shaft. Drive the bearing onto the shaft using a length of metal tube on the inner track (photo). Do not support the shaft on the plastic lubrication disc.

73   On the 4-speed gearbox, locate the washer on the end of the shaft. Rest the circlip on the tapered end of the shaft, and use a socket to drive it into the groove. Check that the circlip is seated correctly by squeezing it with pliers.

Differential bearings (type 2CA transmission) - renewal

74   Lever off the speedometer drive worm (photo).

75   Pull the bearings from both sides of the differential unit using a suitable puller. Identify them for location if they are to be re-used.

76   Drive the new bearings into position using a length of metal tube on their inner tracks.

77   Press the speedometer drive worm into position.

Selector fork shafts (type 2CA transmission) - dismantling and reassembly

78   Support the 3rd/4th selector fork shaft in a soft-jawed vice, then drive out the roll pin using a suitable punch. Slide off the selector fork, noting which way round it is fitted.

79   Similarly drive out the roll pin, and remove the 1st/2nd selector fork and the reverse control relay from the other shaft.

80   Reassembly is a reversal of dismantling, but use new roll pins.

Synchro units (type 2CA transmission) - dismantling and reassembly

81   Mark the hub and outer sleeve in relation to each other, to ensure correct reassembly.

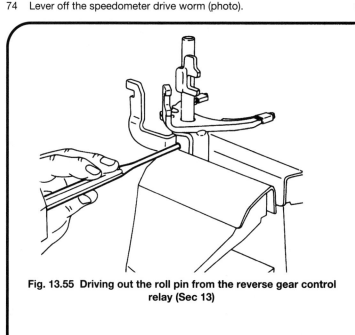

Fig. 13.55 Driving out the roll pin from the reverse gear control relay (Sec 13)

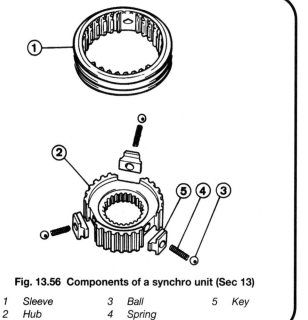

Fig. 13.56 Components of a synchro unit (Sec 13)

1	Sleeve	3	Ball	5	Key
2	Hub	4	Spring		

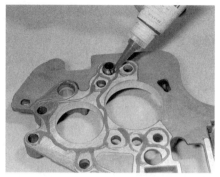

13.87A Applying adhesive to the intermediate plate

13.87B Guiding the gate lever through the intermediate plate

13.88A Applying locking fluid to the bolt threads

13.88B Tightening an intermediate plate bolt

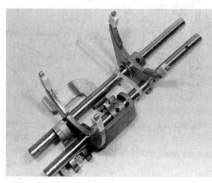

13.89 Selector fork shaft assemblies tied together with a cable tie

13.90 Geartrains and selector forks assembled in clutch/final drive housing

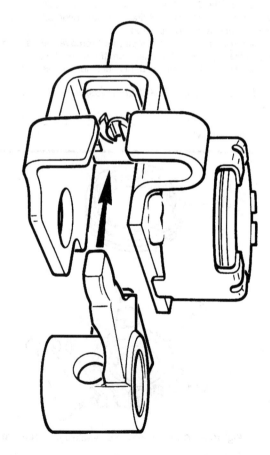

Fig. 13.57 Locating the selector finger in the interlocking key (Sec 13)

82   Wrap the unit in a cloth, then slide the sleeve from the hub. Recover the three balls, three springs, and three sliding keys.
83   To reassemble the units, first insert the hub in the sleeve. The rocker slots in the hub and sleeve must be in alignment.
84   Pull out the hub until the keys, springs and balls can be inserted, then press in the balls and push the hub fully into the sleeve. A large worm-drive clip, piston ring compressor, or three narrow strips of metal may be used to press in the balls.

Type 2CA transmission - reassembly

85   With the clutch/final drive housing on the bench, lower the differential unit into position.
86   Insert the reverse locking spring and plunger.
87   Apply Loctite Autoform 549 adhesive or similar to the contact area on the intermediate plate, then lower the plate onto the clutch/final drive housing, at the same time guiding the gate lever through the hole provided (photos).
88   Apply locking fluid to the bolt threads. Insert the bolts and progressively tighten them to the specified torque (photos). Clean the excess adhesive from the bearing locations.
89   Tie the two selector fork shaft assemblies together (photo).
90   Engage the selector forks in the synchro unit grooves, and mesh the input and output shaft assemblies together. Using both hands, lower the complete assembly into the clutch/final drive housing (photo).
91   Locate the selector finger within the interlocking key, then lift the gate lever and insert the key assembly in the clutch/final drive housing. Make sure that the selector finger engages the fork gates, and that the gate lever engages the outer plate of the interlocking key.
92   Engage the plastic cups with the neutral return spring, and insert them between the interlocking key and intermediate plate (photos).
93   Fit the rubber boot on the selector shaft. Insert the shaft through the intermediate plate, interlocking key and selector finger, align the holes, and drive in the locking pin (photos).
94   Insert the reverse selector arm in the intermediate plate, press down on it to depress the plunger, and insert the shaft. Make sure that the stud on the arm enters the cut-out on the control relay.
95   Engage the reverse idler gear with the selector arm, with the pro-

13.92A Neutral return spring and plastic cups correctly fitted

13.92B Gate lever (arrowed) engaged with interlocking key

13.93A Inserting the locking pin

13.93B Driving the pin through the selector shaft

13.97 Applying jointing compound to the clutch/final drive housing

13.103 Squeezing the circlip into the input shaft groove

13.107 Tightening the output shaft nut

13.108 Driving in the 5th speed selector fork locking pin

jecting shoulder uppermost, and insert the shaft, cut-out end downwards. Turn the shaft until the cut-out drops in the recess.
96   Fit the plastic ring on the shaft.
97   Apply a thin, even, coat of a silicone-based jointing compound to the mating face of the clutch/final drive housing (photo).
98   Lower the gearbox housing onto the clutch/final drive housing, at the same time guiding the input and output shaft bearings and selector fork shafts through their holes.
99   Insert the bolts in their previously-noted locations, and tighten them evenly to the specified torque.
100 Fit the retaining half-rings in the bearing grooves with the chamfers uppermost, then insert and tighten the bolts.

5-speed gearbox only
101 Locate the 5th speed drive gear on the input shaft splines, support the opposite end of the shaft on a block of wood, and fully drive the gear on the splines using a metal tube.
102 Fit the washer on the input shaft with its convex side uppermost.
103 Fit the circlip using a suitable socket and hammer. Check that it is

fully entered in the groove by squeezing with pliers (photo).
104 Fit the thrustwasher to the output shaft (oil groove uppermost) followed by the sleeve, needle bearing, 5th speed driven gear and the 5th synchro ring.
105 Engage the selector fork with the 5th synchro unit, then lower them onto the output shaft and selector fork shafts. Make sure that the projections on the synchro ring are aligned with the rockers in the synchro unit.
106 Fit the special lockwasher and nut (finger-tight).
107 Engage both reverse and 5th speed gears with reference to Fig. 13.52. Tighten the output shaft nut to the specified torque (photo), then return the gears to neutral.
108 Align the holes in the 5th speed selector fork and shaft, and drive in the locking pin (photo).

4- and 5-speed gearboxes
109 Fit the dry rubber gasket to the pressed-steel housing. Locate the housing on the gearbox housing, then insert the bolts and tighten them to the specified torque.

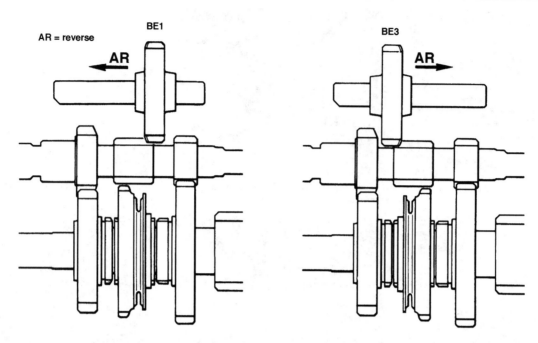

Fig. 13.58 New position of reverse idler gear and 1st/2nd gear synchro unit on the BE3/5 gearbox (Sec 13)

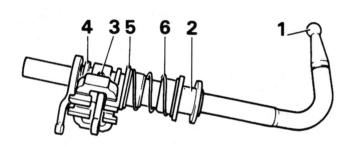

Fig. 13.59 Gear selector shaft and selector finger assembly -
BE3/5 gearbox (Sec 13)

1	One-piece selector shaft/lever	3	1st/2nd, 3rd/4th and 5th selector finger
2	Sleeve assembly with reverse finger	4	Interlock key
		5	Cups
		6	Spring

110 Refit the speedometer drive pinion. Insert and tighten the bolt.
111 Apply a little grease to the guide sleeve, then refit the clutch release bearing, and engage the spring clips with the fork ends.

BE3/5 transmission - general description
112 The BE3/5 gearbox is a refined development of the BE1/5 gearbox, and was introduced to the Citroën BX range in 1989, to progressively replace its predecessor.
113 Most of the procedures described in Chapter 6 for the BE1/5 gearbox are equally applicable to the BE3/5 type, although many of the components have been modified, as detailed in the following paragraphs.
114 When ordering spare parts, ensure that the correct new components are obtained, as many of the BE1/5 and BE3/5 gearbox components are not interchangeable.
115 BE3/5 gearboxes can be identified by the revised gearchange pattern, with reverse positioned opposite (behind) 5th gear.

Reverse idler gear (BE3/5 transmission) - modification
116 A modified reverse idler gear is fitted to the BE3/5 gearbox, and the idler gear is repositioned on the reverse idler shaft (see Fig. 13.58).

Gear selector components (BE3/5 transmission) - modifications
117 On the BE3/5 gearbox, the gearchange pattern has been revised so that reverse is positioned opposite 5th gear.
118 The cable-operated reverse gear stop has been deleted, and a breather plug is fitted in its place.
119 Reverse gear is engaged by an additional selector finger on the selector shaft, which acts on the reverse selector fork.
120 All of the gear selector components have been modified in detail, but the dismantling and reassembly details given in Chapter 6 for the BE1/5 gearbox components are still generally applicable.
121 Note that the gear selector shaft and selector finger assembly components are accurately matched, and no attempt should be made to dismantle the selector finger assembly, as no spares are available. If any of the components are worn or damaged, the complete selector shaft finger assembly must be renewed as a unit.

Primary shaft (BE3/5 transmission) - modification
122 A modified primary shaft is fitted to the BE3/5 gearbox, to allow for the revised position of the reverse idler gear, but the overhaul procedure described in Chapter 6 remains unchanged.

1st/2nd gear synchro unit (BE3/5 transmission) - modification
123 A modified 1st/2nd gear synchro unit is fitted to the BE3/5 gearbox, which fits on the secondary shaft the opposite way round to that described for the BE1/5 gearbox in Chapter 6; i.e. the synchro unit fits with the chamfer on the external teeth *facing away* from 1st gear. The remainder of the secondary shaft dismantling and reassembly procedure described in Chapter 6 remains unchanged.

BE3/5 transmission - modifications
124 Since its introduction in 1989, the BE3/5 transmission has undergone the following modifications in production. Refer to your Citroën dealer for further information.
January 1990 - on GTi 16 valve models, an oil deflector plate is fitted to the inside of gearbox casing to improve lubrication. The plate is fixed to the casing by two crimped fixings.
January 1991 - the gearbox casing filler/level aperture is modified. A web is fitted to the inside of the aperture to alter the transmission oil capacity.

NEW ARRANGEMENT   FORMER ARRANGEMENT

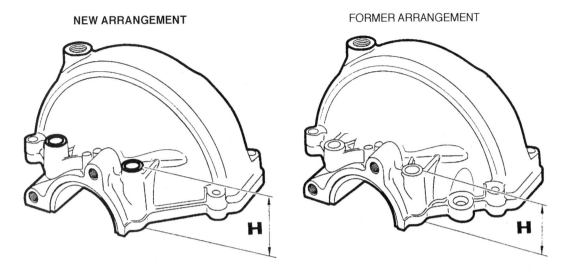

Fig. 13.60 Modified differential housing (from September 1991) - BE3/5 transmission (Sec 13)

New arrangement - H = 49 mm (70 mm retaining bolts)   *Former arrangement - H = 44 mm (65 mm retaining bolts)*

June 1991 - the oil deflector plate previously fitted to only the GTi 16 valve model is fitted to all transmission units.

September 1991 - a modified differential housing and retaining bolts is fitted. The new housing is 5 mm taller (see Fig. 13.60) and is retained by 70 mm long bolts in place of the 65 mm long bolts used to retain the earlier housing. Ensure that the correct length bolts are used when re-fitting the differential housing. Note that under no circumstances should the early-type bolts be used to retain the modified housing, and *vice-versa*.

September 1992 - from serial number 3 859 471 onwards, modified second gear pinions are fitted (23 teeth/43 teeth in place of the earlier 20/37 tooth arrangement). This new arrangement involves the fitting of a new input shaft along with the modified second gear pinions. Note that the complete modified second gear and input shaft assembly can be fitted to earlier gearboxes, but components of the original and modified assemblies must not be mixed.

2CA transmission - modifications

125 Since its introduction, the 2CA transmission has undergone the following modifications in production. Refer to your Citroën dealer for further information.

May 1989 - the helix angle of the second gear pinion teeth is altered. The new modified pinions can be identified by the grooves cut in the pinion teeth (see Fig. 13.61).

October 1989 - the differential assembly and housing are modified. Changes include the pinion shaft diameter being increased from 13 mm to 14 mm, and guide sleeves being machined onto the satellite pinions to allow the fitting of thrustwashers. A modified reversing light switch incorporating a sealed wiring connector is also fitted.

September 1990 - the diameter of the output shaft differential end bearing is reduced from 66 mm down to 62 mm, and the gearbox casing modified to suit. The ignition timing aperture on the casing is also increased, to allow better access to the flywheel marks.

September 1991 - the angle of entry of the reverse gear pinion teeth is modified to 85°, instead of the previous 110°, and the width of the reverse gear idler is increased from 12 mm to 13 mm. The reverse gear selector fork jaw gap is also widened to 13 mm, to take into account the increased width of the idler gear. The output shaft end bearing and gearbox casing are also modified. The bearing has a groove machined in its outer race to accept a circlip; the circlip rests against a recess which is machined in the gearbox casing (see Fig. 13.62). Another minor modification is to the design of the selector shaft oil seal and its casing aperture, which are both reshaped (Fig. 13.63).

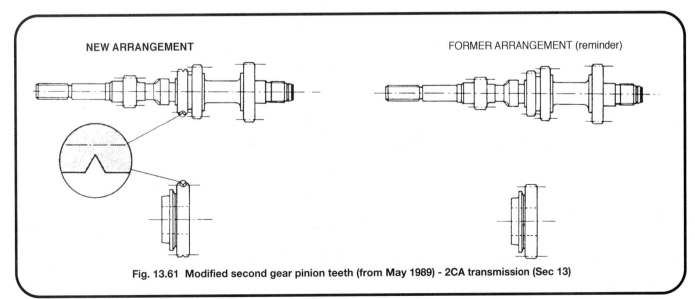

NEW ARRANGEMENT   FORMER ARRANGEMENT (reminder)

Fig. 13.61 Modified second gear pinion teeth (from May 1989) - 2CA transmission (Sec 13)

396

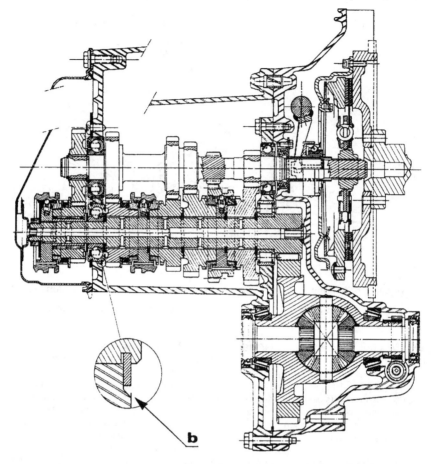

Fig. 13.62 Output shaft bearing modification "b" (from September 1991) - 2CA transmission (Sec 13)

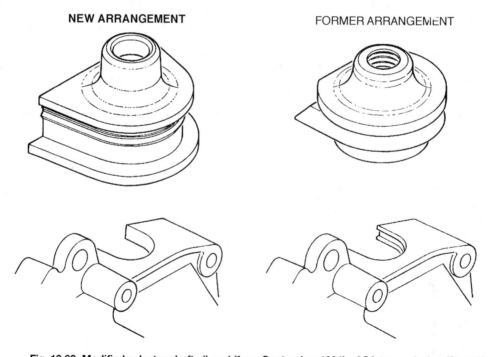

NEW ARRANGEMENT

FORMER ARRANGEMENT

Fig. 13.63 Modified selector shaft oil seal (from September 1991) - 2CA transmission (Sec 13)

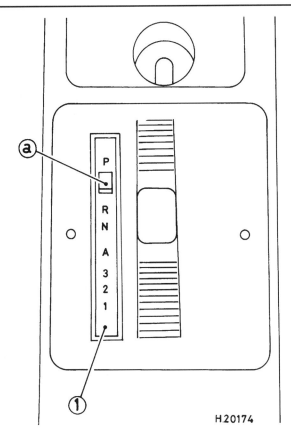

Fig. 13.64 Later type of automatic transmission selector gate (Sec 14)

1   *Plastic indicator*

a   *Depress when setting to avoid marking face plate*

14   Automatic transmission

Selector lever gate - BX 16 models from January 1985

1   A new selector lever gate is fitted to later models, in which a curtain replaces the brushes used in previous models. The new gate allows an improved view of the selected gear, the selected position being illuminated in red.

2   The new- and earlier-type gates are interchangeable. When setting the later type, loosen the gate, then move the plastic indicator so that the gear selected and indicated are aligned, then retighten the gate (Fig. 13.64).

Kickdown cable (BX 16 and BX 19 from September 1988) - adjustment

3   The operations are similar to those described in Chapter 6, Section 26, but note that the movement (C) of the cable crimped stop shown in Fig. 6.50 is now 39.0 mm.

15   Driveshafts

Driveshaft rubber bellows - renewal

1   With the driveshaft removed, loosen the clips on the outer rubber bellows. If plastic straps are fitted, cut them free with snips (photo).

2   Prise the bellows larger diameter end from the outer joint housing (photo), then tap the centre hub outwards, using a soft metal drift in order to release it from the retaining circlip. Slide the outer joint complete from the driveshaft splines.

3   Extract the circlip from the groove in the driveshaft (photo).

4   Prise off the rubber bellows. If necessary, remove the plastic seating from the recess in the driveshaft (photos).

5   Loosen the clips on the inner rubber bellows. If plastic straps are fitted, cut them free.

6   Prise the bellows larger diameter end from the inner joint housing, and slide the rubber bellows off the outer end of the driveshaft (photo).

15.1 Plastic ratchet-type clips used to secure driveshaft joint bellows

15.2 Outer joint with bellows larger diameter end released

15.3 Driveshaft outer joint circlip (arrowed)

15.4A Removing driveshaft outer joint bellows

15.4B Plastic seating (arrowed) for outer joint bellows

15.6 Removing the inner joint bellows

15.7 Inner joint rollers (arrowed)

15.8 Left-hand driveshaft with rollers retained with adhesive tape

15.9 Removing the pressure pad and spring from the inner joint housing

15.11 Injecting grease into the inner joint housing

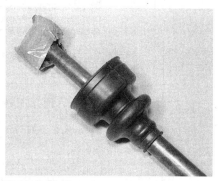

15.12 Inner joint rubber bellows located on driveshaft

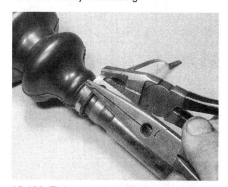

15.16A Tightening the bellows clip

7   Mark the driveshaft and inner joint housing in relation to each other, then separate them, keeping the rollers engaged with their respective spigots (photo).
8   Clean away the grease, then retain the rollers using adhesive tape (photo).
9   Remove the pressure pad and spring from inside the inner joint housing (photo).
10   Clean away the grease, then commence reassembly by inserting the pressure pad and spring into the inner joint housing, with the housing mounted upright in a soft-jawed vice.
11   Inject one-third of the sachet of grease (supplied in the new bellows repair kit) into the inner joint housing (photo).
12   Locate the new inner joint rubber bellows halfway along the driveshaft (photo).
13   Remove the adhesive tape, and insert the driveshaft into the housing.
14   Inject another third of the grease in the joint.
15   Keeping the driveshaft pressed against the internal spring, refit the rubber bellows. The distance between the inner ends of the bellows (Fig. 13.65) is 166.0 mm for vehicles built before June 1987, and 154.0 mm for later models.
16   Tighten the clips. Metal-type clips can be retightened using two pairs of pliers, by holding the buckle and pulling the clip through. Cut off the excess, and bend the clip back under the buckle (photos).

17   Fit the plastic seating in the driveshaft recess, and refit the new rubber bellows smaller diameter end on it.
18   Refit the circlip in the driveshaft groove.
19   Inject the remaining grease in the outer joint, then insert the driveshaft, engage the splines, and press in until the circlip snaps into the groove.
20   Ease the rubber bellows onto the outer joint, and fit the two clips, tightening them as previously described.

16 Braking system

Anti-lock braking system (ABS) - description

1   An anti-lock braking system (ABS) is fitted to the BX 19 GTi from November 1986. The function of the ABS is to prevent the brakes from locking up the roadwheels when applied (retaining steering control), but equally giving the shortest-possible stopping distance for emergency braking. The system operates at speeds in excess of 5 mph, but when in operation, controls the vehicle deceleration until it is brought to a halt.
2   The ABS monitors the rotational speed of each roadwheel during braking. If any wheel begins to slow at a faster rate than the others, showing that it is on the point of locking, the ABS reduces the hy-

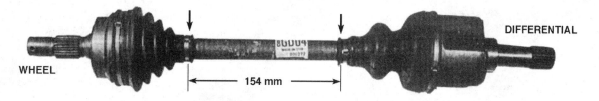

WHEEL   154 mm   DIFFERENTIAL

Fig. 13.65 Driveshaft bellows setting diagram (Sec 15)

Dimension shown is for later models only - see text

15.16B Bellows clip finally secured

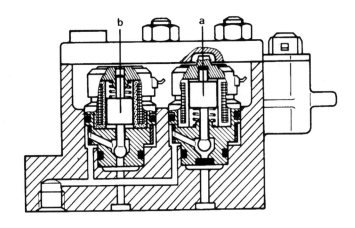

Fig. 13.66 ABS electro-valves at Phase 1 position (Sec 16)

Inlet valve (a) open, return valve (b) shut

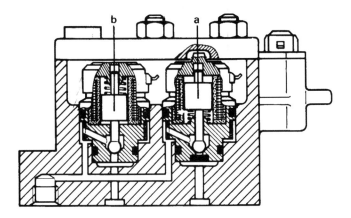

Fig. 13.67 ABS electro-valve at Phase 2 position (Sec 16)

Inlet valve (a) shut, return valve (b) shut

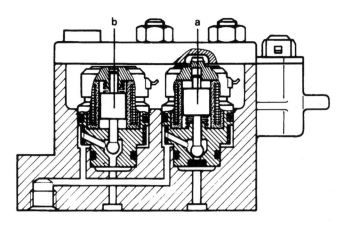

Fig. 13.68 ABS electro-valve in Phase 3 position (Sec 16)

Inlet valve (a) shut, return valve (b) open

draulic pressure to that wheel's brake caliper. (In fact, both rear calipers receive the same hydraulic pressure, even if only one rear wheel is locking). As the wheel grips again, its rotational speed matches the others, and hydraulic pressure to the caliper is restored. This cycle can be repeated several times per second.

3   The ABS is operated by the following hydraulic and electronic components, which are complementary to the otherwise conventional brake system.

(a) *The front and rear wheel sensor units, on the driveshaft joints/wheel hubs.*
(b) *The hydraulic control block unit, located on the left-hand wheel arch in the engine compartment.*
(c) *The electronic control unit (ECU), located under the front passenger seat.*

4   In common with other models in the BX range, the front and rear brake hydraulic circuits are separate, but the ABS differs in also separating the right and left-hand front brake circuits. The remaining brake system components and layout are otherwise the same as on standard models.

5   The hydraulic control block unit contains six electro-valves, each of the three brake circuits having its own inlet and return electro-valve. Each pair of valves work as follows in accordance with the electrical control unit.

Phase 1: Under normal braking, as the pressure rises, the inlet valve is open and the return valve is shut; the hydraulic supply pressure to the brake unit is normal (Fig. 13.66).

Phase 2: Under steady braking, both the inlet and return valves close to give a constant and carefully-regulated supply of hydraulic pressure to the brake in question (Fig. 13.67).

Phase 3: If a brake starts to lock up, the pressure to it is released by the return valve opening (inlet still closed); the hydraulic pressure to that brake is then released (Fig. 13.68).

6   The electronic part of the system comprises a speed sensor unit for each roadwheel, and the central control unit (under the passenger seat). Each front driveshaft outer CV joint and each rear wheel hub has a toothed rotor (or wheel), the speed of which is recorded by the adjacent sensor unit; this in turn relays the signal to the ECU. From the signals received by the ECU from each roadwheel, the average road speed is calculated, and any sudden acceleration or deceleration accounted.

7   An automatic checking device is built into the electronic control unit. Any faults in the ABS will illuminate the yellow warning light on the instrument panel and cancel the ABS (but still allow normal braking). The yellow warning light will also light up when the ignition is initially switched on, but will cancel as soon as the engine is started.

8   If a fault develops or is suspected in the ABS, have it checked out by a Citroën dealer at the earliest opportunity.

Brake hydraulic system bleeding (with ABS)

9   When bleeding the brake hydraulic system on models fitted with ABS, the procedures are the same as for the standard braking system

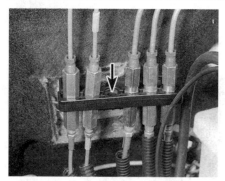

16.9 Brake hydraulic line connection bracket at bulkhead. Arrow indicates position for compensator valve bleed screw on some models

16.10 ABS hydraulic control block unit

16.16A ABS wheel sensor - front brake
1 Wiring
2 Retaining bolt
3 Adjuster screw (shear type)
4 Toothed wheel
5 Air gap

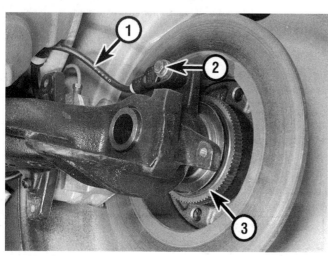

16.16B ABS wheel sensor - rear brake
1 Wiring   3 Toothed wheel
2 Retaining bolt and sensor

models described in Chapter 9. Note that on some models, the bleed nipple for the brake compensator control valve is located in the hydraulic line connection bracket on the bulkhead (photo).

Hydraulic control block (ABS) - removal and refitting
10   If the hydraulic control block unit develops a malfunction, it must be renewed as a unit, as it cannot be repaired (photo).
11   Detach the wiring connections from the control block unit.
12   Disconnect the hydraulic pipes from the control block unit with reference to Chapter 8, Sections 2 and 6.
13   Undo the retaining bolts and remove the hydraulic control block.
14   Refitting is a reversal of the removal procedure. On completion, the brake hydraulic system will need to be bled as described in Chapter 9.

ABS wheel sensor - removal and refitting
15   Raise and support the vehicle at the front and/or rear as applicable. Removal of the appropriate roadwheel will provide improved access.
16   Disconnect the sensor wiring plug, and free the wiring from any clips or ties (photos).
17   Undo the sensor retaining bolt and remove the sensor.
18   Refitting is a reversal of the removal procedure, but note the following additional procedure when fitting a new sensor to the front hub swivel.
19   Fit the sensor with the adjuster screw loosened off. Position a feeler blade, of a thickness corresponding to the specified air gap, be-

tween the tip of the sensor and the toothed wheel. Tighten the retaining bolt to the specified torque. Make sure that the sensor tip, feeler blade and toothed wheel are in contact, then tighten the adjuster screw until its head shears off. Withdraw the feeler blade.
20   Refit the roadwheel and lower the vehicle.

ABS electronic control unit - removal and refitting
21   Unbolt and remove the front passenger seat for access to the electronic control unit (ECU).
22   Unbolt the ECU and its cover plate from the brackets (photo).
23   Disconnect the multi-plug and remove the ECU.
24   Refit by reversing the removal operations.

ABS (from September 1987) - modifications
25   Later models are fitted with a modified ECU and hydraulic unit.
26   The brake stop-light switch is connected to the ECU by means of pin No. 12, as shown in the relevant wiring diagram at the end of this manual.

Rear disc pads (all models) - inspection
27   When inspecting the rear pads, it is strongly recommended that they be removed and cleaned (Chapter 9, Section 4) even if they appear unworn. Rear pad wear is very slow if the vehicle is driven mostly unladen, and it is possible for the pads to seize in place if they are not removed periodically.

Rear brake disc (all models) - removal
28   If the brake disc is difficult to separate from the hub, remove the backplate and tap the disc off from behind. Be careful not to fracture or distort the disc, if it is to be re-used.

Rear brake discs and pads (all models) - modifications
29   From October 1988, modified rear brake calipers and disc pads are fitted.
30   The brake calipers are modified to provide increased clearance for the disc (now 12.2 mm). The thicknesses of the disc pad backing plate and friction material are modified accordingly; the pad backing plate is now 5 mm thick, instead of 4 mm previously, and the friction material thickness is now reduced by 1 mm.
31   Vehicles with the early-type calipers can be fitted with the later-type pads, and it is possible to fit the later-type calipers to early vehicles, in which case the later-type pads must be fitted. Note that the early-type pads **must not** be fitted to models with the later calipers.

Front brake discs - BX 19 GTi 16 valve
32   The discs on these models are of ventilated type. The operations described in Chapter 9 otherwise apply (photos).

Brake control valve/compensator - from October 1988
33   From October 1988, all models are fitted with a new type control

16.22 ABS electronic control unit

16.32A Ventilated type brake disc

16.32B Locating pip (arrowed) on inboard pad

valve, which incorporates three slide valves instead of the previous two.

34   If the new type valve is being fitted as a replacement for the two slide valve assembly, then remove the calibrating plug (V) shown in Fig. 13.69, and connect the rear brake pipe to the tapped port.

35   If a three slide valve assembly is being renewed, the new valve will be supplied with a bleed valve screwed into the rear brake pipe connecting port. Remove the bleed screw.

Control valve - bleeding (two slide valves)

36   Have the engine running, and the hydraulic circuit pressurised with the brake pedal depressed.

37   Bleed at each of the three bleed screws.

 (a) Control valve.

 (b) Front brakes.

 (c) Rear brakes.

Control valve - bleeding (three slide valves)

38   Bleed at the two bleed screws. Refer to detailed bleeding procedure in Chapter 9, Section 14.

17   Suspension and steering

Front suspension - modifications from September 1985

1   From the above date, all models are fitted with a modified front suspension arm, having a revised type of flexible pivot bush fitted. In

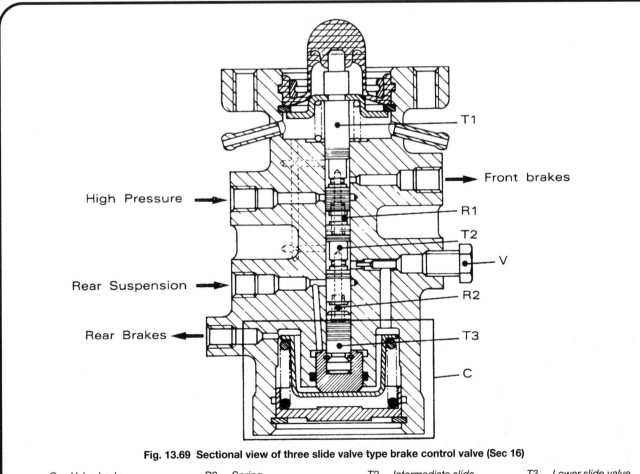

Fig. 13.69 Sectional view of three slide valve type brake control valve (Sec 16)

| C | Valve body | R2 | Spring | T2 | Intermediate slide valve | T3 | Lower slide valve |
| R1 | Spring | T1 | Upper slide valve | | | V | Calibrating plug |

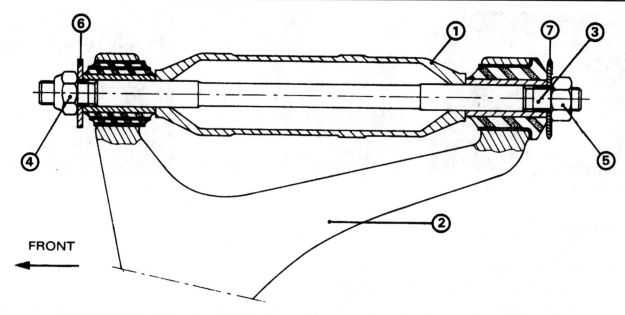

Fig. 13.70 Sectional view of modified front suspension arm and associated components (Sec 17)

1	Subframe	3	Pivot shaft	5	Rear nut	7	Rear washer
2	Suspension arm	4	Front nut	6	Front washer		

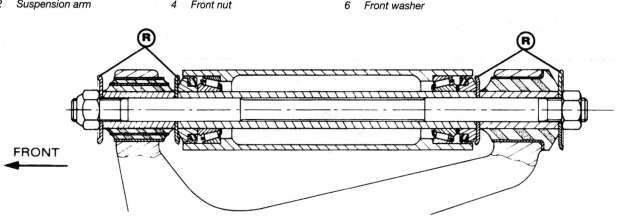

Fig. 13.71 Special replacement suspension arm with 14.0 mm diameter pivot shaft (Sec 17)

R   Washers

addition to the suspension arm, the following associated items are also modified.

   (a) **Subframe:** of modified design, and no longer fitted with taper-roller bearings (photo).
   (b) **Suspension arm bushes:** Redesigned bushes are fitted to suit the new subframes.
   (c) **Spindle (pivot) shaft:** Increased in diameter from 14 mm to 16 mm.
   (d) **Suspension spheres:** The capacity of the front suspension spheres is 500 cc on BX 16 and BX 19 after January 1988.

2   The spheres on all models are colour-coded for identification purposes after January 1988.

3   The geometry of the subframe remains the same as the type fitted to earlier models.

4   Subframes for the earlier models are no longer being produced, and if renewal of the earlier type is necessary, it may therefore be necessary to renew the lower arms and their respective associated fittings in accordance with the model type. Your Citroën dealer will advise accordingly.

5   When renewing a suspension arm on early models fitted with the original-type subframe, a special replacement arm is necessary, which has the 14 mm spindle (pivot) shaft rubber bushes and washers

(Fig. 13.71).

6   When fitting the later-type suspension arms and subframe assemblies to early models, the suspension geometry remains the same, and the original suspension spheres can be used.

7   Renewal of the suspension arm bushes on the later types is identical to that described in Chapter 10 for the early-type arm.

Front anti-roll bar - modification

8   The front anti-roll bar bearings on models from 1987 incorporate a rubber bush instead of the earlier plastic half-shells.

9   The rubber bush-type bearings may be fitted to earlier anti-roll bars, but both bearings must be renewed at the same time.

10   When fitting an anti-roll bar using the later-type rubber bushes, make sure that the bushes and bar are dry. Centre the bar within the subframe, and only tighten the bearing fixing bolts when the vehicle is at normal driving height, with its roadwheels in contact with the ground.

11   The torque wrench setting for the bearing-to-subframe bolts is as given in the Specifications for Chapter 10.

Front suspension spheres (BX 19 GTi 16 valve) - general

12   From March 1989, the capacity of the front suspension spheres on BX 19 GTi 16 valve models is 400 cc.

17.1 Later type of front suspension arm and subframe

17.17A Removing centre pad from steering wheel

17.17B Steering wheel retaining nut (arrowed)

17.19 Upper steering column oil seal (arrowed)

17.23 Steering intermediate shaft universal joint (arrowed)

17.24 Steering column upper retaining nut (arrowed)

Rear suspension spheres (Estate) - general

13   The capacity of the rear suspension spheres on Estate versions is 500 cc.

Rear anti-roll bar (BX 19 GTi 16 valve) - modification

14   From March 1989, the rear anti-roll bar on BX 19 GTi 16 valve models is increased in diameter, and the ends of the bar are located by splines instead of flats. Procedures are unaffected.

Rear suspension spheres (BX 19 GTi 16 valve) - general

15   From March 1989, the capacity of the rear suspension spheres on BX 19 GTi 16 valve models is 400 cc.

Steering wheel (later models) - removal and refitting

16   Set the front wheels in the straight-ahead position.
17   Prise out the centre pad, then use a socket to unscrew the retaining nut (photos).

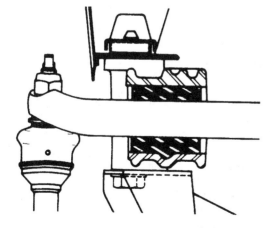

Fig. 13.72 Later type front anti-roll bar bushes (Sec 17)

18   Mark the hub in relation to the inner column, then pull off the steering wheel. If it is tight, a rocking action may release it from the splines.
19   If required, the upper column oil seal can be prised free for renewal. Note the seal fitting position and orientation (photo).
20   Refitting is a reversal of removal, but check that the steering wheel is correctly centred with the front wheel straight-ahead. Tighten the nut while holding the steering wheel rim.

Steering column and lock (later models) - removal and refitting

21   Disconnect the battery earth lead, then undo the retaining screws and remove the lower steering column cover. As the cover is removed, detach the wiring connector from the dimmer switch and relay unit. Remove the upper column cover.
22   If required, the steering wheel can be removed as described in paragraphs 16 to 19.
23   Unscrew and remove the column clamp bolt from the intermediate shaft universal joint (photo).
24   Undo the upper column retaining bolts/nuts (photo), and carefully lower the column from its mountings. To fully withdraw the column, it will be necessary to detach the column switch wiring harness connectors.
25   If necessary, the intermediate shaft can be removed after prising out the grommet and unscrewing the bottom clamp bolt.
26   To remove the steering lock, unscrew the retaining bolt then, with the ignition key turned to position A (first position), depress the plunger in the housing.
27   Refitting is a reversal of removal.

18   Bodywork and fittings

Door trim panels - later models

1   Later models fitted with electrically-operated windows have the switches mounted in the door panels. When removing the trim panels on these models, it is necessary to prise free the switches from the

18.1A Window regulator switch prised from door

18.1B Window regulator switches withdrawn to expose wiring

18.2 Extracting a screw from the window regulator mounting panel

18.4 Removing a plastic cover for access to a centre console retaining bolt

18.13 Prising out tailgate strut balljoint clip - Estate

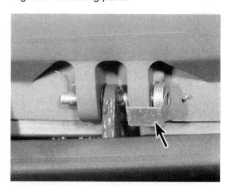

18.14 Tailgate hinge pin retaining clip (arrowed) - Estate

18.17A Unscrewing a rear bumper lower screw - Estate

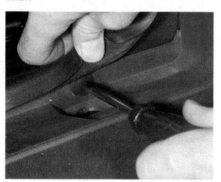

18.17B Unscrewing a rear bumper upper screw - Estate

18.17C Rear bumper end clip viewed from underneath vehicle - Estate

panel using a thin-bladed screwdriver, then disconnect the wiring from the switches (photos).

2   The window regulator switches are mounted in a secondary panel attached to the main door panel. If required, the panels can be separated by undoing the retaining screws from the rear face (photo).

3   If door-mounted speakers are fitted, the wires for these will also have to be disconnected to allow the door panels to be removed (see Section 19).

Floor-mounted centre console - later models

4   The floor-mounted centre console on later models is secured to the floor by two bolts on top, and a screw each side at the front. The bolts are recessed in the upper face of the panel, and are accessible after removal of the plastic covers. These can be prised free (photo).

5   When removing the console, it may be necessary to detach the wiring connectors from any switches mounted in the console. Some models also have radio headphone jack points mounted in the rear of the console, and these will also have to be detached.

Dashboard - later models

6   While the dashboard layout differs on later models, the main differences concerning its removal are the associated components at-

tached to it, such as the revised heater controls, and the later-type steering column and facia switches.

7   The removal of the associated components is dealt with elsewhere in this Chapter. The removal procedures for the dashboard are otherwise similar to those described for earlier models in Chapter 11.

Door windows (all models) - general

8   On early models, the window lift channels are glued to the side of the glass. Later models have slotted channels with rubber inserts.

9   If problems are experienced with early-type channels coming unstuck, purchase a modification kit from a Citroën dealer, and fit the later-type channels.

10   Mark the position of the old lift channels before removal (saw or prise them off), and fit the new ones in the same position. Measuring horizontally from the front bottom corner of the glass, the front edge of the lift channel should be 207 mm from the corner on the front windows, 124 mm from the corner on the rear.

Tailgate (Estate) - removal and refitting

11   Disconnect the battery.

12   Open the tailgate fully. Disconnect the electrical wiring (heated glass element, rear wiper and central locking) and the washer hose.

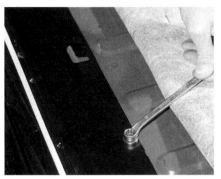

18.22 Unscrewing rear seat back hinge bolt

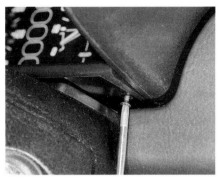

19.7 Unscrewing a trim panel retaining screw

19.8 Unscrewing a clock/upper facia tray securing screw

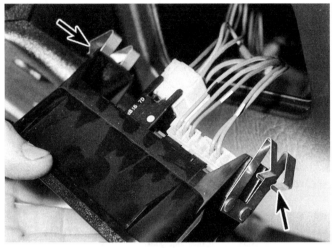

19.9 Withdrawing the switch panel - retaining clips arrowed

19.10 Instrument panel lower retaining screw

Extensive dismantling of the interior side trim panels and window surrounds will be required in order to gain access to the wiring connecting plugs.

13   With an assistant supporting the tailgate, prise out the spring clips from the strut balljoints (photo), and pull the struts off their ball studs.

14   Prise off the retaining clips, and tap the hinge pins out. Lift the tailgate from the vehicle (photo).

15   Refitting is a reversal of removal.

Rear bumper (Estate) - removal and refitting

16   The rear bumper comprises a centre section secured to the tailgate by screws, and two end sections held by screws and clips.

17   Remove the screws and withdraw the bumper. The end sections slide rearwards off the clips (photos).

18   Refitting is a reversal of removal.

Rear seat (Estate) - removal and refitting

19   Pivot the seat cushion forwards.

20   Pull the seat back downwards.

21   Prise up the hinge cover flap to expose the seat hinge bolts.

22   Unscrew the hinge bolts and remove the seat back (photo).

23   The seat cushion can be removed after disconnecting the hinges in a similar way.

24   Refitting is a reversal of removal.

---

19   Electrical system

Starter motor (BX 19 GTi) - removal and refitting

1   Access to the starter motor on this model is poor, and the vehicle is best raised and supported at the front end to give a suitable working

area underneath. On 16 valve versions, it is possible to remove the starter motor after first taking out the radiator and working through the front grille opening (cover flap removed).

2   Working from underneath, unclip and detach the three crankcase breather hoses from the engine (near the oil filter). Unscrew and remove the oil filter as described in Chapter 1. Take care if the engine is still warm, as any oil spillage will be hot.

3   Detach the battery earth lead.

4   Undo the starter motor bracket bolts at the filter end. Unscrew and remove the starter motor-to-clutch housing securing bolts, then withdraw the starter motor, detach the wiring connections and remove the starter motor from the car.

5   Refitting is a reversal of the removal procedure. In view of its relatively low cost, the oil filter is best renewed. Refer to the relevant Section in Chapter 1 for refitting the oil filter.

Instrument panel (later models) - removal and refitting

6   Disconnect the battery earth lead.

7   Undo the single screw each side, and remove the trim panel located between the instrument panel and the steering column upper shroud (photo).

8   Undo the two screws and withdraw the clock/upper facia tray (photo). Disconnect the wiring connector and remove the tray.

9   Release the switch panel located on the right-hand side of the facia, by reaching up behind and depressing the retaining clips each side (photo). Withdraw the panel as far as possible to allow access through the aperture.

10   Undo and remove the two instrument panel retaining screws from the front lower edge of the panel (photo).

11   Reach through the clock/upper facia tray aperture and, using an 11 mm spanner, undo the upper left-hand instrument panel retaining nut. The "spire"-type nut is threaded onto a plastic stud at the rear of

19.11A Working through the facia aperture with an 11 mm spanner . . .

19.11B . . . to remove the left-hand upper retaining nut . . .

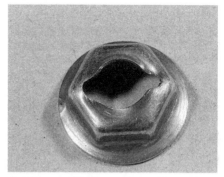

19.11C . . . which is a self-threading "spire" type . . .

19.11D . . . threaded onto the stud at the rear of the instrument panel

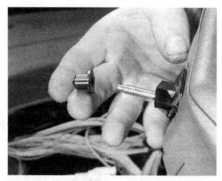

19.11E Instrument panel wing nut

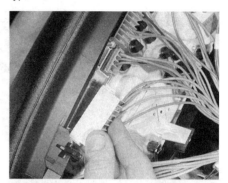

19.12A Instrument panel wiring connectors

19.12B Speedometer cable connector

19.18 Removing a facia switch

19.22 Detaching the wiring plug from the instrument lighting rheostat

the instrument panel; later models have wing nuts. Working through the right-hand side switch panel aperture, undo the right-hand side upper retaining nut using the same procedure (photos).

12   Partially withdraw the instrument panel until the wiring connecting plugs can be detached and the speedometer cable disconnected. To do this, pull the sleeve on the connector away from the speedometer head. To reconnect, simply push the sleeve towards the speedometer (photos).

13   The various instrument panel bulbs and their holders are easily accessible in the rear face of the unit. Untwist the holder, and then remove the bulb from it. Take care not to damage the printed circuit on the rear face of the panel.

14   To remove the instrument panel from the surrounding facia panel, remove the two side screws, and prise free the two clips from the pegs at the lower rear face. Separate the instrument panel from the facia panel.

15   If removing the surrounding facia panel, disconnect the wiring from the four switches, noting the wiring locations given below.

   (a) Grey to the heated rear window switch.
   (b) Black to the hazard warning switch.
   (c) Yellow to the rear window washer/wiper.
   (d) Blue to the rear foglight switch.

16   Refitting of both the instrument panel and its surround is a reversal of the removal procedure. Check the operation of the various switches and controls on completion.

Instrument panel facia switches (later models) - removal and refitting

17   Disconnect the battery earth lead.

18   Although it is possible to remove a switch from the facia with it *in situ*, we found it difficult, due to the lack of access to the retaining clips on each side of the switch. It may be easier to remove the facia (see previous sub-Section), and then push out the switch from the rear whilst compressing the clip each side (photo).

19   Detach the wiring connector from the switch and remove it.

20   Refit in the reverse order of removal.

Steering column switches (later models) - removal and refitting

21   Disconnect the battery earth lead.

22   Undo the seven retaining screws, and remove the column lower shroud. As it is withdrawn, detach the wires from the instrument lighting rheostat and relay unit (photo).

19.23A Removing the steering column upper shroud

19.23B Removing the steering column upper shroud side panel

19.24A Removing a steering column switch

19.24B Steering column switch wiring connectors

19.28A Disconnecting the wiring from the front foglight switch

19.28B Front foglight and electric mirror switches and panel

19.29 Refitting the front foglight switch

19.32 Removing the door warning panel

19.33 Removing the bonnet-open warning switch

23   Undo and remove the column upper mounting nuts, then loosen the lower mounting bolts to lower the column enough to allow the upper shroud to be removed. The upper shroud has a detachable side panel, which is removed sideways by withdrawing it from the windscreen wiper control stalk (photos).

24   To remove either of the column switches, undo the retaining screws and remove them from the brackets. Detach the wiring connectors from the switches (photos).

25   Refitting is a reversal of the removal procedure. Check the switches for satisfactory operation on completion.

Front foglight and mirror switches (BX 19 models) - removal and refitting

26   Disconnect the battery earth lead.

27   Reach up behind the facia panel, depress the combined switch panel retaining clip each side, and push the panel out of its recess in the facia.

28   Disconnect the wiring connector from the rear of the appropriate switch, then push the switch unit(s) out of the panel. The foglight switch has retaining clips which must be depressed to allow its removal (photos).

29   Refit in the reverse order of removal. If preferred, the panel can be fitted first, then the switches connected and pushed into position (photo).

Door-open warning panel - removal and refitting

30   Disconnect the battery earth lead.

31   Tilt, pull and withdraw the coin tray for access to the retaining clip on the left side of the door warning panel.

32   Release the door warning panel retaining clip, then withdraw the panel (photo). To renew a warning bulb, twist and remove the holder from the rear face of the panel, then withdraw the bulb. To remove the panel completely, pull free the wiring multi-connector.

33   As well as indicating if any of the doors are open, this warning panel will also indicate if the bonnet and tailgate are not closed properly. If required, the bonnet warning switch can be removed by carefully prising it free from its aperture (photo) and the wiring disconnected.

34   Refitting is a reversal of the removal procedure. Check for satisfactory operation on completion.

Clock - removal and refitting

35   Disconnect the battery earth lead.

19.37 Clock unit rear details - unclip to remove

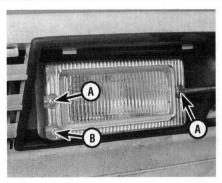

19.41 Front foglight retaining screws (A) and adjuster screw (B)

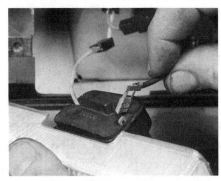

19.42A Disconnecting the foglight wiring

19.42B Front foglight bulbholder

19.43 Extracting the front foglight bulb

19.46 Centre vent grille retaining clip (grille removed for clarity)

19.47 Withdrawing the grille panel

19.49A Map reading light switch and roof console retaining screw (arrowed)

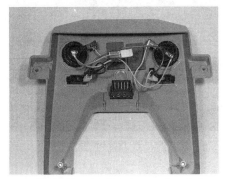

19.49B Map reading light/sunroof console removed

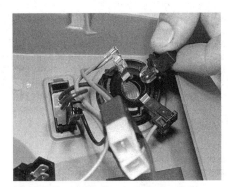

19.49C Removing the map reading light bulb

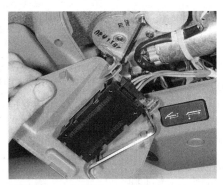

19.52 Removing the remote control door locking receiver unit

19.54 Fuel injection system relays (GTi with Bosch LE3 Jetronic fuel injection)

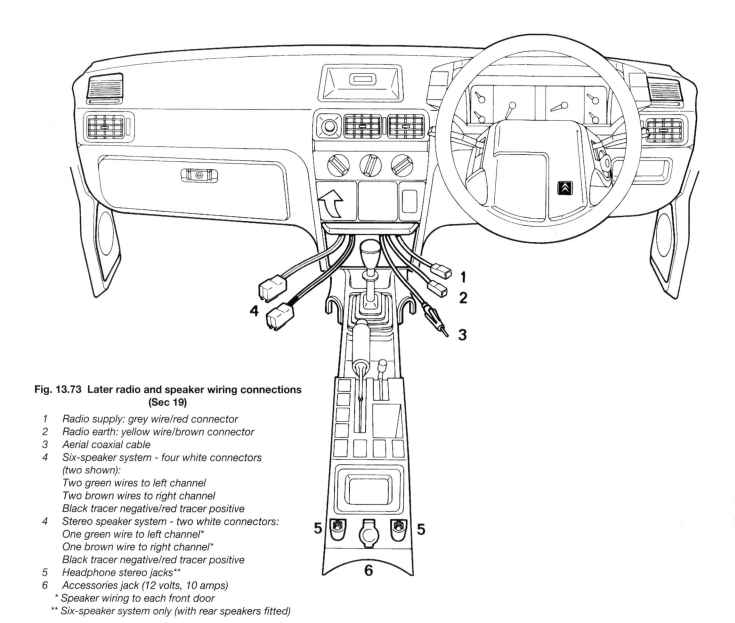

Fig. 13.73 Later radio and speaker wiring connections (Sec 19)

1   *Radio supply: grey wire/red connector*
2   *Radio earth: yellow wire/brown connector*
3   *Aerial coaxial cable*
4   *Six-speaker system - four white connectors*
    (two shown):
    Two green wires to left channel
    Two brown wires to right channel
    Black tracer negative/red tracer positive
4   *Stereo speaker system - two white connectors:*
    One green wire to left channel*
    One brown wire to right channel*
    Black tracer negative/red tracer positive
5   *Headphone stereo jacks***
6   *Accessories jack (12 volts, 10 amps)*
   * Speaker wiring to each front door
  ** Six-speaker system only (with rear speakers fitted)

36   Undo the retaining screws and remove the clock/upper facia tray.
37   To remove the clock illumination bulb, twist and remove the holder, then withdraw the bulb from it. To remove the clock unit, detach the wiring connector, then unclip and remove the clock from the tray (photo).
38   Refit in the reverse order of removal, and reset the clock on completion.

Windscreen and rear window washer units - later models
39   Although the location and general details concerning the washer reservoir units remain the same as earlier models, the reservoir pump units are now separate, mounted on the side of the reservoirs rather than being an integral part of the cap as with earlier models.

Front foglight - bulb renewal
40   Disconnect the battery earth lead.
41   Undo the retaining screws and remove the light unit (photo).
42   Detach the wiring and withdraw the cover (photos).
43   Release the retaining clip and extract the bulb (photo).
44   Refit in the reverse order of removal (avoid touching the new bulb glass with your fingers), then check for satisfactory operation and ad-

justment. If required, the light beam can be adjusted by turning the adjuster screw ("B" in photo 19.41).

Cigar lighter (later models) - removal and refitting
45   Disconnect the battery earth lead.
46   Using a suitable screwdriver as a lever, pass it through the centre vent grille on the right-hand side, and depress the grille panel retaining clip whilst pulling on the panel (photo).
47   With the grille panel withdrawn from the facia (photo), detach the wiring from the cigar lighter, compress the retaining clips and withdraw the lighter unit from the panel.
48   Refit in the reverse order of removal.

Interior map reading light - bulb renewal
49   The information given in Section 19 of Chapter 12 remains the same, but the accompanying photos clarify the procedures for this light type (photos).
50   Note that to remove the roof console complete, it will be necessary to detach the sunroof control switch wiring as well as the map reading light wiring (where applicable).

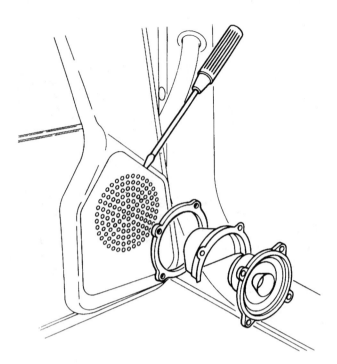

Fig. 13.74 Using a screwdriver to prise the radio speaker grille from the door (Sec 19)

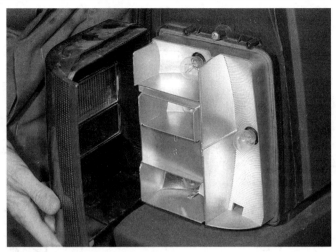

19.74 Rear light assembly (Estate)

Remote control door locking system

Control unit battery renewal
51   To renew the batteries in the control unit, depress the battery holder retaining clip each side and withdraw the holder. The batteries can be extracted and removed, but ensure that the correct battery type is used (battery reference V13GA).

Receiver unit
52   This is located in the roof console. It is not repairable, and if suspect, must be renewed. Prise free the inspection panel from the roof console, detach the wiring from the receiver unit, then unclip and remove the receiver (photo).
53   Refitting is a reversal of the removal procedure. Check for satisfactory operation on completion.

Relay units - BX 19 GTi
54   Further relay units are located in the engine compartment, under a plastic cover (photo).
55   If suspect, these units should be checked by a Citroën dealer. They are easily renewed by detaching the wiring connector and then unscrewing the retaining bolt. Refit in reverse order.

Radio equipment - later models
56   Depending on model, later variants are fitted with a wiring harness and connections for a stereo or a six-speaker radio system, even though the radio and speaker units may not be fitted as standard.
57   The wiring connections are shown and identified in Fig. 13.73.
58   With the stereo system, there are facilities provided in each front door panel for speaker fitting, the wiring being already provided. The speaker grille can be removed from the door panel by prising it free using a screwdriver as a lever (Fig. 13.74).
59   When refitting the grille to the door, locate it at the bottom edge, and press it into position at the top.
60   The six-speaker system has a speaker (tweeter) at each end of the dashboard, one speaker in each front door, and one each side at the rear, either in the rear quarter panel or above the wheel arches (Estate model). Headphone sockets and an accessories jack may be fitted to the rear face of the centre console, for use by rear passengers. Note

that the headphone sockets will only work when the rear speakers are fitted and connected.

Central locking control unit (all models) - location
61   The central locking control unit is located next to the handbrake lever. It is accessible after removing the handbrake console.

Control units and relays (models from 1987) - location
62   Refer to Fig. 13.75. Not all the items shown are fitted to UK petrol-engined models.

Low-maintenance batteries - description and precautions
63   These are fitted to later models; from time to time, such batteries may require the addition of de-mineralised water when the electrolyte level falls.
64   If this type of battery is to be charged from the mains electric supply, use a charger which has a regulated output of between 14.8 and 15.5 volts, and which has the ability to adjust the charge rate according to battery condition and capacity.
65   Always disconnect the battery leads before charging.

Speedometer - removal and refitting
66   The speedometer can be removed from the instrument panel only after the panel has been withdrawn as described in paragraphs 6 to 12, or in Chapter 12, Section 22, according to the date of vehicle production.

Speedometer cable - removal and refitting
67   Disconnect the speedometer drive cable from the rear of the speedometer after sliding back the plastic locking sleeve. The instrument panel will have to be partially withdrawn for access to the connector (refer to paragraphs 6 to 12, or to Chapter 12, Section 22).
68   Disconnect the cable from the transmission by pulling out the tapered rubber cotter pin. Before withdrawing the cable any further, note how it is routed within the engine compartment, as the new cable must be installed in identical fashion to ensure correct operation.
69   Release the bulkhead grommets, and withdraw the cable into the engine compartment.
70   Fitting the new cable is a reversal of the removal operations, but make sure that its routing is as originally taken, and avoid bending the cable sharply.

Side repeater lights - bulb renewal
71   Direction indicator side repeater lights are fitted to later models, from 1987 model year.
72   To renew the bulb, carefully twist the lens anti-clockwise, and

withdraw the light unit from the wing. Take care not to allow the wiring to fall back inside the wing - tape it to the wing if necessary. Pull the bulbholder from the back of the light unit for access to the bulb.

Rear light bulbs (Estate) - renewal

73   Open the tailgate.

74   Extract the lens securing screws and remove the lens. Note the positioning lug at the base of the lens (photo).

Dim-dip lighting system - general information

75   From late 1986 onwards (1987 model year), all models are equipped with a dim-dip lighting system to comply with UK regulations. The function of the system is to prevent the vehicle being driven with only the sidelights illuminated.

76   The system uses a relay-controlled resistor circuit. When the sidelights are on, with the ignition also on, the headlights are automatically illuminated at approximately one-sixth their normal dipped beam power.

Key to Fig. 13.75

Ref	Position	Description	Exact location
44	f5	On-board computer display	In the centre of the instrument panel (apparent)
54	k7	ABS control unit	Under the driver's seat
57	f4	Fuel calculator (interface unit)	On the inside of the instrument panel, under the top glove compartment, towards console
75	e7	Ignition module	On LH side of bulkhead, near ignition coil
76	i9	Impulse-operated window winder	unit Inside driver's door
84	a3	Water level indicator unit	On RH panel of radiator
85	f7	Oil level indicator unit	In instrument cluster
87	f5	Water temperature warning unit (Diesel with air conditioning)	On RH side of steering bracket
90	k5	Door lock control unit	Beside the handbrake lever
91	j5	Remote control door lock unit "PLIP"	Roof panel apparent front part
110	b8	Preheating timer unit	LH front wheel arch
142	b7	IEI control unit	Connected to the airflow meter, LH air inlet tube
145	f8	Direction indicator unit	On junction box, C; behind the cassette box
302	b7	Airflow meter	On air intake tube
312	f6	ABS (brake) diode	On electrical wiring behind the instrument clusters
658	f6	Blower speed module	In the steering bracket
660	95	On-board computer keyboard and module	Console apparent bottom section
731	d7	Fuel injection relay	On LH side of battery tray
734	d7	Injector relay	On LH side of battery tray
737	b8	Two relays for day running lights (Sweden, Norway, Finland)	LH front wheel arch
742	d7	Four relays for air conditioning	On LH side of battery tray
745	f5	Blower motor max. speed relay	On RH side of steering bracket
750	b8	Foglight relay	On LH front wheel arch
756	f5	ABS relay	On RH side of steering bracket
760	f7	Heated rear window relay	Junction box: R4, behind the cassette box
761	f7	Front window winder relay	Junction box: R3, behind the cassette box
762	f8	Rear window winder relay	Junction box: R2, behind the cassette box
765	f8	Windscreen intermittent wipe	Junction box: 1, behind the cassette box
766	f4	Rear screen intermittent wipe	On the inside of the instrument panel, under the top glove compartment, towards console
767	9	Headlight washer relay (Sweden, Norway, Finland)	In the steering gear housing lower cover
774	f8	Engine cooling fan relay	Connection box: R1, behind the cassette box
775	d7	Starter motor safety relay	On LH side of battery tray
777	b8	Fuel heater relay	LH front wheel arch

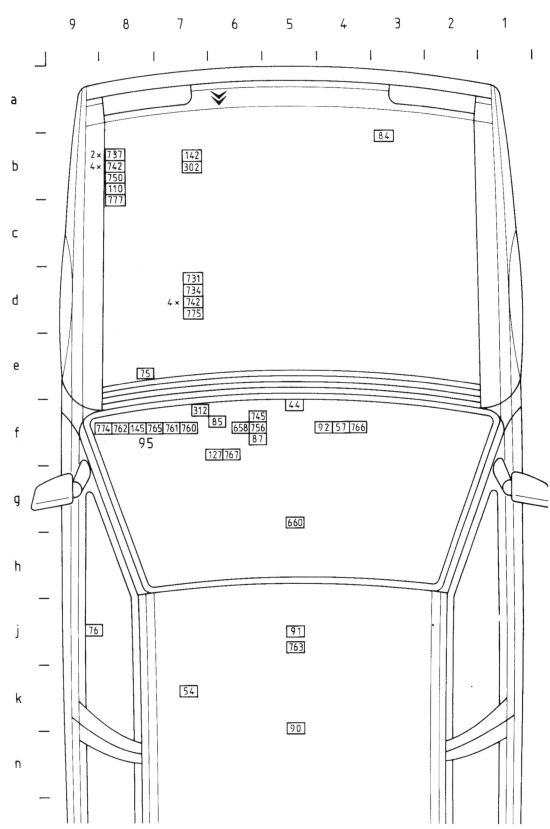

Fig. 13.75 Location of electronic control units and relays for all models from 1987

Key to Fig. 13.76

No	Description	Circuit No	Location	No	Description	Circuit No	Location
1	Front cigar lighter/illumination	VII	26 to 28	386	RH rear number plate light	VI	6
5	Ignition distributor	V	1 to 5	430	LH front brake caliper	III	11 to 12
10	Alternator	II	1 to 6	431	RH front brake caliper	III	13 to 14
25	Horn	VI	26 to 27	440	LH front sidelight	VI	14
44	Digital display	V	20 to 23	441	RH front sidelight	VI	15
45	Battery	I	5	442	LH rear light	VI	8
46	Instrument panel	III	1 to 25	443	RH rear light	VI	9
46	Instrument panel	IV	4 to 6, 18	447	LH front foglight	VI	19
46	Instrument panel	VI	5 to 7	448	RH front foglight	VI	20
47	Hydraulic control unit for anti-lock braking system	IV	19 to 29	457	LH stop-light	IV	13
				458	RH stop-light	IV	14
50	Ignition coil	V	3 to 4	460	LH rear foglight	VI	11
57	Fuel calculator unit	V	18 to 19	461	RH rear foglight	VI	12
75	Ignition module	V	3 to 5	462	LH reversing light	IV	11
76	LH front window winder control unit	VIII	2 to 9	463	RH reversing light	IV	12
84	Coolant level indicator unit	III	6 to 8	470	Fuses F1, F2, F3, F7	I	15, 12, 34, 46
90	Door locking control unit	IX	15 to 25	470	Fuse F4	II	9
91	Remote control door locking unit	IX	14 to 16	470	Fuse F5, F14	IV	8, 28
92	Interior light timer	IX	6 to 10	470	Fuse F8, F10, F11, F12, F13	VI	8, 9, 10, 11, 25
140	Distance sensor	V	19				
142	Electronic control unit for injection	V	6 to 14	470	Fuse F6, F9	VIII	7, 21
145	Direction indicator unit (C)	IV	8 to 9	480	LH front direction indicator	IV	7
146	LH front wheel sensor	IV	18 to 19	481	RH front direction indicator	IV	8
147	RH front wheel sensor	IV	24 to 25	482	LH rear direction indicator	IV	9
148	LH rear wheel sensor	IV	20 to 21	483	RH rear direction indicator	IV	10
149	RH rear wheel sensor	IV	22 to 23	488	LH headlight	VI	1 to 2
168	Battery connector	I	2 to 6	489	RH headlight	VI	3 to 4
170	Boot light switch	IX	26	500	LH front loudspeaker	X	12
180	Reversing light switch	IV	11	501	RH front loudspeaker	X	14
185	Stop-light switch	IV	13	502	LH rear loudspeaker	X	11
190	Handbrake switch	III	10	503	RH rear loudspeaker	X	14
192	Throttle spindle switch	V	11 to 12	506	LH front tweeter loudspeaker	X	10
229	Ignition switch	I	7 to 34	507	RH front tweeter loudspeaker	X	16
230	LH front door switch	IX	11	510	Front foglight switch	VI	17 to 19
231	RH front door switch	IX	12	511	Rear foglight switch	VI	11 to 13
232	LH rear door switch	IX	10	519	RH window winder switch on driver's door	VIII	12 to 15
233	RH rear door switch	IX	13				
234	Glovebox switch	V	27	520	LH window winder switch on driver's door	VIII	5 to 10
235	Hydraulic fluid flow pressure switch	III	8	521	RH front window winder switch	VIII	13 to 14
236	Hydraulic fluid level switch	III	9	522	LH rear window winder switch	VIII	20 to 22
237	Coolant level switch	III	6 to 7	523	RH rear window winder switch	VIII	23 to 25
238	RH front door lock switch	VII	22	530	Sunroof switch	IX	3 to 4
239	LH front door lock switch	VII	20	532	Heated rear window switch	VI	21 to 23
241	RH rear door lock switch	VII	23	551	Rear screen intermittent wiper switch	VII	3 to 9
242	LH rear door lock switch	VII	21				
243	Boot lock switch	VII	24	570	Hazard warning light switch	IV	1 to 9
244	Bonnet lock switch	VII	19	576	Injectors	V	10, 11, 12, 13
253	Screen wiper/washer and computer switch	V	24 to 25				
				580	Fuel gauge	III	14 to 15
253	Screen wiper/washer and computer switch	VII	11 to 15	600	Windscreen wiper motor	VII	12 to 18
				601	Rear screen wiper motor	VII	1 to 5
260	Lighting/direction indicator/horn switch	IV	7 to 8	610	Sunroof motor	IX	3 to 6
				615	LH front window winder motor	VIII	4 to 7
260	Lighting/direction indicator/horn switch	VI	4 to 7, 26	616	RH front window winder motor	VIII	13 to 14
				617	LH rear window winder motor	VIII	21
276	Rear view mirror switch	VII	20 to 27	618	RH rear window winder motor	VIII	24
278	Blower motor speed control	II	13 to 19	625	LH front door lock motor	IX	18 to 20
280	Additional air control	V	15	626	RH front door lock motor	IX	21
300	Starter motor	II	3 to 5	627	LH rear door lock motor	IX	18
302	Airflow meter	V	11 to 14	628	RH rear door lock motor	IX	20
312	Anti-lock braking system diode	IV	16 to 17	629	Boot lid lock motor	IX	20 to 21
370	Boot light	IX	26	635	LH engine cooling fan motor	II	9
375	Glovebox light	V	27	650	Engine oil pressure switch	III	5
385	LH rear number plate light	VI	7	658	Blower fan control module	II	13 to 15
				660	On-board computer	V	19 to 26

Key to Fig. 13.76 (continued)

No	Description	Circuit No	Location	No	Description	Circuit No	Location
680	Windscreen washer pump	VII	11	762	Rear window winder motor relay (R2)	VIII	20 to 21
681	Rear screen washer pump	VII	8	763	Sunroof motor relay	IX	3 to 6
683	Fuel pump	V	17	765	Windscreen wiper relay (1)	VII	14 to 17
691	LH interior light	IX	10 to 11	766	Rear screen wiper relay	VII	2 to 7
692	RH interior light	IX	12 to 13	774	Engine cooling fan relay (R1)	II	9 to 11
695	Interior spotlights	IX	9	788	Cooling fan first speed resistor	II	8
698	Headphone sockets (2)	X	1 to 9	795	Lighting rheostat	I	19
710	Supply socket	VIII	1	815	RH front exterior mirror	VIII	21 to 23
721	Radio connections (12V and speakers)	X	11 to 16	835	Engine oil level gauge	III	19 to 20
731	Fuel injection relay	V	7 to 8	840	Coolant temperature sensor	III	18
734	Injector relays	V	9 to 10	841	Coolant temperature sensor (injection)	V	10
745	Blower motor high speed relay	II	13 to 16	842	Oil pressure sensor	III	17
750	Foglight relay	VI	17 to 20	843	Oil temperature sensor	III	16
756	Anti-lock braking system solenoid relay	IV	27 to 29	850	Cooling fan thermal switch	II	8 to 9
760	Heated rear screen relay (R4)	VI	23 to 25	855	Water temperature switch	III	3
761	Front window winder motor relay (R3)	VIII	7 to 9	935	Air conditioning fan	II	13
				940	Door closed label	VII	19 to 25
				945	Heated rear screen	VI	25

Harness code

A	Front	RE	Rear screen wiper
C	Switches	RV	Rear door locking
CN	Battery negative cable	SR	Radio (rear section)
CP	Battery positive cable	SV	Radio (front section)
E	Window wiper	T	Instrument panel
F	Rear light cluster connection	U	Brake pad wear
FP	Fuel pump	V	RH side tailgate
G	LH side tailgate	Y	Anti-lock braking system
H	Interior	Z	Ignition
IM	Injection		
J	Fuel gauge		
L	Boot lighting		
M	Engine		
M-B	Junction box earth		
M-F	Rear light cluster earth		
M-P	Fuel pump earth		
O	On-board computer		
P	Interior lighting		
PC	Driver's door		
PP	Passenger's door		
R	Rear		

Note: *Letter/number codes appearing in small boxes on the diagrams convey multi-plug connector information. For example - "3M1": the first number is the number of wires at that connector (three), the letter is a connector colour code (M - Brown, as given below), and the last number is the wire number within the group of wires at the connector (one in a group of three).*

Earthing points

m1	Behind battery
m2	Along LH side of the steering column
m3	Roof lighting
m4	Behind console
m5	RH rear lights
m6	LH rear lights
m7	LH front wheelarch

Colour code

B	White
Bl	Blue
G	Grey
Ic	Transparent
J	Yellow
M	Brown
Mv	Mauve
N	Black
Or	Orange
R	Red
V	Green

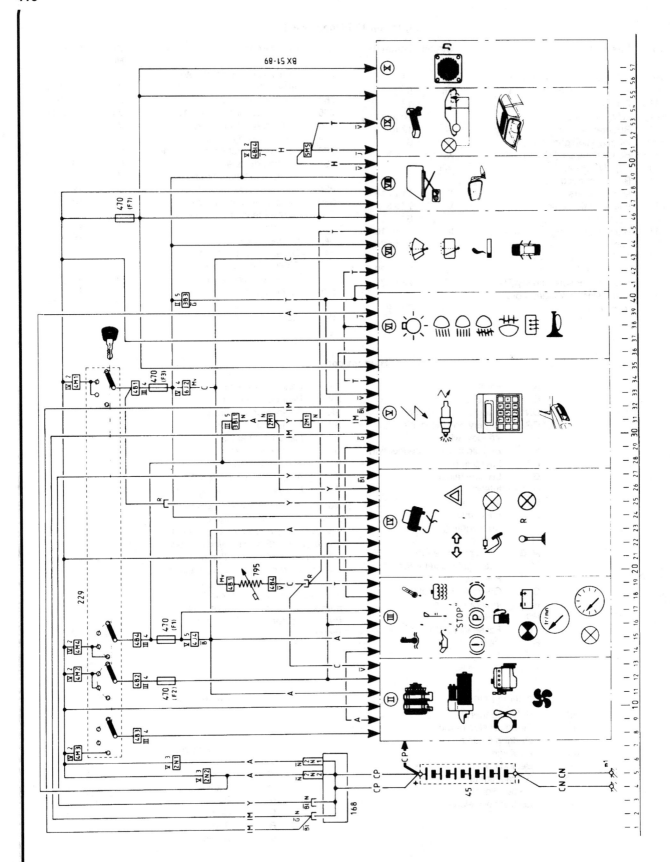

Fig. 13.76 Wiring diagram for all models from 1987 - circuit I

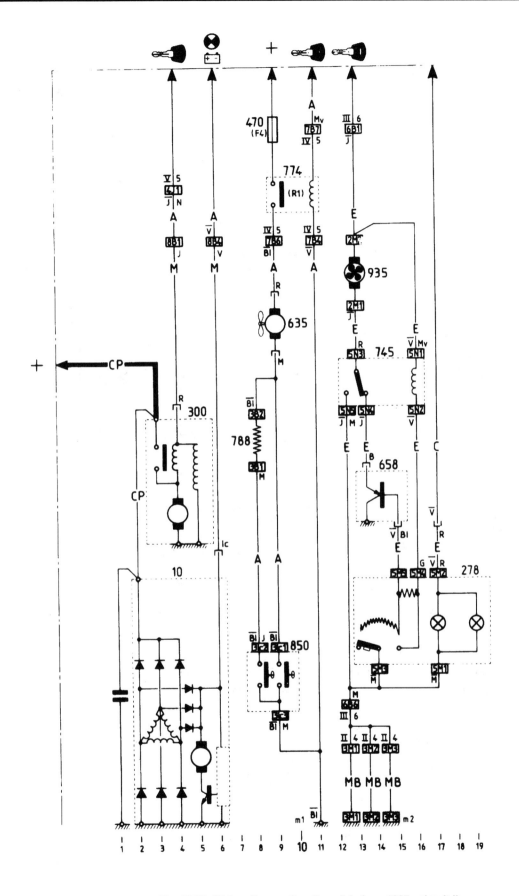

Fig. 13.76 Wiring diagram for all models from 1987 - circuit II

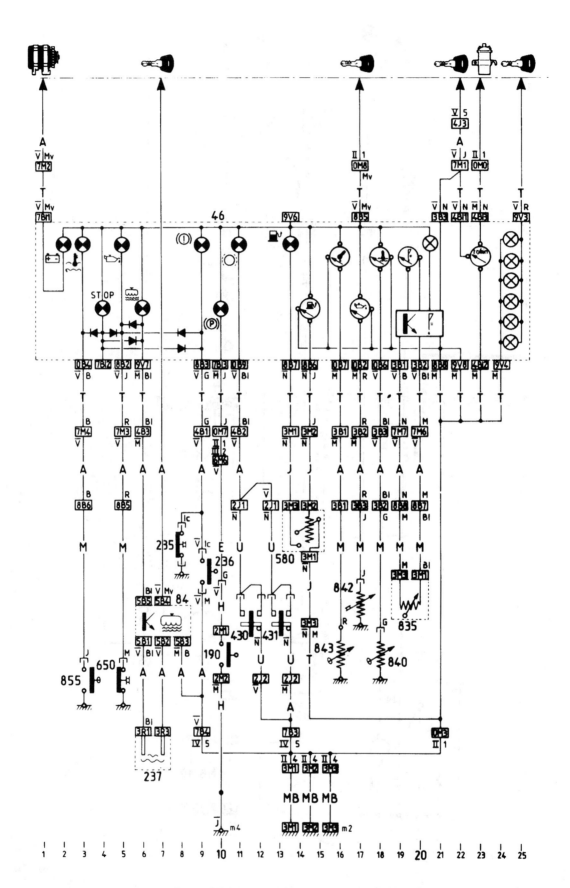

Fig. 13.76 Wiring diagram for all models from 1987 - circuit III

419

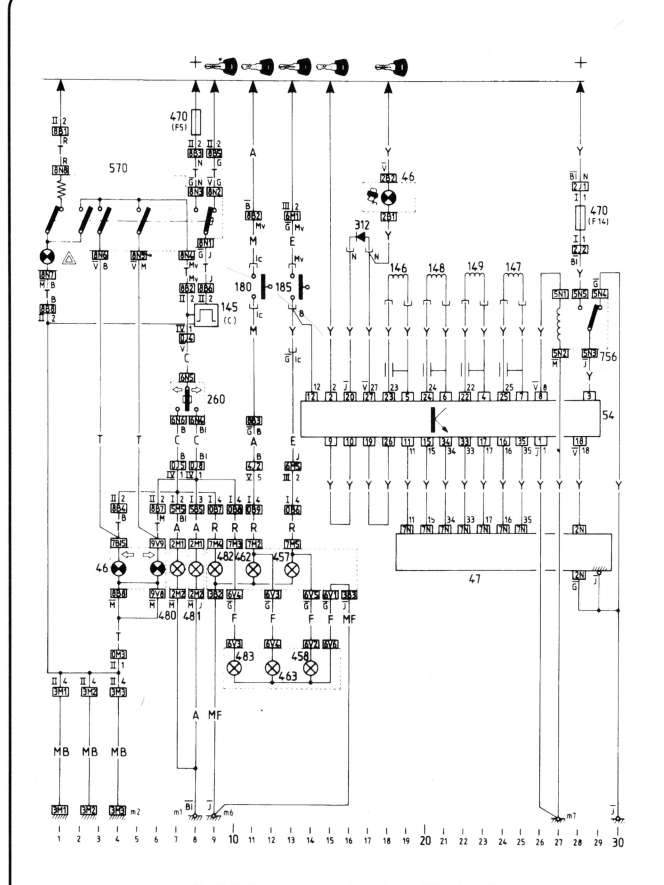

Fig. 13.76 Wiring diagram for all models from 1987 - circuit IV

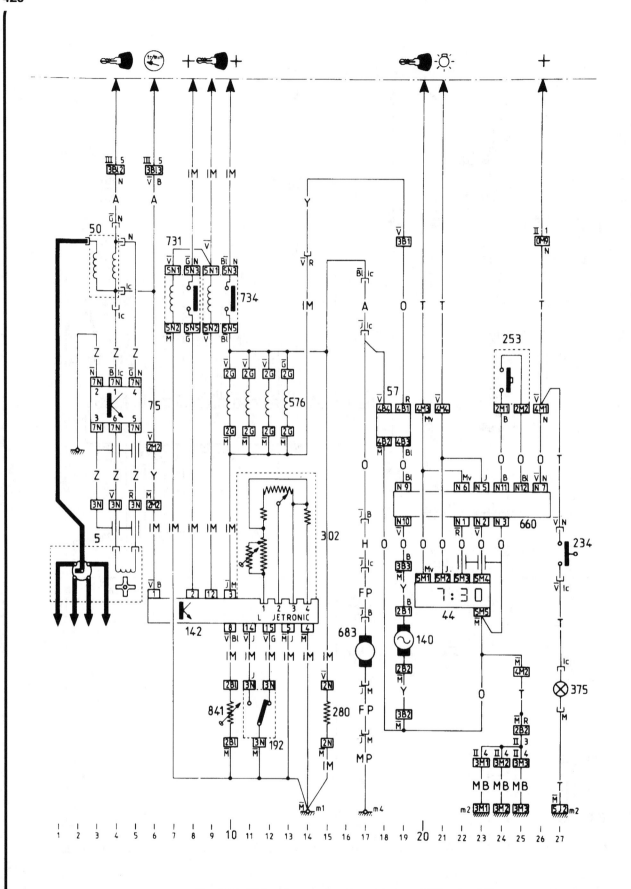

Fig. 13.76 Wiring diagram for all models from 1987 - circuit V

421

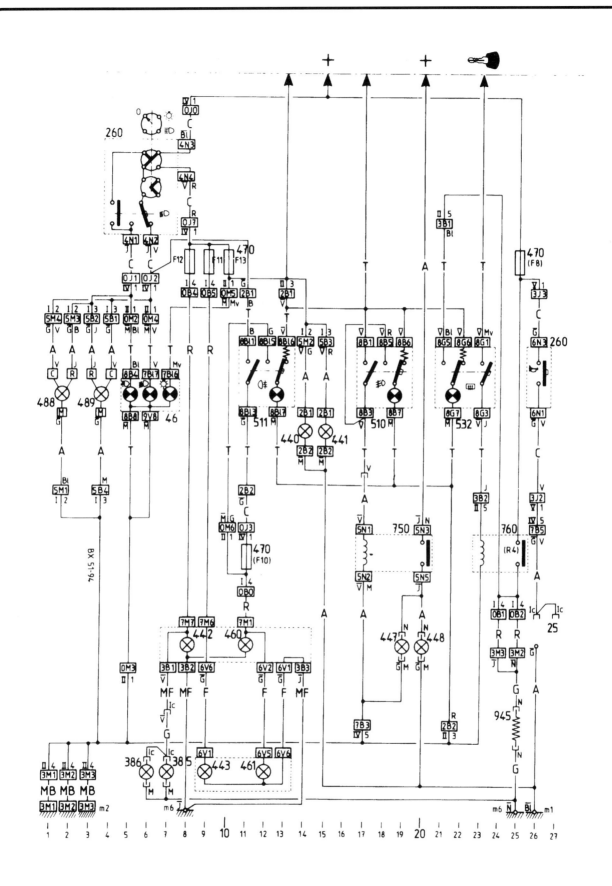

Fig. 13.76 Wiring diagram for all models from 1987 - circuit VI

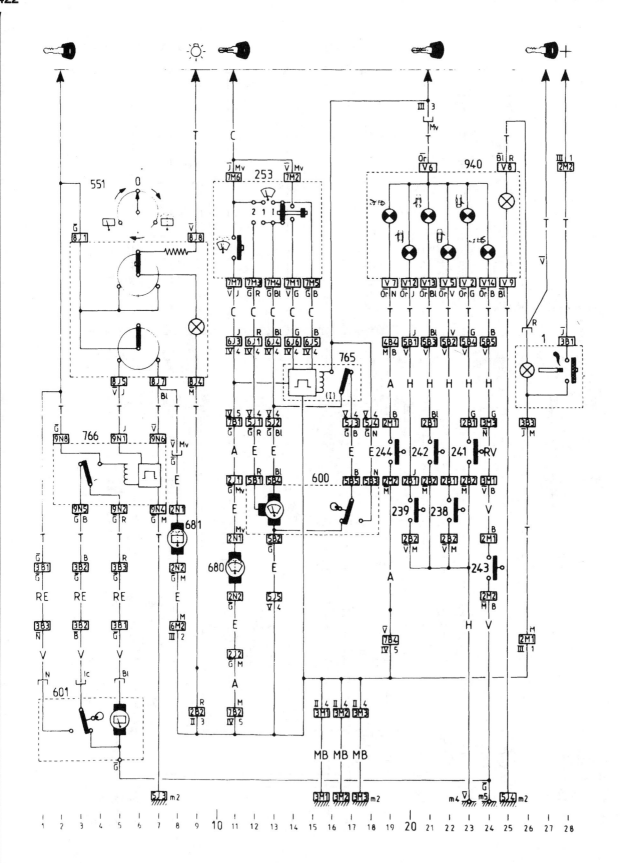

Fig. 13.76 Wiring diagram for all models from 1987 - circuit VII

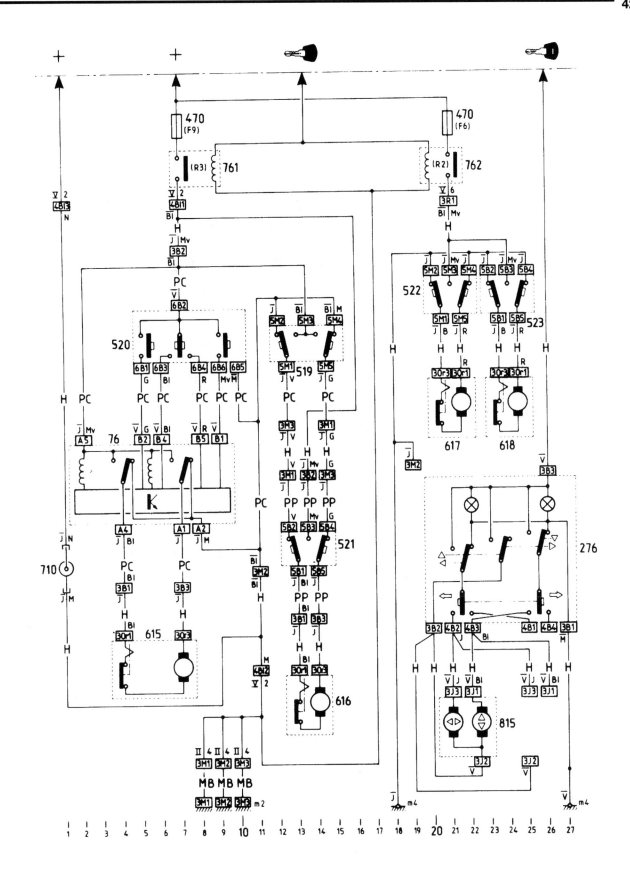

Fig. 13.76 Wiring diagram for all models from 1987 - circuit VIII

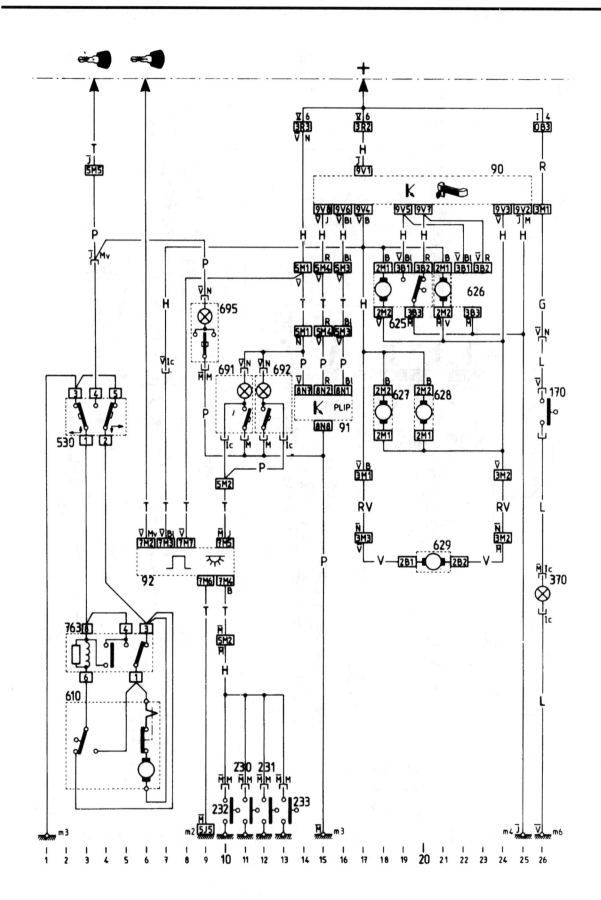

Fig. 13.76 Wiring diagram for all models from 1987 - circuit IX

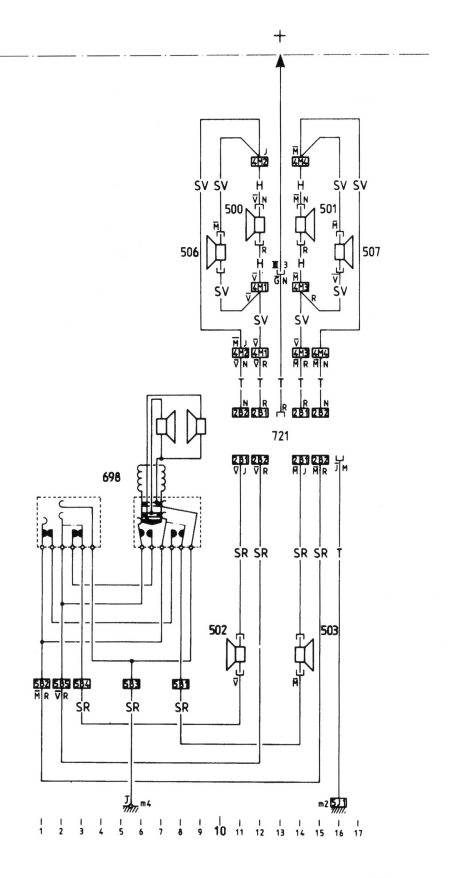

Fig. 13.76 Wiring diagram for all models from 1987 - circuit X

Key to Fig. 13.77
For colour code and other information, see key to Fig. 13.76

No	Description
35	Battery
40	Instrument cluster
50	Supply box
52	Power supply connector box
211	LH combination switch
300	Ignition switch
391	LH number plate light
392	RH number plate light
492	LH sidelight
493	RH sidelight
506	LH tail light
507	RH tail light
786	LH headlight

No	Description
787	RH headlight
827	Dim-dip relay
858	Dim-dip resistor unit

Harness code

AV	Front
CN	Battery negative cable
CP	Battery positive cable
ES	Windscreen wiper
FR	Rear lights
MF	Lighting earth
PB	Dashboard
RG	Left-hand rear
VG	Left-hand tailgate

Key to Fig. 13.78
For colour code and other information, see key to Fig. 13.76

No	Description
47	Hydraulic unit
54	ECU
146	LH front wheel sensor
147	RH front wheel sensor
148	LH rear wheel sensor
149	RH rear wheel sensor
185	Brake stop-light switch
229	Ignition switch
312	Diode
457	LH stop-light
458	RH stop-light

No	Description
470	F14 fuse
756	Control relay
963	ABS warning light

Harness code

A	Front
E	Screen wiper
F	Rear light interconnection
MF	Rear light earth
R	Rear

No reference: ABS

Key to Fig. 13.79
For colour code and other information, see key to Fig. 13.76

No	Description	Circuit No	Location
1	Front cigar lighter/illumination	VII	25 to 25
5	Ignition distributor	IV	7 to 11
10	Alternator	II	1 to 6
25	Horn	III	21
45	Battery	I	2
46	Instrument panel	II	13 to 15
46	Instrument panel	IV	4 to 6
46	Instrument panel	V	1 to 26
50	Ignition coil	IV	3 to 5
75	Ignition module	IV	5 to 8
84	Coolant level indicator unit	V	6 to 8
90	Door locking control unit	VII	17 to 25
145	Direction indicator unit (C)	VI	8 to 9
168	Battery connector	I	2 to 3
170	Boot light switch	VIII	26
180	Reversing light switch	VI	11
185	Stop-light switch	VI	13
190	Handbrake switch	V	10
225	Choke warning light switch	V	12
229	Ignition switch	I	4 to 36
230	LH front door switch	VIII	11
231	RH front door switch	VIII	13
235	Hydraulic fluid flow pressure switch	V	8
236	Hydraulic fluid level switch	V	9
237	Coolant level switch	V	6 to 7
260	Lighting/direction indicator/horn switch	II	9 to 13
260	Lighting/direction indicator/horn switch	III	21
260	Lighting/direction indicator/horn switch	IV	7 to 8
263	Front wash/wipe switch	II	18 to 22
278	Blower motor speed control	VII	8 to 12
285	Ignition coil capacitor	IV	1
300	Starter motor	II	3 to 5
370	Boot or interior light	VIII	26
385	LH rear number plate light	II	19
386	RH rear number plate light	II	18
430	LH front brake caliper	V	10 to 11
431	RH front brake caliper	V	12 to 13
440	LH front sidelight	II	16
441	RH front sidelight	II	17
442	LH rear light	II	20
443	RH rear light	II	21
457	LH stop-light	VI	13
458	RH stop-light	VI	14
460	LH rear foglight	III	11
461	RH rear foglight	III	12
462	LH reversing light	VI	11
463	RH reversing light	VI	12
470	Fuses	I	23, 24, 35, 39
470	Fuses	II	15, 20, 21
470	Fuses	III	11, 19
470	Fuse F5	VI	8
470	Fuse F4, F9	VII	1, 19
480	LH front direction indicator	VI	7
481	RH front direction indicator	VI	8
482	LH rear direction indicator	VI	8
483	RH rear direction indicator	VI	10
488	LH headlight	II	9 to 10
489	RH headlight	II	11 to 12
500	LH front loudspeaker	VII	29 to 30

For colour code and other information, see key to Fig. 13.76

Key to Fig. 13.79 (continued)

No	Description	Circuit No	Location	No	Description	Circuit No	Location
501	RH front loudspeaker	VII	29 to 30	635	LH engine cooling fan motor	VII	1
511	Rear foglight switch	III	11 to 13	650	Engine oil pressure switch	V	5
519	RH window winder switch on driver's door	VII	20 to 23	658	Blower fan control module	VII	6
520	LH window winder switch on driver's door	VII	15 to 18	680	Windscreen washer pump	II	18
				681	Rear screen washer pump	III	7
521	RH front window winder switch	VII	21 to 22	691	LH interior light	VIII	11 to 12
530	Sunroof switch	VIII	3 to 4	692	RH interior light	VIII	14 to 15
532	Heated rear window switch	III	16 to 18	695	Interior spotlights	VIII	9
551	Rear screen intermittent wiper switch	III	3 to 8	721	Radio connections (12V and speakers)	VII	28 to 30
570	Hazard warning light switch	VI	1 to 9	745	Blower motor high speed relay	II	5 to 10
580	Fuel gauge	V	14	760	Heated rear screen relay (R4)	III	17 to 19
600	Windscreen wiper motor	II	19 to 25	761	Front window winder motor relay (R3)	VII	13 to 19
601	Rear screen wiper motor	III	1 to 5	763	Sunroof motor relay	VII	3 to 6
610	Sunroof motor	VIII	3 to 6	765	Windscreen wiper relay	II	21 to 24
615	LH front window winder motor	VII	15 to 18	774	Engine cooling fan relay (R1)	VII	1 to 3
616	RH front window winder motor	VII	21 to 22	795	Lighting rheostat	I	35
625	LH front door lock motor	VIII	18 to 20	850	Cooling fan thermal switch	VII	1
626	RH front door lock motor	VIII	21 to 23	855	Water temperature switch	V	3
627	LH rear door lock motor	VIII	18	935	Air conditioning fan	VII	5
628	RH rear door lock motor	VIII	27	945	Heated rear screen	III	19
629	Boot lid lock motor	VIII	20 to 21				

Harness code

A	Front		M-B	Junction box earth
C	Switches		M-F	Rear light cluster earth
CN	Battery negative cable		P	Interior lighting
CP	Battery positive cable		PC	Driver's door
E	Window wiper		PP	Passenger's door
F	Rear light cluster connection		R	Rear
G	LH side tailgate		RE	Rear screen wiper
H	Interior		T	Instrument panel
J	Fuel gauge		U	Brake pad wear
L	Boot lighting		V	RH side tailgate
M	Engine		Z	Ignition

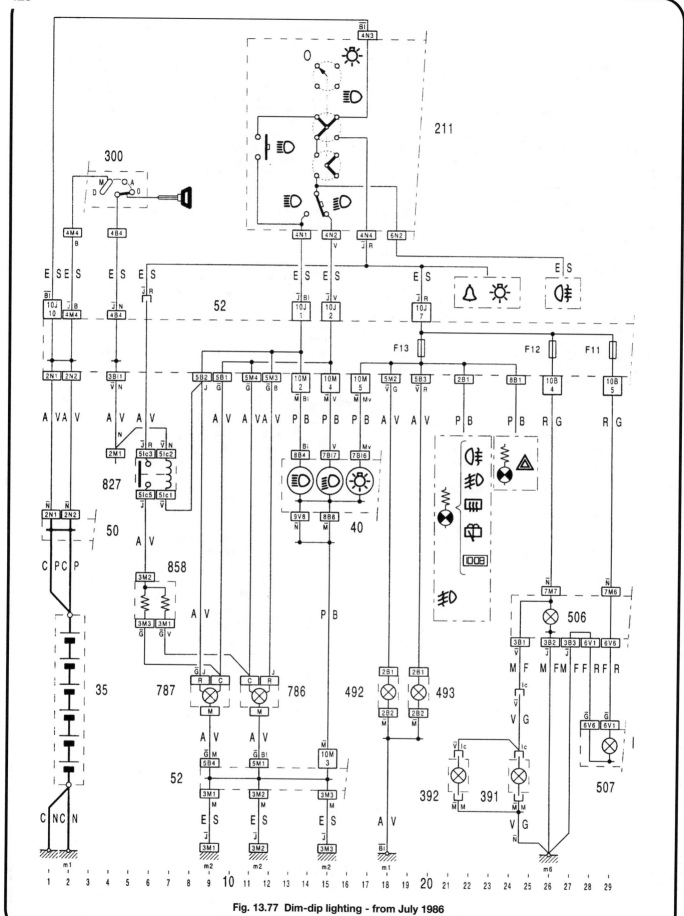

Fig. 13.77 Dim-dip lighting - from July 1986

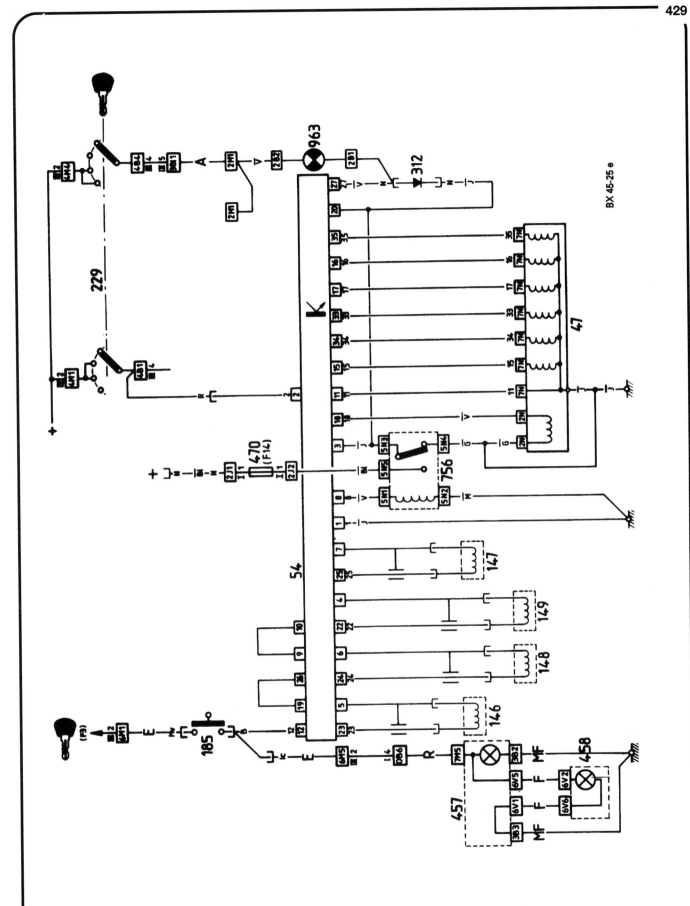

BX 45-25 e

Fig. 13.78 Anti-lock Braking System (ABS) - from September 1987

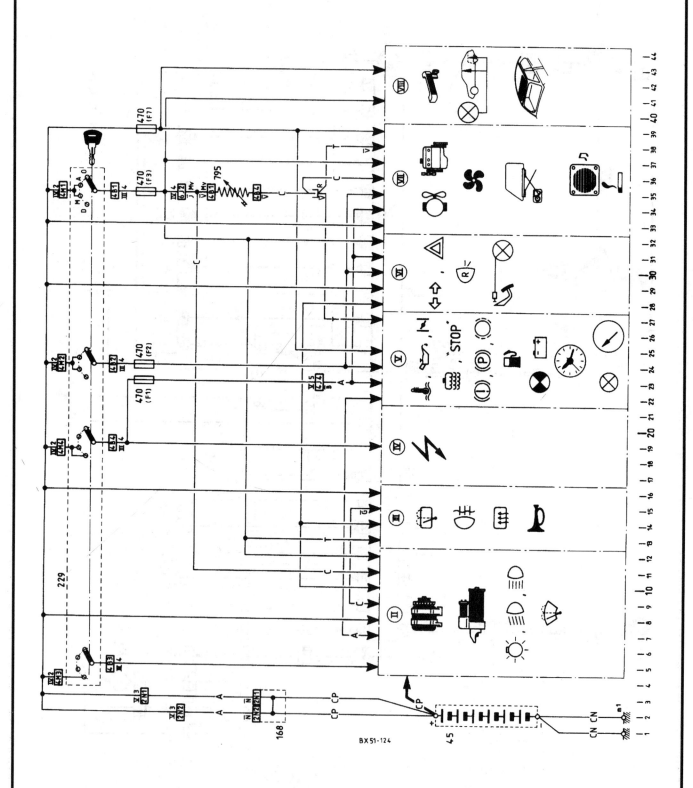

Fig. 13.79 Wiring diagram for BX and BX 14 models from October 1988 - circuit I

BX 51-124

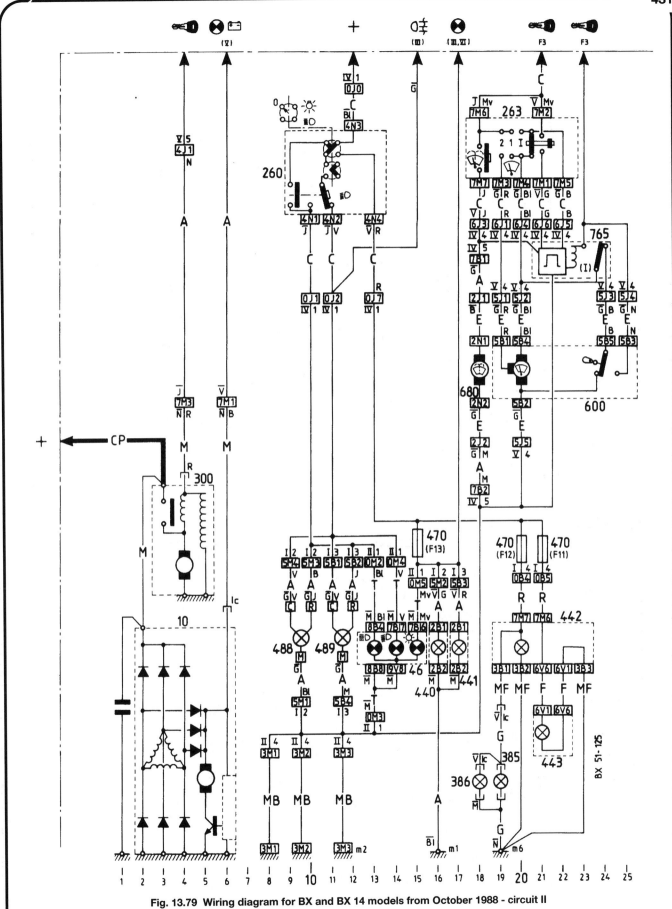

Fig. 13.79 Wiring diagram for BX and BX 14 models from October 1988 - circuit II

432

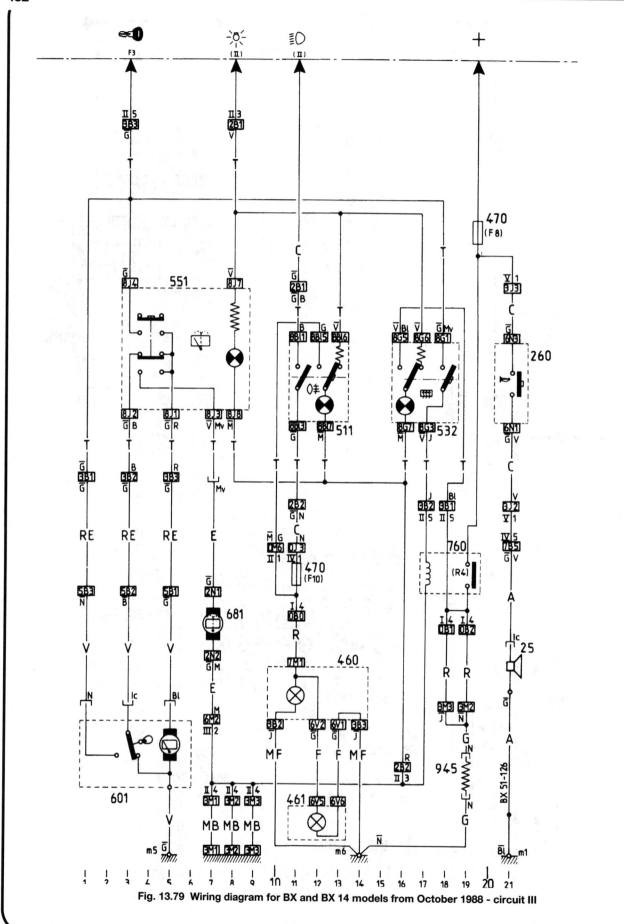

Fig. 13.79 Wiring diagram for BX and BX 14 models from October 1988 - circuit III

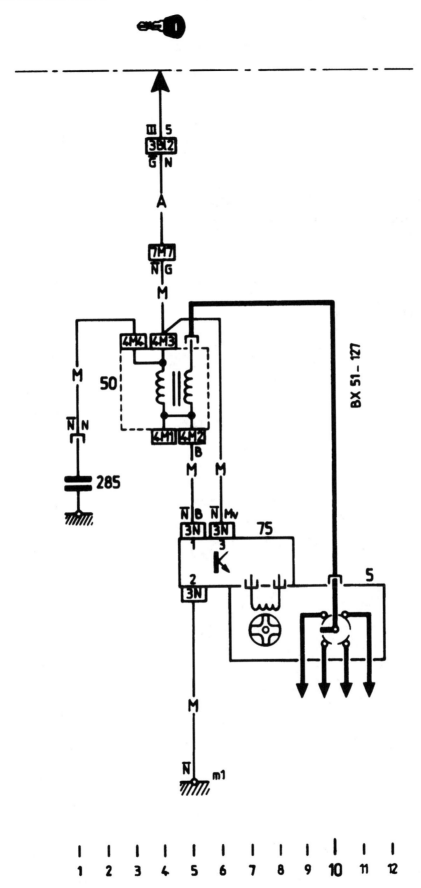

Fig. 13.79 Wiring diagram for BX and BX 14 models from October 1988 - circuit IV

434

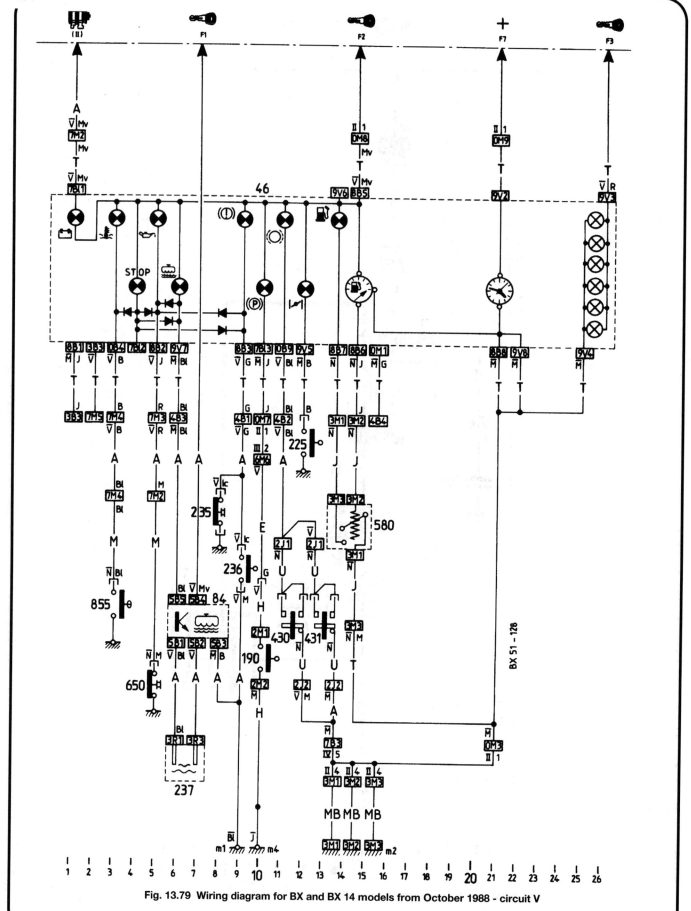

Fig. 13.79 Wiring diagram for BX and BX 14 models from October 1988 - circuit V

435

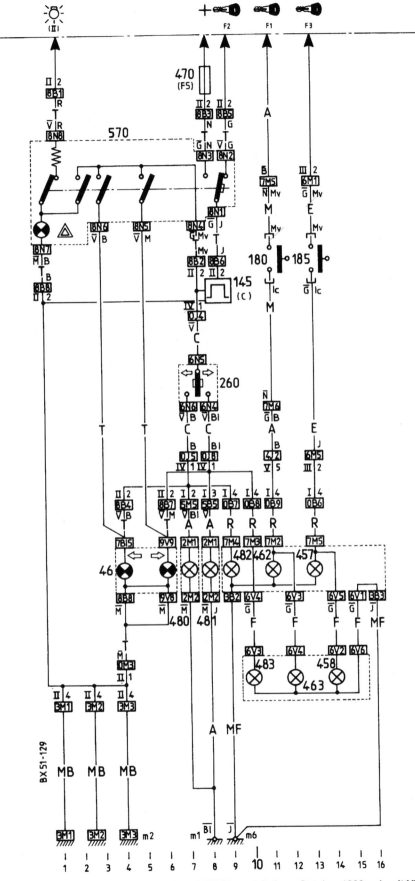

Fig. 13.79 Wiring diagram for BX and BX 14 models from October 1988 - circuit VI

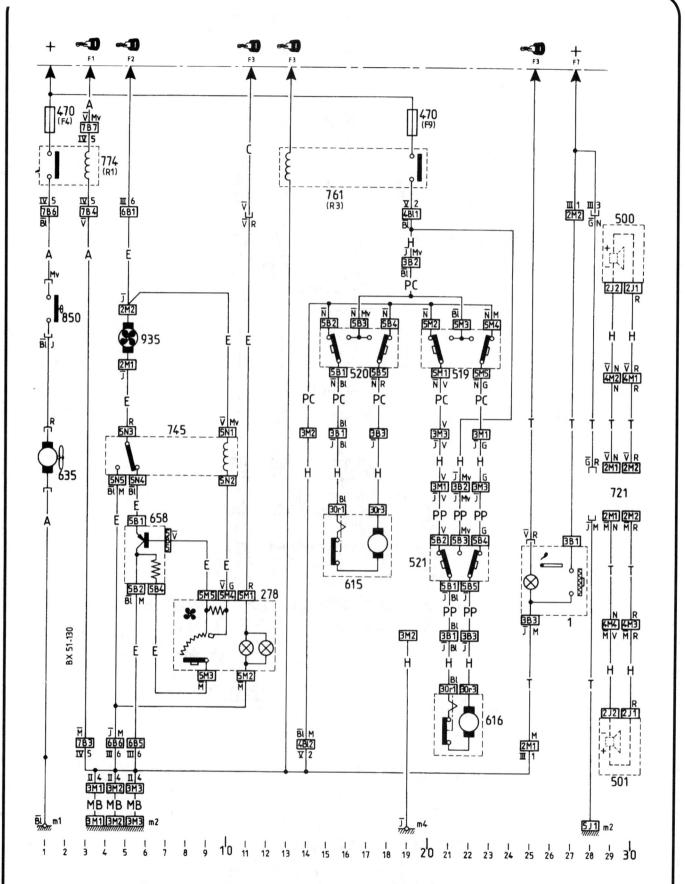

Fig. 13.79 Wiring diagram for BX and BX 14 models from October 1988 - circuit VII

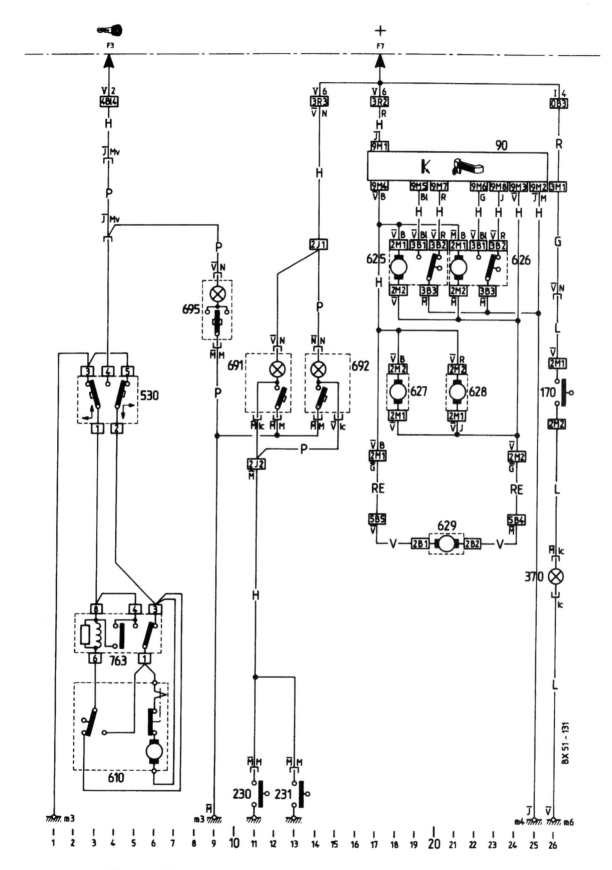

Fig. 13.79 Wiring diagram for BX and BX 14 models from October 1988 - circuit VIII

Key to Fig. 13.80
For colour code and other information, see key to Fig. 13.76

No	Description	No	Description
5	Distributor	285	Ignition coil suppressor
45	Battery	302	Airflow meter
46	Instrument panel	332	Idling actuator
50	Ignition coil	470	Fuse
75	Ignition module	576	Injectors
131	TDC sensor	683	Fuel pump
142	ECU	720	Diagnostic plug
168	Battery connector	731	Injector relay
192	Throttle position switch	749	Fuel pump relay
229	Ignition switch	841	Coolant temperature sensor

Harness code

A	Front
CN	Battery negative
CP	Battery positive
P	Fuel pump lead
IC	Injection, body section
IM	Injection, engine section
MB	Battery earth
MP	Fuel pump earth
T	Dashboard
Z	Ignition

Key to Fig. 13.81
For colour code and other information, see key to Fig. 13.76

No	Description	No	Description
35	Battery	498	Left-hand reversing light
40	Instrument cluster	499	Right-hand reversing light
45	Ignition coil	570	Injectors
50	Power supply connector block	680	Ignition module
52	Junction box	721	Right-hand cooling fan
142	Injection ECU	755	Fuel pump
150	Knock sensor	770	Throttle valve potentiometer
152	TDC sensor	772	Mixture adjustment potentiometer
180	Supplementary air device	775	Pressostat
216	Automatic gearbox switch	783	Injection diagnostic socket
255	Air conditioning compressor	801	Automatic gearbox relay
270	Ignition coil suppressor	807	Injection relay
300	Ignition switch	816	Fuel pump relay
318	Throttle position switch	822	Injection air conditioning compressor cut-off relay
340	Airflow meter	838	Automatic gearbox idling relay
350	Starter meter	839	Cooling fan relay (air conditioning)
375	Distributor	907	Injection air temperature sensor
431	Idle actuator	909	Injection coolant temperature sensor

Harness code

AA	Ignition
AV	Front
CN	Negative cable
CP	Positive cable
FR	Rear lights
JC	Injection (body part)
JM	Injection (engine part)
LP	Pump junction
MB	Earth for junction box
MF	Earth for lights
MP	Earth for fuel pump
MT	Earth for engine
PB	Dashboard
RG	Left rear
RS	Starter relay

Key to Fig. 13.82
For colour code and other information, see key to Fig. 13.76

No	Description	No	Description
5	Distributor	300	Starter motor
45	Battery	302	Airflow sensor
46	Instrument panel	334	Fuel vapour purge valve
50	Coil	470	Fuse
75	Ignition module	576	Injectors
131	TDC sensor	683	Fuel pump
142	Injection ECU	720	Diagnostic plug
168	Battery connector	731	Injection relay
192	Throttle position switch	749	Fuel pump relay
229	Ignition switch	833	Oxygen sensor
280	Supplementary air device	841	Coolant temperature sensor
285	Coil capacitor		

Harness code

A	Front
CN	Battery negative cable
CP	Battery positive cable
FP	Fuel pump
IC	Injection, body part
IM	Injection, engine part
M	Engine
MB	Module earth
MP	Fuel pump earth
T	Dashboard
Z	Ignition

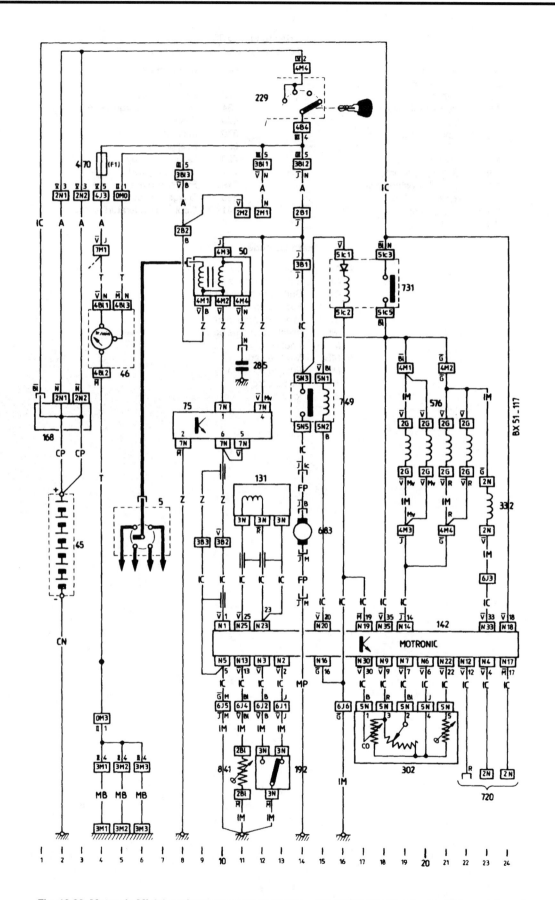

Fig. 13.80 Motronic ML4.1 engine management system - BX 19 GTi 16 valve (up to 1991 model year)

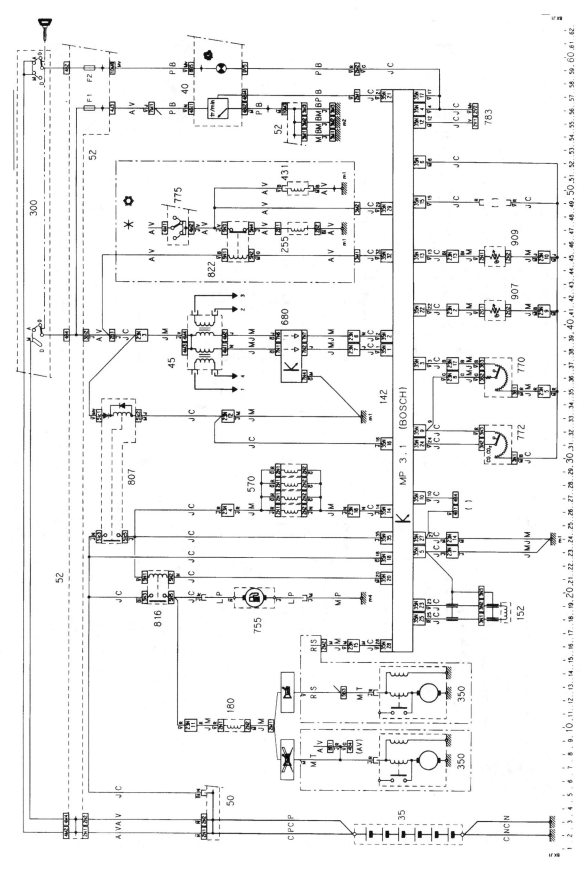

Fig. 13.81 Motronic MP3.1 engine management system - BX 19 GTi (from 1991 model year)

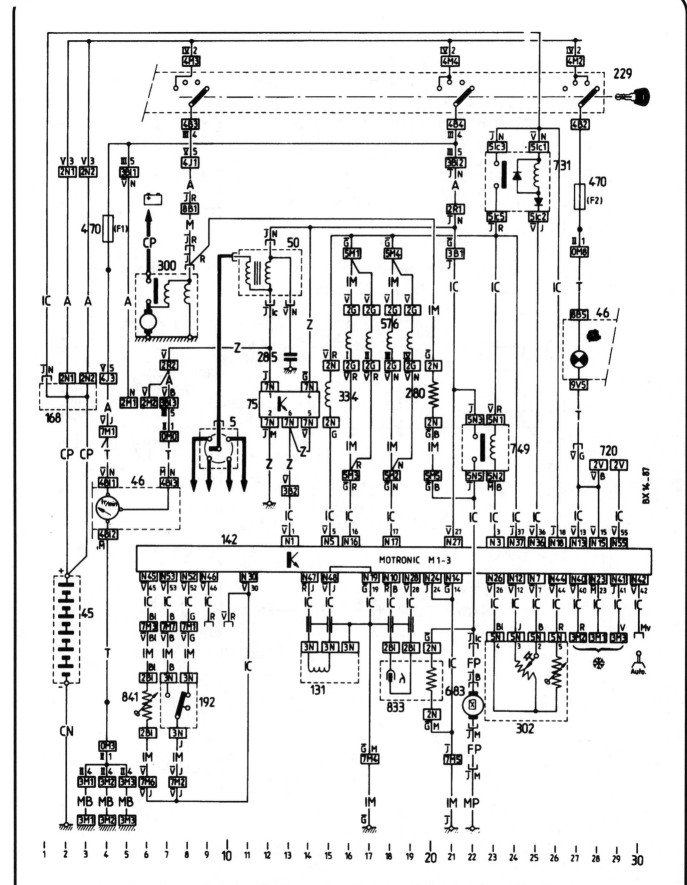

Fig. 13.82 Motronic M1.3 engine management system - BX 19 TZi with catalytic converter

Index